Communications
in Computer and Information Science   1312

More information about this series at http://www.springer.com/series/7899

Andrew R. Ruis · Seung B. Lee (Eds.)

Advances in Quantitative Ethnography

Second International Conference, ICQE 2020
Malibu, CA, USA, February 1–3, 2021
Proceedings

 Springer

Editors
Andrew R. Ruis ⓘ
University of Wisconsin–Madison
Madison, WI, USA

Seung B. Lee ⓘ
Pepperdine University
Malibu, CA, USA

ISSN 1865-0929   ISSN 1865-0937 (electronic)
Communications in Computer and Information Science
ISBN 978-3-030-67787-9   ISBN 978-3-030-67788-6 (eBook)
https://doi.org/10.1007/978-3-030-67788-6

This Springer imprint is published by the registered company Springer Nature Switzerland AG
The registered company address is: Gewerbestrasse 11, 6330 Cham, Switzerland

Preface

At the conclusion of the First International Conference on Quantitative Ethnography (ICQE19), the nascent QE community came up with a wish list of sorts, a set of action items, goals, and plans for 2020. Well, "everybody has a plan until they get punched in the mouth," to quote pugilist and philosopher of the sweet science Mike Tyson, and 2020 has not stopped pummeling us. Yet while we have had to adapt many of our plans due to the COVID-19 pandemic, most notably holding ICQE20 entirely online—and in 2021—we have nonetheless achieved many of our goals over the past year.

Since the inaugural conference, the QE community has founded a professional association, the International Society for Quantitative Ethnography (http://qesoc.org/). The society, in turn, has developed resources and hosted events to support QE scholarship and community development. There is now a monthly QE Webinar Series, which showcases emerging research and new developments in quantitative ethnography, as well as a QE Zotero Library, which provides a complete list of QE publications with links to the full-text version of each item. Last spring, the society hosted the QE-COVID Data Challenge, which brought together nearly 100 researchers from 16 countries to collaboratively analyze data and generate insights with the potential to make a difference in public policy or deepen understanding of the social and cultural dimensions of the pandemic. And last fall, when ICQE20 would otherwise have taken place, the society hosted the QEurious Meetup, a week-long event to help scholars learn QE research techniques, meet potential collaborators, and get feedback on work in progress.

A significant number of the submissions to ICQE this year were the direct result of activities organized by the QE community. Collectively, they reflect the impressive range and depth of scholarship that the QE community is producing, and also the new collaborations and research directions that have been fostered by the events described above.

This volume contains the proceedings of the Second International Conference on Quantitative Ethnography (ICQE20), and it continues the conversation begun at ICQE19 about the affordances, challenges, and potential of applying unified methods to qualitative data. We received 56 submissions, which were each evaluated by two primary reviewers and one meta-reviewer from the conference's international Program Committee using a double-blind review process. Based on this review process, we accepted 28 papers for inclusion in this, the second volume of Advances in Quantitative Ethnography.

The contributions in this volume come from diverse fields and perspectives, and consist of empirical studies as well as methodological and theoretical advances. Collectively, these papers exemplify the advantages of using QE methods and techniques to understand human thought, behavior, and interaction in a number of different domains and contexts, as well as the ways in which scholars are wrestling with the challenges—both practical and philosophical—of unifying ethnography and statistics, human interpretation and machine processing.

As with ICQE19, our goal for ICQE20 was to facilitate a discussion of quantitative ethnography as a field of research, to support continued development of the QE community, and to address fundamental questions about how to make meaning from large sets of rich qualitative data. We have thus organized both the conference and these proceedings so as to promote meaningful intellectual engagement and maximize opportunities for scholars with different interests and backgrounds to interact—through the papers collected here, and at the conference through paper and poster presentations, symposia, workshops, panels, and keynotes that represent both the state of the art and future directions for scholarship in quantitative ethnography.

We believe that the papers included in this volume, and the content of the conference more generally, represent the breadth and depth of current scholarship in quantitative ethnography and also the development of a community of researchers eager to share ideas, resources, and inspiration—even when they cannot do so in person.

January 2021

A. R. Ruis
Seung B. Lee

Organization

Program Committee Chairs

Andrew R. Ruis   University of Wisconsin-Madison, USA
Seung B. Lee   Pepperdine University, USA

Program and Conference Committee Members

Golnaz Arastoopour Irgens   Clemson University, USA
Ryan Baker   University of Pennsylvania, USA
Simon Buckingham Shum   University of Technology Sydney, Australia
Brendan Eagan   University of Wisconsin-Madison, USA
Danielle Espino   Pepperdine University, USA
Moira Faul   University of Geneva, Switzerland
Karin Frey   University of Washington, USA
Eric Hamilton   Pepperdine University, USA
Sarah Jung   University of Wisconsin-Madison, USA
Adam Lefstein   Ben-Gurion University of the Negev, Israel
Leanne Ma   University of Toronto, Canada
Nadine Melzner   Technical University of Munich, Germany
Morten Misfeldt   University of Copenhagen, Denmark
Toshio Mochizuki   Senshu University, Japan
Larry Nucci   University of California, Berkeley, USA
Jun Oshima   Shizuoka University, Japan
Vitaliy Popov   University of Michigan, USA
Daniel Spikol   Malmö University, Sweden
Barbara Wasson   University of Bergen, Norway
David Williamson Shaffer   University of Wisconsin-Madison, USA
Bian Wu   East China Normal University, China
Szilvia Zörgő   Semmelweis University, Hungary

Conference Management Team

Alex George   University of Wisconsin-Madison, USA
Hyunju Park Johnson   University of Wisconsin-Madison, USA
Karen Hill   University of Wisconsin-Madison, USA

Contents

Theory and Methodology

Scoping the Emerging Field of Quantitative Ethnography: Opportunities, Challenges and Future Directions

Rogers Kaliisa[1]([⊠]) [iD], Kamila Misiejuk[2] [iD], Golnaz Arastoopour Irgens[3] [iD], and Morten Misfeldt[4] [iD]

[1] Department of Education, University of Oslo, Oslo, Norway
rogers.kaliisa@iped.uio.no
[2] Centre for the Science of Learning and Technology, University of Bergen, Bergen, Norway
Kamila.Misiejuk@uib.no
[3] Department of Education and Human Development, Clemson University, Clemson, South Carolina, USA
garasto@clemson.edu
[4] Department of Computer Science, University of Copenhagen, Copenhagen, Denmark
misfeldt@ind.ku.dk

Abstract. Quantitative Ethnography (QE) is an emerging methodological approach that combines ethnographic and statistical tools to analyze both Big Data and smaller data to study human behavior and interactions. This paper presents a methodological scoping review of 60 studies employing QE approaches with an intention to characterize and establish where the boundaries of QE might and should be in order to establish the identity of the field. The key finding is that QE researchers have enough commonality in their approach to the analysis of human behavior with a strong focus on grounded analysis, the validity of codes and consistency between quantitative models and qualitative analysis. Nonetheless, in order to reach a larger audience, the QE community should attend to a number of conceptual and methodological issues (e.g. interpretability). We believe that the strength of work from individual researchers reported in this review and initiatives such as the recently established International Society for Quantitative Ethnography (ISQE) can present a powerful force to shape the identity of the QE community.

Keywords: Quantitative Ethnography · Epistemic network analysis

1 Introduction

The increasing use of technology in many areas of society and life has led to an increasing amount of Big Data about human behavior and interaction [1]. However, this volume of data is usually too large and strains the capabilities of human interpretation and the traditional social science research approaches. In response to this challenge, a number of theoretical and methodological approaches have been suggested. Quantitative ethnography (QE) [2], is one of these approaches, and is the focus of this paper. QE links the

© Springer Nature Switzerland AG 2021
A. R. Ruis and S. B. Lee (Eds.): ICQE 2021, CCIS 1312, pp. 3–17, 2021.
https://doi.org/10.1007/978-3-030-67788-6_1

power of statistics with the power of in-depth, ethnographic approaches, and examines both "Big data" and smaller data sets to understand the breadth of human behavior [3]. QE varies from other approaches to big data analysis with its focus on validity and the linkages and consistency between quantitative models and qualitative analysis, both of which are sound on their own, and both of which are attending to the same mechanisms at work in the same set of data. Simply put, unlike the traditional mixed-methods approach, QE brings two broad approaches to fair sampling together into a single solution of research techniques other than two separate but related analyses. Thus, providing researchers with a thicker and richer description of the data as it yields quantifiable information about the network and visualization of discourse over time for individuals and groups [4]. The result is a more unified mixed-methods approach that uniquely links qualitative and quantitative approaches to data by treating them as two sides of the same coin and results in a valid and robust understanding of human behavior [5].

This paper reports the first scoping review of research that employs QE approaches and techniques to study human behavior and interaction. A scoping review is a process of summarizing a range of evidence in order to convey the breadth and depth of a field [6]. This approach has been reported as appropriate for reviewing educational research across a range of domains, particularly those 'breaking new ground' [7] as is the case with QE. In the following sections, we provide a brief description of the central conceptual and theoretical underpinnings of QE, research questions, review methodology, presentation and discussion of findings, and future directions of the QE approach.

2   Theoretical Foundations of QE

The QE methodology is grounded in several theoretical and epistemological assumptions. For example, QE is based on the premise that any culture of learning is characterized by a Discourse (with a big D) which [8] defines as a particular way of "talking, listening, writing, reading, acting, interacting, believing, valuing, and feeling" (p. 25) within some community. In this regard, the notion of "Big 'D' Discourse" sets a larger context for the analysis of "discourse" (with a little "d"), which describes how people interact (e.g. the flow of language-in-use across time and the patterns and connections across this flow of language) [8]. Moreover, for researchers to characterize learning and behavior and make sense of Discourse, they derive codes (with a small c) and Codes (with a big C). Using this parallel terminology, a Code is the culturally relevant meaning of some action or an interpretation of something that happens, while a code is a warrant to justify the claims made based on a discourse (e.g. the things a group of people could say as evidence for that interpretation) [2]. However, in order to create Thick Descriptions, QE seeks to find connections between the different Codes into what [9] calls 'Cultures' which consist of symbols that interact to form a web of meanings. It is from this background that QE researchers are interested in modelling Codes in their data to see how they are systematically related to one another in a broader Discourse. In addition, QE researchers tend to make use of existing theories to explain the observed phenomena and to close the interpretive loop by making it possible to search for understanding in a corpus of data, selection of appropriate analytic methods and the interpretation of a model against the original data [10].

3 Tools and Techniques of QE

QE uses a range of conceptual and practical tools for sensibly analyzing big data and human behavior. One common tool used for the model specification is Epistemic Network Analysis (ENA), a network analysis technique for analyzing the structure of connections among coded data by quantifying and modeling the co-occurrence of codes. The co-occurrences are modeled as dynamic, weighted node-link networks. Such networks can be compared visually and statistically, allowing for comparisons between groups or samples. The tool also allows the researcher to view the original qualitative data to close the interpretative loop. ENA stems from the operationalization of epistemic frame theory, a learning theory that models learning as ways of thinking, acting, and being in the world of some community of practice [11]. This theory suggests that any community of practice has a culture and that culture has a grammar, a structure composed of skills, knowledge, identity, values and epistemology, which forms the epistemic frame of the community [12]. Using ENA, researchers analyze the development of learners' epistemic frames by modeling connections in student discourse [13] and measuring the co-occurrence of concepts within the conversations, topics, or activities that take place during learning [11, 12].

Beyond ENA, the QE community has continued to develop new tools that align with the epistemological assumptions of QE. For example, to support inter-rater reliability (IRR), [16] developed a statistic called Shaffer's rho to improve on the measurement of percent agreement and to reach valid theoretical saturation. Moreover, to aid QE researchers with the coding of large datasets, [17] developed nCoder, a tool that helps researchers to discover and code key concepts in text data with minimum human judgements and as a theoretical warrant that their codes were theoretically saturated. Moreover, to deal with the shortcomings of existing tools, QE researchers have developed additional tools. For example, to address the presence of false negatives due to codes that occur infrequently, [18] recently created nCoder+, which is an add-on to nCoder equipped with a semantic component that helps to solve low recall. [19], developed the Reproducible Open Coding Kit (ROCK) a tool that eases manual coding of QE data sets, while [20] suggested a multimodal matrix approach to support the modeling of QE data.

4 Purpose of this Scoping Review and Research Questions

To the best of our knowledge, there are no studies that have mapped the landscape of QE to characterize this emerging field and how it differs from traditional qualitative, quantitative, and mixed methods approaches. Thus, in this methodological review, we identified and mapped the available evidence and the current progress and trends in the emerging approach of QE. We argue that a scoping review of QE studies is needed (i) to characterize and conceptualize the existing body of work, and establish where the boundaries of QE might and should be in order to develop the identity of the field; and to (ii) identify the opportunities, challenges and future directions of the QE approach. Against this background, the research questions in this study are:

1. Which research areas (e.g. learning sciences) and settings (e.g. educational situations) have been investigated using QE approaches.

2. What are the methodological characteristics (e.g. data, tools, visualizations, coding, and analysis) of studies employing QE approaches?
3. How are studies employing QE theoretically grounded (e.g. what theoretical approaches are commonly used) and what role does theory play in QE studies?

5 Methodology

The methodological framework of undertaking a scoping review by [6] and used in previous scoping reviews [21] underpinned this review. The review followed the following five stages: (i) identifying the research questions (ii) identifying relevant studies; (iii) study selection; (iv) charting data; (v) collating, summarizing and reporting results. To identify relevant studies, we used the following digital sources: ProQuest; ERIC; Web of Science; Scopus; Google Scholar; Science Direct; and PubMed. In addition, we performed manual searching through reference lists of some QE papers, as well as conference proceedings (e.g. the International Conference on Learning Analytics & Knowledge [LAK], and the first International Conference on Quantitative Ethnography [ICQE]). The search string used was "Quantitative Ethnography" OR "Epistemic Network Analysis" OR "ncoder" OR "ncoder+". The initial search resulted in 1,231 studies that were filtered based on our inclusion criteria (e.g. study applies QE as defined by Shaffer, presents empirical findings and published in English between 2009 and April 2020). The screening was based on titles, abstracts and full-text skimming, and began on 1 February 2020 until 30 April 2020. The final dataset included 60 papers: 34 conference papers and 26 journal articles (see appendix I, and others indicated by * in the reference list). Editorials, theoretical papers, and posters were excluded from the analysis but where applicable, these have been used in the background and discussion of the empirical studies.

The coding was performed through several stages. Initially, two coders took a grounded approach and reviewed 10 studies for training purposes and to gain familiarity with the literature. In this case, initial codes were formed based on the descriptions and contextual information provided in the papers. Next, each of the coders independently coded a further 10 papers and then discussed coding challenges to refine the coding scheme. As other QE researchers [22], we used social moderation where two raters coded all the papers and then discussed all the areas where ratings differed until an agreement was reached. Finally, the coders split the papers and proceeded with coding the full sample following the revised codes. We undertook a narrative analysis of the identified studies using individual papers as the unit of analysis. We tabulated the included studies to provide an overview of the different codes. The full coding details can be found at [https://onedrive.live.com/view.aspx?resid=E3B64EB830502E3E!119&ith int=file%2cxlsx&authkey=!Ao6IIVyrsFLIcgI].

6 Results

6.1 Descriptive Information of Included Studies

The 60 studies included in this review consist of conference papers (n = 34) and journal articles (n = 26) published by 9 different conferences and 18 journals. The analysis also showed that the number of studies employing QE approaches has been growing steadily between 2009 and 2020 with a significant spike of studies in 2019 (n = 28) (Fig. 1). This is partly explained by the fact that the first international conference on QE was held in October 2019 [23], which resulted in an increase, in the number of QE studies. The steady increase in both conference and journal publications imply that the field is maturing and reaching a larger audience. The findings further revealed that QE studies are generally applying small sample sizes with most papers (n = 44) having a sample size of less than 100. Only six studies had a sample size between 100–1000 participants, yet only one study had a sample size higher than 1000 participants did. Nine papers were not explicit with the actual sample size

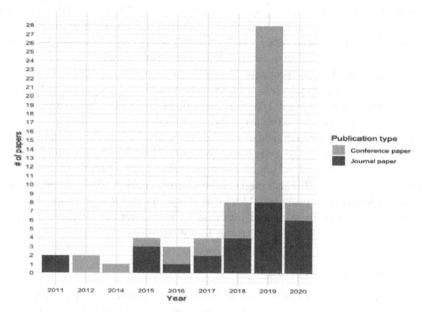

Fig. 1. The trend and type of QE publications

6.2 Discipline and Contextual Diversity in QE

The coding showed that the bulk of current QE studies are overwhelmingly within the learning sciences (n = 53) and specifically in domains such as engineering education; science education; teacher education; collaborative learning; educational and epistemic games; language learning; and learning design. Beyond the learning sciences, six studies were from the health sciences in domains such as surgery [15], medicine [24] and care transitions [25]. The review found one study within the behavioral sciences [14], which examined adolescents' self-evaluative emotions and judgements towards aggression. Overall, studies employing QE draw on a diverse range of research fields, which could imply that QE caters to the sensitivity of different ontologies and worldviews.

The findings showed that formal learning settings (n = 31) such as university (n = 21) and K-12 (n = 10), are a major site for QE research. These are closely followed by studies conducted in informal settings (n = 27) such as work-place learning environments, online/virtual learning environments including simulations and games, and social media sites. Non-formal settings were only represented in one study [40]. These findings suggest that QE is broadening its reach across different settings beyond formal educational organizations and gaining attention in other contexts, such as informal learning settings.

6.3 Text and Non-text Data Sources in QE Studies

The coding revealed that the most frequently utilized types of data were online discussion forums (n = 19) mainly used to gain insights into students' cognitive presence; interviews (n = 10) used to get a sense of the emic codes that people in a culture use to make sense of the world; and Third-party data (n = 10) such as gaming environments/simulations used to evaluate students' learning products. The other forms of data used but less prominent include audio (n = 6) and video (n = 3); assessment (n = 3) such as grades, and pre-post test scores; institutional data (n = 2) such as lesson plans from LMSs; observation (n = 2); as well as reflection journals, literature review, social media interaction data, eye tracking, students essays and survey each used in one study respectively. Overall, QE studies utilize a number of sources of data to study human behavior. Nonetheless, it is surprising that observation, which is one of the key ethnographic data collection approaches, was used by only two QE studies. This area might require further consideration to strengthen the study of human behavior using QE. Moreover, it was noted that most of the data used in QE studies are originally text-based (discussion forums), yet other non-text data such as videos are always converted to text forms for QE analysis.

6.4 Common Coding Approaches

Coding of the data is an essential part of the QE process since it "should accurately reflect something that is meaningful in the discourse" [26]. The articles in this review were coded by the following aspects of the coding process: 1) Coding type: approaches to data coding (top-down, bottom-up, hybrid); 2) Data coding: techniques used for data coding (automated, manual, mixed); 3) Raters: number of human and non-human raters coding and/or validating the data; 4) Coding validation: methods used to validate the coding scheme.

The most popular coding type method is top-down coding, that is, using predefined codes to code the data, used by 25 articles. Eighteen articles used bottom-up coding, where codes emerge from the data. Eleven articles used hybrid coding that combines both top-down and bottom-up coding methods. Six articles did not specify their coding type.

In 30 articles, a human or humans coded the data manually. Three articles used qualitative data analysis software, MAXQDA, for manual coding. Eighteen articles coded their data automatically: using Latent Dirichlet Allocation (LDA) (n = 2), agent identification system (n = 1), BeGaze software that annotates gaze targets (n = 2), nCoder (n = 5), or an automated coding algorithm similar to nCoder (n = 7). [27] used topic modeling, word frequencies and n-grams to develop the codes used for the automated data coding with nCoder, while [28] used a mixed-method (manual + automated) approach. First, two human coders manually coded for cognitive presence, and then, LDA was applied to detect topics in the discussion messages. Eleven articles did not specify the data coding method.

Twenty-six articles coded and/or validated their codes with the help of two human raters. Another popular method was two human raters + machine adopted by 10 articles, while five articles relied only on automated methods. Two papers coded and/or validated their data by four raters. [29] used nine raters, whereas [30] used only one rater.

The most popular statistics used to validate the codes was Cohen's kappa reported in 30 articles. Shaffer's rho was reported in nine articles. [31] used Krippendorff's alpha. [32] and [33] mentioned using interrater reliability without specifying the exact statistics applied. Two papers used social moderation to validate their codes, while one paper used verbal agreement. [34] reported accuracy as their validation measure. Twenty-three papers did not specify their coding validation method. Overall, 30 articles specified all the aspects (coding type, data coding, raters, and validation methods), which constitutes only 50% of all papers included in this literature review. Two articles did not report any aspects of their coding process (Fig. 2).

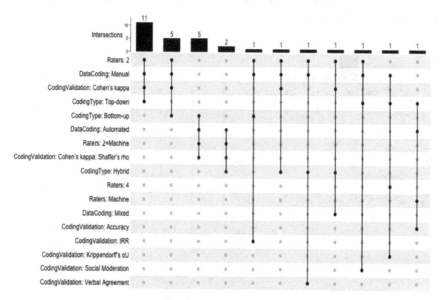

Fig. 2. Coding patterns.

The most popular coding pattern is manual top-down coding validated by two raters using Cohen's kappa (n = 11), and a variation of this pattern, where the coding is bottom-up (n = 5). Another popular pattern is automated bottom-up coding, where the codes are validated by two raters and a machine, and reporting Cohen's kappa and Shaffer's rho as validation statistics (n = 5). Two papers used hybrid automated coding validated by two raters and a machine using Cohen's kappa and Shaffer's rho. The main finding is that only half of the papers reported on all steps of the coding and the coding validation process. Moreover, we discovered two main patterns of data coding: 1) two raters would manually code the data using either bottom-up or top-down method and validate the coding with Cohen's Kappa; 2) data would be automatically coded using either bottom-up or top-down method, and validated by two raters and the machine by applying Shaffer's rho and Cohen's Kappa.

6.5   ENA as a Dominant Analysis Method in QE Studies

All articles included in this literature review used ENA as one of their data analysis methods, and 31 articles used ENA as their only data analysis method. To complement the ENA findings, 12 articles used descriptive statistics, whereas eight articles reported both descriptive and inferential statistics. [35] used ENA in combination with cluster analysis and descriptive statistics. [36] applied Principal Component Analysis and descriptive statistics in addition to ENA. ENA and time series were used by both [37] in combination with descriptive statistics, and [38], who visualized the time series with a CORDTRA diagram. Some articles compared the insights gained by using ENA to other data analysis methods. [39] compared ENA and process mining, and complemented the analysis with descriptive statistics. [29] used both ENA and time series (FRIEZE representation) to analyze temporal patterns (Fig. 3).

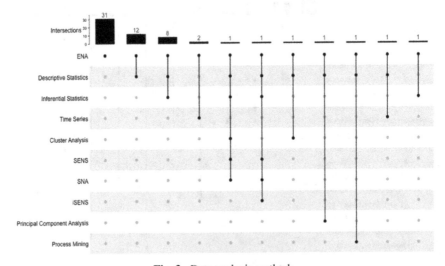

Fig. 3. Data analysis methods.

[40] did innovative work trying to expand ENA with social network analysis (SNA) to develop social and epistemic network signature (SENS). They also applied descriptive statistics, inferential statistics, and cluster analysis in their study. Building upon their findings, [41] compared ENA, SNA, SENS and social-epistemic network signature (iSENS) by using inferential statistics – hierarchical linear models – and descriptive statistics, such as effect size (Cohen's d). In summary, most papers use only ENA as their

data analysis method. Other papers complemented ENA with other methods, compared ENA to other methods, or tried to expand ENA by using other methods.

6.6   The Dynamics of Theory Integration in QE Studies

Theory plays a crucial role in QE by supporting the selection of relevant variables, development and interpretation of models, and converting those interpretations to meaningful and scientifically justified actions. The coding in this study revealed 44 studies that either used a theoretical framework (n = 36) or/and some disciplinary concepts (n = 11) to frame the research and in some cases support the coding, and interpretation of the results. In addition, the analysis revealed 16 studies, which were atheoretical. That is, the studies were not explicitly linked to any specific theoretical framework meaning that they took a data-driven approach. Of those studies that used theoretical frameworks, they mainly grounded their research in the epistemic frame theory (n = 14) which was used as an approach to conceptualize and characterize the structure of connections that students make among elements of authentic practice [42]. The next most used theoretical frameworks were the collaborative learning framework (n = 10); Engineering design thinking (n = 4); the community of inquiry framework (n = 3) and projective reflection (n = 4).

The analysis further revealed that the role played by the theoretical frameworks varied. Some studies used the frameworks as a basis to position their work and as a lens to interpret their findings but did not use them for coding. For example, [33] used epistemic frames to explore the relationship between beginning readers' Dialog about their thinking and ability to self-correct oral reading. However, the author took a more grounded approach to the segmentation of the data without necessarily using epistemic frame elements as [43] did. On the other hand, some QE studies used theoretical frameworks in an inductive way by using theoretical insights as a basis to support the filtering of data to develop relevant codes and later for closing the interpretative loop. For example, [44] used the community of inquiry framework as an analytical lens to understand the association between the individual phases of cognitive and social presences in communities of inquiry and at the same time, used the same framework to code the presence or absence of each dimension and to make sense out of the resulting models. Moreover, it was noticed that in some QE studies the theoretical frameworks are neither strictly deductive nor inductive, but represent a combination of both. In other words, theory was used as an analytical lens and for the development of codes but in combination with data-driven approaches. For example, [27] used a computational thinking-STEM taxonomy as a guiding framework but at the same time employed thematic analysis to identify student-constructed computational thinking practices that fit under the broader taxonomy categories. In sum, the findings suggest that QE is not aligned to a single theoretical perspective, but rather underpinned by different theoretical outlooks. In addition to employing a diverse catalog of perspectives, QE researchers also use theoretical frameworks to inform various stages of the analytical process.

7 Discussion

This methodological review was set out to map the available evidence and trends in the emerging approach of QE with an intention to characterize and establish the boundaries of QE in order to shape the identity of the field. First, in relation to RQ1 on research fields and settings of QE implementation, the findings indicated that QE researchers are overwhelmingly associated with the learning sciences. The findings also noted that QE is slowly being adopted in other fields such as health and behavioral sciences. Consequently, the majority of QE studies are implemented within formal educational settings but with a steady increase in other contexts such as informal and non-formal settings. The diversity of research fields and settings imply that QE is broadening its reach and caters to the sensitivity of different ontologies, worldviews, and contexts, something that provides hope for the future of this emerging field.

Second, in response to RQ2, which identified the methodological characteristics of QE studies, findings revealed that QE studies utilize a number of data sources to study human behavior with discussion forums, interviews and Third-party data from virtual learning environments being the most common. However, only two QE studies used observation as a source of data for QE analysis, despite this being one of the key ethnographic data collection approaches and a key premise of QE. More importantly, even though QE provides tools for analysis of Big data, currently few QE studies have analyzed Big data from platforms such as Twitter with most studies relying on data from very small sample sizes which could lead to challenges of drawing conclusions and integrating statistical approaches on too little ethnographic data as also noted by [2]. This implies that any conclusions made from QE studies employing small samples are limited to that of the sample population, which could affect the application of QE at scale, yet an indication of maturity of research and applied methods relates to the scale of the studies in research and practice [45]. Moreover, it was noted that most of the data used in QE studies are originally text-based (discussion forums), yet other non-text data such as videos are always converted to text forms for QE analysis. This raises a question as to whether QE data always need to be in a text form for analysis to take place. Therefore, given the increasing use of non-text data in QE studies, the QE community should develop tools specific to non-text data to avoid the possibility of describing such data as *what it is not* rather than *what it is*.

In addition, only half of the papers in this review reported on all steps of the coding and the coding validation process. This is despite the emphasis that QE places on data coding and validation [46]. Of those papers that did report on the coding process, two main patterns of data coding emerged: 1) a traditional approach in which two raters manually coding the data and validating the coding with Cohen's Kappa; 2) as recommended in the QE foundational book [2], using automated classifiers to code the data that would be validated against two raters and the machine by applying Shaffer's rho and Cohen's Kappa. Though the bottom-up approach to coding is central to grounded analysis that plays a significant role in QE, articles in our literature review apply different coding approaches depending on the context.

Moreover, even though QE is positioned as a field encompassing ENA, we found few mentions of QE in the papers with more emphasis being on ENA. For example, only two papers described QE as a field [34, 47]. Five papers mentioned QE while describing the ENA method, whereas other 53 papers do not mention QE at all, though they usually cite [2]. This suggests a conflation between QE as a broader methodological approach and ENA as a tool used within QE. Perhaps, this is one area where the QE community should be more explicit as it strives to build an identity.

Lastly, in response to RQ3 on the theoretical grounding of QE studies, the findings revealed that the majority of QE studies integrated theory in their research practice. However, even though some QE papers highlight theoretical frameworks, they were not used to inform the analysis and interpretation of results. Moreover, 16 studies were entirely atheoretical which can lead to different, but equally troubling analytical weaknesses in QE since researchers may lack critical distance from the data and merely report findings based on preconceived notions and categories of discourse [10]. This may result in making macro-level claims that are not well supported by data and identifying emic concepts from the bottom-up without necessarily defining a set of categories in advance. In sum, since the definition of QE emphasizes the use of statistical techniques with the interpretive power of qualitative and grounded analysis to warrant claims about the quality of thick description, a hybrid approach as that taken by [27] who concurrently used a theoretical framework and thematic analysis to support the framing, coding and interpretation of data could be a better approach for QE researchers to promote coherence and ensure validity.

8   Implications and Conclusions

Overall, it is possible to conclude from this study that most of the QE researchers study human behavior in line with Shaffer's definition of QE. There is an observed effort among QE researchers to ensure the validity of their codes through IRR, model development and closing the interpretive loop. The review identified that most studies have a strong focus on validity and the linkages and consistency between quantitative models and qualitative analysis without necessarily treating them as separate. This is a promising trend towards the development of an identity for the QE community.

Nonetheless, our premise in this paper is that, as a new field trying to develop an identity, QE researchers need to attend to a number of conceptual and methodological issues. First, the over dominance of ENA in QE studies at the expense of QE could limit the clear understanding and development of the QE community if overshadowed by one of its tools of analysis. It is, therefore, necessary that QE researchers put the principles of QE at the center of their research before introducing the specific tools of analysis. In addition, the papers reviewed for this paper suggests that the QE field has yet to define the standards, which would indicate the identity of the field. For example, even though the key principle of QE is to ensure 'validity', some QE studies still pay little attention to providing explicit details regarding the coding and validation processes. We argue that this is one of the areas where QE researchers should place more attention. Moreover, as a way to extend the QE methodology to a larger audience, it is important for the QE community to attend to technical aspects such as attendability and interpretability since some of the tools and outputs from QE analysis currently require sophisticated mathematical reasoning and prior experience and training in both qualitative and statistical analysis [48]. One possible approach is to develop simple tools with an interface as those suggested by [49] and [50] that support the sharing of QE outputs with the broader public to encourage uptake of QE in other fields of practice that are inherently less quantitative. We believe that the strength of work from individual researchers reported in this review and initiatives such as the recently established International Society for Quantitative Ethnography (ISQE) can present a powerful force to shape the identity of the QE community.

Appendix I

List of studies included in the scoping review but not cited in the main text (n = 36)

Authors	Authors
Andrist, Collier, Gleicher, Mutlu, Shaffer (2015)	Orrill, Shaffer (2012)
Andrist, Ruis, Shaffer (2018)	Peters-Burton (2015)
Arastoopour Irgens, Shaffer, Swiecki, Ruis, Chesler (2015)	Peters-Burton, Parrish, Mulvey (2019)
Arastoopour Irgens, Shaffer (2015)	Phillips, Kovanović, Mitchell, Gašević (2019)
Barany, Foster (2019)	Ruis, Rosser, Nathwani, Beams, Jung, Pugh (2019)
Bressler, Bodzin, Eagan, Tabatabai (2019)	Ruis, Rosser, Quandt-Walle, Nathwani, Shaffer, Pugh (2018)
Brown, Nagar, Orrill, Weiland, Burke (2016)	Ruis, Siebert-Evenstone, Pozen, Eagan, Shaffer (2019)
Cai, Eagan, Dowell, Pennebaker, Shaffer, Graesser (2017)	Shah, Foster, Talafian, Barany (2019)
Chesler, Ruis, Collier, Swiecki, Arastoopour Irgens, Shaffer (2015)	Siebert-Evenstone, Shaffer (2019)
Csanadi, Eagan, Shaffer, Kollar, Fischer (2017)	Sinclair, Ferreira, Gašević, Lucas, Lopez (2019)
Espino, Lee, Van Tress, Baker, Hamilton (2020)	Sung, Cao, Ruis, Shaffer (2019)
Fisher, Hirshfield, Siebert-Evenstone, Arastoopour Irgens, Koretsky (2016)	Talafian, Shah, Barany, Foster (2019)
Fougt, Siebert-Evenstone, Eagan, Tabatabai, Misfeldt (2018)	Wakimoto, Sasaki, Hirayama, Mochizuki, Eagan, Yuki, Kato (2019)
Foster, Shah, Barany, Talafian (2019)	Whitelock-Wainwright, Tsai, Lyons, Kaliff, Bryant, Ryan, Gašević (2020)
Knight, Arastoopour Irgens, Shaffer, Buckingham Shum, Littleton (2014)	Wooldridge, Carayon, Shaffer, Eagan (2018)
Lim, Dawson, Joksimović, Gašević (2019)	Yi, Lu, Leng (2019)
Nachtigall, Sung (2019)	Yue, Hu, Xiao (2019)
Oner (2020)	

References

1. Brown, B., Chui, M., Manyika, J.: Are you ready for the era of 'big data'. McKinsey Q. **4**(1), 24–35 (2011)
2. Shaffer, D.W.: Quantitative Ethnography. Cathcart Press, Madison (2017)

3. Wu, B., Hu, Y., Ruis, A., Wang, M.: Analysing computational thinking in collaborative programming: a quantitative ethnography approach. J. Comput. Assist. Learn. **35**(3), 421–434 (2019)

4. Shaffer, D.W., Collier, W., Ruis, A.: A tutorial on epistemic network analysis: analyzing the structure of connections in cognitive, social, and interaction data. J. Learn. Anal. **3**(3), 9–45 (2016)

5. Misfeldt, M., Spikol, D., Bruun, J., Saqr, M., Kaliisa, R., Ruis, A., Eagan, B.: Quantitative ethnography as a framework for network analysis–a discussion of the foundations for network approaches to learning analysis. In: LAK 2010 Companion Proceedings (2020)

6. Levac, D., Colquhoun, H., O'Brien, K.K.: Scoping studies: advancing the methodology. Implement. Sci. **5**(1) (2010). https://doi.org/10.1186/1748-5908-5-69

7. Munn, Z., Peters, M.D., Stern, C., Tufanaru, C., McArthur, A., Aromataris, E.: Systematic review or scoping review? Guidance for authors when choosing between a systematic or scoping review approach. BMC Med. Res. Methodol. **18**(1) (2018). https://doi.org/10.1186/s12874-018-0611-x

8. Gee, J.P.: Discourse, small d, big D. In: Tracy, K., Sandel, T., Ilie, C. (eds.) The International Encyclopedia of Language and Social Interaction, pp. 1–5 (2015)

9. Geertz, C.: Deep play: notes on the Balinese cockfight. In: Crothers, L., Lockhart, C. (eds.) The Interpretation of Cultures. Selected Essays, pp. 412–453. Palgrave Macmillan, New York (1973)

10. Wise, A.F., Shaffer, D.W.: Why theory matters more than ever in the age of big data. J. Learn. Anal. **2**(2), 5–13 (2015)

11. Shaffer, D.W., Ruis, A.R.: Epistemic network analysis: a worked example of theory-based learning analytics. In: Lang, C., Siemens, G., Wise, A.F., Gašević, D. (eds.) Handbook of Learning Analytics, pp. 175–187. Society for Learning Analytics Research (2017)

12. Rupp, et al.: Modeling learning progressions in epistemic games with epistemic network analysis: principles for data analysis and generation. In: LeaPS 2009 Proceedings (2009)

13. Arastoopour Irgens, G., Shaffer, D.W.: Measuring social identity development in epistemic games. In: CSCL 2013 Proceedings, pp. 42–48 (2013)

14. Frey, K.S., Kwak-Tanquay, S., Nguyen, H.A., Onyewuenyi, A.C., Strong, Z.H., Waller, I.A.: Adolescents' views of third-party vengeful and reparative actions. In: ICQE 2019 Proceedings, pp. 89–105 (2019)

15. D'Angelo, A.L.D., Ruis, A.R., Collier, W., Shaffer, D.W., Pugh, C.M.: Evaluating how residents talk and what it means for surgical performance in the simulation lab. Am. J. Surg. **220**(1), 37–43 (2020)

16. Eagan, B.R., Rogers, B., Pozen, R., Marquart, C., Shaffer, D.W.: rhoR: Rho for inter-rater reliability (Version 1.1.0) (2016)

17. Shaffer, D.W., et al.: The nCoder: A Technique for Improving the Utility of Inter-Rater Reliability Statistics. Epistemic Games Group Working Paper 2015-01 (2015)

18. Cai, Z., Siebert-Evenstone, A., Eagan, B., Shaffer, D.W., Hu, X., Graesser, A.C.: nCoder+: a semantic tool for improving recall of nCoder coding. In: ICQE 2019 Proceedings, pp. 41–54 (2019)

19. Zörgő, S., Peters, G.J.Y.: Epistemic network analysis for semi-structured interviews and other continuous narratives: Challenges and insights. In: ICQE 2019 Proceedings, pp. 267–277 (2019)

20. Buckingham Shum, S., Echeverria, V., Martinez-Maldonado, R.: The Multimodal Matrix as a quantitative ethnography methodology. In: ICQE 2019 Proceedings, pp. 26–40 (2019)

21. Major, L., Warwick, P., Rasmussen, I., Ludvigsen, S., Cook, V.: Classroom dialogue and digital technologies: a scoping review. Educ. Inf. Technol. **23**(5), 1995–2028 (2018)

22. Espino, D., Lee, S., Eagan, B., Hamilton, E.: An initial look at the developing culture of online global meet-ups in establishing a collaborative, STEM media-making community. In: CSCL 2019 Proceedings, pp. 608–611 (2019)

23. Eagan, B., Misfeldt, M., Siebert-Evenstone, A. (eds.): Advances in Quantitative Ethnography: First International Conference, ICQE 2019, Madison, WI, USA, 20–22 October 2019, Proceedings, vol. 1112. Springer Nature (2019)

24. Sullivan, S., et al.: Using epistemic network analysis to identify targets for educational interventions in trauma team communication. Surgery **163**(4), 938–943 (2018)

25. Wooldridge, Abigail R., Haefli, R.: Using epistemic network analysis to explore outcomes of care transitions. In: Eagan, B., Misfeldt, M., Siebert-Evenstone, A. (eds.) ICQE 2019. CCIS, vol. 1112, pp. 245–256. Springer, Cham (2019). https://doi.org/10.1007/978-3-030-33232-7_21

26. Shaffer, D.W.: Big data for thick description of deep learning. In: Millis, K., Long, D., Magliano, J., Wiemer, K. (eds.) Deep Comprehension, pp. 265–277. Routledge, New York (2018)

27. Arastoopour Irgens, G., et al.: Modeling and measuring high school students' computational thinking practices in science. J. Sci. Educ. Tech. **29**(1), 137–161 (2020)

28. Ferreira, R., Kovanović, V., Gašević, D., Rolim, V.: Towards combined network and text analytics of student discourse in online discussions. In: AIED 2018 Proceedings, pp. 111–126 (2018)

29. Lund, K., Quignard, M., Shaffer, D.W.: Gaining insight by transforming between temporal representations of human interaction. J. Learn. Anal. **4**(3), 102–122 (2017)

30. Nash, P., Shaffer, D.W.: Mentor modeling: the internalization of modeled professional thinking in an epistemic game. J. Comput. Assist. Learn. **27**(2), 173–189 (2011)

31. Bauer, E., et al.: Using ENA to analyze pre-service teachers' diagnostic argumentations: a conceptual framework and initial applications. In: Eagan, B., Misfeldt, M., Siebert-Evenstone, A. (eds.) ICQE 2019. CCIS, vol. 1112, pp. 14–25. Springer, Cham (2019). https://doi.org/10.1007/978-3-030-33232-7_2

32. Hu, S., Torphy, K.T., Chen, Z., Eagan, B.: How do US teachers align instructional resources to the common core state standards: a case of Pinterest. In: SMSociety 2018 Proceedings, pp. 315–319 (2018)

33. Pratt, S.M.: A mixed methods approach to exploring the relationship between beginning readers' dialog about their thinking and ability to self-correct oral reading. Read. Psychol. **41**(1), 1–43 (2020)

34. Karumbaiah, S., Baker, R.S., Barany, A., Shute, V.: Using epistemic networks with automated codes to understand why players quit levels in a learning game. In: Eagan, B., Misfeldt, M., Siebert-Evenstone, A. (eds.) ICQE 2019. CCIS, vol. 1112, pp. 106–116. Springer, Cham (2019). https://doi.org/10.1007/978-3-030-33232-7_9

35. Peters-Burton, E.E.: Outcomes of a self-regulated learning curriculum model. Sci. Educ. **24**(7–8), 855–885 (2015)

36. Swiecki, Z., Ruis, A.R., Farrell, C., Shaffer, D.W.: Assessing individual contributions to collaborative problem solving: a network analysis approach. Comput. Hum. Behav. **104** 105876 (2020)

37. Zhang, S., Liu, Q., Cai, Z.: Exploring primary school teachers' technological pedagogical content knowledge (TPACK) in online collaborative discourse: an epistemic network analysis. Br. J. Educ. Technol. **50**(6), 3437–3455 (2019)

38. Siebert-Evenstone, A., Arastoopour Irgens, G., Collier, W., Swiecki, Z., Ruis, A.R., Shaffer, D.W.: In search of conversational grain size: Modelling semantic structure using moving stanza windows. J. Learn. Anal. **4**(3), 123–139 (2017)

39. Melzner, N., Greisel, M., Dresel, M., Kollar, I.: Using Process Mining (PM) and Epistemic Network Analysis (ENA) for Comparing Processes of Collaborative Problem Regulation. In: Eagan, B., Misfeldt, M., Siebert-Evenstone, A. (eds.) ICQE 2019. CCIS, vol. 1112, pp. 154–164. Springer, Cham (2019). https://doi.org/10.1007/978-3-030-33232-7_13
40. Gašević, D., Joksimović, S., Eagan, B.R., Shaffer, D.W.: SENS: network analytics to combine social and cognitive perspectives of collaborative learning. Comput. Hum. Behav. **92**, 562–577 (2019)
41. Swiecki, Z., Shaffer, D.W.: iSENS: an integrated approach to combining epistemic and social network analyses. In: LAK 2010 Proceedings, pp. 305–313 (2020)
42. Bagley, E., Shaffer, D.W.: Epistemic mentoring in virtual and face-to-face environments. In: ICLS 2012 Proceedings, pp. 256–260 (2012)
43. Svarovsky, G.N.: Exploring complex engineering learning over time with epistemic network analysis. J-PEER **1**(2), 4 (2011)
44. Rolim, V., Ferreira, R., Lins, R.D., Gašević, D.: A network-based analytic approach to uncovering the relationship between social and cognitive presences in communities of inquiry. Internet High. Educ. **42**, 53–65 (2019)
45. Ognjanović, I., Gašević, D., Dawson, S.: Using institutional data to predict student course selections in higher education. Internet High. Educ. **29**, 49–62 (2016)
46. Shaffer, D.W.: QE-COVID data challenge. Why QE? [White paper]. (2020). https://sites.google.com/wisc.edu/qe-covid-data-challenge/why-qe
47. Wu, B., Hu, Y., Ruis, A., Wang, M.: Analysing computational thinking in collaborative programming: a quantitative ethnography approach. J. Comput. Assist. Learn. **35**(3), 421–434 (2019)
48. Swiecki, Z., Shaffer, D.W.: Toward a taxonomy of team performance visualization tools. In: ICLS 2018 Proceedings, pp. 144–151 (2018)
49. Swiecki, Z., Marquart, C., Sachar, A., Hinojosa, C., Ruis, A.R., Shaffer, D.W.: Designing an Interface for sharing quantitative ethnographic research data. In: ICQE 2019 Proceedings, pp. 334–341 (2019)
50. Herder, T., et al.: Supporting teachers' intervention in students' virtual collaboration using a network based model. In: LAK 2008 Proceedings, pp. 21–25 (2018)

Using Topic Modeling for Code Discovery in Large Scale Text Data

Zhiqiang Cai$^{(\boxtimes)}$ (ID), Amanda Siebert-Evenstone (ID), Brendan Eagan (ID),
and David Williamson Shaffer (ID)

University of Wisconsin-Madison, Madison, WI 53706, USA
zhiqiang.cai@wisc.edu

Abstract. When text datasets are very large, manually coding line by line becomes impractical. As a result, researchers sometimes try to use machine learning algorithms to automatically code text data. One of the most popular algorithms is topic modeling. For a given text dataset, a topic model provides probability distributions of words for a set of "topics" in the data, which researchers then use to interpret meaning of the topics. A topic model also gives each document in the dataset a score for each topic, which can be used as a non-binary coding for what proportion of a topic is in the document. Unfortunately, it is often difficult to interpret what the topics mean in a defensible way, or to validate document topic proportion scores as meaningful codes. In this study, we examine how keywords from codes developed by human experts were distributed in topics generated from topic modeling. The results show that (1) top keywords of a single topic often contain words from multiple human-generated codes; and conversely, (2) words from human-generated codes appear as high-probability keywords in multiple topic. These results explain why directly using topics from topic models as codes is problematic. However, they also imply that topic modeling makes it possible for researchers to discover codes from short word lists.

Keywords: Coding · Grounded coding · A priori coding · Automatic coding · Grounded theory · Qualitative analysis · Quantitative analysis · Latent semantic analysis · Topic modeling · Code discovery

1 Introduction

One of the most important steps in a quantitative ethnographic analysis is linking evidence to meaning. In general, coding is an analytic process that searches for relevant features within a dataset and assigns meaning to a given piece of evidence [8, 29]. There are both many traditions of coding as well as many ways that researchers engage in the process of coding. Researchers may generate codes from data, theory, or a literature review of a field. In this process, researchers engage in a number of steps and make many decisions. For example, in a single analysis, researchers make decisions about the underlying data including choosing, cleaning, segmenting, assigning meta data, and other choices that affect the resulting data and codes. Further, researchers perform many

© Springer Nature Switzerland AG 2021
A. R. Ruis and S. B. Lee (Eds.): ICQE 2021, CCIS 1312, pp. 18–31, 2021.
https://doi.org/10.1007/978-3-030-67788-6_2

operations on a code or a set of codes including identifying, naming, organizing, categorizing, aggregating or disaggregating, refining, validating, and applying the codes. Throughout this process, the ultimate goal of coding is to engage in a rigorous procedure to warrant a meaningful story about the data [33].

The process of developing codes thus depends on reading data deeply; this is what allows researchers to discover what is happening in a given context. However, this process is quite difficult and time-consuming [24]. Machine algorithms, in contrast, can read data quickly and discover patterns that researchers may have missed. However, machine algorithms read data without understanding its meaning deeply, and thus may produce codes that don't describe the data in useful ways [32].

Fundamentally, we argue that because coding is a process of searching for *meaningful* patterns in data, it may be best suited by combining the talents of humans and machines. In this paper, we explore the iterative process of identifying and developing codes. Then we explore how machine learning methods can supplement code discovery and refinement rather than replace meaning-based processes of coding.

2   Background

2.1   What are Meaningful Patterns?

Building on the idea of *thick description*, or explanations of action in terms of their socially-situated meanings, Geertz (1973) argues that, fundamentally, data analysis "is sorting out the structures of signification" and then "determining their social ground and import" (p. 9) [17]. Consequently, researchers sort and interpret their observations to discover what is happening in a given context, in light of how participants would understand and describe it. As Ryle and Geertz [17, 31] argue, one common way to engage in this process is by creating codes.

Many researchers may employ a *grounded approach* to coding: intensively reading and rereading qualitative data to discover and construct theory and codes from it [18, 32]. Researchers engage in a rigorous and systematic search for meaning [25] to find *patterns*, where some phenomenon repeats in a predictable way. Only by finding and comparing such patterns can a researcher begin to identify and distinguish codes.

Many factors influence how a researcher makes sense of data. Each researcher brings a different set of experiences and identities to their work, which may help them find certain descriptions and miss or disregard others. To address this problem, a common heuristic for developing codes is to start by describing each line of data, which, as Charmaz argues, "helps you to refrain from inputting your motives, fears or unresolved personal issues to your respondents and to your collected data" (p. 37) [10].

A grounded coding process iterates through open, axial, and selective coding. *Open coding*, or coding line by line, breaks down data to identify preliminary concepts. These early descriptions provide the basis for future interpretations [33]. Next, researchers begin making connections between ideas while comparing concepts and categories during *axial coding*. In this step, there is more emphasis on identifying features and conditions that may explain what is happening or provide contextual information. Interpretations become clearer during *selective coding* where researchers build a conceptual framework to understand the relationships among the codes.

Successful coding, then depends of researchers' ability to construct interpretations and build meaningful models. But that ability, in turn, depends on the ability to find systematic patterns in data, and in this aspect of coding, computers are often much more efficient than human coders. A machine can quickly go through a large volume of data to identify patterns or group similar patterns together.

At the same time, the machine learning algorithms often used for such pattern finding suffer from different problems. Chen and colleagues [11] outlined various challenges in using machine learning for qualitative data analysis: such methods are often unable to build useable models, use decontextualized features, require large amounts of data and in some cases prelabeled data, and tend to perform better on high frequency codes in comparison with more sparse codes. Thus, a machine learning approach to pattern-finding may not result in good codes or interpretations of data: patterns may be systematic, but they may not be meaningful.

In this paper, we argue that good storytelling, and thus good coding, requires identifying meaningful patterns in your data. By combining the systematic pattern-finding abilities of computers with the human ability for meaning-making, we explore how researchers can combine qualitative data analysis with machine-learning to discover codes and refine our coding process.

2.2 Computer-Facilitated Coding

Large scale text-based data is increasingly easier to find. In the field of education, large scale text data is often collected from online learning environments, such as MOOCS [14, 22, 28, 36–38], intelligent tutoring systems [1, 6, 9, 19], virtual internship systems [12, 13, 35], and others.

Broadly speaking, two classes of computational tools have been developed to help researchers code large scale data. One class of tools copy manual, paper-and-pencil-based processes into a screen-and-mouse environment. Manual coding systems such as NVIVO and MAXQDA support coding through better data organization, quicker data navigation, more convenient ways of highlighting data segments, and visual displays of the coding process and results. While it is more convenient to use such tools then paper-and-pencil, researchers still have to go through the data line-by-line to mark all possible instances of a code.[1] Coding systems like the Reproducible Open Coding Kit [27] help users prepare and annotate data for future modeling, including data that was manually coded using one of the systems listed above.

A second class of computational approaches includes tools such as the nCoder [8, 15] and LightSide [23], which augment the coding process by introducing statistical and machine-learning tools. In the next section we explore how this class of tools affects the coding process by describing the functionality of nCoder.

2.3 Coding and Validating Through nCoder

nCoder is a tool that helps researchers develop, validate, and apply automated classifiers to their data. It uses an active machine learning approach aimed at maximizing the impact

---

[1] Some of these systems also include rudimentary keyword-based searches to support coding.

of human coding expertise while minimizing the researchers' effort. nCoder has been used in analyses in an array of fields including studies of engineering [2], naval warfare teams [34] as well as on a variety of data types, such as chat logs [12], interviews [21], and training session transcripts [30]. nCoder augments the coding process in 4 important ways.

1. *nCoder scaffolds the generation of classifiers.* As in traditional qualitative analyses, a researcher names and defines conceptual ideas or patterns. Users then create a procedural (algorithmic) definition of a given code using *regular expressions* (regexes): words, word stems, or more complex patterns of words. For example, a user interested in how students define ideas may search for "definition", look for all words that contain the stem "defin", or explicitly search for words that start with "defin" but do not include the common colloquialism "definitely": ^(?!definitely)*\bdefin. Next, nCoder provides data samples taken from a training set for the rater to use as a guide when they apply and revise their regexes.

2. *nCoder modifies the coding process by changing the way data is sampled.* Specifically, nCoder draws a test set of size n from the holdout set using a conditional sampling method called *base rate inflation*. nCoder randomly selects items one at a time and codes them. Selection and coding continue until $20\% \times n$ of the items match one of the regexes for the code. These positively coded items are added to the test set. Then nCoder randomly selects an additional $80\% \times n$ items, codes them, and adds them to the test set. This ensures that even with small test sets and/or low frequency codes, raters will see instances that represent the concept being coded. Once the human rater has coded the test set and inter-rater reliability has been computed, the test set items are added to a training set for users to refine the regexes.

3. *nCoder provides a three-way validation process to ensure that codes are both procedurally and conceptually valid.* This coding process involves three raters – two human raters and a machine rating codes using regex matching. One human rater starts the coding process by defining codes. For each code, the rater creates a classifier for the code by specifying a set of regexes. The human rater then codes a test set to see whether or not the examples of the code that were found using the regexes match their understanding of that concept. Cohen's kappa is calculated between the human rater and the machine establishing reliability or procedural validity. After achieving validity for this procedural definition of the code, the rater measures their agreement about the code with a second rater, establishing conceptual validity. Only when all three raters are in agreement by achieving an acceptable kappa and rho (described next), the classifier is validated.

4. *nCoder calculates Shaffer's ρ to warrant interrater reliability of codes on a large dataset from small test sets.* Shaffer's ρ is a Monte Carlo rejective method that tests whether an interrater reliability statistic is over a given threshold at a specified α level [15, 32]. That is, Shaffer's ρ tests whether it is possible to claim that the population κ is above some threshold τ based on the κ value in a test set.

These features allow a researcher to use nCoder to manually code a small amount of data and develop reliable and valid classifiers to automatically code large scale data.

2.4 Using Topic Modeling for Code Development

While existing tools help researchers *code* their data, they may lack the power of discovering *potential codes* in large scale data. Advances in *machine learning* and *natural language processing* (NLP) make it possible to automatically discover patterns that humans cannot see in data, or specific instances of existing codes that humans might miss. Topic modeling [5, 7] is one of the most popular NLP methods for automated coding. Topic modeling uses a large corpus of data to generate groups of words, called *topics*, each of which is represented by a probability distribution assigned to the words in the data. The words with highest probabilities are used to interpret the "meaning" of the found topics, where we put meaning in quotation marks to indicate that this is a post-hoc description, assigned by a researcher, to one of the groups of words identified by the topic model. Topic modeling also assigns *topic proportion scores* to each document which are often used as non-binary codes.

The problem is that topics from topic modeling are not always easy to interpret and topic model-based coding is hard to validate. There has been research comparing human coding with topic model based coding [3, 4, 26]. But while the goal of such studies is to improve topic interpretability, no study has been able to match human coding well enough that human coding can be replaced. Topic modeling was originally designed to be a *generative method* to help researchers find and describe what is in large numbers of text documents [5]. That is, it was intended to help surface underlying and undiscovered patterns in data. However, as Bakharia [3] and others argue topic modeling only produces "buckets of words" that may not help researchers tell meaningful stories.

However, the fact that topic models cannot replace human coders does not mean the method has no role to play in developing meaningful codes. Researchers have identified several ways that topic modeling could a "valuable aids within the quantitative ethnography process" (p. 297) [3]. In this study, we use topic modeling as a discovery tool for researchers to identify and refine codes and then develop reliable and validated classifiers to code data. Our work is closely related to the nCoder coding process. We ask:

RQ1: Are human created codewords (words that match the regexes) grouped by topics? This question asks whether or not a set of code words for a given code appear together at the top (sorted by probability from high to low) of a single topic.
RQ2: Do high-probability keywords in topics include codewords identified by human coders? This question asks whether or not human created codewords emerge at the top of the topics (not necessarily grouped together).

To answer these questions, we used two existing datasets for which researchers have established and validated regex-based coding classifiers through nCoder. We then ran topic models on the same datasets and find human created codewords that appear as high-probability words within the topics identified.

3 Methods

3.1 Data

Our study examined two existing datasets. The first dataset was from a study by Ruis and colleagues (2019), which we will refer to as the *medical dataset* [30]. Their study investigated the use of procedural simulation in continuing medical education short course. The study included 58 surgeons who participated in a one-day course on laparoscopic inguinal and ventral hernia repair. Participants were assigned to groups based on their reported experiences. Their group discussions were recorded and transcribed. The transcribed data was coded with six codes (see Table 1), which were defined based on ethnographic observations and conventional content analysis. Regex-based classifiers were created and validated through the nCoder tool. Table 1 shows the definition of the codes, the number of codewords involved, and the validation results.

Table 1. Definition and validation of codes in the medical dataset

Code	Description	Codewords (74)	Human 1 vs Human 2	Human 1 vs Computer	Human 2 vs Computer
			κ*	κ*	κ*
REAL WORLD CASE	Referencing real bodies, patients, or other cases	8	0.80	0.95	0.73
MESH REPAIR	Referencing mesh, tacking, or suturing	27	1.00	1.00	0.97
GENERAL ANATOMY	Referencing the anatomy of the abdomen	12	1.00	1.00	0.96
PATHOLOGICAL ANATOMYA	Referencing the anatomy of a hernia	27	0.95	0.98	1.00
REQUSTING ADVICE	Asking what surgeons should do in a given situation	–	0.86	0.86	0.75
TROUBLE- SHOOTING	Managing or negotiating complications	–	0.85	0.89	0.80

* All kappas are statistically significant for $\rho(0.65) < 0.05$.

The second dataset was collected from the engineering virtual internship Nephrotex which we will refer to as the *engineering dataset* [12,·13, 16]. The data was collected

Table 2. Definition and validation of codes in the engineering dataset

Code	Description	Codewords (232)	Human 1 vs Human 2 κ^*	Human 1 vs Computer κ^*	Human 2 vs Computer κ^*
TECH CONSTRAINTS	Referring to inputs: material, processing method, surfactant, and CNT %	33	0.96	1.00	0.96
PERFORMANCE PARAMETERS	Referring to attributes: flus, blood cell reactivity, marketability, cost, or reliability	87	0.88	0.93	0.84
COLLABORATION	Facilitating a joint meeting or the production of team design products	13	0.76	0.87	0.76
REDESIGN REASONING	Referring to design and development prioritization, tradeoffs, and design decisions	33	0.89	0.86	0.84
DATA	Referring to or justifying decisions based on numerical values, results tables, graphs, research papers, or relative quantities	34	0.94	0.9	0.89
REQUESTS	Referring to or justifying decisions based on internal consultant's requests or patient's health or comfort	32	0.88	0.94	0.94

* All kappas are statistically significant for $\rho(0.65) < 0.05$.

from novice engineering design teams participating in an educational simulation. Previous analyses of the engineering dataset used nCoder to develop and validate six codes and regex-based classifiers. Table 2 shows the definition of the six codes, number of codewords, and the validation results.

3.2 Extracting Codewords

Codewords for both sets were extracted by matching the words in the dataset with the regex-based classifiers. For the medical dataset, the codes "Requesting Advice" and "Trouble-shooting" were removed because they used multiple word classifiers. From the remaining four codes, a total of 74 codewords were found in the data (see Table 1). For the engineering dataset, all six codes were used in this study. The code "data" matched many numbers which were excluded from the codeword list. A total of 232 codewords were found (see Table 2).

3.3 Generating Topic Models

We used the LDA function in the R package *topicsmodels* [20] to create topic models. The models depend on several parameters which has impact to the performance of the models. However, we were interested in seeing how well topic modeling works with non-optimal choices, as these are the parameters most likely to be chosen by expert coders who are not expert topic modelers. Thus, instead of optimizing performance, we chose to construct a *naïve topic model*, meaning a model with choices that are reasonable and easy to implement.

Document Segmentation. The average size of the documents and the total number of documents are two competing parameters in tension with one another. On one hand, larger document size results in more accurate probability estimation within documents. On the other hand, larger numbers of documents result in better probability estimation across documents. Data lines can thus be split or merged to get the optimal balance of average document size and number of documents. We chose to use the lines of data without alteration as documents input to the topic model.

Word Filtering and Word Lemmatizing. Word exclusion and lemmatizing are two standard practices in topic modeling. *Word exclusion* leaves out commonly occurring words such as conjunctions, articles, and prepositions. We used word exclusion by removing standard function words (of, the, in, etc.). *Lemmatizing* converts words into their root or *lemma form*: for example. *Chairs* becomes *chair*, *seeing* becomes *see*, etc. However, we used the original words rather than their lemmatized form because lemmatizing is time intensive, particularly when the computational power is limited and data size is large.

Number of Topics. Researchers often struggle to determine an appropriate number of topics when trying to optimize a topic model. We chose 10 topics for both models for practical considerations. Ten is larger than the number of codes (4 for medical and 6 for engineering) we were investigating, we anticipated that some subset of topics could represent the different codes. Ten topics was also small enough for us to easily review for this study.

Based on these choices, topic models were generated for the medical and engineering datasets. For each topic in each model, a word list was generated by sorting the words in the topic by word probabilities and choosing the top 15.

4   Results

Table 3 shows the top 15 keyword lists for the topics in the medical dataset. The highlighted words are codewords developed with human input using nCoder. Four different colors represent the four different codes. Similarly, Table 4 shows top 15 keyword lists for topics from the engineering dataset, with six different colors representing six different codes.

Table 3. Codewords in top 15 topic words for the medical dataset

n	T 1	T 2	T 3	T 4	T 5	T 6	T 7	T 8	T 9	T 10
1	yeah	ll	inaudible	mesh	pull	camera	ah	defect	ve	left
2	don	suture	alright	tack	mesh	balloon	don	mesh	hernia	hand
3	bit	cut	sac	sutures	hard	space	uh	close	patient	feel
4	move	grab	mhm	don	guys	port	peritoneum	midline	inguinal	model
5	yup	hold	push	positioning	ten	lateral	um	time	costal	cooper
6	pretty	needle	laughs	tacks	roll	start	lot	size	margin	dissect
7	angle	measure	didn	position	twenty	trocar	real	hole	repair	scope
8	knife	wall	supposed	tacking	nice	incision	stuff	people	ventral	yep
9	finger	abdominal	easier	system	centimeters	oblique	vas	top	lap	fat
10	lower	bring	white	correct	fifteen	rectus	vessels	tie	patients	scissors
11	trouble	spinal	guy	flat	meshes	perfect	easy	bigger	bowel	thirty
12	table	mesh	cord	fixation	pulling	medial	direct	leave	haven	tacker
13	glove	coming	ring	people	middle	trocars	epigastric	grasper	omentum	ahead
14	knot	mark	demonstrates	stay	makes	external	tapp	piece	lot	pubis
15	spot	inside	guess	bit	centimeter	internal	fascia	tension	laparoscopically	won

Color codes: real word case | mesh repair | general anatomy | pathological anatomy

Table 4. Codewords in the top 15 topic words for engineering dataset.

n	T 1	T 2	T 3	T 4	T 5	T 6	T 7	T 8	T 9	T 10
1	consultants	flux	batch	steric	surfactant	list	guys	notebook	prototype	shared
2	prototype	reliability	team	cnt	steric	notebook	im	task	1	space
3	prototypes	cost	design	phase	agree	internship	yeah	submit	cost	write
4	material	marketbility	attach	vapor	hindering	entry	process	alex	2	information
5	internal	bcr	submit	process	surfactants	alex	report	email	prototypes	posted
6	meet	reactivity	testing	prototype	choice	questions	padma	notebooks	3	notebook
7	test	blood	notebook	surfantant	negative	check	time	due	design	consultants
8	agree	cell	team's	dry	graph	deliverable	manufacturing	complete	met	internship
9	design	low	prototype	hindrance	performed	submitted	alan	5	4	alex
10	results	rate	rest	20	charge	nephrotex	guess	team	5	time
11	decide	11	option	jet	attributes	deliverables	rudy	submitted	pmma	meeting
12	cosultant	lower	specifications	material	cost	summary	supposed	send	agree	michelle
13	attributes	lowest	results	2	research	submit	meeting	time	choices	analysis
14	requirements	43.33	time	pespvp	meeting	clicking	5	forget	standards	engineering
15	5	pmma	prototypes	10	hydrophilic	email	hey	deliverable	attributes	similar

Color codes: tech constraints | performance | collaboration | design decisions | data | requests

4.1 RQ1: Are Codewords Grouped by Topics?

In an ideal topic grouping each topic keyword list should contain either no codewords or only codewords from the same code. In practice, if a list contains a large proportion of codewords from a single code, the topic could represent that code well.

For the medical dataset (see Table 3) the topic T_4 contains the largest proportion of codewords: 40% of the 15 most probable words for the topic are from the code MESH REPAIR. Other topics contain smaller proportions of codewords from any single code.

In the engineering dataset the performance of the topic model on this criterion is even worse. No topic has more than 27% of the 15 most probable words from a single code.

Thus, in both cases, topic keyword lists only contain a small proportion of codewords from a single code; most of the most probable topic keywords are either not codewords for any code, or codewords from multiple codes. This suggests that naïve topic modeling does not do a good job of identifying clusters of codewords.

4.2 RQ2: Do High-Probability Topic Keywords Include Human Identified Codewords?

From Table 3 and Table 4, we see that for both datasets, every code has at least 2 codewords included in the most probable words across all topics. This suggests that these naïve topic models identify some codewords from all of the human-identified codes.

5 Discussions

The goal of this study is to investigate whether or not topic modeling could help in discovering codes. That is, assuming that a researcher does not already have a set of codes in mind, could a naïve topic model help to discover useful codes to describe the data?

The common practice of using topic modeling is to "label" the topics by reviewing the top keywords. Our study shows that, topic keywords do not group together words that from classifiers that humans developed using traditional approaches to code identification. Thus "labelled" topics from topic modeling are unlikely to replicate codes that a human would identify as meaningful. Using topics as codes, then, may result in misleading conclusions.

However, our results did show a different potential use for topic modeling in code identification. Although the topic modeling keyword lists cannot be used as codes, they may provide keywords that could be used for code discovery.

In our study, all human identified codes had far more codewords included in the keyword lists than would be likely due to chance alone. For example, the code REAL WORLD CASE had 8 codewords in the medical dataset. The medical dataset had 4581, unique words, so the likelihood of choosing a codeword that indicates a REAL WORLD CASE is 8/4581 = 0.17% or 1 in 573. We examined 10 lists of 15 keywords for the medical dataset. At chance we would expect to find $150 \times 0.17\% = 0.26$ codewords that indicate a REAL WORLD CASE. In fact, we found two such codewords—that is, codewords for a REAL WORLD CASE were 8 times more likely than at random. Moreover, the 150 high-probability keywords from the topic model identified 27 codewords from the human-identified codes—that is, 18% of the keywords were meaningful for codes in the dataset. This, in turn, suggests that the high-probability keywords from a topic model provide a good source of words that a human coder should consider investigating as possible keywords for codes.

Whether or not a code can be actually found through these codewords is still a problem. It depends on how sensitive a researcher is to the codewords and how strong the codewords signal a code to the researcher examining them. The topic keyword lists could be more useful if the actual data containing the keywords could be easily reviewed. A *topic modeling utility* could create a naïve topic model and let a researcher click on a keyword to see sample of data lines that contain it. The data lines may provide much richer information about whether a particular keyword is a clue to a meaningful code.

This work has the obvious limitation of only investigating two datasets with validated regex classifiers. Also, we deliberately chose naïve topic models. It is possible that other algorithms could be developed to improve topic model performance by automatically choosing more effective parameters for a non-technical user, or using more sophisticated supervised topic modeling. Finally, the work here is based on *post hoc* analysis of codewords as they appear in topic keywords. Future work needs to examine the conversion rate of topic keywords to new codes.

These limitations notwithstanding, this work confirms previous findings that topic modeling is not a good substitute for human coding; however, it also suggests that topic modeling can potentially supplement manual and automated coding methods by helping researchers discover potential keywords for new codes or to augment existing codes.

Acknowledgements. The research was supported by the National Science Foundation (DRL-1661036, 1713110; LDI-1934745), the Wisconsin Alumni Research Foundation, and the Office of the Vice Chancellor for Research and Graduate Education at the University of Wisconsin-Madison. The opinions, findings, and conclusions do not reflect the views of the funding agencies, cooperating institutions, or other individuals.

References

1. Anderson, J.R., Corbett, A.T., Koedinger K.R., Pelletier, R.: Cognitive tutors: lessons learned. J. Learn. Sci. (1995). https://doi.org/10.1207/s15327809jls0402_2
2. Arastoopour, G.I.: Connected design rationale: modeling and measuring engineering design learning. Unpublished Doctoral Dissertation. University of Wisconsin-Madison (2017)
3. Bakharia, A.: On the equivalence of inductive content analysis and topic modeling. In: Eagan, B., Misfeldt, M., Siebert-Evenstone, A. (eds.) ICQE 2019. CCIS, vol. 1112, pp. 291–298. Springer, Cham (2019). https://doi.org/10.1007/978-3-030-33232-7_25
4. Baumer, E.P.S., Mimno, D., Guha, S., Quan, E., Gay, G.K.: Comparing grounded theory and topic modeling: extreme divergence or unlikely convergence? J. Assoc. Inf. Sci. Technol. **68**(6), 1397–1410 (2017). https://doi.org/10.1002/asi.23786
5. Blei, D.M., Ng, A.Y., Jordan, M.I.: Latent Dirichlet allocation. J. Mach. Learn. Res. **3**, 993–1022 (2003)
6. Cai, Z., Graesser, A.C., Hu, X.: ASAT: AutoTutor script authoring tool. In: Sottilare, R., Graesser, A.C., Hu, X., Brawner, K. (eds.) Design Recommendations for Intelligent Tutoring Systems: Authoring Tools, pp. 199–210. Army Research Laboratory, Orlando (2015)
7. Cai, Z., Li, H., Hu, X., Graesser, A.C.: Can word probabilities from LDA be simply added up to represent documents? In: Proceedings of the 9th International Conference on Educational Data Mining, pp. 577–578 (2016)
8. Cai, Z., Siebert-Evenstone, A., Eagan, B., Shaffer, D.W., Hu, X., Graesser, A.C.: nCoder+: a semantic tool for improving recall of nCoder coding. In: Eagan, B., Misfeldt, M., Siebert-Evenstone, A. (eds.) ICQE 2019. CCIS, vol. 1112, pp. 41–54. Springer, Cham (2019). https://doi.org/10.1007/978-3-030-33232-7_4
9. Cai, Z., et al.: Trialog in ARIES: user input assessment in an intelligent tutoring system. In: Proceedings of the 3rd IEEE International Conference on Intelligent Computing and Intelligent Systems, pp. 429–433 (2010). https://doi.org/10.13140/2.1.4284.5446
10. Charmaz, K.: Constructing Grounded Theory: A Practical Guide Through Qualitative Analysis. SAGE, Thousand Oaks (2006)
11. Chen, N.: Challenges of applying machine learning to qualitative coding. In: ACM SIGCHI Workshop on Human-Centered Machine Learning (2016)
12. Chesler, N.C., Ruis, A.R., Collier, W., Swiecki, Z., Arastoopour, G., Shaffer, D.W.: A novel paradigm for engineering education: virtual internships with individualized mentoring and assessment of engineering thinking. J. Biomech. Eng. **137**(2), 1–8 (2015). https://doi.org/10.1115/1.4029235

13. D'Angelo, C., Arastoopour, G., Chesler, N., Shaffer, D.W.: Collaborating in a virtual engineering internship. In: Connecting Computer-Supported Collaborative Learning to Policy and Practice: CSCL 2011 Conference Proceedings - Short Papers and Posters, 9th International Computer-Supported Collaborative Learning Conference (2011)

14. Dowell, N.M., et al.: Modeling learners' social centrality and performance through language and discourse. In: Educational Data Mining – EDM 2015, pp. 250–257 (2015)

15. Eagan, B.R., Serlin, R., Ruis, A., Arastoopour, G., Shaffer, D.W.: Can we rely on IRR? Testing the assumptions of inter-rater reliability. In: CSCL 2017 Proceedings, Cim, pp. 529–532 (2017)

16. Eagan, B.R., Swiecki, Z., Farrell, C., Shaffer, D.W.: The binary replicate test: determining the sensitivity of CSCL models to coding error. In: Computer-Supported Collaborative Learning Conference, CSCL (2019)

17. Geertz, C.: The Interpretation of Cultures. Basic Books, New York (1973)

18. Glaser, B.G., Strauss, A.L.: The Discovery of Grounded Theory: Strategies for Qualitative Research. Aldine de Gruyter, New York (1967)

19. Graesser, A.C.: Conversations with AutoTutor help students learn. Int. J. Artif. Intell. Educ. **26**(1), 124–132 (2016). https://doi.org/10.1007/s40593-015-0086-4

20. Grün, B., Hornik, K.: Topicmodels: an R package for fitting topic models. J. Stat. Softw (2011). https://doi.org/10.18637/jss.v040.i13

21. Hardy, M.: Career Interview with Ian Shaw. Qualitative Social Work. (2019). https://doi.org/10.1177/1473325017727342

22. Liu, M., et al.: Understanding MOOCs as an emerging online learning tool: perspectives from the students. Am. J. Dist. Educ. (2014). https://doi.org/10.1080/08923647.2014.926145

23. Mayfield, E., Adamson, D., Rosé, C.P.: LightSide Researcher's Workbench (Version 2.1.2)[Computer Software]. LightSide, Pittsburgh (2013)

24. Miles, M.B., Huberman, A.M.: Qualitative Data Analysis (Second Edition) (1994)

25. Ngulube, P.: Qualitative data analysis and interpretation: systematic search for meaning. In: Addressing Research Challenges: Making Headway for Developing Researchers (2015)

26. Nikolenko, S.I., Koltsov, S., Koltsova, O.: Topic modeling for qualitative studies. J. Inf. Sci. 1–15 (2015). https://doi.org/10.1177/0165551515617393

27. Peters, G., Zörgő, S.: Introduction to the Reproducible Open Coding Kit (ROCK). Psyarxiv (2019). https://doi.org/10.31234/osf.io/stcx9

28. Rezaei, E., Zavaraki, E.Z., Hatami, J., Abadi, K.A., Delavar, A.: The effect of MOOCs instructional design model based on students' learning and motivation. Man in India. **97**, 115–126 (2017)

29. Miles, M.B., Huberman, A.M., Saldana, J.: Qualitative Data Analysis: A Methods Sourcebook. SAGE, Thousand Oaks (2019)

30. Ruis, A.R., Rosser, A.A., Nathwani, J.N., Beems, M.V., Jung, S.A., Pugh, C.M.: Multiple uses for procedural simulators in continuing medical education contexts. In: Eagan, B., Misfeldt, M., Siebert-Evenstone, A. (eds.) ICQE 2019. CCIS, vol. 1112, pp. 211–222. Springer, Cham (2019). https://doi.org/10.1007/978-3-030-33232-7_18

31. Snowdon, P.F.: What Is Le Penseur Really Doing? In: Dolby, D. (ed.) Ryle on Mind and Language. PD, pp. 116–125. Palgrave Macmillan UK, London (2014). https://doi.org/10.1057/9781137476203_7

32. Shaffer, D.W.: Quantitative Ethnography. Cathcart Press, Madison (2017)

33. Strauss, A., Corbin, J.: Basics of qualitative research: techniques and grounded theory procedures for developing grounded theory. (1998). https://doi.org/10.2307/328955

34. Swiecki, Z., Ruis, A.R., Gautam, D., Rus, V., Shaffer, D.W.: Understanding when students are active-in-thinking through modeling-in-context. Br. J. Edu. Technol. (2019). https://doi.org/10.1111/bjet.12869

35. Theelen, H., Willems, M.C., van den Beemt, A., Conijn, R., den Brok, P.: Virtual internships in blended environments to prepare preservice teachers for the professional teaching context. Br. J. Edu. Technol. (2020). https://doi.org/10.1111/bjet.12760
36. Wang, Y., Baker, R.: Content or platform: why do students complete MOOCs? J. Online Learn. Teach. (2015)
37. Wang, Y., Baker, R.: Grit and Intention: why do learners complete MOOCs? Int. Rev. Res. Open Dist. Learn. (2018). https://doi.org/10.19173/irrodl.v19i3.3393
38. Yousef, A.M.F., Chatti, M.A., Schroeder, Ul, Wosnitza, M., Jakobs, H.: MOOCs a review of the state-of-the-art. In: Proceedings of the 6th International Conference on Computer Supported Education – CSEDU 2014, pp. 9–20 (2014)

Epistemic Frames and Political Discourse Modeling

Eric Hamilton$^{(\boxtimes)}$ (ID) and Woodson Hobbs (ID)

Pepperdine University, Malibu, CA 90263, USA
`eric.hamilton@pepperdine.edu`

Abstract. This paper proposes an analytic framework for political discourse that takes place over digital social media. It focuses largely on hostile or acrimonious discourse and why much of that discourse should be considered dysfunctional. The framework applies principles of epistemic frame theory and quantitative ethnography to classify and investigate relationships in political discourse patterns, to situate and visualize broad discourse patterns, and to facilitate ethnographic analysis that incorporates emotion as paramount to explaining these patterns. Commentary threads following political articles from two legacy news outlets are modeled with the Epistemic Network Analysis (ENA) software tool, for purposes of illustrating the viability of a political discourse coding system for the proposed framework. The paper also introduces the constructs of discursive transactions and emotional grammars to extend the explanatory value of the proposed framework. The framework is meant to contribute to a broader dialog on functional discourse patterns, and to help researchers articulate both the spiraling nature of dysfunctional political discourse and the profound damage it inflicts on social goals of fairness, well-being, and prosperity.

Keywords: Quantitative ethnography · Epistemic network analysis · Epistemic frames · Political discourse

1 Introduction and Purpose

This paper proposes an analytic framework for political discourse that takes place over digital social media. The framework applies principles of epistemic frame theory and quantitative ethnography to classify and investigate political discourse patterns; it incorporates emotion as paramount to explaining these patterns. It defines and situates appraisal theory and emotion generation as foundational to examining how individuals contribute to political discourse, especially including acrimonious or hostile discourse.

This framework and overall approach suggest that digital social media can harm discourse significantly through inflammatory emotional provocation at the expense of constructive dialog around issues of public urgency. This suggestion corresponds to popular contemporary assessments of digital social media sites as a collective internet outrage factory [2]. Such assessments highlight the concern that current political discourse has devolved in spiraling ways that inflict profound and irreversible damage on social goals of fairness, well-being, and prosperity.

© Springer Nature Switzerland AG 2021
A. R. Ruis and S. B. Lee (Eds.): ICQE 2021, CCIS 1312, pp. 32–46, 2021.
https://doi.org/10.1007/978-3-030-67788-6_3

Dysfunctional discourse is a term that lends itself to multiple interpretations. In this context, it refers to discordant or hostile conversational threads on social media whose hostility is traceable to the discordance already present in the thread or in the broader discourse it represents. That is, it is hostility related to discourse rather than to underlying substance. Dysfunctional discourse minimizes the substantive importance of public debate issues, directing the attentional cycles those issues require in a deliberative democracy with attention to conflict maintenance tasks such as responding to defending or attacking others.

Acrimonious political discourse, of course, did not begin with the Internet. It has a long and colorful history in the US [5], but the advent of digital social media has fundamentally altered the underlying conditions of discourse significantly [6]. This in part may be due to the heavy attraction and often addictive nature of screen-mediated content, and to the related rapid feedback that is often associated with such content [7]. Additionally, political division and tribalism increase social media viewership and thus incentivize greater financial returns, both for social media organizations and individual social media influencers. The extraordinary capital flows associated with the ubiquity of and attention to social media can reasonably be implicated as an intrinsic accelerant to social division [8, 9].

This paper and the framework it proposes do not tease out such factors. In a political landscape reeling from discord, however, they are noted as part of a larger intention of this paper that may be likened to the use of cognitive-behavioral therapy (CBT) in clinical psychology [10]. CBT is a method to step back to recognize, dispassionately examine, and make sense of emotionally charged conflict in order to facilitate productive growth aligned with, in this context, the aspirations of a democratic and just society.

While the framework is meant to be relevant in any society that supports the free exercise of political speech, data collection as a partial illustration of application of the framework involves digital social media in the United States.

2 Four Framework Components

Figure 1 depicts four components of this analytic framework for political discourse. It includes two new constructs the paper defines (discursive transactions and emotional grammars). The subsequent sections describe each of these four components in detail.

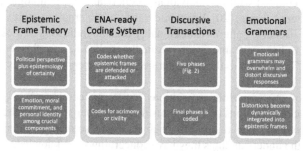

Fig. 1. Four components of proposed model for political discourse analysis.

1. ***Epistemic frame theory*** [11, 12] serves as a set of organizing principles for describing the formation and nature of an individual political belief system. The term "political epistemic frame" or simply "epistemic frame" in this paper refers to an individual's political perspective. It is a complex, dynamic, and multifaceted construct. Epistemic frame theory provides language and a means to integrate important considerations underlying political discourse, including how and why individuals build certainty, moral commitment, and personal identity [13] around their political perspectives. The terminology also invites integration of emotion as a paramount consideration in the analysis of political perspectives.

2. Epistemic frame theory naturally leads to the use of epistemic network analysis, or ENA [14–16], as a means to model discourse patterns. ENA, like any systematic approach to classifying discourse, requires a coding system (Table 1) for classifying discourse patterns. An ***ENA-ready coding system*** is the second component of this framework. Figure 3 depicts application of the coding system to a limited number of digital social media exchanges.

3. The framework's third component is a construct called a ***discursive transaction*** (Fig. 2). The construct blends epistemic frame theory with appraisal theory [17–19] from scholarship on the relationship between cognition and emotion. A discursive transaction refers to the multiphase process of assimilating political commentary or input; appraising that input as precursor to emotional and cognitive response; generating emotional response; converting emotional response into response consistent with and/or modifying the individual's political epistemic frame, and then actually representing the response (orally, via tweet, blog post, etc.).

4. Discourse coding via ENA modeling can only directly apply to the actual utterances (the final phase of discursive transactions that Fig. 2 depicts). Yet ENA models can scaffold ethnographic study of the earlier phases leading to those utterances. The framework's treatment of emotion as a paramount consideration of political discourse leads to a fourth component of ***emotional grammars*** (defined below as a cascade of emotions or responses that are perceived, appraised, and generated by the respondent) to facilitate ethnographic analysis.

3 Epistemic Frame Theory

Epistemic frame theory [11, 12] treats an individual's configuration of knowledge, skills, and experience, coupled with the individual's beliefs and epistemologies, as a unit of analysis (an epistemic frame) [20]. Epistemic frames are internal structures that can modeled by treating discourse patterns as reasonably reliable indicators of those beliefs and epistemologies. Epistemic frames were originally applied to articulate conceptual and belief systems of individuals as they acculturate to learning communities or communities of practice (e.g., [21]).

The theory of epistemic frames positions "epistemic commitments" as a blend of guiding beliefs about positions or viewpoints that can either spur or hinder academic or professional growth. Frames relating to a subject area also incorporate an individual's epistemology – the understandings they have concerning what knowledge is and how it is formed in that area.

This emphasis on individual epistemology or **understanding about knowledge** renders epistemic frame theory as especially suitable for analysis of political discourse. This paper proposes using the construct of an epistemic frame (Fig. 1) to represent an **individual's political perspective, their political beliefs, understandings, and commitments.** An individual's political epistemic frame should thus be understood as providing *an interpretive lens* both for making sense of incoming events, political information, news, arguments, and opinion, and as the basis for contributing to political discourse.

The term *epistemology* has historically referred variously to the study, understanding, or philosophy of knowledge, as a *cognitive* functionality. Several research community developments, beginning in the late 20th century, sought to blend or integrate cognition and emotion – including in 1987, with the founding of the eponymous journal *Cognition and Emotion* – in ways that are essential to investigating the highly charged and intellectually complicated world of political discourse in social media. This relatively recently explored connection and its relevance to political discourse scholarship is widely noted (e.g., [22]), especially through Affective Intelligence Theory [23]. Its two most direct applications in this proposed framework involves appraisal theory and the overload of emotional grammars in the discursive transaction construct.

4 ENA Coding for this Application

ENA provides a mathematized means of representing an individual's epistemic frame as a holistic network of beliefs and epistemologies, and particularly, the relationships between them. Relationships between elements of an epistemic frame become evident by constructing epistemic network models. The ENA software tool [24, 25] uses discourse transcripts that investigators code according to constructs of interest. Each code represents a node on a network graph; connections between the nodes represent co-occurrences of constructs in discourse segments. A limitation of any effort to apply ENA to political discourse is one that is common to all political discourse analytics: emotion considerations are essential to political discourse analysis, yet emotions are ambiguous to code, especially when converted to the written word or expressed in short social media postings. Among countless variables that can be analyzed as a part of epistemic frames, four are especially useful for discourse analysis:

4.1 Self and Identity

Epistemic frames are inextricably bound to one's sense of self and identity. It is canonical that individuals will defend a political viewpoint at almost all costs [26, 27]. The sense of self and identity does generally lead to gravitating both to individuals and to social media that share and reinforce one's political epistemic frame [26].

Threats to the tenets of one's political perspective are thus often treated in research literature as threats to one's identity [26, 27]. A lynchpin of deliberative democracy is that discourse not only gives voice, but also implies the opportunity to shift positions. The more that considering alternative viewpoints threatens identity, the less likely it is that an individual benefits from those alternative viewpoints. Dynamics referred to below – the high cost of admitting errors and insistence on the validity of one's perspective, should be considered among the most compelling factors in political discord.

Table 1. Fifteen discourse codes for political article comment threads

Affective or Emotional Description	Reference to political perspective (epistemic frame)
Acrimony (hostility, contempt, scorn, name-calling, dismissiveness, etc.)	Assertion of one's epistemic frame with no further argument. Statement of position.
Anger (hurt, sadness, fury, etc.)	Assertion against another individual's or group's epistemic frame or perspective.
Moral distancing from other persons or groups	Advancing one's epistemic frame with at least one supporting argument.
Advocacy of canceling, shunning, ostracizing (maybe a step beyond distancing)	Opposing perspective of another individual's or group's epistemic frame, with at least one supporting argument
Fear (anxiety, stress, despair, etc.)	**Political spectrum**
Irony and/or Sarcasm (usually coded with acrimony)	Perceived or stated positioning on politically left spectrum
Proactively civic (often paired with but not fully intersecting civil dialog)	Perceived or stated positioning on politically right spectrum
Civil (tone does not convey acrimony)	Position on spectrum is non-inferrable

4.2 Certitude and the Epistemology of Mutual Exclusion

A second relevant characteristic of political epistemic frames is a belief about the nature of certainty. This involves a sense that as the certainty of one's belief increases, the potential validity of opposing beliefs decreases, a judgement formed by an epistemology of mutual exclusion: two opposing things cannot be simultaneously true. In other words, as epistemic frames take form and develop internal consistency and clarity consistent with perceived or established facts, the more likely it is that opposing points of view seem less viable or morally objectionable. As a result, a reasonable explanation for why others have differing political viewpoints is that they possess some kind of moral deficiency (for example, interest in financial or political power cloaked in language to hide that interest).

4.3 Moral Distancing

An epistemology of mutual exclusion can lead to positioning of one's point of view as morally acceptable and other points of view as morally unacceptable [28, 29] (even though they may be held with similar intensity and the same level of perceived or internal coherence). This epistemology may be considered a key driver in defending one's point of view at all costs, including refusal to admit errors, and seeking to deconstruct or otherwise falsify the potential validity of opposing points of view. It manifests itself in gravitation to like-minded political outlets, scorn placed by a political community on opposing viewpoints, perceived threat to one's identity, and the very high cost of admitting error or even uncertainty. Each of these contributes pressure to avoid legitimizing opposing views with neutral analysis, which then leads to further polarization when differing views are summarily stigmatized without consideration. In social media, algorithms that monetize political controversy and division in order to increase viewership and revenue intensify the polarization vectors, which intensifies a perceived moral imperative to distance one from and to deny legitimacy to opposing views. Yet when political viewpoints are summarily delegitimized or treated as morally inferior, those who hold those points of view may reasonably be expected to find means to respond. Such polarization dynamics may contribute to the multiple and intensifying political shifts emerging in twenty-first century United States.

4.4 Emotional Grammars

The phenomenon of emotion overwhelming reason is a common part of life, though it may be expressed or described in different terminologies. Emotion research includes study of how emotions can outbalance reason in political discourse (Yu and Lin, 2015), resulting in a combination of what is referred to as emotion exaggeration and cognitive reduction. With digital social media, incoming articles or messages may trigger emotions such as outrage or fear once they are appraised, even though the appraisal may be instantaneous. Emotionally exaggerated and cognitively reduced responses, that is, responses that might realistically benefit from information processing, play a crucial role in fostering discord in this proposed analytic framework.

The construct of an emotional grammar is defined here as a sequence of cognitive appraisal of an incoming message and emotion generation to the message in order to underpin a response that may be cognitively reduced. A simple example might be hostility. When one perceives or appraises that another party communicating with them is hostile, the evolutionarily favored response is hostility. Another example might be an unfair or untruthful attack by another. This can lead to outrage and intention to inflict harm. A third example might be a fair or truthful attack, which may lead to guilt or fear, or to efforts to divert attention. Each of these examples is not meant to be determinative, but rather suggestive of emotion-rich patterns that shape how an individual contributes to political discourse.

Table 2 proposes a sample of candidate emotional grammars that might be clarified or studied as political discourse components. Some of these are intuitive; all of them have standing as themes in emotion research. The potential value of emotional grammars as a construct is that they can identify areas of dysfunctionality in discourse, especially in light of research that explores emotionally exaggerated and cognitively reduced discourse patterns [30]. As emotional grammars "pile up" in the discursive transactions described below, they may exceed an individual's allotted time or capacity to manage. This is especially the case when complex perspectives are filtered into characters-limited tweets of comment threads under short response times [23]. This may result in instinctively hostile or defensive social media contributions, contributions that skirt, scorn, or delegitimize opposing viewpoints without assessing those viewpoints fully. Importantly, an understanding of the distorting role that dysfunctional management of emotional grammars can play may help change perceptions of what issues are at stake in political discord.

Coding in the system this paper proposes will not reveal emotional grammars, but can generate models that are consistent with the grammars that emotion research would predict, such as those appearing in Table 2.

Table 2. Six sample emotional grammars

Predicate (the cognitive appraisal of incoming commentary)	→ Emotion generation and preliminary formulation of response
1. *My position (my community's position) on issue A is xyz. These are the reasons it is so. When you do not agree with me, you are disregarding the logic, factual basis, and moral appeal of my position. That is reprehensible.*	*→ You are reprehensible.*
2. *You have attacked or insulted me; you are hostile to me.*	*→ I will be hostile to you. [1]*
3. *You have claimed something about me that is unfair and untrue.*	*→ I am going to attack you in return. [3, 4]*
4. *You have claimed something about me or my beliefs that might be true but that puts me in a bad light.*	*→ I am going to attack you or divert the discussion to an area where you are vulnerable; I am going to build even more defenses to my position to make me feel better about my position, because if my position is more broadly correct, yours cannot be.*
5. *You are intentionally stating that which you know to be false.*	*→ You deserve scorn and to be attacked.*
6. *You are right or mostly right, but admitting that is too costly.*	*→ Divert attention to an area more favorable to defending my point of view.*

5 Discursive Transactions

Modeling epistemic frames entails collecting discourse samples that can then be coded to enable visual depiction and quantitative characterization of the relationships between the coded constructs. This approach is inferential, relying on the coding process and researchers' interpretations of both the samples themselves and the codes. In the case of modeling political discourse with heavy emphasis on emotion, the process is especially inferential; the semantic structure of the utterance translates into an emotion-rich and often emotionally overloaded message. More accurately, the affective intensity of social media discourse varies between and within messages in ways that are often difficult to detect from short written utterances. Yet these utterances are the only representation of sentiments that are shared in the media, and extracting the nature of what is shared is crucial to mapping political discourse in digital social media.

The framework this paper proposes includes a coding scheme for such utterances t epistemic frame theory. The coding scheme does not classify specific positions or perspectives, but as least initially, whether the utterance being coded expressed arguments supporting a particular epistemic frame or sought to falsify a generic epistemic frame the individual opposed. The scheme also sought to identify an affective valence – acrimonious or civil. Within the boundaries of intercoder reliability, these broad baseline aspects of discourse can be quantified and modeled. They can then supplement a more detailed analysis of how political discourse unfolds from an affective point of view. An overall line of inquiry of this research follows is whether affect or emotion are prominent drivers of discourse and epistemic frame development, independent of underlying political positions.

Positioning discourse utterances and the emotional dimensions of the utterances for this analysis has entailed formulation of a five-phase structure based on emotion research. This structure, referred to here as a discursive transaction, may enable clarity on if, how, or why emotion can have such an outsized and distorting effect on discourse.

Fig. 2. Five phases of a Discursive Transaction. A primary thesis of this framework is that emotion exaggeration and cognitive deprivation in Phases 3–4 lead to dysfunctional discourse. ENA modeling of discourse contribution in Phase 5 scaffolds inferences about epistemic frames in the prior phases.

Figure 2 depicts the five phases. The first involves perception of an input event such as a news report, a social media posting, or a conversation. The second phase involves appraisal of the event, by which socio-affective and cognitive faculties interpret the event through the lens of the individual's epistemic frame. Cognitive appraisal theory positions this process as the immediate precursor to emotion generation [31], the third phase. As noted elsewhere, emotion science increasingly treats cognition and emotion either as integrated mechanisms or different parts of the same mechanism that activates particular neural resources for adapting to external conditions, such as threats [31]. Whether integrated functionalities or part of the same mechanism, though, cognition and emotion are no longer treated as meaningfully separate. Appraisal theory originally bridged cognition and emotion [18, 32]. It also bridges epistemic frame theory to this study. Emotion can be regarded as a self-regulatory tool that stimulates an adaptive response that cognition modulates [33]. The response may be considered a modification, adaptation, or extension of the individual's epistemic frame – the input and the emotions it triggers following appraisal may result in creating more connections or create new questions about existing ways of thinking.

The three steps of perceived input, appraisal, and emotion response generation, a commonly recognized sequence in emotion research literature [34, 35], precede adaptive response (Luo and Yin, 2015), treated here as the fourth phase of a discursive transaction. How are feelings, ideas, beliefs, or commitments in the epistemic frame altered as a result of the input event of reflection? The individual may become more convinced of their position, or may gravitate toward the closest pole. If there is an outward response, it may take the form of oral or written utterances, along with other forms (e.g., political protest). The proposed framework focuses on written utterances in the context of digital social media, phase 5 of Fig. 2.

6 Research Method

This study seeks to articulate an analytic and explanatory approach to dysfunctional political discourse. It rests on recent research that has sought to emphasize and define the relationship between emotion and cognition in political discourse, treating appraisal and emotion generation as crucial precursor phases of a discursive transaction (Fig. 2).

Epistemic Network Analysis treats discourse as a proxy or indicator for internal processes. Coding discursive transactions entails classifying both affect and cognition in discourse and as a means for exploring the prior phases of the transaction. A review of sample Twitter exchanges and political blog exchanges led to the initial development of a codebook which includes both affect and cognition.

6.1 ENA Codebook and Discourse Selection

This study applied ENA [36–38] to data using the ENA1.7.0) [39] Web Tool (version 1.7.0) [40]. This study used a collection of Facebook user comments to specific social media posts from four different publications (units) in the United States. The study analyzed two sources that often represent moderate left and moderate right perspectives, *Politico* and *The Hill* as well as two semi-local publications with politically diverse readership, the *Miami Herald* and the *Chicago Tribune*. For each unit a highly commented upon article (minimum of 100 comments) was selected from each publication, using the DataMiner tool (https://data-miner.io/). Comments were scraped from each publication and stored in an Excel spreadsheet. The first forty comments from each publication were chosen and each categorized by identifying if the commenter's relative position on a political spectrum. Both the codebook and specific coding for these commentary threads were carried out in multiple rounds of negotiated coding [41] in order to give a first order approximation of a potential coding system.

Table 1 identifies codes applied to the commentary threads, along with the abbreviations that appear in the ENA models in Figs. 3A, 3B, and 3C.

We defined the units of analysis as all lines of data associated with a single value of as Source subsetted by Spectrum. For example, one unit consisted of all the lines associated with Left, Right, or Neutral/Both.

The purpose of identifying the political spectrum as left, right, and neither/both was to create a whole conversation as the stanza in the ENA tool [40], rather than looking at each comment as a relation to the previous comment. It was challenging to identify each comment in terms of responses to the other as the users only see relevant comments in their Facebook feed thus this could have an alternate impact on their commenting. Additionally, by identifying spectrum, we could analyze the possibility of emotions driving certain responses by political spectrum.

The ENA algorithm uses a moving window to construct a network model for each line in the data, showing how codes in the current line are connected to codes that occur within the recent temporal context [42], defined as 4 lines (each line plus the 3 previous lines) within a given conversation. The resulting networks are aggregated for all lines for each unit of analysis in the model. In this model, networks were aggregated using a binary summation in which the networks for a given line reflect the presence or absence of the co-occurrence of each pair of codes.

The ENA model included codes appearing in Table 1. Conversations were defined as all data lines associated with a single value of Spectrum. For example, one conversation consisted of all the lines associated with Spectrum and Left.

The ENA model normalized the networks for all units of analysis before they were subjected to a dimensional reduction, which accounts for the fact that different units of analysis may have different amounts of coded lines in the data. For the dimensional

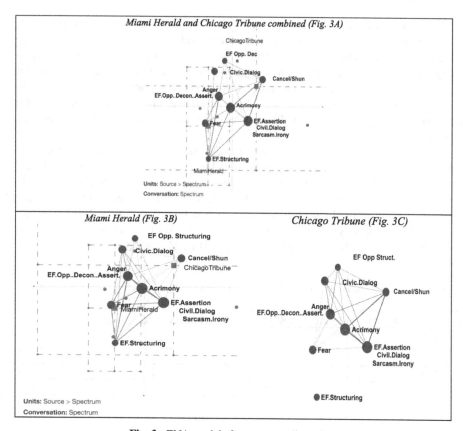

Fig. 3. ENA models from two media outlets

reduction, a singular value decomposition was used to produce orthogonal dimensions that maximize the variance explained by each dimension. (See [37] for a more detailed explanation of the mathematics; see [43] and [44] for examples of this kind of analysis.)

Networks were visualized using network graphs where nodes correspond to the codes, and edges reflect the relative frequency of co-occurrence, or connection, between two codes. The result is two coordinated representations for each unit of analysis: (1) a plotted point, which represents the location of that unit's network in the low-dimensional projected space, and (2) a weighted network graph. The positions of the network graph nodes are fixed, and those positions are determined by an optimization routine that minimizes the difference between the plotted points and their corresponding network centroids. Because of this co-registration of network graphs and projected space, the positions of the network graph nodes—and the connections they define—can be used to interpret the dimensions of the projected space and explain the positions of plotted points in the space. Our model had co-registration correlations of 1 (Pearson) and 1 (Spearman) for the first dimension and co-registration correlations of 1 (Pearson) and 1 (Spearman) for the second. These measures indicate that there is a strong goodness of fit between the visualization and the original model.

ENA can be used to compare units of analysis in terms of their plotted point positions, individual networks, mean plotted point positions, and mean networks, which average the connection weights across individual networks. Networks may also be compared using network difference graphs. These graphs are calculated by subtracting the weight of each connection in one network from the corresponding connections in another. To test for differences, we applied a two-sample t-test assuming unequal variance to the location of points in the projected ENA space for units in *Miami Herald* and *Chicago Tribune*.

Along the X axis, a two sample t test (Table 3) assuming unequal variance showed *Chicago Tribune* (mean = 1.31, SD = 0.63, N = 3 was statistically significantly different at the alpha = 0.05 level from *Miami Herald* (mean = −0.93, SD = 0.98, N = 3; t(3.41) = −3.34, p = 0.04, Cohen's d = 2.73). Along the Y axis, a two sample t test assuming unequal variance showed *Chicago Tribune* (mean = 0.98, SD = 1.64, N = 3 was not statistically significantly different at the alpha = 0.05 level from *Miami Herald* (mean = −0.98, SD = 1.15, N = 3; t(3.59) = 1.69, p = 0.18, Cohen's d = 1.38).

Table 3. T-test of means of means of networks partitioned by source in x- and y-dimension.

X　　Axis:　　SVD1 ;t(3.41)=-3.34p=0.04*		Effect Size:d=2.73	
	Chicago Tribune		*Miami Herald*
Mean:		1.31	-0.93
Standard Deviation:		.63	.98

To test for differences, we applied a two-sample t-test assuming unequal variance to the location of points in the projected ENA space. This modeling is for the purpose of demonstrating application of a coding system alignment with the use of the emotional grammar and discursive transaction constructs; they are thus exploratory and intended to outline the articulation of coding with the broader proposed framework. Results from the *Miami Herald* and the *Chicago Tribune* are selected for display and discussion because they also depict statistically significant relationships.

7　Results

Overall, the results comparing the networks of user discourse on both *Miami Herald* and *Chicago Tribune* were surprisingly different, although the code **Acrimony** was the center for each conversation. For example, Fig. 3A shows the comparative networks of both publications; while there was some variance among the specific codes of each network, the center of both networks as seen in *Chicago Tribune* Fig. 3C and *Miami Herald* Fig. 3B is Acrimony. Acrimony co-occurred frequently with Anger and Fear, though represented slightly different sentiments. Anger and Fear codes were applied to note evident wrath or alarm in addition to the hostility or derision applied with the Acrimony code. Additional observations from this modeling:

- Acrimony (scorn, derision, disgust) was not only consistently the most prominent affect, it was usually the strongest relationship for any other code;
- Anger and Fear frequently co-occurred with arguments support epistemic frames, but infrequently with arguments against opposing epistemic frames;
- *Miami Herald* readers more frequently voiced arguments supporting viewpoints in contrast to *Chicago Tribune* readers whose acrimony was less frequently supported by argument;
- Civic. Dialog, expressing open willingness or appreciation of opposing viewpoints, were rarely in evidence; and
- When the network models were created using the political spectrum, the strength of code acrimony in each network intensified in both the *Herald* and *Chicago Tribune*.

8 Future Directions

The framework this paper proposes seeks to bring the combined analytic power of quantitative ethnography, epistemic frames and epistemic network analysis to understanding discourse patterns that are, at least in part, defining a profoundly conflicted political era. Unsurprisingly, as tools for discourse analysis more generally, the conceptual and software tools that these fields offer may contribute meaningfully to seeing our political discourse patterns more clearly. This proposed framework is preliminary; it seeks to build a rigorous ethnographic foundation that is both descriptive and explanatory while enabling discourse coding, only previewed in this paper, that eventually may provide analytic traction and visual models for the ethnography. Next steps in the quest to break down and understand political discourse include five suggestions:

- **Detail and dimension.** One important next step will entail filling out detail, adding analytic dimensions, and improving framework conceptualizations. For example, this framework considers only a single lane of digital social media discourse, does not address malevolent actors, and has a limited repertoire of emotional grammars as explanatory aspects of dysfunctional discourse. Each of these aspects merits expansion and clarity.
- **Upgrade the framework with examples**. Outside of applying the coding system to several social media conversation threads, this framework outline has deliberately avoided examples from contemporary discourse. Yet each aspect of the framework can be illustrated richly from digital social media across political spectra. One future direction is to furnish examples of how emotional grammars play out.
- **Articulate norms and conventions for functional political discourse**. Consistent with the note above, the framework is not meant to serve as a tool of any political perspective. It is offered to further the interest of encouraging or enabling functional political discourse across all perspectives. No political perspective can function effectively in the absence of such discourse. The norms of classical liberal discourse (not as a political orientation but rather as a foundational disposition of intellectual humility, tolerance, and respect (e.g., see [45]) may be an effective starting point. From there, one future direction is to articulate a twenty-first century set of norms or conventions that are tech-savvy for functional discourse, norms that can appeal to a diverse and large majority of the population.

- **Uncover monetary dimensions of social media algorithms that promote dysfunctional discourse.** Another direction is to investigate who benefits financially from dysfunctional discourse on social media, and whether or how political discord is intensified by algorithmic manipulation in service of financial gain. What portion of dysfunctional discourse in social media is attributable to corporate entities monetizing dysfunctionality, in which case division is not only a function of underlying differences on critical issues, but is a function of the quite arguably artificial and irrelevant factor (to the US polity) of increasing value to social media shareholders?
- **Develop metaphors from the arts.** The suggestion to explore the role of monetary rewards in stimulating political division steps outside of academic avenues, but is relevant in uncovering one of the ways deteriorating discourse can be self-fulfilling and self-accelerating. Another pathway outside of academic lanes for illustrating elements of this framework may be in metaphors from the performing arts. An example to illustrate might be the storyline underlying the musical *Wicked,* and the storyline behind the depression-era *Wizard of Oz.* The latter contains dozens of small details that contribute to an overall narrative that paints "the wicked witch of the west" as an unsympathetic and evil character whose demise was celebrated. The Broadway play *Wicked* creates an alternative interpretation. It treats each detail in the original storyline as truthful, yet viewers see a completely different picture from the same datapoints. The wicked witch was not wicked at all. Details that in one telling were significant become trivial in another telling, and in the end, the epistemic frame of viewers who have seen or read the original *Wizard of Oz* is transformed. The story was not really so much about Dorothy, it was about a woman who fell in love with a character who played a scarecrow. Details considered factual in the original screenplay were subjected to presentation in an entirely different frame of reference. The epistemology of certainty and mutual exclusion (the "good witch" versus the "wicked witch") was overcome when the so-called good witch and the so-called wicked witch were reconciled. Distrust and scorn gave way to profound friendship. In this case, the value of considering the arts is in giving permission to the imagination to consider alternatives to the designation of others as wicked, once a fuller story is known. A second example involves the 1990s era movie *Crimson Tide.* Dialog takes place between the captain (played by Gene Hackman) of a submarine poised to launch nuclear warheads on a perceived enemy, and the submarine's executive officer (played by Denzel Washington) who declined orders to concur with the launch. Earlier in the story, the Denzel Washington character challenges the captain's identification of the enemy, presumably the Russian Federation. The Washington figure reflects, "In the nuclear world, the true enemy can't be destroyed... in my humble opinion, in the nuclear world, the true enemy is war itself." It may be that dysfunctional political discord itself in our current era is a greater enemy of society than the issues that discord represents. The suggestion is not to disavow strides that discord or dissension produce. To the contrary, it is to find ways to preserve discord and dissension as invaluable elements of a functioning democratic society, without devolving into self-sabotaging dysfunction and deterioration.
- There are other examples; they may point to different interpretations than these two scenarios represent, though blending artistic interpretations with scholarship around political discourse, may help us understand ourselves with more clarity and grace.

Acknowledgements. The authors gratefully acknowledge the assistance Dr. Andrew Hurford and Ms. Chen Huang in coding media commentary threads and in reviewing the text of the paper.

References

1. Karadenizova, Z., Dahle, K.-P.: Analyze this! Thematic analysis: hostility, attribution of intent, and interpersonal perception bias. J. Interpers. Viol. p. 0886260517739890 (2017)
2. Hamblin, J.: My outrage is better than your outrage. Atlantic **31** (2015)
3. Sanfey, A.G., et al.: The neural basis of economic decision-making in the ultimatum game. Science **300**(5626), 1755–1758 (2003)
4. Dawes, C.T., et al.: Neural basis of egalitarian behavior. Proc. Nat. Acad. Sci. **109**(17), 6479–6483 (2012)
5. Iyengar, S., et al.: The origins and consequences of affective polarization in the United States. Ann. Rev. Polit. Sci. **22**, 129–146 (2019)
6. Klofstad, C.A.: Enchanted America: How Intuition and Reason Divide Our Politics. Public Opinion Quarterly, University of Chicago Press. (2018)
7. Khalili-Mahani, N., Smyrnova, A., Kakinami, L.: To each stress its own screen: a cross-sectional survey of the patterns of stress and various screen uses in relation to self-admitted screen addiction. J. Med. Internet Res. **21**(4), e11485 (2019)
8. Tucker, J.A., et al.: Social media, political polarization, and political disinformation: a review of the scientific literature (2018). https://dx.doi.org/10.2139/ssrn.3144139
9. Bail, C.A., et al.: Exposure to opposing views on social media can increase political polarization. Proc. Nat. Acad. Sci. **115**(37), 9216–9221 (2018)
10. Zettle, R.D., Hayes, S.C.: Rule-governed behavior: A potential theoretical framework for cognitive-behavioral therapy (2016)
11. Shaffer, D.W.: Epistemic frames for epistemic games. Comput. Educ. **46**(3), 223–234 (2006)
12. Murphy, P.K., et al.: Examining epistemic frames in conceptual change research: implications for learning and instruction. Asia Pacific Educ. Rev. **13**(3), 475–486 (2012)
13. Hart, W., et al.: Feeling validated versus being correct: a meta-analysis of selective exposure to information. Psych. Bull. **135**(4), 555 (2009)
14. Shaffer, D.W., et al.: Epistemic network analysis: a prototype for 21st century assessment of learning. Int. J. Learn. Media **1**(1), 1–21 (2009)
15. Wooldridge, A.R., et al.: Quantifying the qualitative with epistemic network analysis: A human factors case study of task-allocation communication in a primary care team. IISE Trans. Healthc. Syst. Eng. **8**(1), 72–82 (2018)
16. Marquart, C., et al.: Epistemic network analysis (2019)
17. Koole, S.L., Rothermund, K.: Revisiting the past and back to the future: Horizons of cognition and emotion research. Cogn. Emot. **33**(1), 1–7 (2019)
18. Gratch, J., Marsella, S.: A domain-independent framework for modeling emotion. Cogn. Syst. Res. **5**(4), 269–306 (2004)
19. Scherer, K.R., Schorr, A., Johnstone, T.: Appraisal Processes in Emotion: Theory, Methods Research. Oxford University Press, Oxford (2001)
20. Nash, P., Shaffer, D.W.: Epistemic Youth Development: Educational Games as Youth Development Activities. American Educational Research Education, Vancouver (2012)
21. Shaffer, D.W.: Epistemic games to improve professional skills and values. Organisation for Economic Cooperation & Development: Paris (2007)
22. Crigler, A.N.: The affect effect: Dynamics of emotion in political thinking and behavior. University of Chicago Press (2007)

23. Brader, T.: The political relevance of emotions: "reassessing" revisited. Polit. Psychol. **32**(2), 337–346 (2011)
24. Orrill, C.H., Shaffer, D.W.: Exploring connectedness: applying ENA to teacher knowledge. In: International Conference of the Learning Sciences (2012)
25. Shaffer, D.W., Ruis, A.R.: Epistemic network analysis: A worked example of theory-based learning analytics. In: Handbook of Learning Analytics (2017)
26. Resnick, P., et al.: Bursting your (filter) bubble: strategies for promoting diverse exposure. In: Proceedings of the 2013 Conference on Computer Supported Cooperative Work Companion (2013)
27. Lane, D.S., et al.: Social media expression and the political self. J. Commun. **69**(1), 49–72 (2019)
28. Annoni, M.: *Reasons and Emotions.* In: Boniolo, G., Sanchini, V. (eds.) Ethical Counselling and Medical Decision-Making in the Era of Personalised Medicine: A Practice-Oriented Guide, pp. 39–48. Springer, Cham (2016). https://doi.org/10.1007/978-3-319-27690-8
29. Wheatley, T., Haidt, J.: Hypnotic disgust makes moral judgments more severe. Psychol. Sci. **16**(10), 780–784 (2005)
30. Luo, J., Yu, R.: Follow the heart or the head? The interactive influence model of emotion and cognition. Front. Psychol. **6**(573) 2015
31. Gross, J.J., Feldman Barrett, L.: Emotion generation and emotion regulation: one or two depends on your point of view. Emot. Rev. **3**(1), 8–16 (2011)
32. TenHouten, W.D.: Anger, social power, and cognitive appraisal: application of octonionic sociocognitive emotion theory. J. Polit. Power **12**(1), 40–65 (2019)
33. Zinchenko, A., et al.: Moving towards dynamics: emotional modulation of cognitive and emotional control. Int. J. Psychophysiol. **147**, 193–201 (2020)
34. Roseman, I.J.: A model of appraisal in the emotion system. In: Appraisal Processes in Emotion: Theory, Methods, Research, pp. 68–91 (2001)
35. Cacioppo, J.T., et al.: The psychophysiology of emotion. In: Handbook of Emotions, vol. 2, pp. 173–191 (2000)
36. Shaffer, D.W.: Quantitative Ethnography. Cathcart Press, Madison (2017)
37. Shaffer, D.W., Collier, W., Ruis, A.: A tutorial on epistemic network analysis: analyzing the structure of connections in cognitive, social, and interaction data. J. Learn. Anal. **3**(3), 9–45 (2016)
38. Shaffer, D.W., Ruis, A.R.: Epistemic network analysis: A worked example of theory-based learning analytics. In: Lang, C., et al.: Handbook of Learning Analytics, pp. 175–187. Soc. for Learning Analytics Research (2017)
39. Marquart, C.L., et al.: ncodeR: Techniques for automated classifiers (2018)
40. Marquart, C.L., Hinojosa, C., Swiecki, Z., Eagan, B., Shaffer, D.W.: Epistemic Network Analysis (Version 1.7.0) [Software]. (2018). http://app.epistemicnetwork.org
41. Garrison, D.R., et al.: Revisiting methodological issues in transcript analysis: Negotiated coding and reliability. Internet High. Educ. **9**(1), 1–8 (2006)
42. Siebert-Evenstone, A.L., et al.: In search of conversational grain size: modeling semantic structure using moving stanza windows. J. Learn. Anal. **4**(3), 123–139 (2017)
43. Arastoopour, G., et al.: Epistemic Network Analysis as a tool for engineering design assessment. American Society for Engineering Education (2015)
44. Sullivan, S., et al.: Using epistemic network analysis to identify targets for educational interventions in trauma team communication. Surgery **163**(4), 938–943 (2018)
45. Chamlee-Wright, E.: Classical liberalism #1: What is classical liberalism? (2020). https://www.youtube.com/watch?v=hVNgLEvhL5Y

Establishing Trustworthiness Through Algorithmic Approaches to Qualitative Research

Ha Nguyen(✉) ⓘ, June Ahn ⓘ, Ashlee Belgrave, Jiwon Lee, Lora Cawelti, Ha Eun Kim, Yenda Prado, Rossella Santagata, and Adriana Villavicencio

University of California-Irvine, Irvine, USA
thicn@uci.edu

Abstract. Establishing trustworthiness is a fundamental component of qualitative research. In the following paper, we document how combining natural language processing (NLP), with human analysis by researchers, can help analysts develop insights from qualitative data and establish trustworthiness for the analysis process. We document the affordances of such an approach to strengthen three specific aspects of trustworthiness in qualitative research: credibility, dependability, and confirmability. We illustrate this workflow and shed light on its implications for trustworthiness from our own, recent research study of educators' experiences with the 2020 COVID-19 pandemic; a context that compelled our research team to analyze our data efficiently to best aid the community, but also establish rigor and trustworthiness of our process.

Keywords: Natural language processing · Trustworthiness · Qualitative research

1 Introduction

"We need to really study what other districts are doing and and how it's working, how it's working at their district. So working collaboratively with other school leaders at other districts ...." – [Principal, Local Elementary School, Interview Transcript].

The global, COVID-19 pandemic in 2020 brought about tremendous distress and disruption in social life, economic systems, and civic institutions such as schooling and government (and as of this writing, continues to threaten societies around the world). As a team of education researchers in the United States (U.S.), we faced a unique situation of wanting to collect data on how educators, parents, and families were experiencing this crisis while also providing rapid information to inform the questions that our local educator partners were facing. The consequences of our research in this time were substantial. Key decisions such as how to bring students back to physical campuses, or

The original version of this chapter was revised: The author's name has been changed as Ashlee Belgrave. The correction to this chapter is available at
https://doi.org/10.1007/978-3-030-67788-6_29

A. R. Ruis and S. B. Lee (Eds.): ICQE 2021, CCIS 1312, pp. 47–61, 2021.
https://doi.org/10.1007/978-3-030-67788-6_4

support learners and their families in remote learning, had dire repercussions for public well-being.

Within this context, we conducted in-depth interviews with educators, school staff, and parents in California school districts. Many interviewees articulated the need for fast turnaround of research analysis to help them understand a wide variety of topics, from how to differentiate instruction to addressing pandemic-induced community trauma. These needs brought us to consider computational approaches for analyzing a rapidly evolving qualitative data corpus. This experience of utilizing computational approaches to aid our analysis, heightened by the context of the pandemic, brought enduring issues in qualitative research into stark relief. Qualitative research is typically suited for *slow scholarship*, where an analyst can take their time to explore data, and undertake a rigorous process to find relationships and develop deeper, theoretical understandings of a phenomenon.

Instead, to address the fast timelines needed by educators who would use our research, we sought an algorithmic approach by utilizing natural language processing (NLP) to provide an initial parsing, categorizing, and clustering of our qualitative data. Then, we introduced *humans in the loop*, as our research team worked with the outputs of different NLP approaches to analyze and synthesize potential insights. We were inspired by prior frameworks for bringing computation into both deductive (i.e., theory-grounded) and inductive (i.e., data-grounded) analysis workflows [2, 3, 20].

This paper documents what these frameworks may look like in educational research contexts for analysts conducting the research. In the process, we contribute to the emergent research on algorithmic analyses in qualitative work in two main ways. First, we illustrate how different, NLP approaches to parsing, organizing, and presenting raw qualitative data substantially influence the sensemaking and research directions that researchers may take. Understanding how this mutual influence between computation and human insight may intersect, is important to map out methodological transparency in future studies.

Second, our analyses illuminated how combining NLP and algorithmic approaches has potentially major implications for establishing three specific facets of trustworthiness: **credibility, dependability, and confirmability**, which are fundamental aspects of qualitative methods. We describe a set of guidelines for reporting research processes to establish trustworthiness; particularly to map the relationship between data sources, algorithmic choices, development of data patterns, the human sensemaking process, and triangulation of information from both computer and human analysis. This discussion is vital because how researchers make public all facets of their research, is key to establishing rigor in qualitative analyses [1].

2   Theoretical Framework

2.1   Algorithmic Approaches to Qualitative Research

Researchers across fields – such as digital humanities, psychology, communication studies, and education – have applied computational techniques to uncover insights through analysis of texts [4, 19, 25]. A common workflow is to use natural language processing (NLP) to extract aggregate counts of parts of speech (e.g., pronouns, nouns, verbs), word usage, and topics, and map them to predefined categories [11, 25]. The mapping of words to categories is often grounded in prior theories and researcher assumptions. Researchers can come in with preexisting libraries or code categories [23, 25]. Alternatively, researchers can read through several manuscripts, directly refine the code categories, and search for the exact words or phrases in the data corpus [19]. An advantage of using keyword matches is that researchers can automate the analysis and establish inter-rater reliability between the researchers and the classifiers [6].

A limitation to finding exact matches for pre-defined codes, however, is that this approach requires intensive researcher labor to carefully examine raw qualitative data, establish themes, and validate new categories. In rethinking this workflow, researchers have suggested analytic pipelines to automatically search for words with related meanings; for example, using NLP to conduct a search of keywords based on semantic similarity [3]. Researchers in this area suggest use of contextual word embedding to create word vectors from the contexts of the vocabulary (i.e., based on its relation to the surrounding words) and search for semantically similar words based on the contexts.

Researchers have also proposed computational techniques for bottom-up analyses, where keywords and themes can emerge from data without relying on predefined categories. Emergent work has suggested the intersection of computation and ethnography [20]. Both unsupervised machine learning and qualitative methods – such as grounded theory – are inductive and driven by the data [8]. Both approaches value the importance of data contexts in informing interpretation [20]. For example, machine learning researchers have emphasized the role of *human experts in the loop*: while computation can identify semantic patterns, the meaning-making of these patterns depends on human judgment [9].

There is emergent education research that uses computation in inductive analyses. Traditionally, qualitative researchers conduct content analyses by reading the text manually and identifying themes and categories. Recently, researchers have proposed use of topic modeling to discover latent topics in education data corpus [2, 14]. Although topic modeling has shown potential in uncovering broad-based themes, researchers maintain that there is a need for human's domain knowledge to define more fine-grained topics [2]. However, there is limited research that details the analysis workflow for combining human sensemaking and computational outputs, or discusses the implications of presenting these workflows to the public to establish trustworthiness in data interpretation.

2.2 Trustworthiness, A Key Element of Qualitative Research

One critique of qualitative research is that researchers often fail to provide clear justifications for their study designs, analyses trails, interpretations, and claims [7]. In response, qualitative methodologists have suggested several standards for evaluating quality and rigor. For example, Lincoln and Guba [15] translate validity criteria found in quantitative work – internal validity, external validity, reliability, and objectivity – to facets of **trustworthiness**. In place of internal validity (i.e., the extent to which researchers can infer a relationship between variables), qualitative researchers probe for **credibility**, or the extent to which the data and interpretations are plausible and accurate. To establish credibility, researchers can make use of strategies such as triangulation among multiple researchers and data sources, member checks of one's interpretations with participants, and constant comparisons of emerging patterns and data. In place of internal reliability (i.e., the extent to which data collection and analyses are consistent), researchers establish **dependability** by communicating the consistency of the research process. Potential practices to address dependability include use of inter-rater reliability, strong and logical mapping of study designs to research questions, and multiple checks of analysis between researchers. Finally, while research in positivist and post-positivist traditions seek to establish objectivity, qualitative researchers who work in more interpretive traditions, instead strive to establish evidence of **confirmability** in their studies; or "audit trails" of how analyses can be traced back to original data sources.

Despite these guidelines, "there is a lack of will and/or means" to make public the research collection and analysis processes in many qualitative studies [1] (p. 29). If researchers do not spend time explaining how the themes in their findings emerged, readers may have difficulties verifying whether the findings bear congruence with the actual phenomenon under investigation [7]. Even though researchers frequently mention triangulation and member checks to establish credibility, they may not detail how these processes are achieved. Consequently, Anfara et al. [1] propose that researchers need to clearly document the iterations of study design and analysis. Examples of these forms of documentation are mappings of interview protocols to research questions and mappings of emergent themes from analyses to initial codes grounded in data [1, 17].

In the following paper, we argue that computational approaches **can help sharpen notions of trustworthiness in conducting qualitative research**. For example, computational outputs play a role in developing insights into the major themes and sentiments in the text [20]. One might also conceptualize computational algorithms as an external coder, in collaboration with a team of human researchers, and as such might provide evidence to establish credibility and dependability [4, 6, 25]. By establishing practices of explaining different algorithms, and their potential influence on the qualitative sensemaking process, we argue that researchers might also strengthen the confirmability of their studies. In essence, aligning computational models, the data used, and human interpretation–a process known as *closing the interpretive loop* [24]–is key to checking the validity of the model and its interpretation for researchers.

To illuminate this link between algorithms and qualitative analysis, and its implications for strengthening trustworthiness in the analytic process, we present a self-study narrative of the initial stages of a recent, research endeavor [5]. As a self-study, we note that we are not presenting a traditional research study (with the expected paper sections such as methodology, findings etc.). Instead, our documentation represents a layer of *meta-awareness and reflection* of our methodological process itself. The self-narrative we share serves to shed light on how computational approaches can strengthen qualitative research, as we explore the following question:

What are the affordances of algorithmic approaches for developing and examining research directions, analyses, and consistency of findings?

3   Setting the Study Context

Our methodological insights derived from a research study that occurred in Spring-Summer 2020. Our research team was situated in an educational partnership between university researchers, schools, and school districts in California, U.S. To support our partners to prepare plans for schooling and supporting students and families in a time of crisis, throughout May and June 2020, we conducted in-depth interviews with 35 district administrators, principals, teachers, school staff, and parents from our network. Each interview lasted approximately 45 min. The need for efficient turnaround of research led us to consider the potential of computational analyses in highlighting key data patterns.

In our initial phase of analysis, we sought to examine the feasibility of computational approaches in parsing the raw interview transcripts and aiding the research team in identifying areas to focus our analysis. We selected a subset of the interviews with school and district administrators (10 interviews; 48,567 words). Interviewees came from an array of instructional contexts (e.g., elementary, middle, high school; public and charter).

We then applied different NLP algorithms to provide an initial parsing, categorizing, and clustering of our interview corpus. Our research team in this phase, included the co-authors of this paper (6 PhD students in Education, and 3 faculty members who served as the principal investigators of the project). All members of the research team were involved in conceptualizing the research study, as well as recruiting and conducting interviews. Thus, everyone on the research team had prior knowledge that they brought to the analysis process.

In the next sections, we outline the steps we undertook to categorize, cluster, and interpret the data. As we progress through this self-study narrative, we illuminate the key implications for qualitative methodology that emerged and became clear in different stages of the process: selecting and running algorithms, engaging the human researchers in the analytic loops, checking for inter-rater reliability, and triangulating findings.

4 Algorithmic Transparency as a Step Toward Trustworthiness

The first insight we derived from our process can be described as follows:

> Communicating key information about our algorithm choices is vital for understanding how insights and findings are ultimately derived from the research process. The design and implications of algorithms provide evidence for stronger **credibility, dependability and confirmability**.

We illustrate this insight by describing our use of two NLP approaches on the same data corpus: (1) a deductive approach, where codes are generated from the interview design and word clusters are automatically identified based on keyword similarity; (2) and an inductive approach using a pre-trained text model to create topic clusters without researcher keywords.

4.1 Deductive Approach

Word Embedding. The overarching idea of our *deductive* approach is to first identify keywords based on *researcher input* (i.e., the interview questions in our research protocol). For example, our interview questions asked about remote learning, supporting students, equity issues during the pandemic etc. We then parsed the data to select the words that co-occurred with the keywords in similar contexts. We used Word2Vec [18] to train word vectors (representation of words as feature vector) based on the data contexts. The learning model used a Continuous Bag-of-Words (CBOW) approach, which created the embedding by predicting the target word based on its surrounding words. This approach is based on the Distributional Hypothesis that words that appear in similar contexts are likely to have related meanings [13]. In particular, the local contexts of the words were defined by a sliding window of its neighboring words. Consider an example sentence: "Families can pick up meals at the schools around noon". In our case of a sliding window of size 5, the context for the word "meal" in the example was created using the 5 words before ("families", "can", "pick", "up") and the 5 words after the target word ("at", "the", "schools", "around", "noon"). The size of the sliding window influences the vector similarities: smaller windows produce more syntactic closeness, while large windows (e.g., commonly of size 5) generate broader topical groupings [12].

Keyword Search through Semantic Similarity. We then created word clusters by identifying the most similar words to a list of a priori keywords. The keywords were picked by us from the themes in our interview questions. Our keywords covered the following topics: technology access (e.g., "technology access", "devices"), approaches to distance learning (e.g., "distance learning", "online learning"), parental responses (e.g., "parents", "challenging families"), teacher collaboration (e.g., "teachers collaborate"), district policies (e.g., "district policies"), and responses to vulnerable populations (e.g.,"ela", "homeless").

4.2 Inductive Approach

Part-of-Speech Tagging and Word Embedding. We also analyzed our interview corpus using an *inductive, algorithmic* approach. The strategy of our inductive coding is to identify the noun phrases from the interview corpus, and cluster these phrases into topical groupings.

Table 1. Example output from deductive

Keywords	Words
School closure	Facebook, school sites, providing, wifi, ap, six weeks, two weeks, packets, instruction, decisions, game, ideas, open, were trying, small group, email
Food insecurity	Businesses, relevant, successful, complaints, member, income, tried best, dilemma, gift, guy, separated, unprecedented grader, laptops, vulnerable students, administrator, collaboration, finish, we talked, impose, yelling
Distance learning	Face, put together, model, local, brick mortar, feel, eight, scheduling, thursday, mental health, terms, person, grading, devices, make sure, work home, world
Teachers collaborate	Before, days, expectations, daily, create, activity, virtual, grading, students learning, brick mortar, try, staff, pandemic, social, deliver, translate, facebook, job, mandated, ed services, problem
School district	Policy, pd, problem, make, virtually, promotion, scheduled, level, daily, phone, bring, meetings, virtual, packets, creating, enrichment, speakers, offering

We obtained the noun phrases from each sentence of the interview corpus through part-of-speech tagging (POS). POS classifies a word in a text as corresponding to a noun, adjective, or adverb, etc., based on its definition and its adjacent words. We then used Python spaCy's dependency parser to identify the nouns and define their modifiers (e.g., adjective, adverb, or another noun). For example, in the example sentence "I prefer breakfast food", "food" will be identified as the noun, and "breakfast" as the modifier. In total, we identified 1833 unique noun phrases from the corpus.

Upon identifying the phrases, we used the large pre-trained model from spaCy to create a word embedding model for the phrases. The model contains 300 dimensional word vectors that were trained on a vocabulary of 2 million words from web page data (Common Crawl dataset; GloVe, [21]). We then worked to cluster words together using the word embedding developed with spaCy.

Table 2. Example output from inductive

Group	Words
1	Worksheets activities, pamphlets resources, resource guide, family response, stick Chromebook, follow guidelines
2	**Distance learning**, mastery learning, emergency learning
3	Roofs head, avenue support, corporations part, textbook students, taxpayers money, terms work, terms food, terms collaboration, hotel connectivity, family access, kids opportunity, brick mortar
4	Grading policy, learning format, learning school, pacing guide, teaching learning, giving vision, address learning, supervisor vision
5	**School closures**, school districts, school sites, phone calls, budget cuts, work students, contact students, support families, disinfect schools, respond students, check ins, vento liaison, school program, school closing, school community, school homework, summer school, counseling school, community facilitator, lunch community, school model, school board, school level, district office, district sign, partnership district

Notes. Bold text highlights the keywords from the deductive coding

Clustering. We created word clusters based on the Cosine similarity between the word vectors, using DBSCAN (Density-Based Spatial Clustering of Applications with Noise; [10]). DBSCAN is an unsupervised clustering method that has been used with high-dimensional data such as text vectors [26]. The algorithm was chosen because it did not enforce that all samples group into a certain cluster (i.e., allowing for noise and single-word cluster outliers).

The algorithm worked as follows: DBSCAN first divided the data set into n dimensions and formed an n dimensional shape for each data point. DBSCAN iteratively refined the clusters by going through each data point to determine if (1) the distance between points was within a user-specified radius (i.e., Eps) and (2) the clusters met the predetermined minimum number of points (i.e., MinPts). To create a manageable workload of word clusters, we created the clusters from the most frequent 500 noun phrases in the dataset.

The clustering generated 26 clusters, whose word counts ranged from 3 to 27 (Eps = .11, MinPts = 3). To select the optimal value for Eps, we followed the procedures outlined in [22]. We calculated the distance between a data point and its nearest neighboring points, plotted the distance in a k-dist plot, and selected the point of maximum curvature in the plot as the Eps value.

4.3   Algorithm Outputs and its Contributions to Establishing Trustworthiness

The outputs from the two computational approaches were quite different (see Table 1 and 2). Take an example of the phrase "distance learning". Results from deductive analyses yielded terms such as "face", "scheduling", "devices", "grading", and "mental health". Although "distance learning" appeared in a cluster in the inductive codes, this cluster contained a different set of words, grouped together with the terms "emergency learning" and "mastery learning".

Our documentation of the inner workings of our algorithm choices, along with the influence of the parameters on the final output, have implications for establishing credibility, dependability, and confirmability.

Credibility. Being transparent about the algorithm's functionality provides a form of member check to allow the research team (and readers) to understand the interpretation process. Interestingly, we are implicitly treating an algorithm as "another set of eyes" and almost like another member of the research team. Credibility is strengthened if readers can hopefully examine whether the interpretations that emerge from the data and computational output are plausible, given the internal design and implications of a given algorithmic approach.

Dependability. Some ways to strengthen the dependability argument in a qualitative study is to record the methodological and interpretive process of the researchers. We observe that an algorithm – in essence – is acting as another coder.

Thus, being transparent about the algorithm's process is a key element of establishing dependability. In addition, one affordance of algorithmic approaches could be in establishing criteria such as inter-rater reliability (IRR) between researchers. We delve into the opportunities for considering IRR in more detail, below, when we bring the human in the analysis loop.

Confirmability. One common strategy for establishing confirmability in qualitative research is to provide readers with an "audit trail" of steps and process that a research team undertook. This audit trail, when successful and strong, allows other scholars to follow the process and evaluate its logic, match to research aims, and links to findings. Here we note that transparently explaining algorithmic approaches in the process provides a synergistic way to describe an audit trail, and even potentially strengthen ways for other researchers to trace the analysis steps and replicate the interpretation.

5 The Human-Computer Analytic Loop: Strengthening the Trustworthiness Argument

Any given algorithmic output substantially influences the analysis directions of the research team.

We illustrate this insight by describing the process of engaging the entire research team to continue with the analysis process, now aided by an initial look from different NLP algorithms, as a first pass to parse and organize the data.

We randomly divided ourselves into two groups, with each group focusing on understanding the word clusters that were derived by the two algorithms. The first two authors, who took the lead in developing the algorithmic process, also facilitated and took observation notes of the analysis groups. We observed that two sense making activities were occurring as our groups continued to analyze the word clusters: deriving new questions that could focus analyses and developing conjectures for what might be happening in the interview transcripts.

5.1 Algorithmic Output Influences Researcher Sense Making

We observed that the research team readily built conjectures around the data when encountering the word lists. Team members noted that the clusters helped to reduce their cognitive load, as "all the words were on screen" [Member 2]. We attempted to make sense of the word clusters based on their face values as well as prior experiences in educational settings. Member 4 reflected:

> I came up with the themes not purely from the grouping [of words] but because of the added knowledge and experience about each word that emerged. I had to make sense of 2 or more words together and draw on my experience to then come up with the theme. Other themes probably exist that I cannot see because I haven't had related experiences.

Relying on the different word clusters that came about from different algorithm choices resulted in varying conjectures and questions. The key insight here is that the analysis direction that a research team goes down can be substantially influenced by the algorithm choices that are made.

For example, when looking at a word cluster related to "distance learning" from the inductive approach (Table 2), members of our team observed that the relations between "distance learning", "mastery learning", and "emergency learning" could depend on the school's infrastructure to support these different types of learning. Another member voiced that maybe interviewees were talking broadly about different learning models. Another researcher proceeded to propose research questions from this inductive approach: "What types of learning responses are being offered? How do responses vary with different school representations in the dataset?" We note that these types of questions lean towards categorizing responses in a cross-sectional way, using broader descriptors.

Meanwhile, when observing the word clusters that came from a deductive, algorithmic approach, the words associated with "distance learning" included: face, put together, model, brick and mortar, scheduling, mental health, grading, devices etc. Some research team members conjectured that the interviews might reveal the challenges in transitioning to this form of learning. Other members observed that the word clustering here, oriented our thinking to asking the "how" questions, or the details of implementing distance learning.

5.2   Strengthening Credibility and Confirmability

This vignette of how our research team interacted with the algorithmic output have implications for establishing credibility and confirmability.

Credibility. Using algorithmic approaches in the initial analysis phases, may provide qualitative researchers with an additional building block to establish credibility arguments. One simple way to illustrate this affordance is by explaining, as we did above how different algorithmic approaches connected to the varying, iterative interpretive processes of sense-making our research team members undertook.

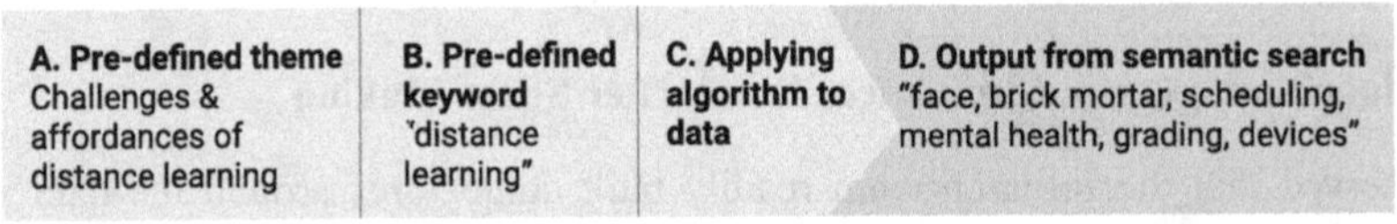

A. Pre-defined theme Challenges & affordances of distance learning	B. Pre-defined keyword "distance learning"	C. Applying algorithm to data	D. Output from semantic search "face, brick mortar, scheduling, mental health, grading, devices"

Fig. 1. Code Mappings for "Distance Learning", Deductive Approach. Blue (Steps A,B,C): Human; Pink (Step D): Computer. (Color figure online)

Tables 1, 2 and Fig. 1 serve as one potential example for how to align researchers' assumptions, data computational output, and interpretative cycles to identify emergent patterns for analyses. We note that researchers should clearly denote where in the process computational analyses come in to shape their assumptions around data and show whether the iterations of interpretations between the researchers and the algorithms are believable and logical. Furthermore, to establish transparency in mapping research questions and analyses, researchers can preregister the expected data outputs to justify why they select certain computational and interpretative strategies. Lastly, we were intrigued by the different conjectures that arose from merely looking at the algorithmic output. As our team delves back into the actual interview transcripts, documenting how subsequent interpretations related to, confirmed, or ran counter to the conjectures created from algorithmic output would greatly enhance credibility.

Confirmability. A key strategy to establish confirmability in qualitative work is to present an "audit trail", explicitly mapping how original data sources link to subsequent research choices. We note here that algorithms and their output represent another source, and a clearly documented trail of how decisions linked back to raw interview transcripts and algorithmic decisions, in an iterative way. In addition, a potential affordance of combining algorithmic approaches with qualitative reporting is to provide a roadmap for other scholars to follow through the steps of interpretive analysis. Fig. 1 provides an example roadmap, where other scholars can clearly trace our steps from pre-defined themes (Fig. 1.A) and keywords (Fig. 1.B) to the computational output (Fig. 1.D).

6   Algorithmic Affordances for Inter-rater Reliability

Communicating the nuances in refining automated classifiers is key to establishing dependability–the extent to which research processes are consistent and reliable.

To establish dependability, qualitative researchers examine inter-rater reliability (IRR) in their coding process. We observed that the codes and their associated keywords from our algorithms (Tables 1 and 2) could be used as keywords for an automated classifier, which can then act as a second coder in collaboration with a researcher. The classifier would identify whether a code is present in the text based on the occurrence of the keywords. Emergent research has suggested the potential of automated classifiers to establish IRR [6, 16].

To determine the feasibility of using an automated classifier for IRR, we selected three themes and their associated words from our team's discussion: distance-learning, teaching-learning, and district-policies. We provided a classifier (nCoder, [16]) with the codes and keywords, "trained" the classifier through human coding of a training set (80 lines/code), had the classifier automatically code the data corpus, and compared codes from a test set to establish IRR. In practice, the process of establishing IRR between researchers, or researchers and computational approaches is iterative. The small size of the training set is only to explore the potential of using the automated classifier for dependability.

The IRR between the classifier and the researcher varied, $\kappa = (.35–.72)$, $\rho > .05$. For codes with low reliability, we found that clusters with fewer keywords (e.g., "distance learning" in deductive code) were harder to establish high reliability for, $\kappa = .35$; $\rho(.65) = 1$. Common phrases (e.g., "project", "expectations") could appear in multiple contexts, and thus there were high rates of false positives for codes that contained these words as identifiers (i.e., precision $< .60$).

Strengthening Dependability. We found that establishing high inter-rater reliability between the automated classifier and researchers was challenging when the training keywords from the algorithms were not unique to the codes. Prior work recommends that in the event of low agreement, the researchers can include more regular expressions for training, while updating the code definitions [6]. Developing and refining keywords is a nuanced process that is rarely documented in study write-ups. To strengthen notions of dependability in leveraging automated classifiers, instead of reporting only the final inter-rater statistics, researchers should document the changes to the code definitions as they work on establishing substantial agreement in automated analyses.

7   Triangulating Findings with Visual Analytics

Visual analytics techniques can serve as another way to show triangulation of data and interpretive process.

Our next insight toward establishing trustworthiness concerns use of visual analytics techniques, such as Epistemic Network Analysis (ENA) [24], to triangulate findings from algorithmic approaches. To illustrate this workflow, we took "themes" that arose after our research team analyzed the word clusters from the two NLP algorithms. For example, one theme was teaching-and-learning and another was distance-learning. We then performed an ENA analysis to examine whether these themes were present, for a given interview excerpt.

For each sentence in the text, ENA counts the occurrences of the themes' related keywords in a window of conversational turns. To bound excerpts, we chose a moving window of 4 sentences. If two or more themes (via their keywords) are present in a text excerpt, they are co-present and reflected as connected in the network graph (see Fig. 2). ENA then normalizes the networks and projects them onto a lower dimensional space. Each node represents a theme (e.g., distance learning); thicker and darker lines represent higher frequencies of occurrences; and subtracting the networks results in comparison graphs that illustrate the differences between networks.

The ENA visualizations allowed us to confirm that different algorithmic approaches to parsing and categorizing words, led to different types of connections between themes. For example, the differences between the two approaches (Fig. 2, A and B) appeared in the positions of specific educator roles (i.e., nodes). This suggests that the conceptualization of each role by the three themes (teaching and learning, distance learning, and district intervention) appeared to differ between the two approaches.

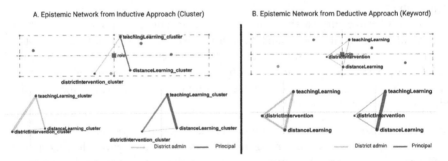

Fig. 2. Epistemic Networks for each Analysis Approach. *Notes.* Top: differences between principal-district networks; bottom: district (green) and principal (purple). (Color figure online)

Notably, ENA allowed for comparisons of different connections of themes based on whether a district administrator or a school principal was voicing these ideas. For example, Fig. 2.A shows ENA graphs based on the inductive, algorithmic model we used. On the lower left (green graph) we see that district administrators talked about teaching and learning and district interventions, more often together. On the lower right (purple graph), we observe that school principals often mentioned teaching and learning and distance learning, more often together. Could these utterances occur because of the roles that these staff play in a school system? These questions helped our team to revisit our qualitative data corpus, from different lenses, and combined with previous approaches offer multiple layers from which to develop insights.

Strengthening Credibility. Using other analysis strategies and visual analytics such as ENA, can strengthen arguments for credibility in qualitative research. Specifically, algorithmic and ENA approaches can be seen as other forms of triangulation – of looking at data from different viewpoints – and develop more rigorous claims and interpretations from data to strengthen the overall analysis.

8   Conclusions

In this paper, we examine how combining output from NLP algorithms, or what one research collaborator playfully described as "word vomit from the machine", with human interpretations can offer insights for establishing trustworthiness for the research process. We document our algorithmic processes to provide transparency to the analysis pipelines. Our experiences shed light on how different approaches influenced disparate research directions and analyses. We also highlight strategies to triangulate findings with visual analytics tools and establish inter-rater reliability (IRR) with an automated classifier. The iterativity in triangulating findings and establishing IRR implies an interdependence between the human and the algorithms that is crucial to the final interpretations.

Table 3. Algorithmic affordances to establish trustworthiness.

Facets	Definition	Use of computation	Our study
Credibility	Are the presented data plausible?	Algorithmic transparency triangulation Constant comparisons	2 algorithmic approaches Visual analytics
Dependability	Are the processes consistent & reliable?	Inter-rater reliability Pre-register analyses	Automated classifier
Confirmability	Are the findings traceable to original data?	Code Mapping	Human-algorithm interpretation

We return to our original premise: How can we establish trustworthiness in qualitative research when adopting human-computer analytic approaches? Table 3 summarizes several strategies for reporting and interpreting human-computer qualitative work. While process of triangulation, constant comparisons, establishing IRR, code mapping, and pre-registering analyses are geared towards analysts conducting the research, we also discuss how algorithmic transparency can help readers confirm the work's validity and bring in researchers who understand trustworthiness and the theoretical underpinnings of qualitative work, but may not be familiar with algorithmic workflows.

The current work is limited to our data contexts and participant insights, and we only explored two ways to code data in our illustrative example. Still, our processes of data collection, analyses, and human interpretation illuminate how different algorithmic approaches can aid interpretations of large qualitative data corpus. Directions for future research include efforts to build synergistic interfaces for researchers to conduct data exploration, interpretation, and triangulation with different computational techniques.

References

1. Anfara Jr, V.A., Brown, K.M., Mangione, T.L.: Qualitative analysis on stage: Making the research process more public. Educ. Res. **31**(7), 28–38 (2002)
2. Bakharia, A.: On the equivalence of inductive content analysis and topic modeling. In: Eagan, B., Misfeldt, M., Siebert-Evenstone, A. (eds.) ICQE 2019. CCIS, vol. 1112, pp. 291–298. Springer, Cham (2019). https://doi.org/10.1007/978-3-030-33232-7_25
3. Bakharia, A., Corrin, L.: Using recent advances in contextual word embeddings to improve the quantitative ethnography workflow. In: Eagan, B., Misfeldt, M., Siebert-Evenstone, A. (eds.) ICQE 2019. CCIS, vol. 1112, pp. 299–306. Springer, Cham (2019). https://doi.org/10.1007/978-3-030-33232-7_26
4. Boyd, R.L.: Psychological text analysis in the digital humanities. In: Hai-Jew, S. (ed.) Analytics in Digital Humanities. Multimedia Systems and Applications, Springer, Cham (2019). https://doi.org/10.1007/978-3-319-54499-1_7
5. Bullough, R.V., Jr., Pinnegar, S.: Guidelines for quality in autobiographical forms of self-study research. Educ. Res. **30**(3), 13–21 (2001)
6. Cai, Z., Siebert-Evenstone, A., Eagan, B., Shaffer, D.W., Hu, X., Graesser, A.C.: nCoder+: a semantic tool for improving recall of nCoder coding. In: Eagan, B., Misfeldt, M., Siebert-Evenstone, A. (eds.) ICQE 2019. CCIS, vol. 1112, pp. 41–54. Springer, Cham (2019). https://doi.org/10.1007/978-3-030-33232-7_4
7. Charmaz, K., Denzin, N.K., Lincoln, Y.S.: Handbook of qualitative research. Sage Publications, Thousand Oaks (2000)
8. Chen, N.C., Drouhard, M., Kocielnik, R., Suh, J., Aragon, C.R.: Using machine learning to support qualitative coding in social science: shifting the focus to ambiguity. ACM Trans. Interact. Intell. Syst. (TiiS) **8**(2), 1–20 (2018)
9. DiMaggio, P., Nag, M., Blei, D.: Exploiting affinities between topic modeling and the sociological perspective on culture: application to newspaper coverage of US government arts funding. Poetics **41**(6), 570–606 (2013)
10. Ester, M., Kriegel, H.P., Sander, J., Xu, X.: A density-based algorithm for discovering clusters in large spatial databases with noise. KDD **96**(34), 226–231 (1996)
11. Fekete, J. D., Dufournaud, N.: Compus: visualization and analysis of structured documents for understanding social life in the 16th century. In: Proceedings of the Fifth ACM Conference on Digital Libraries, pp. 47–55 (2000)
12. Goldberg, Y.: Neural network methods for natural language processing. Synth. Lect. Hum. Lang. Technol. **10**(1), 1–309 (2017)
13. Harris, Z.S.: Distributional structure. Word **10**(2–3), 146–162 (1954)
14. Li, H., Schnieders, J.Z.Y., Bobek, B.L.: Theme analyses for open-ended survey responses in education research on summer melt phenomenon. In: Eagan, B., Misfeldt, M., Siebert-Evenstone, A. (eds.) ICQE 2019. CCIS, vol. 1112, pp. 128–140. Springer, Cham (2019). https://doi.org/10.1007/978-3-030-33232-7_11
15. Lincoln, Y.S., Guba, E.G.: But is it rigorous? Trustworthiness and authenticity in naturalistic evaluation. New Direct. Program Eval. **1986**(30), pp. 73–84 (1986)
16. Marquart, C.L., Swiecki, Z., Eagan, B., Shaffer, D.W.: ncodeR (Version 0.1.2) (2018). https://cran.r-project.org/web/packages/ncodeR/ncodeR.pdf
17. Marshall, C., Rossman, G.B.: Designing Qualitative Research. Sage Publications, Thousand Oaks (2014)
18. Mikolov, T., Sutskever, I., Chen, K., Corrado, G. S., Dean, J. Distributed representations of words and phrases and their compositionality. In: Advances in Neural Information Processing Systems, pp. 3111–3119 (2013)

19. Muralidharan, A., Hearst, M. A.: Supporting exploratory text analysis in literature study. Liter. Linguist. Comput. **28**(2), 283–295 (2012)
20. Ophir, Y., Walter, D., Marchant, E.R.: A collaborative way of knowing: bridging computational communication research and grounded theory ethnography. J. Commun. **70**(3), 447–472 (2020)
21. Pennington, J., Socher, R., Manning, C.D.: Glove: global vectors for word representation. In: Proceedings of the 2014 Conference on Empirical Methods in Natural Language Processing (EMNLP), pp. 1532–1543 (2014)
22. Rahmah, N., Sitanggang, I.S.: Determination of optimal epsilon (eps) value on DBscan algorithm to clustering data on peatland hotspots in sumatra. In IOP Conference Series: Earth and Environmental Science, vol. 31, no. 1, p. 012012. IOP Publishing (2016)
23. Robinson, R.L., Navea, R., Ickes, W.: Predicting final course performance from students' written self-introductions: a LIWC analysis. J. Lang. Soc. Psychol. **32**(4), 469–479 (2013)
24. Shaffer, D. W. Quantitative ethnography (2017). Lulu.com
25. Tausczik, Y.R., Pennebaker, J.W.: The psychological meaning of words: LIWC and computerized text analysis methods. J. Lang. Soc. Psychol. **29**(1), 24–54 (2010)
26. Verma, M., Srivastava, M., Chack, N., Diswar, A.K., Gupta, N.: A comparative study of various clustering algorithms in data mining. Int. J. Eng. Res. Appl. (IJERA) **2**(3), 1379–1384 (2012)

How We Code

David Williamson Shaffer$^{(\boxtimes)}$ (iD) and A. R. Ruis (iD)

University of Wisconsin-Madison, Madison, WI 53706, USA
dws@education.wisc.edu

Abstract. Coding data—defining concepts and identifying where they occur in data—is a critical aspect of qualitative data analysis, and especially so in quantitative ethnography. Coding is a central process for creating meaning from data, and while much has been written about coding methods and theory, relatively little has been written about what constitutes best practices for *fair* and *valid* coding, what justifies those practices, and how to implement them. In this paper, our goal is not to address these issues comprehensively, but to provide guidelines for good coding practice and to highlight some of the issues and key questions that quantitative ethnographers and other researchers should consider when coding data.

Keywords: Coding · Automated classifiers · Inter-Rater Reliability (IRR) · Fairness · Validity

1 Introduction

Although it goes by many names—*classifying, annotating, categorizing, rating, indexing, linking, labeling, tagging, marking up*—the process of coding data is a critical part of data analysis, and particularly of data analysis in *quantitative ethnography*. In brief, *coding* refers to the process of (a) defining concepts of interest ("Codes") and (b) identifying places in a dataset where they occur.

Despite the central role coding plays in interpreting data and testing claims—and the extensive literature on coding methods (e.g., [19]) and theory (e.g., [23])—there has been relatively little written about what constitutes best practices for fair and valid coding, what justifies those practices, and, equally important, how one should implement them.[1] The result is a set of coding practices that range from merely inconsistent to wholly inappropriate, leading to mistakes and misunderstandings in non-standard situations.

There are many reasons for this state of affairs. Different fields have different goals and assumptions about coding, and thus sometimes use different practices. Existing measures for the reliability of coding are problematic, and for historical reasons are used in ways that are not statistically sound. And the theoretical underpinnings of the

---

[1] Because we conceive of this contribution as an overview of key issues in coding theory and practice for QE researchers, both novice and advanced, and due to the limitations of space, we do not include a comprehensive review of the literature on coding and qualitative discourse analysis. We will address this shortcoming in a future, expanded version of this paper.

© Springer Nature Switzerland AG 2021
A. R. Ruis and S. B. Lee (Eds.): ICQE 2021, CCIS 1312, pp. 62–77, 2021.
https://doi.org/10.1007/978-3-030-67788-6_5

processes of coding are actually quite complex, covering everything from hermeneutics and linguistics to statistics and computer science.

In this paper, we are not attempting to resolve all of these issues, nor to provide a complete accounting of all of the conceptual machinery that explains how and why we code. Rather, our hope is to provide some guidelines for good coding practice, and suggest some of the questions that quantitative ethnographers and other researchers need to consider when coding data.

2 Background

In simplest terms, a Code is a label that we assign to some piece of data. For example, coding a photograph means asserting that it has some particular property of interest (perhaps that it contains the IMAGE OF A PERSON). However, in making what seems like a simple assertion such as this, a researcher is actually engaging in a far more complex process. In particular, Codes have five key properties that need to be accounted for in any sound coding process.

1. **Codes are contextual.** For example, it is easier to identify whether a photograph contains the IMAGE OF A PERSON than it is to determine whether that person is KAT-SUNGNGAITTUQ. Katsungngaittuq is an Utkuhikhalingmiut word that means something like "pleading" or "whining"—but not exactly. A child whining to have sugar in her tea when there is no sugar in the house is being KATSUNGNGAITTUQ, but so too is a friend who asks you for a favor that makes the you uncomfortable, even if no whining or pleading is involved.[2] Thus, coding is situated within some cultural context: we cannot code without first understanding that context.

2. **Codes are theoretical.** When a researcher codes data, the Codes are no longer situated only in the cultural context from which the data arose. They are also situated in the context within which the research is taking place. This is the well-known distinction between *emic* and *etic* understanding, where the former refers to categories that are meaningful in the community from which the data came, and the latter refers to categories that are meaningful within some theoretical framework. KATSUNGN-GAITTUQ is an Utkuhikhalingmiut word, but it was used by an anthropologist to create a theory of *emotion concepts* as a way of understanding how children learn the emotional context of life in Utkuhikhalingmiut culture [1].

3. **Codes are contestable.** Like any claims, claims about whether something contains the IMAGE OF A PERSON or that a person is KATSUNGNGAITTUQ are also inherently *contestable*. That is, we could argue about whether or not any one picture does or does not contain a person, or whether (hypothetically, of course) David is being KATSUNGNGAITTUQ when he asks Andrew to "pick up some sushi for me while you are getting lunch." Moreover, because Codes are contestable, a researcher must be able to provide specific *evidence* to support the claim that a Code applies to some piece of data. The gesture of *pointing* to some specific feature in some specific piece of the data *is* the process of coding, and in simplest terms, every claim about a Code implies some act of pointing, and every act of pointing is a claim about some Code.

---

[2] This example is drawn from the work of Briggs [1], but see also Shaffer [20].

4. **Data is constructed**. The pieces of data that we code do not represent natural categories or distinctions. They represent a selection of events in the world that were both *recorded* and *transformed* into individual items to be coded. Identifying *segments of data* to be coded also involves some choice. Even the choice to take something as simple as "turns of talk" as individual segments of data is quickly revealed to be a choice and not a natural parsing of the data if one takes a conversation analytic perspective (see, e.g., [12]). This process of breaking data into such pieces, or *segmentation*, raises its own set of questions about how and why it should be done. While the choices that go into segmentation clearly have implications for any coding process, we choose to bracket those questions here and take it as given that data to be coded has been segmented in some defensible way.

5. **Data is finite**. It is only ever possible to code, at any one time, some finite number of specific segments of data. This means that our Codes are not only situated in the culture from which the data came and within some theoretical framework, they are also *anchored* within the data itself. When we code for KATSUNGNGAITTUQ, we are coding for some *cultural phenomenon* (a particular kind of awkward social interaction) that plays a role in some *theoretical framework* (a theory of emotion concepts). But those meanings are also manifest in some particular way or ways *in the specific set of data* that we have. When we code, we are trying to make claims about a Code *as it appears in the data at hand*.

We use Codes because in order to understand something, we have to know what they *mean*. Meaning is fundamental to any human endeavor, but it is particularly salient in the analysis of human behavior. The problem is that the meaning of any single data point is hard to ascribe. And if we are not sure that the underlying data mean what we think they mean, then the patterns that we find do not have much practical use.

In his theory of Discourse [8], Gee makes the distinction between what he calls *small-d [d]iscourse* and *Big-D [D]iscourse*. [d]iscourse is the things that some person or people actually said and did in the world at some point in time—that is, the things we want to understand. [D]iscourse, on the other hand, is the way that some *group* of people—some community—behave in the world: the *kinds of* things they say, actions they take, tools they use, clothes they wear, and so on. We thus have two parallel processes: a process by which data is constructed from [d]iscourse produced by some community of people, and a process by which a theoretical understanding of that community is construed in terms of its [D]iscourse. One exists in the realm of observing and recording events, and the other is a process of interpreting events situated in theory and praxis.

Coding is the key step in the unraveling (and subsequent re-raveling) of meaning because it is the process of bridging these two worlds: the *world of events* and the *world of interpretation*. We refer to the *constructs that make up a [D]iscourse*—the kinds of things that some group of people say and do, to which we attend as researchers and to which they attend as members of some community—as [C]odes: the cultural meanings that some group of people construe, and that we as researchers, in turn, call out to make our theoretical interpretations of that culture. [C]odes are the parts of a [D]iscourse that we want to understand. [c]odes, then, are the *features of the data* we use to identify these constructs: the specific pieces of *evidence* and rules that we use to warrant our [C]odes.

A [c]ode is the collection of features (rules, examples, properties) in the data that we use to claim that the [C]ode is present.

It follows that all coding is an application of *power*. When we attach a [C]ode to some segment of data, we are saying to the data and to the people about whom it was recorded that we are the arbiters of its meaning—at least for the purposes of our analysis. Similarly, we are saying to some theory that we determine whether, when, and how its constructs apply in some setting (and, indeed, which constructs are worth applying).

Our only defense for such an act is that we believe we are doing so *fairly*. That is, the representations we make are such that members of a community we are discussing, proponents of a particular theory or theories, and informed perusers of the data would all feel that our [C]odes are not inaccurate or misleading–that is, we claim what Charmaz [2] refers to as *resonance*.

In this we are also following the work of Goodman [10] (re-elaborated in Shaffer [20]) that all data analysis aims to present some *fair sample* of the world. The concept of a fair sample is based on the idea that all analytical claims are, in fact, re-presentations of some events in the world, a recasting of some original experiences in some digestible form. Such a re-presentation is *fair* if others would feel that (a) it resembles the key features of events in the world, and (b) the things it resembles are not isolated instances, but are similar to some larger pool of events and experiences.

The question then, is how we can (a) choose a set of [C]odes and (b) operationalize them into a set of [c]odes that are fair in this sense. In other words...

3   How Should We Code?

We address this question by starting at the end of the coding process, because beginning with the final product of coding clarifies some of the criteria that guide earlier steps.

3.1   Coded Data

Fairness. The end result of coding is a set of coded data: data with fair claims about some set of Codes for each of its segments. In some cases, this will be data that has been coded by a human rater or raters. In other cases, the data is coded by some automated process.

In human-coded (sometimes called *hand-coded*) data, there are three possibilities: (1) a single rater codes the data alone; (2) two or more raters code some of the data jointly and then one or more of them code some or all of the rest of the data alone; (3) two or more raters code all of the data. In each of these cases, we have to ask the question: What evidence do we have that the Codes are fair?[3] There are two kinds of evidence that are usually marshalled.

The first is that for each [C]ode we provide a *definition* and *examples*. The definition, of course, *is* the [C]ode. The name of the [C]ode is, ideally, descriptive and evocative, but the definition determines the meaning of the [C]ode. That meaning is always enacted

---

[3] We do not ask: Are the Codes fair? There is no absolute or objective sense in which Codes can be fair or not. But we can ask what evidence we have to support a claim that they are.

within the confines of the data at hand, so the examples provide segments of data to which the [C]ode applies. Expressed in the language of psychometrics, the definition provides evidence of *construct validity* (does the [C]ode relate to underlying theory?) and the examples provide evidence of *face validity* (does the [C]ode make assertions we expect it to make about segments of data?).

The second kind of evidence that [C]odes are fair (in the case of multiple raters) is some measure of *inter-rater reliability* (IRR). There are many measures of IRR that researchers use, and the pros and cons of different measures have been discussed elsewhere [6, 14, 15, 20]. Here we will use Cohen's kappa (κ), as it is common in quantitative ethnography, but whenever we refer to κ we are making a claim about any IRR measure a researcher might choose.

Technically, κ measures the *level of agreement* between two raters taking into account features of the data, or in the language of psychometrics, *concurrent validity* (do two measures of the same construct produce the same results?). But it is easier to think of κ as measuring the *distance* between two raters' understanding of the data. A *high* value of κ indicates that the raters' understandings are close to one another; a low value of κ indicates they are far apart. The distance is proportional to $1/\kappa$.

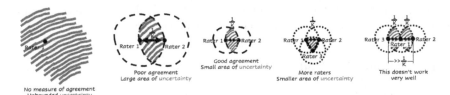

Fig. 1. Low values of κ reflect larger areas of uncertainty about the meaning of a [C]ode than high values of κ; there are diminishing returns for adding additional coders; if there are more than two coders, pairwise measures of agreement are needed.

We can think of this visually as if each rater had a circle around their understanding of the [C]ode, where the radius of the circle is $1/\kappa$ (see Fig. 1). The understandings overlap in the area that is less than $1/\kappa$ away from both raters. Thus, although we never know the "correct" understanding of a [C]ode (since there is no one correct understanding), κ gives us a way of *bounding the uncertainty* about the meaning of a [C]ode: It is likely to be somewhere in the area of uncertainty between the raters. Thus, a high value of κ gives us confidence that the uncertainty in the [C]ode is small.

This visual representation of how an IRR measure like κ bounds uncertainty also explains why there are diminishing returns to using additional coders. The area of uncertainty will surely be smaller at the intersection of three circles then at the intersection of two—and smaller still at the intersection of 4 or 5 or 6 hyperspheres. But while the area of uncertainty becomes smaller as we add more raters, it still exists. When we go from one rater to two, we go from unbounded uncertainty (that is, we have no measure) to uncertainty that we can quantify and thus choose to accept or reject. Figure 1 also shows why, if there are more than two raters, it is essential to get good agreement between every pair. Otherwise, the uncertainty becomes less bounded rather than more.

Code Validation. Determining fairness is often referred to as a *validating* a [C]ode, although we want to emphasize that fairness implies multiple forms of validation, and how we assess fairness varies depending on how the data has been coded.

All Data Coded by a Single Human Rater. This is most often seen in qualitative studies, and the logic is that any qualitative description of events is inherently perspectival, so adding a second rater (or more raters) does not make the account any more "objective."

In the case of a single rater, the only forms of evidence available are the description of a [C]ode and the examples given. In such a case:

1. Fairness of a [C]ode to existing theory can be warranted by comparing the definition to explanations of the theoretical construct(s) to which it relates.
2. Fairness of a [C]ode to the community that produced the data can be warranted by a positionality statement of the rater, and any other evidence that shows the rater understands the emic perspective of the community.
3. Fairness of a [C]ode to the data can be warranted by the examples given, and by the fact that a single rater has coded all of the data.

All Data Coded by Multiple Human Raters. There are two different ways in which this can be done. Using *social moderation,* each rater codes all of the data and then disagreements are discussed until the raters come to consensus (i.e., $\kappa = 1$) [11, 20]. If social moderation is not used, then κ is computed between the raters.

When multiple raters code all of the data, the warrants for fairness that apply to a single rater can (and should) be used. But we also have information about IRR:

1. Fairness to theory is warranted if the raters come from the same field or theoretical framework. If two raters who understand a theory agree on a [C]ode with (say) $\kappa = 0.90$, then although we do not know that any one segment of data is coded in complete accord with the theory, there is a bound on how far from the theory the [C]ode might be.
2. Fairness to the community is warranted if one (or more) of the raters comes from the community that produced the data. There are circumstances where it might not be possible to have the data coded by a member of the community, and so often community triangulation is done with the analysis as a whole rather than each individual [C]ode. But when possible, including members of the community in the coding process is a strong warrant for fairness to the community.
3. Fairness to the data is warranted by the fact that all of the coders have coded all of the data. κ is an accurate measure of the raters' agreement *for this set of data.*

Multiple Human Raters Code Some Data Jointly and Some Alone. For data coded jointly, all of the warrants apply as when multiple raters code all of the data (and thus also the warrants that apply to a single coder). However, the circumstances become more complex for the data that is only coded by a single rater.

For the *data that is coded by both raters* (DBR), we can measure the rate of agreement *for that data.* If $\kappa(DBR) = 0.91$, then we know that the rate of agreement for the DBR was 0.91. Notice, however, that the DBR is only a subset of all of the coded data. We cannot simply assume that because κ(DBR) = 0.91 that κ for all of the data—if we measured it—would be 0.91. That would be as statistically unsound as measuring the heights of 100 students at the University of Wisconsin, taking the average (which when we did it was 1.75 m), and then concluding that the average height of everyone in Wisconsin is 1.75 m.

We have taken a sample from some population (all people in Wisconsin or all the coded data), computed a statistic (either average height or κ), and then assumed that the value of the statistic for the population is the same as for the sample. Instead, we need to control for Type I error (false positives). With height data we might do this using a t-test on the sample. But IRR statistics in general, and κ in particular, have distributions whose shapes vary based on the characteristics of a sample; thus it is impossible test them analytically.

We recommend controlling for Type I error using *Shaffer's* ρ, which is an empirical rejective method designed to warrant claims about the κ for a population based on the κ for a sample [6, 7, 20]. The ρ statistic functions much like a p-value in a t-test: if it is below some critical value (typically $\alpha = 0.05$ or $\alpha = 0.01$), then we conclude that κ for all of the coded data is above some threshold.[4] That is, we use κ and ρ to warrant that the coding done by single raters is fair to the data in the sense that bounding uncertainty now takes into account the fact that our measure was only on a sample of the data.

If we have such a warrant for the rate of agreement over all the data, then we can treat the data coded by a single rater as if it were coded by both raters with a rate of agreement at or above the threshold we specified, with all of the warrants that entails.

Automated Coding. If one of the raters is some automated process—more commonly referred to as an *automated classifier*—then the above still applies, with one exception.

Fairness to theory and fairness to the community are *impossible to achieve with only one human rater and an automated classifier*. The automated classifier does not *understand* the theory and is not a member of the community. Thus, two human raters and one automated classifier are required to use IRR to warrant fairness. The human raters provide warrants to fairness; then acceptable κ and ρ between the automated classifier and each human warrant that the classifier can code the remainder of the data fairly.

Once an automated coding process is determined to be fair, it might be used to code more data that is similar to the data on which it was developed. Technically, this requires a claim of exchangeability: namely, that the original data and the new data are not different in any way that impacts the classifier. We can warrant such a claim by (1) explaining why we think the conditions are the same, or (2) showing that the classifier performs fairly on the new data. Using the first approach means that the fairness of the new coding depends on the accuracy of the assertion of exchangeability. The second requires repeating the coding process: two humans need to code the new data and test agreement with each other and with the classifier.

---

[4] The ρ statistic can be applied to any measure of IRR with raters using binary codes. There are other statistics that can be used for raters when using non-binary codes.

3.2   Coding Practices

Definition and Examples. The definition of a [C]ode is the claim that is being made about the meaning of a segment of data. We sometimes see brief and relatively uninformative definitions (for example, defining a [C]ode for FRIEND as "any reference to a friend or friendship"). But brief definitions make weak or vague claims. We recommend more robust definitions, such as:

> FRIEND: *Explicit reference to a being a friend or any related terms (e.g., buddy, pal, chum, bestie), or to the general concept of friendship; could include familial terms in relation to a non-family-member, for example, calling someone "my sister" when they are not actually a sister; referring to a platonic relationship of mutual respect, trust, loyalty, and/or honesty using a single term or phrase.*

The definition of a [C]ode should always be accompanied by examples from the dataset. Examples show instances where the definition of the [C]ode clearly applies in a case or cases that are not trivial or obvious. So, in that sense, a segment of data where someone says "You're a good friend" is not a good example of the [C]ode FRIEND. Examples should show no more of the context than is needed to see that the [C]ode applies.

Transcription. When coding some kinds of data (for example, video or audio), a researcher has a choice of coding the original data directly, or producing a text transcript before coding. Coding directly from a source like video or audio has several advantages: (1) there is no widely-accepted standard for transcription of the visual content of video data; (2) there is no concern about transcription error; and (3) any transcription is a data reduction, so coding from video or audio data directly preserves context. However, when coding directly from audio or video: (1) segmentation can be more difficult than from transcribed data, and (2) developing automated classifiers, at least with current technology, is difficult. In the ideal case, transcript and original source can be co-registered (for example, using time stamps), so researchers can code from the transcript but preserve the original context. However, we believe that best practice is *not* to code from audio or video data directly but to *add to the transcript information need for coding* (e.g., actions, gestures, intonation). Adding information to the transcript makes the evidence for a [C]ode clear, and thus provides a stronger warrant.

Segmentation. As we argue above, segmentation is a vital part of coding. There is not space here to discuss all of the considerations that go into segmentation, but we do want to make three observations.

Meaningful Breaks. Segmentation is the process of dividing data into *meaningful* pieces. While some researchers segment data by time (e.g., coding 2-s or 1-min intervals of the data), this is not best practice for most contexts. Phenomena of interest can span an arbitrary break in the data, so data should be segmented based on break points that correspond with breaks in the activity being coded: for example, turns of talk in conversation, questions and responses in an interview, sentences or paragraphs in text, or peaks or valleys in a record of galvanic skin response.

Open Coding. One alternative to segmentation is *open coding*, or identifying evidence for a [C]ode in un-segmented data, a practice sometimes used in ethnography. However, it is difficult to achieve good IRR with open coding, and without pre-identified segments of data, it is difficult to account for even simple variables, like duration or frequency of [C]odes. Open coding thus precludes meaningful quantification.

Equivalency. To make quantification possible, segmentation should a divide data into pieces that are exchangeable—that is, equivalent for the purpose of counting.

[C]ode Representation. Researchers also need to decide how to record information about a [C]ode for each segment of data. *Binary representation* is the most common, where a 1 indicates that the [C]ode applies to the segment of data and a 0 indicates that it does not. A *continuous representation* describes a [C]ode by some continuous measure of its intensity or certainty in a segment of data. For example, a value of 0.5 might indicate that the [C]ode applies, but not strongly, or that the rater is 50% confident that the [C]ode applies. Binary representations are more common because people generally have difficulty estimating probabilities of their certainty or intensity of meaning. Some automated classifiers report continuous values, and if a binary and continuous score are being compared, a *cut score* is typically applied: for example, if an automated classifier reports more than 60% certainty, that becomes the equivalent of a human coding positive.

It is possible to construct categorical classifiers: for example, {"[C]ode definitely does not apply," "[C]ode probably does not apply," "[C]ode probably applies," "[C]ode definitely applies"}. These are not recommended because using them usually means converting the categories to a continuous value, and it is difficult to warrant that the intervals between categories are numerically equivalent. Some researchers use a *stacked binary* representation: indicating the binary for each [C]ode using the presence or absence of the label, and listing the labels together. We recommend against this because it is more difficult to conduct IRR or to use quantitative models on a stacked binary representation.

The IRR Loop. The fundamental process of achieving good IRR for a [C]ode involves an iterative cycle of coding, testing, and refining.

Subsets. At any point in the IRR loop, the data to be coded consists of three non-overlapping subsets: (1) A *holdout set*, which consists of all of the segments of data that have not yet been seen by any rater, human or machine, in any way; (2) a *test set*, which consists of any data that has been coded by one or more raters where (a) no rater has seen another's coding, and (b) no test for IRR has been performed; and (3) a *training set*, which consists of any data not in the holdout or test sets.

IRR Principles. IRR can only be warranted by (a) establishing that a test set produces a κ for the whole dataset that is above some threshold, τ, at alpha level, α (typically 0.05 or 0.01), where (b) the test set was sampled from the holdout set. The first principle is discussed above (Sect. 3.1). The second addresses *information leakage* [13, 16]. Coding is a process of *model development*: a mental model for a human rater or a predictive model for an automated classifier. These models are created using the training set and tested using the test set. Information leakage in coding comes about when information about the test set is contained in the training set—that is, when a rater has access to information about the test set prior to coding. Such leakage can lead to biased estimates of IRR. Thus, the IRR loop works as follows:

1. Rater 1 codes segments of data chosen at random from the holdout set.
2. N items from step 1 are chosen for a test set; remaining items are added to the training set.
3. Rater 2 codes the test set.
4. Values are computed for κ and ρ.
5. If $\kappa(N) > \tau$ and $\rho(\tau) < \alpha$, then we can warrant that κ(full dataset) $> \tau$, and the IRR loop is done; or
6. If $\rho(\tau) \geq \alpha$, then the test fails and the test set becomes part of the training set.

    a. Raters examine the segments of data on which there was disagreement.
    b. If necessary, the definition of the [C]ode is changed.
    c. The raters return to step 1.

Threshold Selection. The choice of threshold depends on the statistic chosen, but historically researchers have chosen thresholds that are lower than is desirable. For example, Cohen argued that κ values of 0.61–0.80 indicate *substantial* agreement [4]. However, raters could disagree on 20% of the data and still achieve $\kappa > 0.60$. It would be difficult to argue that such a [C]ode is fair. To achieve fair [C]odes, researchers should set higher thresholds, as high as $\tau = 0.90$ when using κ.

Eagan and colleagues [5] developed a *binary replicate test* for determining appropriate IRR thresholds. In this approach, once coding is complete and a statistical model has been made, the binary replicate test introduces random error into the coding. The level of κ at which the original result becomes insignificant provides an empirical threshold for acceptable error.

Separability of [C]odes. While there are studies that report an "overall κ" or "κ across all codes," any criteria of fairness has to apply *to each [C]ode individually*. [C]odes can be related to one another; however, it makes no sense to assert that if one [C]ode is manifestly unfair but the rest are fair, that the [C]odes are fair "overall." In applying a [C]ode, we assert that a segment of data *means* something. If that assertion is not defensible, then conclusions drawn from it are not defensible either.

Test Set Size. The optimal size of a test set will vary depending on the IRR statistic being used and the frequency, or *base rate*, of the [C]ode in the data. For κ, we have found that test sets of $80 \leq N \leq 100$ are typically large enough to get acceptable agreement. In early iterations of the coding loop, however, when the raters are just starting to come to a consensus on the meaning of the [C]ode, smaller test sets are more efficient, as raters can more quickly see differences in their understanding.

Test Set Construction. The traditional approach to IRR is to construct a test set by randomly selecting items from the holdout set. (In step 2 of the IRR loop, all of the items from step 1 are included in the test set.) This random selection is necessary for generalizing from the test set to the full set of data. However, researchers who control for Type I error using ρ can also use *conditional sampling*. This is possible because ρ is an empirical rejective method: it constructs multiple test sets and uses them to determine the likelihood that the actual test set came from data with $\kappa < \tau$.

Specifically, in step 2 of the IRR loop, researchers can select some number, g, of the items from step 1 that Rater 1 coded positive and include those in the test set; the remaining $N - g$ items are chosen at random from the rest of the items coded in step 1. The result is a test set with an *inflated base rate*, or minimum frequency of items that Rater 1 coded positive. This is useful because: (1) more items coded positive provide more information for raters when they disagree; and (2) κ and many other IRR statistics are more sensitive at higher base rates. Taken together, these advantages of conditional sampling—made possible by ρ—make it easier to get high levels of agreement.

Reporting [C]odes. [C]odes should always be described with the *name or label* for the [C]ode, its *definition, examples*, and a report of the *results of any IRR* that was conducted. Results of IRR for each [C]ode should include the *statistic* used, the *threshold* chosen, the *statistic value* for the final test set, the *method for controlling for Type I error and its value*, as well as the *size of the test set.* Table 1 shows an example codebook entry for the [C]ode FRIEND.

Table 1 Example codebook entry for the [C]ode FRIEND. IRR columns report Cohen's κ computed on a test set of $N = 80$ items and the result of the ρ test to determine whether $\kappa > \tau = 0.90$. Values are reported for comparison between two human raters (H1/H2) and each human and an automated classifier (H1/AC and H2/AC). Bold entries indicate significance at the $\rho < \alpha = 0.05$ level. *Because κ is not statistically higher than τ for all pairs of raters, the [C]ode is not fair,* and a choice to include such a [C]ode in any analysis would require careful justification.

Code	Definition	Examples	IRR $\kappa(80)/\rho(0.90)$		
			H1 H2	H1 AC	H2 AC
FRIEND	Explicit reference to a being a friend or any related terms (e.g., buddy, pal, chum, bestie), or to the general concept of friendship; could include familial terms in relation to a non-family-member, for example, calling someone "my sister" when they are not actually a sister; referring to a platonic relationship of mutual respect, trust, loyalty, and/or honesty using a single term or phrase	*We're like family, I'll always be there for you What are friends for? You totally get me, that's why we're BFFs. Wuddup cuz?*	0.91 0.06	**1.00** 0.01	**0.96** 0.02

Derived Coding. Thus far, we have been discussing what Shaffer [20] terms *primary [C]odes.* With a primary [C]ode, segments of data can be coded using only evidence from within a segment itself. In contrast, coding a segment of data with a *derived [C]ode* requires combining two or more pieces of evidence, which may or may not come from the segment being coded. When it is difficult for raters to come to agreement on a complex [C]ode, they can often identify simpler primary [C]odes that can be fairly coded, and then use their combination to make assertions about more complex meaning.

Derived [C]odes are also essential when addressing issues of *context* in coding. Coding a segment of data *in context* means that a decision about the meaning of the segment uses (points to) evidence from elsewhere in the data. As discussed above (see Sect. 2), this act of pointing is always equivalent to some primary [C]ode; thus coding in context can always be accounted for, in principle, using a derived [C]ode.

When using derived [C]odes, it is sometimes effective to use the primary [C]odes directly and let a model of the [D]iscourse connect them into more complex [C]odes. If derived [C]odes are used, however, they need to be validated: it is not the case that if primary [C]odes are fair, any combination of them will be as well.

Automated Coding. There are three types of automated classifiers in use today.

Supervised Machine Learning. Supervised machine learning methods take a set of human-coded segments of data as input. The algorithm identifies a set of *features* in the data (for text data, these could be words, bigrams, trigrams, length of segments, etc.) and then finds the combinations of features that best predict the human coding. Such models use *cross validation* to test the accuracy of the classifiers: the algorithm creates a holdout set and a training set from the human-coded data, then develops a classifier from the training set and tests it on the holdout set. These methods are easy to use; the only human intervention required is the input of the initial coded data. However, supervised machine learning methods require large amounts of data to produce accurate classifiers—often on the order of thousands of segments. Moreover, supervised machine learning models lack transparency: the combination of features is often a complex calculation that cannot be inspected or explained by a human researcher. The warrants for fairness from supervised models may thus appear weaker than other approaches.

Unsupervised Machine Learning. Unsupervised machine learning algorithms, such as *topic modeling*, take a set of *uncoded* text data and extract groups of keywords that are related to one another. These groups can be taken as [c]odes, and human researchers can inspect the keywords to try to discern the [C]odes to which they refer. Unsupervised models are often tempting for researchers to use, especially in exploratory analyses, as they work quickly and require no initial coding. They also provide a transparent model by producing explicit groups of keywords for each [C]ode. However, unsupervised models cannot be used as fair classifiers *unless the implied [C]odes are defined and a complete process of IRR is carried out.* IRR in these circumstances is often problematic because one of the raters (the automated classifier) cannot change its coding. Moreover, from experience we have found that validating unsupervised models requires human raters to code a substantial number of segments of data.

Active Machine Learning. In active machine learning, the algorithm selects segments of data to present to a human rater so as to minimize the number of excerpts that a human rater has to code. For example, *nCoder* [17, 21] automatically constructs test sets with inflated base rates based on its current classifier, including segments that contain high-frequency words that the human rater has not seen before. When a test set does not result in acceptable IRR, the system shows the segments where raters disagreed and asks the human rater to identify what features they used to make their coding decision. As a result, active machine learning systems can be substantially more efficient than supervised or unsupervised methods. Such systems also represent [c]odes as explicit descriptions of words or patterns of words, and are thus fully transparent.

Advantages of Automated Classifiers. Automated classifiers, once developed, can code large amounts of data quickly and do not suffer from *coding fatigue*: the phenomenon where human raters become less attentive after coding many segments of data. Automated classifiers are consistent and can potentially be applied to new data collected under similar conditions to the original.

Subgroup Fairness. Because many datasets contain subgroups that have low numerical representation in the data—such as populations defined by demographic data such as race or disability status—bias can result when that dataset is used to develop a [C]ode: for example, training facial recognition software using predominantly white faces, and as a result misidentifying the faces of people of color [3, 18]. Many of the methods used to assess fairness depend on the frequency with which events occur in the data. If a subgroup is underrepresented in a dataset, then data from that group may be underrepresented in the test set used to compute IRR and warrant fairness. Attention should be paid to examining the discourse of subgroups relative to any [C]ode. If the code occurs more or less frequently in a subgroup than in the discourse of the community as a whole *without any theoretically-sound reason*, or if disagreements in IRR occur more or less frequently in segments of data from the subgroup, then the coding process should be examined with some care.

3.3   Generating [C]odes

Grounded Generation Cycle. The *grounded generation cycle* is the fundamental process for identifying [C]odes and warranting that the choice of [C]odes is grounded simultaneously in theory, community, and data [2].

1. [C]odes must reflect understanding generated from close reading of the data. Glesne [9] describes coding as a process of sorting and defining, in which a researcher progressively puts similar segments of data together to identify common themes. Shaffer [20] suggests looking for striking or interesting segments of data and using those to identify meaningful categories in the [D]iscourse. In these approaches, the researchers' understanding of the data and the community it represents helps generate a set of fair [C]odes.
2. [C]odes must be fair to some theoretical framework. In qualitative approaches, the researchers' understanding of the setting needs to relate to existing research.

These two perspectives—understanding the data and understanding relevant theory—are sometimes described as *bottom-up* versus *top-down* coding. However, developing good [C]odes is never entirely either a bottom-up or top-down process. Rather, it is an iterative process of moving back and forth between data and theory.

Quantitative Tools. The grounded generation cycle can be supported using quantitative techniques. One common approach is to construct a table of word frequencies that can help researchers check that they have not overlooked some key term of art. Some use *word stemming* to gather together variations on the same word (e.g., command, commands, commander, commanding). Other *natural language processing* approaches can identify words (or N-grams) that occur more frequently in the corpus of data than in common usage, and others (e.g., *latent semantic analysis, topic modeling,* or *skip-grams*) use the frequencies with which words co-occur in common usage to identify families of words that occur together in the data. Any of these approaches are appropriate tools to augment the qualitative process of code generation, *as long as all segments of data that are measured quantitatively are placed in the training set,* and are not used to measure IRR. This includes any summary information about the data, which should exclude information from the holdout set. Thus, a holdout set should be created *at the beginning of the code generation process.*

Automated Approaches to Code Generation. As discussed above, there are algorithms that can identify groups of related words and phrases in uncoded data (topic modeling is one of the best known). Such automated approaches can be useful in identifying potential topics that might be used as [C]odes, and it is possible to use such topics and/or keywords as input to the grounded generation cycle. However, ***there is no way to generate fair [C]odes using only an automated process.*** A [C]ode is not only a claim that some topic exists in the data, but that it is a *meaningful* part of the [D]iscourse of some community. This can only be warranted by a process that understands the meaning of segments of data, which existing automated processes cannot do.

Iterativity. This description of creating fair [C]odes might suggest that it is a linear process, however, the iterativity in coding goes beyond the grounded coding cycle and the IRR loop. In practice, the stages of [C]ode identification, implementation, and validation are not independent. For example, the process of getting IRR with one [C]ode might lead to the realization that the definition of the [C]ode needs to change (step 6b in the IRR loop). One persistent question in managing the iterative process of coding is whether to start with broad or narrow [C]odes. We recommend starting with broad [C]odes and progressively making them narrower. It is notoriously hard to get good IRR for very specific [C]odes because fine distinctions between [C]odes are often hard for both human and machine raters to identify. Subdividing an initial broad [C]ode has the advantage of only requiring consideration of segments already identified by the broad [C]ode. Thus, it is generally easier to break a broad code into more specific [C]odes than it is to aggregate very specific [C]odes into a broader category.

Huis Clos. It is sometimes tempting to use existing tools for making claims about data: *sentiment analysis,* for example, or *reading level analysis.* However, whatever their source, and however well established the algorithms that produce them, they are systems for making claims about segments of data. Therefore *all* of the concerns above regarding fairness apply. Consider, for example, a measure like the number of words in a segment of data. This is easy to calculate, but in the context at hand, is the number of words *meaningful*? And if so, *what does it mean*—and *how do we know* what it means?

Thus, any claim about data is a [C]ode, and the process of coding—and concerns about warranting code fairness—are not only universal, but unavoidable.

4 Discussion

We have argued here that coding is a process fundamental to the analysis of data, because coding is the bridge between the world of data and the world of interpretation. The central question in coding, then, is how to make sure that the linkages between data and analysis are valid, in the sense that our interpretation of the analysis and our interpretation of the data are both consistent with one another and fair.

We have consistently addressed this question in terms of *fairness* rather than *validity*, not because quantitative ethnographers can ignore questions of validity, but because we think that the term itself is used in ways that are complex and sometimes contentious. In the end, validity is about meaning. As researchers we care that the meanings we assert respect the communities we are describing, the theoretical constructs we are using, and the data we have collected. In this sense, validity as it is sometimes formally construed is necessary but insufficient. Thus, quantitative ethnographers care not only about cross-validation of coding algorithms, but also about IRR between humans, and between humans and automated classifiers. They care not just about whether coding can be done quickly, but that it is the result of a process that manages [C]ode generation, IRR, coding, and code reporting, all within the framework of best practices for assuring that the results are fair.

Of course, there is room in quantitative ethnography for exploratory analyses. Quantitative ethnographers can, do, and should at times conduct preliminary analyses that use unvalidated codes, or put data into a model as a way of gaining insight into its meaningful structure. It is absolutely possible to start with such approaches and validate them later. But in doing so, we must remember that an exploratory analysis that takes these approaches is, by definition, making claims that may be unfair, and therefore we need to use the utmost caution in using them in any public-facing analysis of data.

We hope that the considerations we have explored above provide a helpful framework for coding data fairly, but we recognize that issues arise in any analysis that cannot be addressed with simple reference to general guidelines. We thus believe that Siebert-Evenstone's Maxim [22] is the best guide for coding in a way that is consistent with theory, community, and the evidence available: *When in doubt, read your data.*

Acknowledgements. This work was funded in part by the National Science Foundation (DRL-1661036, DRL-1713110), the Wisconsin Alumni Research Foundation, and the Office of the Vice Chancellor for Research and Graduate Education at the University of Wisconsin-Madison. The opinions, findings, and conclusions do not reflect the views of the funding agencies, cooperating institutions, or other individuals.

References

1. Briggs, J.L.: Emotions have many faces: inuit lessons. Anthropologica **42**(2), 157–164 (2000)
2. Charmaz, K.: Constructing Grounded Theory: A Practical Guide through Qualitative Analysis. Sage, Thousand Oaks (2006)
3. Chouldechova, A., Roth, A.: The frontiers of fairness in machine learning. arXiv:1810.08810 (2018)
4. Cohen, J.: Kappa: coefficient of concordance. Educ. Psych. Meas. **20**, 37 (1960)
5. Eagan, B., et al.: The binary replicate test: determining the sensitivity of CSCL models to coding error. In: International Conference on Computer Supported Collaborative Learning (2019)
6. Eagan, B.R. et al.: Can we rely on reliability? Testing the assumptions of inter-rater reliability. In: Smith, B.K. et al. (eds.) Making a difference: Prioritizing equity and access in CSCL: 12th International Conference on Computer-Supported Collaborative Learning. pp. 529–532 (2017)
7. Eagan, B.R., et al.: rhoR: Rho for inter rater reliability (2016)
8. Gee, J.P.: An Introduction to Discourse Analysis: Theory and Method. Routledge, London (1999)
9. Glesne, C.: Becoming Qualitative Researchers: An Introduction. Pearson, Boston (2015)
10. Goodman, N.: Ways of Worldmaking. Hackett, Indianapolis (1978)
11. Herrenkohl, L.R., Cornelius, L.: Investigating elementary students' scientific and historical argumentation. J. Learn. Sci. **22**(3), 413–461 (2013)
12. Hutchby, I., Wooffitt, R.: Conversation analysis. Polity (2008)
13. Kaufman, S., et al.: Leakage in data mining: formulation, detection, and avoidance. ACM Trans. Knowl. Discov. Data (TKDD) **6**(4), 1–21 (2012)
14. Kurasaki, K.S.: Intercoder reliability for validating conclusions drawn from open-ended interview data. Field Methods **12**(3), 179–194 (2000)
15. Lombard, M., et al.: Content analysis in mass communication: assessment and reporting of intercoder reliability. Hum. Commun. Res. **28**(4), 587–604 (2002)
16. Lukács, G., Ansorge, U.: Information leakage in the response time-based concealed information test. Appl. Cogn. Psychol. **33**(6), 1178–1196 (2019)
17. Marquart, C.L. et al.: ncodeR: techniques for automated classifiers [R package] (2018)
18. Mehrabi, N., et al.: A survey on bias and fairness in machine learning. arXiv:1908.09635 (2019)
19. Saldaña, J.: The Coding Manual for Qualitative Researchers. SAGE Publications, Thousand Oaks (2015)
20. Shaffer, D.W.: Quantitative Ethnography. Cathcart Press, Madison (2017)
21. Shaffer, D.W., et al.: The nCoder: A Technique for Improving the Utility of Inter-Rater Reliability Statistics. Epistemic Games Group, Madison (2015)
22. Siebert-Evenstone, A.: Personal communication (n.d.)
23. Thornberg, R., Charmaz, K.: Grounded theory and theoretical coding. In: Flick, U. (ed.) The SAGE Handbook of Qualitative Data Analysis, pp. 153–169 SAGE Publications, London (2014)

Exploring the Effects of Segmentation on Semi-structured Interview Data with Epistemic Network Analysis

Szilvia Zörgő[1]([✉]) [ID], Zachari Swiecki[2] [ID], and A. R. Ruis[3] [ID]

[1] Institute of Behavioral Sciences, Semmelweis University, Budapest, Hungary
zorgoszilvia@gmail.com
[2] Faculty of Information Technology, Monash University, Melbourne, Australia
[3] Wisconsin Center for Education Research, University of Wisconsin−Madison, Madison, USA

Abstract. Quantitative ethnographic models are typically constructed using qualitative data that has been segmented and coded. While there exist methodological studies that have investigated the effects of changes in coding on model features, the effects of segmentation have received less attention. Our aim was to examine, using a dataset comprised of narratives from semi-structured interviews, the effects of different segmentation decisions on population- and individual-level model features via epistemic network analysis. We found that while segmentation choices may not affect model features overall, the effects on some individual networks can be substantial. This study demonstrates a novel method for exploring and quantifying the impact of segmentation choices on model features.

Keywords: Epistemic network analysis (ENA) · Semi-structured interviews · Quantitative ethnography (QE) · Methodology · Data segmentation

1 Introduction

Quantitative ethnography (QE) is a nascent field aiming to unify quantitative and qualitative research methodologies in order to facilitate thick description at scale [1]. Most QE studies involve coding raw qualitative data with constructs relevant to the research question(s) and segmenting the data into meaningful parts to explore the interactions of codes [2]. These acts are integral to modelling cognition or behavior and identifying significant patterns. While QE researchers have begun to explore the effects of coding and window length on model features [3–5], the effects of segmentation more broadly have not been similarly examined. In this study, we explored how different approaches to segmentation affect models of patient narratives constructed with Epistemic Network Analysis (ENA), a technique for modelling the structure of connections among codes in qualitative datasets.

© Springer Nature Switzerland AG 2021
A. R. Ruis and S. B. Lee (Eds.): ICQE 2021, CCIS 1312, pp. 78–90, 2021.
https://doi.org/10.1007/978-3-030-67788-6_6

2 Theory

Research in QE is conducted on various kinds of *discourse data* [2, 6], including log files of online activity, recordings of conversations or interviews, published writing, photographs, field notes, and many others. To facilitate analyses of discourse, QE researchers not only collect or record data that document people thinking, acting, and being in the world, they also *transform* those data into a representation that makes quantification possible.

This transformation can involve a number of critical decisions. Transcribing video recordings of conversations, for example, might involve: associating spoken sounds with the appropriate word or other verbal expression; identifying which sequences of words should be grouped into utterances; converting utterances into sentences by including punctuation; assigning those sentences to speakers; documenting gestures, facial expressions, or other visual information using consistent notation; applying time stamps; and so on. These processes entail both reducing and standardizing audio-video data into text data for subsequent analysis.

One of the most critical transformation processes that researchers perform is *segmentation*: the division of data into consistent and meaningful parts. In QE analyses, there are two key levels of segmentation. The first involves segmentation into *items* or lines (represented as rows in a qualitative data table[1]), which are the most elemental units of data. This is the level on which codes are applied, so most researchers choose relatively short segments, such as sentences or paragraphs in formal prose, turns of talk in conversations, or questions and responses in structured interviews. The second level of segmentation involves establishing *relational context*: groupings of items that are linked for the purposes of interpretation. Defining the recent temporal context—some span of items within temporal or conceptual proximity to one another—is one way of establishing interpretive segmentation. This is the level on which interactions among codes are considered meaningful.

For example, many QE studies use ENA to model the structure of connections among codes in discourse. To operationalize the relational context for each unit of analysis, ENA uses two parameters: conversation and stanza window. *Conversations* define groupings of items that *can* be connected in a model. For example, in a dataset that documents the interactions of different project teams on different days, the conversations might be defined by "Team" and "Day." This would group items (say, turns of talk) such that each segment contains all the items from one team's interaction on one day. This means that individuals can make connections only to contributions from their own team, and for a given team, only within a single day's interaction.

Stanza windows define *how* connection structure is computed within conversations for a given unit of analysis. There are three main types of stanza window:

- *Moving stanza* windows compute the connection structure of each line in a conversation relative to every line that comes before it *within the window*. With a moving

---

[1] Qualitative data tables contain various kinds of data where rows and columns exhibit ontological consistency. Rows contain the same categories of values (data and metadata), while each column contains one type of information (e.g., age of participants).

stanza window of length 4, for example, each line is connected to the three lines that precede it. The connections in each window for which a given unit contributes the referring line (the last line in the window) are then aggregated across all conversations, reflecting the connections contributed by that unit.

- *Infinite stanza* windows compute the connection structure of each line in a conversation relative to every line that comes before it *within the conversation*. Thus, the infinite stanza works in the same way as a moving stanza, but there is no limit on the number of previous lines that are included in the window (except for the length of the conversation itself).
- *Whole conversation* stanzas use the entire conversation as the stanza window, but only connect codes contributed by the same unit. The whole conversation model identifies whether or not a connection occurred in the unit's lines in a given conversation, then aggregates connections across all conversations.

Thus, the operationalization of relational context may have a significant impact on resulting models of connection structure.

Despite the importance of relational context in ENA models, relatively few studies have examined the extent to which different choices of conversation and stanza window affect model features. Ruis and colleagues, for example, found that for one dataset documenting the interactions of engineering student project teams, statistical discrimination between two sub-populations was fairly robust to window length once a minimum length was reached (in their study, that minimum was four lines) [7]. However, they also found that model features and interpretation were more sensitive to window length, and did not stabilize until a window length of seven.

Operationalizing relational context is also particularly challenging with some types of data, e.g. semi-structured interviews, as alternations between interviewer speech and interviewee speech do not necessarily denote meaningful segments for the purpose of analysis. An interviewee may answer one question by addressing various topics relevant to the research objectives in a single turn of talk, which may need to be segmented and analyzed separately. While some researchers choose to parse an interview transcript according to questions and responses when the interview is more clearly structured [8], this may not be a viable option when the interview allows for organic digressions, distal or implicit connections, and the interweaving of several relevant sub-topics. Yet, because many exploratory research initiatives utilize semi-structured interviews for data collection, this form of qualitative data is quite common. Consequently, it is important to understand the effects of different approaches to segmentation on analyses of such discourse.

One approach to assessing the impact of different model parameters—in this case, different conversation and stanza window selections—is through a *sensitivity analysis*. In a sensitivity analysis, researchers examine whether alteration of one or more parameters invalidates a given inference [9]. In this study, we used a well-studied dataset documenting patient decision-making regarding choice of therapy to explore the effects of segmentation on model outputs. We then used this dataset to address two research questions:

RQ1: Do different segmentations produce significantly different ENA models?

RQ2: Do different segmentations affect the interpretation of individual ENA networks?

3 Empirical Data

3.1 Study Design and Data Collection

The empirical data we utilized was derived from a previous study on how patients make decisions regarding their choice of therapy. In that project, we were interested in why patients choose to employ biomedicine only or non-conventional medicine (i.e., Complementary and Alternative Medicine, CAM) either instead of or in addition to biomedicine. The study took place in Budapest, Hungary; data was collected via semi-structured interviews conducted with patients primarily included based on diagnosis group (diabetes, musculoskeletal, digestive, and nervous system diseases). Interviews covered three overarching themes: (i) trusted sources of health-related information, (ii) lay etiology (theories of illness causation), and (iii) patient journey (decisions and experiences). Interviews lasted 60 minutes on average and were sound-recorded and transcribed verbatim. Zörgő & Peters give a full description of the study, focusing on methodological considerations [10]. We included a total of 26 interviews in the present study; each interview was considered a separate source of data.

3.2 Coding

Our deductive code system comprised three levels of abstraction, containing a total of 52 low-level codes. We had three clusters of codes, based on the interview structure: Epistemology (sources of health-related information, appraisal of information; $N = 16$), Ontology (concepts of illness and health; metaphors of illness and health; $N = 23$), and Behavior (choices of therapy, evaluation of therapeutic efficacy; $N = 13$). Sentences constituted the lowest level of segmentation (i.e., utterances); coding was performed manually on this level. The analysis below contains the six codes from the Ontology cluster that we used in this study; each code pertains to a lay theory of etiology (see Table 1).

Table 1. Codes capturing patient theories of illness causation (etiology)

Code name	Label	Description
Psychosocial/ Neurological	E.e.psych	Emotions, stress, trauma, nerves, nerve damage
Psychosocial vitalist	E.e.vital	Energy/qi/prana, block, "law of attraction", spiritual teleology
Ecological	E.e.eco	Environmental toxins, chemicals, "electro-smog"
Immunological	E.e.immun	Weakness or susceptibility of immune system
Nutritional	E.e.nutri	Quality or type of food, additives, toxins in food
Genetic	E.e.gene	Inherited illness or susceptibility, genetic causes

4   Methods

4.1   Constants and Variables of Segmentation

To explore the effects of segmentation on model features, we used two forms of conversation (source-based and delimiter-based) and three stanza window definitions (whole conversation, infinite stanza, and a moving stanza window of 4 lines). All other model parameters were held constant. Units were defined as individual patients, each of whom was associated with one interview (i.e., one source), and all lines were coded as described above.

4.2   Forms of Segmentation

Source-Based Segmentation. For source-based segmentation, the conversation was defined as one interview transcript, and each source is uniquely associated with one patient. In this type of segmentation, all utterances within an interview were considered relevant context. Source-based segmentation connotes one of the few "naturally" occurring choices for segmenting semi-structured interview data on the conversation level.

Delimiter-Based Segmentation. For delimiter-based segmentation, the conversation was defined according to a coding process in which two independent raters segmented

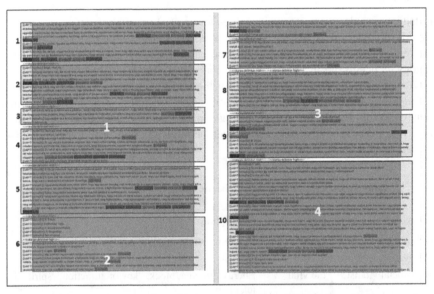

Fig. 1. Delimiter-based segmentation with the same definition of stanza (i.e., recent temporal context) manually performed by two independent raters. The first version (DelimiterV1) is represented by green boxes within the narrative, numbered in black (1–10). The second version (DelimiterV2) is displayed with overlaying red boxes, numbered in white (1–4). Coding is utterance-based (utterance = sentence); codes are depicted within the text representing three code clusters (yellow = epistemology, blue = ontology, red = behavior). (Color figure online)

each source manually to identify shifts in topic within the patient's narrative. This process yielded two versions of the same type of segmentation: DelimiterV1 and DelimiterV2. The former was performed by a research assistant with some prior knowledge of the research topic, the latter by the principal investigator with extensive knowledge of the topic.

As Fig. 1 shows, although there are some instances when both versions of segmentation (DelimiterV1 and DelimiterV2) agree where a delimiter should occur in the narrative (e.g., after green 7 and red 2), and there are times when the red delimiter is exactly the double of the green (e.g., green 8–9 = red 3), in many cases, delimiting stanzas differ substantially, such as red 1 ending in the middle of green 6.

4.3 Model Comparison

To compare the ENA models constructed with different segmentation parameters, we first constructed a "gold standard" model—that is, the model that aligned best with our qualitative understanding of the data.[2] Source-based segmentation with an infinite stanza window provided good interpretive alignment with the qualitative data. The codes pertain to lay etiology, allowing us to model how a patient conceptualizes illness causation. Previous studies have observed that these explanatory models exhibit a high level of intrapersonal congruence, despite the fact that an individual's narrative may contain references to a variety of illnesses. In other words, regardless of how many comorbidities a patient exhibits, from a certain analytical perspective, their theory of illness causation will be consistent or integrated to include all experienced phenomena. Thus, to examine an explanatory model that encompasses the illness with which we included the patient into the study and its comorbidities as well, we chose a segmentation where each individual's narrative is considered a separate, bounded entity within which codes may co-occur, and we regarded every utterance from an individual as closely connected. Code co-occurrences within aggregated interview narratives and mean networks were produced for the two main groups in the study: users of biomedicine and users of CAM.

Following the approach described in [11], we compared each patient's gold standard ENA model to their corresponding model under eight combinations of conversation/stanza window by computing the pairwise correlations (Pearson's r) between the normalized adjacency vectors (i.e., the vectors representing the normalized connection strengths between each unique pair of codes) of each unit. A high-magnitude correlation between normalized adjacency vectors suggests that the structure of connections associated with each unit was similar in both models. A low-magnitude correlation between

---

[2] The method we describe below can be used to compare any two ENA models that use the same units and codes, and thus does not require a gold standard model. We chose to use one here to reduce the number of comparisons made and simplify the presentation of the results. In many cases it may be difficult to justify a gold standard model. However, if one is justified, an alternate approach is to project all other models into the metric space produced by the gold standard model. Such an approach has the advantage of comparing units of analysis along fewer dimensions, rather than making comparisons in a high-dimensional space. We applied both approaches to these data and our results were consistent between them. Here we present only the high-dimensional comparisons to demonstrate the most general approach.

Table 2. The nine models created to test the effects of segmentation on network structure

Model	Unit	Conversation	Stanza window
Gold standard	Individual (source)	Source	Infinite stanza
Model 1			Whole conversation
Model 2			Moving window (4)
Model 3		Source + DelimiterV1	Whole conversation
Model 4			Infinite stanza
Model 5			Moving window (4)
Model 6		Source + DelimiterV2	Whole conversation
Model 7			Infinite stanza
Model 8			Moving window (4)

normalized adjacency vectors suggests that the models produced different connection structures.

Prior to computing the correlations, individuals with no connections in one of the two models compared in a given correlation were excluded. This situation was relatively rare—only six patients had no connections under one or more of their models.

To evaluate how the networks changed overall for a given comparison, we averaged the correlations. Prior to averaging, we transformed the correlations using Fischer's Z transformation, which allows for meaningful averages of correlation coefficients and the calculation of confidence intervals. To test for significant differences between models, we tested whether the average correlation between models was significantly different from a high correlation value (0.90) using the 95% confidence intervals.

To inspect individual differences, we constructed boxplots of the (untransformed) correlation values. This enabled us to explore the extent to which individual networks might change substantially even if the average correlation between two models is high.

Finally, to explore model differences due to segmentation in more detail, we compared ENA network graphs from the gold standard model to network graphs from the other models for individuals whose vectors were substantially different. In these network graphs, the nodes correspond to the codes in the analysis, and the edges reflect the relative frequency of co-occurrence between codes. Thicker and more saturated edges indicate higher relative co-occurrence.

5   Results

Figure 2 shows the pairwise correlations between the eight models generated with differing segmentation parameters (mod1-8) and the gold standard model (gsmod).

All of the models generated with different segmentations (i.e., different combinations of conversation and stanza window) are highly correlated with the gold standard model (gsmod). That is, for no model is the upper bound of the 95% confidence interval below the critical value of 0.90. Furthermore, no model's confidence interval had a lower bound

Adjacency Vector Comparisons

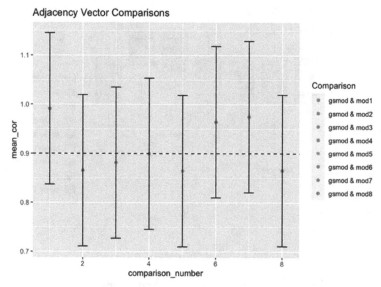

Fig. 2. Mean pairwise correlations (Pearson's r) between the normalized adjacency vectors of models created with different types of segmentation (mod1–8) and the gold standard model (gsmod). The upper bounds of the 95% confidence intervals for all comparisons are above the critical value of 0.90, suggesting that the models are highly correlated with the gold standard.

less than 0.70, indicating that all models were highly correlated with the gold standard model.

While there are no statistically significant differences between the adjacency vectors of the gold standard model and the other models, some comparisons show that certain individuals changed substantially (see Fig. 3). In particular, 97 comparisons yielded correlations below 0.90, and some are as low as 0.20. This suggests that while the models as a whole are highly correlated, some individuals have very different networks under models constructed with different segmentations.

To explore the extent to which interpretation of patient networks changed due to segmentation, we chose two examples: Patient 25 and Patient 16. Source 25 is the interview transcript of a patient in the CAM group, a female in her twenties, suffering from Crohn's disease and ulcerative colitis; she was diagnosed at the age of 14. Source 16 is the interview transcript of a patient in the biomedicine group, also a female in her twenties, suffering from type 1 diabetes; she was diagnosed at the age of 2. Both patients require biomedical treatment, but Patient 25 employs complementary therapies as well. Both Crohn's disease and type 1 diabetes are chronic conditions, and in the current biomedical understanding, their causes are unknown. In instances of chronic conditions of unknown origin, lay explanatory models of illness may play an even more significant role in patient decision-making regarding choice of therapy. This was also why these specific patients were selected for closer scrutiny. The source-based moving stanza model of Source 25 exhibited one of the most substantial changes compared to the gold standard, while Source 16's same two models remained very similar.

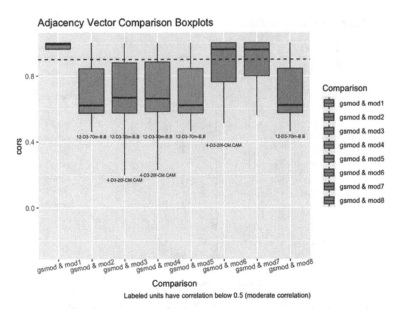

Fig. 3. Box plots showing the distribution of pairwise correlations for each model comparison. Although mean pairwise correlations between models were uniformly high, many individual pairwise correlations were substantially lower.

The graphs in Fig. 4 compare the co-occurrence of etiology codes within the narratives of the two individuals. Both network models were generated with source-based segmentation, the graphs on the left with an infinite stanza window (gold standard), the ones on the right with a moving stanza window of 4 utterances. While the basic structure of the biomedical patient's network (bottom models in red) stays consistent in the two versions of segmentation (and all other types of models in our study), the CAM individual's network exhibits substantial differences. In both versions of segmentation, the biomedical patient makes connections among psychological, ecological, and nutritional factors within their theory of illness causation. The CAM patient, on the other hand, makes connections among psychological, vitalist, immunological, and nutritional factors in the infinite stanza version of the model, but only a fraction of these remain in the moving stanza version: the connection among psychological, vitalist, and nutritional factors remains (with different edge weights), but the connection to immunological factors disappears, as well as the connection between codes Vital and Nutri.

The first third of Patient 16's discourse does not contain any etiology codes, these only appear in the remainder of the interview; Patient 25's narrative, in contrast, contains etiology codes in the first and second third only. The average distance between two etiology codes in Source 16 is much less than in Source 25 (once every 7.6 lines and once every 40.8 lines, respectively). Compared to the entire length of the interview, the number of utterances spanning the first and last coded utterance is proportionally similar in the two patients' discourse (Source 16: 88 out of 371 utterances, which is 23.7% of the total number of utterances; Source 25: 451 out of 2126 utterances, which is 21.2% of the total number of utterances). Thus, etiology codes spanned about the same length

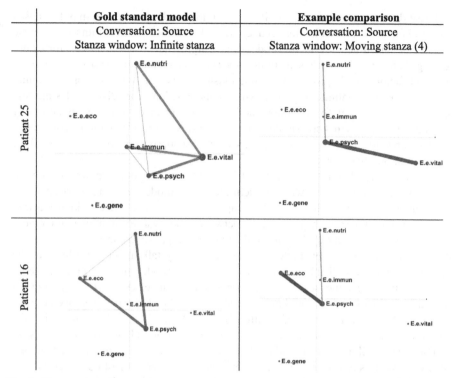

Fig. 4. The network models of two patients in two different model comparisons. Unit 25 (top, teal) is an individual in the CAM group, while Unit 16 (bottom, red) belongs to the biomedicine group. The networks were generated using an interview transcript (source) as conversation, and the stanza window was defined as infinite stanza (left) and moving stanza (right). The former is how we defined the gold standard model. The figure illustrates the extent to which a network structure can change with segmentation (Source 25) or remain roughly similar (Source 16), compared to the gold standard. (Color figure online)

in both interviews proportionally, yet there were marked differences in the position of these codes within the interview and relative to each other. These features may explain a unit's sensitivity to changes in model parameters.

Our employed R scripts, disclosed results, and extra visualizations can be openly accessed at our Gitlab repository: https://gitlab.com/szilvia/icqe20-segmentation.

6 Discussion

We compared the normalized adjacency vectors of units in eight different ENA models to our gold standard in order to assess the extent to which varying segmentation affects overall network structure. As our results show, different segmentation choices did not produce models with significantly different features in aggregate, but for some individuals, there were substantial differences in their ENA networks under models produced with different segmentations.

These differences in unit sensitivity to changing model parameters may be caused by several factors. Apart from their frequency, the location of codes within the discourse seems to be an influencing factor; codes appearing earlier in an interview, for example, might increase the unit's sensitivity to varying segmentation. Another potentially important factor is code proximity, as relationships between codes in close proximity may look similar in infinite and fixed window models, but more distal codes are less likely to be connected in fixed window models. Further research is needed to more fully understand the factors that contribute to a unit's sensitivity to varying model parameters and to understand what segmentation choices are most appropriate for different kinds of data and research questions.

The source-based infinite stanza and whole conversation models capture the broadest range of possible connections, while the delimiter-based models and source-based model with a moving stanza window of 4 lines capture code co-occurrences taking place in more recent temporal context. Yet, distance between codes (varying number of utterances between two codes) may or may not reflect cognitive proximity in a semi-structured interview. In our specific example, an interviewee may talk about one illness at the beginning of a narrative that may receive a set of etiology codes, then go on to talk about a comorbidity with another set of etiology codes, and alternate between these throughout the interview. This situation could indeed lead to a larger distance between two etiology codes, but there is a latent variable affecting that distance: the illness to which the codes refer. Thus, it may be beneficial to segment a narrative based on an underlying variable, such as illness in this particular case, and examine the relationship among codes vis-a-vis this type of segmentation. Naturally, other clusters of codes (pertaining to other phenomena or research questions) may be influenced by a different variable. For example, our study also worked with a cluster of codes relating to the patient's trusted sources of information; this cluster may be less meaningful in an illness-based narrative structure and more adequately understood with a discourse segmentation determined by stages in a patient journey (e.g., before diagnosis/after diagnosis or according to various employed treatments).

From a pragmatic point of view, one could assert that each of our nine models (gold standard plus comparisons), highlights a different aspect of our data. In the source-based segmentation, the whole conversation model (mod 1) showed us all possible connections among all codes in the given source, but only whether they occurred or not, while the infinite stanza model (gsmod) provided insights into the relative frequency of those connections. Finally, the source-based moving stanza window of 4 model (mod 2) indicated which of those weighted connections were among codes that are spatially/temporally closer to each other within the interview. The delimiter-based models depicted the same basic principles, but within segments of narrative that were manually determined to be closely connected (according to a certain definition of stanza: i.e., topic of discussion). Depending on the analytical goal, all of these models are potentially useful. The method we present here for comparing models with different segmentation parameters allows researchers to assess whether and to what extent any two models are significantly different, but it does not indicate which model is better. That decision remains one that must be based on the research questions being asked and deep qualitative engagement with the data and the context in which they were collected.

Even if segmentation has little effect on model features overall, this study suggests that individual networks may vary substantially under different segmentation parameters, and thus other factors may be important when defining the conversation and stanza window. For example, the (relative) frequency of codes can have a significant impact on model features, as whole conversation models are sensitive only to the presence or absence of a code in the conversation, while infinite stanza windows are also sensitive to how often codes occur and where in the conversation they appear. Additional studies are needed to explore the relationship between segmentation and the (relative) frequency and distribution of codes.

7 Limitations

Our study had several limitations. First, to reduce the number of comparisons for simplicity of presentation, we selected a gold standard model (source-based, infinite stanza), yet in reality, such "gold standards" do not exist for a given dataset, much less for datasets in general. The method we present here does not require a gold standard—it can be used to compare any two models with the same units and codes, and thus has significant advantages over projecting one model into the metric space defined by another model—but all comparisons are still pairwise, and thus there are a large number of possible comparisons. In addition, the lowest correlations do not necessarily reflect networks with the most significant differences (for any two models), as the overall structure of connections could be similar even if all the edge weights are different. Many small changes to the line weights could result in a poorer correlation than one large change (e.g., a connection present in one model and not present in another), but the impact on interpretation may be greater in the latter case. Furthermore, correlating the normalized adjacency vectors is merely one way to compare network structures; other modes of comparison, such as correlating the eigenvectors, might yield different results. Lastly, as discussed above, the frequency of code occurrence may be a significant factor, particularly if code frequencies are low, as many were in this dataset. Further research is needed on the effects of segmentation on datasets with different frequencies and distributions of codes.

8 Closing Remarks

Our study aimed to investigate the effects of different segmentation parameters on model features, and in particular to explore whether and to what extent different conversation and stanza definitions changed network structure or interpretation. We present a method that can be used to compare any two models with the same units and codes, which can guide model parameterization, but this study also shows that more research is needed to address several key questions: Under what conditions will the choice of segmentation start to have large effects? How do these effects occur? and What influences their magnitude? We believe that inquiry in this domain can aid the construction of more accurate (network) models of qualitative data, which in turn, will facilitate our understanding of human cognition and behavior.

Acknowledgements. The authors are grateful to collaborator GJY Peters and to research assistants Anna Geröly, Anna Jeney, and Krisztina Veres for their rigorous work in the project that provided our empirical data. This work was funded in part by the National Science Foundation (DRL-1661036, DRL-1713110), the Wisconsin Alumni Research Foundation, and the Office of the Vice Chancellor for Research and Graduate Education at the University of Wisconsin-Madison. The opinions, findings, and conclusions do not reflect the views of the funding agencies, cooperating institutions, or other individuals.

References

1. Williamson Shaffer, D.: Big data for thick description of deep learning. In: Millis, K., Long, D., Magliano, J., Wiemer, K. (eds.) Deep Comprehension: Multi-Disciplinary Approaches to Understanding, Enhancing, and Measuring Comprehension, pp. 262–275, 1st ed. Routledge (2018)
2. Williamson Shaffer, D.: Quantitative Ethnography. Cathcart Press, Madison
3. Cai, Z., Siebert-Evenstone, A., Eagan, B., Shaffer, D.W., Hu, X., Graesser, A.C.: nCoder+: a semantic tool for improving recall of nCoder coding. In: Eagan, B., Misfeldt, M., Siebert-Evenstone, A. (eds.) ICQE 2019. CCIS, vol. 1112, pp. 41–54. Springer, Cham (2019). https://doi.org/10.1007/978-3-030-33232-7_4
4. Bakharia, A.: On the equivalence of inductive content analysis and topic modeling. In: Eagan, B., Misfeldt, M., Siebert-Evenstone, A. (eds.) ICQE 2019. CCIS, vol. 1112, pp. 291–298. Springer, Cham (2019). https://doi.org/10.1007/978-3-030-33232-7_25
5. Eagan, B., Swiecki, Z., Farrell, C., Williamson Shaffer, D.: The binary replicate test: determining the sensitivity of CSCL models to coding error. In: Wide Lens: Combining Embodied, Enactive, Extended, and Embedded Learning in Collaborative Settings, pp. 328–335. International Society of the Learning Sciences, Lyon, France (2019)
6. Gee, J.: An Introduction to Discourse Analysis: Theory and Method. Routledge, London (2014)
7. Ruis, A.R., Siebert-Evenstone, A.L., Pozen, R., Eagan, B.R., Williamson Shaffer, D.: Finding common ground: a method for measuring recent temporal context in analyses of complex, collaborative thinking. In: A Wide Lens: Combining Embodied, Enactive, Extended, and Embedded Learning in Collaborative Settings. International Society of the Learning Sciences, Lyon, France, pp. 136–143 (2019)
8. Wooldridge, A.R., Haefli, R.: Using epistemic network analysis to explore outcomes of care transitions. In: Eagan, B., Misfeldt, M., Siebert-Evenstone, A. (eds.) ICQE 2019. CCIS, vol. 1112, pp. 245–256. Springer, Cham (2019). https://doi.org/10.1007/978-3-030-33232-7_21
9. Frank, K., Min, K.: Indices of Robustness for Sample Representation. Sociol. Methodol. **37**, 349–392 (2007)
10. Zörgő, S., Peters, G.: Epistemic network analysis for semi-structured interviews and other continuous narratives: challenges and insights. In: Eagan, B., Misfeldt, M., Siebert-Evenstone, A. (eds.) Advances in Quantitative Ethnography, pp. 267-277. Springer, Cham (2019). https://doi.org/10.1007/978-3-030-33232-7_23
11. Swiecki, Z.: Modeling interdependence in collaborative problem-solving. Doctoral dissertation, University of Wisconsin–Madison (2020)

The Mathematical Foundations of Epistemic Network Analysis

Dale Bowman[1], Zachari Swiecki[2], Zhiqiang Cai[3], Yeyu Wang[3], Brendan Eagan[3], Jeff Linderoth[3], and David Williamson Shaffer[3]([⊠])

[1] Institute for Intelligent Systems, University of Memphis, Memphis, TN 38111, USA
[2] Monash University, Melbourne, Vic 3800, Australia
[3] University of Wisconsin–Madison, Madison, WI 53711, USA
`zcai77@wisc.edu, dws@education.wisc.edu`

Abstract. *Epistemic network analysis* (ENA) has been used in more than 300 published studies to date. However, there is no work in publication that describes the transformations that constitute ENA in formal mathematical terms. This paper provides such a description, focusing on the mathematical formulations that lead to two key affordances of ENA that are not present in other network analysis tools or multivariate analyses: (1) summary statistics that can be used to compare the differences in the *content* rather than the *structure* of networks and (2) network visualizations that provide information that is mathematically consistent with those statistics. Specifically, we describe the mathematical transformations by which ENA constructs matrix representations of discourse data, uses those representations to generate networks for units of analysis, places those networks into a metric space, identifies meaningful dimensions in the space, and positions the nodes of network graphs within that space so as to enable interpretation of those dimensions in terms of the content of the networks. We conclude with a discussion of how the mathematical formalisms of ENA can be used to model networks more generally.

Keywords: Epistemic network analysis · ENA · Discourse · Dimensional reduction · Network visualization · Quantitative ethnography

1 Introduction

Quantitative ethnographic approaches to data analysis are currently being used by more than 400 researchers in 21 countries, and the quantitative ethnographic method of *epistemic network analysis* (ENA) in particular has been used in more than 300 published studies at the time of this writing. In the context of the International Conference on Quantitative Ethnography (ICQE)—of which this paper is a part—we argue that we can take it as a shared understanding that ENA is a useful tool for modeling human activity.

© Springer Nature Switzerland AG 2021
A. R. Ruis and S. B. Lee (Eds.): ICQE 2021, CCIS 1312, pp. 91–105, 2021.
https://doi.org/10.1007/978-3-030-67788-6_7

There already exist papers that describe ENA in broad conceptual terms [17], and papers that place the logic of ENA within the broader epistemological framework of *quantitative ethnography* [15]. Other work has provided worked examples of ENA analyses, including descriptions and illustrations of some of the mathematical transformations that ENA uses to produce quantifications and visualizations of patterns of discourse [16]. And, of course, the rENA package [9] makes it possible to examine one set of specific computational algorithms that can be used to conduct ENA analyses.

However, to our knowledge, there is no work in publication that describes the *mathematical formulation* of ENA: that is, a description of ENA as a set of mathematical transformations, independent of any specific conceptual framework, example, or algorithm.

In what follows, we provide such a description, and we argue that this is valuable for two reasons. First, and most transparently, precise mathematical formulations are objects to think with. Our own experience of describing ENA in such terms has led to new insights about the ENA algorithm, and more generally, mathematical formalisms are a powerful language for communicating and interrogating complex processes. But we also present this mathematical formulation of ENA with the idea that future expansions, changes, and even challenges to the existing technique could be more precisely and clearly described in terms of the changes they make to this formal description of ENA as a mathematical transformation.

Our hope is that such a description will thus be a valuable contribution to the ICQE conference and the to field of quantitative ethnography more broadly.

2   Background

ENA is an analytic method that was originally developed to model discourse networks based on theories of cognition that suggest connections between ideas and actions are more important to the learning process than ideas or actions in isolation [4,14]. ENA was therefore designed to model the structures of connections (edges) among discourse elements (nodes, or vertices), and a central premise of any ENA analysis is that the connections between categories of interest (edges) are more important than the categories (nodes) themselves.

ENA has been used extensively to model discourse networks (see, for example, [2,7,11]). It has also been used to model network trajectories of cognitive networks and social networks [10], social gaze coordination [1], performance of surgeons [3,13] and healthcare teams [18,19], patient and clinician interviews [20], and semantic properties of historical records [12].

Motivation for the development of a network approach to address analytical questions such as these came from limitations of existing tools. For example, multivariate analysis is a classical approach that has been used to model the interaction between cognitive elements. However, in contexts with a large number of variables, the number of possible interaction terms increases exponentially. Traditional multivariate methods thus require large amounts of data—and even in the presence of a large amount of data, the traditional methods focus primarily on the variables. Interaction terms are typically of secondary interest.

Network analysis is a logical alternative for modeling contexts where interactions are of primary interest. However, most network analysis methods have been developed to analyze relatively large networks: often with tens or hundreds of nodes, but sometimes with thousands, millions, or even billions [5]. Moreover, in many network analytic contexts, the nodes are not consistent from network to network. Thus they can only be efficiently analyzed using summary statistics such as structural cohesion, clustering coefficients, or density (e.g., [8]).

Importantly, summary statistics from traditional network analyses are *structural* in the sense that they describe *how* nodes are connected without reference to *which* nodes are connected. For example, *structural cohesion* measures the minimal number of edges that need to be removed to disconnect the remaining nodes from each other. *Clustering coefficients* calculate the ratio of the number of closed triples (three nodes connected with three edges) to the total number of triples (three nodes connected with two or three edges) in order to assess the degree to which nodes in a graph cluster together. *Network density* is the portion of potential connections in a network that are actual connections.

Because traditional summary statistics are structural measures, describing a network using them can obscure important differences between networks. For example, two networks can both have densities of 0.5 (half of the possible connections are actually present), but have no overlapping connections. The same nodes may be connected by two completely different "halves" of the possible connections.

A second persistent problem with traditional network analytic approaches is visualization [6]. More specifically, it is difficult to compare two networks if the nodes and edges are not in the same location in the visualizations of the networks. However, there is no deterministic way to arrange the nodes and edges of networks using traditional approaches. Network layouts thus may—or may not—produce visual intuitions that align with the mathematical differences between any two networks.

ENA addresses these problem by using a different set of mathematical formalisms to analyze networks, specifically taking advantage of three properties of discourse networks in the context of quantitative ethnography. First, because of their grounding in ethnographic techniques, where it is difficult to analyze a hundred different elements of discourse, discourse networks in quantitative ethnography tend to have *relatively small sets of nodes*. Second, discourse networks are typically characterized by *dynamic and differentially weighted connections*—that is, the analysis focuses on changes or differences in the weights (rather than just the presence) of connections. And finally, in a given context, networks typically *contain the same discourse elements of interest*. Thus, ENA can take advantage of mathematical techniques that would be impossible (or at least unwieldy) to use to for networks with large numbers of nodes that change from network to network.

As a result, the mathematical formulation is able to provide network representations that:

1. Produce summary statistics that can be used to compare the differences in the *content* rather than the *structure* of networks—that is, to compare which nodes are more or less strongly connected; and
2. Produce network visualizations that are *co-registered* with the summary statistics—that is, the information conveyed in the network visualization is always mathematically consistent with the summary statistics.

Central to this approach is recognizing that the mathematical representation of a network is a square matrix Ω such that matrix element w_{ij} represents the strength of the connection from node i to node j.

The primary questions in understanding the mathematics of ENA are thus:

1. How are summary statistics that allow comparison of the content of matrices computed from Ω; and
2. How are nodes positioned calculated from Ω such that the resulting network graphs are co-registered with those summary statistics?

It is these questions that we attempt to answer in the next section.

3   Mathematical Formulation of ENA

We begin by describing the method for constructing an Ω matrix for each discourse network in a model.

3.1   Utterances and Codes

Let $\Theta = (\theta_1, \ldots, \theta_n)$ be a sequence of utterances and $A = \{a_1, \ldots, a_m\}$ be a set of codes.

3.2   Coding

For each utterance $\theta_i, i = 1, \ldots, n$, there is an associated coding vector $\boldsymbol{w}^i = (w_1^i, \ldots, w_m^i)$ where w_j^i is the weight for code a_j associated with utterance θ_i for $i = 1, \ldots, n$ and $j = 1, \ldots, m$. We assume that the strength of association between code a_j in utterance θ_i and code a_k in utterance θ_ℓ is the product of their weights, $w_j^i w_k^\ell$.

3.3   Conversations and Units

We divide Θ into subsequences called conversations. Let C be the set of subsequences of Θ defined as $C = \{c^1, \ldots, c^N\}$ for $c^k = (\theta_{\pi_1}, \ldots, \theta_{\pi_k})$ where $\theta_{\pi.} \in \theta$ and $(\pi_1, \ldots, \pi_k)$ is a sequence of the indices $(1, \ldots, n)$ such that when $i < j$ we have $\pi_i < \pi_j$. That is, a conversation c^k for $k = 1, \ldots, N$ is a subsequence of Θ. These subsequences can be mutually exclusive or they may have non-empty intersections.

Similarly we can divide Θ into subsequences called units that can represent individual people or students, etc. Let $\Upsilon = \{v^1, \ldots, v^M\}$ be the set of units, where $v^k = (\theta_{\nu_1}, \ldots, \theta_{\nu_k})$ for $\theta_\nu. \in \Theta$, and $(\nu_1, \ldots, \nu_k)$ is a subsequence of indices $(1, \ldots, n)$ for $k = 1, \ldots, M$.

Further define $\lambda^{xy} = c^x \cap \nu^y$ for $x = 1, \ldots, N$ and $y = 1, \ldots, M$. Let $\Lambda = \{\lambda^{xy} : x = 1, \ldots, N, y = 1, \ldots, M\}$. That is, λ^{xy} is the sequence of utterances in conversation x belonging to unit y.

Finally, we may (optionally) divide Υ into discrete subsets (groups of units) $\Xi = \xi^1, \ldots, \xi^n$, such that $v^\eta \in \xi^\psi \implies v^\eta \notin \xi^{\phi \neq \psi}$. These subsets might be used to compare groups of units statistically.

3.4   Associations

Let $s > 0$ be an integer indicating the size of the *stanza window* being used. For utterance θ_i in conversation c^x, construct two vectors $\mathbf{p}^{xi}$ and $\mathbf{q}^{xi}$ defined as

$$\mathbf{p}^{xi} = \begin{cases} \mathbf{0} & s = 1 \\ \sum_{n=(i-s+1)}^{i-1} \mathbf{w}^n & s > 1 \end{cases} \tag{3.1}$$

$$\mathbf{q}^{xi} = \sum_{n=i-s+1}^{i} \mathbf{w}^n. \tag{3.2}$$

The vector $\mathbf{p}^{xi}$ is a conversation memory weight. For cases where $i < s$, the index of summation, n, in 3.1 and 3.2 may be less than or equal to zero. In this case, we define $\mathbf{w}^n \equiv 0$ when $n \leq 0$. Defining $\mathbf{X}'$ as the transpose of matrix $\mathbf{X}$, let

$$\mathbf{G}^{xi} = \mathbf{p}^{xi}(\mathbf{p}^{xi})', \tag{3.3}$$

and

$$\mathbf{F}^{xi} = \mathbf{q}^{xi}(\mathbf{q}^{xi})', \tag{3.4}$$

and let $\mathbf{H}^{xi}$ be the $m \times m$ symmetric matrix defined as

$$\mathbf{H}^{xi} = \mathbf{F}^{xi} - \mathbf{G}^{xi}. \tag{3.5}$$

Here, $\mathbf{G}^{xi}$ is the cumulative weight of all connections in the $s - 1$ utterances preceding utterance θ_i in conversation c^x, while $\mathbf{F}^{xi}$ is the cumulative weight of all connections in the $s - 1$ utterances preceding utterance θ_i *and* in utterance θ_i. Then, $\mathbf{H}^{xi}$ is a matrix that gives, for each utterance $\theta_i \in c^x$, the strength of association between pairs of codes. $\mathbf{H}^{xi}$ can also be constructed using the following

$$\mathbf{H}^{xi} = \boldsymbol{w}^i \left(\boldsymbol{w}^i\right)' + \left[\boldsymbol{w}^i \left(\mathbf{p}^{xi}\right)' + \mathbf{p}^{xi} \left(\boldsymbol{w}^i\right)'\right]. \tag{3.6}$$

With this formulation the first term in the sum measures the strength of associations between codes in utterance θ_i and the second two terms measure the strength of association between the referring utterance θ_i and the s leading utterances in the conversation.

A $1-1$ transformation is then applied to elements of $\mathbf{H}^{xi}$. The most common transformation applied to the $\mathbf{H}$ matrix is a binary model where $\mathbf{H}^{xi*}$ is defined as

$$\mathbf{H}^{xi*}_{jk} = \begin{cases} 1 \ h^{xi}_{jk} > 0 \\ 0 \ \text{otherwise.} \end{cases} \tag{3.7}$$

for $j = 1, \ldots, m$ and $k = 1, \ldots, m$.

When weighted models are used, $\mathbf{H}^{xi*}$ is defined as

$$H^{xi*}_{ij} = \log(H^{xi}_{jk}) \quad \text{or} \quad H^{xi*}_{ij} = \sqrt{(H^{xi}_{jk})}. \tag{3.8}$$

The square root transformation has the advantage of returning the elements of the association matrix back to the units of the original weights. Both transformations reduce the magnitude of the associations, de-emphasizing the impact of large weights in the data.

For example, if two codes have weights of 3 in adjacent utterances in the data, then their un-transformed connection strength would be 9. This would have an association strength equivalent to codes co-occuring with weights of 1 *nine different times*. Thus, small increases in weight of individual utterances can have large impacts on the adjacency matrices for units of analysis. Applying the square root transform decreases the potential disproportional impact of multiplying weights.

3.5   Accumulation for Units

For each unit v^y, construct matrix

$$\boldsymbol{\Omega}^y = \sum_{x=1}^{N} \sum_{i \in \lambda^{xy}} \mathbf{H}^{xi*}. \tag{3.9}$$

Here, Ω^y_{ij} is the cumulative strength of association between codes a_i and a_j for unit v^y over all conversations in C. Since the interaction of codes with themselves is not of interest when studying connections between codes in the symmetric association matrices $\mathbf{H}^{xi*}$, the diagonal elements of the association matrices, $\boldsymbol{\Omega}^y$, are set to zero: $\Omega^y_{ii} = 0 \ i = 1, \ldots, m$.

For symmetric association matrices constructed in this way with diagonal elements set to zero, there is redundant information in the matrix $\boldsymbol{\Omega}^y$. We define a new operation *vecsym* to retain only the non-redundant information from the association matrices as follows. If the association matrix has components

$$
\Omega^y = \begin{bmatrix}
\Omega^y_{11} & \Omega^y_{12} & \Omega^y_{13} & \cdots & \Omega^y_{1m} \\
\Omega^y_{21} & \Omega^y_{22} & \Omega^y_{23} & \cdots & \Omega^y_{2m} \\
\vdots & \vdots & \vdots & \vdots & \vdots \\
\Omega^y_{m-1,1} & \Omega^y_{m-1,2} & \Omega^y_{m-1,3} & \cdots & \Omega^y_{m-1,m} \\
\Omega^y_{m1} & \Omega^y_{m2} & \Omega^y_{m3} & \cdots & \Omega^y_{mm}
\end{bmatrix},
$$

then $vecsym(\Omega^y)$ is defined as

$$
vecsym(\Omega^y) = (\Omega^y_{12}, \Omega^y_{13}, \Omega^y_{23}, \ldots, \\
\ldots, \Omega^y_{1\chi}, \Omega^y_{2\chi}, \ldots, \Omega^y_{\chi-1,\chi}, \ldots, \Omega^y_{1m}, \ldots, \Omega^y_{2m-1,m})'. \quad (3.10)
$$

Thus, the association vector is formed by concatenating the upper diagonal matrix by column.

We will use the notation $\mathbf{z}^y$ to denote the association vector of unit v^y and Z to denote the set of association vectors for all units, that is

$$
\mathbf{z}^y = vecsym(\Omega^y), \quad (3.11)
$$

and

$$
Z = (\mathbf{z}^1, \ldots, \mathbf{z}^M). \quad (3.12)
$$

3.6 Normalization of Adjacency Vectors

The adjacency vectors may be normalized by

$$
\mathbf{N}^y = \frac{\mathbf{z}^y}{\| \mathbf{z}^y \|} \quad \text{for } y = 1, \ldots, M. \quad (3.13)
$$

The normalization step is performed if the magnitude of the vectors from each unit should be removed, for example, if networks represent different amounts of data. Normalization returns the proportions of each code pair or connection within a given unit. The adjacency vectors (normalized or not) are then centered as

$$
\mathbf{N}^y = \mathbf{N}^y - \bar{\mathbf{N}} \quad y = 1, \ldots, M \quad (3.14)
$$

where $\bar{\mathbf{N}} = \dfrac{\sum_{y=1}^{M} \mathbf{N}^y}{M}$ is the mean of the (normalized) adjacency vectors.

3.7 Projection

We next construct a projection from $\mathbf{N}$ into a lower-dimensional space for analyzing units Υ.

If the units Υ have been divided into discrete subsets Ξ—and particularly if the units have been divided into exactly 2 discrete subsets—then ENA typically uses a *means rotation*, which, to our knowledge, is a unique projection developed for ENA (although it could be used with other analytical techniques).

To construct a means rotation, construct vector $\boldsymbol{\mu}$ as

$$\boldsymbol{\mu} = \frac{\bar{\xi}^1 - \bar{\xi}^2}{\|\bar{\xi}^1 - \bar{\xi}^2\|} \tag{3.15}$$

where

$$\bar{\xi}^\psi = \frac{\displaystyle\sum_{v \in \xi^\psi} \mathbf{N}^v}{|\xi^\psi|}. \tag{3.16}$$

That is, $\boldsymbol{\mu}$ is a unit vector whose direction is from the mean of ξ^1 to the mean of ξ^2.

Then, remove from each point its projected component on $\boldsymbol{\mu}$ to produce

$$\tilde{\mathbf{N}} = \mathbf{N} - \mathbf{N}\boldsymbol{\mu}\boldsymbol{\mu}' \tag{3.17}$$

and apply *singular value decomposition*[1] (SVD) to $\tilde{\mathbf{N}}$.

The dimensions of $\tilde{\mathbf{N}}$ are $M \times \ell$ where $M = |U|$ and ℓ is $\dfrac{m^2 - m}{2} - 1$. If $rank(\mathbf{N}) = k$, then we can factor $\tilde{\mathbf{N}}$ as

$$\tilde{\mathbf{N}} = \mathbf{UDV}', \tag{3.18}$$

where $\mathbf{U}$ is an $M \times k$ matrix whose columns are the eigenvectors of $\tilde{\mathbf{N}}\tilde{\mathbf{N}}'$, $\mathbf{V}$ is an $\ell \times k$ matrix whose columns are the eigenvectors of $\tilde{\mathbf{N}}'\tilde{\mathbf{N}}$, and $\mathbf{D}$ is a diagonal matrix whose elements are the non-zero eigenvalues of $\tilde{\mathbf{N}}\tilde{\mathbf{N}}'$ (also the eigenvalues of $\tilde{\mathbf{N}}'\tilde{\mathbf{N}}$) arranged in descending order. This decomposition is known as the full rank single decomposition.

The columns of $\mathbf{U}$ and $\mathbf{V}$ are orthonormal vectors, that is $\mathbf{U}'\mathbf{U} = \mathbf{V}'\mathbf{V} = I$. Thus we can show that the columns of $\mathbf{V}$ are an orthonormal set of basis vectors for the column row space of $\tilde{\mathbf{N}}$.

Let $\mathbf{R} = (\boldsymbol{\mu}, \mathbf{V})$ be a *rotation matrix* such that

$$\mathbf{N_r} = \mathbf{NR} = (\mathbf{N}\boldsymbol{\mu}, \mathbf{NV}). \tag{3.19}$$

---

[1] SVD is related to other commonly used dimension reduction/visualization techniques, such as *principal component analysis* (PCA) and *factor analysis*. SVD decomposes the original (non-symmetric) data matrix, Z, without centering, while PCA standardizes the columns of the original matrix and decomposes the data into a set of ordered, orthogonal components using the eigenvalues of the symmetric sample covariance matrix, thus centering the data prior to decomposition. Factor analysis derives a set of influential factors by decomposing the sample covariance matrix of a set of centered variables into two additive components, one of which is attributed to the set of common factors and the other is specific to each observation.

Then $\mathbf{N_r}$ is a projection of $\mathbf{N}$ such that the first dimension of $\mathbf{N_r}$ passes through $\bar{\xi}^1$ and $\bar{\xi}^2$, and subsequent dimensions are orthogonal to the first dimension[2] and to each other, sorted by their eigenvalues in descending order.

That is, the first dimension of $\mathbf{N_r}$ shows the differences between the means of ξ^1 and ξ^2, and the remaining dimensions each account for the most remaining variance in $\mathbf{N}$ after removing the previous dimensions.

In cases where there are not two groups to compare (or if the analysis does not call for comparing two groups), set $\tilde{\mathbf{N}} = \mathbf{N}$ and construct an SVD.

Notice that $\mathbf{N_r}$ describes each unit, v, such that $\mathbf{N_r^v}$ is based on the *connections* the unit makes between codes $A = a_1, \ldots, a_m$. Furthermore, the differences between connections of any two units, v^k and v^l, are modeled by the difference between $\mathbf{N_r^k}$ and $\mathbf{N_r^l}$.

Thus, the dimensions of $\mathbf{N_r}$ constitute *summary statistics* that can be used to compare the differences in the content (rather than the structure) of network——that is, to compare which nodes are more or less strongly connected. These dimensions can show what linear combination of connections most strongly distinguish between two groups in the data, and what connections account for the most variance among units in the data.

It follows, of course, that these summary statistics function as numerical representations of the content of the networks. One can compare groups of units using these summary statistics using a variety of statistical models to test the significance of differences between networks, or one can predict outcome variables based on the content of networks, including models that control for possible confounds.

3.8   Placement of Nodes

Let $\mathbf{B}$ be a $m \times \frac{m^2 - m}{2}$ matrix, where m is the number of codes, $|A|$, such that β_{ij} represents the position of code a_j on the ith dimension of $\mathbf{N_r}$.

Let $\tilde{\mathbf{w}}^k$ be the normalized vector of weights for unit v^k, such that

$$\tilde{\mathbf{w}}_i^k = \frac{1}{2} \left(\frac{\displaystyle\sum_{j=1}^{m} \Omega_{ij}^k}{\displaystyle\sum_{i=1,j=1}^{i=m,j=m} \Omega_{ij}^k} \right). \tag{3.20}$$

---

[2] Briefly, we prove orthogonality of V and μ by $V'\mu = 0$. By Eqs. 3.17 and 3.18, and because μ is a unit vector $\mu'\mu = 1$,

$$V'\mu = D^{-1}U'(\mathbf{N} - \mathbf{N}\mu\mu')\mu$$
$$= D^{-1}U'\mathbf{N}\mu - D^{-1}U'\mathbf{N}\mu\mu'\mu$$
$$= D^{-1}U'\mathbf{N}\mu - D^{-1}U'\mathbf{N}\mu$$
$$= 0$$

That is, the ith component of the $\tilde{\mathbf{w}}^k$ is $\frac{1}{2}$ of sum of the normalized weights of connections to/from code a_i.[3]

For any unit v^k, the location of the *centroid*, $\mathbf{c}^k$, of its weighted network graph with node positions from $\mathbf{B}$ is thus:

$$\mathbf{c}^k = \mathbf{B}\tilde{\mathbf{w}}^k \tag{3.21}$$

That is, along any dimension j of $\mathbf{N_r}$, the coordinate of the centroid c_j^k is the average of node positions $\mathbf{B_j}$ weighted by $\tilde{\mathbf{w}}^k$.

We seek to minimize the total sum of the squared distances between centroids, $\mathbf{c}^k$, and projected points, $\mathbf{N_r^k}$. That is, we want to find $\mathbf{B}$ that minimizes

$$\sum_{k=1}^{|U|} (\mathbf{N_r^k} - \mathbf{B}\mathbf{w}^k)'(\mathbf{N_r^k} - \mathbf{B}\mathbf{w}^k). \tag{3.22}$$

Because the dimensions of $\mathbf{N_r}$ are orthogonal, we can solve this equation independently for each dimension. Notice that for any dimension j, this equation is equivalent to a linear regression[4]

$$\mathbf{N_{r,j}} = \sum_{i=1}^{m} \beta_{ij}\tilde{\mathbf{w}_i} + \epsilon_j \tag{3.23}$$

which can be solved using *linear least squares* as

$$\hat{\mathbf{B}_j} = (\tilde{\mathbf{w}_i}'\tilde{\mathbf{w}_i})^{-1}\tilde{\mathbf{w}_i}'\mathbf{N_{r,j}}. \tag{3.24}$$

Notice that positioning the nodes for codes A such that the jth coordinate of $a_i = \beta_{ij}$ thus aligns the network graph of each unit v^k with its projected point such that $\mathbf{c}^k$ approximates $\mathbf{N_r^k}$.

3.9   Goodness of Fit

Let F^j be a function on a matrix $\mathbf{M}$ that returns the *pairwise directed differences* between elements in the jth column of $\mathbf{M}$:

$$f_{i,k}^j(\mathbf{M}) = m_{i,j} - m_{k,j}.$$

Further, let $\bar{\mathbf{e}}$ indicate the mean value of vector $\mathbf{e}$, and $corr_{\mathbf{e}_1\mathbf{e}_2}$ be the correlation of any two vectors $\mathbf{e}_1$ and $\mathbf{e}_2$.

---

[3] We use $\frac{1}{2}$ of the normalized weights because for any pair of codes a_i and a_j, one half of the normalized weight of their connection is associated with each code. Thus the total normalized weights are preserved and $\sum_i \tilde{\mathbf{w}}_i^k = \sum_i \mathbf{N_i^k}$.

[4] There is no intercept term included in Eq. 3.23. This is because the columns of $\tilde{\mathbf{w}_i}$ (which function as the independent variables in the regression) are not linearly independent. In particular, by Eq. 3.20, $\forall k, \sum_j \tilde{\mathbf{w}}_{ij}^k = 1$. Thus, adding an intercept term would make the equation ill-defined—that is, without a unique solution.

We define a *goodness of fit* measure γ^j between $\mathbf{N_r}$ and $\mathbf{C}$ on dimension j:

$$\gamma^j = r(vecsym(F^j(\mathbf{N_r})), vecsym(F^j(\mathbf{C}))). \tag{3.25}$$

As $\gamma^j \to 1$, network visualizations are co-registered with summary statistics in the following sense: given networks for any two units, v^k and v^l,

$$(c_j^k - c_j^l) \sim (n_{r,j}^k - n_{r,j}^l). \tag{3.26}$$

Because the positions of c_j^k and c_j^l are determined by the weights of their connections and the positions of the nodes of the network graphs, if $c_j^k < c_j^l$, then v^k has stronger connections to nodes positioned toward the negative side of dimension j than v^l, and v^l has stronger connections to nodes positioned toward the positive side of dimension j than v^k. If $\gamma^j \to 1$, then by Eq. 3.26, we can make the same claim for $n_{r,j}^k$ and $n_{r,j}^l$.

That is, if $\gamma^j \to 1$, the information conveyed in the network visualization is mathematically consistent with the summary statistics, and the positions of nodes can be used to *interpret the meaning* of dimensions of $\mathbf{N_r}$.

4   Example

There are, of course, many examples of ENA analyses, including elsewhere in this volume. Here we show one very brief example to illustrate the mathematics of ENA.

Our example is from an analysis of two Shakespeare plays: *Romeo and Juliet* and *Hamlet*.

In this example:

$\Theta = $ (Lines of the plays)

$A = \{$MEN, WOMEN, HONOR, LOVE, DEATH$\}$

$C = \{$Each scene of each act of each play$\}$

$\Upsilon = \{$Characters in the plays$\}$

$\Xi = \{$Characters from *Hamlet*, Characters from *Romeo and Juliet*$\}$

Because our model is only illustrative, we will not describe the construction of $\mathbf{W}$ (the matrix of coding vectors for each utterance), except to say that an automated coding process based on regular expression matching identified lines where characters were talking about MEN ($\mathbf{W_1}$)—and similarly for WOMEN ($\mathbf{W_2}$), HONOR ($\mathbf{W_3}$), and so on. The stanza window was four lines ($s = 4$), and we used a binary model (i.e, Eq. 3.7, not Eq. 3.8). The data was normalized (Eq. 3.13), and we performed a means rotation (Eqs. 3.15 through 3.19) using the groups ξ_1 (Characters from *Hamlet*) and ξ_2 (Characters from *Romeo and Juliet*).

The results are shown in Fig. 1, which illustrates networks for Romeo's friend, Mercutio (green, left) and Hamlet's friend, Horatio (purple, right). Notice that

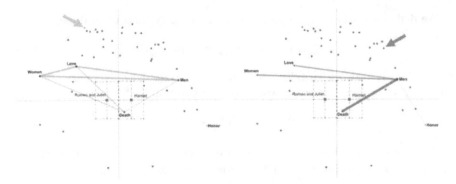

Fig. 1. Two ENA networks: Mercutio from *Romeo and Juliet* (green, left) and Horatio from *Hamlet* (purple, right). Arrows indicate projected points corresponding to each network. Projected points for other characters are shown in red (*Hamlet*) and blue (*Romeo and Juliet*). Red and blue squares and dashed lines show the mean and associated 95% confidence intervals for projected points for each group. (Color figure online)

the plotted point for Mercutio (indicated by a green arrow) has a negative value on the x-axis, and Mercutio's network makes strong connections to the codes WOMEN and LOVE, both of which have negative x coordinates. In contrast, Horatio's plotted point (indicated by a purple arrow) has a positive x value, and his strongest connections are to the code MEN, which has a positive x coordinate.

For those familiar with the respective plays, these networks and their associated summary statistics make sense. Although Mercutio is best known for his death in a duel (hence connections to DEATH), he spends much of the play before that telling Romeo to forget his unrequited love for Rosaline, and making lewd jokes about Juliet's nurse (hence WOMEN and LOVE). Horatio is best known from Hamlet's soliloquy over a dead jester's skull ("Alas, poor Yorick! I knew him, Horatio"). Horatio tries to communicate with the ghost of Hamlet's father, and talks about the death of Hamlet's friends, Rosencrantz and Guildenstern—thus, his connections between DEATH and MEN.

The remaining plotted points (red for characters in *Hamlet*, blue for characters in *Romeo and Juliet*) and their associated means and confidence intervals show that characters in the two plays have different networks overall. Both plays are about DEATH, but characters in *Romeo and Juliet* have lower x values, meaning they talk more about DEATH connected to WOMEN and LOVE. In *Hamlet*, characters have higher x values, and thus their talk is of death connected more to MEN and HONOR.

These differences are statistically significant. Along the x axis (the means rotation), a Mann-Whitney U test showed that *Hamlet* (Mdn = 0.13, N = 34) was statistically significantly different at the alpha = 0.05 level from *Romeo and Juliet* (Mdn = −0.16, N = 37; U = 870.00, p = 0.00, r = −0.38).

5   Discussion

We have thus shown how the mathematical foundations of ENA facilitate two key features of such analyses. First, summary statistics are generated by:

1. Constructing a matrix representing the connections between codes made by each line in the data (Eqs. 3.1 to 3.8);
2. Summing matrices to form a network for each unit in the data (Eq. 3.9);
3. Placing those networks in a space where each dimension represents the connection between a unique pair of codes (Eqs. 3.10 to 3.14); and
4. Using a means rotation and/or SVD to project those networks from the original matrix space to a space where the dimensions correspond to differences between groups or to variance among the matrices (Eqs. 3.15 to 3.19).

The result is a set of dimensions that can be used to compare the differences in the *content* rather than the *structure* of networks—that is, to compare which nodes are more or less strongly connected.

Next, network graphs are constructed by aligning the projected points in this new space and the centroids of the network graphs by using a linear regression to position the nodes in the space (Eqs. 3.20 to 3.24). The result is a set of network visualizations that are *co-registered* with the summary statistics—that is, the information conveyed in the network visualizations reflects the underlying summary statistics, and vice versa.

Finally, because ENA uses a means rotation, the summary statistics it produces (namely, the first dimension in the projected space) are often able to find differences between groups that other projection methods (such as SVD alone) may not. Moreover, the co-registration of projected matrices and their associated network graphs makes it possible to interpret differences between groups in terms of the relative strengths of the connections in their mean networks. In the example above from *Hamlet* and *Romeo and Juliet*, there is no significant difference between the two plays when the networks are projected using only SVD. Taken together, these affordances of ENA's mathematical foundation makes it possible to create summary statistics and associated network visualizations that identify interpretable differences in content between groups of networks.

Before we conclude, we want to highlight one further conclusion from this examination of the mathematical formalisms of ENA. Specifically, we note that the key network analytic properties of ENA (content-based summary statistics and co-registered network graphs) *do not require construction of adjacency matrices for units through lines, conversations, stanza windows, and the rest of the mathematical machinery described in Eqs. 3.1 through 3.8*. ENA can begin with any set of adjacency matrices, place them in a space, project them onto meaningful dimensions, and construct coordinated network graphs. This means that ENA can be applied to any set of network matrices *as long as the nodes are consistent across all networks*.

There are, of course, some practical limitations. For example, the number of columns in the matrix space, $\mathbf{N}$, is equal to $\frac{m(m-1)}{2}$, where m is the number of nodes in the networks. As a result, models with many nodes require large numbers of networks so that the number of rows of **N** is larger than the number of columns. Otherwise the linear regressions in Eq. 3.23 will have more parameters than data points and the solutions will not be unique. As a result, node placements will not provide reliable interpretations of the dimensions of the projected space. Moreover, network graphs with a large number of nodes are difficult to read, and can make interpretation of the dimensions of the projected space difficult as well.

These limits notwithstanding, this ability for ENA to operate on any set of adjacency matrices means that the technique is not limited to analysis of spoken conversations or chat messaging. ENA allows modeling, visualization, and interpretation of any data that can be described in terms of network matrices, whatever the source of the data and the method of construction of those matrices.

As a result, the mathematics of ENA provides a powerful toolkit for analyzing discourse data, text data of many kinds, and indeed data on any phenomena where connections between codes of interest are of primary importance.

Acknowledgements. This work was funded in part by the National Science Foundation (DRL-1661036, DRL-1713110), the Wisconsin Alumni Research Foundation, and the Office of the Vice Chancellor for Research and Graduate Education at the University of Wisconsin–Madison. The opinions, findings, and conclusions do not reflect the views of the funding agencies, cooperating institutions, or other individuals.

References

1. Andrist, S., Ruis, A.R., Shaffer, D.W.: A network analytic approach to gaze coordination during a collaborative task. Comput. Hum. Behav. **89**, 339–348 (2018)
2. Arastoopour, G., Shaffer, D.W., Swiecki, Z., Ruis, A.R., Chesler, N.C.: Teaching and assessing engineering design thinking with virtual internships and epistemic network analysis. Int. J. Eng. Educ. **32**(3), 1492–1501 (2016)
3. D'Angelo, A.L.D., Ruis, A.R., Collier, W., Williamson Shaffer, D., Pugh, C.M.: Evaluating how residents talk and what it means for surgical performance in the simulation lab. Am. J. Surg. (2020, in Press)
4. DiSessa, A.A.: Knowledge in pieces. In: Forman, G., Pufall, P. (eds.) Constructivism in the Computer Age, pp. 47–70. Erlbaum, Hillsdale (1988)
5. Dorogovtsev, S.N., Mendes, J.F.F.: Evolution of Networks: From Biological Nets to the Internet and WWW. Oxford University Press, Oxford (2003)
6. Herman, I., Melancon, G., Marshall, M.: Graph visualization and navigation in information visualization: a survey. IEEE Trans. Vis. Comput. Graph. **6**, 24–43 (2000)
7. Knight, S., Arastoopour, G., Shaffer, D.W., Shum, S.B., Littleton, K.: Epistemic networks for epistemic commitments (2014)
8. Krause, A.E., et al.: Adaptations in a hierarchical food web of southeastern lake Michigan. Ecol. Model. **220**(22), 3147–3162 (2009)
9. Marquart, C.L., Swiecki, Z., Collier, W., Eagan, B.R., Woodward, R., Shaffer, D.W.: rENA: epistemic network analysis [r package]. https://cran.r-project.org/web/packages/rENA/index.html

10. Nash, P., Shaffer, D.W.: Epistemic trajectories: mentoring in a game design practicum. Instruc. Sci. **41**(4), 745–771 (2013)
11. Quardokus Fisher, K., Hirshfield, L., Siebert-Evenstone, A.L., Arastoopour, G., Koretsky, M.: Network analysis of interactions between students and an instructor during design meetings. In: Proceedings of the American Society for Engineering Education, p. 17035. ASEE (2016)
12. Ruis, A.R.: 'Trois empreintes d'un même cachet': toward a historical definition of nutrition. In: Ewing, E.T., Randall, K. (eds.) Viral Networks: Connecting Digital Humanities and Medical History, pp. 179–212. VT Publishing, Blacksburg (2018)
13. Ruis, A.R., Rosser, A.A., Quandt-Walle, C., Nathwani, J.N., Shaffer, D.W., Pugh, C.M.: The hands and head of a surgeon: modeling operative competency with multimodal epistemic network analysis. Am. J. Surg. **216**(5), 835–840 (2018)
14. Shaffer, D.W.: Models of situated action: computer games and the problem of transfer. In: Steinkuehler, C., Squire, K.D., Barab, S.A. (eds.) Games, Learning, and Society: Learning and Meaning in the Digital Age, pp. 403–431. Cambridge University Press, New York (2012)
15. Shaffer, D.W.: Quantitative Ethnography. Cathcart Press, Madison (2017)
16. Shaffer, D.W., Collier, W., Ruis, A.R.: A tutorial on epistemic network analysis: analyzing the structure of connections in cognitive, social, and interaction data. J. Learn. Analytics **3**(3), 9–45 (2016)
17. Shaffer, D.W., et al.: Epistemic network analysis: a prototype for 21st century assessment of learning. Int. J. Learn. Media **1**(1), 1–21 (2009)
18. Sullivan, S.A., et al.: Using epistemic network analysis to identify targets for educational interventions in trauma team communication. Surgery **163**(4), 938–943 (2018)
19. Wooldridge, A.R., Carayon, P., Eagan, B.R., Shaffer, D.W.: Quantifying the qualitative with epistemic network analysis: a human factors case study of task-allocation communication in a primary care team. IISE Trans. Healthcare Syst. Eng. **8**(1), 72–82 (2018)
20. Zörgő, S., Peters, G.-J.Y.: Epistemic network analysis for semi-structured interviews and other continuous narratives: challenges and insights. In: Eagan, B., Misfeldt, M., Siebert-Evenstone, A. (eds.) ICQE 2019. CCIS, vol. 1112, pp. 267–277. Springer, Cham (2019). https://doi.org/10.1007/978-3-030-33232-7_23

Trajectories in Epistemic Network Analysis

Jais Brohinsky[1,2](✉) ⓘ, Cody Marquart[1,2], Junting Wang[1,2], A. R. Ruis[1,2] ⓘ,
and David Williamson Shaffer[1,2] ⓘ

[1] University of Wisconsin – Madison, Madison, WI, USA
brohinsky@wisc.edu
[2] Wisconsin Center for Education Research, Madison, WI, USA

Abstract. While quantitative ethnographers have used epistemic network analysis (ENA) to model trajectories that show change in network structure over time, visualizing trajectory models in a way that facilitates accurate interpretation has been a significant challenge. As a result, ENA has predominantly been used to construct aggregate models, which can obscure key differences in how network structures change over time. This study reports on the development and testing of a new approach to visualizing ENA trajectories. It documents the challenges associated with visualizing ENA trajectory models, the features constructed to address those challenges, and the design decisions that aid in the interpretation of trajectory models. To test this approach, we compare ENA trajectory models with aggregate models using a dataset with previously published results and known temporal features. This comparison focuses on interpretability and consistency with prior qualitative analysis, and we show that ENA trajectories are able to represent information unavailable in aggregate models and facilitate interpretations consistent with qualitative findings. This suggests that this approach to ENA trajectories is an effective tool for representing change in network structure over time.

Keywords: Epistemic network analysis (ENA) · ENA trajectories · Time-Series analysis · Longitudinal research

1 Introduction

Research that focuses on processes, as opposed to only outcomes, must account for change over time. *Trajectories*, or models showing a particular path or movement over time, are used in a wide range of process-oriented research. Phenomena like disease progression or transmission, growth and decay, and learning are inherently temporal, and so trajectories have been employed in a number of fields, from medicine [6] and business [14] to sociology [12] and educational research. For example, Van Den Heuvel-Panhuizen [24] examined how middle-school students' mathematical understanding of percentages progresses from developing context-dependent, informal solutions to generalized, formal solutions.

Although quantitative ethnographic (QE) researchers work extensively with process data, trajectory analyses have been relatively rare [8, 10, 17]. This is due in part to the

© Springer Nature Switzerland AG 2021
A. R. Ruis and S. B. Lee (Eds.): ICQE 2021, CCIS 1312, pp. 106–121, 2021.
https://doi.org/10.1007/978-3-030-67788-6_8

challenge of effectively visualizing and interpreting temporal trajectories in complex multivariate models. For example, epistemic network analysis (ENA) is widely used in QE research to model the structure of relationships among Codes in a Discourse, but accounting for change in network structure over time involves interpreting changes in individual or mean network locations in a multidimensional space whose dimensions are defined by complex connection patterns. Thus, ENA has predominantly been used to build aggregate models, which obscure any changes that occur in connection structure over time.

In this study, we developed and tested a new approach to visualizing ENA trajectories. In what follows, we describe the obstacles introduced by these representations, the features built to overcome those obstacles, and design decisions that make the models easier to interpret. We then compare the use of ENA trajectory models to ENA aggregate models using one dataset with published results and known temporal features, focusing on intelligibility and consistency with prior results.

2 Theory

2.1 ENA Trajectories

Trajectory models require *time units*, or temporal segmentation. Indeed, aggregate models can be considered a special case of trajectory models where the temporal segmentation is defined as the largest possible time unit. As such, aggregate models simplify or obscure patterns and anomalies that otherwise require finer time units to capture. For instance, Siebert-Evenstone et al. [21] studied student discourse in an engineering simulation to demonstrate how an analysis that divides conversations into multiple moving stanza windows shows patterns not found in an analysis of conversations in aggregate. Ruis et al. [19] show that the size of these moving stanza windows is an important factor affecting results.

However, while ENA uses temporal features to identify connections among Codes, those connections are ultimately aggregated into single networks. Thus, the structure of ENA allows for the construction of trajectories by aggregating connections among codes over smaller time units.

QE researchers have used ENA to track changes in discourse patterns over time [8, 10, 17]. However, visualizing trajectories in ENA is complicated by an affordance ENA was designed to offer: each dimension in ENA space can be used to interpret the differences between networks, and the position of any point is therefore interpretable based on its x and y coordinates. Moreover, researchers often use information from *both* dimensions to draw conclusions. For example, Fisher et al. [9] investigated a virtual engineering laboratory and showed that a coach's discourse networks relative to high-performing teams had both high x-values *and* low y-values (Fig. 1) and therefore required a multidimensional interpretation.

In a trajectory model, each ENA point needs to be interpreted by *three* variables: its x-value, its y-value, and time. This added variable increases complexity, which can make models difficult to read [2]. Given these constraints, previous ENA trajectories have been limited to representations with small numbers of time units. For instance,

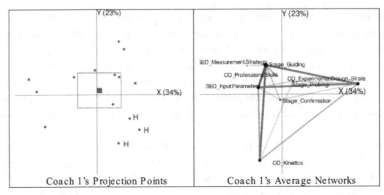

Fig. 1. Fisher et al. [9] found that a coach's discourse networks for high-performing teams (H-points) had both high x-values *and* low y-values and, therefore, required a multidimensional interpretation.

Espino et al. [8] and Nash and Shaffer [17] both display changes over three time units (Fig. 2).

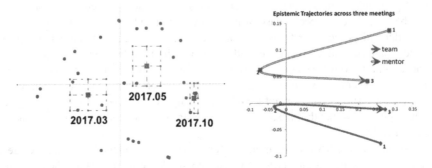

Fig. 2. These examples of previous ENA trajectories include only three time units. The plot on the left shows the change in discourse patterns of online student groups across three months [8]. The plot on the right compares a mentor and a team of students in a game design practicum [17].

2.2 Design Challenges

The core design challenge in ENA is to find a set of design principles that can be used to increase the *legibility* of ENA trajectory models: that is, *the ease with which a user can read and understand* the relationships between the three crucial variables of x-value, y-value, and time.

For instance, organizing models based on important variables can surface patterns and anomalies that may otherwise be illegible [11]. In ENA, the two interpretable axes can be separated and ordered by time, thus individually representing trajectories across each ENA dimension. Rogers et al. [18] employed this method to demonstrate changes between acts in Shakespeare's *Romeo and Juliet* (Fig. 3). In this case, time is substituted for the y-dimension. Moving from top to bottom, the plot shows progressive changes in ENA x-values for different characters throughout the play.

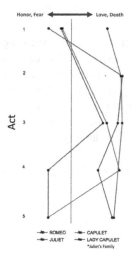

Fig. 3. Rogers et al. [18] modeled a single ENA dimension by time to represent discourse changes in *Romeo and Juliet* over five acts. Plotted points on the left have greater connections to HONOR and FEAR, while points on the right have greater connections to LOVE and DEATH.

However, as seen in Fisher et al. [9], interpretations of ENA space can rely on relationships *between* the original axes. Thus, the change in x-values in a re-ordered plot like Fig. 3 might need to be considered in relation to the corresponding change in y-values, and vice versa. Tufte [22] advocates decomposing complex visualizations into a series of smaller images and simultaneously displaying these images to allow for comparison. Such a comparison can permit simpler representations to be grasped and then added together to illustrate a larger story.

To accomplish this, a re-ordered plot can be shown alongside the original ENA space and *co-register*, or mathematically and graphically align, such that change in one model corresponds with change in the other. Co-registration between three variables requires three coordinated models: two re-ordered plots and the main ENA space. Thus, complex temporal information is decomposed to show simultaneous change in *pairs* of variables, making changes easier to interpret [23].

In Fig. 3, lines connecting ENA networks at successive time points combine to visualize the overall shape of a trajectory. However, connecting points in sequence requires a shape that is as legible between any two successive points as it is for the whole. Straight lines are legible between two points, but sharp changes in direction from one line segment to another create trajectories that can fail to read as continuous shapes [4]. Smooth forms like curves confer continuity, which Lemon et al. [15] demonstrate to aid in the interpretation of complex diagrams.

Using three co-registered plots and curves to connect time units, we propose to construct ENA trajectories that can accommodate an increased number of time units while legibly representing relationships among three variables.

2.3 Temporal Data

In order to construct ENA trajectories and test their legibility, we used a dataset that affords meaningful time units, incorporates changes that we would expect to see in a trajectory model, and was previously analyzed, which enables comparison of aggregate and trajectory models. Brohinsky et al. [3] explored argumentation in a collaborative, problem-based learning activity that was organized in rounds and constructed to catalyze a conceptual shift [7]. Therefore, we use this dataset to ask two questions:

1. Can ENA trajectory models legibly represent complex information that is unavailable in aggregate models?

2. Will ENA trajectory models yield interpretations consistent with a qualitative analysis of the activity?

3 Methods

3.1 Data

As part of a program evaluation for an experiential science curriculum, five groups participated a team-based archeological mystery activity. Group consisted of 5–7 university students and were divided into teams of 2–3 students. Teams were asked to determine the subject of an unknown text – an anatomy and physiology textbook that describes the human body with an architectural metaphor [1] – using only fragments of its pages. Each team was asked to answer two questions: (a) What is the document about, and (b) Who is its intended audience?

The activity was structured in three rounds. Each round was divided into a presentation and discussion section, with time between rounds for silent study. In the first round, teams received 4–8 fragments containing diagrams, chapter headings, and prose that focused on the architectural metaphor. In the second round, students passed half of their fragments to a different team, and in the third round, 'newly discovered' fragments containing words like *anatomy*, *physiology*, *bones*, and *teeth* were introduced.

Each session was audio recorded, transcribed, and timestamped to the minute. Codes were created using an iterative, grounded approach [5] that yielded two overarching categories, one in which ideas were generated and one dissenting against them. Based on the data, each main category was divided into three subcategories, yielding three generative/dissenting pairs: Hypothesis/Refutation, Supporting Evidence/Falsifying Evidence, Agreement/Disagreement (Table 1).

Transcripts were segmented by turn of talk, and three were coded by two raters. Social moderation was used to reconcile divergent interpretations [13]. Coding of the remaining transcripts was then done by a single rater.

Table 1. Codebook

Code	Definition	Example
Hypothesis	A new explanation regarding the text's subject or audience	… we thought this was about constructing houses
Refutation	A new statement or question challenging a hypothesis	I'm thinking that it's not necessarily an instruction manual on how to build a house
Supporting Evidence	Empirical data or inference used to support a hypothesis	There's a picture of a house on another of the fragments
Falsifying Evidence	Empirical data or inference that challenges a hypothesis or supports a refutation	But it's in first person a lot
Agreement	A statement reiterating or supporting the validity of a 'generative' statement	I guess that goes with our mission theory
Disagreement	A statement supporting the validity of a 'dissenting' statement	The palace I think was referencing other places

3.2 ENA

The ENA Web Tool [16] was used to model the coded discourse of the different groups in aggregate. ENA visualizes patterns of coded talk as weighted network plots [20] that display co-occurrences of the codes in Table 1.

We chose to model connections between codes within each activity round but not between rounds. The ENA algorithm employed a sliding window that registered the co-occurrence of codes within recent temporal context [21], which we defined as four lines of talk. Thus, for every utterance, ENA created a network connecting codes for that particular line with codes in the three previous lines, which, our qualitative analysis suggests, captures the majority of pertinent connections for a given line.

Networks were aggregated for each student and normalized to account for the fact that some people talk more than others. Normalized networks were then decomposed through a singular value decomposition (SVD) and represented as points in a coordinate space formed by the first two SVD dimensions, which together explained 39.3% of the variance in the data[1].

To compare the discourse of different groups, we analyzed the positions of group means in the ENA space. To account for non-normality, we used a two-sample Mann-Whitney U test. In addition, we compared group means and networks using a difference graph, which was calculated by subtracting weighted connections in one network from the corresponding connection in the other.

3.3 Trajectory ENA

To create trajectories, we divided the activity into six time units: the presentation and discussion for each of the three rounds. Time unit means were projected into the aggregate ENA space described above. Thus, a given group was represented by six means. These group means were plotted and sequentially connected by cubic splines, which were chosen because the function produces curves between successive time points. Earlier time unit means were represented as triangles and were bisected by the splines.

To simplify these trajectories, we constructed two smaller representations, each ordered by a single ENA dimension and time. These subplots were added below and to the side of the main ENA model. Subplot means were connected by splines and were co-registered with means in the main plot. To this end, subplots were arranged such that the y-axis for the plot tracking change along the x-dimension aligned with the y-axis of the original ENA space, and the x-axis for the plot tracking change along the y-dimension aligned with the x-axis of the original ENA space (Fig. 4).

---

[1] Readers already familiar with ENA may notice that this is conceptually similar to constructing 6 different ENA models (one for each activity round): a network is constructed for each student in the data for each round. However, projecting each round in its own ENA space would make it difficult to compare one round to another. Instead, networks for six rounds were included in the same projection, and nodes were positioned so as to interpret the resulting space. SVD is a rigid-body rotation, which means it preserves betweenness, so the interpretation of any single student's network will be the same in any projection. As with any change in projection, different projections may highlight different statistical properties of networks; however, we did not conduct statistical tests in the trajectory space—although we note that such a modeling approach inherits the constraints and affordances of longitudinal data generally in terms of sample sizes, effect sizes, and issues of covariance when data from individual students are recorded at multiple time points. A detailed discussion of these issues is beyond the scope of this paper, which aims to examine one format for visualizing trajectory data in ENA.

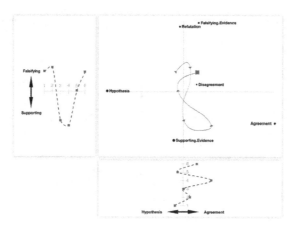

Fig. 4. Trajectory model for Group 4 at Time 6 showing coordinated main plot and subplots

4   Results

4.1   ENA

Figure 5 shows aggregate plots for Group 1 (hereafter Red Group) and Group 2 (hereafter Blue Group), as well as their difference graph (bottom), which subtracts corresponding weighted connections between codes. The colored squares represent group activity means averaged across all six time units.

We understand the x-axis in terms of the HYPOTHESIS and AGREEMENT codes: namely, the left end of the axis is defined by connections to the generation of new ideas, while the right end is defined by connections to agreeing with previously stated ideas. Similarly, we understand the y-axis to differentiate between using evidence to support or falsify ideas.

The networks for the two groups appear similar. Group means are close together, and while the Red Group shows stronger connections between falsifying evidence and hypothesis, the prominence of lightly saturated lines in the subtraction plot indicates that strength of connection between most codes is nearly equal.

Moreover, using a Mann-Whitney U test, we found no significant difference between the Red Group mean (Mdn $= -0.01$) and the Blue Group mean (Mdn $= 0.10$) on the x-dimension ($U = 478.5$, $p = 0.43$, $r = 0.11$). We also found no significant different between the Red Group mean (Mdn $= 0.20$) and the Blue Group mean (Mdn $= 0.06$) on the y-dimension ($U = 596.5$, $p = 0.47$, $r = -0.1$).

A qualitative analysis, however, suggests that the groups differed in important ways.

4.2   Qualitative Analysis

Red Group. The aggregate ENA plot captures the Red Group's strong connections between two dissenting codes, FALSIFYING EVIDENCE and REFUTATION, and the generative codes HYPOTHESIS and SUPPORTING EVIDENCE. For example, in her very first presentation, Jane argues against an idea put forward by the previous speaker:

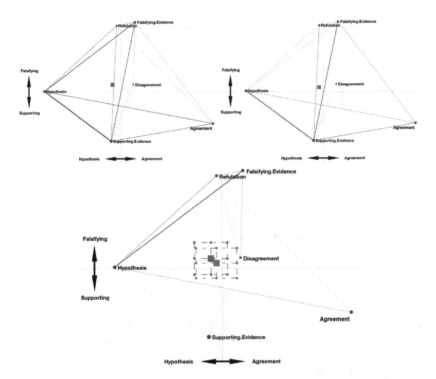

Fig. 5. Individual plots for Red Group (left) and Blue Group (right) with interpreted axes, along with their difference graph (bottom). (Color figure online)

1	Jane:	[We] also concluded that these are pieces of a book written about houses,	HYPOTHESIS
2	Jane:	but we do not think it was solely about wood.	REFUTATION
3	Jane:	There are parts that talk about pieces of a frame,	SUPPORTING EVIDENCE
4	Jane:	but we also have a chapter that starts with 'The motion of the bellows.' So, we concluded that there's something going on with metal there.	FALSIFYING EVIDENCE

Jane begins in line 1 by offering a HYPOTHESIS ("these are pieces of a book written about houses"), followed immediately by a REFUTATION of the previous group's claim that this book was "solely about wood" (line 2). She cites "parts that talk about pieces of a frame" (line 3) as SUPPORTING EVIDENCE that the book is about houses. In line 4, she points to "a chapter that starts with 'The motion of the bellows' as FALSIFYING EVIDENCE, warranting her conclusion that "there's something going on with metal there" and substantiating her REFUTATION that the book is not "solely about wood."

In other words, at the beginning of the discussion, Jane used FALSIFYING EVIDENCE and REFUTATION as key components for justifying her HYPOTHESIS, and indeed, throughout their deliberations, Jane and the other members of the Red Group argued against each other's claims using contradicting information.

In the final discussion of the activity, the tenor of the discussion changed. The group was still hypothesizing about the subject of the book, but after 40 min of argument, the students were no longer addressing each other's claims with FALSIFYING EVIDENCE or REFUTATION. For example, in the final discussion, Mary and Jane propose:

1	Mary:	I think the audience is some sort of either like academic space or government, and they're giving this journal or observation to some sort of body of people.	HYPOTHESIS
2	Mary:	I think it's about some sort of civilization and observations of the civilization.	HYPOTHESIS
3	Jane:	I think it was written in the 19th century.	HYPOTHESIS
4	Jane:	I think it's a scholarly work.	AGREEMENT
5	Jane:	The audience is people who want to learn about this sort of stuff whether that's students or other people in the field.	HYPOTHESIS

Mary begins in line 1 by offering a HYPOTHESIS that the book is written for an "academic space or government." In line 2, she adds another HYPOTHESIS that the book is about a "civilization and observations of the civilization." Jane then puts forth a HYPOTHESIS that the book "was written in the 19th century" (line 3). She expresses AGREEMENT with Mary in line 4 that "it's a scholarly work" and continues in line 5 with a HYPOTHESIS about the book being written for "people who want to learn about this sort of stuff": namely, architecture "students or other people in the field."

In other words, Jane and her other group members began the activity by using FALSIFYING EVIDENCE and REFUTATION to justify a HYPOTHESIS. At the end, however, they stopped dissenting and simply supported or agreed with a preferred HYPOTHESIS.

Blue Group. The aggregate ENA plot also captures the Blue Group's strong connections between the generative codes HYPOTHESIS and SUPPORTING EVIDENCE. For example, in the first discussion, Cam and Ben propose:

1	Cam:	But overall the working hypothesis would be a textbook meant for students of probably early adolescence on comparative architecture.	HYPOTHESIS
2	Cam:	We saw that there were questions posed to the reader, which seemed like a reflective activity to prompt learning.	SUPPORTING EVIDENCE
3	Ben:	It could just be fiction. Might be a Thomas Pynchon novel.	HYPOTHESIS

Cam starts in line 1 by offering a HYPOTHESIS that the book is "a textbook meant for students of probably early adolescence on comparative architecture." He cites "questions posed to the reader" (line 2) as SUPPORTING EVIDENCE substantiating his textbook idea. In line 3, Ben then uses this same evidence to offer his own HYPOTHESIS that the book "could just be fiction."

In other words, at the start of the activity, the Blue Group used SUPPORTING EVIDENCE as a key component for justifying a new HYPOTHESIS.

As the activity continued, however, the conversation changed. Instead of generating new ideas and substantiating them with SUPPORTING EVIDENCE, students began winnowing out old ideas using REFUTATION and coming to AGREEMENT around a single proposal: the book uses the metaphor of architecture to talk about the human body. For example, in the final discussion, Cam asks:

1	Cam:	Do you think the metaphor is wrong?	
2	Ben:	I mean, it's for sure a metaphor,	AGREEMENT
3	Ben:	but it's not straightforward instructional. It's in that genre, but we don't know what the corresponding commentary ties into.	REFUTATION

Cam begins in line 1 by asking if Ben thinks the HYPOTHESIS about the "metaphor is wrong." Ben responds by expressing AGREEMENT, that the text is "for sure a metaphor" (line 2). Ben continues in line 3 by issuing a REFUTATION of a previous proposal about the book being "straightforward instructional."

In other words, the Blue Group began the activity generating one HYPOTHESIS after another using SUPPORTING EVIDENCE. However, they then used REFUTATION to winnow out most of these ideas as they came to AGREEMENT around a single proposal.

Thus, although these two groups both had similar connections in the aggregate models, the ways in which they made these connections were very different over time. The Red Group used dissenting codes like FALSIFYING EVIDENCE and REFUTATION in the beginning but not at the end, while maintaining connections to HYPOTHESIS throughout. The Blue Group, on the other hand, replaced initial connections to HYPOTHESIS with connections to AGREEMENT and increased their use of dissenting codes like REFUTATION.

4.3 Trajectories

Figure 6 shows a trajectory model for the two groups. The red and blue squares show group means for the current time unit, in this case, the final discussion in the activity, and colored triangles show group means for previous time units.

Some differences between the overall trajectories are immediately apparent. For instance, the groups begin and end in different locations. Moreover, the Blue Group's trajectory spans a wider range of x-values, and more of its means fall on the Agreement end of the x-axis. However, while the Blue Group's starting location is quickly legible, the Red Group's is not, and further interpretation of the plot requires disentangling three crucial variables: change in x-value, change in y-value, and progression in time.

Figure 7 shows the groups at Time 3. As described above in the methods section, these models include separate x- and y-subplots showing change in the x- and y-dimensions as functions of time.

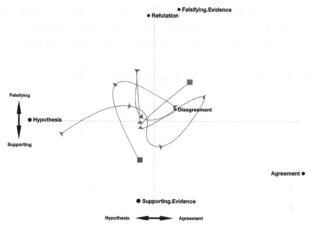

Fig. 6. Trajectory model for the Red Group and Blue Group with interpreted axes (Color figure online)

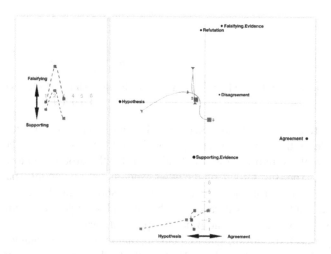

Fig. 7. Trajectory model for the Red Group and Blue Group at Time 3 (Color figure online)

As noted in our qualitative analysis, the Red Group began the activity with strong connections to dissenting codes like FALSIFYING EVIDENCE and REFUTATION. The Blue Group, on the other hand, did not start with strong connections to these codes. Aligning with this analysis, the y-subplot (left) shows all of the Red Group's time means to be higher in the falsifying part of the space than the Blue Group's corresponding means.

Our qualitative analysis also indicates that the Blue Group replaced strong initial connections to HYPOTHESIS with connections to AGREEMENT, whereas the Red Group maintained its connections to HYPOTHESIS. The x-subplot (bottom) shows that the Blue Group's trajectory moves from HYPOTHESIS toward AGREEMENT, while the Red Group's maintains the same position.

Hence, across the first three time units of the activity, the trajectory plots are consistent with our qualitative understanding of the Red Group's initial use of FALSIFYING EVIDENCE and REFUTATION, as well as the Blue Group's transition from HYPOTHESIS to AGREEMENT.

In Fig. 8, the final three time units are added to the models.

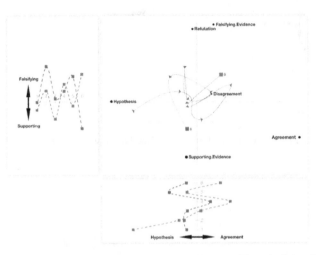

Fig. 8. Trajectory model for the Red Group and Blue Group at Time 6 (Color figure online)

Our qualitative analysis showed that the Red Group stopped making connections to dissenting codes at the end of the activity. Consistent with this analysis, the line graph on the left side of the figure shows the final mean for the group drop away from the falsifying space. The Blue Group, on the other hand, moves up into this space.

In addition, results from our qualitative analysis showed the Blue Group making connections to AGREEMENT as it came together around a single idea in the latter half of the activity. The x-position of the Blue Group's final mean on the agreement side of the space aligns with this result. The Red Group, on the other hand, maintained strong connections to the HYPOTHESIS code, and indeed, the final mean for this group is located in almost the same x-position as the starting mean.

In sum, the trajectory plots demonstrate distinctions between the two groups that were not shown in the aggregate models and that align with our qualitative analysis.

While this study focuses on comparing ENA trajectories to aggregate models, trajectories also offered interpretations beyond those of the original qualitative analysis. The increased connections to HYPOTHESIS at time unit five align with the intent of the activity as described above in the methods section: new data was introduced to catalyze a conceptual shift. However, the y-positions suggest a crucial difference between the two groups. The Red Group's presentations at time five are the only presentations (odd time units) with more connections to dissenting codes than the subsequent discussions (even time units). When considered in relation the Blue Group's AGREEMENT around a single proposal and the Red Group's lack thereof, this may suggest that, when working toward consensus, new ideas benefit from a period of support in order for argument to be productive.

5 Discussion

The ENA trajectories we designed afford interpretations that align with important qualitative distinctions missing from the aggregate ENA models. For example, the trajectories showed how the Red Group made strong connections to dissenting codes like FALSIFYING EVIDENCE and REFUTATION at the start of the activity, but not the end, while maintaining connections to HYPOTHESIS throughout. Also, they showed how the Blue Group replaced initial connections to HYPOTHESIS with connections to AGREEMENT and increased their use of dissenting codes.

These differences were only visible in the ENA model once the activity was divided into appropriate time units. However, the overall group trajectories were difficult to interpret due to the three-variable relationship of time and ENA dimensions. The distinctions were made legible by constructing separate x- and y-subplots ordered by time. Subplots displayed a successive series of time unit means that were connected by splines and co-registered with the main plot. Co-registration allowed changes in the subplots to be interpreted using, and simultaneously tracked in, the dimensions of the main ENA space.

These results have some clear limitations, however. First, this study was only conducted with a single dataset. A variety of datasets is needed to more generally determine the extent to which these ENA trajectories legibly represent information unavailable in aggregate models. Moreover, while the main and subplots are capable of displaying many trajectories at once, visualizing more than two or three quickly becomes illegible. This is exacerbated if the trajectories cross paths multiple times. Future work will consider this issue in more detail. We will also develop an R package for ENA trajectories. This package will include features reported here as well as animated transitions between time units. We hypothesize that animations will improve the legibility of the trajectories.

Despite these limitations, this study demonstrates an effective method for visualizing ENA trajectories that enhances legibility and preserves co-registration of the statistical properties and graphical representations of the networks. This increased legibility offers quantitative ethnographic researchers an improved tool for analyzing process data in ENA models.

Acknowledgments. This work was funded in part by the National Science Foundation (DRL-1661036, DRL-1713110), the Wisconsin Alumni Research Foundation, and the Office of the Vice Chancellor for Research and Graduate Education at the University of Wisconsin-Madison. The opinions, findings, and conclusions do not reflect the views of the funding agencies, cooperating institutions, or other individuals.

References

1. Alcott, W.A.: The house I live in: Or the human body. George W. Light, Boston (1839)
2. Aigner, W., Miksch, S., Schumann, H., Tominski, C.: Visualization of Time-Oriented Data. Springer, London (2011)

3. Brohinsky, J., Sonnert, G., Sadler, P.: Dynamics of dissent in the classroom. Paper presented to the Learning Sciences Graduate Student Conference, Chicago (2019)
4. Chang, D., Nesbitt, K.V.: Developing Gestalt-based design guidelines for multi- sensory displays. In: Proceedings of the 2005 NICTA-HCSNet Multimodal User Interaction Workshop, vol 57, pp. 9–16. Australian Computer Society, Sydney (2006)
5. Corbin, J.M., Strauss, A.: Grounded theory research: procedures, canons, and evaluative criteria. Qualitative Sociol. 13(1), 3–21 (1990)
6. Corbin, J.M., Strauss, A.: A nursing model for chronic illness management based upon the trajectory framework. Scholarly Inquiry Nursing Practice 5(3), 155–174 (1991)
7. Duit, R., Treagust, D.F.: Conceptual change: a powerful framework for improving science teaching and learning. Int. J. Sci. Educ. 25(6), 671–688 (2003)
8. Espino, D., Lee, S., Eagan, B., Hamilton, E.: An initial look at the developing culture of online global meet-ups in establishing a collaborative, STEM media-making community. In: Lund, K., Niccolai, G.P., Lavoué, E., Hmelo-Silver, C., Gweon, G., Baker, M. (eds.) 13th International Conference on Computer Supported Collaborative Learning, vol 2, pp. 608–611. International Society of the Learning Sciences, Lyon (2019)
9. Fisher, K.Q., Hirshfield, L., Siebert-Evenstone, A., Arastoopour, G., Koretsky, M.: Network analysis of interactions between students and an instructor during design meetings. In: Proceedings of the American Society for Engineering Education, ASEE, New Orleans (2016)
10. Foster, A., Shah, M., Barany, A., Talafian, H.: Tracing identity exploration trajectories with quantitative ethnographic techniques: a case study. In: Eagan, B., Misfeldt, M., Siebert-Evenstone, A. (eds.) International Conference on Quantitative Ethnography, vol. 1112, pp. 77–88. Springer, Cham (2019)
11. Friendly, M., Kwan, E.: Effect ordering for data displays. Comput. Stat. Data Anal. 43(4), 509–539 (2003)
12. Healy, K., Moody, J.: Data visualization in sociology. Ann. Rev. Sociol. 40, 105–128 (2014)
13. Herrenkohl, L.R., Cornelius, L.: Investigating elementary students' scientific and historical argumentation. J. Learn. Sci. 22(3), 413–461 (2013)
14. Katz, J.A.: The chronology and intellectual trajectory of American entrepreneurship education: 1876–1999. J. Bus. Venturing 18(2), 283–300 (2003)
15. Lemon, K., Allen, E.B., Carver, J.C., Bradshaw, G.L.: An empirical study of the effects of gestalt principles on diagram understandability. In: First International Symposium on Empirical Software Engineering and Measurement, pp. 156–165. IEEE, Madrid (2007)
16. Marquart, C.L., Hinojosa, C., Swiecki, Z., Shaffer, D.W.: Epistemic Network Analysis. http://app.epistemicnetwork.org/login.html (2018)
17. Nash, P., Shaffer, D.W.: Epistemic trajectories: mentoring in a game design practicum. Instructional Sci. 41(4), 745–771 (2013)
18. Rogers, M., Eagan, B., Siebert-Evenstone, A., Shaffer, D.W.: Trajectories with epistemic network analysis. Poster session presented to the annual UW–Madison education research poster fair. Madison (2019)
19. Ruis, A.R., Siebert-Evenstone, A.L., Pozen, R., Eagan, B., Shaffer, D.W.: Finding common ground: a method for measuring recent temporal context in analyses of complex, collaborative thinking. In: Lund, K., Niccolai, G., Lavoué, E., Hmelo-Silver, C., Gwon, G., Baker, M. (eds.) 13th International Conference on Computer Supported Collaborative Learning. vol 1, pp. 136–143. International Society of the Learning Sciences, Lyon (2019)
20. Shaffer, D.W.: Quantitative Ethnography. Cathcart Press, Madison (2017)
21. Siebert-Evenstone, A.L., Irgens, G.A., Collier, W., Swiecki, Z., Ruis, A.R., Shaffer, D.W.: In search of conversational grain size: modelling semantic structure using moving stanza windows. J. Learn. Anal. 4(3), 123–139 (2017)

22. Tufte, E.R.: The Visual Display of Quantitative Information. Graphics Press, Cheshire (1983)
23. van den Elzen, S., van Wijk, J.J.: Small multiples, large singles: a new approach for visual data exploration. In: Computer Graphics Forum, vol 32, pp. 191–200. Blackwell Publishing Ltd, Oxford, UK (2013)
24. Van Den Heuvel-Panhuizen, M.: The didactical use of models in realistic mathematics education: an example from a longitudinal trajectory on percentage. Educ. Stud. Math. **54**(1), 9–35 (2003)

Directed Epistemic Network Analysis

Ariel Fogel[1]([⊠]) [iD], Zachari Swiecki[2] [iD], Cody Marquart[1], Zhiqiang Cai[1] [iD],
Yeyu Wang[1] [iD], Jais Brohinsky[1] [iD], Amanda Siebert-Evenstone[1] [iD],
Brendan Eagan[1] [iD], A. R. Ruis[1] [iD], and David Williamson Shaffer[1] [iD]

[1] University of Wisconsin–Madison, Madison, WI, USA
ajfogel@wisc.edu
[2] Monash University, Melbourne, VIC, Australia

Abstract. Quantitative ethnographers across a range of domains study complex collaborative thinking (CCT): the processes by which members of a group or team develop shared understanding by making cognitive connections from the statements and actions of the group. CCT is difficult to model because the actions of group members are interdependent—the activity of any individual is influenced by the actions of other members of the group. Moreover, the actions of group members engaged in some collaborative tasks may need to follow a particular *order*. However, current techniques can account for either interdependence or order, but not both. In this paper, we present directed epistemic network analysis (dENA), an extension of epistemic network analysis (ENA), as a method that can simultaneously account for the interdependent and ordered aspects of CCT. To illustrate the method, we compare a qualitative analysis of two U.S. Navy commanders working in a simulation to ENA and dENA analyses of their performance. We find that by accounting for interdependence but not order, ENA was not able to model differences between the commanders seen in the qualitative analysis, but by accounting for both interdependence and order, dENA was able to do so.

Keywords: Complex collaborative thinking · Directed epistemic network analysis (dENA) · Epistemic network analysis (ENA)

1 Introduction

Many quantitative ethnographers study *complex collaborative thinking* (CCT) [12, 8, 17], often conceptualized as the process by which members of a group develop shared understanding. Researchers attempting to model CCT face the challenge of accounting for *interdependence*, or the direct influence of group activity on the actions of individual members. Interdependence implies that the relationship between events are inherently *temporal*—that is, individual actions are more strongly influenced by immediately preceding actions than by more distant ones [21]. The concurrent interdependent and temporal aspects of CCT make assessing individuals difficult, as models must account for individual contributions in the context of group contributions within recent temporal context. Additionally, some collaborative tasks require group members to perform a series of actions in a specific *order* to accomplish the shared goal. Current modeling

© Springer Nature Switzerland AG 2021
A. R. Ruis and S. B. Lee (Eds.): ICQE 2021, CCIS 1312, pp. 122–136, 2021.
https://doi.org/10.1007/978-3-030-67788-6_9

approaches can account for some combinations of interdependence, temporality, and order, but no extant techniques can account for all three simultaneously. In this paper, we propose a new technique, *directed epistemic network analysis* (dENA), an extension of epistemic network analysis (ENA) [18], that can construct models of CCT that account for interdependence, temporality, and order. We tested this novel technique on a well- dataset for which there are published findings on CCT, and we compared dENA models of CCT with ENA models. We found that by accounting for interdependence but not order, ENA was not able to model differences between individuals seen in the qualitative analysis, but by accounting for both interdependence and order, dENA was able to do so.

2   Theory

Quantitative ethnographers study tasks involving CCT across a wide range of domains, from collaborative problem solving by students learning social science research methods [12] to interactions between children and robots [8]. This prior works suggests that CCT involves three key elements: interdependence, temporality, and order.

In collaborative contexts, *interdependence* has been defined in terms of the coordination of behavior and information between group members [3]. In particular, as individuals participate in collaborative activities, they add information to the *common ground*, or the set of shared knowledge and experiences resulting from interactions with other members [1]. Group members then respond to information in the common ground, which influences subsequent actions and interpretations [4]. Thus, interdependence can be more generally defined as the influence of the group's actions on those of a given member of the group.

The interdependence of group processes also means that CCT has an important *temporal* aspect: events at any given point in time are influenced by events that occurred previously. Suthers and Desiato [21] argue that the *recent temporal context*, or immediately preceding events, have the greatest influence on the interpretation of subsequent actions and interactions. That is, actions taken by some group members affect the likelihood of actions taken by others in the near future [5]. For example, if one individual asks a question, another will likely respond in short order.

In addition, the *order* in which events unfold in the recent temporal context affects group members' future actions and interactions [15]. Some collaborative tasks require groups to follow a particular sequence of events, such as the specific order of actions naval navigation teams need to take to accurately track the position of their ships [6].

Thus, it may be important to simultaneously account for all three of these elements in models of CCT. However, existing approaches account for some, but not all, of these characteristics. For example, Sequential Pattern Mining and Lag Sequential Analysis account for order and temporality by using sliding windows to identify sequences of discourse moves occurring in the same recent temporal context [7, 14]. A key limitation of both methods is that while they can model the interdependence of a team as a whole, neither technique models *individual CCT in relation* to the contributions of collaborators; that is, they do not account for the how one specific individual's actions depend on others in a team or group.

Epistemic network analysis (ENA), on the other hand, models temporality and inter-dependence in collaborative activity [23] but does not explicitly represent the order of events in the model. That is, it can account for how he how one specific individual's actions depend on recent actions of others in a team or group, but not the order in which events occurred within a window of time. The algorithm accumulates *codes*, or indicators of meaningful discourse moves made by group members that occur *cotem-porally*—that is, within the same recent temporal context. The algorithm visualizes the relative co-occurrence of codes using weighted network diagrams, with each node in the network corresponding to a code. The network diagram for each unit of analysis, or group member, is summarized using an ENA score and plotted in the same metric space. This enables researchers to directly compare the actions of specific individuals in the context of the group.

Recent work comparing ENA to Sequential Pattern Mining found that, in at least one context, ENA outperformed Sequential Pattern Mining as a measure of CCT [22]. This suggests that accounting for order may be less important than accounting for co-temporality, but there are contexts where accounting for order in CCT has been shown to be important, as in Hutchin's study of naval navigation teams [6].

Some studies have sought to use ENA to accomplish this goal. D'Angelo and col-leagues [2] used ENA to model order by using two nodes for each code instead of one. One node represented instances when an individual was responding *to* the code; the other represented instances when an individual responded *with* the code. While D'Angelo et al. [2] were able to use this method to compare the operative discourse of surgical residents as they performed simulated procedures, there are drawbacks to this approach. In par-ticular, the resulting ENA visualizations are difficult to interpret: it is hard to keep track of the difference between responding *to* and responding *with* the same code. Also, this approach doubles the number of codes, which can cause overfitting problems in models with fewer units of analysis.

Others have accounted for order by including only those connections that occurred in a particular sequence [16]. However, this approach only works if there is a strong justification for defining one or more connections as meaningful only in one order; and doing so makes the interpretation of resulting visualizations more difficult, as the network graphs do not indicate the directionality of the connections.

In what follows, we propose an approach to account for the ordering of events within an ENA framework. The technique, directed ENA (dENA), tracks both what individuals respond *with* and what they respond *to* as they act within the context of a group. Rather than accomplishing this by representing each code with two nodes, dENA represents the directionality of a response using triangles between each set of codes. An individual's network is then summarized with two ENA scores, drawn as a vector, to represent their overall responses as well as the common ground to which they responded. Thus, dENA provides a method to compare the discourse of individuals within a group, accounting simultaneously for interdependence, temporality, and order.

To test this technique, we use data on Navy air defense warfare teams that has previously been analyzed by quantitative ethnographic researchers using a variety of methodologies, including ENA [22, 23]. We compared ENA and dENA to address the following research questions:

1. What differences does *ENA* show between two units of analysis that are qualitatively different?

2. What differences does *dENA* show between two units of analysis that are qualitatively different?

3 Study 1

3.1 Methods

Data. We analyzed discourse data collected from U.S. Navy air defense warfare teams engaging in training scenarios. Each team's goal was to perform the *detect-to-engage* sequence, in which they must detect and identify nearby vessels, or *tracks*, and assess whether these tracks pose a threat to the Navy ship.

The detect-to-engage sequence typically begins with the detection and identification of a track. When a track's identity is uncertain, team members continue monitoring its behavior and make an assessment as to whether its behavior is threatening. Based on these assessments, teams decide to warn tracks of imminent attach or engage them in combat.

Every team participated in the same four training scenarios, with each scenario testing how the team handled a different set of tracks. Each team consisted of six participants: two commanders and four support roles. In this analysis, we focused on interactions between one of the command roles, the Tactical Action Officer (TAO), and other members of the team.

Coding. We analyzed the transcripts using the codes in Table 1, which were developed by Swiecki et al. [23] using a grounded approach informed by prior qualitative analyses on similar data [11] as well as existing air defense warfare literature [13]. The nCodeR package for the R statistical programming language was used to develop an automated classifier for each code in Table 1 [10]. All codes were validated at a kappa threshold of 0.65 and a rho threshold of 0.05.

Epistemic Network Analysis. We used ENA [18] to visualize and test differences in the discourse of commanders in both conditions. We conducted the analysis using the rENA package [9] for the R programming language.

The data were segmented by team and scenario. This segmentation defined the ENA *conversations*, or the set of utterances made by the team members over the course of the scenario. The ENA algorithm slid a moving window [20] of 5 lines over the conversations to identify co-occurrences between codes for each unit of analysis (i.e., for each commander). Once the co-occurrences were accumulated, they were transformed into high-dimensional vectors for each unit of analysis and normalized and centered. Next, the algorithm performed a dimensional reduction on the unit vectors via singular value decomposition. This process resulted in an ENA score for each unit of analysis on each dimension.

Each unit's score was visualized by projecting the resulting values from the first two dimensions of the dimensional reduction into a lower dimensional space. In addition

Table 1. Qualitative codes, definitions and examples.

Code	Definition	Example
DETECT/IDENTIFY	Talk about radar detection of a track or the identification of a track, (e.g., vessel type)	IR/EW NEW BEARING, BEARING 078 APQ120 CORRELATES TRACK 7036 POSSIBLE F-4
TRACK BEHAVIOR	Talk about kinematic data about a track or a track's location	AIR/IDS TRACK NUMBER 7021 DROP IN ALTITUDE TO 18 THOUSAND FEET
SEEKING INFORMATION	Asking questions regarding track behavior, identification, or status	TAO CO, WE'VE UPGRADED THEM TO LEVEL 7 RIGHT?
DETERRENT ORDERS	Giving orders meant to warn or deter tracks	TIC AIR, CONDUCT LEVEL 2 WARNING ON 7037
DEFENSIVE ORDERS	Giving orders to prepare defenses or engage hostile tracks	TAO/CO COVER 7016 WITH BIRDS

to scores, the method produces a weighted network graph for each unit of analysis whose nodes represent the codes and whose edges represent the relative frequency of co-occurrence between those codes. Thicker and more saturated lines indicate more frequent co-occurrence.

ENA uses an optimization routine to *co-register* each ENA score with its associated weighted network graph. By projecting each unit's ENA score and weighted network graph into the same metric space, ENA enabled us to compare which connections were stronger between different units of analysis, as well as define the dimensions along which units of analysis differed. The algorithm positions the nodes in the metric space by minimizing the distance between the plotted points and the centroids of each network. ENA also computes a representation to visually compare two networks in the same space by subtracting the connection weights of one unit's network from the other network and plotting the network difference.

3.2 Results

Qualitative Results. Previous analyses [22] suggested that a key issue for commanders in these scenarios is maintaining awareness of tactical information.

For example, the following excerpt shows part of one team's activity (Team 1) as they dealt with a hostile combat helicopter (which they refer to as "TRACK 7023"). The excerpt begins when the TAO orders the team to issue a warning to the helicopter ("LEVEL 3 WARNING") and to track it with onboard weapons.

Line	Team member	Utterance
6447	TAO	AIR TAO, COVER TRACK 7023 LEVEL 3 WARNING, SAY AGAIN, LEVEL 3 WARNINGS
6448	ADWC	AIR, COVERING INSIDE TRACK 7023
6449	TAO	ASK HIM TO VECTOR TO 000
6450	IDS	WHERE IS 23?
6451	TAO	THEY BEAR 047, 12 MILES

The action unfolds as follows:

6447. The TAO issues two orders. The first is a DEFENSIVE ORDER to the ADWC to "COVER TRACK 7023" the second is a DETERRENT ORDER to the IDS to warn the track to move away from the area.

6448. In response, the Air Defense Warfare Coordinator (ADWC) begins tracking the hostile helicopter with the onboard ship weapons.

6449. The TAO tells the Identification Supervisor (IDS) what the content of the warning should be: specifically, to tell the helicopter to turn to 0°, or due north, away from the ship.

6450. The IDS responds by SEEKING INFORMATION on the position of the helicopter, asking "WHERE IS 23?"

6451. The TAO, in turn, responds by describing the relevant part of the TRACK BEHAVIOR, which in this case is the helicopter's most recent position: "THEY BEAR 047, 12 MILES," meaning they are 12 miles north-east of the ship—and thus, turning north will lead them away.

In other words, Team 1 maintained tactical awareness because when a supporting member of the team (the IDS) was SEEKING INFORMATION about TRACK 7023's recent behavior, the TAO responded with the relevant information about the TRACK BEHAVIOR.

In the next excerpt, a second team (Team 2) also maintained awareness of tactical information about the helicopter designated as TRACK 7023, albeit in a different way than Team 1. The excerpt begins after the TAO orders the ADWC to attack the hostile helicopter, and a news helicopter is shot down by mistake:

Line	Team member	Utterance
4857	TAO	AWC/TAO HOW DO WE KNOW THAT WE SHOT DOWN THE NEWS HELO?
4858	ADWC	BECAUSE COUPLE OF SECONDS AFTER I FIRED A SHOT IT FLEW RIGHT ACROSS OUR BOW AND TOOK THE HIT
4859	TAO	AND THEN DISAPPEARED OFF THE SCREEN?
4860	ADWC	THAT'S AFFIRMATIVE YOU MIGHT WANT TO GO UP TO BRIDGE AND ASK

The action unfolds as follows:

4857. The TAO is SEEKING INFORMATION about how the ADWC knows the team had hit a news helicopter: "HOW DO WE KNOW THAT WE SHOT DOWN THE NEWS HELO?"

4858. The ADWC responds by describing the TRACK BEHAVIOR of NEWS HELO: shortly after the ADWC fired on Track 7023 ("COUPLE OF SECONDS AFTER I FIRED A SHOT") the news helicopter flew into the line of fire ("FLEW RIGHT ACROSS OUR BOW AND TOOK THE HIT").

4859. The TAO, now SEEKING INFORMATION to confirm that the news helicopter was actually hit, asks whether the helicopter disappeared off the screen.

4860. The ADWC responds that the helicopter did disappear (TRACK BEHAVIOR).

In other words, unlike the TAO on Team 1, who *responded* to SEEKING INFORMATION by *providing* TRACK BEHAVIOR, the TAO from Team 2 was SEEKING INFORMATION *from others* in order to *discover more* about the TRACK BEHAVIOR that led to the downing of a non-combatant.

Epistemic Network Analysis. In the ENA model shown in Fig. 1, the top of the space contains connections to SEEKING INFORMATION. The bottom of the space contains DETECT/IDENTIFY and TRACK BEHAVIOR, codes most associated with generating information about the tracks. This suggests that the commanders' discourse was most distinguished on the vertical dimension in terms of *Providing Information* and *Seeking Information*.

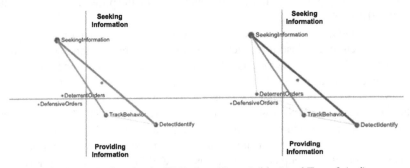

Fig. 1. ENA plots for the TAOs from Team 1 (blue) and Team 2 (red).

The ENA scores for both Team 1's TAO (Fig. 1, left) and Team 2's TAO (Fig. 1, right) are positioned toward to the top of the space. This means their discourse focused on connections to Seeking Information. For both TAO's, the strongest connections were between SEEKING INFORMATION and DETECT/IDENTIFY as well as SEEKING INFORMATION and TRACK BEHAVIOR.

Comparing the networks of the two TAOs using a network difference graph shows that the TAOs' networks are very similar (see Fig. 2). The ENA scores for both TAOs overlap, meaning there is little difference in the summary of these networks' connections. Additionally, the strong connections in the individual plots between SEEKING INFORMATION and DETECT/IDENTIFY as well as SEEKING INFORMATION and TRACK BEHAVIOR are thin and desaturated, suggesting that there is little difference in the weight or strength of those connections between the networks. The network difference graph thus suggests little difference in the discourse of the two teams' TAOs.

Fig. 2. Network difference graph for the TAOs from Team 1 (blue) and Team 2 (red).

These results suggest that both commanders were involved in exchanges in which DETECT/IDENTIFY and TRACK BEHAVIOR information was missed or incomplete and had to be clarified. These findings are consistent with those of Swiecki et al. [22], who found that teams often had to ask explicitly for Tactical Information to be repeated.

3.3 Discussion

The qualitative results show that both TAOs were involved in situations in which connections were made between SEEKING INFORMATION and TRACK BEHAVIOR. However, the TAO in Team 1 *responded* to SEEKING INFORMATION with TRACK BEHAVIOR while the TAO in Team 2 was SEEKING INFORMATION *in order to understand* TRACK BEHAVIOR. That is, the Team 1 TAO was providing information about TRACK BEHAVIOR *after* another team member was SEEKING INFORMATION. The Team 2 TAO did the opposite: they were responding when another team member described TRACK BEHAVIOR by SEEKING INFORMATION (that is, *additional* information) about the tactical situation.

In other words, although the ENA plots show that both TAO's made connections between SEEKING INFORMATION and TRACK BEHAVIOR:

1. What the two TAOs were doing was actually quite different;
2. These differences can be seen in the order in which the codes occur in the discourse; and
3. These differences are not apparent because the unordered ENA model treats as identical: (a) the TAO *providing* information to other team members who are asking about the tactical situation, and (b) the TAO *seeking* additional information from other team members to clarify the tactical situation.

4   Study 2

4.1 Methods

Directed Epistemic Network Analysis. We conducted the second study using the same data and coding scheme as the first. For this study, we developed and implemented *directed epistemic network analysis* (dENA), an extension of ENA that accounts for the order in which a connection between two codes occurred.

The ENA algorithm uses a moving window to identify connections formed from a current line of data (e.g., turn of talk), or *response*, to the preceding lines within the window, or *common ground*. These connections counts are then accumulated into a *symmetric adjacency matrix* for each unit of analysis: the number of connections from any code A to code B are the same as the number of connections from B to A.

Rather than produce a symmetric adjacency matrix for each, unit of analysis, dENA accounts for the order in which the connection occur by constructing an *asymmetric adjacency matrix* for each unit of analysis: the number of connections from any code A to code B may be different than the number of connections from B to A. Figure 3 highlights how this matrix is created using coded data from the first qualitative example in Study 1. With a moving window of 5 lines, dENA collapses code occurrences from the common ground (lines 2–5) and response (line 6) using a binary summation. The binarized summation of the ground and response code occurrences are then represented as vectors and multiplied to construct an asymmetric adjacency matrix.

Line	Seeking Information	Detect/ Identify	Track Behavior	Deterrent Orders	Defensive Orders
1	0	1	0	0	0
2	0	0	0	1	1
3	0	0	0	0	0
4	0	0	0	0	0
5	1	0	0	0	0
6	0	0	1	0	0
Ground Summation	1	0	0	1	1
Response Summation	0	0	1	0	0

Fig. 3. The top section shows a moving window (indicated by the red dashed line) on coded data. Line 6 represents the current turn of talk, or the *response* line. The portion of the window shaded gray represents the recent temporal context, or the *ground* lines. The bottom section shows the ground and response summation vectors for the indicated window.

The asymmetric adjacency matrices are then transformed to create two high-dimensional vectors for each unit of analysis, the ground vector and the response vector. The ground vector represents the connections formed from the codes in the common ground to the codes in the unit's responses. The response vector represents the connections formed from the unit's contributions back to the contributions in the common ground. Put another way, the ground vector summarizes what a given unit *responds to*, while the response vector summarizes what a given unit *responds with*.

The ground and response vectors for all units are normalized and centered and the algorithm performs a dimensional reduction via a singular value decomposition of the matrix of either the ground or response vectors. This process, which involves the same mathematics used in ENA, results in a pair of dENA scores for each unit of analysis in the lower dimensional space: a *ground score* and a *response score*.

The scores are visualized by plotting them in the lower dimensional space resulting from the dimensional reduction (see arrow in Fig. 4). For each unit, its scores are represented by a vector with its head at the response score and tail at the ground score. Subpopulations within the data are summarized by independently calculating the mean response and ground scores. The scores are then connected by a vector from ground mean to response mean.

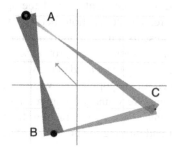

Fig. 4. Sample unit's dENA network. The overall size of the nodes represents the relative response strength with each code. The red dot in the middle of CODE A represents self-connections. The triangles represent directed connections: more saturated and opaque connections mean stronger connections. The network is summarized by two scores, connected as a vector. The tail of the vector is a ground score summarizing the ground connections and the head is the response score representing the response connections.

To help interpret these vectors, the algorithm co-registers *directed and weighted network graphs* in the same low dimensional space. For each unit, its graph shows the strength and directionality of the connections it made.

The nodes of the network correspond to the codes, and node size is proportional to the number of occurrences of that code *as a response* in the data, with larger nodes indicating more responses. The color and saturation of the circle within each node is proportional to the number of self-connections for that code: that is, when a code appears in both the response and ground of a given window. Colored circles that are larger and more saturated reflect codes with more frequent self-connections. For example, Fig. 4 suggests that roughly a quarter of responses made with code A were responding to code A.

The relative frequency of connections between any two codes are represented by two triangles. The connections between code A and code C, for example, are represented by one triangle with its base at code A pointing towards code C and the other with its base at code C pointing towards code A. Thicker and more saturated triangles indicate more frequent connections. Each triangle represents an ordered connection between two codes. The base of the triangle represents the common ground that a code was responding to and the opposite vertex of the triangle represents the response. Thus, in a given unit's network, the triangle with a base at code C and vertex directed towards code A would be interpreted as that unit's relative response to code C with code A.

The location of the tapered point where two triangles meet indicates the relative proportion of responses of one code to the other. For example, if the two triangles meet closer to code A's node, connections of A in response to C were more frequent than the reverse.

Network nodes in dENA are positioned in the space using the same optimization routine used in ENA, except that in dENA, the algorithm minimizes the distance between the *means of the ground and response scores* and the centroids of the corresponding networks. As a result, the dENA metric space can be interpreted based on the location of the nodes. Units with vectors on the right side of the space have more frequent connections between the codes on the right side of the space. Similarly, units with vectors on the left have more frequent connections between the codes on the left side of the space. The vector that represents a unit of analysis shows the directionality of the network: which nodes the unit is responding to (ground score, or tail of the vector) and what responses are made (response score, or head of the vector). Like the unit vectors, the network graphs can be averaged for subpopulations within the data to view their overall patterns of directed connections. We visually compared the dENA network graphs of two units of analysis in the same space by subtracting the connection weights of one unit's network from the other and plotting the network difference.

4.2 Results

Qualitative Results. Recall that the qualitative results from Study 1 show that the TAO on Team 1 responded to SEEKING INFORMATION with TRACK BEHAVIOR to help the team maintain tactical awareness of the situation. In contrast, the TAO on Team 2 responded to TRACK BEHAVIOR by SEEKING INFORMATION to understand the tactical situation.

Directed Epistemic Network Analysis. We examined the directed epistemic networks of the TAOs from Team 1 and Team 2. The left side of the space contains DETECT/IDENTIFY and TRACK BEHAVIOR, codes associated Providing Information. The right side of the space contains connections to SEEKING INFORMATION. This means the TAOs' discourse was most distinguished in terms of Providing Information and Seeking Information (Fig. 5).

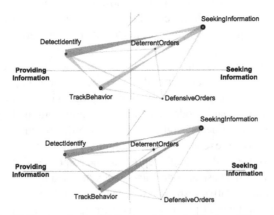

Fig. 5. dENA plots for the TAOs from Team 1 (blue) and Team 2 (red).

The strongest directed connections in each TAO's network were between SEEKING INFORMATION and TRACK BEHAVIOR and SEEKING INFORMATION and DETECT/IDENTIFY: the triangles with the widest base, darkest saturation, and heaviest opacity are based at TRACK BEHAVIOR and DETECT/IDENTIFY and point towards SEEKING INFORMATION. This means that relative to other directed connections, each TAO responded more to TRACK BEHAVIOR and DETECT/IDENTIFY with SEEKING INFORMATION.

Each TAO's vector summarizes the information in their respective networks. Overall, both TAOs were responding to Providing Information with Seeking Information. The ground scores, or tails of the summary vectors, are positioned closer to the side associated with Providing Information. The response scores, or heads of the summary vectors, are closer to the side associated with Seeking Information.

The network subtraction shows that the greatest difference in their networks was the connection between SEEKING INFORMATION and TRACK BEHAVIOR (Fig. 6). The TAO on Team 1 (blue) responded strongly *to* SEEKING INFORMATION *with* TRACK BEHAVIOR relative to the TAO on Team 2. In contrast, the TAO on Team 2 responded strongly *with* SEEKING INFORMATION *to* TRACK BEHAVIOR compared to the other TAO.

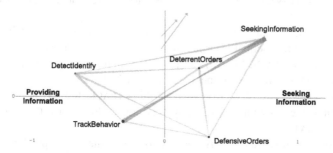

Fig. 6. dENA network difference plot for the TAOs from Team 1 (blue) and Team 2 (red).

The two triangles meet at a point approximately midway between SEEKING INFORMATION and TRACK BEHAVIOR. This means that the TAO on Team 1 responded to SEEKING INFORMATION with TRACK BEHAVIOR with approximately the same relative frequency as the TAO on Team 2 (red) responded to TRACK BEHAVIOR with SEEKING INFORMATION.

Taken together, this suggests that the key difference in how the two TAOs made connections between TRACK BEHAVIOR and SEEKING INFORMATION was the order of the connections rather than their relative frequency.

4.3   Discussion

The dENA results show that both TAOs were involved in situations where tactical information was missed and needed to be clarified. Each TAO's dENA plots shows strong responses between TRACK BEHAVIOR and DETECT/IDENTIFY, on one hand, and SEEKING INFORMATION on the other. Comparing the differences between the TAOs shows that the

Team 1 TAO responded to SEEKING INFORMATION *with* TRACK BEHAVIOR while the TAO on Team 2 was SEEKING INFORMATION *in response to* TRACK BEHAVIOR. These results align with the qualitative results of Study 1—the Team 1 TAO was providing tactical information to other team members while the TAO on Team 2 was SEEKING INFORMATION about TRACK BEHAVIOR to better understand the tactical situation.

5 General Discussion

In this paper, we compared the results of a qualitative analysis with those of two quantitative analyses leveraging ENA. Using data on U.S. Navy air defense warfare teams, we focused on the discourse of two tactical officers (TAOs) on two different teams that participated in the same training simulations. Our qualitative analysis showed that both teams were involved in situations where information was reiterated to maintain awareness of the tactical situation. However, the TAO on Team 1 *provided* tactical information *to* team members about hostile track behavior, while the TAO on Team 2 *requested* information *from* team members to gain a better understanding of the situation. This suggests a need to consider the order in which the two TAOs made connections between SEEKING INFORMATION and TACTICAL INFORMATION to evaluate their performance and give relevant feedback.

The ENA model (Study 1) showed that both TAOs were *involved* in situations requests were made for tactical information. However, the model showed little difference between the two TAOs. In contrast, the dENA model (Study 2) was aligned with the qualitative findings: relative to the TAO on team 2, the TAO on Team 1 responded more often *to* SEEKING INFORMATION by describing TRACK BEHAVIOR; relative to the TAO on Team 1, the TAO on Team 2 responded more often to TRACK BEHAVIOR by SEEKING INFORMATION.

These results demonstrate dENA's ability to model the interdependent, temporal, *and* ordered aspects of Complex Collaborative Thinking (CCT). Like ENA, dENA uses a moving window to account for the ways group members respond to events in the recent temporal context [20], and accounts for interdependence by measuring connections within that window to model individuals' responses to information in the common ground [1]. But unlike ENA, dENA preserves the order of events, enabling the algorithm to model the influence of information *from* the common ground *on* individuals' responses [4].

This approach builds on, but also extends, the visual affordances of ENA. ENA represents networks in two ways: (1) as network graphs, where the strength of connections between nodes is represented by line thickness and saturation; and (2) as a set of points in a metric space that allows networks to be compared statistically in terms of their content. Crucially, ENA co-registers a statistical model of networks with their individual network graphs such that the dimensions of the statistical model can be interpreted using the positions of nodes in the network. dENA retains these key properties but adapts them to account for the order in which the events that generate the networks occur. First, the network graphs in dENA account for directionality between nodes by representing each pairwise connection with a pair of triangles, such that the thickness and saturation of the triangles represents the total strength of the pairwise connection, and the relative heights of the triangles represent the proportion of connections going in each direction. The number of times each node is part of a response is modeled by the size of the node, and self-references are represented as a proportion of the node size. Second, each network is represented a *vector* in the metric space pointing from the position of its accumulated ground to the position of its accumulated response. dENA co-registers the network graphs with the vector corresponding to each network such that the dimensions of the metric space can be interpreted in terms of the flow of information in the networks.

This study has several limitations. The analysis was conducted using a single dataset. However, the data we used—and the analysis we provided—was only meant to provide an example of how dENA can model interdependent, temporal, and ordered elements common in a CCT context. Future work will, of course, explore using this approach to model other domains of CCT. Second, we have yet to develop a method for testing whether differences between network vectors are significant. We intend to incorporate significance testing in future work. Additionally, the current implementation of dENA does not yet account for sequences of more than two events. Our future work will explore extensions of dENA to account for and represent longer sequences.

These limitations notwithstanding, this work shows dENA is a method that can analyze the CCT of individuals in the context of a group, representing ordered connections in a way that visually captures qualitative differences that unordered models cannot. Unlike other approaches, dENA is thus able to present an interpretable visualization capable of simultaneously accounting for interdependence, temporality, *and* order.

Acknowledgements. This work was funded in part by the National Science Foundation (DRL-1661036, DRL-1713110), the Wisconsin Alumni Research Foundation, and the Office of the Vice Chancellor for Research and Graduate Education at the University of Wisconsin-Madison. The opinions, findings, and conclusions do not reflect the views of the funding agencies, cooperating institutions, or other individuals.

References

1. Clark, H.H.: Using Language. Cambridge University Press, Cambridge (1996)
2. D'Angelo, A.-L.D., Ruis, A.R., Collier, W., Shaffer, D.W., Pugh, C.M.: Evaluating how residents talk and what it means for surgical performance in the simulation lab. American Journal of Surgery. In press (2020)
3. DeChurch, L.A., Mesmer-Magnus, J.R.: The cognitive underpinnings of effective teamwork: a meta-analysis. J. Appl. Psychol. **95**(1), 32–53 (2010)
4. Dillenbourg, P.: Collaborative Learning: Cognitive and Computational Approaches. Advances in Learning and Instruction Series. Elsevier Science Inc, New York (1999)
5. Halpin, P.F., von Davier, A.A.: Modeling collaboration using point processes. In: von Davier, A.A., Zhu, M., Kyllonen, P.C. (eds.) Innovative Assessment of Collaboration, pp. 233–247. Springer, Cham (2017)
6. Hutchins, E.: Cognition in the Wild. MIT Press, Cambridge (1995)
7. Kapur, M.: Temporality matters: advancing a method for analyzing problem- solving processes in a computer-supported collaborative environment. Int. J. Comput. Supported Collaborative Learning **6**(1), 39–56 (2011)

8. Kim, Y., Tscholl, M.: The dynamic interaction between engagement, friendship, and collaboration in robot children triads. In: Eagan, B., Misfeldt, M., Siebert-Evenstone, A. (eds.) ICQE 2019. CCIS, vol. 1112, pp. 307–314. Springer, Cham (2019). https://doi.org/10.1007/978-3-030-33232-7_27

9. Marquart, C.L., Swiecki, Z., Collier, W., Eagan, B., Woodward, R., Shaffer, D. W. rENA: Epistemic Network Analysis (Version 0.1.3) (2018)

10. Marquart, C.L., Swiecki, Z., Eagan, B., Shaffer, D. W.: ncodeR (Version 0.1.2) (2018)

11. Morrison, J.G., Kelly, R.T., Moore, R.A., Hutchins, S.G.: Tactical decision making under stress (TADMUS) decision support system, vol. 13 (1996)

12. Nachtigall, V., Sung, H.: Students' collaboration patterns in a productive failure setting: an epistemic network analysis of contrasting cases. In: Eagan, B., Misfeldt, M., Siebert-Evenstone, A. (eds.) ICQE 2019. CCIS, vol. 1112, pp. 165–176. Springer, Cham (2019). https://doi.org/10.1007/978-3-030-33232-7_14

13. Paris, C., Johnston, J.H., Reeves, D.: A schema-based approach to measuring team decision making in a Navy combat information center. The Human in Command, pp. 263–278 (2000)

14. Perera, D., Kay, J., Koprinska, I., Yacef, K., Zaïane, O.R.: Clustering and sequential pattern mining of online collaborative learning data. IEEE Trans. Knowl. Data Eng. 21(6), 759–772 (2009)

15. Reimann, P.: Time is precious: variable- and event-centred approaches to process analysis in CSCL research. Comput. Supported Learn. 4, 239–257 (2009)

16. Ruis, A.R., Rosser, A.A., Quandt-Walle, C., Nathwani, J.N., Shaffer, D.W., Pugh, C.M.: The hands and head of a surgeon: modeling operative competency with multimodal epistemic network analysis. Am. J. Surgery 216(5), 835–840 (2018)

17. Ruis, A.R., Siebert-Evenstone, A.L., Pozen, R., Eagan, B., Shaffer, D.W.: Finding common ground: a method for measuring recent temporal context in analyses of complex, collaborative thinking. In: Lund, K., Niccolai, G., Lavoué, E., Hmelo-Silver, C., Gwon, G., Baker, M. (eds.) 13th International Conference on Computer Supported Collaborative Learning (CSCL), vol. 1, pp. 136–143. International Society of the Learning Sciences, Lyon, France (2019)

18. Shaffer, D.W., Collier, W., Ruis, A.R.: A tutorial on epistemic network analysis: analyzing the structure of connections in cognitive, social, and interaction data. J. Learn. Analytics 3(3), 9–45 (2016)

19. Shaffer, D.W.: Quantitative Ethnography. Cathcart Press, Madison (2017)

20. Siebert-Evenstone, A., Arastoopour Irgens, G., Collier, W., Swiecki, Z., Ruis, A.R., Shaffer, D.W.: In search of conversational grain size: Modelling semantic structure using moving stanza windows. J. Learn. Anal. 4(3), 123–139 (2017)

21. Suthers, D.D., Desiato, C.: Exposing chat features through analysis of uptake between contributions. In: 2012 45th Hawaii International Conference on System Sciences, pp. 3368–3377. IEEE, Hawaii (2012)

22. Swiecki, Z., Lian, Z., Ruis, A., Shaffer, D.W.: Does order matter? Investigating sequential and cotemporal models of collaboration. In: Lund, K., Niccolai, G.P., Lavoué, E., Gweon, C.H., Baker, M. (eds.) 13th International Conference on Computer Supported Collaborative Learning (CSCL), vol. 1, pp. 112–119. International Society of the Learning Sciences, Lyon, France (2019)

23. Swiecki, Z., Ruis, A.R., Farrell, C., Shaffer, D.W.: Assessing individual contributions to collaborative problem solving: a network analysis approach. Comput. Hum. Behav. 104 (2020)

Simplification of Epistemic Networks Using Parsimonious Removal with Interpretive Alignment

Yeyu Wang$^{(\boxtimes)}$ (ID), Zachari Swiecki (ID), A. R. Ruis (ID), and David Williamson Shaffer (ID)

University of Wisconsin – Madison, Madison, WI, USA
ywang2466@wisc.edu

Abstract. A key goal of quantitative ethnographic (QE) models, and statistical models more generally, is to produce the most *parsimonious* model that adequately explains or predicts the phenomenon of interest. In epistemic network analysis (ENA), for example, this entails constructing network models with the fewest number of codes whose interaction structure provides sufficient explanatory power in a given context. Unlike most statistical models, however, modification of ENA models can affect not only the statistical properties but also the *interpretive alignment* between quantitative features and qualitative meaning that is a central goal in QE analyses. In this study, we propose a novel method, Parsimonious Removal with Interpretive Alignment, for systematically identifying more parsimonious ENA models that are likely to maintain interpretive alignment with an existing model. To test the efficacy of the method, we implemented it on a well-studied dataset for which there is a published, validated ENA model, and we show that the method successfully identifies reduced models likely to maintain explanatory power and interpretive alignment.

Keywords: Model comparison · Model refinement · Unified methods · Epistemic network analysis (ENA) · Interpretive alignment

1 Introduction

Quantitative ethnography (QE) is a method for studying cultural and behavioral patterns that facilitates thick description of qualitative data at scale [8]. To do this, QE unifies qualitative and quantitative approaches with the goal of achieving *interpretive alignment* between qualitative meaning-making and the features of quantitative models. For example, *epistemic network analysis* (ENA), a widely used QE technique, models the structure of connections among key concepts, behaviors, or other elements (i.e., Codes) to represent complex phenomena [9]. Critically, ENA maintains linkages between model features (i.e., weighted connections between Codes) and the original qualitative data that produced them, enabling researchers to warrant interpretive alignment.

However, a model that achieves interpretive alignment might not be the most *parsimonious* one. In statistics, model parsimony is often operationalized as the inclusion of the fewest number of variables that sufficiently explain or predict the phenomenon

© Springer Nature Switzerland AG 2021
A. R. Ruis and S. B. Lee (Eds.): ICQE 2021, CCIS 1312, pp. 137–151, 2021.
https://doi.org/10.1007/978-3-030-67788-6_10

of interest [7]. The variables in an ENA model are the connections among Codes, but because QE unifies qualitative and quantitative perspectives, the most parsimonious ENA model is not necessarily the model with the fewest Codes. Rather, parsimony in ENA involves constructing a model with the fewest Codes that maintains both explanatory power and *interpretive alignment*.

To identify the most parsimonious ENA model while maintaining interpretive alignment, QE researchers typically take a trial-and-error approach. However, this process involves iterative confirmation across qualitative and quantitative perspectives, and there is no reliable method for determining whether two ENA models with different Codes have equivalent explanatory power.

To address this challenge in QE model refinement, we propose a novel method, *parsimonious removal with interpretive alignment* (PRIA), for removing Codes to identify more parsimonious models likely to maintain interpretive alignment. We tested this method on a well-studied dataset for which there are published QE findings, and our results suggest that the PRIA method can reliably find the most parsimonious ENA model that maintains explanatory power. While researchers still need to verify interpretive alignment, PRIA provides a principled method for testing the effects of removing one or more Codes from an existing model.

2 Theory

2.1 Properties of QE Models

Quantitative ethnography unifies ethnographic and computational methods to understand culture, behavior, cognition, and other aspects of human activity at scale. Unlike mixed method studies, in which the qualitative and quantitative analyses are only minimally interdependent, QE studies generate thick descriptions of big data using processes that "inseparably" combine qualitative and quantitative approaches [8].

For example, one frequently-used modeling technique in QE is *epistemic network analysis* (ENA). ENA models the structure of connections among Codes by quantifying the co-occurrence of Codes within recent temporal context. ENA analyses begin when researchers perform a close reading of some discourse data to generate theories about the situated meaning of events, which are then operationalized as Codes. ENA constructs network graphs of the coded data that can be used to explore hypotheses about the relationships among them, as well as summary statistics that can be used to compare the relationships among Codes statistically. Then researchers *close the interpretive loop* [8], validating the features of the model by re-examining the original data that contributed to those features.

In particular, ENA supports the unification of qualitative and quantitative methods in at least five ways. ENA models:

1. Represent the connections among Codes that were developed and validated by researchers grounded in the empirical data.
2. Generate an *ENA score* in a projected metric space. ENA score is defined as a summative measure for an individual network that can be used to conduct statistical tests.

3. Position nodes in the ENA space such that network graphs can be used to interpret the meaning of ENA scores in terms of the network structures they represent.
4. Provide a *goodness of fit* measure that indicates how well the projected metric space and weighted network models are coordinated. High goodness of fit indicates that the network graphs provide a reliable interpretation of the dimensions of the projected metric space.
5. Preserve the *interpretive alignment* between quantitative features (statistical significance between groups and interpretation of the dimensions based on node positions) and a qualitative understanding of the data.

For example, [10] explored collaborative problem-solving in a military training exercise on air defense warfare, using qualitative analysis on the discourse data and ENA to model the patterns in discourse. They compared the behavior of commanders with and without access to a tactical scaffolding system, which provided detailed information about *tracks* (ships and aircraft detected on radar) and a record of actions taken toward them. [10] found that commanders without access to the scaffolding system focused more on seeking information about behaviors of incoming aircraft to understand the tactical situation; commanders using the scaffolding system integrated information about the tactical situation to issue deterrent orders. The ENA space they created showed that network nodes for information seeking were on the negative side of the first dimension of the ENA space, and commanders working without the scaffolding system had low values on that dimension. Network nodes for tactical decision making were on the positive side of the first dimension, and commanders working with the scaffolding system had high values on that dimension. There was a statistically significant difference between commanders in the control and experimental conditions on the first dimension of the ENA space. Thus, the interpretation derived from the quantified ENA model was consistent with the situated hypothesis and Code generation based on thick description of the discourse data.

2.2 Model Parsimony

A common challenge that researchers face when using ENA is deciding whether one or more codes can be removed from a model without affecting interpretive alignment. For example, researchers may construct a model in which one or more Codes—or more specifically, the connections involving one or more Codes—do not provide significant explanatory or discriminative power. That is, the model refinement process may involve exploring whether a more parsimonious model can be constructed that does not change the interpretation of the data, but that tells the story more clearly by removing Codes that do not play a significant role in the model. However, the unification of qualitative and quantitative methods in QE poses a particular challenge for refining QE models in this way.

In statistics, *parsimony*—the idea that a model is better when fewer variables have the same explanatory power—is one of the most important factors in model selection and evaluation. As [11] argue, the primary benefit of a more parsimonious model is that it increases the predictive power by better distinguishing the signal from noise.

Parsimony balances variance explained and model complexity, and reduces the likelihood of overfitting, or over-parametrization in model selection [6].

However, [2] examined studies of qualitative parsimony and failed to find a universal definition due to the complexity and diversity of social science research. Although they claimed that "one 'size' of parsimony does not appear to fit all qualitative methods" (p. 1403), parsimony involves the simplest expressions of qualitative findings grounded in thick description.

The problem for QE researchers is that unlike pure statistical models, which can be reduced to the most parsimonious form by systematically removing variables until the amount of variance explained drops too low [7], modification of QE models can affect not only the *statistical* properties of a model but also the *interpretive alignment* between quantitative features and qualitative meaning that is a central goal in QE analyses.

From a QE perspective, then, parsimony needs to unify two points of view. From a quantitative perspective, a parsimonious model needs to involve the fewest parameters or variables to achieve the same level of explanatory power. Connections between Codes are the variables in an ENA model, so the more parsimonious ENA model thus has fewer Codes (and hence, fewer connections). From an ethnographic perspective, QE researchers are concerned with capturing the "right" amount detail to explain the phenomenon at hand. Adding more Codes does not always provide a better or more clear interpretation of events, and in fact can obscure the most central features of a situation.

2.3   Current Approach to Identifying Parsimonious ENA Models

In practice, researchers using ENA take an exploratory approach to refining models, trying to achieve parsimony while maintaining explanatory power and interpretive alignment. Typically, researchers examine their existing "best" model to determine whether one or more Codes are contributing significantly to meaningful interpretation. Codes that are weakly connected, especially those located toward the center of the model, are a common target for removal. A researcher selects one or more Codes to remove, produces a deflated model, and then checks whether the deflated model maintains (a) high goodness of fit, (b) statistical significance, and (c) interpretive alignment. Needless to say, this process is time-consuming, and there is no extant technique for comparing two models with different Codes in a principled way.

2.4   The PRIA Approach to Identifying More Parsimonious ENA Models

To address this issue, we propose a method, Parsimonious Removal with Interpretive Alignment (PRIA), to identify deflated models that are likely to maintain explanatory power and interpretive alignment. This method has five steps:

Step 1: Generate deflated models. We construct a set of *deflated models* by generating all possible ENA models with fewer codes using the same parameters as the *original model*.

Step 2: Determine which deflated models have high goodness of fit. We conduct a goodness of fit test on all deflated models, which measures the extent to which the interpretation of dimensions is reliable.

Step 3. Correlate ENA scores. We compute the correlation of ENA scores between each deflated model and the original model. This correlation measures the extent to which the summary statistics for individual units of analysis in the deflated model vary from the original model.

Step 4. Correlate node positions. We compute the correlation of node positions between each deflated model and the original model. Node positions are used to interpret the meaning of ENA scores in terms of the network structures they represent. A high correlation of the node positions between the deflated model and the original model suggests that the underlying patterns described by the networks are aligned.

Step 5: Confirm interpretive alignment for *candidate models*. Deflated models that pass tests for goodness of fit and correlation of ENA scores and node positions become *candidate models*. We sort the set of candidate models by the number of codes removed, from most codes removed to least. Then, we check interpretive alignment one candidate model at a time until we find the most parsimonious model that has good interpretive alignment. To ensure that interpretive alignment is conserved, we examine each candidate model from two perspectives:

1. From the quantitative perspective, we re-run any statistical tests from the original model to determine whether differences remain significant. Additionally, we examine the network graphs to verify that the node positions preserve the interpretation of the dimensions.
2. From the qualitative perspective, we once again close the interpretive loop, re-examining the original data to see if it is aligned with the candidate model.

The candidate model with the most codes removed that meets these alignment criteria becomes the *reduced model*.

2.5   Data and Research Questions

We thus propose five steps for generating a reduced model and confirming interpretive alignment. To examine the feasibility of PRIA, we analyzed a dataset collected from the Tactical Decision Making Under Stress (TADMUS) project [1]. We chose this dataset because prior work has developed and validated a coding scheme and ENA models [10]. In what follows, we use this data to address the following research questions:

1. Can candidate models be constructed that have high goodness of fit, ENA score correlation, and node position correlation?
2. Do any of the candidate models preserve the statistical results of the original?
3. Do any of the candidate models preserve the interpretation of the dimensions of the original?
4. Are any of the candidate models that meet all of the above criteria also well aligned with the original data?

3   Method

3.1   Dataset and Codebook

In this study, we tested the Code removal procedure using data collected in the TADMUS project. The dataset includes the discourse of 16 Navy Air Defense Warfare (ADW) teams working collaboratively to make tactical decisions in a military training simulation [4]. In these training simulations, teams were tasked with identifying, tracking, and assessing potentially hostile air or surface vessels called tracks. Each team consisted of up to six members, two in command roles, and four in supporting roles. Those in command roles made tactical decisions based on the information reported by the supporting members of the team. A decision-support system was developed to scaffold the decision-making process of the commanders by providing detailed information about tracks and a record of actions taken toward them [3]. To test the effectiveness of the system, eight teams were randomly assigned to the experimental group, who had access to the support system, while the other eight teams were assigned to the control group, with access only to the regular watch station. The regular watch station is a device that provides basic tracking and identification information. In this study, we made use of the discourse data for each team in the training project for 94 participants. The transcripts of their discourse are segmented to 12,027 turns of talk in total.

Table 1. Codes, definitions, and examples developed by [10]

Code	Definition	Examples
DETECT/IDENTIFY (DI)	Talk about radar detection of a track or the identification of a track, (e.g., vessel type)	IR/EW NEW BEARING, BEARING 078 APQ120 CORRELATES TRACK 7036 POSSIBLE F-4
TRACK BEHAVIOR (TB)	Talk about kinematic data about a track or a track's location	AIR/IDS TRACK NUMBER 7021 DROP IN ALTITUDE TO 18 THOUSAND FEET
ASSESSMENT (A)	Talk about whether a track is friendly or hostile, the threat level of a track, or indicating tracks of interest	TRACKS OF INTEREST 7013 LEVEL 5 7037 LEVEL 5 7007 LEVEL 4 TRACK 7020 LEVEL 5 AND 7036 LEVEL 5
STATUS UPDATES (SU)	Talk about procedural information, e.g., track responses to tactical actions, or talk about tactical actions taken by the team	TAO ID, STILL NO RESPONSE FROM TRACK 37, POSSIBLE PUMA HELO
SEEKING INFORMATION (SI)	Asking questions regarding track behavior, identification, or status	TAO CO, WE'VE UPGRADED THEM TO LEVEL 7 RIGHT?

(continued)

Table 1. (*continued*)

Code	Definition	Examples
RECOMMENDATIONS (R)	Recommending or requesting tactical actions	AIR/TIC RECOMMEND LEVEL THREE ON TRACK 7016 7022
DETERRENT ORDERS (DTO)	Giving orders meant to warn or deter tracks	TIC AIR, CONDUCT LEVEL 2 WARNING ON 7037
DEFENSIVE ORDERS (DFO)	Giving orders to prepare ship defenses or engage hostile tracks	TAO/CO COVER 7016 WITH BIRDS

We adopted this dataset and coding scheme because the Codes were grounded in the qualitative understanding of researchers familiar with the data, and automated classifiers were developed validated by two expert human raters. To understand the differences in team discourse with and without the supporting system, [10] analyzed the transcripts and developed the eight behavior codes in Table 1. For each code, pairwise inter-rater reliability between two human raters and the automated classifier was Cohen's $\kappa > 0.84$ and Shaffer's $\rho(0.65) < 0.05$, indicating that all codes met a minimum threshold of $\kappa = 0.65$.

3.2 Epistemic Network Analysis

Using the same parameters reported in [10], ENA models were constructed with participants subdivided into training scenarios as the units, scenario as the conversation variable, and a moving window of 5 turns of talk, using rENA 0.2.0.1 [5]. We included all eight codes listed in Table 1. To create a projected ENA space, we used a means rotation to maximize the differences between control and experimental conditions, followed by a singular value decomposition, to define the first and second dimensions, respectively, of the projected metric space. On the other hand, we calculate the arithmetic means of the network edges, defined as *centroids*. To test the reliability of the interpretation on the means rotation dimension, we computed the goodness of fit using Pearson's r between the ENA scores with centroids for the same individual ($r = 0.95$).

3.3 Code Removal Procedure and Criteria

As described above in the theory section, we constructed all possible reduced models by extracting potential combinations of code removal[1]. Then, we measured each one on three criteria: (a) its goodness of fit, (b) the correlation of its ENA scores with the original model, and (c) the correlation of its node positions with the original model (see Table 2). Then, we compared the computed correlations (Criteria 1–3 in Table 2) with

---

[1] In this study, the original model includes eight Codes. We took combination of k Codes ($k = 1$, 2, ..., 5) to be removed from the original model. The maximum value of k is 5 since ENA needs at least three Codes to be constructed.

a given threshold, 0.95. Deflated models significantly above the threshold on all three criteria were classed as candidate models, which were rank-ordered by number of codes, with the model having the least number of codes listed first.

Table 2. Goals and criteria for generating deflated models

Goals		Criteria
Model fitting	The interpretation of dimensions is reliable	Criterion 1: Goodness of Fit for deflated model
Model alignment	The interpretation of individuals is aligned with the original model	Criterion 2: Correlation of ENA scores between the original and deflated models
	The interpretation of dimensions is aligned with the original model	Criterion 3: Correlation of node positions between the original and deflated models

To ensure that the interpretation of dimensions in a deflated model is reliable, we computed the goodness of fit by calculating the pairwise correlation (Pearson's r) of the ENA scores with their corresponding network centroids. We then calculated the 95% confidence interval (C.I.) and compared the lower bound of the C.I. with the threshold of 0.95 (Criterion 1), to maintain the same goodness of fit as the original model. If the lower bound is above the threshold, the fit of the deflated model is significantly higher than the threshold, which indicates that the deflated model is well fitted and reliable for interpretation. Of the deflated models that satisfied Criterion 1, we selected deflated models whose ENA scores and node positions are highly correlated with the original model (Criteria 2 and 3). High correlation of ENA scores indicates that the interpretation of the individuals in the model is consistent with the original model, and high correlation of node positions maintain the interpretation of the dimensions in the network. We calculated the C.I. of correlations for both ENA scores and node positions between each deflated model and original model and returned the deflated models whose lower bounds of the C.I. were above the threshold. The models that satisfied all criteria were considered candidate models, and we sorted them by the number of Codes removed.

After the PRIA algorithm output the candidate models, we confirmed the statistical results and interpretive alignment of the most parsimonious candidate model. To do this, we first determined whether there is a significant difference between the two conditions on the first dimension of the candidate model, using two-sample t-test. We then checked the interpretation of the first dimension based on the locations of the nodes to determine whether it was consistent with the original model. Lastly, we compared the transcripts of two teams in the same training scenario that had similar tactical decision-making processes and results, except that one team's discourse contained a removed Code and the other team's discourse did not. The first candidate model to achieve interpretive alignment was confirmed as the reduced model.

4   Results

4.1   Code Removal Results

Of the 218 possible deflated models, the PRIA algorithm returned 3 that satisfied Criteria 1–3 (see Table 3). The three candidate models in Table 3 all have a high goodness of fit and high correlations of ENA scores and node coordinates with the original model. We chose the candidate model with most Codes removed to assess first for interpretive alignment. The model includes five Codes: "Seeking Information", "Detect/Identify", "Track Behavior", "Status Updates", and "Deterrent Orders.

Table 3. Candidate models with correlations (confidence intervals) significantly higher than 0.95

Codes removed	C1: Goodness of Fit	C2: Correlation of ENA scores	C3: Correlation of node positions	Number of codes removed
Assessment, defensive order, recommendation	**0.9562** **(0.9556, 0.9567)**	**0.961** **(0.953, 0.9677)**	**0.9986** **(0.9785, 0.9999)**	**3**
Defensive order, recommendation	0.957 (0.9564, 0.9575)	0.9738 (0.9683, 0.9783)	0.9997 (0.9968, 1)	2
Defensive order	0.9511 (0.9505, 0.9517)	0.9953 (0.9943, 0.9961)	0.9985 (0.9892, 0.9998)	1

4.2   Quantitative Confirmation

To compare the original model and the most parsimonious candidate model, we plotted both models (see Fig. 1). We examined whether the model interpretation changed in the following two respects: 1) statistical comparison of the two conditions; 2) network interpretation based on the node positions.

Statistical Testing Between Conditions. In the Original Model, There is a Significant Difference Between the Control Condition (Mean $= -0.25$, N $= 211$) and the Experimental Condition (Mean $= 0.25$, N $= 211$) According to a Two-Sample t-test ($t = 10.52$, $P < 0.005$, $D = 1.02$) on the First (Means Rotated) Dimension. In the Candidate Model, There is a Significant Difference Between the Control Condition (Mean $= -0.27$, N $= 211$) and the Experimental Condition (Mean $= 0.27$, N $= 211$) According to a Two-Sample t-test ($t = 9.36$, $P < 0.005$, $D = 0.91$). Thus, the Most Parsimonious Candidate Model Maintains the Significant Difference Between the Two Conditions.

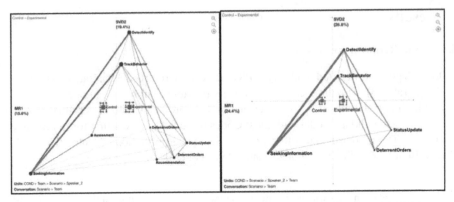

Fig. 1. The original model (left) and the most parsimonious candidate model (right)

Node Positions in ENA. In the Original Network, Codes Related to Tactical Decision Making (DETERRENT ORDERS and STATUS UPDATE) Are Located on the Positive Side of the First Dimension, While SEEKING INFORMATION is Located on the Negative Side. In the Most Parsimonious Candidate Model, the Relative Location of Major Codes Along the Means Rotation Space Are in Relative the Same Positions as the Original Model.

4.3 Qualitative Confirmation

We identified two teams (hereafter, Team 1 and Team 2) working on the same training scenario with a similar distribution of ENA scores in the original model. The distribution of ENA scores were not significantly different according to a Mann-Whitney U Test ($U = 25, p = 0.31$, Cliff's $d = 0.39$) and suggest that the two teams made similar connections between codes. However, Team 2 made connections between ASSESSMENT and other codes, but Team 1 did not. The removal of ASSESSMENT in addition to DEFENSIVE ORDER and RECOMMENDATION is what differentiated the most parsimonious candidate model from the next most parsimonious one. In the examples below, we look at each team at the beginning of a training session involving the same potential attack.

Example 1: Decision Making Without Explicit Assessment of Threats. At the Beginning of the Task, Team 1 is Told by the SSES that There is an Iranian F-4 in Their Airspace ("IN VICINITY") on a Training Mission ("FOR APPARENT LOCAL TRAINING"):

Line	Speaker	Utterance
1	SSES	TAO/SSES WE HAVE INDICATIONS OF AN IRANIAN F-4 AIRCRAFT UP IN VICINTIY BUSHEHR AIRBORNE FOR APPARENT LOCAL TRAINING

That is, the SSES points out a plane in the area (DETECT/IDENTIFY) and describes its behavior (TRACK BEHAVIOR).

Almost immediately, the team sees radar contacts for another fighter plane:

Line	Speaker	Utterance
2	EWS	TIC/EW I HAVE AN APS-115 CORRELATES TO P-3 BEARING 025
3	TAO	TRACK 7023 BEARING 025 40M
4	TIC	EW/TIC WE COPY WE GOT THAT CORRELATED TRACK 7023
5	IDS	THIS IS IDS, 7023 NO MODES NO CODES

In line 2, the Electronic Warfare Supervisor (EWS) identifies it as a P-3 (DETECT/IDENTIFY) and gives its bearing (TRACK BEHAVIOR). In line 4, the TIC designates as "TRACK 7023" (DETECT/IDENTIFY), and in line 5, the IDS reports "NO MODES NO CODES" (DETECT/IDENTIFY), indicating that the plane is not responding to automatic tracking. In other words, the plane is not identifying itself, and thus could be hostile.

The team subsequently identifies three other radar tracks, and then almost immediately (line 14) the EWS acquires the Iranian F-4 on radar (DETECT/IDENTIFY and TRACK BEHAVIOR). The TIC marks it as "TRACK 7036" in line 15 and gives its updated bearing (DETECT/IDENTIFY and TRACK BEHAVIOR):

Line	Speaker	Utterance
14	EWS	TIC/EWS APQ-120 BEARING 077 CORRELATES F-1 MIRAGE CORRECTION F-4 PHANTOM
15	TIC	F-4 CORRELATES TO TRACK 7036 BEARING 078 RANGE 50NM

Then, the SSES then notifies the team that there are multiple aircraft departing from the Iranian coast on the way toward the ship (DETECT/IDENTIFY and TRACK BEHAVIOR).

Line	Speaker	Utterance
16	SSES	TAO/SSES WE HAVE INDICATIONS OF MULTIPLE AIRCRAFT DEPARTING IRANIAN COAST, EXACT COMPOSITION UNKNOWN, LOCATION UNKNOWN

In other words, the team has taken a series of actions to DETECT/IDENTIFY tracks and designate track behavior. Collectively, these actions suggest there are hostile aircraft preparing to attack the ship, even though the Iranian F-4 (now TRACK 7036) was supposedly on a training mission:

1. There are multiple planes in the airspace,
2. At least one of them is not identifying itself (TRACK 7023 has "NO MODES NO CODES in line 5), and
3. There are multiple airplanes departing from Iran toward the ship (line 8).

In response to this tactical situation, the TAO issues a level 1 warning (DETERRENT ORDER, giving orders to warn or deter tracks) for the F-4 (TRACK 7036), which is "FEET WET", or flying from land to the water and approaching the ship:

Line	Speaker	Utterance
17	TAO	AWC/TAO TRACK 7036 GOING FEET WET ISSUE LEVEL 1 WARNING PLEASE

Team 1 thus identified a series of tracks and recorded their behavior, leading the TAO to (a) conclude that the tracks were hostile and (b) issue a deterrent order as a "LEVEL 1 WARNING". However, this process of deciding to issue a deterrent order does not show explicit ASSESSMENT of the threat level of the planes.

Example 2: Decision Making with Explicit Assessment of Threats. The Second Team, Working on the Same Training Scenario, Receives the Same Notification from SSES at the Beginning of the Exercise. The SESS Detects an "IRANIAN F-4 AIRCRAFT" (DETECT/IDENTIFY) is "IN VICINITY" (TRACK BEHAVIOR):

Line	Speaker	Utterance
1	SSES	TAO/SSES WE HAVE INDICATIONS OF AN IRANIAN F-4 AIRCRAFT UP IN VICINTIY BUSHEHR AIRBORNE FOR APPARENT LOCAL TRAINING

The TIC acknowledges the intelligence provided by the SSES and, using that information, asks the AWC to investigate a track that might be the F-4:

Line	Speaker	Utterance
2	TIC	TIC AYE
3	TIC	AWC/TIC TRACK 7020 WE NEED TO PROBABLY INTERROGATE THEM AND SEE IF WE GET ANY EW, THAT MIGHT BE THE F-4. HE'S AT 3,000FT, UH ACTUALLY I TAKE THAT BACK IT'S PROBABLY A HELO AT 80KNTS 3,000FT THERE ABOUT 40M

In line 3, the TIC initially identifies "TRACK 7020" as the Iranian F-4 (DETECT/IDENTIFY), but quickly changes the identification to a helicopter ("IT'S PROBABLY A HELO") based on the TRACK BEHAVIOR, including altitude ("3,000FT"), distance ("40M"), and speed ("80KNT").

Next, the IDS identifies a new track, TRACK 7023:

Line	Speaker	Utterance
4	IDS	TIC/IDC TRACK 7023 NO MODES NO CODES
5	TIC	TAO/TIC 7023 SPEEDING UP AND TURNING WEST. SHE IS ALSO CLIMBING. SHE IS AT 1800FT RIGHT NOW AND TURNING SOUTH ON 239 250KNTS
6	IDS	TIC/IDC TRACK 7023 UPDATED UNKNOWN ASSUMED HOSTILE

The IDS notes (line 4) that the new track has no radar information indicating whether it is friendly or hostile ("NO MODES NO CODES"). Immediately after this

DETECT/IDENTIFY from the IDS, the TIC (line 5) reports that the track is exhibiting unusual TRACK BEHAVIOR, including changing speed ("SPEEDING UP"), direction ("TURNING WEST"), and height ("CLIMBING"). Using that information, the IDS makes an explicit ASSESSMENT: TRACK 7023 is "ASSUMED HOSTILE" (line 6).

Soon after, the SSES identifies (line 10) multiple aircraft taking off from the Iranian coast "FEET WET" (DETECT/IDENTIFY and TRACK BEHAVIOR):

Line	Speaker	Utterance
10	SSES	TAO/SSES WE HAVE INDICATIONS OF MULTIPLE AIRCRAFT DEPARTING IRANIAN COAST, EXACT COMPOSITION UNKNOWN, LOCATION UNKNOWN

Moments later, given the information from the SSES, the TAO issues "LEVEL 1 WARNINGS" to Track 7036 (DETERRENT ORDER):

Line	Speaker	Utterance
15	TAO	AWC/TAO ISSUE LEVEL 1 WARNINGS TO TRACK 7036

Thus Team 2, like Team 1, identifies a series of tracks and records their behavior, leading the TAO to conclude that the tracks are hostile and issue a DETERRENT ORDER—the same level 1 warning that the TAO from Team 1 ordered.

Along the way, in Team 2 the IDS makes an explicit ASSESSMENT of the tactical situation (line 6). However, this assessment does not appear to have influenced the Team's tactical decision making or behavior: in both teams, the TAO reaches the same conclusion. In other words, although Team 2 makes an explicit ASSESSMENT of the situation, it appears that the assessment served only to make explicit the interpretations the team was already making—which, in turn, provides qualitative evidence that removing the code from the model does not significantly change the model of team behavior or our interpretation of it.

5   Discussion

In this paper, we proposed the PRIA method and successfully reduced an existing ENA model to a more parsimonious model with fewer Codes but equivalent explanatory power and interpretive alignment. We propose this method based on five properties of ENA that support the unification of qualitative and quantitative approaches. Based on each property, we generated corresponding criteria and confirmatory procedures.

1. ENA models generate the ENA scores, a summative measure for individuals, projected as points in the ENA space. PRIA correlates the ENA scores between the original model and the reduced model, to ensure the interpretation of individuals in the space is maintained.
2. ENA models provide an interpretation of the dimensions of the ENA space based on the node positions. PRIA correlates the original node position between the original and the reduced, to ensure the interpretation of dimension is maintained.

3. ENA models generate a goodness of fit measure to test how well the projected metric space and the weighted network models are coordinated—and thus whether the interpretation of the dimension is reliable. PRIA computes the goodness of fit test on the reduced model to ensure the qualified candidate models are also reliable.

Based on these properties and criteria, PRIA deflates the original model and generates the candidate models with Codes removed that maintain both good model fit and alignment with the original model.

PRIA then has two additional confirmatory procedures that validate the interpretive alignment between quantitative metrics (statistical tests and node positions) and qualitative analyses.

4. ENA performs the statistical tests on the ENA scores and enables interpretation of those results based on node positions. PRIA performs the same tests on the reduced model to confirm significance remained and checks that the node positions in the reduced model do not result in a different interpretation from the original model.
5. ENA closes the interpretive loop by enabling researchers to confirm that the results of a model conform to the original qualitative data. PRIA re-closes that loop to ensure that the reduced model is consistent with the qualitative data as well.

We tested the PRIA method on a data from a military training project that already had validated Codes and an existing ENA model aligned with qualitative analyses. For this data, PRIA suggested it was possible to construct a reduced model with three Codes removed that met all of these criteria.

The PRIA method has some limitations. First, *this approach requires an existing ENA model, with validated Codes and good interpretive alignment*, to generate and evaluate more parsimonious candidate models. That is, the PRIA method provides a principled way for researchers to *refine an existing validated model*, rather than providing a technique to automatically generate an optimal model from a large set of Codes. Second, we only tested the PRIA method on one dataset. To test the generalizability of PRIA method, we will need to conduct the same procedure on other datasets with different properties. Finally, we chose an arbitrary threshold of 0.95 for our correlation criteria. Methods to determine appropriate minimum thresholds need to be developed.

Despite these limitations, the PRIA method shows that it is possible to generate parsimonious reduced models that have good interpretive alignment and explanatory power equivalent to the original model. This suggests that the PRIA approach can provide a principled method for identifying more parsimonious ENA models.

Acknowledgments. This work was funded in part by the National Science Foundation (DRL-1661036, DRL-1713110), the Wisconsin Alumni Research Foundation, and the Office of the Vice Chancellor for Research and Graduate Education at the University of Wisconsin-Madison. The opinions, findings, and conclusions do not reflect the views of the funding agencies, cooperating institutions, or other individuals.

References

1. Cannon-Bowers, J.A., Salas, E.E.: Making decisions under stress: implications for individual and team training. Acta Physiol. **103**, 337–341 (1999)
2. Cutcliffe, J.R., Harder, H.G.: The perpetual search for parsimony: enhancing the epistemological and practical utility of qualitative research findings. Int. J. Nursing Stud. **46**(10), 1401–1410 (2009)
3. Hutchins, S.G., et al.: Principles for aiding complex military decision making. In: Proceedings of the Second International Command and Control Research and Technology Symposium, p. 22 (1996)
4. Johnston, J.H., et al.: Application of cognitive load theory to develop a measure of team cognitive efficiency. Mil. Psychol. **25**(3), 252–265 (2013)
5. Marquart, L.C., et al.: rENA. https://cran.r-project.org/web/packages/rENA/citation.html. Accessed 29 June 2020
6. Mees, A.: Parsimonious dynamical reconstruction. Int. J. Bifurcat. Chaos. **3**(03), 669–675 (1993)
7. Raykov, T., Marcoulides, G.A.: On desirability of parsimony in structural equation model selection. Struct. Equ. Model. Multidisc. J. **6**(3), 292–300 (1999)
8. Shaffer, D.W.: Quantitative Ethnography. Cathcart Press, Madison (2017)
9. Shaffer, D.W., Ruis, A.R.: Epistemic network analysis: a worked example of theory-based learning analytics. In: Handbook of Learning Analytics, pp. 175–187. Society for Learning Analytics Research (SoLAR) (2017)
10. Swiecki, Z., et al.: Assessing individual contributions to collaborative problem solving: a network analysis approach. Comput. Hum. Behav. **104**, 105876 (2020)
11. Vandekerckhove, J., et al.: Model Comparison and the Principle of Parsimony. Oxford University Press, Oxford (2015)

Case Studies

Case Studies

Connecting Curricular Design and Student Identity Change: An Epistemic Network Analysis

Amanda Barany[1]([⊠]) [iD], Mamta Shah[2], and Aroutis Foster[1] [iD]

[1] Drexel University, Philadelphia, PA 19104, USA
amb595@drexel.edu
[2] Elsevier Inc., Philadelphia, PA 19103, USA

Abstract. This paper reports findings from session 3 of the play-based course *Virtual City Planning*, which supported the exploration of environmental science identities. The Projective Reflection theoretical framework structured course design and implementation as well as assessment of student data for 18 middle schoolers in a local science museum. Epistemic Network Analysis was used to visualize different processes of identity exploration enacted each week as supported by curricular activities, supported by in-depth qualitative examinations of student reflections. Results illustrated connections between the design of each week's activities and the facets of identity on which students focused, highlighting the potential of such intentionally designed environments for supporting identity exploration and the potential future acquisition of science careers. Implications for curricular design and identity assessment are discussed.

Keywords: Identity exploration · STEM · Epistemic network analysis · Design-based research · Quantitative ethnography

1 Introduction

Research on science, technology, engineering and mathematics (STEM) education has increasingly referenced ways to develop learner skills in identity exploration, or a student's "deliberate internal or external action of seeking and processing information in relation to the self" [1, p. 250]. Processes of self-directed learning can promote identity changes in targeted directions over time, such as taking steps to attain a future STEM career [2]. Experiences that support learning as identity exploration are therefore particularly valuable in a 21st century context in that they can support adaptive skill development and career preparation for emerging and under-accessed STEM careers [3]. Identity exploration processes hold promise for increasing participation in and eventual acquisition of STEM careers among underrepresented gender [4] and racial groups [5].

Research has highlighted the value of STEM learning ecosystems that include schools, community settings such as after-school and summer programs, science centers and museums, and informal experiences at home and in a variety of environments that

© Springer Nature Switzerland AG 2021
A. R. Ruis and S. B. Lee (Eds.): ICQE 2021, CCIS 1312, pp. 155–169, 2021.
https://doi.org/10.1007/978-3-030-67788-6_11

together constitute a rich array of learning opportunities for young people [6]. There is an upward trend in formal (e.g. university) and informal (e.g. museums) learning institutions partnering (often with support from federal agencies) to offer programs for K-12 students with a shared commitment to expand students' access to STEM pathways. This paper contributes to this growing body of work as an example of such a partnership: researchers at a university funded by a National Science Foundation CAREER grant partnered with a local science museum to offer situated, targeted and intentional opportunities for exploration of environmental science and urban planning roles. The Projective Reflection (PR) theoretical and pedagogical framework was used to design Virtual City Planning (VCP), a play-based course designed to promote identity exploration around urban planning and environmental science careers. VCP was implemented in a museum classroom context with a diverse sample of middle school students. This paper examines group identity exploration trajectories over time in the third offering of VCP using Epistemic Network Analysis to model connections students drew between facets of their identities as supported by curricular activities across four weeks. Findings (a) illustrate how VCP session 3 built upon the strengths of two prior iterations to optimally support situated, targeted and intentional identity exploration over time, and (b) revealed group trends in how students reflected on different facets of the self as supported by each week's activities. Implications of these findings for games and education practitioners, designers and researchers are discussed. The research question asks: How did the design of Virtual City Planning Session 3 support student exploration of science career identities?

2 Literature Review

Researchers have proposed that educators should strive for designing learning environments, and by extension curricula, that enable students to become 'committed learners' [7]. This kind of learning is characterized by activities that students find important and personally rewarding. Furthermore, diSessa argued for the design of learning activities that meaningfully string together over time, allowing students to accomplish them with a sense of competence, build mastery of skills, and align with their goals and interests. These propositions are relevant to curricular interventions designed for promoting students that are committed to science. Findings from Relevance of Science Education, an international comparative project, indicated students' sense of self played a major role in how they engaged in learning about STEM disciplines in school. Researchers argued that it may be worthwhile for science curricula to afford students opportunities to explore personal relevance, particularly in terms of the role of science and how students could use science for the benefit of society [8]. Others studied the evolution of students' interest in science and scientific careers over a 5-year period, seeking to identify, understand and address barriers to participation, engagement and achievement in science and mathematics, particularly as it begins to drop around the age of 14 years [9]. Using the lens of identity, findings emphasized the need for educational endeavors to support articulation and bridging of learners 'doing science' and 'being a scientist'.

Recent studies have demonstrated the value of specific curricular elements that support students' science identities. For instance, studies on the use of Citizen Science, a role-playing digital game centered on limnology and environmental advocacy, illustrated how the game encouraged the development of player identities as citizen scientists within the domain of lake ecology [10]. Through their implementation studies, researchers found that game literacy or technical literacy mediated content knowledge. Thus, educators could adopt novel activities for students to make sense of the social and technical symbols embedded in a play-based curriculum to facilitate students' understanding of the narrative, and by extension, support their participation in identity exploration activities. More recently, researchers argued that in addition to content knowledge, students must also be encouraged to adopt the social and cultural practices enacted by real-world scientists to fully explore and enact science identities [11]. They designed EcoXPT, an immersive virtual science curriculum intended to offer authentic and situated learning experiences for 7th graders. Students found the EcoXPT afforded them agency and found the experience relevant to their future work. Engagement in the curriculum also increased students' self-efficacy and understanding of scientists' work. On fostering science identity exploration and change, most students described changes in what they thought scientists did for their work and the ways in which scientists approach problems they want to solve. Students discussed the tools and approaches that scientists use; students expressed their surprise at the amount of experimentation and work scientists must do to test their hypotheses and solve problems, often due to multiple possible explanations. In students' descriptions of what it means to be a science professional, they described several characteristics that were based on types of knowledge or skills that a scientist must have, they emphasize being able to think and approach problems in a certain way- emphasizing a growth mindset. They also brought in the role of affect, passion, and interest as central to embodying the role of a scientist. Finally, researchers engaged high school students in an authentic geoscience problem-based inquiry at a local urban park in partnership with undergraduate students and geoscience faculty at a local higher education institution. They found that place-based pedagogical approaches positively influenced students' science identities, particularly their interest in science [12]. The project also found that engaging students in their communities and affording them an opportunity to work with stakeholders in those personally relevant places was favorable to students' identity development.

While this literature underscores the value of learning experiences that support identity exploration in authentic, place-based settings, research is needed to 1) connect specific features of the course design to student outcomes over time and 2) understand identity exploration processes in an intentional and theoretically comprehensive way. This work leveraged the Projective Reflection (PR) theoretical framework as a tool for designing a play-based experience around authentic urban planning and environmental science career roles, and used epistemic network analysis to visualize student identity exploration as connections drawn between PR constructs in each week of the course.

2.1 The Projective Reflection Theoretical Framework

Projective Reflection (PR) is a theory and methodology of learning that integrates a focus on content (situated identity anchored in a specific community of practice and enacted locally) and on the self (identity engaged in role-possible selves inspired by the community of practice reflecting an individual goal) in an integrated manner. Projective

Reflection defines learning as an intentional process of exploring role-possible selves in digital and non-digital play-based environments as a learner projects forward and reflects on who they are in relation to specific domains and careers [13]. Projective Reflection builds upon seminal research in interest and motivation, 21st century skills and knowledge, self-regulation and self-efficacy research, and conceptualizations of identity related to possible selves in order to conceptualize learning as a situated, intentional, and targeted exploration of career or content-specific roles [14].

Four theoretical constructs support exploration of identities through role-possible selves in PR to enable an integrated change in learners over time: (1) Knowledge (foundational, meta, humanistic) [15], (2) Interest (situated/perceptual, epistemic/personal) and Valuing [16], (3) patterns of Self-organization and Self-control [17]; and (4) Self-perceptions and Self-definitions [18] (See Table 1). The model conceptualizes identity exploration as not just the manifestation of each construct, but as the integration of these processes (e.g. when a student can connect role-specific knowledge to personal interests and values, perceptions of self, etc.) Identity exploration as a process is valuable for learners to give them experience trying on a specific role (whether they select it for their future or not), and as a way to practice the flexibility and adaptability they might need to continue exploring possible identities across their lives and careers.

Table 1. Projective reflection construct definitions.

PR constructs	Definitions	Examples
Knowledge	Shifts in what learners know about environmental science/urban planning: • *Foundational knowledge*: awareness of complex and domain-specific content and processes • *Meta-knowledge*: awareness of how to use foundational knowledge in relevant socially situated contexts • *Humanistic knowledge*: awareness of the self and one's situation in a broader social and global context	Philadelphia "Lost 26% of job opportunities between 1997–2000 because less industrial jobs. To make up city raised property taxes…"
Interest and valuing	• Caring about environmental science and urban planning issues and viewing them as personally relevant or meaningful • Shifts in identification with environmental science • Viewing environmental science and urban planning as being relevant to the community or the world • Seeing utility for environmental science beyond school	"I care a lot about having plenty of green areas for kids to play in and explore… I feel like we should have a lot of places like that"

(*continued*)

Table 1. (*continued*)

PR constructs	Definitions	Examples
Self-organization and self-control	Shifts in behavior, motivation, and cognition toward a goal: • *Self-regulation:* goal setting and achievement conducted independently • *Co-regulation*: self-regulation processes supported by experts/mentors • *Socially shared regulation*: self-regulation is socially shared and defined in collaboration with peers	To meet stakeholder needs: "We made sure the housing and industrial zones were away from the rivers"
Self-perceptions and self-definitions	Shifts in how a participant sees the self in relation to science: • *Self-efficacy*: confidence in one's ability to achieve future goals/roles • *Self-concept*: awareness of current aspects of self (i.e. skills, preferences, characteristics, abilities, etc.) • Specific roles one wants or expects to become in future	"In the future, I plan to major in some type of art form… I'm leaning towards becoming an illustrator but that may change over time"

The Play Curricular activity Reflection Discussion (PCaRD) pedagogical model for play-based learning (See [19] for more information) can be used to enact Projective Reflection in a game and game-based curriculum through Play, and outside the game through Curricular activities that include opportunities for Reflection and Discussion. This process can provide students with opportunities to intentionally construct knowledge, cultivate interest and valuing for the academic domain, develop competence with the learning content and context, and explore possible selves in relation to the domain in an explicit manner [20]. While CaRD activities are anchored in the game and build on students' play experiences, they are also designed to align with target knowledge and attitudes within chosen academic domains.

3 Methods

This research was conducted as part of a 5-year (2014–2019) NSF CAREER project awarded to advance theory and research on promoting identity exploration and change in science using Projective Reflection as a theoretical framework for curricular design, implementation and assessment [13]. Building on this broader agenda, Virtual City Planning (VCP), a play-based course, was designed, developed, implemented, and refined using design-based research [21] across three iterations to help a total of 54 8th grade students engage in situated, targeted, and intentional exploration of urban planning and environmental science careers.

Over one academic year, VCP was offered to students who participated in weekly STEM career programming at their local science museum. This research focuses on the third iteration of VCP, which was implemented with 18 students across four weekly three-hour classes. VCP Session 1 and 2 were enacted across a greater number of weeks, and as such included the use of more activities and digital tools (including the virtual learning environment Philadelphia Land Science). Given the shortened time frame of Session 3, and limitations of Wi-Fi accessibility in the museum space, Session 3 involved analogous real-world roleplay experiences and design activities instead of virtual engagement. Session 3 also benefited from the refinement of activities based on what was learned from the prior two sessions about optimally supporting identity exploration in this context, and as such was selected as the unit of analysis for this study.

Design-based research supported cycles of design, enactment, analysis, and redesign across three iterations of Virtual City Planning (see [22]). This process helped ascertain what designed changes would lead to students exploring urban planning and environmental science identities in an intentional and an integrated manner. Design of each weekly session for VCP was also informed by the PCaRD model, so that each week offered opportunities for uninterrupted play or exploration of the environment and the roles as supported by curricular activities that encouraged explicit reflection and discussion. Play, Curricular activities, Reflection, and Discussion opportunities were designed around Projective Reflection to encourage repeated engagement with changing facets of the self as they explored the environmental science and urban planning roles.

3.1 VCP Session 3 Design

In week 1, students' baseline information was collected through a pre-survey that included 5-point Likert style questions and short-answer reflections, as well as demographic information. Students then rezoned downtown Philadelphia on paper maps to better meet their interests, goals, and desired future roles. For instance, a student who hoped to become a chef might zone downtown with more green spaces for farming, and commercial spaces for restaurants. This activity improved on prior iterations to make design more personal, as prior sessions encouraged students to design for the needs of community stakeholders. Written questions encouraged students to reflect about who they want to be in future and how that would impact their vision for the city.

In week 2, students engaged in the Know, Want-to-Know, and Learned (KWL) activity. They were provided with fictional brochures from four Philadelphia stakeholder groups to learn about the issues facing the city and the design changes hypothetical residents might be seeking. They were then asked to document what they knew about urban planning and the city stakeholders at this point in the intervention. Students were then encouraged to write and share what questions they had or what they wanted to explore further related to environmental science and urban planning, and were then provided real-world printed resources (i.e. Philadelphia development reports) so that they could research the answers to their questions. This explicit focus on interest-driven exploration of environmental science and urban planning information was intentionally included in this iteration, because students in the past had only briefly engaged with urban planning reports in the virtual space, and had only focused on narrow topics that were not explicitly connected to their personal interests. Students concluded by sharing what they discovered with the class in short presentations.

In week 3, students engaged in iterations of the Poster Map Design activity. Each student chose two stakeholder groups they wanted to explore in further detail based on their initial exploration in week 2. This built on a feature of Session 2 design that assigned stakeholder groups to students based on their affirmed interests but made the process even more self-directed. Teams were then each given a poster board printed with a detailed map of downtown Philadelphia and 10 rectangular blocks of the city outlined in black marker. The group had to fill each rectangular space with a different zone color so that the city design would best meet the needs of their stakeholder group. In the second iteration, all groups competed and negotiated on a single new poster board to fill the zones in ways that would best meet the needs of all stakeholder groups. In-class discussions and written reflections encouraged explicit exploration of urban planning roles and processes as they completed each round of design.

In week 4, students were given a city zoning proposal template upon which to build their own final urban planning proposals. This activity prompted them to introduce themselves as urban planners, state their design processes across the weeks, explain and justify their city design changes, and reflect on aspects of self (i.e. confidence in the role, future career goals, etc.). Students concluded with a post-survey that asked similar questions to the pre-survey from week 1.

3.2 Data Collection

Data sources included 1) pre-post assessments consisting of demographics questions, short-answer reflections, and 5-point Likert style questions (pre $\rho' = .969$, post $\rho' = .993$), 2) written student reflections based on in-class prompts, and 3) researcher observations, which focused on recording statements and reflections linked to specific students as they shared with their peers or engaged in group discussion and negotiation. Artifacts such as map designs were also collected and referenced for context on student processes over time. Collected data was organized chronologically by student to track their processes of exploration over time, then coded deductively for the presence (1) or absence (0) of explicit reflection on aspects of the self - one or more of the four Projective Reflection constructs [23]. Coding was conducted independently by two graduate-level coders using the qualitative analysis software MAXQDA 2018. The independently coded datasets were then merged to check for inconsistencies, which were reviewed and discussed until mutual agreement was reached.

3.3 Data Analysis

In this study, we applied Epistemic Network Analysis (ENA) [24] to our data using the ENA1.7.0 Web Tool (version 1.7.0) [25]. ENA is a quantitative ethnographic technique which can be used to model the structure of connections enacted in complex thinking processes over time - in this case, patterns of identity change enacted across weeks of participation in VCP Session 3. The algorithm uses a moving window to construct a network model for each line in the data, showing how codes in the current line are connected to codes that occur within the recent temporal context [26], defined as 4 lines (each line plus the 3 previous lines) in a given conversation. From an identity perspective, chronological assessment of associations over time is appropriate when considered from a developmental understanding of identity that conceptualizes current and future self as necessarily influenced by understanding of the past self.

Networks were generated for each week of reflective data, subset by each student. The resulting networks are aggregated for all lines for each unit of analysis in the model. In this model, we aggregated networks using a binary summation in which the networks for a given line reflect the presence or absence of the co-occurrence of each pair of codes. Conversations in the VCP data were bounded by student and by week (class) but were not bounded by the activities enacted each week. A review of the data revealed that students would refer back to their reflections from earlier in the class period, even if they were enacted during a different activity. The codes visualized in the network align with the four Projective Reflection constructs.

The ENA model normalized the networks for all units of analysis before they were subjected to a dimensional reduction, which accounts for the fact that different units of analysis had different amounts of coded lines in the data. For the dimensional reduction, we used a singular value decomposition, which produces orthogonal dimensions that maximize the variance explained by each dimension. (i.e. [27]). Our model had co-registration correlations of 0.96 (Pearson) and 0.95 (Spearman) for the first dimension and co-registration correlations of 0.96 (Pearson) and 0.97 (Spearman) for the second. These measures indicate that there is a strong goodness of fit between the visualization and the original model. ENA offered a unique way to recognize the patterns of identity exploration at both the group and individual levels for engaging in Projective Reflection as a result of the play-based course. Networks for each week of participation illustrated the strength of association students drew between different identity constructs, while the subset means for each student illustrate individual nuance in their exploration processes. We referred back to the interactions and activities coded in the data as part of a multi-level process of case study development [28] to help close the interpretive loop and thus fully understand the phenomena visualized in the network models. While not described in detail in this work, qualitative understandings of student outcomes are leveraged here to contextualize student outcomes by week with attention to the curricular design and implementation (see [13] for a detailed report).

4   Results

Epistemic networks for students' identity exploration help to illustrate differences in the associations students draw between the four Projective Reflection constructs. Epistemic networks visualize VCP Session 3 connections by week to showcase how the play-based course supported different facets of the identity exploration process over time. A summative network helps to reveal insights into the overall effects of Virtual City Planning on students' exploration of urban planning and environmental science career identities. To lend descriptive depth to the network findings, qualitative discussions of student outcomes are discussed. Student names listed below are pseudonyms.

4.1 Epistemic Networks

Epistemic networks for students' identity exploration help to illustrate differences in the associations students draw between the four Projective Reflection constructs. The epistemic networks in Fig. 1 provide summative visualizations of student reflections by week to showcase how the play-based course supported different facets of the identity exploration process over time. The network for student data in week 1 illustrates that students were most likely to associate discussions of their Self-perceptions and Self-definitions to their existing Knowledge (.71) and their Interests and Valuing (.50) (See Fig. 1a). Network data for students in week 2 revealed strongest associations between students' emerging Knowledge and their Interests and Valuing (.74) (See Fig. 1b). The Poster Map Design activity in week 3 allowed students to use their emerging Knowledge of environmental science and urban planning topics as part of their active Self-organization and Self-control strategies (.59). A relatively strong association was also visualized between Knowledge and Interests and Valuing (.29) (See Fig. 1c). In week 4, students most strongly associated Self-perceptions and Self-definitions to Knowledge (.57) and to Interests and Valuing (.54), but also Knowledge to Interests and Valuing (.47) (See Fig. 1d).

The Centroids for networks of student reflection data summarize the differences by week in terms of what activities supported reflection on which Projective Reflection constructs (See Fig. 2). This figure shows the centroid and network for a summative variable (orange) showing student connections across all four weeks in VCP session 3. Overlaid is the centroid for all students by week (squares) as well as centroids for each student by week (circles). This allows for a visual comparison across weeks, highlighting how the centroids for weeks 1 and 4 are pulled toward Self-perceptions and Self-definitions, the centroid for week 2 is pulled toward the Interest variable, and the week 3 centroid is pulled toward Self-organization and Self-control. Student centroids for weeks 1 and 4 are also clustered more tightly together, illustrating the potential impact of the more structured survey activities on student identity exploration patterns compared to the more open-ended exploration activities enacted in middle weeks.

4.2 Interpretive Qualitative Examinations

Most students in week 1 had clear ideas about the careers or areas in which they would like to pursue in future (i.e. illustrator, electrical engineer, model, neurosurgeon, etc.), which aligns with the stronger associations to Self-perceptions and Self-definitions in week 1. In some cases, these roles were connected to situational Interests (i.e. Jamila wanted to become an electrical engineer "because my engineering teacher is fun, and urban planning is not"). A few students (i.e. Catherine, Bethany) were unsure what they wanted to be in future but had general areas of interest (i.e. Bethany enjoyed art and could see herself using it). Most students did not see urban planning as a potential future career, but students such as Dominic and Emil recognized the value of urban planning for affecting their desired careers (i.e. designing parks and museums to use).

In week 2, students demonstrated increased detail in their meta Knowledge of urban planning processes as they engaged in their roles. For example, Sharon, who initially

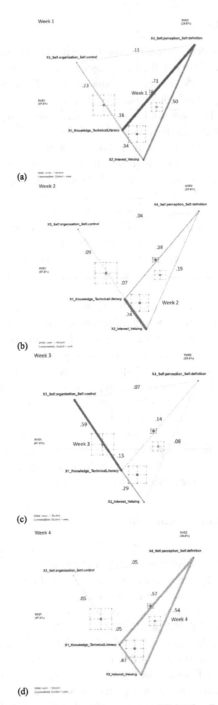

Fig. 1. The network of the group's associations across Projective Reflection constructs for (a) Week 1 (red), (b) Week 2 (blue), (c) Week 3 (purple), and (d) Week 4 (green). (Color figure online)

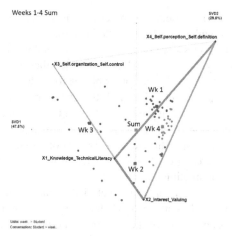

Fig. 2. The network of associations and centroid for the summary variable (orange) of weeks 1–4 which reveals an overall balanced process of identity exploration over time. (Color figure online)

wrote "I don't know" for many knowledge questions, now explained that urban planners are "People who zone cities to fit the needs of the citizens," and recognized that stakeholders "each focus on specific issues to lobby for." Students such as Jamila were able to describe increasing foundational knowledge of issues that affect Philadelphia residents: "Pollution from "developed areas" go into lakes and stuff and harm people and animals." Many students also actively built their humanistic Knowledge of issues facing Philadelphia citizens through inquiry-based research (i.e. Caiden researched that Philadelphia "Lost 26% of job opportunities between 1997–2000 because less industrial jobs. To make up city raised property taxes made it hard for people to afford living downtown. People moved to suburbs which made problems harder").

Students identified specific issues facing their city that they found important, relevant, or meaningful as a result of engaging with the KWL activity in week 2, which offers an explanation for the higher levels of association made to Interest and Valuing. Emil assessed the value of water clarity from an urban planning perspective: "water quality is most prominent in environmental issues. I believe this is because most stakeholder teams included some people that analyzed water quality. Also, a report said that "In general, trends show many air pollutants in Philadelphia to be decreasing."".

Students engaged actively with their group and with other groups to negotiate map design changes in week 3, and to make sure that the needs of stakeholders were met. This resulted in opportunities for students to engage in different strategies of Self-organization and Self-control. In some cases, this involved friendly debate between peers (i.e. Rahim and Isabel). Most students were able to detail the design changes, either as a strategy for meeting stakeholder needs (i.e. Sharon wrote "We made sure the housing and industrial zones were away from the rivers"), or from a procedural standpoint (i.e. Caiden described the chronological design process: "Rechange zone 1 to open space, Change 2 to high density, Change 3 to medium housing, and commercial business, 4 to commercial, 5 to commercial and open spaces, 6 to medium, 7 to wetland, Commercial for 8, High and open, Wetlands CO"). Several observation notes described instances in which peers verbally negotiated design together. This culminated in a final, student-led debate recorded in observation notes: There was a pretty big debate in the end where [one group] wanted industry (mostly argued by Mariah and Shane) and the other 3 tables… Wanted green spaces. One argument was that there are other places for industry besides Center City, whereas Shane argued that without industry all things will get more expensive because they are not locally produced and argued that you can have greenery around industrial areas. In some cases, their continued research, advocacy in group discussions, and map design centered around these specific interests. In a whole-class debate on city design, for example, Shane advocated strongly for the value of industrial areas for keeping the costs of products down (by making them locally).

A review of the qualitative data from week 4 illustrated how students were now more readily able to connect their new Knowledge of urban planning and environmental science to their Interests and views of the self. For example, Students such as Bethany demonstrated new awareness of issues facing Philadelphia ("Some economic issues are not enough jobs, and not enough low-density homes. Some residents can't find jobs to afford the homes, which is why we need low density homes."). Oliver wrote that "I care a lot about having plenty of green areas for kids to play in and explore. Nature is a beautiful thing, I've found some places with overgrown grass and trees in Philadelphia. Exploring those places with friends is an amazing thing, and I feel like we should have a lot of places like that." Some students did not express personal interests in the topic but were able to explain in detail why urban planning and city design were important. For example, Emil wrote that "I have barely any [interests in learning about cities and the environment] (sorry)," but detailed issues he felt were globally relevant: "I'm very scared for the health of not only our city, but our planet. We destroy natural ecosystems to create businesses and heat up the Earth just to run our cars. I'm hoping by adding more green open spaces, we will create a better Philadelphia."

While many students completed VCP Session 3 maintaining the careers they hoped to pursue in future, students such as Bethany reflected that this was the first time she had been prompted to think about future careers or roles (Self-perceptions and Self-definitions). Several students remained unsure whether they would pursue future roles related to urban planning but could see themselves in a career that uses environmental science, while others reflected that their current desired role could shift. For example, Emil wrote "In the future, I plan to major in some type of art form. At the moment, I'm leaning towards becoming an illustrator but that may change over time." Student reflections showed how VCP encouraged situated, targeted, and intentional exploration of urban planning and environmental science roles: "My name is Sharon and over the past couple weeks, we have talked about an urban planner's responsibilities in their job. Depending on what your company cares most about, you have to figure out which zones of the city you should adapt to fit your needs. You also have to work with other companies and compromise on what works best for each organization and the citizens."

5 Discussion and Conclusion

Results illustrate the utility of educational experiences designed to facilitate identity exploration as defined by Projective Reflection [13] and using the Play Curricular activity Reflection Discussion (PCaRD) model [20] for supporting students' personalized processes of identity exploration related to STEM domains (i.e. environmental science and urban planning). The Centroids for networks of student reflection data in weeks 1–4 summarize the differences by week in terms of what activities supported reflection on which Projective Reflection constructs. The positionality of these means aligns with the qualitative student outcomes described above: students initially connected their early knowledge and interests to a starting self in the survey reflection and map design activity, then were more likely to connect their emerging knowledge of Philadelphia issues to the questions they found interesting in the KWL activity. The whole-group Poster Map Design activity then allowed students to connect their emerging interests and knowledge to self-regulation and socially shared regulation related to the negotiation of city design to meet the needs of the entire community. Finally, students summed up the experience in their surveys and final reports, connecting specific and contextualized knowledge and interests to a newly developed sense of self.

These findings align with existing research on how curricular interventions can support such processes, most notably descriptions of how activities can meaningfully string together over time to create valuable summative experiences [7]. The network in Fig. 5 shows that even though activities by week emphasized different aspects of the identity exploration process, the overall result was a relatively balanced or integrated process of connection-making across all four features of Projective Reflection. The network also shows how activities that support more open-ended exploration and negotiation promote a wider spread of student reflective outcomes, while more constrained activities (such as the survey questions in weeks 1 and 4) result in student identity outcomes that tend to cluster together more tightly. These findings offer valuable insights into the relationship between curricular activities (and their affordances and constraints), and suggest that multi-modal opportunities for reflection and discussion might both support student autonomy in their exploration processes as well as ensure that key opportunities are experienced universally.

Limitations of this study relate to the highly specialized and tailored nature of study design and implementation, which limits generalizability of findings. The study also tracks a relatively small sample of purposively sampled students across a relatively short period of time; more long-term assessments of identity exploration as a result of curricular experiences are therefore essential next steps. This study also only examines identity exploration as a individual, developmental process; social-Epistemic Network Analysis may prove useful in future to examine identity exploration as both an individual/developmental and collective/situational process of change over time.

Quantitative Ethnographic [24] techniques such as Epistemic Network Analysis served as a valuable and innovative approach for understanding whole-group trajectories of identity exploration on a week-by week basis as operationalized by Projective Reflection. ENA not only allowed researchers to examine large quantities of student data related to identity exploration by providing a nuanced view of the relationships between identity constructs (integration), but also allowed for a tighter connection to be drawn between the design intentions and outcomes of curricular elements. Future reports will expand on this inquiry to connect curricular design to student outcome in other sessions and contexts, as well as test and refine new virtual learning environments that can facilitate Projective Reflection in different contexts.

Acknowledgements. This project was funded by the National Science Foundation (DRL-1350707). The views expressed are those of the authors. Thank you to the Epistemic Analytics Group for access to *Land Science* and existing student data (DRL-1661036, DRL-1713110).

References

1. Kaplan, A., Sinai, M., Flum, H.: Design-based interventions for promoting students' identity exploration within the school curriculum. In: MotivationalInterventions, pp. 243–291. Emerald Group Publishing Limited (2014)
2. Stets, J.E., Brenner, P.S., Burke, P.J., Serpe, R.T.: The science identity and entering a science occupation. Soc. Sci. Res. **64**, 1–4 (2017)
3. Callahan, J., Ito, M., Campbell R., Wortman, S., Wortman, A.: Influences on occupational identity in adolescence: a review of research and programs. In: Connected Learning Alliance Proceedings, Irvine, CA (2019)
4. Vincent-Ruz, P., Schunn, C.D.: The nature of science identity and its role as the driver of student choices. Int. J. STEM Educ. **5**(1), 1–12 (2018). https://doi.org/10.1186/s40594-018-0140-5
5. Johnson, L., Becker, S.A., Cummins, M., Estrada, V., Freeman, A., Hall, C.: NMC horizon report: 2016 higher education edition, pp. 1–50. The New Media Consortium (2016)
6. Traphagen, K., Traill, S.: How cross-sector collaborations are advancing STEM learning. Noyce Foundation, Los Altos, CA (2014)
7. diSessa, A.A.: How should students learn? J. Comput. Documentation **23**(2), 14–18 (1999)
8. Schreiner, C., Sjøberg, S.: Science education and youth's identity construction-two incompatible projects? In: Corrigan, D., Dillon, J., Gunstone, R. (eds.) The Re-emergence of Values in the Science Curriculum, pp. 231–247. SensePublishers, Rotterdam (2007)
9. Aschbacher, P.R., Li, E., Roth, E.J.: Is science me? High school students' identities, participation and aspirations in science, engineering, and medicine. J. Res. Sci. Teach. **47**(5), 564–582 (2010)
10. Gaydos, M.J., Squire, K.D.: Role playing games for scientific citizenship. Cult. Sci. Edu. **7**(4), 821–844 (2012)
11. Reilly, J.M., McGivney, E., Dede, C., Grotzer, T.: Assessing science identity exploration in immersive virtual environments: a mixed methods approach. J. Exp. Edu. 1–22 (2020)
12. Defelice, A., Pieroni, P., Adams, J.D., Branco, B.: Engaging underrepresented high school students in an urban environmental and geoscience place-based curriculum. J. Geosci. Educ. **62**(1), 49–60 (2014)
13. Foster, A.: CAREER: projective reflection: learning as identity exploration within games for science. National Science Foundation, Drexel University, Philadelphia, PA (2014)
14. Foster, A., Shah, M., Barany, A.: Facilitating learning as identity change through game-based learning. In: Baek, Y. (ed.) Game-Based Learning: Theory, Strategies, and Performance Outcomes. Nova Publishers, New York (2017)
15. Kereluik, K., Mishra, P., Fahnoe, C., Terry, L.: What knowledge is of most worth: Teacher knowledge for 21st century learning. J. Digital Learn. Teach. Educ. **29**(4), 127–140 (2013)

16. Wigfield, A., Eccles, J.S.: Expectancy–value theory of achievement motivation. Contemp. Educ. Psychol. **25**(1), 68–81 (2000)
17. Vygotsky, L.S.: Mind in Society: The Development of Higher Psychological Processes. Harvard University Press, Cambridge (1978)
18. Kaplan, A., Flum, H.: Achievement goal orientations and identity formation styles. Educ. Res. Rev. **5**(1), 50–67 (2010)
19. Foster, A., Shah, M.: The play curricular activity reflection and discussion model for game-based learning. J. Res. Technol. Educ. **47**(2), 71–88 (2015)
20. Foster, A., Shah, M.: Knew me and new me: facilitating student identity exploration and learning through game integration. Int. J. Gaming Comput.-Mediated Simul. **8**(3), 39–58 (2016)
21. Cobb, P., Confrey, J., DiSessa, A., Lehrer, R., Schauble, L.: Design experiments in educational research. Educ. Res. **32**(1), 9–13 (2003)
22. Barany, A., Foster, A., Shah, M.: Design-based research iterations of a virtual learning environment for identity exploration. In: Economou, D., Klippel, A., Dodds, H., Peña-Rios, A., Lee, M. J.W., Beck, D., Richter, J. (eds.) Immersive Learning Research Network. Proceedings of 6th International Conference. iLRN 2020 Online (2020)
23. Krippendorff, K.: Content Analysis: An Introduction to Its Methodology. Sage Publications, Thousand Oaks (2004)
24. Shaffer, D.W., Collier, W., Ruis, A.R.: A tutorial on epistemic network analysis: analyzing the structure of connections in cognitive, social, and interaction data. J. Learn. Anal. **3**(3), 9–45 (2016)
25. Marquart, C.L., Hinojosa, C., Swiecki, Z., Eagan, B., Shaffer, D.W.: Epistemic Network Analysis (Version 1.7.0) [Software] (2018)
26. Siebert-Evenstone, A.L., Irgens, G.A., Collier, W., Swiecki, Z., Ruis, A.R., Shaffer, D.W.: In search of conversational grain size: modelling semantic structure using moving stanza windows. J. Learn. Analytics **4**(3), 123–139 (2017)
27. Arastoopour, G., Swiecki, Z., Chesler, N.C., Shaffer, D.W.: Epistemic network analysis as a tool for engineering design assessment. Presented at the American Society for Engineering Education, Seattle, WA (2015)
28. Stake, R.E.: The Art of Case Study Research. Sage Publications, Thousand Oaks (2020)

Socio-semantic Network Analysis of Knowledge-Creation Discourse on a Real-Time Scale

Ayano Ohsaki[1,2]([✉]) [ID] and Jun Oshima[2] [ID]

[1] Advanced Institute of Industrial Technology, 1-10-40, Higashi-ooi, Shinagawa-ku, Tokyo 1400011, Japan
ohsaki-ayano@aiit.ac.jp
[2] Research and Education Center for the Learning Sciences, Shizuoka University, 836 Ohya, Suruga-ku, Shizuoka-shi, Shizuoka 4228529, Japan

Abstract. This study discusses the temporal analysis method with data on collected on a real-time scale to investigate learning as knowledge-creation. During collaborative learning, collaboratively building ideas is important for learners. Thus, collaborative learning strategies must consider learners' discourses temporally. Therefore, this study used data collected in real-time and two analysis methods: the combination of socio-semantic network analysis (SSNA) and in-depth dialogical discourse analysis. Especially, the authors used the SSNA combined with the moving stanza window method and the network lifetime in this study. The goal of this study was to examine the possibility of analyzing data with timestamp information. For this goal, the authors conducted a comparative study by analyzing the same dataset using the following steps. First, the authors visualized the data gathered from collaborative learning. Second, the authors conducted a comparison between the analyzed results of the ordered data and of data with timestamp information. Third, the authors detected the pivotal points from the results of analyzing data with timestamp information using the SSNA combined with the moving stanza window method and the network lifetime, and the discourse data was analyzed in great depth. The first finding of this study is that the proposed analysis method can effectively represent the process of ideas improvement. The second finding is that analysis using timestamp information is effective for assessing the similarities and differences between each group. This study suggests the effectiveness of temporal analysis and analyzing data gathered in real-time.

Keywords: Knowledge-creation · Temporal analysis · Discourse analysis · Network analysis · Socio-semantic network analysis

1 Introduction

The purpose of this study is to establish an analysis method to determine how learners engage in learning as knowledge-creation. In knowledge-creation metaphors for learning, learners are expected to create and improve ideas rather than memorize a fixed

© Springer Nature Switzerland AG 2021
A. R. Ruis and S. B. Lee (Eds.): ICQE 2021, CCIS 1312, pp. 170–184, 2021.
https://doi.org/10.1007/978-3-030-67788-6_12

set of knowledge [1–4]. Furthermore, educators have to assess learners' process of knowledge-creation to design educational materials, instructions, and learning environments that effectively support learners. Studies on knowledge-creation have been a part of the research on computer-supported collaborative learning (CSCL) as educators and researchers have tried to design and assess computerized learning environments [1, 4].

CSCL research has paid attention to temporal analysis to assess details relevant to learning [5]. During collaborative learning, it is important for learners to share their own ideas and build on those ideas with each other. These conditions often appear in learners' discourses, i.e., in the relationships between activities, and cannot be confirmed with only the analysis of independent activities. In addition, although aggregate analysis of entire datasets has demonstrated results related to learning activities, temporal analysis has been found to be useful for visualizing and assessing learning activities at any given time [6]. In other words, analyses of collaborative learning should focus on analyzing learners' discourse temporally rather than categorizing utterances and counting them as a whole.

To study learning as knowledge-creation, practical analysis methods such as discourse analysis have been required, and a recent study has reported the usefulness of the combination of socio-semantic network analysis (SSNA) and in-depth dialogical discourse analysis to solve both practical and theoretical problems [7]. However, most SSNA research studies have used ordered data, and little is known about using data on a real-time scale in analyses. Hence, there is a need to develop and examine methods that use data on a real-time scale in combined quantitative and qualitative approaches to study learning as knowledge-creation. This study attempts to position the temporal analysis method for studying learning as knowledge-creation by comparing the analysis results of ordered data and data that includes timestamp information.

2 Theoretical Background

2.1 Socio-semantic Network Analysis (SSNA)

In this study, the authors adopted SSNA, which is based on the social network analysis (SNA) method with an added semantic perspective. SNA is a method used to conduct network analysis on human behaviors by representing a person as a node and the relationship between persons as a link. In studies on learning as knowledge-creation, SNA is regarded as one of the most effective analysis tools [4, 8–10], and SSNA has also been effectively used to study knowledge-creation [4]. The most important benefit of using the latter in this study is that it can directly analyze ideas from the discourse data.

In SSNA, a network is constructed using keywords as nodes. Several studies [7, 11] have suggested that the network of keywords used in discourse could be an appropriate tool for evaluating the idea improvement in knowledge-creation practices based on two assumptions. First, learners' ideas are represented as clusters of keywords used in the discourse. Second, their improvement may be represented as structural changes in the keyword network over time because learners attempt to assimilate and accommodate their ideas in new contexts. Under these assumptions, the total value of degree centralities for nodes in the network could be metrics to be calculated. The metrics can represent the expansion of the network structure (i.e., the increase in nodes over time) and its restructuring (i.e., the increase in the links between nodes). By referring to previous studies, the same metrics are used in the present study, while also taking the temporality of the real-time scale into consideration.

When using SSNA to analyze ideas, the total value of the degree centralities (C_d) was used as a measurement of ideas improvement [11]. The C_d score shows the relationship between keywords in discourses by calculating how many observed keywords connect to a given keyword. The score for the normalized degree centrality for a cluster consisting of m keywords, $C'_d(i)$, can be calculated using Formula (1), where a_{ij} is the adjacency matrix for each pair of nodes i and j [11].

$$C'_d(i) = \frac{1}{m-1} \sum_{j=1}^{m} a_{ij} \tag{1}$$

For measurements, the authors used C_d to represent the sum of C'_d in any interval from x to y, which was calculated using Formula (2) using the results of Formula (1) [11]. Most studies have used this measure for aggregative analysis and have set x to 1 and y to the number of the last utterance.

$$C_d = \sum_{i=x}^{y} C'_d(i) \tag{2}$$

The higher the C_d score, the greater the indication that keywords are interrelated. However, the C_d score may be lowered because the probability of linkages in keywords decreases as the number of keywords that appear increases. Thus, assessing not only scores but also their transitions through the discourse is necessary to trace improvement of ideas.

Following previous studies, this study used C_d as a measure. In addition, this study discusses what can be deduced by the transition of C_d when considering temporality.

2.2 Temporal Analysis

The importance of temporality in the analysis of activities has been indicated by many research studies across disciplines. In CSCL research, the problem of ignoring temporality has often been discussed. For example, Siebert-Evenstone et al. [12] pointed out that organizing a network of whole conversations involves the possibility of unrelated nodes linking to each other. Furthermore, through a comparison of the traditional method and epistemic network analysis (ENA) [13], Csanadi et al. [5] reported that the results of the traditional coding-count method, which neglects temporality, can be misleading. In the network science field outside of the CSCL field, ignoring temporality has been recognized as a problem that can result in fallacious information because most of the interactions in networks are finite in duration [14–17]. Especially in fields such as epidemiology and information technology, studies that have been conducted on "temporal networks" have focused on the moment two nodes link [16, 17]. Based on previous studies, generating an analysis method that considers temporality is a critical research endeavor when studying knowledge-creation.

Having clarified the importance of this study, the technique used to take temporality into account during analysis is explained below. This study used a procedure that had been suggested in a recent study that the authors had conducted. This includes a combination of two concepts from research on CSCL and network science [6]. The first concept of "the moving stanza window method," which can model discourse consisting of utterances in close temporal proximity [12, 18]. The second concept is "the network lifetime," which is concerned with the calculation of the duration of nodes from the network science field [14]. This concept contributes to the implementation of temporality in analysis by limiting the periods in which interactions between nodes can occur in a network.

To examine the effectiveness of the proposed methods for temporal analysis, the authors conducted a phased approach [6]. Figures 1, 2, and 3 show the differences among the three analysis methods. In these figures, utterances are on the left, networks of keywords are on the right, and small letters signify keywords. Figure 1 shows the example results of aggregative SSNA, which has been used in many previous studies on knowledge-creation. Figure 2 shows the example results of aggregative SSNA with the moving stanza window method. Then, Fig. 3 shows the example results of SSNA combined with the moving stanza window method and the concept of the network lifetime.

Basically, the aggregative SSNA as the general analysis method shows only the temporal nature of how the network structure develops but not how the structure is restructured. In the first calculation, a network is created from keywords in the first utterance (Fig. 1a). Second, a network is created from keywords in the first and second utterances (Fig. 1b). In this manner, the number of utterances constituting the cluster gradually increases, and eventually, a network of keywords from all utterances is created (Fig. 1d).

Next, how SSNA with the moving stanza window method operates is shown in Fig. 2. In this example, the window size is two, and one window consists of two utterances based on the assumptions regarding the dialogism of human conversation. Hence, the first network is created from keywords in the first window built from two utterances (Fig. 2a). The second network is created from keywords in the first and second windows (Fig. 2b). Then, the number of windows increases, and the last network is created by using keywords in all the windows (Fig. 2d). A striking difference is observed in the presence or absence of the moving stanza window method when comparing Figs. 1a and 2a. This analysis method can compute discourse temporality but not show how the structure is restructured. Therefore, the authors call this analysis method the aggregative SSNA with the moving stanza window method.

Figure 3 shows how the combination of the SSNA with the moving stanza window method and the network lifetime operates. To compare the analysis methods, the window size is set to two, which is the same as the aggregative SSNA with the moving stanza window method. In this study, the lifetime is set to two to create a network for two windows. This setting is based on the assumptions that not all interactions are independent and past dialogue may influence new ones. Thus, comparisons of Figs. 2 and 3 confirm the results of implementing the network lifetime. On the one hand, the results of the first and second networks in Fig. 3 are the same as the aggregative SSNA with the moving stanza window method (Fig. 2a, Fig. 2b) because these networks are within their lifetime. On the other hand, the network in Fig. 3c is different from the network in Fig. 2c. The third network in Fig. 3 is created out of keywords from only the second and third windows after the second network is broken because the first window is outside of the lifetime. The last network is also created from only the last two windows (Fig. 3d). Therefore, this analysis method can indicate discourses' temporality and how the structure has been restructured.

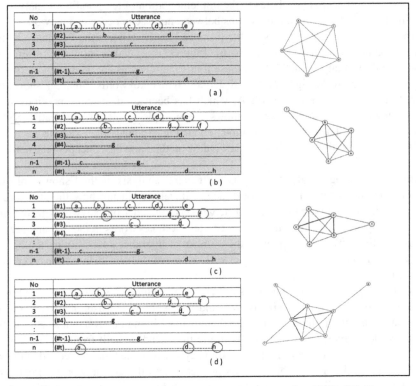

Fig. 1. Example results demonstrating the usage of the aggregative SSNA [6]. Utterances are on the left, and networks of keywords are on the right. The small letters signify keywords. (a) A network is created from the first utterance in the first calculation of the discourse data. (b) A network is created from the first and second utterances in the second calculation of the discourse data. (c) A network is created from the first to third utterances in the third calculation of the discourse data. (d) A network is created from the first to last utterances in the last calculation of the discourse data.

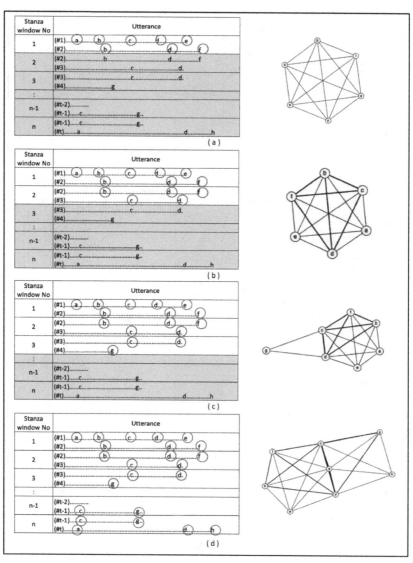

Fig. 2. Example results demonstrating the usage of the aggregative SSNA with the moving stanza window method (window size = 2) [6]. Utterances are on the left, and networks of keywords are on the right. The small letters signify keywords. (a) A network is created from the first window in the first calculation of the discourse data. (b) A network is created from the first and second windows in the second calculation of the discourse data. (c) A network is created from the first to third windows in the third calculation of the discourse data. (d) A network is created from the first to last windows in the last calculation of the discourse data.

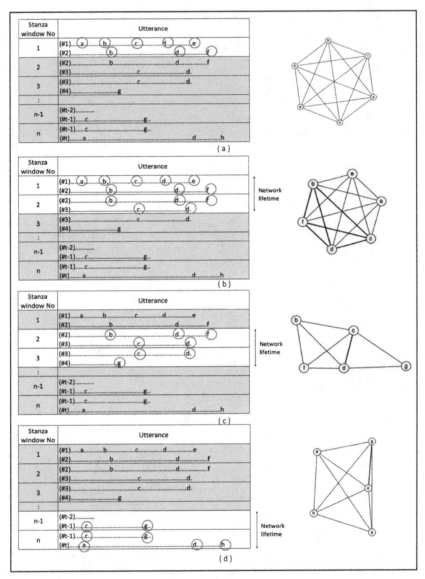

Fig. 3. Example results demonstrating the usage of SSNA combined with the moving stanza window method (window size = 2) and the network lifetime (lifetime = 2) [6]. Utterances are on the left, and networks of keywords are on the right. The small letters signify keywords. (a) A network is created from the first window in the first calculation of the discourse data. (b) A network is created from the first and second windows in the second calculation of the discourse data. (c) A network is created from the second and third windows in the third calculation of the discourse data. (d) A network is created from the last two windows in the last calculation of the discourse data.

3   Research Questions

While studies have taken advantage of SNA to evaluate social interactions in collaborative learning discourses [4, 8–10], recent studies have developed other analytics to evaluate ideas themselves [7, 11]. Recent studies have analyzed ideas by using SSNA, which incorporates temporality, and have allowed for more detailed analysis from the perspective of improvements of ideas [6]. However, the study dealt with ordered data that has no time information. To the best of the authors' knowledge, no studies thus far have tried to develop and examine methods to analyze discourse data on a real-time scale. Therefore, this study used data on a real-time scale to conduct analysis by combining SSNA and in-depth dialogical discourse analysis and by combining SSNA with the moving stanza window method and the network lifetime; then, this study discussed the following research questions as the first phase of the research.

RQ1: What insight can be gained from temporal analysis of discourse data with timestamp data compared to analysis without it?

To answer this question, the authors conducted comparisons between temporal analysis using timestamp information and temporal analysis using only ordered data. In this investigation, the authors were not concerned with the aggregative SSNA, which had been used in previous studies, to concentrate on how to deal with differences in the two kinds of data. The authors hypothesize that analyzing data on a real-time scale using the SSNA combined with the moving stanza window method and the network lifetime will show how ideas improve in a way that analyzing ordered data cannot indicate.

RQ2: Can differences between high- and low-learning outcome groups be found by analyzing data on a real-time scale?

To investigate this question, the authors analyzed two datasets: one pertaining to a high-learning outcome group and the other to a low-learning outcome group. These groups were selected by evaluating the results of the post-tests on their conceptual understanding of the topic [19]. The authors hypothesize that the results of analyzing data on a real-time scale will show activity patterns related to time instead of only to the total value of degree centrality.

4   Methods

4.1   Data

We used datasets on tenth-grade students' collaborative discourse on the human immune system that was gathered during their regular biology class, which was designed in a jigsaw instruction format [20]. Jigsaw instruction is a method for collaborative learning that features two activities. First, each learning group during the "expert activity" portion studies different educational materials (e.g., group A members study educational material A, and group B members study educational material B). Members from the different groups create a new group for the second "jigsaw activity" where they develop their ideas to address the main problem by using information gained from the expert activity position. In this class, 39 students participated, and there were 12 groups of three or four students. The problem they discussed was "Can you explain how vaccinations protect us from infections?" The transcribed conversations from both the high- and low-learning outcome groups were selected, and their conceptual understanding of the topic were evaluated in their post-tests [19]. The high-learning outcome group had 205 utterances, and the low-learning outcome group had 282 utterances.

4.2 Analysis

To examine the research questions, the authors conducted a comparative study by analyzing the same dataset using the following three steps. First, the authors visualized the data in collaborative learning by using the following two approaches. Approach 1: ordered data was analyzed using the SSNA combined with the moving stanza window method (window size = 2) and the network lifetime (lifetime = 2); Approach 2: data with timestamp information was analyzed using the SSNA combined with the moving stanza window method (window size = 2) and the network lifetime (lifetime = 2). In this step, the authors used an application called KBDeX [11] to calculate how the total value of the degree centralities of the 23 nodes (words representing students' conceptual understanding of the human immune system) in the network transitioned. In the second step, the authors conducted a comparison of the results of Approaches 1 and 2. Finally, in the third step, the authors detected the pivotal points from the results of Approach 2 and analyzed discourse data in-depth. After, the authors analyzed the results of Approach 2 to investigate RQ2.

5   Results

In step 1, the authors analyzed the data on both the low and high-learning outcome groups using the Approaches 1 and 2. The results of the visualization are shown in Fig. 4. In Fig. 4, the upper image illustrates the results of Approach 1: analyzing ordered data using the SSNA combined with the moving stanza window method and the network lifetime. The bottom image shows the results of Approach 2: analyzing data on a real-time scale using the SSNA combined with the moving stanza window method and the network lifetime. In these images, the black dotted lines show the results for the low-learning outcome group, and the red solid lines show the results for the high-learning outcome group. The vertical axes of the two images signify the total values of degree centralities, and the horizontal axes signify order in Fig. 4a and time in Fig. 4b. The results of Approach 2 show two-phase activities because 10–25 min was break time (Fig. 4b).

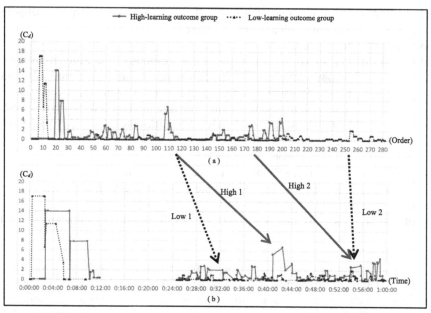

Fig. 4. The transitions of the total value of degree centralities (C_d) of discourses during learning activities (a) The transitions of the result of calculating ordered data using the SSNA combined with the moving stanza window method (window size = 2) and the network lifetime (lifetime = 2). (b) The transitions of the result of calculating data with timestamp information using the SSNA combined with the moving stanza window method (window size = 2) and the network lifetime (lifetime = 2).

The step-2 analysis was conducted to answer RQ1. Comparisons of Figs. 4a and 4b show that Approach 1 did not correctly illustrate learning activities. In Fig. 4, the four arrows show the gap between the ordered data and data with timestamp information. Take the "Low 1" arrow in Fig. 4 as an example. This utterance was made at around #110 in Fig. 4a, although the utterance was actually spoken near the 32-min mark (Fig. 4b). Likewise, in the case of the "High 1" arrow, this utterance was made at around #110 in Fig. 4a, but the utterance was spoken close to the 44-min mark (Fig. 4b). In Fig. 4a, both utterances were shown at the same time. These results show they were not shown when analyzing the ordered data, which was revealed by the data with timestamp information.

For the step-3 analysis, a dialogue analysis was conducted to extract the points that were considered pivotal in the results of Approach 2 and to determine whether these points were "pivotal points" or not. This procedure is based on a mixed method approach including in-depth dialogical discourse analysis by tracing the discourse back from the candidates for the pivotal points. The authors picked example points for each group in this study. The original discourse was in Japanese and was translated into English by the first author (keywords in SSNA are shown in bold). The utterances from the high-learning outcome group were as follow:

Student D (#46)   **B cell** is activated. The **B cell** release **antibodies**. Then, **antibodies** combine with **antigens**. Combine?

Student E (#47)   It's in here.

Student D (#48)   Oh, so, so, so. The name of this **response** is an **antigen-antibody response**. It's based on the flow to remove **antigenic antibody** complexes. **Responses** and complexes, isn't it? After the second time, it can make **antibodies** sooner because the first **infected cell** infected by the measles virus already made **antibodies**. Ah… it's like a **T cell**.

Student E (#49)   I think so.

Student D (#50)   And, how about document B?

Student F (#51)   It's about a **primary response** and a **secondary response**.

Student D (#52)   Yes, yes. And the **C cell** is the **T cell**'s version of this.

Student E (#53)   Right.

Student D (#54)   Then, we can summarize this result on that (web document). That means…

This point was detected near 28 min, as can be seen in Fig. 4b, because it was where the network happened frequently over a short period of time and where the shape (i.e., in the graph) of changes in scores was different from other points. The starting utterance number was #46. The dialogical discourse analysis confirmed that constructive ideas developed at this point; student D shared ideas, student E supported ideas, and student F helped to create ideas with student D. Similarly, the utterances from the low-learning outcome group were as follow:

Student G (#197)   **Cellular immunity** is…

Student H (#198)   **Primary response** and **secondary response**.

Student G (#199)   Is this a **primary response**?

Student H (#200)   Well… Like a **primary response**. The **primary responses** may involve fewer **antibodies**.

Student G (#201)   It's really difficult.

Student H (#202)   Right.

Student H (#203)   During the **primary response**, it takes less time to make **antibodies**.

Student G (#204)   When, well…First, for now, it makes **immune memory cells**.

Student H (#205)   To make.

Student H (#206)   In **cellular immunity**, uh, the **primary response** of **cellular immunity**?

Student G (#207)   Eh? Isn't this both the **primary response**?

Student H (#208)   Yeah…

Student G (#209)   Eh? Is the **primary response** only this one?

Student H (#210)   Eh?

Student G (#211)   The **primary response** is…

Student H (#212)   The **primary response** and, well, **antibodies** are made, but it takes a long time, and the amount is small.

Student G (#213)   Is the **primary response** a system of only this? Ah, a space for writing is… it is a mistake.

Student H (#214)   But antibodies are made, ah, well, memory, eh, what? **Antibody memory cell**...
Student G (#215)   I want to delete it, but I cannot.
Student H (#216)   Hmm.

This point was detected near 47 min, as shown in Fig. 4b, because it was where the net-work occurred frequently over a short period of time and where the shape of changes in scores was different from other points. The starting utterance number was #197. The dialogical discourse analysis confirmed the students' confusion at this point, with student G guessing ideas, student E wondering about ideas, and the third student not contributing to this idea exchange.

In addition, to answer RQ2, the authors focused on the differences and the similarities in the groups during transitions, as seen in Fig. 4b. On the one hand, differences are especially observable in the later phase. The transitions in the low-learning outcome group moved at a low altitude and marked the highest point of the later phase at the end of class. The transitions in the high-learning outcome group oscillated up and down and marked the highest point of the later phase in the middle of class.

On the other hand, similar patterns were shown in both groups during the first 12 min and at around the 54-min point. The former phase was for a time of knowledge-sharing designed by jigsaw instruction. To determine the reason for the similarity at 54 min, the authors referred to the teacher's instructions. As a result, this study confirmed that at the 54-min point the teacher informed the class that the activity was ending.

6   Discussions

RQ1: What insight can be gained from temporal analysis of discourse data with timestamp data compared to analysis without it?

First, from the results of the analysis, this study identified the peaks and troughs of idea improvement as well as when they happened. At some times, learners created new and revised existing ideas, whereas at other times they maintained existing ideas. When analyzing the ordered data, the results did not show this situation because the data was plotted at regular intervals. By employing data that contains timestamp information, the density of several nodes' positions could be observed. This representation is more in accordance with the realities faced by learners and allows for a more appropriate and detailed analysis of how they engage in learning during classes.

Second, our analysis provided further important information for considering idea improvement through discourse: the duration of peaks and troughs. In this study, the authors proposed adding time dimensions to data. Consequently, it became possible to evaluate how long the critical phases of idea improvement continued over time. For example, Fig. 4b illustrates that the degree centrality of the two groups remained high for a long time at the start phase. As a result, the differences between high- and low-learning outcome groups could be represented clearly.

RQ2: Can differences between high- and low-learning outcome groups be found by analyzing data on a real-time scale?

RQ2 required the idea improvement process pattern to be compared between the high- and low-learning outcome groups. The present findings confirmed that the peaks of idea improvement in the high-learning outcome group were more frequent and longer than in the low-learning outcome group by analyzing data on a real-time scale. This is because, since timestamp information is a common indicator for multiple groups, using data on a real-time scale allowed comparison of the groups on the same scale. Concretely, at the phase from 24 min to the end in Fig. 4b, the red line illustrates how the degree centralities of the high-learning outcome group rose regularly and maintained a high score, and the black dotted line shows how the degree centralities of the low-learning outcome group rarely rose and would fall immediately when they did. Therefore, these results suggest that continuous idea improvement is critical for the high-learning outcome group, as shown in a previous study [1].

7   Limitations and Conclusion

Of course, this study is limited and is a work in progress as the authors analyzed only two groups of contrastive data. There is a need for further research to develop a more well-defined analysis method. The goal of this study was to examine the possibility of analyzing data using timestamp information. In this aspect, the authors conclude with two suggestions.

The main finding of this study that analyzed data on a real-time scale showed that the proposed method is an effective means of visualizing transitions of ideas during learning activities. This visualization can illustrate the "bursty" [21] characteristic of the process of ideas improvement, learners' activity time, break times, and differences and similarities in different groups. These factors are not indicated in the analysis results for ordered data. Furthermore, the mixed-method approach that combines visualization and in-depth dialogical discourse analysis also detected pivotal points to indicate how learners engage in improvement of ideas. This study suggested the effectiveness of temporal analysis and analyzing data on a real-time scale.

The second finding of this study is that analyzing data with timestamp information is effective for assessing between-group similarities and differences. The results of investigating RQ2 corroborate this assertion. By adopting the real-time data, the common scale for activities was set. It allows the authors to assess each group on the same scale and compare them. Consequently, the results of the analysis suggest that learners' continuous engagement in the idea improvement is characteristic of high-learning outcomes group. One of the purposes of researching analysis methods for learning is to identify the characteristics of processes related to the quality of learning outcomes to support learners. As such, the results of this study are significant.

Acknowledgments. This work was supported by JSPS KAKENHI Grant Numbers JP16H0187, JP18K13238, and JP19H01715.

References

1. Scardamalia, M.: Collective cognitive responsibility for the advancement of knowledge. In: Smith, B. (ed.) Liberal Education in a Knowledge Society, pp. 67–98. Open Court, Chicago (2002)
2. Paavola, S., Lipponen, L., Hakkarainen, K.: Models of innovative knowledge communities and three metaphors of learning. Rev. Edu. Res. **74**, 557–576 (2004)
3. Hakkarainen, K., Paavola, S., Kangas, K., Seitamaa-Hakkarainen, P.: Socio-cultural perspectives on collaborative learning: toward knowledge creation. In: Hmelo-Silver, C., Chinn, C.A., Chan, C., O'donnell, A. (eds.) The International Handbook of Collaborative Learning, pp. 57–73. Routledge, New York (2013)
4. Scardamalia, M., Bereiter, C.: Knowledge building and knowledge creation: theory, pedagogy, and technology. In: Sawyer, K. (ed.) The Cambridge Handbook of the Learning Sciences, 2nd edn., pp. 397–417. Cambridge University Press, New York (2014)
5. Csanadi, A., Eagan, B., Kollar, I., Shaffer, D.W., Fischer, F.: When coding-and-counting is not enough: using epistemic network analysis (ENA) to analyze verbal data in CSCL research. Int. J. Comput.-Support. Collab. Learn. **13**, 419–438 (2018)
6. Ohsaki, A., Oshima, J.: A socio-semantic network analysis of discourse using the network lifetime and the moving stanza window method. In: Eagan, B., Misfeldt, M., Siebert-Evenstone, A. (eds.) ICQE 2019. CCIS, vol. 1112, pp. 326–333. Springer, Cham (2019). https://doi.org/10.1007/978-3-030-33232-7_29
7. Oshima, J., Oshima, R., Fujita, W.: A mixed-methods approach to analyze shared epistemic agency in jigsaw instruction at multiple scales of temporality. J. Learn. Anl. **5**, 10–24 (2018)
8. Zhang, J., Scardamalia, M., Reeve, R., Messina, R.: Designs for collective cognitive responsibility in knowledge-building communities. J. Learn. Sci. **18**, 7–44 (2009)
9. Hong, H.Y., Chen, F.C., Chai, C.S., Chan, W.C.: Teacher-education students' views about knowledge building theory and practice. Instr. Sci. **39**, 467–482 (2011)
10. Chen, B., Scardamalia, M., Bereiter, C.: Advancing knowledge-building discourse through judgments of promising ideas. Int. J. Comput. Support. Collab. Learn. **10**, 345–366 (2015)
11. Oshima, J., Oshima, R., Matsuzawa, Y.: Knowledge building discourse explorer: a social network analysis application for knowledge building discourse. Edu. Tech. Res. Dev. **60**, 903–921 (2012)
12. Siebert-Evenstone, A.L., Irgens, G.A., Collier, W., Swiecki, Z., Ruis, A.R., Shaffer, D.W.: In search of conversational grain size: modeling semantic structure using moving stanza windows. J. Learn. Anl. **4**, 123–139 (2017)
13. Shaffer, D.W.: Quantitative Ethnography. Cathcart, Madison (2017)
14. Barabási, A.: Network Science. Cambridge University Press, Cambridge (2016)
15. Morris, M., Kretzschmar, M.: Concurrent partnerships and transmission dynamics in networks. Soc. Netw. **17**, 299–318 (1995)
16. Masuda, N., Holme, P.: Predicting and controlling infectious diseases epidemics using temporal networks. F1000 Prime Rep. 5,6 (2013)
17. Holme, P., Saramäki, J.: Temporal networks. Phys. Rep. **519**, 97–125 (2012)
18. Dyke, G., Kumar, R., Ai, H., Rose, C.: Challenging assumptions: using sliding window visualizations to reveal time-based irregularities in CSCL processes. In: the Future of Learning: Proceedings of the 10th International Conference of the Learning Sciences (ICLS 2012), vol. 1, pp. 363–370, International Society of the Learning Sciences, Sydney (2012)
19. Oshima, J., Ohsaki, A., Yamada, Y., Oshima, R.: Collective knowledge advancement and conceptual understanding of complex scientific concepts in the jigsaw instruction. In: Making a Difference: Prioritizing Equity and Access in CSCL, 12th International Conference on Computer Supported Collaborative Learning (CSCL) 2017, vol. 1, pp. 57–64. International Society of the Learning Sciences, Philadelphia (2017)

20. Miyake, N., Kirschner, P.A.: The social and interactive dimensions of collaborative learning. In: Sawyer, K. (ed.) The Cambridge Handbook of the Learning Sciences (Second edition), pp. 418–438. Cambridge University Press, New York (2014)
21. Barabási, A.: The origin of bursts and heavy tails in human dynamics. Nature **435**, 207–211 (2005)

Using Epistemic Networks to Analyze Self-regulated Learning in an Open-Ended Problem-Solving Environment

Luc Paquette[1]($\boxtimes$), Theodore Grant[1], Yingbin Zhang[1], Gautam Biswas[2], and Ryan Baker[3]

[1] University of Illinois at Urbana Champaign, Champaign, IL 61820, USA
lpaq@illinois.edu
[2] Vanderbilt University, Nashville, TN 37235, USA
[3] University of Pennsylvania, Philadelphia, PA 19104, USA

Abstract. The micro-level analyses of how students' self-regulated learning (SRL) behaviors unfold over time provides a valuable framework for understanding their learning processes as they interact with computer-based learning environments. In this paper, we use log trace data to investigate how students self-regulate their learning in the Betty's Brain environment, where they engage in three categories of open-ended problem-solving actions: information seeking, solution construction and solution assessment. We use Epistemic Network Analysis (ENA) to provide us with an overall understanding of the co-occurrences between action types both within and between the three action categories. Comparisons of epistemic networks generated for two groups of students, those with low and high performance, provided us with insights into their self-regulated behaviors.

Keywords: Self-regulated learning · Open-ended problem-solving · Epistemic network analysis · Betty's Brain

1 Introduction

Self-regulated learning (SRL) refers to the process where learners actively and adaptively adjust their cognition, emotion, and behavior toward their goals [1]. SRL processes, in general, consist of three cyclical phases: (1) preparatory, where learners analyze the task, set goals, and make plans, (2) performance, where learners execute the plan, monitor and control the processes, and (3) appraisal, where learners evaluate their performance based on self- or external feedback and adapt their goal and plans [2]. SRL provides a valuable theoretical framework for understanding the interactions between cognition, metacognition, motivation, and emotion during learning [2].

Increasingly, researchers are viewing SRL as events that unfold over time rather than static skills [3–5]. Understanding and researching SRL from this conceptual perspective requires fine-granularity learning activity data which can be provided by computer-based learning environments (CBLE), due to their capability to record each of the learners' actions unobtrusively. Approaches for micro-level analyses are necessary to obtain

© Springer Nature Switzerland AG 2021
A. R. Ruis and S. B. Lee (Eds.): ICQE 2021, CCIS 1312, pp. 185–201, 2021.
https://doi.org/10.1007/978-3-030-67788-6_13

insights about SRL from such moment-to-moment data [4, 6, 7]. Researchers have explored SRL using multiple approaches, such as knowledge engineering [8], sequential pattern mining [9], lag-sequential analysis [10], statistical discourse analysis [11], and process mining [12, 13]. The current study employs an emerging method, epistemic network analysis (ENA) [14], for the in-depth analyses of SRL processes.

We apply ENA to trace data captured from Betty's Brain, a CBLE designed to foster student self-regulation [15]. We aim to investigate the relationship between students' self-regulated behavior in Betty's Brain and their performance, and the affordances of ENA for the study of student behaviors in CBLEs. Results illustrated how students engage in three main categories of actions required to regulate their open-ended problem-solving [16]: information seeking, solution construction, and solution assessment. ENA highlighted differences in behaviors between low and high performers, allowing us to identify opportunities for further analyses and refinements of Betty's Brain.

2   Related Work

2.1   Investigation of Self-regulated Learning Using Trace Data

Much of the work measuring and studying SRL relies upon self-reported, out-of-context questionnaires (e.g., [17]). Such methods assume that SRL involves static skills. It may capture the global level of self-regulation, but trace data, such as computer action logs and think-aloud data, may better reflect specific SRL strategies in context [18].

Various analytical approaches have been applied to the micro-level analysis of SRL using trace data. Knowledge engineering was used to identify the different help-seeking strategies students employ while using an intelligent tutor [8]. Sequential pattern mining was applied to evaluate the effectiveness of SRL scaffolding during the study of scientific phenomena [9]. Lag-sequential analyses were used to understand the differences in self-directed speech and self-regulated behaviors for children with language disorders [10]. Statistical discourse analysis was utilized to investigate how sequences of cognitive, metacognitive, and relational activities impact later cognition in a collaborative writing task [11]. These methods have shown potential in revealing the micro-processes of SRL. However, their results only highlight local behavior patterns.

In contrast, process mining depicts a holistic SRL process, where actions have directional connections [12]. This technique has been applied [13] to compare processes between groups who did/did not receive metacognitive prompts when studying topics in educational psychology. However, process mining does not allow a global statistical test for the difference between groups and different weighting for individuals [19]. These shortcomings may be overcome by ENA, which provides both networked visualizations of the data, facilitating qualitative interpretation, and statistical tests.

2.2   Using ENA to Study SRL with Trace Data

ENA has been used to investigate SRL behaviors using a range of data types including trace data [20, 21], qualitatively coded questionnaires [19] and interviews [22]. ENA was combined with process mining and clustering, to provide a rich interpretation of SRL [19–21]. We limit our discussion to studies that used trace or analogous data.

Gamage, et al. [22] used ENA to compare participation of two groups of MOOC takers: multiple MOOC completers, and first-time MOOC taker. They applied ENA to qualitative coding of log sheets and interviews to identify cognitive (e.g. watching a video) and social (e.g. use or discussion tools) tasks students performed. While they did not use trace data, their codes were analogous to trace data produced by MOOCs.

Trace data produced by LMSs has been used to conduct ENA analyses [20, 21]. ENA was used to compare the use of SRL related actions, e.g., goal setting, making plans, work on a task, evaluation, and reflection, between the top and bottom decile of students using assessment performance [20]. Another use of ENA was to compare student behaviors for different course taking strategies (e.g. reading the e-book, viewing learning resources, taking quizzes and assignments) [21]. In both studies, ENA was combined with process mining [20, 21] or agglomerative hierarchical clustering [21].

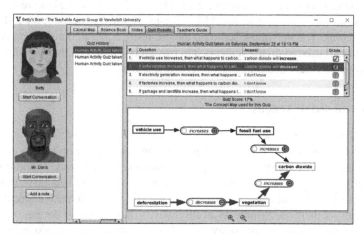

Fig. 1. The Betty's Brain interface. Here the student is looking at a quiz's results.

3 Betty's Brain

Betty's Brain (Fig. 1) is an open-ended CBLE that provides students opportunities to develop and apply SRL processes as they build causal models of scientific phenomena [16]. Trace data in Betty's Brain captures the performance and appraisal phases, i.e., how learners process the task, evaluate their performance, and adjust strategies [2, 23].

Students create a causal map of scientific concepts with associated links to model a scientific phenomenon (e.g., climate change), to teach a computer agent, generically called Betty. This causal map represents Betty's Brain, i.e., what she has learned about the topic. To produce this map, students acquire knowledge of the subject by using hypertext resources, translate that knowledge into causal links between selected concepts (e.g., *global temperature* increases *ocean temperature*) and test their map by having Betty take quizzes (see Sect. 4.2 for more details about possible student actions).

4 Methods

4.1 Participants and Procedures

Data for this analysis were collected from 98 sixth graders in an urban public school in south-eastern United States. This school serves 700 students in grades 5–8 (40% underrepresented minorities, and 8% enrolled in the free and reduced lunch program). The study was conducted in classrooms in December 2018 and lasted seven school days (50 min per day). Students answered a pre-test (1), received Betty's Brain training (2), used the system to study climate change (3–6), and answered a post-test (7).

The pre- ($M = 6.26$; $SD = 2.66$) and post-tests ($M = 9.18$; $SD = 3.28$) assessed students' knowledge of climate change and causal relationships. They were identical in form and content and consisted of seven multiple choice items and three short answer items with a maximum score of 18. Learning gains ($M = 0.25$; $SD = 0.24$) were calculated as (post-test scores − pre-test scores)/(18 − pre-test scores) to account for differences in pre-test scores. The maximum score on the pre-test, 13, showed no ceiling effect. A median split was used to divide students into two groups based on their learning gains: low performers (<0.26) and high performers ($>= 0.26$).

4.2 Contextualizing Actions

In Betty's Brain, students can perform a set of actions to build their causal map. They can *read* a hyperlink resource, work on their causal map by *adding* or *deleting* a concept, *adding a causal link* between two concepts, or *editing an existing link*. In addition, they can ask Betty to *take a quiz* (generated by the system) which Betty will answer using the students' causal map. Students can then *view the quiz's results* to make inference about the correctness of their causal map. As an alternative to having Betty take a quiz, students can use dropdown menus to ask Betty to explain the causal relationship between two concepts. While Betty's answers to such questions are not graded, they allow students to better understand how concepts are related to each other in their map.

To study SRL behaviors, the different types of actions were further contextualized based on their duration and coherence. First, quiz result viewing and resource reading actions were contextualized as short vs. Long, where a short action is usually too short for the student to acquire the information presented by the resource. Quiz result viewing actions were labeled as long or short, based on whether their duration was higher than 2 s. Reading actions were labeled long or short, based on whether their duration was greater than 10 s. Both time thresholds were selected based on prior research [24]. In addition, long readings were labeled as old or new based on whether the page has been previously accessed; providing insights about whether the student was exposed to new information (new reading) or was revisiting information (old reading).

Long reading of old pages and links edits were labeled coherent vs. Incoherent, based using Coherence Analysis [24]. The students' actions generate information that can be used to guide subsequent actions. For example, reading a hypertext resource provides information about the causal links between different concepts, and quiz results provides information about missing or incorrect links. If a student performs a sequence of actions where first action informs a second one, the second action is considered "coherent".

For example, if, after reading a resource discussing two concepts, the student adds (or edits) a link connecting those concepts, the add (or edit) link action is considered coherent with the reading action. In contrast, if a student adds a link between two concepts without previously reading a resource related to those concepts, this addition is considered "incoherent". Similarly, viewing a quiz result provides information that can lead to reading a related resource (coherent reading) or editing a related link (coherent addition, or coherent editing). Coherence analysis is operationalized based on information stored within the students' log trace data and does not rely on human judgement.

It is important to note that a coherent action does not necessarily imply that the action is part of the correct solution, only that it is informed by a prior action. In addition, neither short reading or short viewing of quiz results counted towards considering a future action as coherent since short action are indicative of searching for relevant information rather than acquiring new information.

Each action type was classified as part of one of three categories of actions reflecting processes relevant to SRL (Table 1): information seeking, solution construction and solution assessment. Those categories were taken from a model aligning Betty's Brain's actions to a framework for problem-solving in open-ended learning environments [16]. Any action not related to one of the three categories was excluded from our analyses.

Table 1. Selected action types, their classification as one of the three categories of open-ended problem-solving actions and frequency of occurrences across student groupings.

Action type	All (N = 98)		Low perf. (N = 48)		High perf. (N = 50)	
	Mean	%	Mean	%	Mean	%
Information seeking						
new_read	9.33	2.25%	8.98	2.25%	9.66	2.25%
short_read	88.39	21.34%	87.17	21.87%	89.56	20.86%
coherent_read	25.73	6.21%	23.77	5.96%	27.62	6.43%
incoherent_read	13.36	3.22%	13.44	3.37%	13.28	3.09%
Solution construction						
add_concept	30.50	7.36%	32.13	8.06%	28.94	6.74%
delete_concept	14.10	3.40%	18.10	4.54%	10.26	2.39%
coherent_addition	26.43	6.38%	23.69	5.94%	29.06	6.77%
incoherent_addition	11.32	2.73%	11.88	2.98%	10.78	2.51%
coherent_revision	13.66	3.30%	12.08	3.03%	15.18	3.54%
incoherent_revision	3.38	0.82%	3.52	0.88%	3.24	0.75%
Solution assessment						
taking_quiz	24.45	5.90%	22.65	5.68%	26.18	6.10%
long_view_quiz_result	52.09	12.58%	47.54	11.93%	56.46	13.15%
short_view_quiz_result	24.14	5.83%	20.94	5.25%	27.22	6.34%
view_ungraded_quiz_question	1.83	0.44%	2.42	0.61%	1.26	0.29%
ask_Betty_causal_question	4.29	1.03%	4.38	1.10%	4.2	0.98%

Information seeking includes all action types related to reading one of the hypermedia resource pages provided within Betty's Brain. It includes new reading, short reading, and coherent and incoherent reading actions. *Solution construction* includes action types related to building or editing the causal map. It includes adding or deleting a concept, coherent or incoherent additions and revisions of a causal link. *Solution assessment* includes actions related to evaluating the correctness of the causal map. It includes asking Betty to take a quiz, long and short viewing of a quiz result, viewing an ungraded quiz question, and asking Betty a causal question.

4.3 Epistemic Network Analysis

We applied Epistemic Network Analysis (ENA) [14] to our data using the webtool (version 1.7.0) [25]. Each data point corresponded to one of the 98 participants in our study who were grouped into high or low performers, as discussed earlier.

Our ENA models used a moving window of three actions (each action plus the two previous actions) to generate the networks. This window size was selected to account for situations where students might perform an intermediate action between two connected actions. For example, a student might perform a coherent reading followed by an incoherent reading before adding a link related to the first reading. In such a case, there should be a link between the first coherent reading and the following coherent addition of a link, regardless of the superfluous incoherent reading. Initial exploration of the data investigated the use of a larger window size of four. This change did not affect general trends in the networks and the smaller window size was selected.

ENA was used to investigate the relationships between action types both within each of the three categories of open-ended problem-solving actions, across each pair of categories and over the three categories combined. In each case, we first generated a network including all 98 participants to describe the average co-occurrence of action types. Then analyses were conducted to investigate differences in behaviors between the low and high performing students. Results from these analyses were interpreted to provide insights about how behavioral patterns relate to performance within Betty's Brain.

First, networks were generated for each of the categories of problem-solving actions: information seeking; solution construction; and solution assessment. Each network was analyzed to identify how different groups of students might approach each category. Second, networks combining two categories were generated to investigate differences when transitioning between categories of actions: information seeking and solution construction; solution construction and solution assessment; solution assessment and information seeking. Finally, networks including all three categories were generated to investigate patterns spanning the full problem-solving process.

For all analyses, a means rotation was applied to align the means of both student grouping (low and high performers) along the X axis. Statistical significance in network differences between the groups were computed using Mann-Whitney on the X axis.

5 Results

5.1 Information Seeking

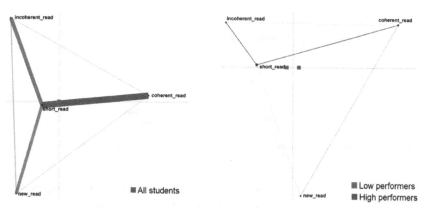

Fig. 2. Information seeking networks for all participants (left) and performance groups (right).

As the network including all participants illustrates (left of Fig. 2), short reading actions are central to information seeking behaviors. They often co-occur with coherent, incoherent, and new reading actions. This is unsurprising as short readings are both very frequent (21.34% of all actions) and indicative of a student searching through resources for the page(s) that may contain information they currently seek. The network also suggests it is somewhat rare for long reading actions (coherent, incoherent, and new reading) to co-occur with each other. Suggesting that actions of other types, whether short readings to search for information or actions related to other categories of actions (e.g. solution construction), act as intermediate actions between long readings.

Comparison of information seeking networks (right of Fig. 2) showed no statistically significant difference between low (Mdn = −0.04) and high (Mdn = 0.28) performers (U = 1340, p = 0.32, r = 0.12) despite short readings more often co-occurring with coherent readings for high performers and with incoherent readings for low performers.

5.2 Solution Construction

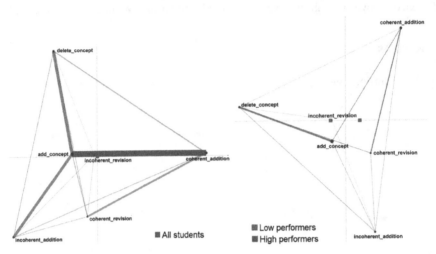

Fig. 3. Solution construction networks for all participants (left) and performance groups (right)

Co-occurrences of solution construction actions are centered around adding new concepts to the map (left of Fig. 3). Adding a new concept is most strongly connected to deleting a concept and adding a new causal link (coherent and incoherent). The network shows few other strong connections, besides the connection between coherent revisions of a link and the coherent addition of a link. Most cases of co-occurring actions can be interpreted as one edit that requires multiple actions; e.g., adding a new link to the map might first require adding new concepts or deleting incorrect links (coherent revision).

A significant difference was observed in networks (right of Fig. 3) between low (Mdn = −0.19) and high (Mdn = 0.37) performers (U = 1750, p < 0.01, r = 0.46). Adding a new concept is central to building the causal map, however high performers showed stronger connections to coherent addition of new links, whereas low performers showed more behaviors combining adding and deleting concepts, indicating they might be unsure of how to build their map. This suggests that low performers have more difficulty in identifying the appropriate concepts to build their map, which may partially explain their lower performance: adding and deleting concepts rather than adding links and testing them. High performers show more behaviors combining coherent revisions (i.e., making corrections to their map) and additions of links (both coherent and incoherent – indicating that high performers also made mistakes when building their maps).

5.3 Solution Assessment

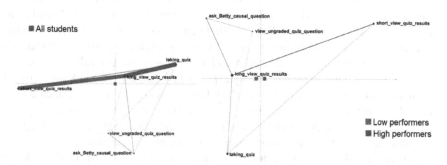

Fig. 4. Solution assessment networks for all participants (left) and comparing groups (right)

Co-occurrences of solution assessment actions (left of Fig. 4) show a strong connection between having Betty take a quiz and long quiz views. Interestingly, it was rare for short quiz views to co-occur with quiz taking, suggesting that after having Betty take a quiz, students often spend a reasonable amount of time viewing the quiz's results. Actions related to quickly browsing results (short viewing) are most strongly connected to long views of quiz results and might indicate students going back to quickly review a previously studied results or searching for some results that they wanted to study in more detail. No significant difference was found between networks (right of Fig. 4) for low (Mdn = −0.04) and high (Mdn = 0.19) performers (U = 1023, p = 0.21, r = 0.15).

5.4 Information Seeking and Solution Construction

Figure 5 (left) shows the co-occurrence of information seeking and solution construction behaviors for all students. While adding a concept to the causal map appears to be

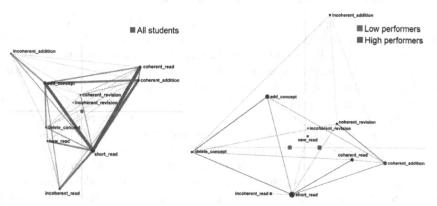

Fig. 5. Networks combining information seeking and solution construction for all participants (left) and performance groups (right)

connected to all types of reading actions to some degree (with its strongest connection to short readings and its weakest to new readings), deleting a concept is weakly linked to information seeking (with its connection to short readings being the strongest).

For actions related to adding a causal link to the map, both coherent and incoherent addition are connected to short readings, but the connection is stronger for coherent addition. As expected, coherent addition is connected to coherent reading, but this connection is not as strong as the one to short reading. Incoherent addition is rarely connected to incoherent reading. This might be partially explained by the fact that a link added based on an incoherent reading would still be labeled as coherent since it is informed by the content of that incoherent reading. However, co-occurrence of incoherent reading and coherent addition also appear to be uncommon, therefore, it is generally less frequent for an incoherent reading action to co-occur with solution construction.

As expected, coherent and incoherent additions of a link are connected to adding concept actions, which are themselves strongly connected to information seeking (both coherent and incoherent). Adding a concept appears to be an intermediate step between reading and adding a link to the causal map. In some cases, this process might lead to adding an incoherent link, implying the link did not appear in the pages the student read. Revisions of causal links generally have weak connections to information seeking actions, with the strongest connection between coherent revision and short readings.

A significant difference was observed (right of Fig. 5) between low (Mdn $= -0.32$) and high (Mdn $= 0.53$) performers ($U = 713$, $p < 0.01$, $r = 0.41$). High performers showed stronger connections between coherent solution construction (addition and revision of links) and information seeking (short and coherent readings). No differences in incoherent solution construction actions (incoherent addition/ revision of a link) were observed. Behaviors related to adding and deleting concepts co-occurred more frequently with short readings for low performers. They also showed slightly stronger connections between deleting a concept and coherent reading. This suggests low performers did not understand what they were reading, and this lack of surety resulted in adding and deleting concepts more often instead of adding links after adding concepts.

5.5 Solution Construction and Solution Assessment

Co-occurrences of solution assessment and solution construction actions (left of Fig. 6) are centered around the actions of having Betty take a quiz and long quiz viewing. Both action types are well connected to most of the solution construction actions. This could be related to either students validating their map by having Betty take a quiz or students modifying their map based on their interpretation of the quiz results.

There was a significant difference (right of Fig. 6) between low (Mdn $= -0.41$) and high (Mdn $= 0.52$) performers ($U = 614$, $p < 0.01$, $r = 0.49$). High performers showed stronger connections between coherent additions and revisions of causal links, and the main solution assessment actions (having Betty taking a quiz and long view of quiz results). Network connections for incoherent addition or revision of a link appeared to be stronger for low performers. However, these differences were small. Low performers showed stronger connections between adding or deleting a concept and the main solution assessment actions. They showed stronger connections between asking Betty a causal question and all solution construction actions. However, none of those connections were strong. This might be partially explained by the low frequency of asking Betty a causal question throughout the problem-solving process (1.03% of actions).

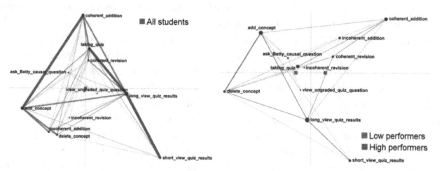

Fig. 6. Networks combining solution construction and solution assessment for all participants (left) and performance groups (right)

5.6   Solution Assessment and Information Seeking

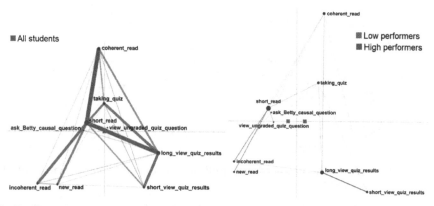

Fig. 7. Networks combining solution assessment and information seeking for all participants (left) and performance groups (right)

Co-occurrences of solution assessment and information seeking actions (left of Fig. 7) were mainly associated with three solution assessment action types (having Betty take a quiz, and short and long viewing of quiz results) and two information seeking actions (short and coherent readings). All three solution assessment action types show a similar pattern where the strongest connection is to short reading, followed by coherent reading. However, the strength of those connections varies across action types. The strongest connections to short or coherent reading are from long viewing of quiz results, followed by having Betty take a quiz, with the weakest for short viewing of quiz results.

Overall, those patterns are consistent with expected behaviors. Having Betty take a quiz is expected to lead to actions related to viewing its results, which then informs information seeking behaviors, especially if Betty answered a question incorrectly or could not answer a question that was asked of her. Information seeking may start with short readings as the students search for a resource aligning with the quiz results, which should then lead to a coherent reading action. Few connections were observed between solution assessment actions and incoherent reading. It may be that short readings (i.e., searching for relevant information) act as an intermediate action between viewing quiz results and incoherent readings (indicating the students end up on the wrong page because of their lack of understanding). Actions related to asking Betty to answer a causal question did not appear to frequently co-occur with information seeking actions.

A significant difference was observed between networks (right of Fig. 7) for low (Mdn = −0.03) and high (Mdn = 0.27) performers (U = 892, p = 0.03, r = 0.26). However, a visual inspection of the networks did not reveal any important differences in connections bridging solution assessment and information seeking. Rather, differences appear to be local with high performers showing strong connections within solution assessment and within information seeking for low performers.

5.7 Combined Analysis of Open-Ended Problem-Solving Processes

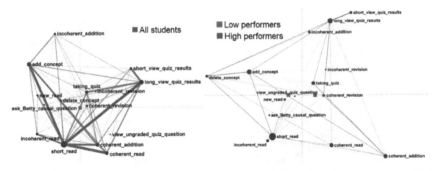

Fig. 8. Networks combining all actions for all participants (left) and performance groups (right)

While the network (left of Fig. 8) provides a global view of the co-occurrences of action types it does not highlight any particular set of multiple strongly connected actions spanning the three categories of actions. The most strongly connected actions are short readings and long viewing of quiz results. This might be because they are the two most common action types, both are central to their own category (information seeking and solution assessment respectively) and are actions that can be repeated multiple times to achieve a goal – for example, browsing multiple resources (short reads) to find the appropriate one and viewing the results of many different questions (long view of quiz results) for the same quiz. Both short readings and long viewing of quiz results are also actions that we expect students would perform regardless of whether they make coherent use of the information they acquire. In contrast, there doesn't appear to be one central solution construction action with most of them well connected in the network.

There was a significant difference (right of Fig. 8) between low (Mdn $= -0.31$) and high (Mdn $= 0.44$) performers (U $= 1686$, p < 0.01, r $= 0.40$). The difference mainly aligns with the expected strategic problem-solving behavior rather than unexpected behaviors. High performers showed stronger connections for many of the expected interactions across action categories. They showed stronger connections between short and coherent readings, which were in turn connected to coherent additions of links. While information seeking actions did not show stronger connection with adding a concept in the map for high performers, they showed a stronger connection between adding a new concept and coherent link addition. Coherent link addition was also more strongly connected to having Betty take a quiz and to long viewing of quiz results; themselves more strongly associated with coherent revision of a link and coherent readings.

Low performers showed stronger connections related to a few unexpected problem-solving behaviors. In general, they showed stronger connections spanning the three categories of actions for adding and removing concepts. Both were connected to short readings (information seeking) and long viewing of quiz results (solution assessment).

Two action types, short readings and long viewing of quiz results, appears to be points of divergence in the behaviors of the two groups. Both co-occurred more frequently with adding and deleting a concept for low performers and with the expected coherent problem-solving behaviors for high performers.

6 Discussion

6.1 SRL Behaviors of Low and High Performers in Betty's Brain

In this paper, we generated a set of epistemic networks to illustrate the co-occurrences of actions related to three main categories of open-ended problem-solving actions: information seeking, solution construction and solution assessment and interpreted them as SRL processes used by the students. Our analyses investigated overall co-occurrence for all students as well as differences across students based on their performance.

In line with prior studies [12, 26], ENA revealed that high performers showed stronger connections related to the expected SRL problem-solving process. Searching through resources (short readings) was more often connected to finding the relevant one (coherent readings). When constructing the causal map, high performers showed stronger connections between adding a new concept and adding coherent links. They showed stronger connections to coherent revisions of existing links. When assessing their solution, they showed stronger connections between quiz taking, quiz result views, and coherent responses to those results (readings and adding or revising a link). While it is not surprising that high performers showed stronger connections related to the expected SRL process, ENA was an effective tool for revealing those connections.

Perhaps most surprising was our observation that, while high performers show more connections related to coherent actions, connections for incoherent actions showed no or weak differences between high and low performers. In other words, the high performers were better at implementing efficient problem-solving strategies, but both groups had difficulties inhibiting inefficient behavior.

One way low performers differentiate themselves is their behavior related to adding and deleting concepts from the causal map. ENA showed that the co-occurrence of these actions with both information seeking (short reading) and solution assessment (long quiz result views) was more frequent for low performers. This observation raises questions about the reasons why low performers add and delete concepts in the map. Concepts are well identified in the hyperlink resources and adding a concept is achieved through a fixed menu of concepts that are needed to build a correct map. Unlike causal links, which are inferred by students and might need to be revised, it should not be necessary to delete a concept. One possible explanation m be that low performers are unable to fully understand the resources, leading to uncertainty and therefore, adding and deleting of concepts. Further investigations may be required to better understand this phenomenon and its association with poorer performance.

Our analyses of the networks also suggested differentiations in actions co-occurring with asking Betty a causal question. Because this action type is infrequent (1.03% actions), its connections in the networks are weak. However, low performers showed stronger connections than high performers. This result was surprising considering past research [27], using differential sequence mining, suggested that high performing students were more likely to combine asking Betty a causal question and following up by asking Betty to explain her answer. This raises questions related to how students made use of this feature in our study and why it was mainly associated with low performance.

6.2 Factors Influencing the Interpretation of Epistemic Networks

While ENA was an effective tool in our investigation, there were factors that influenced how each of the networks were interpreted. Most important was the difference in the frequencies of different action types. Some types were either very frequent (e.g. short readings) or uncommon (e.g. asking Betty a causal question). Such differences in frequency can impact the visual representation of the network. For example, short reading actions tend to be central to whichever network includes it and its connections are usually the strongest. Visually, the thickness of the connections between other action types might be impacted by the thickness of the connections associated with short readings. While we decided to include short readings in every relevant network, we also experimented with networks that excluded them. We observed that doing so increased the thickness of other links and made the networks easier to interpret. Mello and Gasevic [28] observed a similar effect where "the exclusion of the dominant code led to an entirely different configuration in ENA." Further research might be necessary to formally investigate when it is acceptable to exclude dominant codes and to assess the impact of such exclusions on ENA results.

Another factor we observed is related to the statistical significance of the difference between networks. In our analyses, we wanted to systematically investigate differences within a specific category of problem-solving actions (e.g. information seeking alone) and across multiple categories (e.g. information seeking and solution construction). For this purpose, we generated multiple networks using different sets of actions types. While analyses of statistical significance allowed us to say whether there was a difference between two networks in their entirety, it did not allow us to identify whether a specific subset of action types had the most impact in driving this difference. For our purpose, this was important when comparing networks across multiple categories.

In such cases, we were interested in knowing whether the connections between those two categories were different across groupings. However, the generated networks would still include connections between actions within the same category. For example, the networks generated to investigate the co-occurrences of solution assessment and information seeking actions (Fig. 7) showed a statistically significant difference. However, visual inspection of the network showed that stronger connections were local to action types within the same category. I.e., the strongest connection for high performers was between two solution assessment actions and the strongest connections for low performers were among three information seeking actions. In such a case, the statistical significance of the difference between the two networks was not a useful tool for us to investigate differences in behaviors that spanned those two categories. Further work should investigate whether masking specific connections in the networks, a feature available in the R version of ENA might allow for a more targeted comparison of how different groups of students navigate the transition between categories of open-ended problem-solving actions. Alternatively, it might be beneficial to complement ENA with other methods focusing on the identification of local behavior patterns such as sequential or differential pattern mining [27]. ENA allows a holistic test between groups, while the other methods can examine differences in single pairs of actions.

Acknowledgments. This research was supported by NSF ECR Award #1561676.

References

1. Schunk, D.H., Greene, J.A.: Historical, contemporary, and future perspectives on self-regulated learning and performance. In: Handbook of Self-Regulation of Learning and Performance, pp. 1–15. Routledge/Taylor & Francis Group (2018)
2. Panadero, E.: A review of self-regulated learning: six models and four directions for research. Front. Psychol. **8**, 422 (2017)
3. Azevedo, R., Moos, D.C., Johnson, A.M., Chauncey, A.D.: Measuring cognitive and metacognitive regulatory processes during hypermedia learning: Issues and challenges. Educ. Psychol. **45**(4), 210–223 (2010)
4. Molenaar, I., Järvelä, S.: Sequential and temporal characteristics of self and socially regulated learning. Metacogn. Learn. **9**(2), 75–85 (2014). https://doi.org/10.1007/s11409-014-9114-2
5. Winne, P.H., Baker, R.S.: The potentials of educational data mining for researching metacognition, motivation and self-regulated learning. J. Educ. Data Mining **5**(1), 1–8 (2013)
6. Azevedo, R.: Issues in dealing with sequential and temporal characteristics of self- and socially-regulated learning. Metacogn. Learn. **9**(2), 217–228 (2014). https://doi.org/10.1007/s11409-014-9123-1
7. Winne, P.H.: Issues in researching self-regulated learning as patterns of events. Metacogn. Learn. **9**(2), 229–237 (2014). https://doi.org/10.1007/s11409-014-9113-3
8. Aleven, V., McLaren, B., Roll, I., Koedinger, K.: Toward meta-cognitive tutoring: a model of help seeking with a cognitive tutor. Int. J. Artif. Intell. Educ. **16**(2), 101–128 (2006)
9. Kinnebrew, J.S., Segedy, J.R., Biswas, G.: Analyzing the temporal evolution of students' behaviors in open-ended learning environments. Metacogn. Learn. **9**(2), 187–215 (2014). https://doi.org/10.1007/s11409-014-9112-4

10. Kuvalja, M., Verma, M., Whitebread, D.: Patterns of co-occurring non-verbal behaviour and self-directed speech; a comparison of three methodological approaches. Metacogn. Learn. **9**(2), 87–111 (2013). https://doi.org/10.1007/s11409-013-9106-7

11. Molenaar, I., Chiu, M.M.: Dissecting sequences of regulation and cognition: statistical discourse analysis of primary school children's collaborative learning. Metacogn. Learn. **9**(2), 137–160 (2013). https://doi.org/10.1007/s11409-013-9105-8

12. Bannert, M., Reimann, P., Sonnenberg, C.: Process mining techniques for analysing patterns and strategies in students' self-regulated learning. Metacogn. Learn. **9**(2), 161–185 (2013). https://doi.org/10.1007/s11409-013-9107-6

13. Sonnenberg, C., Bannert, M.: Using Process Mining to examine the sustainability of instructional support: How stable are the effects of metacognitive prompting on self-regulatory behavior? Comput. Hum. Behav. **96**, 259–272 (2018)

14. Shaffer, D.W., Collier, W., Ruis, A.R.: A tutorial on epistemic network analysis: analyzing the structure of connections in cognitive, social, and interaction data. J. Learn. Anal. **3**(3), 9–45 (2016)

15. Biswas, G., Segedy, J., Bunchongchit, K.: From design to implementation to practice a learning by teaching system: Betty's Brain. International Journal of Artificial Intelligence in Education **26**(1), 350–364 (2015). https://doi.org/10.1007/s40593-015-0057-9

16. Kinnebrew, J.S., Segedy, J.R., Biswas, G.: Integrating model-driven and data-driven techniques for analyzing learning behaviors in open-ended learning environments. IEEE Trans. Learn. Technol. **10**(2), 140–153 (2017)

17. Pintrich, P.R., De Groot, E.V.: Motivational and self-regulated learning components of classroom academic performance. J. Educ. Psychol. **82**(1), 33 (1990)

18. Rovers, S.F.E., Clarebout, G., Savelberg, H.H.C.M., de Bruin, A.B.H., van Merriënboer, J.J.G.: Granularity matters: comparing different ways of measuring self-regulated learning. Metacogn. Learn. **14**(1), 1–19 (2019). https://doi.org/10.1007/s11409-019-09188-6

19. Melzner, N., Greisel, M., Dresel, M., Kollar, I.: Using process mining (PM) and epistemic network analysis (ENA) for comparing processes of collaborative problem regulation. In: Eagan, B., Misfeldt, M., Siebert-Evenstone, A. (eds.) ICQE 2019. CCIS, vol. 1112, pp. 154–164. Springer, Cham (2019). https://doi.org/10.1007/978-3-030-33232-7_13

20. Saint, J., Gasevic, D., Matcha, W., Uzir, N.A.A., Pardo, A.: Combining analytic methods to unlock sequential and temporal patterns of self-regulated learning. In: Proceedings of the Tenth International Conference on Learning Analytics and Knowledge, pp. 402–411 (2020)

21. Uzir, N.A.A., Gasevic, D., Jovanovic, J., Matcha, W., Lim, A., Fudge, A.: Analytics of time management and learning strategies for effective online learning in blended environments. In: Proceedings of the Tenth International Conference on Learning Analytics and Knowledge, pp. 392–401 (2020)

22. Gamage, D., Perera, I., Fernando, S.: Exploring MOOC user behaviors beyond platforms. Int. J. Emerg. Technol. Learn. **15**(8), 161–179 (2020)

23. Zimmerman, B.J.: Attaining self-regulation: a social cognitive perspective. In: Handbook of Self-Regulation, chap. 2, pp. 13–39. Academic Press, San Diego (2000)

24. Segedy, J.R., Kinnebrew, J.S., Biswas, G.: Using coherence analysis to characterize self-regulated learning behaviours in open-ended learning environments. J. Learn. Anal. **2**(1), 13–48 (2015)

25. Marquart, C.L., Hinojosa, C., Swiecki, Z., Eagan, B., Shaffer, D.W.: Epistemic Network Analysis (Version 1.7.0) [Software] (2018). https://app.epistemicnetwork.org

26. Azevedo, R., et al.: Using trace data to examine the complex roles of cognitive, metacognitive, and emotional self-regulatory processes during learning with multi-agent systems. In: Azevedo, R., Aleven, V. (eds.) International Handbook of Metacognition and Learning Technologies. SIHE, vol. 28, pp. 427–449. Springer, New York (2013). https://doi.org/10.1007/978-1-4419-5546-3_28

27. Kinnebrew, J.S., Loretz, K.M., Biswas, G.: A contextualized, differential sequence mining method to derive students' learning behavior patterns. J. Educ. Data Mining **5**(1), 190–219 (2013)
28. Mello, R., Gašević, D.: What is the effect of a dominant code in an epistemic network analysis? In: Eagan, B., Misfeldt, M., Siebert-Evenstone, A. (eds.) ICQE 2019. CCIS, vol. 1112, pp. 66–76. Springer, Cham (2019). https://doi.org/10.1007/978-3-030-33232-7_6

The Value of Epistemic Network Analysis in Single-Case Learning Analytics: A Case Study in Lifelong Learning

Luis P. Prieto[1]([⊠]) [iD], María Jesús Rodríguez-Triana[1] [iD], Tobias Ley[1] [iD], and Brendan Eagan[2] [iD]

[1] Tallinn University, 10120 Tallinn, Estonia
lprisan@tlu.ee
[2] University of Wisconsin-Madison, Madison, WI 53715, USA

Abstract. Certain educational contexts like lifelong learning have been comparatively understudied, due to the uniqueness of such learning processes, which make it difficult to ascertain generalizable models or average intervention effects. The ability to collect large amounts of data from a single learner longitudinally, throughout their lifelong trajectory, and the use of learning analytics (LA), presents novel opportunities in this regard. However, quantitative data and models may not be enough to deeply understand such unique learning processes and their context, without the help of qualitative data and ethnographic methods of collecting and analyzing it. This paper presents an approach to understanding lifelong learning that combines both qualitative and quantitative data (which we have termed single-case learning analytics). We illustrate how these two kinds of longitudinal data can be combined and the role of Epistemic Network Analysis (ENA) in this approach, through a case study in which daily quantitative and qualitative data were gathered about a lifelong learner's social-emotional learning (SEL), for about nine months. Our results show how qualitative data (and ENA outputs) can be used to not only close the interpretive loop but also help interpret and improve the accuracy of quantitative models of a single learner's process and contextual influences. Along with ongoing advances in automated coding, this approach opens the door to user-facing, ENA-enhanced LA to support personalized learning over extended periods of time.

Keywords: Lifelong learning · Social emotional learning · Learning analytics · Epistemic network analysis · Longitudinal data · Single-case research designs

1 Introduction

The longitudinal study of learning that happens throughout a person's lifetime (what is often called lifelong learning, LL) has traditionally been an under-developed area within the educational sciences [1]. This is especially true of learning processes that are informal in nature, or those that happen across and beyond institutional boundaries (e.g., after one's formal education ends, or in ongoing professional development).

© Springer Nature Switzerland AG 2021
A. R. Ruis and S. B. Lee (Eds.): ICQE 2021, CCIS 1312, pp. 202–217, 2021.
https://doi.org/10.1007/978-3-030-67788-6_14

This relative scarcity of research can be attributed to several conceptual and methodological challenges. The uniqueness of each learner's goals after the formal education stage makes it difficult to study LL and draw generalizable and practically-relevant conclusions. Further, three additional difficulties arise when studying any kind of learning, but especially in truly lifelong learning: the critical importance of individual differences, the uniqueness of each learner's contextual influences (which affect deeply such situated processes), and the long-term and cross-boundaries nature of this kind of learning.

Against this comparatively bleak state of affairs, recent trends may offer untapped opportunities. Every human being now generates increasing amounts of data, both in explicitly learning-oriented platforms and apps, as well as general-purpose services, from search engines to self-tracking devices. In parallel, advances in learning analytics (the analysis of machine-readable data about learners and their contexts using automated, big-data techniques [2]), provide opportunities to address this need.

However, the challenges of LL research outlined above remain: every lifelong learner has different goals, uses different tools (which will produce heterogeneous datasets), and is difficult to compare meaningfully with a cohort of similar learners. Furthermore, there exist theoretical and methodological difficulties to the application of learning analytics (LA) in LL: how to ensure these (largely quantitative) data mean what we (and the learner) think so that we can make theoretically-grounded inferences from the data?

As a way to start tackling these challenges in learning settings such as long-term LL, we propose an approach we have termed 'single-case learning analytics' (SCLA), in which data is collected longitudinally about single learners, including data about their context and individual differences. Although LA often focuses on quantitative data (which is more amenable to big-data analysis techniques) [2], in SCLA we also exploit longitudinal *qualitative* data, as this kind of data and their analysis (including ethnographic methods) have traditionally been the main approach to understand meanings and contexts [3].

Yet, how exactly should we analyze and combine these longitudinal quantitative and qualitative data to understand single learners, their processes and contexts? Recent methodological proposals have tried combining quantitative ethnography methods (like epistemic network analysis, ENA) with standard LA techniques such as social network analysis (SNA) [4] or process mining [5]. Still, these methods are designed and require relatively large cohorts to generate enough data for analysis and to enable meaningful comparisons across learners.

The present methodological contribution illustrates how an SCLA approach can be applied to the longitudinal study of (informal) LL, and what are the main benefits of adding qualitative data and analyses (such as ENA) along with quantitative ones, for researchers, and eventually for learners themselves. This illustration is done through the example of a case study in which one learner gathered daily quantitative and qualitative/unstructured data related to his socio-emotional learning and workplace activities, for approximately nine months.

2   Lifelong and Socio-emotional Learning: The Role of Quantitative Ethnography

One of the main purported aims of educational systems is to develop contributing citizens and productive workers, who are also lifelong learners [6]. Indeed, international visions of long-term educational goals (like OECD's Learning Compass 2030 [7]) emphasize the need for citizens that are also lifelong learners, orienting towards long-term wellbeing (of self and others). This long-term orientation also emphasizes an aspect of learning and education that only recently has started to be systematically studied: the social and emotional aspects of learning.

Social and emotional learning (SEL) [6] is an approach promoting educational interventions that focus specifically on skills, competencies and attitudes that are not exclusively cognitive or content-related. SEL interventions often focus on competencies such as self-awareness (e.g., of one's emotions and values), self-management (including emotion and behavior regulation), social awareness (including perspective-taking and empathy), relationship skills (communication, cooperation, help-seeking or conflict negotiation) and responsible decision making (e.g., considering ethics and safety) [6]. SEL interventions have now become widespread in formal education, with SEL interventions/programs now implemented from preschool through higher education. Recent meta-analyses of literature have shown that SEL-focused interventions have remarkably positive effects, not only in addressing issues like aggression or problematic behaviors but also more generally in learners' mental health and academic achievement [8].

Research on SEL implementation beyond K-12 education (e.g., at the university level) is, however, scarce. Nonetheless, more than a hundred studies have examined the effects of different SEL interventions in higher education [9], with uneven results and only initial attempts at design guidelines for effective SEL interventions and programs in higher education. Yet, as Conley puts it, "the need for SEL does not end in high school" (p. 197) – nor in university, we may add. After their initial training, knowledge workers also need to cooperate, deal with emotions, set personal goals and make decisions responsibly. The implicit assumption that, once we reach adulthood, our socio-emotional skills are static, has little empirical basis.

Still, SEL in lifelong or workplace learning settings has barely been studied. Initial research has found correlations between LL and socio-emotional attitudes [10]. Efforts in the field of learning analytics (LA) have tried to use multimodal longitudinal data to extract insights into aspects of young researchers' self-regulated learning related to mental health and wellbeing [11]. And there exists a current within organizational training promoting emotional intelligence and related skills (e.g., [12]). However, despite the potential of LA (specially to foster self-awareness aspects of SEL) these efforts remain fragmentary and isolated, without a strong theoretical foundation.

To start addressing the lack of a theoretical foundation in the study of socio-emotional aspects of lifelong and workplace learning, we can turn our attention to findings in organizational psychology and the study of emotion and creativity at work. In her seminal work studying the diaries of more than 200 knowledge workers over several months, Teresa Amabile and colleagues found different kinds of events that had an impact on the creativity, productivity and emotional charge of a workday. In Amabile's work, *progress* events (and their flip side, setbacks to the work at hand) had the strongest effect on productivity and creativity in the workplace [13, 14].

Furthermore, the problem remains of what sources of evidence and methodological approaches are most suitable for the long-term and boundary-crossing nature of life-long learning. So far, most of the studies on lifelong learning are restricted to a single institution (e.g., one company or training institution) and relatively short timespans or infrequent data gathering, even when studies are labelled as longitudinal (e.g., the five-wave study of emotional competence and work outcomes in [15]). Long-term studies with a higher frequency of data gathering, like the diary studies of Amabile et al. mentioned above, have a higher chance of delving into the contextual and environmental influences of the socio-emotional experience (a well-known factor to pay attention in SEL [9]). Yet, extracting meaning from unstructured data sources such as diaries is very time-consuming.

Quantitative Ethnography (QE) techniques could aid us in exploring the meanings and patterns hiding in such unstructured data, from a variety of theoretical standpoints. Indeed, recent developments and trends in QE lead us to think that such methods could prove especially fruitful in understanding the socio-emotional aspects of LL: a) the increasing interest within the QE community about the time dimension of ethnographic analyses (e.g., in the concept of epistemic "trajectories", or how the networks of learner meanings evolve over time [16]); b) initial work in studying socio-emotional aspects of learning using ENA (e.g., in the context of school classrooms [17]); and c) the use of multiple theories to study a single phenomenon from multiple perspectives (see, e.g., the work of Bauer and colleagues in which additional insights about teachers' learning processes are extracted by applying multiple coding schemes to the analysis of their argumentations [18]). Yet, the question remains of exactly how such ethnographic methods can be introduced along with quantitative ones, and what kind of insights can come from such a fusion. The remainder of the paper delves into these questions, illustrating a potential answer.

3   Single-Case Learning Analytics (SCLA)

The starting point of our proposed approach is the realization that, in certain educational areas (like informal LL), cohorts of comparable learners may not be available, and thus we need to shift our focus to *single* learning processes (hence the name), without the (often implicit) need to compare a learner with others. We can borrow from previous definitions of LA (e.g., in [2]) to posit one for SCLA: "the use of computational means to collect, analyze and report data about a single learning entity and its context over long periods of time, for purposes of understanding and optimizing such learning and the environment(s) in which it occurs, without necessarily comparing it with other learning processes". From this definition, and taking into account the challenges in understanding learning over long periods of time outlined in the introduction, we can identify several key aspects of SCLA:

1. A focus on $N = 1$ analyses, e.g., within-subjects research designs and single-case experiments [19], rather than across-learner comparisons;

2. The use of longitudinal time-series data (and analysis techniques oriented towards that kind of data), in order to have enough data to use statistical and other big-data analysis techniques in LA;
3. The tracking of multiple contextual variables, to understand contextual and situational factors and their influence on the learning process as they interact with the learner's individual characteristics; and
4. The use of both quantitative and qualitative data, to triangulate [20] the inferences made from the limited data that a single learner generates.

SCLA, like any other data science that uses computation to extract insights from data, can be applied for different purposes: (1) to support the bottom-up exploration of data to gain an initial understanding about emergent relationships and patterns that may be of interest; (2) to support the top-down interpretation of data in the light of (learning) theories or models, both to understand the state and history of the learning process, as well as to validate and advance such theories and their operationalization; and (3) to support the enactment of interventions, both in terms of data gathering, inference and meaning-making about the intervention's effects.

In all those kinds of support, SCLA could serve a dual-stakeholder purpose: it aims both at supporting the learner directly by providing insights in-context (which can also be seen as a form of "member checking", often used in ethnographic and qualitative research [21]), as well as helping in the advancement of researchers' understanding of particular learning processes. In this sense, we should not forget the goal of research to elicit knowledge that is useful for learning situations beyond the one at hand. Hence, even if finding generalizable results is not the main aim of SCLA support, the use of this approach with multiple individual learners can eventually provide evidence of the generalizability of our theories, models and interventions (both in terms of average effects, the range/spread of such effects, and the role of contextual variables in them).

4 Case Study: Analyzing Adam's Progress

To illustrate the potential of an SCLA approach to investigate longitudinal data about lifelong learning, we have conducted a case study on the data of a knowledge worker (a researcher), gathered daily during approximately nine months. Through these data, we aim at providing illustrative answers to the following research questions:

- **RQ1**: *What kinds of insights can be drawn from the longitudinal gathering of qualitative and quantitative data (i.e., using an SCLA approach)?*
- **RQ2**: *What is the added value of gathering and analyzing qualitative data (especially, Epistemic Network Analysis) in extracting such insights?*

4.1 Research and Educational Context

The case study presented below is part of a longer-term design-based research (DBR) [22] aiming at the support of informal, lifelong social-emotional learning, concretely its *self-awareness* aspects (see Sect. 2) using SCLA technologies. The initial iterations of this DBR, which has gone on for more than two years, have focused on the basic feasibility of the SCLA approach, using a single lifelong learner (a researcher in a public European university, and one of the authors) as the main focus of analysis. In this sense, these initial iterations of the DBR could be likened to an autoethnography [23] (or, rather, a quantitative autoethnography). In the remainder of the paper, we will refer to the lifelong learner as Adam (fictitious name).

Following the work of Amabile in knowledge worker engagement (see Sect. 2), and the recent concern about disengagement and mental health problems in academics [24], the driving question of inquiry in this exploration of lifelong SEL is: "what makes for a good day in my work?" (i.e., what factors seem to have an influence or correlate with overall satisfaction and engagement at work).

During previous DBR iterations (not detailed here for space reasons), basic technology prototypes have been developed, and the data gathering and analysis means have been tuned, especially to avoid well-known barriers in long-term self-tracking such as tracking fatigue [25] (e.g., making the data to be gathered on a daily basis lightweight enough to be sustained over time), and to iteratively find contextual variables that seem to correlate with the learner's engagement and overall satisfaction. The methodology section below thus describes the data gathering and analysis as they took place in the present iteration on which the illustrative case study is based.

4.2 Methods

Data Gathering. In a similar approach to the diary studies performed by Amabile and colleagues [14], Adam gathered evidence on a daily basis, in the form of structured, quantitative questionnaires (but less exhaustively than in the original research, since this sort of self-tracking would have to be sustained, potentially, indefinitely). This structured part of the questionnaire included the number of hours slept (as an indicator of self-care strongly related with emotion regulation and many mental health outcomes [26]), the number of hours spent doing creative work or learning something new (as creativity and continuous learning had been identified in previous iterations as valuable for Adam, as well as in literature about worker engagement and satisfaction [13]). The questionnaire also inquired about the amount of time that Adam spent on focused work (in the form of "pomodoros" [27], or periods of uninterrupted, undistracted work - a technique that Adam used frequently to encourage himself to avoid multitasking and emails, also related in his experience and in literature with lower work satisfaction [28]). Finally, the quantitative variables contained a Likert-scale self-report measure of the overall satisfaction with that day's work (from −2, very unsatisfied, to +2, very satisfied). This structured data input was complemented with an unstructured, open-text diary entry aimed at recording the main events of the day, along with other reflections and the reporting of feelings and moods.

These daily entries were filled in at the end of each workday. In total, 166 daily entries were recorded in as many workdays, for a period of over nine months (holidays and weekends were not tracked unless Adam chose to work on those days). These unstructured diary entries were not very long, often taken the form of a few sentences:

the dataset analyzed here included 728 sentences in total, an average of 4.38 sentences per entry.

Data Analysis. To illustrate the kinds of insights that can be drawn from an SCLA approach (RQ1), different kinds of analyses have been performed: first, the quantitative data was solely analyzed, to establish a baseline for what can be extracted from such time-series data. More concretely, exploratory visual analyses were performed, as well as bivariate correlations between the different variables (especially, of quantitative contextual variables like the hours slept or worked, with the daily satisfaction score). Also, multivariate models were trained (stepwise linear regression and regression trees, both using the R implementation via the *rpart* and *MASS* packages) of the overall daily satisfaction as a function of the other variables, to understand linear and nonlinear relationships between such quantitative variables. These two kinds of models were chosen due to their higher interpretability, rather than to minimize modelling error (since both Adam and the rest of the research team needed to interpret and get insights from those models).

To illustrate the added value of adding qualitative data to an SCLA approach (RQ2), the open-text diary data was coded at the sentence-level (by Adam himself, to ensure that emic meaning was preserved) using two different coding schemes. First, a very simple coding scheme was used, regarding whether the sentence mentions progress or a setback in Adam's work (as per Amabile's conclusion that those two factors are the most important for worked engagement [14]). A second, more complex open coding scheme, loosely inspired in Amabile's Detailed Event Narrative Analysis (DENA) [29] was used to understand the different contextual influences and patterns that might be affecting the overall satisfaction, beyond those captured in the quantitative variables. As mentioned in Sect. 2, such contextual influences are a crucial component of SEL, and finding out their respective positive/negative influence on the learner's satisfaction and emotional tone can be an important step in developing emotional self-awareness. A total of 62 codes were obtained through this open coding process, but in the analyses below only the ten most-frequently appearing codes have been used, for brevity and visual simplicity's sake. Given that the participant that generated the data was also doing the qualitative coding, for this illustrative example we have foregone the use of multiple raters and inter-rater reliability, as well as member checking techniques.

These two sets of coding schemes were added to the (purely quantitative) multivariate models of overall satisfaction in two different ways: a) a naïve approach that used each of the sentence-level codes as a count variable (i.e., the number of appearances of the code in a certain day, or a value of 0 if the code does not appear that day); and b) the inclusion of a day's centroid using the four first dimensions of a means-rotated ENA [3] of the sentence-level codes (including both the simple coding scheme and the ten most frequent codes from the open coding scheme). The *rENA* R package was used to perform these calculations. These two sets of features were added into stepwise linear regression and regression trees. An additional reason for using these two types of models is the fact that they inherently perform feature selection, eliminating less predictive variables (in this case, of the overall daily satisfaction), aiming for parsimonious (yet reasonably accurate) models.

Finally, to attempt to quantify the added value of introducing such qualitative data and analyses into an SCLA approach, both in-sample and out-of-sample errors (via repeated 10-fold cross-validation) and performance metrics have been calculated on each of the trained models, to triangulate the evidence about which models seem to perform better: root mean squared error, R-squared, Akaike and Bayesian Information Criteria (AIC/BIC, only applicable to the linear models).

4.3   Results

Stage 1 of analysis (baseline quantitative exploration, no unstructured diary data). If we take the multivariate time series of the quantitative data input by Adam during the 166 workdays of the study, we can extract the following insights:

Basic Visualizations. Basic time series visualizations of the data can be provided for visual analysis, both to the researcher (as visual analysis is still a widely-used method in single-case experimental designs [30]) and to the learner, as illustrated in Fig. 1.

Basic Modelling. Aside from simple correlational models (e.g., correlation matrices to answer exploratory questions like "is my length of sleep correlated with my overall satisfaction with a day?"), we can also build multivariate models that relate the overall satisfaction with other quantitative variables tracked. Figure 2 represents two simple kinds of multivariate models (a stepwise linear regression and a regression tree), which reveal trends in the quantitative data that could be interesting both for learners and researchers.

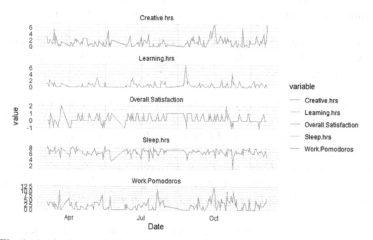

Fig. 1. Basic time-series visualization of Adam's longitudinal quantitative data.

In those models based on the purely quantitative data, interesting trends are already observable: the positive correlation of creative work or learning time (depending on whether we choose the linear or non-linear model) with the day's overall satisfaction.

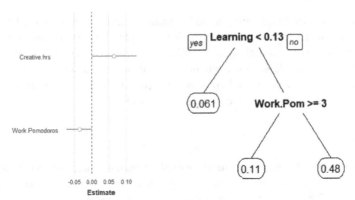

Fig. 2. Graphical representation of stepwise linear regression (left, coefficients and standard errors shown) and regression tree (right) models of a day's overall satisfaction (Likert from −2 to +2), as a function of the other quantitative variables available in the single-case dataset.

We can also observe an initially surprising negative relationship of focused work time (as measured by the amount of "pomodoros" done) in the linear model, which is qualified differently in the non-linear tree model (suggesting that there may be a "sweet spot" of small amounts of focused work that correlate with satisfaction).

Stage 2 of analysis (adding qualitative diary data and its analysis). What new insights or advantages can we obtain by adding and analyzing unstructured, qualitative data, in the form of diary entries?

Closing the Interpretive Loop. Just by having the open-text diary entries, we can get a better intuition of the purely quantitative insights in the previous section.

For instance, we can look at interesting points in the time series, like contrasting the high-satisfaction day in mid-October (see Fig. 1), with the low-satisfaction days that appeared shortly afterwards:

- High-satisfaction day: *"Really good day! Started early [...] working mostly revising and meeting students (good, advances, some creativity even). Lunch with colleagues to celebrate paper submission. [...] I did probably more than any recent day, but did not feel hectic!"*
- Low-satisfaction day: *"Long, tiring day of work as stress for the [journal paper] deadline increases [...]. Lots of meetings in the afternoon [...] and more work until very late. By the end of it, I'm cranky, tired and with a headache."*

"Naive" Inclusion of Qualitative Coding. As mentioned in the Methods section above, we had performed two kinds of qualitative coding on the diary entries, at the sentence level: a very simple coding scheme looking for statements indicating progress or setbacks/blockages, and a more complex bottom-up coding of the day's events.

As a first step in the usage of the qualitative data to complement the quantitative ones, we can naively include the appearance of a code (or counting the appearances of a code) in a particular day's diary entry and use those as additional binary/quantitative predictors in our modelling of a day's satisfaction. In Fig. 3 we can see that our stepwise linear models considered some of the codes (both from the simpler coding scheme and the more complex, open coding) as meaningful predictors.

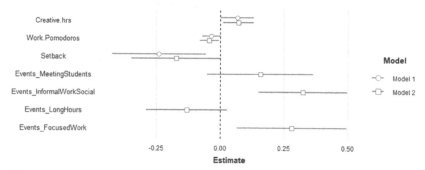

Fig. 3. Coefficients and standard errors of the stepwise linear regression models including qualitative codes "naïvely". Model 1 includes only the progress/setback codes. Model 2 includes both the progress/setback and the 10 most frequent codes of the open coding.

These enhanced models, along with the raw data (to close the interpretive loop) again give a more nuanced view of the effects of how the work is structured (e.g., the tradeoff between being able to do focused work and doing it for too long (as it can be seen in the negative coefficient of both *LongHours* and *Work.pomodoros*); or the positive relation of including informal social events at work (like having lunch with colleagues). For instance, the low-satisfaction day quoted above also exemplifies these trends (notice the absence of an informal social event in the low-satisfaction example, a day which had quantitative values of *Creative.hrs* = 0, and *Work.pomodoros* = 8).

Epistemic Network Analysis (ENA) as a Visualization Device. Once the qualitative coding is in place, we can start using quantitative ethnography methods such as ENA, on the data, to gain insights about the meanings captured by those codes, and how that translates into higher or lower satisfaction days. For instance, looking at the (means rotated, using a day's sentences as whole-conversation stanzas) epistemic network of Adam's diary entries (Fig. 4), we can see an even more nuanced picture of what distinguishes a "good day" from the others. Not only are certain codes more common in certain kinds of days (e.g., the focused work or informal social events at work for good days; the setbacks, long hours and physical exhaustion for non-good days); their connections are also important (e.g., focused work on a particular research project as prominent in the "good day" networks), especially in certain, more ambivalent codes. For example, meetings or generic tasks belong to good/non-good days depending on the other codes that appear that same day (hecticness, meaning no time for rest between tasks/meetings; vs. Informal social events, often done in breaks between tasks). We can further close the interpretive loop by looking at the raw data in two days that exemplify this pattern: *"Another hectic, fragmented day, back-to-back meetings (some of them OK - with students). Still, lunch in front of the computer and general sense of being surpassed by work. [...] End up dead*

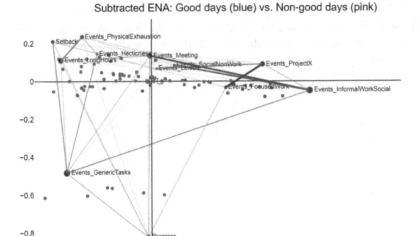

Fig. 4. Epistemic network of the qualitative coding of diary entries (including progress/setback and the 10 most frequent open codes), comparing days with high overall satisfaction (blue network, green points) with medium- and low-satisfaction ones (pink network, red points). (Color figure online)

tired and spent." (*Overall.Satisfaction* = −1) vs. *"Quite focused day of work, started a bit earlier and managed to keep closer to my plans (even if there were still changes and delays). Some good news [...] and lunch with colleagues also helped to get my spirits up."* (*Overall.Satisfaction* = +1).

Epistemic Network Analysis (ENA) to Enhance Modelling. Once the ENA is in place, we can use the main dimensions of the ENA space (i.e., those that explain most of the variance in the data) as quantitative variables in models of the overall satisfaction with a day (as done in the previous section), along with the quantitative variables which further characterize the context of a given day. For instance, adding the four first dimensions of ENA to the other quantitative variables, we find that most of such dimensions are found to be good predictors of overall satisfaction, both in (stepwise) linear and nonlinear (regression tree) models. For example, we can see that the first (means rotated) dimension has a large effect size in predicting whether a given day is a "good day" (MR1 in Fig. 5, left); and that certain smaller values of this ENA dimension, along with higher values of creative work and learning time, also tend to be part of "good days" (right-most branches in Fig. 5, right).

Evaluating/Comparing the Models of Satisfaction. So far, we have seen how data from qualitative analyses can be added to the baseline quantitative longitudinal data, to provide a more nuanced visualization, understanding and modelling of overall satisfaction, and its co-occurrence with a range of contextual factors in Adam's work life. But, to what extent does the addition of qualitative data (based on "naive qualitative" or ENA variables) add meaningful information to the models (vs. adding noise or overfitting to the data)? Given the relatively small size of the dataset analyzed here, and the fact that we do not claim generalizability of these particular models beyond Adam's particular case (cf. [33]), we can compare the different models presented so far, regarding several performance metrics (see the methods section above). The results of such comparison can be found in Table 1.

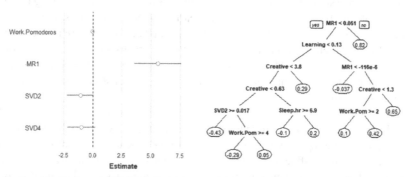

Fig. 5. Graphical representation of the models of overall satisfaction, taking into account the quantitative self-tracked measures and the four main ENA dimensions (labeled MR1, SVD2-4). Coefficients of a stepwise linear regression (left), and regression tree representation (right).

Table 1. Relative performance achieved by the different models of overall satisfaction presented in the paper. iR^2 = in-sample R-squared; AIC = Akaike Information Criterion; BIC = Bayesian Information Criterion; iRMSE = in-sample root mean squared error; oR^2 = out-of-sample R-squared; oRMSE = out-of-sample root mean squared error. Best values highlighted **in bold**.

Model type	Data used	iR2	AIC	BIC	iRMSE	oR2	oRMSE
Stepwise linear	Quantitative	0.034	292.45	304.9	0.57	0.034	0.588
Regression tree	Quantitative	0.1	NA	NA	0.55	0.045	0.573
Stepwise linear	Quantitative + naive progress	0.072	287.78	303.34	0.559	0.041	0.571
Stepwise linear	Quantitative + naive progress + open coding	0.215	**268.12**	296.13	0.514	0.11	0.556
Stepwise linear	Quantitative + ENA	0.166	272.12	**290.8**	0.53	0.087	0.562
Regression tree	Quantitative + ENA	**0.253**	NA	NA	**0.501**	**0.146**	**0.554**

We can observe that, for all model evaluation/comparison metrics, models that include data coming from qualitative data (either naively considered, or in the form of ENA dimensions) perform substantially better. The best-performing model seems to be the regression tree using both quantitative and ENA variables, which also provides a relatively simple set of rules and insights, for both researchers and learners.

5 Discussion and Future Work

The results from the illustrative case study above exemplify some of the main character-istics of an SCLA approach (see Sect. 3), as applied to Adam's lifelong SEL dataset: the triangulation of longitudinal quantitative and qualitative data and the insights obtained from it (e.g., the increasing nuance from the initial models' negative relationship between the *Work.Pomodoros* variable and overall satisfaction vs. The notion of "focused work on project X" as a marker of positive satisfaction, in later models); or the tracking of multi-ple contextual variables through the codes appearing in the diary entries (e.g., meetings or informal social events at work). The insights from these analyses are also congruent with previous research by Amabile et al. (e.g., work setbacks as negative predictors of satisfaction) [14], with an additional layer of contextual specificity and the ability to close the interpretive loop that the availability of the raw unstructured data (i.e., the diary entries) award.

These results and insights, however, should not be taken as generalizable to other lifelong learners (nor was it our intention). Yet, a similar SCLA approach could be used with a cohort of lifelong or workplace learners, to try to tease out more generalizable insights or contextual influences. We are indeed starting a study into PhD students' experiences of progress in their dissertations, using techniques and data related to the ones presented here.

The aforementioned lack of generalizability also poses interesting challenges going forward: how could these analyses and insights be scaled up so that we can support every lifelong learner (potentially, every citizen) out there while taking into account their uniqueness? Aside from the theoretical challenges of learners' variety of goals (and the-ories that may be relevant to each case), technological issues also need to be addressed, such as the development of automated qualitative coding that requires minimal amounts of human labor (while remaining inspectable and improvable), either using rules-based approaches [31] or natural language processing (NLP) techniques. Such automated cod-ing of individual learner data would also have the added benefit of potentially maintaining learners' privacy in a way that current centralized and researcher-driven analyses cannot.

Aside from the generalizability issue, the case study presented here is mainly pro-vided as an illustration of a methodological contribution and exhibits several limitations: the qualitative analyses were performed by a single coder (even if that coder was the author of the diaries himself); the progress/setback coding scheme used is an overly simplified version of Amabile's research on worker satisfaction and productivity, and only the most frequent open codes were used for modeling (to keep the visualizations readable). Furthermore, the time-series nature of the data has not really been exploited in the analyses above, and computational techniques such as sequence analysis or hidden Markov models (HMMs) could have been applied to extract time-dependent patterns and hidden states of Adam's socio-emotional work life. Also, the timespan of the illustrative case study (9 months) is rather limited, compared with our ultimate aim of providing a truly lifelong account of a learner's evolution.

There are other aspects of the SCLA approach that have not been fully explored in this brief account: a more extensive use of "theoretical ecumenism" (i.e., the use of multiple theories and frameworks to analyze the data, to draw epistemic relationships between multiple theories, and better understand the phenomenon at hand, as shown by [18]); the issue of how much data is enough to start drawing inferences and insights about even a single learner (cf. The concept of "theoretical saturation" [3]); or the iterative nature of the SCLA approach, to get the right balance between richer data and a data-gathering scheme that can be sustained over such long periods of time.

In general, we hope this methodological contribution expands the range of settings where QE methods can be applied to the analysis of individual learning, as long as there is the sort of meaning-making (or "dialogue with oneself") that self-tracking and diary data represent. In any case, nothing precludes the quantitative ethnographer to use the SCLA techniques presented here with a group of learners as a "single-case" learner entity, studying their learning process for an extended period of time, without necessarily comparing them with other groups. We also hope that this approach sparks further discussion within the community about how to make QE/ENA analyses available and useful to learners themselves, as our ethical and methodological duty (cf. The concept of "member checking" in qualitative research [32]).

Acknowledgements. This project has received funding from the European Union's Horizon 2020 research and innovation programme under grant agreement No. 669074.

References

1. Field, J.: Is lifelong learning making a difference? Research-based evidence on the impact of adult learning. In: Aspin, D.N., Chapman, J., Evans, K., Bagnall, R. (eds.) Second international handbook of lifelong learning, pp. 887–897. Springer Netherlands, Dordrecht (2012). https://doi.org/10.1007/978-94-007-2360-3_54
2. Ferguson, R.: Learning analytics: drivers, developments and challenges. Int. J. Technol. Enhanced Learn. 4(5/6), 304 (2012). https://doi.org/10.1504/IJTEL.2012.051816
3. Shaffer, D.W.: Quantitative ethnography. Lulu.com (2017)
4. Swiecki, Z., Shaffer, D.W.: iSENS: an integrated approach to combining epistemic and social network analyses. In: Proceedings of the Tenth International Conference on Learning Analytics and Knowledge, pp. 305–313 (2020)
5. Melzner, N., Greisel, M., Dresel, M., Kollar, I.: Using process mining (PM) and epistemic network analysis (ENA) for comparing processes of collaborative problem regulation. In: Eagan, B., Misfeldt, M., Siebert-Evenstone, A. (eds.) ICQE 2019. CCIS, vol. 1112, pp. 154–164. Springer, Cham (2019). https://doi.org/10.1007/978-3-030-33232-7_13
6. Weissberg, R.P., Durlak, J.A., Domitrovich, C.E., Gullotta, T.P.: Social and emotional learning: past, present, and future. In: Handbook of Social and Emotional Learning: Research and Practice, pp. 3–19. The Guilford Press, New York (2015)
7. Learning Compass 2030 - Organisation for Economic Co-operation and Development. https://www.oecd.org/education/2030-project/teaching-and-learning/learning/learning-compass-2030/. Accessed 11 June 2020
8. Corcoran, R.P., Cheung, A.C.K., Kim, E., Xie, C.: Effective universal school-based social and emotional learning programs for improving academic achievement: a systematic review and meta-analysis of 50 years of research. Educ. Res. Rev. 25, 56–72 (2018). https://doi.org/10.1016/j.edurev.2017.12.001
9. Conley, C.S.: SEL in higher education. In: Handbook of Social and Emotional Learning: Research and Practice, pp. 197–212 (2015)

10. Akcaalan, M.: Investigation of the relationships between lifelong learning and social emotional learning. Online Submiss. **1**, 14–20 (2016)
11. Di Mitri, D., Scheffel, M., Drachsler, H., Börner, D., Ternier, S., Specht, M.: Learning pulse: a machine learning approach for predicting performance in self-regulated learning using multi-modal data. In: Proceedings of the Seventh International Learning Analytics and Knowledge Conference, pp. 188–197. ACM (2017)
12. Cherniss, C., Adler, M.: Promoting Emotional Intelligence in Organizations: Make Training in Emotional Intelligence Effective. American Society for Training and Development (2000)
13. Amabile, T.M., Barsade, S.G., Mueller, J.S., Staw, B.M.: Affect and creativity at work. Adm. Sci. Q. **50**(3), 367–403 (2005). https://doi.org/10.2189/asqu.2005.50.3.367
14. Amabile, T., Kramer, S.: The Progress Principle: Using Small Wins to Ignite Joy, Engagement, and Creativity at Work. Harvard Business Press, Boston (2011)
15. Parmentier, M., Pirsoul, T., Nils, F.: Emotional processes in career adaptation: a longitudi-nal study in an adult education program. Presented at the 50th International Conference of EUCEN: Times of Transition – The Role of University Lifelong Learning (2018)
16. Foster, A., Shah, M., Barany, A., Talafian, H.: Tracing identity exploration trajectories with quantitative ethnographic techniques: a case study. In: Eagan, B., Misfeldt, M., Siebert-Evenstone, A. (eds.) ICQE 2019. CCIS, vol. 1112, pp. 77–88. Springer, Cham (2019). https://doi.org/10.1007/978-3-030-33232-7_7
17. Hod, Y., Katz, S., Eagan, B.: Refining qualitative ethnographies using epistemic network analysis: a study of socioemotional learning dimensions in a humanistic knowledge building community. Comput. Educ. 103943 (2020)
18. Bauer, E., et al.: Using ENA to analyze pre-service teachers' diagnostic argumentations: a conceptual framework and initial applications. In: Eagan, B., Misfeldt, M., Siebert-Evenstone, A. (eds.) ICQE 2019. CCIS, vol. 1112, pp. 14–25. Springer, Cham (2019). https://doi.org/10.1007/978-3-030-33232-7_2
19. Kazdin, A.E.: Single-Case Research Designs: Methods for Clinical and Applied Settings. Oxford University Press, Oxford (2011)
20. Fielding, N.G.: Triangulation and mixed methods designs: Data integration with new research technologies. J. Mixed Methods Res. **6**(2), 124–136 (2012). https://doi.org/10.1177/1558689812437101
21. Houghton, C., Casey, D., Shaw, D., Murphy, K.: Rigour in qualitative case-study research. Nurse Res. **20**, 12–17 (2013)
22. Wang, F., Hannafin, M.J.: Design-based research and technology-enhanced learning environ-ments. Educ. Technol. Res. Dev. **53**, 5–23 (2005)
23. Sambrook, S.A., Jones, N., Doloriert, C.: Employee engagement and autoethnography: being and studying self. J. Workplace Learn. **26**, 172–187 (2014)
24. Woolston, C.: Feeling overwhelmed by academia? You are not alone. Nature **557**, 129 (2018)
25. Choe, E.K., Lee, N.B., Lee, B., Pratt, W., Kientz, J.A.: Understanding quantified-selfers' practices in collecting and exploring personal data. In: Proceedings of the SIGCHI Conference on Human Factors in Computing Systems, pp. 1143–1152 (2014)
26. Walker, M.: Why We Sleep: The New Science of Sleep and Dreams. Penguin, Harmondsworth (2017)
27. Cirillo, F.: The pomodoro technique (the pomodoro). Agile Process. Softw. Eng. **54**, 35 (2006)
28. Essiam, J.O., Mensah, M.E., Kudu, L.K., Gyamfi, G.D.: Influence of job stress on job satis-faction among university staff: analytical evidence from a public university in Ghana. Int. J. Econ. Commer. Manag. **3**, 1–5 (2015)
29. Amabile, T.M., Mueller, J.S., Archambault, S.M.: Coding manual for the DENA coding scheme (Detailed Event Narrative Analysis) (2003)
30. Lane, J.D., Gast, D.L.: Visual analysis in single case experimental design studies: brief review and guidelines. Neuropsychol. Rehabil. **24**, 445–463 (2014)

31. Cai, Z., Siebert-Evenstone, A., Eagan, B., Shaffer, D.W., Hu, X., Graesser, A.C.: nCoder+: a semantic tool for improving recall of nCoder coding. In: Eagan, B., Misfeldt, M., Siebert-Evenstone, A. (eds.) ICQE 2019. CCIS, vol. 1112, pp. 41–54. Springer, Cham (2019). https://doi.org/10.1007/978-3-030-33232-7_4

32. Harper, M., Cole, P.: Member checking: Can benefits be gained similar to group therapy. Qual. Rep. **17**, 510–517 (2012)

33. Shaffer, D.W., Serlin, R.C.: What good are statistics that don't generalize? Educ. Researcher **33**, 14–25 (2004)

Counting the Game: Visualizing Changes in Play by Incorporating Game Events

Jennifer Scianna[1]([✉]), David Gagnon[1] [ID], and Mariah A. Knowles[2] [ID]

[1] Wisconsin Center for Education Research, University of Wisconsin-Madison, Madison, WI, USA
{jscianna,djgagnon}@wisc.edu
[2] Information School, University of Wisconsin-Madison, Madison, WI, USA
mariah.knowles@wisc.edu

Abstract. Lakeland is an educational game developed with the intent of exposing secondary science students to complex systems, namely phosphorous cycling. Data collected anonymously through embedded logging structures was sampled to include sessions where players returned to play more than once during December 2019 consistent with classroom play. Using Epistemic Network Analysis, games from the same player were compared to identify significant differences in how players responded to game events. Consistent with prior research around systems thinking, players' ability to think through temporally distant phenomena, as evidenced by changes in their use of time manipulation and short vs. self-sustaining strategies in Game 1 and Game 2, demonstrate the potential for ENA to uncover and even assess complex student behaviors using log data. Furthermore, this study highlights the importance of including computer-generated data alongside the human-generated reactions being logged.

Keywords: Educational games · Systems thinking · Game-Based assessment

1 Introduction

"You set out to form a new town called Lakeland. Your people love to play in the water. Grow your town without ruining the lakes," [1]. Lakeland's players receive quite the edict upon beginning a new game. A relatively open landscape sets the stage as players build their first house near the beloved lake, but despite the serene music and lighthearted graphics, the tone is set. As a player, you have the power to make or break Lakeland; don't mess up.

The decision space afforded to players is sufficiently wide to see a variety of responses to the problem set out before them. This variety creates an opportune moment for us to gain insight into how players begin to piece together the complex systems that underlie the game's simulation, a challenging proposition given that students often fail to capture the dynamics of complex systems [2]. Yet each time a player's action yields some response from the game, there is a new opportunity presented for the student to assemble a causal relationship that underlies the system. The student and simulation go round and

© Springer Nature Switzerland AG 2021
A. R. Ruis and S. B. Lee (Eds.): ICQE 2021, CCIS 1312, pp. 218–231, 2021.
https://doi.org/10.1007/978-3-030-67788-6_15

round creating a "circle of gameplay" that could be likened to a conversation [3]. We can use log data to "eavesdrop" on the player's conversation with the game to better understand how players progress in their ability to navigate the rules of the game.

While prior games-based, quantitative ethnographic (QE) research has focused primarily on user actions in the analysis of learning [4], collaboration [5], and student quit behavior [6] in games, in this study, we propose the addition of computer-generated events. We utilize Lakeland as the context to explore this while answering the question, "How do player responses to in-game feedback change between first and second games played?" Through this process, we demonstrate that the inclusion of game data allows visualization of the interplay between game and player and is useful in understanding student growth. This work directly contributes to the growing body of work taking a QE approach to analyzing user-generated log data. With this approach, we demonstrate that ENA can effectively visualize differences between first-time play sessions and repeat play sessions by focusing the model on the player-feedback game loop and indicators of systems thinking.

2   Relevant Literature

2.1   Systems Thinking in Science

Student success in Lakeland hinges on the students' ability to understand the varied relationships to seek a solution. They must consider more than just a series of causal events to see the problem posed in a more holistic way, a task that may be considered a "wicked problem" [7]. This framing draws a particular definition of system thinking that highlights the unique nature of problems, interplay between attempts to address the problem and how it is framed, and ambiguity of the causality particularly as it related to the temporal distance between an intervention and any direct effects." [8]. Grohs et al. operationalize the "wicked problem" framing in their attempt to assess systems thinking in students by centering their assessment around student ability to work within three dimensions of understanding the problem, recognizing competing perspectives, and ability to think through different points in time incorporating both historic and present considerations [9].

If this seems like a tall order for students, it's because it is. In problem-based contexts, students often fall short of being able to consider varied aspects of the systems at play to propose solutions [3, 10]. The trouble stems from failing to notice aspects of the system that are either temporally distant, varying in impact, or non-obvious, microscopic as a mechanism [3]. The further away a consequence is from the causal agent, whether enacted by a student or occurring in the environment, the less likely a student is to detect the relationship and incorporate it into their understanding of the system. A student has to notice both the cause and the effect with a short enough time passing to connect the two [3]. Despite systems thinking appearing in a significant portion of the cross-cutting concepts in the Next Generation Science Standards [11], the context in which students encounter these concepts tend to be ill-suited for success. Environmental systems in particular have presented challenges for students in perceiving how toxins accumulate in the environment, understanding the intricacies of stock and flow systems, and reconciling the temporal delays between actions and their effect [10].

The persistent appearance of time as a determining factor for student understanding is something well-suited to exploiting in game contexts. In real-time strategy games, the ability to manipulate time is often afforded to the player easing the demand on players to remember events that occurred long ago and tie them to current consequences. Everything becomes more connected for those who know what to look for. Additionally, rules allow designers to assist students in noticing phenomena by forcing spatial proximity, for example encouraging towns to be in close proximity to the lake in Lakeland. Furthermore, the natural scaffolding that exists in game environments perpetually attunes players to the information available to them through tutorials and visual indicators; thus, as students become more comfortable with the "rules of the game," they will likely progress in their ability to engage in relevant systems thinking.

2.2   Educational Games and Assessment

As noted above, educational games are a particularly good format for circumventing many of the issues that inhibit systems thinking because they put players in a situated learning environment that allows for interactions that might not otherwise be cost or time efficient [12]. These environments also provide a unique opportunity to gain insights into or assess how students think about or approach problems. This can happen by accident through the nature of the task given the student, or they can be intentionally designed and embedded. The latter example, known as stealth assessments are named as such because the assessment is tied to the game mechanic itself and imperceptible to the player [13].

Lakeland was not explicitly developed with stealth assessments in mind. However, we can retroactively compare how an expert system engineer would balance competing problems in Lakeland with how a novice student might approach the same task. Using the idea of an epistemic frame [12] to evaluate student actions, the engineer would be more likely to see the connection between feedback from seemingly disparate areas [9] to find long-term solutions whereas novices (secondary science students) would be more likely to employ short term solutions. Analysis of the solutions players seek may serve as a proxy for a designed assessment.

The student's proposed solutions and decisions are not generated in isolation; they are perpetually influenced by the "circle of gameplay" where the "gamer's input and the game's output reciprocally influence each other," [3]. Players are made aware of hidden mechanisms by the game feedback, and the way a player responds to game challenges and feedback provides evidence of their level of understanding of the underlying content [13]. Therefore, it is essential that we consider the dynamic between game and player as proposed by Owen and Baker [14] who advocate for including game feedback events as essential components of logging systems for behavioral modeling in educational video games.

2.3   Games and Quantitative Ethnography

Prior work has centered on the work of epistemic games or quantitative ethnographic approaches to game data, but there are several gaps that have been identified. Arastoopour Irgens and colleagues began looking at in-game data through ENA modeling, but the observed behaviors of the students largely focused on textual data communicated to teammates or non-player characters in the virtual internship [4]. More recently, log data has been analyzed using ENA to identify trends amongst students who quit challenging levels in Physics Playground, but the analysis was limited to students' actions [11]. Feedback provided by the game did not close the loop of player experience. It is within reason then that by connecting player actions to feedback received, we can build a better understanding of the player's decision space. We seek to extend prior assessment work using Epistemic Network Analysis in games as a method for visualizing the shift in the relationship between in-game feedback and student actions from first play session to subsequent sessions.

3   Methods

3.1   Context

Lakeland was designed to teach students about the complex ways nutrient cycles are manifested in agricultural and environmental contexts, and in doing so encourage systems thinking throughout gameplay. Like many real-time strategy games, players are constantly making decisions that have short-term and long-term impacts in the game space. In Lakeland, the primary player decisions include what they can buy and how they use the resources - corn, milk, and manure - from farms and dairies (Fig. 1). Ultimately, success in the game hinges on understanding how to manage soil nutrition for productivity in order to expand without causing algae blooms.

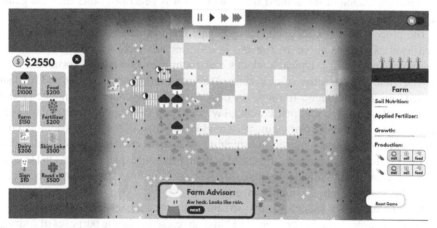

Fig. 1. Player decisions are limited to decisions around what they buy (left) and how they choose to utilize resources, either before or after production (right).

Players are assisted by a near-constant stream of feedback. As play begins, tutorials are presented by different advisors, a manifestation of the different perspectives inherent to wicked problems [9]: the farm advisor introduces players to the logistics of manure replenishing nutrients in the soil, the mayor focuses on expansion of the town, and the business advisor pushes the player to turn products into profits. Each potential avenue for players to focus on is further elucidated in the achievements available that focus on town growth, number of farms, amount of money, and size of algae bloom (for the destructive player). In the town, farmbits (townspeople) report their satisfaction (Fig. 2a) and needs (Fig. 2b) through emojis. Similarly, farm and lake tiles show visual indicators of production (Fig. 2c) and changing nutrient levels (Fig. 2d). However, learning the rules of a game and its underlying system takes time, and it is not uncommon that players will not be successful at deciphering the help that game is trying to provide on their first try.

Fig. 2. Positive and negative feedback provided to players from visual cues comes from Farmbits or Farms. (a) A fed Farmbit. (b) A tired Farmbit. (c) A farm that has produced corn. (d) A nutrient depleted farm (upper left) and nutrient rich farm (lower right).

3.2   Data Collection

CSV files containing both processed and raw user data for December 2019 were downloaded from the Open Game Data website [12]. Data is anonymized and contains no additional indication of the context under which it was generated other than the game itself.

The processed data CSV included aggregate features calculated at the scale of a given level as well as an entire session. Session records were filtered to obtain sessions representative of a typical student's classroom play experience: sessions length between 5 and 45 min, active (user generated) event counts greater than 20, and English selected (original language). To subset the data, the processed data was segmented using the "num_play" feature into first ("num_play" = 1) and subsequent ("num_play" > 1) games played. From those two segments, a random selection of ten first sessions and ten subsequent sessions was obtained to further down sample. Final selection for included sessions was based on whether a player had both first and subsequent sessions in December as we wanted to eliminate possible interference from long spans of time between plays. This yielded eight session for investigation.

The raw data CSV included a live stream of events for each player organized by session ID. In order to make the event data "human readable" for the purposes of coding, a Python script turned the JSON event data from each line into a textual description of the event using the documentation provided by the developers in the associated ReadMe file. For example, Event 7 is a "Buy" event that is sent with JSON metadata including the item selected to buy, tile data including description, nutrition and position in terms of X, Y coordinates on the map, whether the player can build on that tile, and the information of every tile they hovered over when choosing where to place their item.

3.3 Quantitative Analysis

Filtered data was analyzed to both confirm the effectiveness of the filters and to consider similarity of student experience between first and subsequent game play experiences. A paired, two-tailed t-test was used to compare length of play and number of student actions between games. This was essential to ensure that a student simply did not act in the first game, causing their lone farmbit to die, and necessitating a restart of the game. Additionally, paired, two-tailed t-tests were used to confirm that there were no significant differences in how many of the twenty-six possible tutorials players encountered and how many of the sixteen possible achievements they received. Game tutorials occur as students progress through the game introducing them to concepts as they go. The tutorials range in conceptual complexity from simply explaining the buy mechanism to introducing the idea of fertilizer runoff and algae blooms.

3.4 Qualitative Coding

Codes were developed using a grounded approach based on our own play experiences, prior observations of student game play, and special consideration for feedback and behaviors related to systems thinking. To begin, we played through the game considering the feedback given and our actions before referring to the ReadMe files for the game. We considered game events in isolation to simplify how we looked for a given behavior. For example, in considering the meaning of buying corn, we went through all the possible reasons a player would buy corn. We then looked at the game play log and discussed what was happening in each situation that a player was buying corn. Based on those observations, the code of short-term solution was created to represent the observations that players often bought corn when (1) they had farmbits in crisis with no chance of producing corn or (2) they did not have the resources necessary to invest in a self-sustaining solution. We applied a similar method for game event codes deriving them via a combination of developer intent and our response to the feedback during gameplay.

A final pass on the codes and coordinating definitions sought to incorporate the systems thinking literature. Acknowledging the importance of temporal distance in a student's ability to comprehend complex systems, a code was introduced for Time Manipulation with the thought that students who were trying to understand relationships would use the fast-forward tool to shorten the time between interactions. This aligned with our own verbalized use of the fast-forward and pause features during initial game play and student observations.

With the codes completed, we turned our attention to applying the codes to the log file dataset using the nCoder webtool [16]. Since the event text was generated through a uniform script, our collaborative code-defining process yielded high levels of agreement between coders and the automated coder. Individual codes and agreement measures can be seen in Table 1.

Table 1. Codebook (Kappa agreement reported in order of Rater 1 vs Classifier; Rater 2 vs Classifier, and Rater 1 vs Rater 2.)

Code	Definition	Example	Agreement
Positive farmbit	Farmbit (townsperson) expresses contentment or happiness with emojis	Lucy at 26,26; I've got my floatie on. Swimming emoji	1.00** 1.00** 1.00**
Negative farmbit	Farmbit expresses sadness or distress	Sidney at 20,23... I'm tired. Sleepy face	0.96* 0.96* 1.00**
New resources	When a resource is produced and appears on the map	Farmharvested at 25,25; Items marked for use and sell	1.00** 0.92* 0.92*
Time manipulation	When the player changes game speed	current: fast, previous: play, Player Changed	1.00* 1.00* 1.00*
World feedback	When visual feedback indicates a problem with a world tile	Farmfail; farm at 23,23; Items marked for sell and sell	0.95* 0.92* 0.92*
Short term solutions	Player buys resource that doesn't have lasting impact (food, manure, skimmer)	Tile: Growing, Medium nutrition, land at 19,30; buy: food	0.96* 1.00** 0.96*
Self-sustaining solutions	Players buys a long-term solution such as a farm or dairy	Tile: Growing, Medium nutrition; at 29,24; buy farm	1.00** 1.00** 1.00**
Resource management	When players indicate a resource should be used, sold, or consumed	Itemuseselect; item at 27,23; food for use, Previously Sell	1.00** 1.00** 1.00**

*rho ≤ 0.05, **rho < 0.01

3.5 Epistemic Network Analysis

Epistemic Network Analysis [17] was used to explore the data using the ENA Web Tool [18]. Units of analysis were defined as all events associated with a given game (Game 1 or Game 2) subset by Speaker (Player or Game) and Session_id. For example, one unit included all lines associated with player X's first game. The ENA algorithm uses a moving window to judge co-temporality when constructing a network model [19], defined here as 10 events. A window size of 10 was chosen due to the rapid nature of feedback generated from the game and co-occurrence of logging events (i.e. If the game generates new resources, and a farmbit reacts immediately, there may be two more actions before the player has a chance to respond. In order to ensure that we were capturing connections between the game and the player.) The resulting networks are aggregated for the categories of first or second game. Networks for third game or higher were removed due to having too few samples.

The ENA model normalized the networks for all units of analysis before they were subjected to a dimensional reduction using singular value decomposition, which produces orthogonal dimensions that maximize the variance explained by each dimension. A means rotation was performed between the groups to better interpret the axis.

Networks were visualized using network graphs where nodes correspond to the codes, and edges reflect the relative frequency of co-occurrence, or connection, between two codes. These networks were compared using network difference graphs that illustrated differences between first games and second games by subtracting the weight of each connection in the Second Game Played network from the corresponding connections in the First Game Played network. To further test for differences we applied a Mann-Whitney test to the location of points in the projected ENA space for units in each category.

4 Results

4.1 Qualitative Counts

After filtering sessions, eight sessions were identified as having both first and second sessions that occurred in December. The average session durations for Game 1 and Game 2 were 11.6 min and 15.7 min, respectively. Players in Game 1 acted more frequently than those in Game 2 logging one player action for every 3.06 events logged by the game as opposed to a 1 to 3.38 ratio for Game 2. A two-tailed, paired t-test demonstrated no significant differences in the play sessions regarding length of play or number of actions: session duration p = .30, session active events p = .11, and session events p = .11. This indicates that play within each of the selected games was comparable and confirms the effectiveness of the filter in looking for games that fit the typical classroom use. Paired, two-tailed t-tests also compared the number of achievements players received and number of tutorials they encountered in Game 1 and Game 2 and found no significant differences (p = .06, p = .10).

4.2 Quantitative Models

Epistemic Network Analysis of Game One and Game Two yielded an ENA model that had co-registration correlations of 0.98 (Pearson) and 0.98 (Spearman) for the first dimension and 0.99 (Pearson) and 0.99 (Spearman) for the second indicating a strong goodness of fit between the visualization and the original model. Along the X axis (MR1), a Mann-Whitney test showed that Game 1 (Mdn = 0.05, N = 28) was statistically significantly different at the alpha = 0.05 level from Game 2 (Mdn = −0.44, N = 16 U = 124.00, p = 0.01, r = 0.45).

Figure 3 shows the relationships most prominent in Game 1. We choose to specifically focus on relationships between player actions with the game and player actions with themselves. Player-Game connections are dominated by frequent connections between *Positive Farmbit Feedback* and *Resource Management* and *Positive Farmbit Feedback* and *Time Manipulation*. Player-Player connections most often occur between *Resource Management* and *Time Manipulation*.

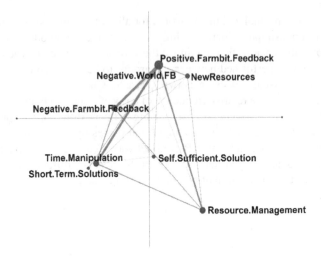

Fig. 3. ENA plot of Game 1 sessions.

In Game 2, shown in Fig. 4, the connection between *Positive Farmbit Feedback* and *Resource Management* dominates the player-game connections with *Time Manipulation* and *Positive Farmbit Feedback* also showing a strong connection. There are not any strong player to player connections.

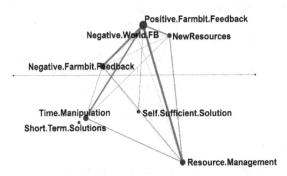

Fig. 4. ENA plot of Game 2 sessions.

In these plots, the Y axis is interpreted as game feedback (positive axis) vs. player events (negative axis). This allows visualization of the connections between player and game as they run vertically through the plot. In the comparison plot, a means rotation of the X axis elucidates the difference between first and second game players (Fig. 5).

Short-term, reactionary actions such as *Time Manipulation* and *Short Term Solutions* fall towards the left on the x axis whereas sustainable, planning actions such as *Resource Management* fall towards the right. First game players tend to manipulate time more in connection to farmbit feedback whereas second game players manipulate time in connection to new resources. Similarly, positive feedback is more often connected to short-term solutions during first games and resource management during second games.

1 – 2

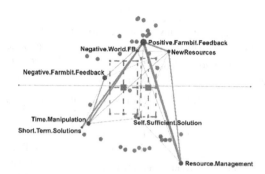

Units: games_played > session_id > speaker
Conversation: games_played

Fig. 5. Comparison ENA plot of Game 1 (red network) and Game 2 (blue network) demonstrate the differences between games. (Color figure online)

4.3 Qualitative Description

To better understand the differences in how players respond to feedback in Game 1 as opposed to Game 2, we can focus on the connections between Time Manipulation in each case. Tables 2 and 3 illustrate narrative differences between how *New Resources* and *Positive Farmbit Feedback* are connected to *Time Manipulation*. The selections chosen include 10 log events to parallel the size of the moving stanza used in the ENA models. Events that were not coded in ways relevant to the model were left in the sequence and marked with "N/A," but they were described in the explanation with possible impact.

The player we observe in the Game 1 event sequence is not showing that they are planning ahead. They have not checked on any of the resources in this section. They have

Table 2. Event sequence of a Game 1 session.

Log event	Coded	Explanation
Farmharvested tile at 24,23, Items marked for use and use	New Resources	The player sees their farm get harvested. Both corn that are produced display on the game board. They are not consumed by a farmbit because they are not hungry. While it was raining, any fertilizer that was placed onto farms by the player moved, but the rain stops. The game slows down the speed of play as another farm produces more food. Sidney goes to the lake to get water to restart the farm. The player pauses the game, likely to take inventory of all the new resources produced after the rain. The rain tutorial ends. The player starts the time back at a normal pace. Noting the abundance of corn, the player selects an item and marks it for sale
Rainstopped	N/A	
Speed: Changed to playfrom fast by game	N/A	
Farmharvested tile at 23,23, Items marked for use and use	New Resources	
Emote Sidney, at 26,26, I've got my floatie on flamingo swim emoji	Positive Farmbit	
Speed: Changed to pause from play by Player	Time Manipulation	
Checkpoint End: Rain	N/A	
Speed to play from pause by Player	Time Manipulation	
Selecti tem item: at 22,22, food for use	N/A	
Itemuseselect item: at 22,22, food for sell, Previously Use	Resource Management	

Table 3. Event Sequence of a Game 2 Session

Log event	Coded	Explanation
Emote Mary, at 21,21, Ive got my floatie on flamingo swim emoji	Positive Farmbit	The player sees their Farmbit enter the water, likely to begin growing another harvest at the farm. The player decides to sell one unit of food, which is not the same resource Mary takes off to sell. The player checks on two other items which lets them see that both are set to be used for food. The player slows time down in preparation for new resources to be produced. Mary continues tending the farm that just produced by getting water with their floatie and taking produce to be sold at the market. The player moves the game back to fast to speed through the production
Itemuseselect item: at 20,24, food for sell, Previously Use	Resource Management	
Emote Mary, at 17,22, Off to market sale	Positive Farmbit	
Selectitem item: at 22,24, food for use	Information Seeking	
Selectitem item: at 23,25, food for use	Information Seeking	
Speed: Changed to fast from play by Player.	Time Manipulation	
Farmharvested: at 22,24, Items marked for use and use	New Resources	
Emote Mary, at 21,21, Ive got my floatie on flamingo swim emoji	Positive Farmbit	
Emote Mary, at 17,24, Off to market sale	Positive Farmbit	
Speed: Changed to play from fast by Player	Time Manipulation	

gotten several pieces of feedback that production is continuing successfully through the farmbit collecting water to restart growth and the new resources now accumulating on the board. It is possible that the player is working towards stockpiling their resources, so they do not need to change their use. However, when the game encourages the player to slow down, calling attention to the changes that have happened after the rain, the player feels it is necessary to slow further and pauses the underlying simulation. It is only in this moment, when the feedback from the game is paused, that the player begins to interact with their resources and plan.

In the selected sequence from Game 2, the player is still changing the speed of the game, but it is not in direct relation to an immediate event. They are responding in order to plan and set up future actions. This is evident through positioning of emotes and actions the player is taking. While the player marks an item for sale at tile 20, 24, the Farmbit takes items to market from tiles 17, 22 and 17, 24 which came from a different farm that previously produced. The player is also checking unrelated items available on the board, likely to confirm their plan.

How players choose to use their ability to manipulate the passage of time in Lakeland differs between Game 1 and Game 2. Through looking at *Time Manipulation* we also are able to see differences in when players manage their resources. The Game 1 player is only able to manage resources in the moment, choosing to pause the game before making decisions, whereas the Game 2 player is able to forecast the needs of their town and manages resources far in advance of when they are needed.

5 Discussion

ENA was an effective tool for capturing the shift in player actions from Game 1 to Game 2. This aligns with prior findings where ENA was used to identify novices and experts in virtual internships [4]. Expert systems-thinkers should be able to predict the causal relationships of the system and be both preemptive in their approach to potential problems as well as know what information is valuable to act on in the moment. By applying a grounded coding approach to the actions that players are taking, we were able to tell a story about how the player's strategy develops between sessions. Grounding the chosen codes in the known challenges of systems thinking (temporal distance in particular), player actions, and game feedback created a sufficient framework for understanding how players are moving through the game in relation to their conceptual understanding of the game and its intended learning objectives.

There are several limitations of this study worthy of further investigation. Primarily, the sample size is small, including only a handful of players; it would be worthwhile to expand the sample for generalizability. The games were also heavily filtered, and it may yield interesting results to include players who experience rapid iteration through quick failed games. Furthermore, the nature of a moving window in ENA creates connections ahead of and behind events. There is no way to determine causality or directionality based on these findings at this time. This provides a potential use case for directional ENA in future iterations.

Moving forward, these exploratory findings indicate the potential application of ENA as a method for assessing students from log data alone. The next steps would include investigating these patterns through both ideographic (comparison of individual to self over time) and nomothetic (comparison of trends within a group) lenses as a test of validity. Here, we have demonstrated the beginnings of this work through the generation of a network based on a group of individuals who share commonalities, in this case being new to Lakeland or a repeat player. Expanding our sample size would allow for nomothetic-like extrapolation to the "general laws that hold across persons" [20].

A next step would include comparing networks that represent an individual's actions over time, such as player 5 at the beginning, middle and end of Game 1, or player 5 over the course of Game 1, Game 2, and Game 3. This would allow an idiographic demonstration should their network shift from session to session demonstrating a change in student behavior and thus understanding.

In this paper, we have focused on the detectable differences between game play sessions, not on their implications. The method demonstrated here could further serve a variety of audiences within the larger educational games community including game designers as a measure of design effectiveness or teachers as a means of assessment. Still, from another angle, the method described serves the larger quantitative ethnography community in furthering the way that we think about data, coding, and models. We have integrated computer-generated actions into our models alongside raw log data in a meaningful way that tells a story of user experience, a contribution that can add to the way we investigate student interactions with digital environments in the future.

Acknowledgments. Lakeland was supported by the United States Dairy Association Innovations at the Nexus of Food, Energy, and Water (USDA INFEWS) grant through Principal Investigator Victor Zivala and the Scalable Systems Lab. Additional support was obtained from the Wisconsin Center for Education Research and Wisconsin Department of Public Instruction.

References

1. Field Day Lab: Lakeland (2019). https://fielddaylab.wisc.edu/play/lakeland/game/iframe.html
2. Grotzer, T.A., et al.: Turning transfer inside out: the affordances of virtual worlds and mobile devices in real world contexts for teaching about causality across time and distance in ecosystems. Technol. Knowl. Learn. **20**(1), 43–69 (2015)
3. Heaton, T.: A Circular Model of Gameplay (2006). https://www.gamasutra.com/view/feature/130978/a_circular_model_of_gameplay.php
4. Arastoopour, G., Shaffer, D.W., Swiecki, Z., Ruis, A.R., Chesler, N.C.: Teaching and assessing engineering design thinking with virtual internships and epistemic network analysis. Int. J. Eng. Educ. **32**(3B), 1492–1501 (2016)
5. Herder, T., et al.: Supporting teachers' intervention in students' virtual collaboration using a network based model. In: Proceedings of the 8th International Conference on Learning Analytics and Knowledge (LAK'2018). Association for Computing Machinery, New York, NY, USA, pp. 21–25 (2018)
6. Karumbaiah, S., Baker, R., Barany, A., Shute, V.: Using epistemic networks with automated codes to understand why players quit levels in a learning game. In: Eagan, B., Misfeldt, M., Siebert-Evenstone, A. (eds.) Advances in Quantitative Ethnography First International Conference, pp 106-116. Springer, Madison, WI (2019)
7. Behl, D.V., Ferreira, S.: Systems thinking: an analysis of key factors and relationships. Procedia Comput. Sci. **36**, 104–109 (2014)
8. Rittel, H.W.J., Webber, M.M.: Dilemmas in a general theory of planning. Policy Sci. **4**, 155–169 (1973)
9. Grohs, J.R., Kirk, G.R., Soledad, M.M., Knight, D.B.: Assessing systems thinking: a tool to measure complex reasoning through ill-structured problems. Thinking Skills Creativity **28**, 110–130 (2018)
10. Doganca Kucuk, Z., Saysel, A.K.: Developing seventh grade students' understanding of complex environmental problems with systems tools and representations: a quasi-experimental study. Res. Sci. Educ. **48**(2), 491–514 (2018)
11. NGSS Lead States. Next Generation Science Standards: For States, by States (2013). http://www.nextgenscience.org/
12. Shaffer, D.W.: Epistemic frames for epistemic games. Comput. Educ. **46**(3), 223–234 (2006)
13. Kim, Y.J., Almond, R.G., Shute, V.J.: Applying evidence-centered design for the development of game-based assessments in physics playground. Int. J. Test. **16**(2), 142–163 (2016)
14. Owen, V.E., Baker, R.S.: Fueling prediction of player decisions: foundations of feature engineering for optimized behavior modeling in serious games. Technol. Knowl. Learn. (2018)
15. Field Day Lab: Open Game Data (2020). https://fielddaylab.wisc.edu/opengamedata/
16. Marquart, C.L., Hinojosa, C., Swiecki, Z., Eagan, B., Shaffer, D.W.: nCoder (Beta) (2018). http://app.epistemicnetwork.org
17. Shaffer, D.W.: Quantitative Ethnography. Cathcart Press, Madison, WI (2017)
18. Marquart, C.L., Hinojosa, C., Swiecki, Z., Eagan, B., Shaffer, D.W.: Epistemic Network Analysis (Version 1.6.0) (2018). http://app.epistemicnetwork.org

19. Siebert-Evenstone, A., Arastoopour Irgens, G., Collier, W., Swiecki, Z., Ruis, A.R., Shaffer, D.W.: In search of conversational grain size: modelling semantic structure using moving stanza windows. J. Learn. Analytics **4**(3), 123–139 (2017)
20. Walker, A.A., Engelhard, G.: Game-based assessments: a promising way to create idiographic perspectives. Measurement **12**, 57–61 (2014)

"What Would Happen if Humans Disappeared from Earth?" Tracing and Visualizing Change in a Pre-School Child's Domain-Related Curiosities

Mamta Shah[1]([✉]) [iD], Amanda Barany[2]([✉]) [iD], and Amanda Siebert-Evenstone[3]([✉]) [iD]

[1] Elsevier Inc., Philadelphia, PA 19103, USA
m.shah@elsevier.com
[2] Drexel University, Philadelphia, PA 19104, USA
amb595@drexel.edu
[3] University of Wisconsin, Madison, WI 53706, USA
alevenstone@wisc.edu

Abstract. The National Research Council reports on science education have discussed how children of preschool age demonstrate readiness for science. However, what is missing is a discussion of mechanisms and practices that can promote deep curiosity over a long period. In this self and quantitative ethnography, we explore family engagement with scientific thinking and content as it unfolded for a mother-son dyad during a 10-month period. Shah and her son Mihir (pseudonym) participated in 'A Bedtime Curiosity' (ABC) routine (designed by Shah) wherein the latter was encouraged to express an idea he was curious about, ask a question, and then co-explore possible answers by watching a short video, followed by discussion if requested. After thematically coding the set of questions (N = 123), we used epistemic network analysis (ENA) to identify and model the connections between his curiosity over time. Thereafter, we took advantage of the self-ethnography to reevaluate the qualitative and quantitative data as well as the entire routine from the perspective of both the parent-researcher and the participating child. This body of work is positioned to extend the literature on examining parent-child interactions to support children's curiosity- a phenomenon that is crucial to child development.

Keywords: Curiosity · Epistemic network analysis · Parent-child interaction · Questioning · Self-Ethnography · Quantitative ethnography

1 Introduction

The National Research Council reports on science education [1, 2] have discussed how children of preschool age demonstrate readiness for science. However, what is missing is a discussion on mechanisms and practices that can promote deep curiosity over a long period. Scholars such as Clark [3], and Gilbert and Byers [4] have pointed to similar gaps in the discussion on the pedagogical practices of promoting curiosity despite its

A. R. Ruis and S. B. Lee (Eds.): ICQE 2021, CCIS 1312, pp. 232–247, 2021.
https://doi.org/10.1007/978-3-030-67788-6_16

widely recognized significance of scientific development and innovation. It may be useful to seek inspiration from educational philosophers such as Rudolf Steiner and John Dewey who have advocated for dialogue and inquiry-based science education [5–7]. Dewey in particular argued for educational practices that foster scientific habits; this goal for scientific thinking could be achieved by providing an environment of active knowledge-making. Furthermore, Bell and colleagues [8] have highlighted the significance of informal, everyday and undesigned environments for fostering self-initiated and long-term engagement in science learning. Family routines (e.g. dinner time talks, walks in the neighborhood) where children can engage in guided interactions or activities can offer valuable opportunities for "occasioned knowledge exploration" [9].

In this paper, we explore one account of family engagement with promoting curiosity, and by extension promoting scientific thinking and content, as it unfolded for a mother-son dyad from November 2018-September 2019. It is novel in that Shah assumed the role of a parent-researcher in this self-ethnography [10] and implemented a quantitative ethnographic (QE) technique. The research question guiding this study was as follows: *"In what ways did a preschool child's domain-related curiosity shift over time as he engaged in a nightly bedtime reading and inquiry routine?"*

2 Review of Literature

Curiosity is central to children's development and is fostered through social interaction. As such, inviting children to explore what they are curious to know can support them in learning science and provide insights about their development [11]. Preschool-aged children, in particular, are inherently curious and wonder about a variety of topics. Lindholm [12] distinguishes between curiosity and wonder. "Wondering and curiosity.... reflect somewhat different modes of questioning and stimulate exploratory joy from different positions. Curiosity remains in the space of terms, concepts, and causality'. Wonder emerges from a wordless experience of something's existence. And while wonder is more ignited by perception, curiosity is more ignited by reflection" (pp.990). Bearing this in mind, Lindholm urged for balancing a reductionist approach (i.e., promoting causal thinking through rational explanations) and a maximist approach (i.e., ontological thinking through activities that enhance imagination) in science education for preschool children.

Although in the context of schools, Engel [11] underscores the role adults can play in scaffolding children's curiosities beyond serving as mere sources of information providers. Their role should also include offering an inviting environment for children to pursue their curiosity, helping children expand and refine their questions, and nurturing children's capacity to undertake explorations in systematic manners. In their study, Crowley and Jacob [13] provided an account of a mother and her 4-year old son's conversation about dinosaur fossils during a museum visit to demonstrate how joint activities with families can help children develop 'islands of expertise'. Through parents' mediation, their choices about family activities, and the cognitive structure welcomed in this conversation (e.g. questioning, explaining, discussing), children can begin to build domain-specific knowledge bases. By pursuing such fundamentally social endeavors, parents can scaffold children's sense of identity as individuals who are motivated to pursue activities that are related to a variety of academic disciplines [13]. Another notion about the value of family routines is referred to as 'opportunities for occasioned knowledge exploration' [9] where children can engage in guided interactions or activities with parents to pursue their curiosity and engage in science learning.

Several researchers have leveraged children's natural affinities for asking questions and learning about their development by cataloguing children's questions. Simultaneously, studies have examined the learning opportunities afforded for children through interactions with parents. For instance, in a study involving four-year-old girls, Tizard and Hughes [14] found that one of the most common forms of conversations involved children asking their mothers questions to seek new information. The resultant discussions, termed as 'passages of intellectual search,' demonstrated children's capacity to pursue knowledge. Chouinard [15] expressed the crucial role that questioning, and information-seeking behaviors play in advancing preschool children's cognitive development. In her monograph, Chouinard reported on findings from four studies, at least two of which involved four-year-old children and parent/child dyads. She concluded that children's questions offer a mechanism for seeking information that are related in topic and structures to their cognitive development. Shifts in development, and by extension concept building, as a result of newly gathered information result in shifts in the content of questions being asked. Furthermore, questions seeking biological information (e.g. how do babies grow) are more frequently observed than those seeking nonbiological information (e.g. what is the name of Z?). Chouinard also found that the nature of stimulus impacts the depth of the concepts they seek information about; real stimuli versus replicas (e.g. drawing) were found to be more impactful. Lastly, children use their existing knowledge and understanding of current situations to generate questions that can help them advance their cognitive state and reconcile a cognitive equilibrium (e.g. to know more about a phenomenon in the world, to solve a practical problem). Lastly, Frazier, Gelman, and Wellman [16] found that children's exploratory orientations and desires to obtain causal explanations motivate them to frequently ask 'what' and 'why' questions of their expert conversational partners (i.e. parents).

One of the core practices of science is learning to ask and refine questions. For example, in the Next Generation Science Standards [17], kindergarteners through second-graders are encouraged to ask questions and define problems. For these younger grades, questioning is often driven by children's experiences in the world. That is, children often ask questions to find out how the world around them works. Further, when students are able to ask questions and work to figure out the answers, their role shifts from a more passive receiver of knowledge into an active agent in their learning [18]. And so, questioning often serves as a way to learn more about what curiosities children have about their experiences.

Ethnographic studies have documented young people's engagement in scientific thinking and content, and at the same time investigated change in curiosity and identification with science as a result of family interactions or in home settings [19, 20]. The research approach is valuable because one goal of ethnographic research is to create a *thick description* [21] of the context, which provides sufficient details and interpretation to allow others to understand the contextual meanings behind the behaviors. Few studies have involved the use of self-ethnography to examine family processes related to science engagement; that is, assuming the role of a parent-researcher who is present at all times documenting a serendipitous activity as it unfolds and the guided participation by parents, followed by a reflection on the outcomes in situ [22]. Self-ethnography affords individuals to examine settings and processes they have 'natural access' to. Unlike auto-ethnographic studies, researchers in a self-ethnography are interested in examining their context instead of themselves or their experiences at the center [10].

In this self-ethnography, we explore family engagement with promoting curiosity, and by extension promoting scientific thinking and content, as it unfolded for a mother-son dyad from November 2018-September 2019. Shah and her son Mihir (pseudonym) participated in 'A Bedtime Curiosity' (ABC) routine (designed by Shah) wherein the latter was encouraged to express an idea he was curious about, ask a question, and then co-explore possible answers by watching a short video (3–7 min), followed by discussion if requested. Videos were the chosen medium because of their affordances as aural and visual explanations, or for the opportunity they presented to vicariously experience the phenomena Mihir was curious about. Guiding principles for the use of technology with early learners from the Office of Educational Technology [23] suggests that the use of videos when combined with interaction and guidance from parents can foster cross-disciplinary learning (e.g. STEM). Every question he asked during the ABC routine was logged chronologically, amounting to 123 questions. Shah also maintained a memo to chronicle the context for Mihir's questions. Shah partnered with two researchers to examine the domain-related curiosities of Mihir using an inductive approach.

The authors employed a *quantitative ethnographic approach* [24] which bridges qualitative and quantitative analyses to make statistical warrants about our thick descriptions. This unified methods approach allowed our team to iterate and reflect on what was happening during the ABC routine at multiple levels. Therefore, in this analysis, we first used a *grounded approach* [25] of intensively reading and rereading the qualitative data to discover codes from the data. Next, we use epistemic network analysis [ENA; 24] to quantify and visualize patterns in our data. After creating and analyzing ENA models, we took advantage of the self-ethnography to reevaluate the data as well as the entire routine from the perspective of both the parent-researcher and the participating child. By analyzing this context using such an iterative and reflective approach, we are able to provide a fuller picture of this particular family curiosity routine. We present the results that compare the first half and second half of questions and then close the interpretive loop with a reflection by Shah and Mihir. We conclude with implications for future research.

3   Methods

3.1   Context

Shah is an academic-corporate parent and like many working parents is constantly finding ways to nurture her child's curiosity. So, on the Thanksgiving night of 2018, Shah decided to introduce a modification to the bedtime routine with her then 4 year and 11-month-old son, Mihir (pseudonym). Reading books was always a part of their nightly routine. Shah selected books based on the recommendations of the local librarian, the time of the year, current events, and Mihir's interests, among other influences. Per the new routine, they read two instead of three books, and after that, they devoted time to uncovering *a bedtime curiosity* (ABC). During ABC, Mihir was encouraged to express an idea he was curious about, ask a question, and then explore possible answers with his father or mother (Shah) by watching a short video (3–7 min), followed by discussion if requested.

3.2   Origin of A Bedtime Curiosity (ABC) Routine and Establishing the Practice

Shah and Mihir were reading the book, 'The Magic School Bus and the Science Fair Expedition' in mid-November, 2018. This time-travel story illustrated the works of Copernicus, Galileo, and Newton, what each scientist was interested in, what some of their contributions were, and how each one carried forward the work of the previous scholar. One illustration in the book caught Shah's attention (see Fig. 1). Mihir and Shah sat talking about how the root of all artistic and scientific advancements can be traced back to questions: things/ideas people (of all ages) are curious about, which leads them to seek new information, make discoveries and inventions. Following the conversation, Shah reflected on how she could learn about what Mihir is curious about, how she could help him develop questions if an idea piqued his interest, and how she could support Mihir to find answers to questions. Their previous schedule gave way to a bedtime curiosity (ABC) routine. Additional resources such as the PBS Kids show, Sid the Science Kid, Mister Rogers' Neighborhood television series, and 'How People Make Things' also helped Shah shape the ABC routine.

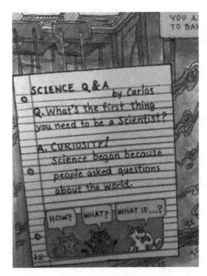

Fig. 1. An illustration from 'The Magic School Bus and the Science Fair Expedition

To establish the ABC routine, Shah started the practice with what Mihir was interested in, what was personally relevant to him, and for him to know that the routine welcomed curiosities of all kinds. It is not surprising that as a pre-Kindergartner, Mihir had many questions about farting, pooping, and peeing. So, over the first few evenings, Shah and Mihir watched videos about how pee is formed, how poop is formed, and why people fart. Needless to say, Mihir quickly grew accustomed to ABC routine. The dyad would then watch a video and talk about the curiosity for a few minutes. Videos were used as a medium for their affordances as aural and visual explanations, or the opportunity to vicariously experience the phenomena Mihir was curious about.

3.3 Memoing

The ABC routine was consistently followed for a period of 10 months; that is, from November 2018 until September 2019 with some exceptions (e.g. Shah was traveling, Mihir went to bed early). Shah concluded the routine right before Mihir began Kindergarten. Every question he asked during the ABC routine was logged chronologically, amounting to 123 questions. Shah also maintained a memo to chronicle the context for Mihir's questions. At times, the context was an educated guess. For instance, a question on 'What does a sunset on Mars look like?' was a result of a trip to the library where he learned about the Mars rovers, and 'What did Ben Franklin do?' was asked after a trip to a science museum dedicated to Ben Franklin. At other times, Mihir explicitly described the context that led him to being curious about a topic. For instance, Mihir wanted to know about how the Dreidel game was played when his school Principal gifted a Dreidel to all children during Hanukkah. For his fifth birthday party, Mihir and his friends screen-printed t-shirts. While he knew about the printing technique, he wanted to know how t-shirts were made. Seasonal changes, important national holidays (e.g. Martin Luther King Day), current events (e.g. a picture of a black hole), and current interests (e.g. LEGO) also inspired additional questions.

There were two events during the ABC routine where Shah intervened to help spark Mihir's curiosity and scaffold the nature of questions he asked. First, Shah explained to Mihir the range of questions he could ask in addition to 'How' questions. She introduced to him some ideas that could be explored when framed with a Why, What, When, Which, Whose kind of question. Second, Shah asked Mihir if he thought about things he uses every day and wondered how those things were made (e.g. crayons, pencils).

3.4 Coding

In total, 123 questions were documented to provide a detailed record of interactions. To identify elements of discourse associated with curiosity, we conducted a thematic analysis approach [26] of the questions to generate a set of qualitative codes representing the nature of questions. Initially, we evaluated the questions to find patterns of topics, ideas, and patterns of meaning. Patterns related to the domain concepts Mihir referenced in his questioning were identified, and a set of nested codes related to emergent topics and subtopics was developed and refined (See Table 1).

Researchers deductively applied the identified codes to each line of data [27]. To address reliability and validity we used *social moderation*, where two raters coded all of the data and then achieved agreement on each code [28]. Questions were coded for the presence (1) or absence (0) of a connection to each of the identified content domains and subdomains. For example, the question "how do plants give us oxygen?" was coded as related to the Science domain and the Botany subdomain.

Table 1. Inductive codes developed through thematic analysis

Domain	Frequency	Example of questions Mihir asked
Science	71	
Anatomy	22*	What happens when bones break?
Zoology	12*	How do fish breathe underwater?
Astronomy	27*	How long would it take for us to travel across the solar system?
Meteorology	4	What causes lightning?
Geology	1	Where does metal come from?
Paleontology	4	Why did dinosaurs go extinct?
Biology	30*	Why is it important to drink water?
Engineering	36	
Manufacturing	29*	How is a carpet made?
Robotics	2	How do you make a talking robot?
Technology	35*	How did Dr. Katie Bouman take a picture of a blackhole?
Other	–	
History	21*	Why was the Eiffel Tower built?
Games	2	How to play the dreidel game?

*Subdomains with greater than five occurrences were selected as codes for the epistemic network visualizations

3.5 Data Analysis

We used *Epistemic Network Analysis* [ENA; described in detail elsewhere 29] to identify and model the connections between his curiosity across domains over the 10-month period. ENA measures connections by quantifying the co-occurrence of domain codes within a defined segment of data. In this case, we used a *moving window* [30] of two questions to measure connections between codes within a given question and to the previous question. This stanza size was selected to account for the fact that Mihir asked no more than a few questions per night during the ABC routine. To gain an understanding of Mihir's shifts in associations across domains over time, the variable Time (which splits the dataset into two chronological halves of 62 and 61 posts) and Units (which splits the questions into sections of 10 chronological questions for more nuanced examination) were developed. These variables were selected as meaningful *units of analysis* for which to develop epistemic network visualizations. On a typical night, approximately 1–2 questions were asked and answered, and while the dates that each curiosity was explored was not recorded, Time 1 and Time 2 each likely represent approximately the same span of time, as well as containing a similar number of data points.

The variable Units was also set as the conversation so that connections could be made within each set of 10 questions but not across sets of 10 in order to observe smaller sets of questions over time. Codes selected for the epistemic network visualizations included subdomains with greater than five occurrences (See Table 1).

Codes that occurred outside of the moving stanza window were not considered connected. Subsequently, ENA creates two coordinated representations for each unit including the weighted network graph, which visualizes these connections as network graphs where the nodes correspond to the codes and edges reflect the relative frequency of the connection between two codes, and a plotted point.

For our analysis, we used a technique called a *means rotation* [31] that combines (1) a hyperplane projection of the high-dimensional points to a line that maximizes the difference between the means of two units and (2) a singular value decomposition. The resulting space highlights any differences between the units by constructing the dimensional reduction that places the means of the two units as close as possible to the X-axis of the metric space. In this study, we rotated the space by the first and second halves of questions to see change over time along the x-axis. Thus, we can quantify and visualize the structure of connections among elements of curiosity and compare differences across questions and time, making it possible to characterize Mihir's curiosities over time. After using ENA, we revisited the qualitative data to further investigate key connections between elements.

4 Results

Below we present the epistemic network visualizations of Mihir's curiosity over time (Time 1 = questions 1–61; Time 2 = questions 62–123). We interpret the results in the context of the memos recorded by Shah, and reflections offered by Shah and Mihir independently about the visualizations and the ABC routine.

4.1 Epistemic Network Analysis

Time 1. An epistemic network visualizing Mihir's connections between topics of curiosity in Time 1 (questions 1–62) revealed the strongest associations between Manufacturing and Technology (.46) and between Biology and Anatomy (.26) overall. An examination of projected points for each chronological unit of 10 questions (Unit 1.1 represents questions 1–10, for example) offers nuance that might help explain these stronger associations. For example, at Time 1.1 (questions 1–10), the projected point is closer to the Biology/Anatomy association, as Mihir repeatedly asked questions related to the nature of bodily functions around this time (i.e. "How is pee formed?"). Projected points for Times 1.2–1.4 (questions 20–40) demonstrate a distinct shift toward questions that associate Manufacturing and Technology, as he asked a series of questions related to how various items he encountered in his daily life were made (i.e. pillow, music box, light bulbs, candy canes, etc.). Projected points for Times 1.5–1.7 illustrate the diversification of his questioning, away from observations related to his immediate personal surroundings (i.e. the biology of the self and of the form and function of household objects), and toward questions that were more diverse, complex, and topically abstract. For example, the projected point for Time 1.5 illustrates an increase in questions related to historical topics, such as curiosity around the authors of his favorite books (i.e. "Who was Dr. Seuss?") and political figures (i.e. "Who is the most famous president of USA?"). Projected points for Times 1.6 and 1.7 illustrate a shift back toward questioning related to Manufacturing and Technology, however, a focus on more abstract items is more apparent (i.e. "How is metal made?"). Mihir also returned to his curiosity of biology topics, in this case more specifically connecting zoology and the behaviors and functions of animals around the world (i.e. "What does a turtle's brain look like?").

Time 2. An epistemic network visualizing Mihir's connections between topics of curiosity in Time 2 (questions 63–123) revealed more balanced associations drawn across domains overall, but with strongest associations between Biology and Anatomy (.30), Biology and Astronomy (.25), Manufacturing and Technology (.22), and Astronomy and History (.21) (See Fig. 2). An examination of the projected points for each chronological unit of 10 questions again offers nuance to illustrate shifts in Mihir's patterns of connection-making over time. Projected points for Times 2.7–2.12 each shift in distinct directions as Mihir began asking questions that were driven by more diverse and complex topics. For example, the projected point for Sect. 2.7 is situated by stronger associations between Astronomy, Biology, Zoology and Anatomy constructs through questions that continue to explore the nature of animal anatomy (i.e. "How does a cow poop?") alongside questions related to space (i.e. "How old is the Earth?"). The projected point for Time 2.8 has stronger connections between Astronomy and Biology, as Mihir began asking questions about the nature of space and of human development (both historically in questions such as "How did people come on Earth?" and biologically in questions such as "How does a baby develop in mommy's tummy?") (Fig. 3).

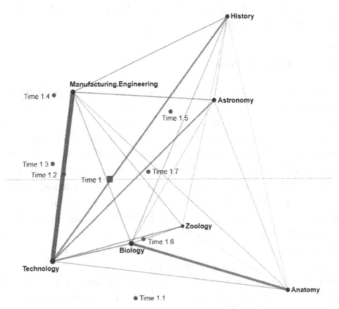

Fig. 2. Network representation of the associations between codes in Time 1 data (questions 1–62). Thicker lines represent more frequent connections.

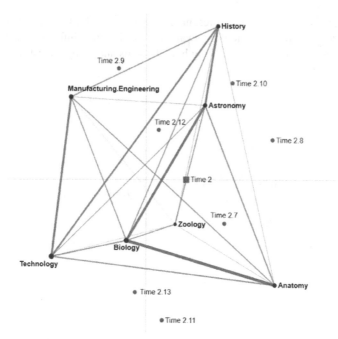

Fig. 3. Network representation of the associations between codes in Time 2 data (questions 63–123). Thicker lines represent more frequent connections.

Interests in History persisted in Time 2.9 in questions such as "Who are our ancestors?" but were interspersed with renewed connections to Manufacturing and Technology as he inquired into the nature of mechanical items (i.e. a AA battery). The projected point for Time 2.10 is situated by a particularly strong association between History and Astronomy, as Mihir began asking more complex questions about the nature of space (i.e. "Why do stars explode?") and about what specific historical figures in space exploration are known for (i.e. "What did Neil Armstrong do?"). Time 2.11 is marked by a series of increasingly complex questions about the nature of human bodily functions, as evidenced by the location of the projected point in the lower quadrant of the network. Questions such as "How does the brain work?" were followed up by "How does the middle portion of the brain work?" and later "How do nerves in the brain work?" illustrating his increasing capacity to follow lines of curiosity with increasing specificity as he gained new understanding on the topic. In his final lines of questioning in the data (points 2.12 and 2.13), Mihir best exemplifies his emerging capacity to maintain several lines of questioning simultaneously, and to build on what he asked and learned in prior questions to narrow his lines of inquiry. For example, questions related to History and Astronomy (i.e. "When was Neil Armstrong born?"), Manufacturing and technology relating to the creation of famous historical monuments (i.e. "Why was the Eiffel Tower built?"), and even hypotheticals about human biology and anatomy (i.e. "What if humans weighed one ton?") are all present. These questions build on interests he mentioned prior, demonstrate an emerging awareness of historical influence, and are more complex in their composition (i.e. asking hypotheticals and "why" questions) (Fig. 4).

Fig. 4. Difference network comparisons between Time 1 (red lines) and Time 2 (blue lines) Thicker lines represent more frequent relative connections for that unit. (Color figure online)

Time 1 vs Time 2. To more clearly compare the two sets of questions, we created a *difference network* (Figure #), which subtracts the edge weights of the mean networks for each unit and then visualizes the differences in weights. Connections represented in red lines were stronger among Time 1 questions, while connections in Blue occurred proportionally more often among Time 2 questions. This difference model shows the increasing complexity of his questioning over time (See Figure X). While associations between Manufacturing and Technology were higher in Time 1 (red lines), the majority of associations across constructs increased in Time 2 (blue lines) as each question was more likely to embody more than one topic (i.e. Astronomy and History) and as Mihir was more likely to maintain continued curiosity in increasingly specific lines of inquiry into several areas of curiosity at once (i.e. Biology/Anatomy and Astronomy/History).

After investigating our ENA model, we were interested in understanding the perspective of one of Mihir's parents to provide additional insights and context for the questions that arose throughout the routine. Next, we walk through Shah's reflections on the goals and results of the ABC routine.

Mihir's Reflection. When the authors would meet to discuss their analysis and write this paper, Mihir would regularly join the virtual sessions to observe and occasionally ask questions. Given Mihir's apparent interest in the research on his questioning, a non-parent researcher shared findings from this study with Mihir and gave him the opportunity to reflect on the ABC routine. During this virtual call, Mihir showed off a space-themed project he had been working on, and volunteered that he planned to start the ABC routine with his mother (Shah) again soon. Mihir described each phase of the ABC routine (reading, asking a question, then watching a video), and explained that he liked each part of the process and would not change any part of it. When Mihir saw the epistemic networks in the call, he initially shared that he did not understand them "at all," but quickly followed up with questions about what the thicker lines in the model meant. A discussion of the constructs in the network led to follow-up questions from Mihir about terms he didn't know (i.e. anatomy). Mihir could not call to mind examples of the kinds of questions he asked or remember why he asked them, and signed off a few minutes later by asking to continue the conversation at another time. Several days later, however, Mihir shared with his mother (Shah) that he learned, for example, that he had asked many questions about manufacturing as evidenced by one of the thicker lines. This suggests that his understanding of the networks had developed through the discussion, and that he had connected the findings to a facet of his own process. Further iterations of reflection with Mihir might strengthen his ability to use ENA as a form of self-examination tool as the ABC routine continues.

Shah's Reflection. After completing the analysis above, Shah dove into her memos and reflected on the ENA visualizations. When she introduced the ABC routine, Shah did not foresee a specific course it would take in terms of the topics Mihir would be curious about. All she wanted to do was guide Mihir's self-led desires to know more about specific topics during a family routine. Mihir started off wanting to know more about things that amused him as a 4-year-old. Mihir's curiosity about these seemed natural to her as everyone experiences farting, pooping, and peeing. However, the processes that result in these physiological outcomes are invisible to us, and may be especially intriguing to a young mind as that of Mihir. As such, Shah saw these initial questions as windows of opportunity to introduce Mihir to how the human anatomy functions. This welcoming space also helped establish the practice for the next 10 months. As mentioned earlier, the only two times Shah intervened during the routine was when she suggested to Mihir additional ways of asking questions, and to wonder about everyday objects. Mihir latched onto the latter suggestion quite instantly. While his curiosity of specific domains shifted from human anatomy to manufacturing/engineering (as evident in the Time 1 network), Shah argued that one underlying idea behind his questions remained constant; that is, his desire to know more about underlying processes and to vicariously observe how everyday objects and functions operated. He learnt that watching videos helped with humanizing these processes and making each topic feel less abstract. The verbal demonstration about additional ways of asking questions manifested overtly in Mihir's questions in Time 2. As is evident both in the memo and the ENA visualizations, Mihir became more comfortable asking complex questions. His maturity with the ABC routine and the events during Time 2 (e.g. Martin Luther King Day, picture of blackhole by Dr. Katie Bouman, a trip to Field Museum and Museum of Science and Industry in Chicago, IL). Shah found the ENA visualizations fascinating. They confirmed her belief in the semi-serendipitous ABC routine in helping Mihir articulate his desire to seek information, ask questions, make observations and connections to events, objects and activities in his daily life.

Reviving and Refining the ABC Routine. Shah and Mihir have resumed the ABC routine as he entered grade 1 in September 2020; they are both interested in continuing the routine longitudinally. Shah has made changes to the memoing process of the ABC routine for this iteration that include 1) documenting the date each question was asked, 2) logging the titles of books that were read, 3) recording the types of multimedia resources used to answer Mihir's questions, 4) noting which of Mihir's parents facilitated the routine during each session, and 5) recording observation notes from each discussion. These changes were included to offer more variables for exploration of Mihir's trajectory of change using ENA in subsequent iterations of the work, and to include more descriptive references to each interaction that can support member-checking and strengthen the socio-temporal dynamics of the self-ethnographic process.

5   Discussion

In this paper, we employed self-ethnography to demonstrate how one family routine (i.e. A Bedtime Curiosity) was designed to nurture a young child's domain-specific curiosity through the act of questioning (N = 123). We employed quantitative ethnography and techniques to visualize and study change over time (November 2018-September 2019). An epistemic network visualizing Mihir's connections between topics of curiosity in Time 1 (questions 1–62) revealed the strongest associations between Manufacturing and Technology (.46) and between Biology and Anatomy (.26) overall (See Fig. 1). An epistemic network visualizing Mihir's connections between topics of curiosity in Time 2 (questions 63–123) revealed more balanced associations drawn across domains overall, but with strongest associations between Biology and Anatomy (.30), Biology and Astronomy (.25), Manufacturing and Technology (.22), and Astronomy and History (.21) (See Fig. 2). The visualized change in Mihir's curiosity over time confirms Chouinard's [15] findings about the evolution of children's questioning as they mature, and the concepts solidify.

Shah is a learning scientist with a background in human development. The ABC routine and the context in which it was designed and implemented extends the work of Crowley and Jacob [13] on the role of parents in making intentional decisions and bringing their empirical knowledge to organize everyday activities and conversations over a period of time for their children to develop the motivation and fluency to seek information about various academic domains. In the case of ABC, Shah designed it to support Mihir's epistemic curiosity - the enduring desire to know for its own sake - which is only fueled by new information. It is essential for rational exploration and resolutions of practical problems, but also for satisfying ontological and epistemological questions [32, 33], resulting in successive loops of questioning and knowledge-seeking [12]. However, it is integral to recognize that curiosity as a virtue is valued and practiced differently across cultures. For instance, the frequency of parents engaging in a dialogue where young children under 5 years are encouraged to question has gained mixed results in eastern and western cultures [15, 34, 35]. The application of the ABC routine and the two minor pivots Shah documented above is in harmony with Engel's [11] arguments on the nuanced roles adults can play in nurturing curiosity; in this case, a family setting.

Using a combination of self- and quantitative ethnography, we were able to generate unique and valuable insights into the nature of development of curiosity in children. One goal of QE is to provide rich, exploratory examinations that capture the nuance of complex thinking. As such, QE provides a pragmatic approach to addressing the entirety of our researcher endeavors, including the design, data collection, analyses, and interpretations. Critical to maintaining the ethnographic nature, this study highlights the importance of closing the interpretive loop to understand the relational and contextual grounding within an analysis [22].

Curiosity is closely linked to interest. The ABC routine and the intentionality of the process as part of the authors' communications with Mihir even beyond the study duration may have deepened his desire to know more about some disciplines more than the others. For instance, as of September 2020, Mihir started 1st grade and will be 7 years old soon. He has an emerging interest in planetary science. 27/123 of Mihir's questions Shah documented from November 2018-September 2019 focused on planetary science (e.g. How long would it take for us to travel through the solar system; How was Earth formed, What if Earth was the size of Jupiter). His interest in planetary science may have sustained even beyond September 2019. The COVID-19 pandemic gave Shah a chance to observe Mihir participate in many activities over a month-long period (March 12-April 13, 2020) which involved Mihir *inquiring* about how the universe works, *constructing* a space fort, and *communicating, and expressing* [ICCE,26]- *his* interest in planetary science through his participation in an online STEAM design challenge. It is beyond the scope of this paper to describe the novel explorations Mihir engaged during this period. However, it provides additional impetus to Shah to support Mihir's readiness for a deeper exploration of topics. Lindholm's (2018) framework on science education that is based on Deweyan ideas of promoting scientific habits may continue to offer valuable insights for understanding Mihir's (and other individuals) trajectory as they from childhood to pre-adolescence to adolescence.

6   Limitations and Implications

First, Shah is a working parent and designed the ABC routine to be semi-serendipitous based on the conditions surrounding the family routine. However, future studies could also examine the relationship between daily activities and questions asked during anytime of the day. This may afford deeper insights into children's emergent curiosity and interest over time. Second, a challenge of self-ethnographic studies is its strong reliance on the primary researcher alone to have the richest funds of knowledge to draw attention to one's cultural context and interpret the findings. However, the collaborative nature of this project allowed researchers to bring in multiple perspectives through their expertise in quantitative ethnography, NGSS, and social work. Third, similar to limitations in the literature, this study focuses on a Mother-Child relationship without including Father-child relationships. While the authors do not claim to have exhausted the literature in this field of study; two opportunities may offer promising directions for advancement: a) studying father-child interactions and b) studying adult-child interactions in families with same-sex parents. Future research may also explore shifts in Mihir's curiosity around these topics using quantitative assessments. In the case of the ABC routine, the authors have decided to explore these avenues moving forward.

Acknowledgments. This work was funded in part by the National Science Foundation (DRL-1661036, DRL-1713110), the Wisconsin Alumni Research Foundation, and the Office of the Vice Chancellor for Research and Graduate Education at the University of Wisconsin-Madison. The opinions, findings, and conclusions do not reflect the views of the funding agencies, cooperating institutions, or other individuals.

References

1. National Research Council. Taking science to school: learning and teaching science in grades K-8. Committee on Science Learning, Preschool Through Eighth Grade. Washington, DC. The National Academies Press (2007)
2. National Research Council. Discipline-based education research: understanding and improving learning in undergraduate science and engineering. Washington DC. The National Academies Press (2012)
3. Clark, S.: Cultivating classroom curiosity: a quasi-experimental, longitudinal study investigating the impact of the question formulation technique on adolescent intellectual curiosity. Dissertation, Boston University, School of Education (2017)
4. Gilbert, A., Byers, C.C.: Wonder as a tool to engage preservice elementary teachers in science learning and teaching. Sci. Educ. **101**(6), 907–928 (2017)
5. Dewey, J.: The Child and the Curriculum. University of Chicago Press, Chicago (1902)
6. Dewey, J.: Science as subject matter and as method. Science **31**(787), 121–127 (1910)
7. Steiner, R.: A Modern Art of Education. Anthroposophic Press, New York (2004)
8. Bell, P., Lewenstein, B., Shouse, A.W., Feder, M.A. (eds.): Learning Science in Informal Environments: People, Places, and Pursuits. National Academies Press, Washington (2009)
9. Goodwin, M.H.: Occasioned knowledge exploration in family interaction. Discourse Soc. **18**(1), 93–110 (2007)
10. Alvesson, M.: Methodology for close up studies-struggling with closeness and closure. High. Educ. **46**(2), 167–193 (2003)
11. Engel, S.: Children's need to know: curiosity in schools. Harvard Educ. Rev. **81**(4), 625–645 (2011)
12. Lindholm, M.: Promoting curiosity?: possibilities and pitfalls in science education. Sci. Educ. **27**, 987–1002 (2018)
13. Crowley, K., Jacobs, M.: Building islands of expertise in everyday family activity. In: Leinhardt, G., Crowley, K., Knutson, K. (eds.) Learning Conversations in Museums, pp. 333–356. Lawrence Erlbaum, Mahwah, NJ (2002)
14. Tizard, B., Hughes, M.: Young Children Learning. Harvard University Press, Cambridge, MA (1984)
15. Chouinard, M.M.: Children's questions: a mechanism for cognitive development. Monographs of the Society for Research in Child Development, 72 (Serial No. 286, v-112) (2007)
16. Frazier, B.N., Gelman, S.A., Wellman, H.M.: Preschoolers' search for explanatory information within adult: child conversation. Child Dev. **80**(6), 1592–1611 (2009)

17. NGSS Lead States. Next Generation Science Standards: For States, By States. Washington, DC. National Academies Press (2013)

18. Berland, L.K., Schwarz, C.V., Krist, C., Kenyon, L., Lo, A.S., Reiser, B.J.: Epistemologies in practice: making scientific practices meaningful for students. J. Res. Sci. Teach. **53**(7), 1082–1112 (2016)

19. Bricker, L.A., Bell, P.: "What comes to mind when you think of science? The perfumery!": documenting science-related cultural learning pathways across contexts and timescales. J. Res. Sci. Teach. **51**(3), 260–285 (2014)

20. Zimmerman, H.T.: Participating in science at home: recognition work and learning in biology. J. Res. Sci. Teach. **49**(5), 597–630 (2012)

21. Geertz, C.: The Interpretation of Cultures. Basic Books, United States (1973)

22. Vedder-Weiss, D.: Serendipitous science engagement: a family self-ethnography. J. Res. Sci. Teach. **54**(3), 350–378 (2017)

23. U.S Department of Education (n.d.). Guiding Principles for Use of Technology with Early Learners. Accessed it from https://tech.ed.gov/earlylearning/principles/

24. Shaffer, D.W.: Quantitative Ethnography. Cathcart Press, Madison, WI (2017)

25. Corbin, J., Strauss, A.: Grounded theory research: procedures, canons, and evaluative criteria. GG(1), 3–21 (1990)

26. Boyatzis, R.E.: Thematic Analysis and Code Development: Transforming Qualitative Information. Sage Publications, London and New Delhi (1998)

27. Krippendorff, K.: Content Analysis: An Introduction to its Methodology. Sage Publications, Thousand Oaks, CA (2004)

28. Herrenkohl, L.R., Cornelius, L.: Investigating elementary students' scientific and historical argumentation. J. Learn. Sci. **22**(3), 413–461 (2013)

29. Shaffer, D.W., Collier, W., Ruis, A.R.R.: A tutorial on epistemic network analysis: analyzing the structure of connections in cognitive, social, and interaction data. J. Learn. Anal. **3** (2016)

30. Siebert-Evenstone, A.L., Arastoopour Irgens, G., Collier, W., Swiecki, Z., Ruis, A.R., Williamson Shaffer, D.: In search of conversational grain size: modelling semantic structure using moving stanza windows. J. Learn. Anal. **4**, 123–139 (2017). https://doi.org/10.18608/jla.2017.43.7

31. Swiecki, Z., Ruis, A.R., Farrell, C., Shaffer, D.W.: Assessing individual contributions to collaborative problem solving: a network analysis approach. Comput. Hum. Behav. October 2018

32. Huff, T.E.: Intellectual Curiosity and the Scientific Revolution: A Global Perspective. Cambridge University Press, Cambridge (2011)

33. Ball, P.: Curiosity. How Science Became Interested in Everything. The Bodly Head, London (2012)

34. Gauvain, M., Munroe, R.L., Beebe, H.: Children's question in cross-cultural perspective: a fourculture study. J. Cross-Cultural Psychol. **44**, 1148–1165 (2013)

35. Harris, P.L.: Trusting What You're Told. How Children Learn from Others. Belknap, Harvard (2012)

36. Shah, M., Foster, A.: Developing and assessing teachers' knowledge of game-based learning. J. Technol. Teach. Educ. **23**(2), 241–267 (2015)

Does Social Presence Play a Role in Learners' Positions in MOOC Learner Network? A Machine Learning Approach to Analyze Social Presence in Discussion Forums

Wenting Zou[(✉)], Zilong Pan, Chenglu Li, and Min Liu

University of Texas at Austin, Austin, TX 78712, USA
ellenzou@utexas.edu

Abstract. Low engagement has been a longstanding problem in MOOCs. However, engagement is crucial in social learning contexts. To further understand learners' engagement in MOOC discussion forum, this study focuses on the perspective of social presence, an important factor that mediates learners' positions within a learning network. To tackle the challenge of analyzing large amounts of text data, we built and tested a machine learning model to automatically classify the student-generated posts into different categories of social presence. We then measured learners' position in the learner network using social networking analysis (SNA) parameters (namely in-degree, closeness and betweenness centrality). Correlation tests showed that certain types of social presence have strong positive correlations with learners' network parameters. We also divided learners into groups based on their network positions to examine the differences of social presence demonstrated across different groups. The findings will inform MOOC learners to strategically present themselves in the discussion forum in order to increase the possibilities of peer interaction and cognitive engagement.

Keywords: MOOC · Discussion forum · Social presence · Text mining · Social Network Analysis (SNA) · Machine learning

1 Significance of the Study

Low course completion rates (typically between 5–10%) has been a common problem across different MOOCs [11, 39]. Research has investigated different possible factors that affect learners' engagement and performance, such as social interaction and rapport, difficulty of content, motivation, pedagogy, the backgrounds of participants and so on [11, 13, 34]. Among them, the social factor plays an important role in learners' engagement and performance in MOOCs [26, 39]. Social interaction is essential for stimulating higher order-thinking and improving learning outcomes [39]. In order to engage learners, a lot of MOOCs seek to develop a sense of learning communities among learners, particularly through the discussion forum [2].

Studying the discussion forum in online courses to understand the dynamics of learners' social interaction has long been a popular research topic. In terms of methodology,

© Springer Nature Switzerland AG 2021
A. R. Ruis and S. B. Lee (Eds.): ICQE 2021, CCIS 1312, pp. 248–264, 2021.
https://doi.org/10.1007/978-3-030-67788-6_17

most existing studies analyzed students' social behaviors in a quantitative way, such as using survey to ask learners to report their level of engagement in forums, or counting the frequency of social behaviors including posting, replying, liking posts, subscribing to threads, and following others etc. [3, 24], whereas other work pointed out that quantitative index of participation does not directly imply the quality of interaction [27]. Some researchers conducted content analyses of thread topics [17] to monitor students' social interaction in discussion forums (e.g., answering questions, self-introduction, complaining about difficulties and exchange of social support, discussing off-task topics etc.). However, few studies honed in on analyzing social presence in relation to learners' position in a learner network. To address this gap in the literature, this study attempts to unpack learners' social presence to understand what particular dimensions of social presence associate with their positions in the learner network in a MOOC. We see it as an essential step to gain an in-depth understanding of learners' engagement in constructivist online learning contexts. The findings will inform MOOC learners on how to strategically present themselves in the discussion forum to increase the possibilities of peer interaction, engage in meaningful discussions and ultimately achieve productive learning outcomes.

2 Theoretical Background

2.1 Social Presence in the Communities of Inquiry (CoI) Framework

Providing online learners with a sense of community is crucial to foster interpersonal communications for students to socially engage in learning. To develop a functional learning community, learners have to be involved in peer interaction and present themselves in a social learning setting. In fact, the importance of online presence has been highlighted by numerous studies [16]. Although the roots of social presence can be traced back to Mehrabian's concept of immediacy [31], the definition of the concept varied across different contexts. Short, Williams, and Christie [33] defined social presence as the "degree of salience of the other person in the interaction and the consequent salience of the interpersonal relationships (p. 65). While Gunawardena and Zittle [18] described social presence as a "measure of the psychological distance that a communicator puts between himself or herself and the object of his/her communication". In contrast, Rourke et al. [31] defined the concept of social presence from a learner's perspective by emphasizing the learner's responsibility and ability to socially and effectively project themselves in communities of inquiry (CoI). The CoI framework was initially proposed by Garrison, Anderson and Archer [14] on the premise that successful online learning requires the development of community, in which higher order thinking occurs when the students share their personal experience and thoughts through interaction with the instructor and peers. Within this framework, three elements are conceptualized as key components to support successful online learning experience, namely social presence, teaching presence, and cognitive presence. The framework aims at establishing an online environment that goes beyond a social community for general social exchange and low-level cognitive interactions, and emphasizes the cultivation of higher-level learning [1, 15]. At the operational level, a CoI integrates the learners' sense of community and belonging, the instructor's role in course design and facilitation, and learners' cognitive engagement with the course content [15]. It could therefore be used as a theoretical guide to assess different educational approaches and strategies in facilitating a community of inquiry [15].

Although social presence, cognitive presence, and teaching presence are equally important components in the CoI framework, this study focuses only on the analysis of social presence in relation to students' learning experience in MOOC. The reasons are: (1) social presence itself provides rich contextual information of the social climate in which learning takes place, which warrants thorough examination in relation to learners' engagement and overall performance; (2) the amount of input from instructors was minimum in this MOOC, which renders the analysis of teaching presence limited and unreliable; (3) analysis on the cognitive aspect of students' posts relies heavily on the course topic, which is complicated and challenging to conduct automatic analysis by a text classifier.

As an important component within the CoI framework, social presence is regarded as the ability of learners to project themselves socially and emotionally, thereby representing themselves as "real" people in a friendly and supportive learning community [15]. Social presence helps learners establish rapport with peers and with the instructor, which is a prerequisite for meaning negotiation, collaborative knowledge construction, and critical thinking. In this sense, it has the potential to enhance cognitive presence [6]. In the CoI framework, social presence can be analyzed from three aspects: affective expression, open communication, and group cohesion [1]. These three aspects in combination help learners develop interpersonal relationships with other members of the community and ultimately establish a trusting environment for learning to unfold [14]. When the climate is conducive to learning, knowledge could be socially constructed rather than transmitted or discovered, because increased opportunities for peer interaction allow for the development of rich and elaborate thinking and exploring, which in turn contributes to students' learning at a deeper level [4]. Previous studies provide ample evidence that raising social presence creates a learning environment that is perceived as warm, collegial, and approachable for all involved [32] and enhances cognition in social learning environments [6, 30]. Further benefits of social presence, according to Rourke et al. [31], are its ability to instigate, sustain, and support cognitive and affective learning objectives by making group interactions appealing, engaging, and intrinsically rewarding. Despites these purported benefits, the existing studies that examined social presence are not in relation to students' engagement in the learner network in MOOCs. Intuitively, as a learner who is situated in a social learning context, the types of social presence he or she exhibits may have more direct impact on the learner's connection and relationship with peers, which can be reflected in his or her position/centrality in the learner network. To test this hypothesis, this study attempts to take an exploratory approach to examine the potential relationship between learners' social presence and their position/centrality in a learning community.

Another gap emerged from the literature of social presence is that, the majority of previous studies of social presence mainly focused on small scale bounded online courses. There is a need to examine learners' social presence in MOOCs where learners have the opportunities to interact with a significantly larger pool of peers and yet still complain about a lack of peer support and a sense of community, as pointed out by some critics of MOOCs [7].

2.2 Social Network Analysis in MOOCs

Social Network Analysis (SNA) is a methodology that becomes increasingly popular in the realm of education research [8]. It provides the theoretical and methodological tools to understand activities and social processes in which learning occurs through extracting the patterns of connections among learners. In the context of MOOCs, SNA is often used to untangle the complex learner network and examine the relationship between social network properties and learning outcomes. For example, Poquet and Dawson [28] applied SNA to understand how social processes unfold in a particular cohort defined by its participants' regularity of forum presence. They analyzed this cohort and its development in comparison to the entire MOOC learner network. Results showed that the cohort, similar to its bounded counterparts in formal online education, could potentially cultivate interpersonal relationships and gradually deepen a shared cognitive engagement. Another study conducted by Yang and her colleagues [38] suggested that learners who participated in the forums early on were more likely to complete the course, whereas those who joined later found it hard to form social connections with peers. However, learners' network positions do not consistently predict their performance in MOOCs. For instance, Jiang, Fitzhugh and Warschauer [20] found a significant correlation between learners' network centrality measures and their final grades in an algebra MOOC, but this pattern did not apply to a finance MOOC. Similarly, Joksimović et al. [21] found that some centrality measures significantly correlated with the learners' completion and distinction status in two offerings of a programming MOOC, while others were useful in one course but not the other. Another study by Houston, Brady, Narasimham, and Fisher [19] found that direct learner interactions on the forums are more often correlated with learners' final grades than indirect measures (e.g., closeness and betweenness centrality).

In summary, using SNA to reveal how learning unfolds in MOOC forums has been relatively sparse in the literature thus far. Moreover, most of the existing studies used a quantitative approach to analyze learners' behaviors in forums. There is a need to use automated computational models to analyze the large scale of discourse in MOOC forums, which will supplement SNA techniques by adding rich contextual information to the structural patterns of learner interactions [10].

While the majority of previous studies focused on how students' network measures predict learning outcomes, the current study seeks to probe what kinds of online social presence contribute to learners' network positions. As a methodological contribution, we also proposed a theoretically grounded computational linguistics model to analyze students' forum posts based on the chosen framework of social presence.

We attempt to answer the following three questions in this study:

(1) What types of social presence are more common among learners in discussion forums?
(2) How do learners' social presence correlate with their positions in the learner network in discussion forums?

(3) What are the differences of social presence demonstrated by learners with different network positions?

3 Methods

3.1 Data Source

Participants were 661 students who participated in the discussion forums in a professional development MOOC titled Data Visualization for Storytelling and Discovery in Journalism, designed by a large research university. This MOOC primarily targeted journalism professionals but it's also open for free to anyone interested in this topic. It was deployed on a Moodle learning management system and launched from June to July 2018. It consisted of course features such as reading materials, video lectures, quizzes, and weekly discussion forums to engage and evaluate participants' performance. The MOOC consisted of four modules and students were required to participate in the forum discussions by the end of each module. A total of 13,210 posts were extracted and analyzed using the social presence categories originally devised by Rourke et al. [31]. We also made some minor modifications to the categories based on the findings of our own dataset.

3.2 Data Analysis

Identifying Different Types of Social Presence. Prior research regarding content analysis in MOOC forums is mostly based on manually coding a small set of learner-generated posts [5, 22]. However, this type of qualitative analysis is time-consuming and labor intensive, thus not practical to deal with large scale dataset. To combat this methodological challenge, we designed and tested different machine learning models in order to automatically classify the forum posts into different categories of social presence based on our selected framework. There are three phases in building and validating the machine learning models: firstly, 1,000 forum posts were randomly selected and manually coded into different categories of social presence (see Table 2). These categories touch upon both the cognitive aspects (e.g., asking questions, agreement and disagreement, providing advice, sharing resources etc.) and social aspects (self-disclosure, expressing emotions, complimenting others, expressing gratitude etc.) in learners' communication within a community of inquiry. Two researchers were involved in this qualitative analysis process. They discussed regularly to compare codes and categories, and re-coded certain posts if needed. Any disagreements were resolved until the inter-rater reliability reached 100%. Secondly, based on the hand-coded data from phase 1, we extracted some linguistic markers (e.g., verbs, adjectives, adverbs, punctuations etc.) for each category of social presence, and used these linguistic markers to search for more posts in our corpus and included them in the training set. The purpose of this step is to enlarge the training set and increase the robustness of our classification model. In the final phase, we built and compared different machine learning models using the training set. To optimize the performance of the machine learning model, seven types of supervised machine learning algorithms were tested in this phase, which are (1) Transfer learning with BERT [9]; (2) One-way RNN with Attention layer [35]; (3) One-way RNN with Mish activation and Attention layer; (4) One-way RNN; (5) Bidirectional RNN; (6) Random Forest and (7) Naive Bayes.

The performance of all the algorithms was evaluated based on training loss and validation loss to evaluate the robustness of the prediction performance. Dataset was split into training, validation, and testing sets with a ratio of 0.6, 0.2, and 0.2 respectively. Metrics such as accuracy, macro precision, macro recall, macro F-measure, and Matthew's correlation coefficient were used to show the actual performance (see Table 1).

Table 1. Evaluation metrics of models.

Model	Accuracy	Precision	Recall	F1	Matthew's corrcoef
BERT*	0.85	0.81	0.84	0.83	0.83
One-way RNN with Attention Layer	0.84	0.81	0.80	0.81	0.81
One-way RNN with Mish Activation and Attention Layer	0.84	0.82	0.81	0.81	0.81
Bidirectional RNN	0.81	0.74	0.78	0.76	0.77
One-way RNN	0.80	0.73	0.76	0.73	0.76
Random Forest	0.66	0.60	0.55	0.56	0.58
Naive Bayes	0.68	0.67	0.50	0.52	0.60

After testing the machine learning model, BERT was selected and applied to analyze the remaining posts to automatically categorize them into different social presences.

Measuring Learners' Positions in the Learning Network. The learners' positions in the forums was measured using three SNA parameters: in-degree centrality, closeness centrality and betweenness centrality. Specifically, in-degree value was determined by the total number of replies one received from others. High in-degree value indicates that others interact frequently with this particular participant in the network. This might imply, for example, that the participant is a popular student in the class or that the nature of her or his posts are in some way interesting or remarkable from the others' point of view. Although out-degree may also be an interesting index that indicates learners' centrality to some extent, it only signals how proactive learners are in terms of initiating conversations with peers. Since this study focuses on exploring how various types of social presence trigger different levels of interaction in a learning community, in-degree is a more suitable index than out-degree to reflect and measure how learners were received by the learning community through demonstrating different types of social presence. Betweenness centrality, on the other hand, shows how often a given participant is found in the shortest path between two other participants in the network, implying how often one learner serves as a bridge of communication between other two learners. By contrast, closeness centrality measures the average distance from one node to all other nodes in the network [36]. Unlike in-degree and betweenness centrality, a learner with low closeness centrality means he or she has closer ties with other learners in the forums. All calculations were completed in Gephi, an open-source network analysis and visualization software.

Before calculating the three network parameters for each individual, we conducted a network density analysis to see the level of connectedness among learners in the whole course. The result suggested that the learner network in this MOOC was relatively sparse ($d = .002$) with many small subgroups isolated from the dominant groups. We then performed a modularity operation on the learner network to detect all subgroups, and removed those with less than five participants. The purpose of this step is to make sure that the network parameters accurately reflect learners' positions in the network.

4   Results

4.1   The Types of Social Presence Learners Exhibited in the Discussion Forums

As shown in Table 2, three types of social presence were dominant in the discussion forums: *Personal opinion/reflection* ($N = 5593$), *Negative emotions* ($N = 2928$), *Expressing gratitude* ($N = 2062$). By contrast, *Asking questions* ($N = 1715$), *Positive emotions* ($N = 1649$), *Complimenting others* ($N = 1460$), *Disagreement/doubts/criticism* ($N = 1215$), and *Offering advice* ($N = 1150$) seem to occur less frequently in the discussion forums. Whereas the least frequent types of social presence are: *Vocatives* ($N = 694$), *Sharing resources* ($N = 542$), *Expressing agreement* ($N = 412$), *Self-disclosure* ($N = 263$), and *Referencing others* ($N = 65$). Interestingly, some categories of social presence, such as *Use of humor, Unconventional emotion expression, Course reflection, Social sharing* etc., are extremely rare ($N < 10$) in our dataset. Since those categories appeared at a negligible level, they were excluded in the correlation analysis in the next phase.

Table 2. Summary of the occurrence of different types of social presence.

Aspects	Category	Examples	Occurrences
Affective	Positive emotions	I think the information is really interesting!	1649
	Negative emotions	I got a bit confused now because i was later working with a lot of similar ones	2928
	Self-disclosure	i'm also from ohio (dayton), so i get your hot water situation	263
Open communication	Referencing others	Like @Becky suggested with 11 countries it could well be displayed on a world map	65

(continued)

Table 2. (*continued*)

Aspects	Category	Examples	Occurrences
	Asking questions	Any improvements to suggest?	1715
	Complimenting others	I find it very informative, also you did a great job with the legends and notes	1460
	Expressing gratitude	Thanks, your comments are valid and important	2062
	Expressing agreement	I think you're right, it seems to describe the relationship better	412
	Disagreement/doubts/criticism	I don't think map chart can add any value for this life expectancy information	1215
	Offering advice	I would suggest creating three charts	1150
	Personal opinion/reflection	my trick was to use the "who won where" map three times to make comparisons easier	5593
	Sharing resources	You can check out some examples here: https://www.tableau.com/learn/articles/best-beautiful-data-visualization-examples	542
Group cohesion	Vocatives (addressing an individual by name)	Hi Chris, I went to the link that you included in your critique	694

4.2 The Correlation Between Learners' Social Presence and Their Positions in the Learner Network

Spearman correlations were chosen to examine the associations between different types of social presence and learners' positions in the learning network of this MOOC. All statistically significant pairs of correlations were flagged in Table 3. It's worth noting that all correlations were significant at the 0.01 level (2-tailed). We hereby interpret the strength of association based on correlation coefficients.

The strongest correlations between social presence and learners' network parameters occur in these four categories: *Complimenting others*, *Personal opinion/reflection*, *Asking questions* and expressing *Positive emotions* (see Table 3). These four types of social presence are strongly correlated with ($r > .6$) all three network parameters (replies received/in-degree, closeness centrality, betweenness centrality) respectively. This means that as learners exhibit more of the above-mentioned four types of social presence, they are more likely to receive replies from peers, establish closer relationships with all other learners in the network, and become connectors who help bridging the communication among other learners.

The categories of social presence that have medium correlations ($.5 < r < .6$) with learners' positions in the network include: *Offering advice*, *Expressing gratitude*, *Sharing*

Table 3. The correlations between social presence and network parameters.

	Replies received (in-degree)	Betweenness centrality	Closeness centrality
Offering advice	.534**	.549**	.561**
Expressing agreement	.386**	.457**	.439**
Complimenting others	.613**	.676**	.704**
Disagreement/doubts/criticism	.499**	.513**	.486**
Expressing gratitude	.546**	.581**	.576**
Personal opinion/reflection	.678**	.679**	.675**
Self-disclosure	.446**	.457**	.459**
Asking questions	.622**	.635**	.612**
Referencing others	.204**	.213**	.221**
Sharing resources	.542**	.555**	.558**
Vocatives	.462**	.481**	.485**
Negative emotions	.548**	.532**	.557**
Positive emotions	.641**	.669**	.695**

**Correlation is significant at the 0.01 level.*

resources, and expressing *Negative emotions*. Although the associations are slightly weaker compared to the top four categories, we can still assume that learners who are keen on providing suggestions to others, showing gratitude, sharing useful materials and expressing negative emotions might attract peers' responses more easily, get closer to other learners, and more likely to bridge others to form a tighter learning community within the MOOC.

The weaker associations ($.2 < r < .5$) between social presence and learners' positions in the network appear in these five categories: *Expressing agreement, Disagreement/doubts/criticism, Self-disclosure, Vocatives, Referencing others*. Interestingly, raising *Disagreement/doubts/criticism* has stronger correlations with learners' network parameters compared to *Expressing agreement*, suggesting that dissenting voices or opposite views attract more attention from peers than seconding others' opinions, and more likely to push the learner towards important positions in the learning network. Surprisingly, *Referencing others* has the weakest correlation ($r < .3$) with learners' role in the network. This is unexpected since explicitly referencing others' messages is a very common way to get peers' attention and give rise to more ensuing interactions. Yet in our case, this type of approach is less effective to trigger responses from others.

4.3 Learners' Exhibited Social Presence in Different Centrality Groups

To further investigate how learners' social presence vary in different groups in terms of their network positions, we classified them based on their in-degree, closeness and betweenness centrality respectively. Kruskal-Wallis H tests were performed to determine if there are statistically significant differences of social presence across groups. Results showed that for each of the three network measures, all 13 types of social presence are significantly different across the low, medium and high centrality groups *(p < .01)*.

Fig. 1. The average frequency of different types of social presence in groups of high reply rate (received >12 replies), medium reply rate (received 1–12 replies) and zero reply rate (received 0 reply).

Fig. 2. The average frequency of different types of social presence in groups of low, medium and high closeness centrality

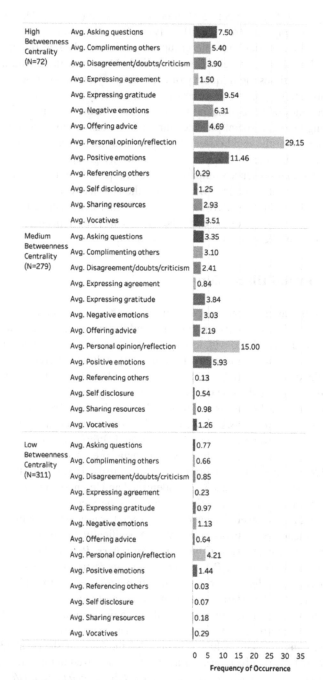

Fig. 3. The average frequency of different types of social presence in groups of high, medium and low betweenness centrality.

Specifically, from the perspective of in-degree measure (see Fig. 1), we found that the group of zero reply rate (received 0 reply) demonstrated significantly less social presence in all 13 categories than the group of medium reply rate (received 1 to 12 replies) and high reply rate (received > 12 replies). Moreover, the medium reply rate group showed 2 to 3 times the frequency of each category of social presence compared to the zero reply rate group, while learners in the high reply rate group exhibited 2 to 3 times in the frequency of those social presence compared to the medium reply rate group. When examining learners' social presence through the lens of closeness centrality (see Fig. 2), it is found that the gap between high and medium closeness centrality groups were even wider in that the medium closeness centrality group showed 3 to 5 times of all categories of social presence compared to the group with high closeness centrality (longer distance to all other nodes). By contrast, the gap between the low and medium closeness centrality group was narrower, with the former demonstrated 2 to 3 times of each type of social presence compared to the latter. This pattern persists when dividing learners based on their betweenness centrality (see Fig. 3).

5   Conclusion and Discussion

This study aims to examine what types of social presence are more common while learners participating in MOOC discussion forums. And further, we investigated what types of social presence are correlated with learners' positions in the learning network, as well as how learners with varied positions in the network exhibit different types of social presence. A trained and validated machine learning model was adopted to automatically classify the posts generated by learners. The results highlighted three types of dominant social presence in the discussion forum: *Personal opinion/reflection, Expressing gratitude* and *Negative emotions*, followed by *Asking questions, Positive emotions, Complimenting others, Disagreement/doubts/criticism*, and *Offering advice*, which appeared less frequently. The most uncommon types of social presence are found to be *Self-disclosure* and *Referencing others*. Correlation tests were used to examine the association between the 13 types of social presence we identified and learners' network parameters: the number of replies they received (in-degree), closeness centrality and betweenness centrality. Our findings showed that each type of social presence has significant positive correlations with learners' network parameters. Specifically, the strongest correlations occurred in these four categories: *Complimenting others, Personal opinion/reflection, Asking questions* and expressing *Positive emotions*, suggesting that these four types of social behaviors are more likely to trigger interaction with peers, help the learner shorten his/her distance to all other learners in the network, and increase the opportunities to serve as a bridge to facilitate communication flows in the learning community. In terms of the frequency of occurrence, open communication appeared to be the dominant aspect of social presence in our results, which is in line with the study of Shea et al. [32]. In contrast, we found that the relatively weaker associations occurred in these five categories: *Expressing agreement, Self-disclosure, Vocatives, Disagreement/doubts/criticism* and *Referencing others*, meaning that although these social behaviors may still improve learners' overall status in the network, they are less effective compared to *Complimenting others*, providing *Personal opinion/reflection, Asking questions* and expressing *Positive emotions.* Another interesting finding is that raising *Disagreement/doubts/criticism* has stronger correlations with learners' network parameters compared to *Expressing agreement,* suggesting that raising opposing views may help a learner attract more attention from peers, and more likely to push the learner towards important positions in the learning network. Another interesting comparison that's worth noting is the positive and negative emotions. In our findings, it seems that disseminating positive emotions in the discussion forum is more effective to help a learner gain popularity in the network than expressing negative emotions. Since emotions are ubiquitous in social learning settings and profoundly affect students' academic engagement and performance [29], it is meaningful to understand how learners' emotions directly or indirectly influence learning by motivating students to engage or disengage in task-related interactions. Our finding suggested that positive emotions, most typically learners' expression of interest and desire to dig deeper into the learning materials, are more conductive than negative emotions in forming social interactions within a learning network. Although we didn't investigate the correlation between emotions and learning outcomes in this study, we speculate that the expression of positive emotions might give rise to more opportunities for meaning negotiation and knowledge construction within the learning community, and ultimately increase learners' overall engagement and reduce the possibility of dropping out. This finding echoes Fredrickson's [12] broaden-and-build metaphor of positive emotions in that positive emotions such as joy and interest is to motivate exploratory behavior and an enlargement of one's action repertoire. However, it is unexpected that *Referencing others,* most typically mentioning the message from a specific individual, has the weakest correlation with learners' role in the network. This might be explained by the relatively lower occurrences of this type of behavior in the discussion forum.

To further understand how learners' social presence vary in different groups in terms of their network status, we divided the learners based on their levels of in-degree, closeness and betweenness centrality. The analysis showed that learners with lower network status (lower in-degree, closeness and betweenness centrality) demonstrated significantly less social presence than those with higher network status. The gaps are particularly wider when grouping them by closeness and betweenness centrality. This finding implies that learners need to invest more efforts to express themselves within a network. Specifically, they need to double or triple their contribution of posts that demonstrate various types of social presence to boost their network status to the next level (e.g., from low to medium level, or from medium to high level in terms of centrality). Since lack of interaction and feeling of isolation is one of the major complaints from students participating in MOOCs [25], it's critical for learners to reflect on their own level of contribution compared to their peers in a learning community, then strategically present themselves to establish more social ties with others and avoid being marginalized. As Whiteman [37] pointed out, students feel more comfortable to learn in an environment when they establish kinship with their community. When the environment is lacking social presence, the participants often see it as impersonal and, in turn, decreases the learners' motivation to contribute and share their knowledge with others [23]. The ultimate goal for creating social presence in MOOCs or any learning contexts, whether it be online or face-to-face, is to create a level of comfort in which people feel at ease to share and learn within a community. Without this goal being achieved, learners might still feel isolated, unfulfilling and more likely to drop out. The findings of this study fill the gap of existing literature by examining learners' social presence and its possible impact on learners' positions in the learning network in a MOOC. It shed light on what particular dimensions of social presence are more effective to establish social ties and facilitate the flows of communication in a learner network. It also informs MOOC learners/instructors in terms of how to strategically present themselves in discussion forums to earn more possibilities to engage in valuable discourse, participate in collective knowledge construction and facilitate the distribution of expertise among all participants in the community.

References

1. Akyol, Z., Garrison, D.R.: The development of a community of inquiry over time in an online course: understanding the progression and integration of social, cognitive and teaching presence. J. Asynchronous Learn. Netw. **12**, 3–22 (2008)
2. Al-Rahmi, W.M., Alias, N., Othman, M.S., Marin, V.I., Tur, G.: A model of factors affecting learning performance through the use of social media in Malaysian higher education. Comput. Educ. **121**, 59–72 (2018)
3. Anderson, A., Huttenlocher, D., Kleinberg, J., Leskovec, J.: Engaging with massive online courses. In Proceedings of the 23rd International Conference on World Wide Web, pp. 687–698. ACM, April 2014
4. Bransford, J.D., Brown, A.L., Cocking, R.R.: How People Learn, vol. 11. National Academy Press, Washington, DC (2000)
5. Barak, M., Watted, A., Haick, H.: Motivation to learn in massive open online courses: examining aspects of language and social engagement. Comput. Educ. **94**, 49–60 (2016)
6. Caspi, A., Blau, I.: Social presence in online discussion groups: testing three conceptions and their relations to perceived learning. Soc. Psychol. Educ. **11**(3), 323–346 (2008). https://doi.org/10.1007/s11218-008-9054-2
7. Clinnin, K.: Redefining the MOOC: examining the multilingual and community potential of massive online courses. J. Global Liter. Technol. Emerg. Pedag. **2**(3), 140–162 (2014)
8. De Laat, M., Lally, V., Lipponen, L., Simons, R.J.: Investigating patterns of interaction in networked learning and computer-supported collaborative learning: a role for social network analysis. Int. J. Comput. Support. Collab. Learn. **2**(1), 87–103 (2007). https://doi.org/10.1007/s11412-007-9006-4
9. Devlin, J., Chang, M.W., Lee, K., Toutanova, K.: Bert: Pre-training of deep bidirectional transformers for language understanding. arXiv preprint arXiv:1810.04805 (2018)
10. Dowell, N.M., et al.: Modeling Learners' Social Centrality and Performance through Language and Discourse. International Educational Data Mining Society (2015)
11. Fidalgo-Blanco, Á., Sein-Echaluce, M.L., García-Peñalvo, F.J.: From massive access to cooperation: lessons learned and proven results of a hybrid xMOOC/cMOOC pedagogical approach to MOOCs. Int. J. Educ. Technol. High. Educ. **13**(1), 1–13 (2016). https://doi.org/10.1186/s41239-016-0024-z
12. Fredrickson, B.L.: The role of positive emotions in positive psychology: the broaden-and-build theory of positive emotions. Am. Psychol. **56**(3), 218 (2001)
13. García-Peñalvo, F.J., Fidalgo-Blanco, Á., Sein-Echaluce, M.L.: An adaptive hybrid MOOC model: Disrupting the MOOC concept in higher education. Telemat. Inform. **35**(4), 1018–1030 (2018)
14. Garrison, D.R., Anderson, T., Archer, W.: Critical thinking, cognitive presence, and computer conferencing in distance education. Am. J. Distance Educ. **15**(1), 7–23 (2001)

15. Garrison, D.R., Arbaugh, J.B.: Researching the community of inquiry framework: review, issues, and future directions. Internet High. Educ. **10**(3), 157–172 (2007)
16. Garrison, D.R., Cleveland-Innes, M.: Facilitating cognitive presence in online learning: Interaction is not enough. Am. J. Distance Educ. **19**(3), 133–148 (2005)
17. Gillani, N., Eynon, R., Osborne, M., Hjorth, I., Roberts, S.: Communication communities in MOOCs. (arXiv preprint arXiv:1403.4640) (2014)
18. Gunawardena, C.N., Zittle, F.J.: Social presence as a predictor of satisfaction within a computer-mediated conferencing environment. Am. J. Distance Educ. **11**(3), 8–26 (1997)
19. Houston, S.L., Brady, K., Narasimham, G., Fisher, D.: Pass the idea please: the relationship between network position, direct engagement, and course performance in MOOCs. In: Proceedings of the 4th (2017) ACM Conference on Learning@ scale, New York, NY, USA, pp. 295–298.ACM (2017)
20. Jiang, S., Fitzhugh, S.M., Warschauer, M.: Social positioning and performance in MOOCs. In: Proceedings of Graph-Based Educational Data Mining Workshop at the 7th International Conference on Educational Data Mining, pp. 55–58. CEUR-WS (2014)
21. Joksimović, S., Manataki, A., Gašević, D., Dawson, S., Kovanović, V., Kereki, D., et al.: Translating network position into performance: importance of centrality in different network configurations. In: Proceedings of the 6th International Conference on Learning Analytics & Knowledge, New York, NY, USA, pp. 314–323. ACM (2016)
22. Kop, R.: The challenges to connectivist learning on open online networks: learning experiences during a massive open online course. Int. Rev. Res. Open Distrib. Learn. **12**(3), 19–38 (2011)
23. Leh, A.S.: Computer-mediated communication and social presence in a distance learning environment. J. Educ. Telecommun. **7**(2), 109–128 (2001)
24. Liu, M., Zou, W., Li, C., Shi, Y., Pan, Z., Pan, X.: Using learning analytics to examine relationships between learners' usage data with their profiles and perceptions: a case study of a MOOC designed for working professionals. In: Ifenthaler, D., Mah, D.-K., Yau, J.Y.-K. (eds.) Utilizing Learning Analytics to Support Study Success, pp. 275–294. Springer, Cham (2019). https://doi.org/10.1007/978-3-319-64792-0_15
25. Liu, M., Zou, W., Shi, Y., Pan, Z., Li, C.: What do participants think of today's MOOCs: an updated look at the benefits and challenges of MOOCs designed for working professionals. J. Comput. High. Educ. **32**(2), 307–329 (2019). https://doi.org/10.1007/s12528-019-09234-x
26. Lu, J., Churchill, D.: The effect of social interaction on learning engagement in a social networking environment. Interact. Learn. Environ. **22**(4), 401–417 (2014)
27. Meyer, K.A.: Evaluating online discussions: Four different frames of analysis. J. Asynchronous Learn. Netw. **8**(2), 101–114 (2004)
28. Poquet, O., Dawson, S.: Untangling MOOC learner networks. In: Proceedings of the 6th International Conference on Learning Analytics & Knowledge, pp. 208–212. ACM (2016)
29. Pekrun, R., Linnenbrink-Garcia, L.: Academic emotions and student engagement. In: Christenson, S., Reschly, A., Wylie, C. (eds.) Handbook of Research on Student Engagement, pp. 259–282. Springer, Boston (2012). https://doi.org/10.1007/978-1-4614-2018-7_12
30. Richardson, J.C., Swan, K.: Examining social presence in online courses in relation to students' perceived learning and satisfaction. J. Asynchronous Learn. Netw. **7**(1), 68–88 (2003)
31. Rourke, L., Anderson, T., Garrison, D.R., Archer, W.: Assessing social presence in asynchronous text-based computer conferencing. J. Distance Educ. **14**(2), 50–71 (1999)
32. Shea, P., et al.: A re-examination of the community of inquiry framework: Social network and content analysis. Internet High. Educ. **13**(1–2), 10–21 (2010)
33. Short, J., Williams, E., Christie, B.: The Social Psychology of Telecommunications. Wiley, Hoboken (1976)

34. Stiller, K.D., Bachmaier, R.: Dropout in an online training for trainee teachers. Eur. J. Open Distance e-Learn. **20**(1), 80–95 (2017)
35. Vaswani, A., et al.: Attention is all you need. In: Advances in Neural Information Processing Systems, pp. 5998–6008 (2017)
36. Wasserman, S., Faust, K.: Social Network Analysis: Methods and Applications, vol. 8. Cambridge University Press, Cambridge (1994)
37. Whiteman, J.A.M.: Interpersonal communication in computer mediated learning (2002)
38. Yang, D., Wen, M., Kumar, A., Xing, E.P., Rosé, C.P.: Towards an integration of text and graph clustering methods as a lens for studying social interaction in MOOCs. Int. Rev. Res. Open Distrib. Learn. **15**(5), 215–234 (2014)
39. Zhang, D.J., Allon, G., Van Mieghem, J.A.: Does social interaction improve learning outcomes? Evidence from field experiments on massive open online courses. Manuf. Serv. Oper. Manage. **19**(3), 347–367 (2017)

Professional Decision Making: Reframing Teachers' Work Using Epistemic Frame Theory

Michael Phillips[1]([✉]) [iD], Amanda Siebert-Evenstone[2] [iD], Aaron Kessler[3] [iD],
Dragan Gasevic[1] [iD], and David Williamson Shaffer[2] [iD]

[1] Monash University, Melbourne, Australia
michael.phillips@monash.edu
[2] University of Wisconsin-Madison, Madison, USA
[3] Massachusetts Institute of Technology, Cambridge, USA

Abstract. For many outside the profession, teaching looks simple and straight-forward; however, for those working in classrooms, it can be a challenging task. In this paper we argue that teaching is a complex profession that requires both novice and expert educators alike to engage students in sets of activities aimed at transforming their understanding of a subject area. This work requires complex planning, enacting instruction, and reflecting on outcomes. In a moment to moment basis teachers must make decisions and iterate on previously made decisions in order to provide effective opportunities for students to engage with the materials, skills or content to be learned.

In this paper, we aim to highlight the complexity of the decision-making process and, in doing so we make the argument that individual teachers' decision-making draws upon a personal epistemic frame which includes factors such as skills, knowledge, identity, values, and epistemology. We provide examples of previous research efforts that have attempted to explore such factors and the limitations, both philosophical and methodological shortcomings of such attempts. Finally, we propose that the use of Quantitative Ethnography and Epistemic Frame Theory provides new opportunities to interrogate teachers' practices and decision-making as a way to better understand the complexity of teacher work.

Keywords: Teachers · Decision-making · Epistemic frame theory

1 Introduction

For decades the work of defining what constitutes a profession has been a topic of active study [1–3]. In this paper, we follow the lead of Evetts [4] in approaching "professions as a generic group of occupations based on knowledge both technical and tacit…Professions are essentially the knowledge-based category of occupations which usually follow a period of tertiary education and vocational training and experience" (p. 397). In line with these ideas of professions, Shaffer [5] suggests that:

profexsionals work on problems that involve uncertainty and that therefore require discretion and judgement. For a professional … no two problems are quite ever the same,

© Springer Nature Switzerland AG 2021
A. R. Ruis and S. B. Lee (Eds.): ICQE 2021, CCIS 1312, pp. 265–276, 2021.
https://doi.org/10.1007/978-3-030-67788-6_18

and no set of routines tell a true professional what to do next. This is as much true for a master carpenter as a transplant surgeon. (p. 95)

Further, people working in these socially constructed professions, and the accrediting bodies that grant the licensure usually associated with such vocations, almost always require professional members to engage in continuing education. Highlighting the importance of always improving, adapting, and developing a deeper understanding of the profession.

While each profession requires their own unique set of practices, engaging in professional activity often requires a series of decisions to be made in the moment of the work being performed that require the professional to quickly synthesize into action prior knowledge, an understanding of their skills and practices, values, beliefs and ethical standards and the goals of the work being completed. These actions are often in service of accomplishing some short term and long-term goals and often require reflection in and on action [6] if the professional is to improve their understanding of the field and improve their own actions.

Given this vision of professional work, we argue that teaching is a complex profession that requires educators, novice and expert alike, to engage students in sets of activities aimed at transforming their understanding of a subject area. The process of teaching requires planning, enacting instruction, and reflecting on outcomes. In a moment to moment basis teachers must make decisions and iterate on previously made decisions in order to provide effective opportunities for students to engage with the materials or content to be learned.

In the sections that follow, we aim to highlight the complexity of the decision-making process. In doing so we argue that individual teachers' decision-making draws upon a personal epistemic frame which includes factors such as knowledge; skills, practices and epistemology; and orientations, and epistemology. We provide examples of previous research efforts that have attempted to explore such factors and the shortcomings of such attempts. Finally, we propose that the use of Quantitative Ethnography and Epistemic Frame Theory provides new opportunities to interrogate teachers' practices and decision-making as never before.

2 Attempts to Better Understand Teacher Decision-Making

Teaching is often cast as something that has been passively observed by students for a long time and therefore appears to many to be relatively straightforward and simple. The stereotypical impression created is that there is a set of routines that help to ensure the delivery of information in class, but that some teachers bring to bear an idiosyncratic edge to their practice that makes them stand out as being good teachers. In essence, then, to the casual observer, teaching looks easy. ([7] p. 119)

In contrast to this often-held perception of teaching, Shulman [8] among many others described the work of educators as an "outrageously complex activity" (p. 11). Researchers have argued that a large part of this complexity results from the myriad of pedagogical decisions that educators need to make (for example, see: [9, 10]). Almost 50 years ago, Shavelson [11] highlighted the centrality of decision-making in the work of educators characterizing it as "the basic teaching skill" [emphasis in original] (p. iii), a perspective supported by Madeline Hunter [12] who suggested that "teaching is decision making" (p. 62), and Fenstermacher [13, 14] argued that the role of teacher education is not to program or train teachers to behave in predetermined ways, but to educate them to reason soundly about their teaching.

While such accounts highlight the importance of pedagogical decision-making, better understanding how such choices are made is important in capturing the sophisticated nature of teaching. Recent attempts to better understand what underpins effective teacher decision-making continue to be reported in the research literature (for example, see: [15–17]) suggesting we are yet to develop a way of effectively interrogating what, why and how teachers make their decisions. Loughran [18] makes the point that many past investigations of teachers' decision-making and their practices examine *what* and *how* teachers do what they do. He argues, however, that to better understand the decisions teachers make, understanding *why* teachers make particular decisions "is crucially important" ([18], p. 526). In support of this argument, the following sections capture just some of the past investigations that have considered three different factors that contribute to the *what* and *how* of pedagogical decision-making: knowledge; skills, practices and epistemologies; and orientations.

2.1 Teacher Knowledge

Developing a clearer sense of what teachers know and how they use their knowledge to enhance their decision-making has been an area of interest for education researchers, teacher educators, and educational policymakers [19]. A great deal of focused research in the 1980s and 1990s considered teachers' knowledge from differing epistemological viewpoints. For example, Tom and Valli [20] developed a philosophically grounded review of professional knowledge, Grimmit and MacKinnon [21] analyzed craft conceptions of teaching and Shulman's [8, 22–26] program of research sought to "show what forms and types of knowledge are required to teach competently" ([27], p. 6). It is this extensive program of research that has led Valli and Tom [28] to suggest that Shulman "probably has gone as far as anyone in his thinking about the forms of teacher knowledge" (p. 6).

Shulman's work resulted in a widely cited 'knowledge base for teaching' which comprised seven categories of knowledge: content knowledge; pedagogical knowledge; curriculum knowledge; knowledge of learners; knowledge of contexts; knowledge of educational ends, purposes, and values; and pedagogical content knowledge. While Shulman's work represented a great leap forward understanding the multi-faceted nature of teacher knowledge, it has largely been discussed in a homogenous way. That is, all educators, irrespective of contextual differences, should aspire to develop all of these forms of knowledge to help them make better pedagogical decisions. Despite the extensive use of these categories in subsequent research efforts, the connections between teacher knowledge and the ways in which particular forms of knowledge influence certain types of decisions remain largely disconnected.

2.2 Skills, Practices and Epistemology

In addition to efforts to better understand the influence of knowledge on decision-making, past research has focused on the skills and practices of educators in different contexts including effective literacy teachers [29], mathematics teachers [30], and science teachers [31]. Interestingly, the findings from such studies differ, sometimes subtly and in other cases markedly, from what is considered effective in particular domains. Bartholomew, Osborne, and Ratcliffe [31] worked with 11 science teachers from the UK and found that teachers' conception and use of learning goals had an impact on a teacher's ability to teach effectively. In contrast, McDonough and Clarke [30] found that "attention given by [Australian] teachers to individual children" (p. 3-267) was particularly important practices for Mathematics teachers of 5 to 7-year-old children, whereas Wray et al. [29] found that effective literacy teachers in England contextualized their teaching which appeared to make it possible for pupils to make active connections between different forms of literacy knowledge.

While these studies contribute to a body of work researching teachers' classroom skills and practices, it quickly becomes clear that what is considered 'effective' is highly contextually dependent and the underlying epistemology of teachers is likely to play a substantial role in the determination of what skills and practices underpin effective teaching. For example, it is reasonable for Chemistry teachers to be interested in the development of skills that allow students to cognitively break down or atomize materials to their constituent components. A Biology teacher, on the other hand, is more likely to be interested in having their students think in 'big picture' ideas or in systems. It is clear that these kinds of epistemological underpinnings have some connection to knowledge and the kinds of skills and practices that need to be concurrently developed but as yet, we do not have a comprehensive understanding of the connections between these different elements and the ways in which they influence educators' pedagogical decisions. A challenge confronting researchers is how to quantify and represent the connections between teachers' epistemology and their skills and practices.

2.3 Orientations

In additional to knowledge and skills, practices and epistemologies, teachers' attitudes, especially the beliefs that form such attitudes [32], have received much attention. Empirical investigations also illustrate the impact of the role of beliefs in a variety of teacher decisions [33] including the integration of technology [34], the way students learn languages [35] or develop music identity and skills [36]. Others have discussed similar findings in relation to teacher attitudes, values, preferences and tastes. Shoenfeld [37] acknowledges that each of these terms provides opportunities to gain insights into what teachers do; however, instead of treating these as separate categories, he employs the term 'orientations' as a broad category that incorporates these often-overlapping constructs.

While there has been some synthesis of the influence of particularly closely aligned components that shape teachers' decision-making (for example Shonfeld's categorization of orientations), researchers have, more often than not, treated these as separate, siloed influences on teacher decision-making. We argue that instead of looking at each of these in isolation, revealing the *what* and *how* of teacher decision-making, we can better explore and explain the complex reasons *why* teachers make the decisions they do by considering the connections between the range of factors that underpin their pedagogical practices. To effectively understand teachers' decision-making, we do not need to quantify individual factors but instead to consider the relationships between teachers' epistemology, skills, values, and knowledge – a collection of factors called an *epistemic frame* [5].

3   Epistemic Frame Theory: A Window into Teachers' Decision-Making

To dive deeper into how people learn to think, Shaffer [5] proposed *epistemic frame theory* to describe the pattern of associations among skills, knowledge, and other cognitive elements that characterize groups of people who share similar ways of framing, investigating, and solving complex problems.

The concept of a frame is from Erving Goffman [38] who argued that people use a set of organizational principles, or what he calls *frames*, that structure our perception of what is happening and what is important during an activity. During our everyday experiences, people filter information, discard certain details, and build frames that organize an understanding of the current situation for future actions. Importantly, these organizational structures exist and are shaped by the person, activity, context, and interactions with other people. When people go to a coffee shop to work, their actions are shaped by individual choices and beliefs about the situation (we enjoy coffee, being around people that are also working is motivating, we want to support local businesses). But this view of the coffee shop is also shaped by the context (there are shared tables and solitary tables, other people are working or not working, the wireless internet connection is reliable). Given this premise, frames are the collections of both individual and social norms, values, and actions that shape how we see the world.

Shaffer [39, 40] builds on Goffman's frame analysis by considering what it means for a person to know something. In this way, *epistemic frames* consider how certain groups of people think. Epistemic frame theory suggests that in specific communities there is a systematic pattern of relationships among skills, knowledge, identity, values, and epistemology that form the epistemic frame for that community. For example, in education, a teacher may learn to develop questions that require students to respond with more than a 'yes' or 'no' answer, therefore revealing not just whether they understand a particular piece of content but also how they came to know this information. Such a response provides the teacher with insights into the emerging metacognitive processes of that individual student. With these new insights, the teacher is able to reconsider how she might shape future learning activities for that student. In this example, the teacher is learning to make decisions by weighing competing factors and eventually justifying why they made those choices.

While frames are core to this theory, another critical component is that these frames are about epistemology. Epistemic frame theory is grounded in Perkins' [41] description of epistemology which he described as "knowledge and know-how concerning justification and explanation" (p. 85). Shaffer [5] extends this notion claiming that epistemology "is a particular way of thinking about or justifying actions, of structuring valid claims.

Epistemology tells you the rules you are supposed to use in deciding whether something is true". (p. 32)

Importantly, Shaffer [5] notes that "epistemology in this sense is domain-specific: Mathematicians make different kinds of arguments than historians do" (p. 32). This challenges the 'straightforward and simple' perception of teaching by suggesting that to be an effective teacher, you have to not only develop particular, discipline-based ways of justifying your actions and structuring valid claims about content knowledge, but you also need to understand the "intellectual and historical justification for the traditional disciplines" ([5], p. 33). To make a decision as a teacher, you need to think in a particular way which is, in part, shaped by the domain or discipline you are teaching as this domain has a particular set of rules that structure valid claims, justify actions and determine whether something is true.

Epistemic frame theory, however, does not solely consider teachers' decisions in light of the underpinning epistemology that teachers bring to their practices. As highlighted earlier, to effectively understand teachers' decision-making we need to consider the relationships between how teachers' skills, knowledge, and values affect their approach to seeing and solving problems.

4 The Multifaceted Nature of Teaching

One way to approach understanding the core practices of teachers is to identify important elements of that culture. Quantitative Ethnography is a way of talking about culture as the ethnographic component of this methodology provides insights into the cultural practices of teaching. Gee [42] describes learning a practice as learning the *Discourse* of that practice, meaning a way of "talking, listening, writing, reading, acting, interacting, believing, valuing, and feeling (and using various objects, symbols, images, tools, and technologies)" (p. 719). As highlighted earlier in this paper, teachers need to develop multiple forms of knowledge to be effective classroom professionals; however, they also need to develop a range of other practices including highly developed interpersonal skills [43] including talking with students in ways that draw upon language that they can comprehend [44], representing content in multiple ways to allow all students access to information while also being inclusive of student opinions but also directing and shaping the classroom culture [45] to name but a few. In the end, learning this Discourse requires developing and transforming their identity as a teacher.

This transformation largely occurs with the help of others. In this way, learning a Discourse involves enculturation into a *community of practice* [46], which is a group of people who see and solve problems in a similar way. Upon entering the workforce as a graduate teacher or newcomer [47], teachers are expected to develop an increasingly sophisticated and diverse range of pedagogical skills through which they can make increasingly complex classroom decisions. This development is often guided by old-timers from within the community [47] and illustrates the power of identity and trajectory as forces that shape teachers' transformations [48].

Importantly, epistemic frame theory shifts the focus of learning from accumulating isolated pieces of cultural knowledge to focusing on the structure of connections among them. Similarly, diSessa [49] argues that deep understanding results from linking basic disciplinary concepts within a theoretical framework. For example, diSessa describes how novices have "knowledge-in-pieces", whereas experts have a deep and systematic understanding of how these disciplinary concepts are connected. Other learning sciences theorists have similarly conceptualized learning as the developing patterns of connections between concepts [50, 51]. As we hypothesize that the linkages between components of teachers' epistemic frames are critical, we choose a methodology that focuses on explicitly modelling such connections.

Taken together, describing the epistemic frame of teachers requires specifying the set of Discourse codes that are core to teachers' way of seeing and problem-solving, but also the relationships between how these codes are connected. The volume of data required to model the relationships between the codes representing components of teachers' epistemic frames is understandably large. This becomes particularly true when using visualizations to explore differences between contexts in which teachers work [52]. Therefore, epistemic frame theory can be a valuable way to understand how teachers learn certain ways of connecting ideas, making decisions, and justifying actions in their teacher training and practice. Consequently, we need a way to view the range of components that shape teacher professional practice.

4.1 The Results of a Pilot Study: Opportunities Offered Through ENA and Quantitative Ethnography

Phillips, et al. [52] conducted a pilot study that considered whether it would be possible to use a quantitative ethnographic approach to reveal relationships between different forms of teacher knowledge and various forms of teacher decision making. This pilot study analyzed the lesson plans of six teachers who worked in a specialist Mathematics, Science and Technology secondary school in Melbourne, Australia. A pair of teachers from each of the specialist areas within the school volunteered to participate in the study, and each of these pairs together taught a co-educational class of approximately 50 Year 10 students (around 16-years old). These six participants provided the initial data for this investigation in the form of 45 lesson plans for the first unit of work that was to be taught in the academic year.

This data was coded using the NVivo12 software program for evidence of teacher knowledge (based on Shulman's knowledge base for teaching described in Sect. 2.1 of this paper) and Shulman's [8] teacher decision making framework known as pedagogical reasoning and action (PR&A). Following the coding of lesson plans in NVivo, we examined the relationship between forms of knowledge and processes of PR&A through Epistemic Network Analysis (ENA) [53]. The results from ENA analysis of teacher lesson plans revealed substantially different connections between knowledge forms and components of the PR&A framework for teachers with differing epistemological backgrounds.

For example, the mathematics teachers involved in this study appear to show greater planned co-occurrences of reflecting, reflection evaluation, and transformation with content knowledge than the science teachers whose lesson plans do not show any evidence of such co-occurrences; however, the nature of the domain is a feature in science teacher lesson plans where it regularly co-occurs with four other knowledge forms and stages of PR&A yet is notably absent from the mathematics teachers lesson plans. Most strikingly, the lesson plans from the IT teachers showed comparatively few co-occurrences between knowledge forms and stages of PR&A, yet had the most codes represented of all three domains.

These co-occurrences were analysed using ENA – a tool which allows for quantitative ethnographic explorations. One of the main aims of Quantitative Ethnography is to use "Big Data to help us transform it into Big Understanding" ([40] p. 398) and an inherent part of this process is taking etic representations, in this investigation the data represented in Figs. 1, 2 and 3, and working with participants in a study to generate emic understandings.

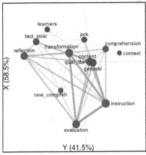 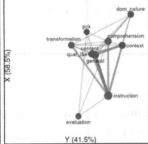 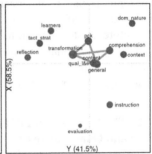

Fig. 1. Co-occurrences between knowledge forms and PR&A in mathematics lesson plans.

Fig. 2. Co-occurrences between knowledge forms and PR&A in science lesson plans.

Fig. 3. Co-occurrences between knowledge forms and PR&A in IT lesson plans

Phillips et al. (in preparation) conducted interviews with each of the teaching teams who indicated that many of the ENA representations reflected their tacit understandings of their practices. Examining the representation of their lesson plans, one of the science teachers commented that "content is kind of in a way the driving force, as a central part of what we have to do, so it makes sense that content would be such a central part of what's in there". The discussion between the mathematics teachers also confirmed that some of the ENA representation reflected conceptions of their shared practice:

> Mathematics teacher 1: The other thing with maths is because they all come in from different schools. At least the first half of the year is really trying to get everyone at the same level, so bringing up the students who might have lower skills up to that so there, I guess, the less connection between the PCK and the learners can be explained that we want to get everyone to the same point so that they're then ready to move into VCE which I guess makes sense.

> Mathematics teacher 2: Which is probably why the faint lines are to the learners because we don't know enough about them, we haven't taught them before, particularly Year 10 it's our first year.

In addition to confirming elements of the ENA representation, this brief discussion between the two mathematics teachers reveals deep emic perspectives of the context for which the lesson plans have been designed. As previously discussed, the school in which these teachers worked was a specialist mathematics, science and technology school only enrolling students in their final three years of secondary schooling. The comments from the two mathematics teachers reveal that, despite recognizing the importance of PCK, the need to ensure that all students in their first year at the school (Year 10) have comparable content knowledge overrides the desire for the development of particular approaches for particular individuals at particular points in time for particular purposes (that is, the essence of PCK).

The two IT teachers expressed some surprise when initially examining the ENA representation of their lesson plans. Both teachers commented on the lack of connections between knowledge forms and decision-making processes. When unpacking this representation, the two IT teachers revealed an important limitation in conclusions drawn simply from representations of lesson planning documents. The intense focus on mathematics and science in this particular school is reflected in large numbers of teachers of these two subjects. As a result, mathematics and science teachers in this particular school are used to working with a variety of different teaching partners. Consequentially, the amount of detail in the lesson plans for these teachers is high as teachers are often working with people who hold varied beliefs and attitudes about teaching. In contrast, there are only two IT teachers in the school who teach all of their classes together. Their desks are also beside one another in the staff room, and they spend a great deal of time outside of class reflecting and discussing previous classes. As a result, the amount of detail recorded in their lesson plans is significantly lower than for the mathematics or science teachers as much of the IT teachers shared practices and understandings are communicated verbally. The importance of presenting etic ENA representations to the teachers to develop deeper emic understandings is, therefore, a vital part of this quantitative ethnographic exploration of teachers' knowledge and decision-making.

Despite the small sample size of teachers involved in this project (n = 6), this study provides what we believe is the first Quantitative Ethnographic [40] account of the co-occurrence of teachers' knowledge forms and PR&A stages. The ENA representations provided in this paper allow researchers to develop new insights into teacher knowledge and decision making that challenge the homogenous nature of these two frameworks that was intimated in many of Shulman's publications. The language that Shulman [8] used to describe his knowledge base for teaching was mostly singular: "*a* codified or codifiable aggregation of knowledge" (p. 4), "*the* knowledge base" (p. 4), "*an* elaborate knowledge base for teaching" [8][emphases added]. While Shulman [8] discussed contextual knowledge, the subsequent applications of his knowledge base for teaching have often been devoid of contextual considerations implying that all effective teachers drew upon all six forms of knowledge irrespective of factors such as discipline taught and age of students.

Shulman's [8] description of stages of PR&A, while helpful with identifying different components of teachers' decision-making processes, did not provide much guidance for researchers or practitioners as these stages "are not meant to represent a set of fixed stages, phases, or steps. Many of the processes can occur in a different order. Some may not occur at all during some acts of teaching. Some may be truncated, others elaborated" (p. 19). The ENA representations presented in this paper provide empirically-based insights into the co-occurrences of the planned PR&A processes of these teachers. While not suggesting that there is a definitive order for these, nor that the findings from this pilot study are broadly generalisable, it is encouraging to see such representations as the process of coding and representing co-occurrences in this manner promises more in-depth insights than have been previously possible.

While adding to our existing understanding of teachers' professional decision making, this investigation and confirming the utility of Epistemic Network Analysis, this work was limited only to teacher knowledge and did not consider other elements of the teachers' epistemic frames.

The next phase in the progression of this work is to expand this pilot study in three important ways. First, using our literature review and situated understanding of this field we hope to further identify and develop culturally relevant codes that capture the ways teachers approach and enact their decision-making practices. Second, we as researchers can bridge our local understanding of teacher-student interactions with larger scale analyses decision-making patterns. Through the use of tools, such as Epistemic Network Analysis, we can measure and visualize how teachers within and across domains, grade-levels, and other contextual factors may make similar or different choices. Finally, and most importantly, we need researchers to analyze and critique these dual analyses to provide better descriptions and interpretations of how teachers think in these contexts.

In the end, using a quantitative ethnographic approach, we as researchers can use our understanding of local connection-making to develop and analyze broader patterns across teachers. We call on colleagues in the teacher education field to join with Quantitative Ethnographers to further this endeavor.

References

1. Greenwood, E.: Attributes of a profession. Soc. Work **2** 45–55 (1957)
2. Freidson, E.: Theory and the professions. Indian Law J. **64**(3), 423–432 (1989)
3. Saks, M.: Defining a profession: The role of knowledge and expertise. Prof. Profession. **2**(1) (2012). https://doi.org/10.7577/pp.v2i1.151
4. Evetts, J.: The sociological analysis of professionalism: occupational change in the modern world. Int. Sociol. **18**(2), 395–415 (2003). https://doi.org/10.1177/0268580903018002005
5. Shaffer, D.W.: How Computer Games Help Children Learn. Macmillan, New York (2006). https://doi.org/10.1057/9780230601994
6. Schön, D.A.: The Reflective Practitioner: How Professionals Think in Action. Routledge, London (2017). https://doi.org/10.4324/9781315237473
7. Loughran, J.J.: Pedagogy: making sense of the complex relationship between teaching and learning. Curricul. Inq. **43**(1), 118–141 (2013). https://doi.org/10.1111/curi.12003
8. Shulman, L.S.: Knowledge and teaching: foundations of the new reform. Harvard Educ. Rev. **57**(1), 1–22 (1987a). https://doi.org/10.17763/haer.57.1.j463w79r56455411
9. Barshay, J.: 20 judgements a teacher makes in 1 minute and 28 seconds. The Hechinger Report (2018). Accessed 17 Nov 2019. https://hechingerreport.org/20-judgments-a-teacher-makes-in-1-minute-and-28-seconds/
10. Westerman, D.A.: Expert and novice teacher decision making. J. Teach. Educ. **42**(4), 292–305 (1991)
11. Shavelson, R.J.: The basic teaching skill: decision making (Research and Development Memorandum No. 104). Stanford University, Stanford Center for Research and Development in Teaching, School of Education, Stanford, CA (1973)

12. Hunter, M.: Teaching is decision making. Educ.l Leader. **37**(1), 62–67 (1979)

13. Fenstermacher, G.: A philosophical consideration of recent research on teacher effectiveness. In: Shulman, L.S. (ed.), Review of Research in Education, vol. 6, pp. 157–185. Peacock, Itasca (1978)

14. Fenstermacher, G.: Philosophy of research on teaching: three aspects. In: Wittrock, M.C. (ed.) Handbook of Research on Teaching, 3rd edn., pp. 37–49. Macmillan, New York (1986)

15. Anderson, L.W.: Classroom Assessment: Enhancing the Quality of Teacher Decision Making. Routledge, London (2003)

16. Eggleston, J. (ed.): Teacher Decision-Making in the Classroom: A Collection of Papers. Routledge, London (2018)

17. Lloyd, C.A.: Exploring the real-world decision-making of novice and experienced teachers. J. Further.High. Educ. **43**(2), 166–182 (2019)

18. Loughran, J.: Pedagogical reasoning: the foundation of the professional knowledge of teaching. Teach. Teach. **25**(5), 523–535 (2019)

19. Guerriero, S.: Teachers' pedagogical knowledge: what it is and how it functions. Educ. Res. Innov. **99–118**, 20 (2017). https://doi.org/10.1787/9789264270695-6-en

20. Tom, A.R., Valli, L.: Professional knowledge for teachers. In: Sikula, J. (ed.) Handbook of Research on Teacher Education, pp. 373–392. Macmillan, New York (1990)

21. Grimmett, P., MacKinnon, A.: Craft knowledge and the education of teachers. In: Grant, G. (ed.) Review of Research in Education. American Education Research Association, Washington DC (1992). https://doi.org/10.2307/1167304

22. Shulman, L.S.: The practical and the eclectic: a deliberation on teaching and educational research. Curricul. Inq. **14**(2), 183–200 (1984). https://doi.org/10.1080/03626784.1984.110 75920

23. Shulman, L.S.: Paradigms and research programs in the study of teaching. In: Wittrock, M. (ed.) Handbook of Research on Teaching, 3rd edn., pp. 3–36. Macmillan, New York (1986)

24. Shulman, L.S.: Those who understand: Knowledge growth in teaching. Educ. Res. **15**(2), 4–14 (1986). https://doi.org/10.3102/0013189X015002004

25. Shulman, L.S.: The wisdom of practice. In: Berliner, D., Rosenshine, B. (eds.) Talks to Teachers: A Festschrift for N.L. Gage, pp. 369–386. Random House, New York (1987)

26. Shulman, L.S.: Toward a pedagogy of substance. AAHE Bull. 8–13 (1989). https://doi.org/ 10.1300/J251v08n02_04

27. Fenstermacher, G.D.: Chapter 1: the knower and the known: the nature of knowledge in research on teaching. Rev. Res. Educ. **20**(1), 3–56 (1994). https://doi.org/10.3102/009173 2X020001003

28. Valli, L., Tom, A.R.: How adequate are the knowledge base frameworks in teacher education? J. Teach. Educ. **39**(5), 5–12 (1988)

29. Wray, D., Medwell, J., Fox, R., Poulson, L.: The teaching practices of effective teachers of literacy. Educ. Rev. **52**(1), 75–84 (2000). https://doi.org/10.1080/00131910097432

30. McDonough, A., Clarke, D.: Describing the practice of effective teachers of mathematics in the early years. Int. Group Psychol. Math. Educ. **3**, 261–268 (2003)

31. Bartholomew, H., Osborne, J., Ratcliffe, M.: Teaching students "ideas-about-science": Five dimensions of effective practice. Sci. Educ. **88**(5), 655–682 (2004). https://doi.org/10.1002/ sce.10136

32. Seufert, S., Guggemos, J., Sailer, M.: Technology-related knowledge, skills, and attitudes of pre- and in-service teachers: the current situation and emerging trends. Comput. Hum. Behav. **115**, 106552 (2020). https://doi.org/10.1016/j.chb.2020.106552

33. Munby, H.: The place of teachers' beliefs in research on teacher thinking and decision making, and an alternative methodology. Instr. Sci. **11**(3), 201–225 (1982). https://doi.org/10.1007/ BF00414280

34. Ertmer, P.A.: Teacher pedagogical beliefs: the final frontier in our quest for technology integration? Educ. Tech. Res. Dev. **53**(4), 25–39 (2005). https://doi.org/10.1007/BF02504683
35. Johnson, K.E.: The emerging beliefs and instructional practices of preservice English as a second language teachers. Teach. Teach. Educ. **10**(4), 439–452 (1994)
36. Kelly-McHale, J.: The influence of music teacher beliefs and practices on the expression of musical identity in an elementary general music classroom. J. Res. Music Educ. **61**(2), 195–216 (2013)
37. Schoenfeld, A.H.: Toward professional development for teachers grounded in a theory of decision making. ZDM **43**(4), 457–469 (2011). https://doi.org/10.1007/s11858-011-0307-8
38. Goffman, E.: Frame Analysis: An Essay on the Organization of Experience. Northeastern University Press, Boston (1974)
39. Shaffer, D.W.: Models of situated action: computer games and the problem of transfer. In: Steinkuehler, C., Squire, K.D., Barab, S.A. (eds.), Games Learning, and Society: Learning and Meaning in the Digital Age, pp. 403–433. Cambridge University, Cambridge (2012). https://doi.org/10.1017/CBO9781139031127.028
40. Shaffer, D.W.: Quantitative Ethnography. Wisconsin, Cathcart Press, Madison (2017)
41. Perkins, D.: Smart Schools. Free Press, New York (1992)
42. Gee, J.P.: Reading as situated language: a sociocognitive perspective. J. Adoles. Adult Literacy **44**(8), 714–725 (2001). https://doi.org/10.1598/JAAL.44.8.3
43. Boak, R.T.R., Conklin, R.C.: Brief notes: the effect of teachers' levels of interpersonal skills on junior high school students' achievement and anxiety. Am. Educ. Res. J. **12**(4), 537–543 (1975). https://doi.org/10.3102/00028312012004537
44. Sparks, D.M., Pole, K.: "Do we teach subjects or students?" Analyzing science and mathematics teacher conversations about issues of equity in the classroom. School Sci. Math. **119**(7), 405–416 (2019). https://doi.org/10.1111/ssm.12361
45. Squire, K.D., MaKinster, J.G., Barnett, M., Luehmann, A.L., Barab, S.L.: De-signed curriculum and local culture: acknowledging the primacy of classroom culture. Sci. Educ. **87**(4), 468–489 (2003). https://doi.org/10.1002/sce.10084
46. Lave, J., Wenger, E.: Situated Learning: Legitimate Peripheral Participation. Cambridge University Press, Cambridge (1991). https://doi.org/10.1017/CBO9780511815355
47. Wenger, E.: Communities of Practice: Learning, Meaning and Identity. Cambridge University Press, Cambridge (1998). https://doi.org/10.1017/CBO9780511803932
48. Phillips, M.: Digital Technology, Schools and Teachers' Workplace Learning: Policy, Practice and Identity. Springer, Cham (2016). https://doi.org/10.1057/978-1-137-52462-1
49. Di Sessa, A.: Knowledge in pieces. Constructivism in the Computer Age, pp. 49–70 (1988)
50. Bransford, J.D., Brown, A.L., Cocking, R.R.: How People Learn: Brain, Mind, Experience, and School. National Academies Press, Washington, DC (1999)
51. Chi, M.T.H., Feltovich, P.J., Glaser, R.: Categorization and representation of physics problems by experts and novices. Cogn. Sci. **5**(2), 121–152 (1981). https://doi.org/10.1207/s15516709cog0502_2
52. Phillips, M., Kovanović, V., Mitchell, I., Gašević, D.: The influence of discipline on teachers' knowledge and decision making. In: Eagan, B., Misfeldt, M., Siebert-Evenstone, A. (eds.) ICQE 2019. CCIS, vol. 1112, pp. 177–188. Springer, Cham (2019). https://doi.org/10.1007/978-3-030-33232-7_15
53. Shaffer, D.W., Hatfield, D., Svarovsky, G.N., Nash, P., Nulty, A., Bagley, E., Mis-levy, R.: Epistemic network analysis: a prototype for 21st-century assessment of learning. Int. J. Learn. Media **1**(2) (2009). https://doi.org/10.1162/ijlm.2009.0013

Negotiating Tensions: A Study of Pre-service English as Foreign Language Teachers' Sense of Identity Within Their Community of Practice

Hazel Vega[(✉)], Golnaz Arastoopour Irgens[iD], and Cinamon Bailey

Clemson University, Clemson, SC, USA
hvegaqu@clemson.edu

Abstract. The dynamic nature of language teacher identity requires an understanding of the processes involved in the formation of teachers' professional identity. In the context of English as a foreign language (EFL), identity formation involves navigating dominant discourses around a hierarchical dichotomy of native and non-native speakers placing non-native teachers in a lesser category. This research presents a qualitative analysis of interview data of 4 pre-service teachers in an EFL teacher education program. Using the community of practice identity negotiation framework, the findings of this study show how pre-service teachers are negotiating practices deemed as valuable by their education program. The findings in this study suggest that EFL pre-service teachers' processes of identity negotiation were mainly characterized by adoption and some degree of tension around ideologies privileging the NS and unmarked speech. This study contributes to the extant conversation about the problematization of the native non-native speaker dichotomy and discusses the unique affordances of Epistemic Network Analysis to examine processes of identity formation and negotiation beyond the context of language teachers.

Keywords: Teacher identity · Pre-service teachers · English as a foreign language · Communities of practice · Epistemic network analysis

1   Introduction

In the last 2 decades, the study of teacher identity has gained prominence in English language teaching [12, 16]. Building on research on teacher identity in mainstream teacher education [3], language teacher identity has been theorized to be negotiated through discourse and characterized as "conflicting, context-bound, and socially constructed" [25, p. 35]. The dynamic nature of language teacher identity indicates a need to understand the processes involved in the formation of teachers' professional identity [7, 18, 29].

In the field of English as a foreign language (EFL), an area that has gained interest in the study of teacher identity is the hierarchy created by native speaker and non-native speaker (NS-NNS) dichotomy, which places the non-native speaker (NNS) at a subordinate position [1, 5, 8, 18]. The native speaker (NS) is valued more, and the NNS is placed in a position of always learning English, and this could affect their identity as teachers,

A. R. Ruis and S. B. Lee (Eds.): ICQE 2021, CCIS 1312, pp. 277–291, 2021.
https://doi.org/10.1007/978-3-030-67788-6_19

especially pre-service teachers who are trying to construct identities reflecting their legitimacy as speakers and practitioners [11, 26]. Despite the theoretical problematization of this dichotomy, it is still pervasive in the English language teaching profession [1, 18], particularly in EFL contexts, where little research has been conducted [26]. Considering the need to contribute to a more nuanced understanding of the construction of language teacher identity, the present study explores the negotiation of identity of four EFL pre-service teachers in an education program in Costa Rica. Building on an earlier study [26], this research uses qualitative interview data in order to analyze and examine how pre-service teachers adopt and negotiate the NS-NNS dichotomy dominant discourses present in their program. Given that pre-service education is a critical period for teacher identity formation, the purpose of the present study is to illuminate the ways in which dominant discourses are initially contested and the ways in which they contribute to tensions in identity development.

2 Theory

2.1 Communities of Practice

This study uses Communities of Practice (CoP) [13] as a theoretical lens to explain the identity process of pre-service teachers in training to become EFL teachers. A CoP framework conceptualizes learning as a process of identification that is a "constant becoming" as the individuals engage in a practice [28, p. 153]. In a CoP, membership is obtained by legitimate participation, which takes two forms: central participation of old-timers, and peripheral participation of newcomers. In an EFL teacher education program, pre-service teachers are newcomers engaging in peripheral participation seeking to find modes of engagement to learn in practice and become legitimate members of the EFL teacher community. Professors and other more experienced professionals are old-timers who model and define legitimate practices for the community. Within the CoP framework, Wenger's [28] duality of identification and negotiation in identity formation account for the agency that newcomers enact when seeking membership in the community. On one hand, identification acts as a process to determine the meanings and "styles and discourses produced by the community" [28, p. 196] relevant for newcomers. On the other hand, negotiation is a form of contestability of existing identifications in the community, involving "the ability, facility, and legitimacy to contribute to, take responsibility for, and shape the meanings that matter within a social configuration" [28, p. 197]. In a teacher education program, pre-service teachers identify with established styles and dominant discourses in coursework and with old-timers. Newcomers decide to what extent those practices are relevant to them. The duality of identification and negotiation captures the dynamic nature of identity formation as an agentive process involving tensions and conflict as pre-service teachers reconcile personal expectations and those of the community.

2.2 The Native Speaker and Non-native Speaker (NS-NNS) Dichotomy

For EFL teachers, the NS-NNS dichotomy is still deeply rooted in the English teaching profession [1, 16]. This NS-NNS binary creates static, mutually exclusive, and hierarchical categories that place the NS in a superior level [18]. Ideologies of native speakerism

[8, 9] constitute the NS as an idealized figure for culture and language and characterize the NNS as inferior, flawed, and a non-White other [1, 8]. Thus, the NS becomes the benchmark against which the NNS's' competence is measured [17, 30].

The present study aligns with views that pursue conceptualizations beyond the NS-NNS dichotomy and account for the dynamic nature of identity negotiation [1, 29]. Although previous studies have reported tensions in identity negotiation [1, 11, 12, 18], there is still a need to characterize such tensions and analyze how they go unnoticed by pre-service teachers and are unaddressed in teacher education programs. The research question addressed in this study is: *How do EFL pre-service teachers make sense of dominant NS-NNS discourses and perceived legitimate practices when negotiating their emerging teacher identities?*

3   Methods

3.1   Context and Participants

This research draws from qualitative interview data from 4 pre-service teachers in an English teaching program for secondary education at one of the largest suburban public universities in Costa Rica. This four-year bachelor's program prepares students to teach English as a foreign language (EFL) in secondary schools. Students complete coursework based on English language and pedagogy content along with a one-semester teaching practicum. Also, one of the last oral communication courses includes the semester-long Global Classroom project, a telecollaboration activity with American students from a midwestern university in the U.S., during which students interact weekly through class oral presentations and discussions. The 4 Spanish-English bilingual participants in this study were in the fourth year of the program and had all met the teaching practicum requirement as well as participated in the telecollaboration project. Three of the participants learned EFL in Costa Rica through elementary, secondary, and college education, and one participant, Vanessa, lived in the U.S. as a child and received English as a second language (ESOL) services at her school. Pseudonyms are used for all participants within this study.

3.2   Quantitative Ethnography

Quantitative ethnography (QE) is an approach that intertwines qualitative and quantitative perspectives [21]. It draws from ethnography in that it seeks practical, functional, and grounded interpretations of data to understand why people in particular cultures or communities do the activities they do and are inclined to certain meaning making. The quantitative perspective allows for making sense of large data sets through data visualizations in order to uncover relationships between codes and to analyze small-d discourse (what participants say) and big-D discourse (the meanings of the community) [21]. In this research, QE facilitated sensible interpretations of the interview data to make sense of small-d discourse of the pre-service teachers in relation to big-D discourse of their community of practice (their teacher education program). The grounded analysis afforded by QE in this study uncovered unexpected patterns that went beyond the frequency with which codes occurred. In other words, such analysis at the discourse level revealed pre-service teachers' making sense of practices from their community in their identity formation.

3.3 Data Collection and Analysis

This paper presents data from a broader study examining the perspectives and learning experiences of pre-service teachers in this English Teaching program and builds on a previous study [26]. After obtaining informed consent from participants, semi-structured, open ended interviews were conducted via video calls. Interviews, which ranged from 45–75 min, were recorded and transcribed. Questions referenced pre-service teachers' experiences and feelings during the teaching practicum and while interacting with NS's, their reflections on accent, and their inquiries regarding what matters to them as future teachers. Additionally, researchers collected syllabi, rubrics of oral performance, and official documentation of the description of the curriculum, objectives, and theoretical principles of the program.

The data analysis consisted of two processes: (1) analysis of documentation, and (2) analysis of the interview data. The first process included thematic analysis of the documentation provided by the program [4] and qualitative deductive coding of the interviews [19] guided by the theory of identity development within CoP's [28]. For the documentation analysis, we looked for evidence of legitimate practices associated with idealized notions of English. In the second process, we identified evidence of participants' identity negotiation in the 143 utterances analyzed. Through discourse analysis, we identified how "situated meanings and Discourses were used to enact and depict identities" [6, p. 150] within a CoP. In 3 iterative rounds of coding, we combined deductive and inductive coding to refine and validate codes. In the first round, we created deductive codes derived from the CoP framework, then we followed an inductive process to extend and add codes. In the third round, for reduction of codes and reaching theoretical saturation, categories generated in the previous round were collapsed into the following codes: adoption, rejection, tension, the NS as a standard, reflections on accents, and NNS less legitimate practices (Table 1).

Using the refined coding scheme, two of the researchers coded the data separately and met to discuss the inconsistencies found in 19 data points. This process served to further refine code definitions and provide systematic procedures for future coding [14, 15, 23].

Table 1. List of generated codes for analysis of teacher interview data

Code	Definition
Adoption	The pre-service teacher (PST) takes on an established practice from the community of practice (CoP). This is reflected in statements in which the participants say that they would take/have taken the practices of the CoP to their teaching and/or their approach to language learning. Interviewer's questions/comments should not include this code. Example: "I would try to implement that [Global Classroom] so that students are going to have a real, um, interaction with the language, with the native speaker"

(continued)

Table 1. (*continued*)

Code	Definition
Rejection	The PST rejects an established practice from the community of practice. This is reflected in statements of disagreement or full dissatisfaction with the CoP. Interviewer's questions/comments should not include this code. Example: "I think that having a strong accent [Spanish accent] means that there has been a really good effort on learning a different language"
Tension	The PST demonstrates a tension when an established practice from the community of practice poses a conflict for the negotiation of their identity. This might be reflected in utterances that do not show full satisfaction with the practices of the community, have mixed negative and positive comments about them, and/or express strong/negative emotions. Interviewer's questions/comments should not include this code. Example: "I don't even know how I'm going to do when I actually have to teach"
The native speaker as the standard	The PST expresses their feelings or perspective about an established practice related to the idealized native speaker, who represent the target language norms against which the non-native speaker measures proficiency. Example: "I have tried to talk like them, but it is almost impossible to achieve their speech or their level"
Reflections on accents	The PST expresses his feelings or perspective about an established practice related to ideas about accent that suggest judgements of legitimacy of accents in relation to a standard language variety. Example: "the important thing is communication. Not the pronunciation, but still I'm very perfectionist about it, so it really frustrates me sometimes"
NNS less legitimate practices	The PST expresses his or her feelings or perspective about an established practice related to his or her own linguistic practices that are perceived as less legitimate than those of they imagine the native speaker would engage in. Example: "I understand that my brain has been always in Spanish mode, so I can't really change all my mindset to the other language"

3.4 Epistemic Network Analysis

Epistemic Network Analysis (ENA) was used [2, 19, 20] to create weighted discourse networks for each participant. In the networks, the nodes represent the codes identified in the data, and the thickness of the links represent how often the participants made connections across the qualitative codes. To identify co-occurrences, we used a moving stanza window [22] that included two lines of talk at a time. This segmentation was chosen given the question-answer format of the interviews and the lengthy utterances of the participants. Connections were operationalized as co-occurrences of codes within a participant's single turn of talk and between the participant's turn of talk and the interviewer's questions. We used the visualizations of the networks rather than relying solely on a coding-and-counting qualitative design [28], which quantifies occurrences of codes within each participants' utterances. This provided more insight into the pre-service teachers' sense of identity by showing an analysis of the temporal proximity and relationships between the processes of adoption, rejection, and tensions, and their connections to ideologies of native speakerism and accents.

4   Results

4.1   Community of Practice: The Teacher Education Program

Taken altogether, the course syllabi, teaching methods, assessment rubrics, and a description of the program characterized *language correctness and non- accented English speaking* as components of legitimate participation and membership in this education program. For example, the Global Classroom telecollaboration project provided pre-service teachers the opportunity to interact with NS's during the last oral communication course. For courses not including telecollaboration, videos and audios, mostly with NS's of English (with American accents), were used to evaluate listening comprehension and as input to complement the contents of the class.

This program placed a strong emphasis on correctness and high levels of teaching proficiency that could be applied to different contexts, and there were strict English-only policies that did not allow students to use Spanish and/or "translation and Spanish-like structures." Moreover, the evaluation of assignments and projects often included a linguistic aspect that assessed the correctness of the language (phonology, grammar, and syntax), which in some instances accounted for 50% of the grade. Oral performance was expected to be fluent and without "choppy sentences, long pauses, and hesitations," and students were expected to monitor the "consonant and vowel sounds" and make correct use of prosodic aspects of English.

4.2   Pre-service Teachers' Negotiation of Identity

In the present study, the data suggest that when negotiating their emerging identities, pre-service teachers adopted practices that their CoP deemed as valuable for competence in English teaching as a foreign language more often than they rejected such practices. However, we identified a zone of tension across their dynamic process of negotiation of identity given that adoption and rejection of practices frequently occurred with some degree of tension for the pre-service teachers in this study. Such tension was manifested in frustration, self-doubt, and developing ideologies, particularly around notions of the idealization of the NS and personal reflections on accents. In this section, we present qualitative and ENA findings organized by these two main notions: (1) the native speaker as a standard; and (2) reflections on accents.

The native speaker as the standard: Pablo and Vanessa

Qualitative Findings. Overall, the 4 participants positioned themselves in an inferior category of the hierarchy of native and nonnative speakers (NS-NNS dichotomy). All of the participants self-identified themselves as NNS's and referred to speakers from the U.S. and the United Kingdom as NS's, which often led them to compare their personal linguistic flaws to the NS's and reflect on advantages of the NS. For example, they expressed a preference for interaction with NS's, indicating it was one of the "best" forms of interaction for meaningful language learning and placed the NS of English as a standard against which they positioned themselves. This pattern was reified in the data when participants recalled a class project (the Global Classroom), which involved frequent interaction via video conferences with a college level class from a university in the U.S. and described it as a significant learning experience. Participants also agreed that they were disappointed that this type of interaction with NS's had been limited during the program.

Particularly, Pablo and Vanessa addressed the dichotomy between NS and NNS more strongly than the other 2 participants. They expressed a desire to incorporate interactions with NS's similar to those of the Global Classroom project in their future teaching practices as such interactions with NS's were a unique channel for students to learn about language and culture. As Vanessa stated, "I would try to implement that [Global Classroom] so that students are going to have a *real*, um, interaction with the language, with the native speaker." In Pablo's case, he went a step further by inviting a NS to his class during his practicum when covering the topic of holidays. He was excited to share his experience, as he explained, "I planned a conversation with a native. It will be a very good opportunity for them to speak [...] to know about U.S. celebrations [...] And I arranged everything so, and it was great, and they [the students] enjoyed that experience." When asked how he would modify this activity, he said that he would include NS's from other places besides the U.S. The commitment and effort in implementing this activity showed that Pablo valued contact with NS's and wanted to provide such an experience for his students.

However, tensions emerged when pre-service teachers positioned the NS as a benchmark for language competence. In the following excerpt, Pablo explained his feelings during the same activity with a NS in his class:

"When she was speaking with my students, I was like, oh my God, she [the guest native speaker] sounds native [...] And I was, Oh my God, I'm not native. But the good thing I think is that [...] I tried to be careful when speaking because you know, when teaching you are kind of exposed to be judged by your students."

Pablo's moment of tension came when he realized that there was a difference between the NS and himself. He acknowledged that his speech did not reach the superior linguistic category of a native speaker. For him, the NS was a benchmark that he used to measure his own proficiency by pointing out that he was *not native*. This was a place for tension for Pablo because on other occasions he acknowledged frustration and self-consciousness when interacting with NS's or comparing himself to them and their accuracy. For example, he stated, "I have *compared myself* listening to videos and audios from the internet, videos from YouTube and *I have tried to talk like them*, but it is almost impossible to achieve their speech or their level." This positioning put Pablo in a vulnerable position of judgement and linguistic insecurity as he felt that his students perceived his speech differently than that of a NS, leading him to become more self-conscious about his English.

Similarly, Vanessa shared the same tension. With her experience as an ESL learner, she expressed conflict regarding target language norms in the program:

"here [in Costa Rica] *you go from Spanish to learning a structured type of English*. And to me, I don't see English that way. I even make a lot of grammatical mistakes that my classmates here in Costa Rica don't make [...] they know a more structured language than I do, and therefore they will teach a more structured language. I don't believe that so much. Like I don't even know how I'm going to do when I actually have to teach, but I don't see myself setting that down and then giving the lesson, just some parts of the sentence or the different tenses of the verb. Like I *just wish to teach the language as it is.*"

Vanessa grappled with the idea that there is a difference between how a NS acquires the language naturally and subconsciously, as opposed to how a NNS requires more effort by consciously thinking about the structure of the language. By saying "you go from Spanish to learning a structured English," she compared how learning Spanish as a native language was a smooth process and learning English in an EFL context was more "structured", thus placing the NNS in a less privileged position of learning. Vanessa's tension challenged the traditional approach when she imagined herself giving less importance to correctness and letting students use "the language as it is". However, this imagined scenario contrasted with expectations of the role of an EFL teacher including deliberate work on linguistic forms, which created a tension for her.

ENA Findings. Using ENA, the qualitative interpretations of Vanessa and Pablo's talk are visualized (Fig. 1). Their strongest connection was between the **NS as a standard** and **adoption**, meaning they predominantly adopted ideologies reflected in the CoP's culture that positioned the NS in a superior level of proficiency. However, they also connected idealized ideas about the NS to **tension**, indicating concerns around their linguistic practices as language learners, although these connections were slightly less frequent. In terms of rejection of practices from their CoP, only Vanessa made a few connections to the **NS as a standard**, and this rejection was also associated with tension. In sum, Pablo and Vanessa's networks are similar in that they adopted their program's ideologies about idealized NS's; however, the perceived NS-NNS dichotomy was also a source of tension as they developed their EFL teacher identities.

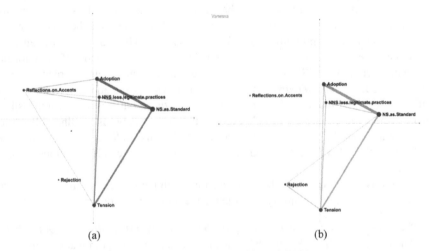

Fig. 1. Discourse networks for (a) Pablo and (b) Vanessa

The Non-native's Reflections on Accents: Laura and Alfonso

Qualitative Findings. The participants in this study adopted and rejected ideologies that associated non-nativeness with a distinctive less legitimate accent, but still expressed tensions with this perspective. Overall, most of the pre-service teachers in this research recognized that their speech had an accent and showed uncomfortable emotions towards not being able to reach the pronunciation level they desired as teachers of English. Specifically, the 2 participants that discussed reflections on their accent were Laura and Alfonso. Although their comments diverged in terms of adoption and rejection of ideas about the type of accent that was deemed valuable for a teacher, they converged in the ambivalence they showed when identifying dissonance between their own accent and the accent they or their CoP expected.

For example, Laura, expressed a desire to achieve a native-like accent and was frustrated with not being able to do so. When asked about how she felt about having an accent in English, she replied:

> *"Frustrated,* but I understand that *my brain has been always in Spanish mode,* so I can't really change all my mindset to the other language. I have to remember [remind] myself that […] I make these kinds of mistakes, that *the important thing is communication.* Not the pronunciation, but still I'm very perfectionist about it, so it really *frustrates* me sometimes."

Laura's feelings of frustration stem from perceiving her Spanish accent as an obstacle when speaking English. She reconciled this by understanding that her "brain has always been in Spanish mode," and that the important aspect of learning English was the ability to communicate with others. However, there was evidence of identity tension as she admitted that she still became frustrated about perceiving traces of Spanish in the way she spoke, and thus was "very perfectionist" about her pronunciation. Her frustration about mistakes in pronunciation, especially the ones related to her Spanish accent when speaking English, also occurred during teaching: "I feel like I'm teaching them something that *I do wrong,* so *I get mad* with myself that I can't really change it and that I know that I'm doing something wrong." She characterized her pronunciation as "wrong" or as less legitimate, and she expressed being "mad" about possibly being a flawed model for her students by teaching them "something wrong". Although Laura generally adopted ideas that privileged native-like English pronunciation coming from her CoP, she experienced tensions in her identity development when she saw her accent as deficient. Laura's tensions led to negative feelings about her accent and a pressure to achieve perfection in phonology.

In contrast, in Alfonso's case, rejection, adoption, and tension collided. He stated that he disagreed with the idea that he needed to have an American Standard accent. This seemed to be influenced by his experience studying in the US for a semester, which exposed him to different accents, so he rejected practices favoring certain varieties of English or judging or comparing accents either from professors or from classmates. The proceeding quote shows how Alfonso was beginning to make a difference between the expected accent for teachers and for EFL students:

"I know that in a context in which I have learned *English for teaching* [...] I might have the idea that it would be important having *a very good accent* or, at least, standardized [American English] accent. But getting out of the teaching context, I think that *having a strong accent [Spanish accent] means that there has been a really good effort on learning a different language and that is of course acceptable to me* [...] *there shouldn't be a judgment in this case.*"

Alfonso disagreed with negative judgement on learners of English with Spanish accents. However, he thought it was desirable for a teacher to have an unmarked "very good... standardized [American English] accent." This distinction indicates that Alfonso was beginning to grapple with notions of differentiated communicative expectations for English teachers and language learners outside the teaching profession. Although that conferred legitimacy to the demand for teachers to have an unmarked accent, his use of uncertain language such as "I might have the idea" denotes that he could be initiating a personal reflection on his ideologies of accent.

In a subsequent comment, he reiterated this perspective by stating that "learning English...is a very valuable process that should be recognized as well and therefore respected. [...] their [English language learners] accent shouldn't be judged." He referred to the commitment and effort that learning a foreign language required, and that in itself should be respected by avoiding judgement on accents. However, this effort was not recognized for English teachers. He said, "we as teachers, we have this idea of using almost perfect English [...] And somehow [...] I think it is also necessary to focus on or to pay close attention on the way we speak." Alfonso oscillated between rejection and tension: he rejected judgement of accents for learners but placed a different expectation for teachers to have a "perfect" English accent, creating a source of tension for him as a teacher-in-training with a Spanish accent. In short, Alfonso and Laura's negotiation of identity speaks to the pressure that they felt as future teachers of English to achieve a "perfect" and "unmarked" accent.

ENA Findings. Through Epistemic Network Analysis (ENA, the qualitative interpretations of Laura and Alfonso's talk are visualized (Fig. 2). Both participants made the strongest connection to **reflections on accents**, but they differed in that Laura made more connections to **adoption**, and Alfonso made more connections to **rejection**. This means that Laura predominately adopted ideologies that associated non-nativeness with less legitimate accents that were reflected in the CoP's culture. For example, she viewed herself as a "perfectionist" and felt frustrated about having a Spanish accent when speaking English. Alfonso rejected this type of ideology saying that accents deserve to be accepted because they are a sign of the effort it takes to learn a whole new language. He opposed judging accents and thought that people should respect the speech of NNS's of English. However, Laura and Alfonso connected **reflections on accents** to **tension**, indicating their concerns around the unmarked pronunciation that their CoP expected from them as future teachers of English. This was evident when Alfonso stated, "we as teachers, we have this idea of using almost perfect English" and that in a teaching context "it would be important having a very good accent or, at least, standardized [American English] accent." In summary, Laura and Alfonso's networks differed in that Laura adopted the ideologies of accent promoted in the CoP more frequently than Alfonso did; however, they converged in perceiving these ideologies as a source of tension in the negotiation of their teacher identities.

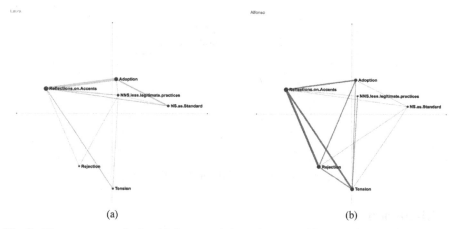

(a)   (b)

Fig. 2. Discourse networks for (a) Laura and (b) Alfonso in which Ideologies of Accent is a central node.

4.3   ENA Findings: Visualization of the Four Participants

Using ENA, the qualitative interpretations of the participant's talk are visualized in an average weighted network (Fig. 3). Overall, a strong relationship is observed across participants between **adoption** and the **NS as a standard** and **reflections on accents**. This means that the pre-service teachers were more likely to accept rather than reject the ideologies from the CoP's culture, positioning the NS as a benchmark and unmarked speech as desirable for English teachers. A moderately thicker line is shown between **adoption** and the **NS as a standard,** suggesting that the figure of the NS is a powerful influence in the identity formation process of these participants. The next strongest connections are made to the node of **tension,** which was linked to all the codes and most strongly to the **NS as a standard**. This suggests that tension was present for all participants across the processes of adoption and rejection of practices of the CoP. This means that although participants were mainly adopting the practices of the CoP, they experienced tensions across all 3 categories of practices, and these tensions also occurred at the same time as participants discussed the adoption or rejection of such practices.

Fig. 3. Discourse network for all participants

5   Discussion

Using Wenger's [28] identity framework in CoP's, this study examined interview data from EFL pre-service teachers to describe their identity development and acceptance or rejection of practices and dominant discourses within their program. The findings in this study suggest that EFL pre-service teachers' processes of identity negotiation were mainly characterized by adoption and some degree of tension around ideologies privileging the NS and unmarked speech. The teachers framed the NS as an idealized figure in their identity formation process leading to feelings of frustration, linguistic insecurity, and inadequacy. More broadly, our results contribute to the understanding of identity as a dynamic social construct in teacher learning by offering a nuanced analysis of the tensions that emerge from the interaction between the individual and social aspects of the construction of identity in a community of practice. For the pre-service teachers in this study, membership to their CoP provided opportunities to engage in practices that they wanted to adopt, but frictions manifested when they realized that their CoP placed expectations that aligned more with a NS, which provoked insecurities and uncomfortable emotions. These expectations of "perfection" and unmarkedness reflected in the CoP, and more broadly in societal language ideologies, came into conflict with the pre-service teachers' own expectations of who they wanted to become as teachers since they perceived a sense of less legitimacy in their personal ways of speaking and learning English. However, the emergence of these tensions indicate that these pre-service teachers were starting to negotiate and contest these dominant discourses present in their CoP by reflecting on the extent to which the idealized NS mattered to them and how it conflicted with their self-perceptions of their existing identities. Possibilities for future research might include sharing ENA visualizations and co-constructing an interpretation of them with participants to inquire on how they are making sense of these contestations.

In this study, we identified three affordances of the QE process and ENA for strengthening the analysis of language teacher identity. First, ENA allowed us to test the deductive categories of adoption and rejection from the CoP framework and the inductive coding category of tension. Through ENA visualizations, it was clear that tension was present and central in all participants' networks. Second, the weights of the links in the ENA visualization helped us iterate through codes and identify salient codes related to tensions in identity development. For example, initial codes such as the native speaker accuracy, the NS as a static/fixed figure, the native speaker as a dynamic figure, and the native speaker as a model for culture were created. Individually, these codes did not show strong connections in ENA visualizations; however, the common theme of the NS indicated that there was an additional code related to the NS, which was a combination of the initial codes. Thus, through further iterations of inductive coding, the code of the NS as a standard was created. This iterative process of interaction between the qualitative data and ENA network visualizations provided grounded evidence of salient codes in our data set and clarity for the story that the data were telling. For the study of language teacher identity negotiation, this process facilitated the relevance of tensions present and in which ways such tensions co-occurred with the adoption and rejection of practices of the CoP. Third, this iterative QE process using ENA and groupings of visualizations allowed us to build on the results of a previous study [26], leading to more detailed insights into teachers' language identity development. After establishing that all participants had connections to tensions, ENA visualizations showed 2 distinct groupings, each with 2 participants. One pair showed strong connections to reflections on accents, and the other pair showed links to the NS as a standard. We also found differences within the groups. For example, one group with 2 participants was concerned with different aspects of the hierarchical dichotomy privileging the NS as a benchmark, thus adopting this dichotomy. However, one of the participants focused more on accepting the NS as an ideal for correctness for his communicative competence, and the other focused more on positioning the NS as an ideal for the learning of English. These distinctions between and within groups revealed tensions at personal, group, and aggregated levels that participants experienced.

6   Conclusion

In this study, Qualitative Ethnography (QE) and Epistemic Network Analysis (ENA) offered unique affordances that might be useful to analyze processes of identity formation and negotiation beyond the context of language teachers. More broadly, QE and ENA can help to identify similar processes of adoption, rejection, and tension embedded in the formation of an identity in a community of practice in formal and informal settings. QE can elucidate how these processes are related to more specific and nuanced aspects that might be leading to emerging negotiations as learners become more central participants of the CoP. Attention to these negotiations is essential to address any problematic tensions that peripheral and more central participants might be experiencing as they learn in practice. In this respect, the affordances of QE and ENA to build and refine theory and iterate and refine codes through exploratory data visualizations, as shown in this paper, assist researchers in identifying strong connections in their data and making grounded interpretations of the sorts of processes that characterize participants' identity formation.

References

1. Aneja, G.A.: Rethinking nativeness: toward a dynamic paradigm of (non) native speakering. Crit. Inq. Lang. Stud. **13**(4), 351–379 (2016)
2. Author
3. Beijaard, D., Meijer, P., Verloop, N.: Reconsidering research on teachers' professional identity. Teach. Teach. Educ. **20**, 107–128 (2004). https://doi.org/10.1016/j.tate.2003.07.001
4. Braun, V., Clarke, V.: Using thematic analysis in psychology. Qual. Res. Psychol. **3**(2), 77–101 (2006)
5. Braine, G.: Non-native-speaker English teachers. Encycl. Appl. Linguist. 1–5 (2012)
6. Gee, J.P.: An Introduction to Discourse Analysis: Theory and Method. Routledge, Abingdon (2011)
7. Gu, M., Benson, P.: The formation of English teacher identities: a cross-cultural investigation. Lang. Teach. Res. **19**(2), 187–206 (2015)
8. Holliday, A.: Key concepts in ELT: native-speakerism. ELT J. **60**, 385–387 (2006)
9. Holliday, A.: The Struggle to Teach English as an International Language. Oxford University Press, Oxford (2005)
10. Huang, I.C., Varghese, M.M.: Toward a composite, personalized, and institutionalized teacher identity for non-native English speakers in US secondary ESL programs. Crit. Inq. Lang. Stud. **12**(1), 51–76 (2015)
11. Huang, Z.: An exploratory study of non-native English-speaking teachers' professional identity construction in a globalizing China. Chin. J. Appl. Ling. **42**(1), 40–59 (2019)
12. Ilieva, R.: Non-native English–speaking teachers' negotiations of program discourses in their construction of professional identities within a TESOL program. Can. Mod. Lang. Rev. **66**(3), 343–369 (2010)
13. Lave, J., Wenger, E.: Situated Learning: Legitimate Peripheral Participation. Cambridge University Press, Cambridge (1991)
14. Miles, M.B., Huberman, A.M.: Qualitative Data Analysis: A Sourcebook of New Methods. Sage Publications, Newbury Park, CA (1984)
15. Miles, M.B., Huberman, A.M.: Qualitative Data Analysis, 2nd edn., pp. 10–12. Sage, Newbury Park, CA (1994)
16. Moussu, L., Llurda, E.: Non-native English-speaking English language teachers: History and research. Lang. Teach. **41**(3), 315–348 (2008)
17. Phillipson, R.: Linguistic Imperialism. Oxford University Press, Oxford, UK (1992)
18. Rudolph, N., Selvi, A.F., Yazan, B.: Conceptualizing and confronting inequity: approaches within and new directions for the "NNEST movement". Crit. Inq. Lang. Stud. **12**(1), 27–50 (2015)
19. Saldaña, J.: The Coding Manual for Qualitative Researchers. Sage Publishing, Thousand Oaks (2015)
20. Shaffer, D.W.: Quantitative Ethnography. Cathcart Press, Madison, WI (2017)
21. Shaffer, D.W., Ruis, A.: Epistemic network analysis: a worked example of theory-based learning analytics. Handb. Learn. Anal
22. Author
23. Strauss, A., Corbin, J.: Basics of Qualitative Research: Grounded Theory Procedures and Techniques. Sage Publications, Beverly Hills, CA (1990)
24. Varghese, M., Morgan, B., Johnston, B., Johnson, K.: Theorizing language teacher identity: three perspectives and beyond. J. Lang. Identity, and Educ. **4**, 21–44 (2005)
25. Varghese, M.M., Motha, S., Trent, J., Park, G., Reeves, J.: Language teacher identity in multilingual settings. TESOL Q. **50**(3), 545–571 (2016)
26. Author

27. Vogel, F., Weinberger, A.: Quantifying qualities of collaborative learning processes. In: Fischer, F., Hmelo-Silver, C.E., Goldman, S.R., Reimann, P. (eds.) International Handbook of the Learning Sciences. Routledge, New York, NY (2018)
28. Wenger, E.: Communities of Practice: Learning, Meaning, and Identity. Cambridge University Press, Cambridge, UK (1998)
29. Yazan, B.: Being and becoming an ESOL teacher through coursework and internship: three teacher candidates' identity negotiation. Crit. Inq. Lang. Stud. **15**(3), 205–227 (2018)
30. Yazan, B., Rudolph, N.: Criticality, Teacher Identity, and (in) Equity in English Language Teaching. Springer International Publishing, Berlin (2018)

How Is Team Membership Change Manifested in Collective Interactions? – Using Epistemic Network Analysis to Explore the Challenges of Contemporary Team Composition

Marta Jackowska[✉]

School of Business and Social Sciences, Aarhus University, Fuglesangs Allé 4,
8210 Aarhus, Denmark
martaj@mgmt.au.dk

Abstract. Work settings characterized by regular team membership changes, where employees often join and leave teams during a project, can lead to significant teamwork challenges. Previous research has focused widely on the individual and group level outcomes of this phenomenon. To date, however, little is known about how teams manage such frequent alterations. To address this, I draw on the anthropological notion of liminality, arguing that team membership change is transitional for individuals due to its uncertainty, and focus on the collective interactions during team meetings in a large Danish multinational corporation (MNC). Investigating the case of a virtual team, I applied Epistemic Network Analysis to explore the changes in the socioemotional- and task-related communication patterns between individuals, before and after a team membership change. Results show that the team's communication has become more complex, as compared to the period before the change, with employees engaging in longer discussions, at the same time being more hesitant to express their opinions. Generally, these findings reflect the team's adjustment to a new situation, and bring attention to the team practices related to team composition. Methodologically, this study extends the application of the Quantitative Ethnography to an organizational field of study.

Keywords: Team composition · Interaction · Team membership change

1 Introduction

Given the dynamic context of contemporary work arrangements, where team membership changes frequently as individuals assemble and dismantle, teams have become increasingly temporary and highly fluid [1–3]. Although team membership changes have become a common practice in various organizations, they may nonetheless be challenging for employees. Previous research on this team phenomenon has already emphasized the imperative of addressing the challenges of team composition [2, 4].

Recent evidence suggests that departing team members may possess distinctive knowledge that stays with them, which in turn can be harmful for team cognition [5, 6].

© Springer Nature Switzerland AG 2021
A. R. Ruis and S. B. Lee (Eds.): ICQE 2021, CCIS 1312, pp. 292–303, 2021.
https://doi.org/10.1007/978-3-030-67788-6_20

Additionally, in her study on professional hockey teams, Stuart [7] found that the loss of a team member with a highly central structural position can adversely influence a team's engagement in a new adaptation process. Although there is a research stream arguing for the beneficial impact of team membership changes [8, 9], it relates primarily to creative teams. However, in teams where work is highly interdependent [7], team membership change poses a risk of disrupting team learning [10, 11] and coordination [12].

While extensive research has been carried out on the outcomes of changes in membership, far too little attention has been paid to the dynamics of this process [13]. Surprisingly, there is still very little understanding of how teams cope with the transitions. Given these points, the following research question arises: *How is the team membership change reflected in the collective interactions of teams?*

I begin by conceptualizing a team membership change as a "significant event in the lifecycle of a team that can alter the course of team functioning" [14]. To theoretically and empirically address this research question, I apply the liminal perspective [15]. Liminality, originally introduced by Van Gennep [15], denotes the temporary period of being "betwixt" and "between" different social states. In other words, individuals are outside their normative structures, yet experience the ambiguity of what awaits [16]. The liminal phase represents the transition, where "the individual does not belong to either the previous or future conditions – but at the same time belongs to both" [17]. Correspondingly, frequent reorganization of work and uncertain encounters inscribed in the nature of team membership changes can facilitate the emergence of the liminal experience among individuals [4, 13]. Applying such a lens enables me to theoretically approach this phenomenon as a dynamic process among individuals.

Empirically, I build on a case of a virtual team, and answer the research question using methods of quantitative- and traditional ethnography, namely Epistemic Network Analysis (ENA) combined with observations. I agree with the authors, who stress the importance of the practices [18–20] and thus argue that the group behavior can help in the further investigation of this phenomenon. In my inductive longitudinal study, I focus on how the members of a virtual team interact with each other before and after a team membership change, and notice how this period influences their socioemotional- and task-related communication.

2   Methods

2.1   Research Setting

To explore the research question of this study, I studied a virtual team in a large multinational corporation (MNC) in Denmark. The team was a part of a bigger project, aimed at the development, maintenance and deployment of the IT solutions to the whole organization. It was common for project members to switch the teams periodically, i.e. join or leave the team, depending on the project needs. In this paper, I zoom in on one of the instances of such team membership changes. I address this change as a liminal phase. In other words, it is a challenging situation prompting the adjustment to a new context [18]. In line with previous research suggesting that such events compel individuals to engage in a construction of a new structure [21, 22], I expect that a change in membership will influence the interaction patterns between team members.

2.2 Data Collection

Data for this study comes from a one-year ethnographic investigation, with particular emphasis on the two months, during which the team was in a process of transition. The primary data used in this study comes from observation of multiple team meetings. Due to the virtual character of team's work, the meetings were held online, hence offering additional information-rich sources of data, such as videos or chat logs, which in turn enhanced the quality of the standard field notes. In total, I performed over 250 h of observation, but for the purpose of this study I focused specifically on 22 team meetings, lasting between an hour and two hours, from the period before and after the membership change.

2.3 Data Analysis

Qualitative Data Analysis. As argued by multiple scholars [23–25], studying team interaction patterns can provide an in-depth understanding of team processes and outcomes. Based on the act4teams coding scheme [20, 26], I identified a set of collective communication patterns occurring in the data and further simplified and adjusted the coding scheme to reflect the content of the team's meetings (see Table 1 for the final coding scheme). I assigned each verbal statement within a meeting to one of the two broader categories, i.e. socioemotional- and task-related communication. The former captures the relational and emotional interaction among team members, while the latter describes how individuals analyze the problems and facilitate decision making.

ENA Analysis. I carried out the analysis with ENA online tool (version 1.7.0) [27]. A unit of analysis was defined as all lines associated with team grouped by date. By examining the co-occurrence of different socioemotional- and task-related statements within the recent temporal context, the final networks were created. The models were primarily tested for 4, 5, 6, and 7 lines as moving stanzas respectively. Drawing on qualitative data as well as comparing the inconsequential differences between the models, I decided to define the recent temporal context as 5 lines, i.e. each line plus the 4 previous lines within a given conversation [28]. These networks were further normalized to account for differing amounts of textual data in each meeting. See Shaffer et al. [29] for a detailed explanation of the mathematics.

Consequently, I examined the graphs to compare the relationships between interactions before and after the membership change that the team experienced, and detect any differences among them. In the model, the node size represents the frequency of the code occurrence, and the thickness of the lines between the nodes relates to the strength of the connection. To outline the major differences, unconnected codes were removed from the model, and the minimum edge weight was set to 0.15.

3 Findings

In this study, I trace a membership change in a virtual team. In what follows, I outline how the new team setup has influenced the team's socioemotional and task-related communication.

Table 1. Socioemotional- and task-related communication.

Function	Collective practice	Definition	ENA abbreviation
Socioemotional statements	Encouraging participation	Addressing quiet participants	SOC_EN
	Providing support	Helping others	SOC_SUP
	Lightening the atmosphere	Improving mood for more cheerful	SOC_LIG
	Expressing opinion	Mentioning opinion	SOC_OP
	Expressing positive feeling	Mentioning explicitly of positive emotion	SOC_POS
	Expressing negative feeling	Mentioning explicitly of negative emotion	SOC_NEG
Task-related statements	Problem	Describing a problem	T_PR
	Solution	Describing a solution	T_SOL
	Question	Asking a question	T_QUE
	Agreement	Expressing agreement	T_AGR
	Disagreement	Expressing disagreement	T_DIS
	Clarifying	Providing a simpler explanation	T_CL
	Procedural suggestion	Suggestion for further procedure	T_SUG
	Elaborating	Providing a thorough explanation	T_ELA
	Informing	Provide essential information/facts	T_INF

3.1 Socioemotional Communication

Team's relations before the change. Employees of the team have been working together for more than three months, and were thus familiar with each other. Although the work of the team was highly virtual, it was also interdependent and required frequent communication, allowing team members to meet on a regular basis to discuss the progress of the tasks. As expected, data analysis of the socioemotional communication before the membership change (Fig. 1a), i.e. expressions relating to individual's emotions and relations with others, indicated that the team's interactions consisted of numerous opinions (SOC_OP). Notably, however, team members have rarely been reluctant to share their point of view, not least the critical one (SOC_NEG). As an example, one of the business consultants in the team, having not heard from his colleague, had no difficulty raising an issue during one of the meetings. *"As some of you know, I was really worried yesterday. If you remember the dashboard task… Then I had a chat with*

Igor, he calmed me down, and I was super excited again. I came in today, nothing has been done and I'm extremely worried again. I would like to hear from you, Igor, I think you owe it to the team".

As team members were observed to be close with each other, they often allowed themselves for sarcastic comments, at the same time remaining friendly and positive about their work (SOC_LIG). To demonstrate, as one employee was not informed about an ad-hoc task, he said mockingly: *"Now I have more work because our amazing manager promised the other team I will do it, even though I told them yesterday I won't"*, to which the manager replied: *"See? We have a great communication!"*, making the team laugh, including the annoyed employee.

Besides, in their discussions, team members were exceptionally helpful to each other, even without an explicit request for help (SOC_SUP). In one of the meetings, a team member stated she felt unsure about a solution due to the missing information. Almost immediately, a remote colleague raised her hand: *"I am not aware of which task this is, but we can sit together after the meeting and figure it out"*.

Generally speaking, the team exhibited supportive and encouraging atmosphere, which is supported by the strong connection between categories reflecting providing support (SOC_SUP), expressing opinion (SOC_OP) and encouraging participation (SOC_EN), as seen in Fig. 1a. Despite working primarily virtually, with few opportunities for physical encounters, team members were comfortable with sharing their viewpoints.

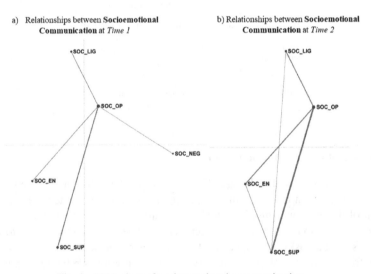

a) Relationships between **Socioemotional Communication** at *Time 1*

b) Relationships between **Socioemotional Communication** at *Time 2*

Fig. 1. ENA plots of socioemotional communication.

Team's Relations After the Change. As soon as the manager received an information about the upcoming change in membership, he gathered the team and explained that the project they were a part of was going through a restructuration phase. I noticed immediately that the team members had become uneasy and uncertain about their future in the project. Although they were promised to stay in the organization, some of them would no longer work on the project, which they expressed as a big loss.

A new team setup, although it did not differ substantially from the previous one, became an evident source of uncertainty, which was reflected in the team's day-to-day interactions. Formerly, what used to come naturally now required more effort and encouragement (SOC_LIG). As an example, in an attempt to get to know team members, one suggested reserved time for a "joke of the day". Further, qualitative analysis revealed that team meetings started with prolonged, compared to before, small talk.

In like manner, sharing opinions was central to social-related communication (Fig. 1b); however, employees needed more encouragement to speak one's mind (SOC_EN). To address that, the manager stated during a meeting: *"As we become a new team, it is important that we share our opinions, so feel free to do so or reach out if you need any help"*.

Employees were slowly adapting for the new situation, at the same time being more cautious to provide an opinion, especially a critical one. For instance, when discussing a solution to one task, one consultant intervened: *"I don't want to be rude, but I think this is wrong. (pause) We should look at what was decided in the previous term and follow"*. She said rather hesitantly, and quickly added: *"I'll be happy to explain further!"*

Remarkably, the team had manifested more support in relation to expressing opinions and addressing other employees as compared to the period before the change (SOC_SUP), which can be seen in Fig. 1b. That had also been reflected in the qualitative data. As an example, seeing that one of the new team members was visibly uneasy about having problems with his task, a colleague said: *"I think it's okay to have problems with it, everyone would feel the same way as you. You can tell us what's wrong and we'll try to help you"*.

3.2 Task-Related Communication

Instructional Interactions Before the Change. The team's interactions related to information about how tasks should be done were rather dynamic (see Fig. 2a). Presumably, since team members knew "who knows what", questions were quickly answered with precise information (T_INF, T_QUE), enabling the team to promptly reach an agreement (T_AGR). Notably, the questions raised during the meetings were not addressed solely by a manager. On the contrary, it was primarily a team member, curious about the progress of a task, who delved deeper into details, often leading to a comprehensive discussion (T_ELA). To demonstrate, as a developer explained the issues she managed to solve, a team member showed interest in getting detailed information on that. *"Nadia, would that configuration bug you solved also help with my task on product ingredients? I would love to hear more about it"*, to which the developer answered with a detailed explanation.

As the Fig. 2a shows, the network appears to be equally distributed across majority of codes, with similar frequencies. In other words, in their communication, team members used comparably equal amount of time when e.g. discussing the problems (T_PR), giving suggestions (T_SUG) or providing explanations (T_CL). One reason for it could be the

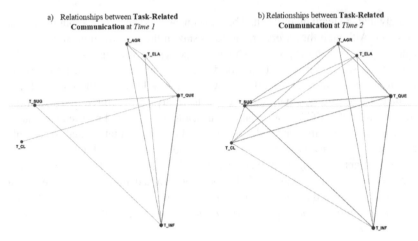

Fig. 2. ENA plots of task-related communication.

fact that the team's tasks were highly interdependent, compelling employees to discuss them thoroughly once they met.

Instructional Interactions After the Change. Reflecting on the observations and the model (Fig. 2b), it can be claimed that the team's task-related communication had become more complex after the change. In particular, team members appeared to be reluctant and nervous when giving suggestions, trying to always back their claims with additional arguments. Talking about a solution to one of the issues, a team member, despite having the most extensive knowledge on that topic, stated: *"Hm... I think this may take some effort to fix it so I would not do this. (pause) My suggestion is that we prepare the solution for configuration, then we clarify with the rest. (pause) Let's talk more about it maybe"*.

Furthermore, as anticipated, employees posed more questions than before, especially in relation to the problems and suggestions put forward. Consequently, task-related interactions became much longer and considerably more detailed. Comparing Figs. 2a and 2b, it can be clearly stated that the newly assembled team had been making stronger connections between task-related constructs (e.g. there is a strong connection between informing T_INF, clarifying T_CL and suggesting T_SUG), which could indicate paying closer attention to each detail, and in turn allowing individuals to slowly adapt to their new tasks.

3.3 Summary of the Findings

As shown above, although the team's encounters look similar, the foci and the way individuals interacted differed significantly when looking at the two time periods (see Figs. 1a,b and 2a,b). A possible reason for the similarity can be due to prior team experiences. Because the team maintained a cooperative atmosphere, it could have promoted similar behavior among the new team members [30]. Examination of epistemic networks and qualitative data suggests that the team's communication had become ambiguous and more complex, with individuals spending more time discussing various topics and engaging in longer conversations, at the same time making more connections between the constructs. These findings suggest that the membership change, compared to the liminal phase, can be captured in the team's communication patterns, offering rich insights into the experience of liminality in organizational settings.

3.4 Quantitative Findings

To evaluate whether differences between the two periods were statistically significant, I applied a Mann-Whitney test for both socioemotional and task-related communication. The results indicated statistically significant differences between the constructs at the alpha $= 0.05$ (Table 2).

Table 2. Parametric tests of significance.

	Axis	Pair	n	Median	U	p	Effect size (r)
Socioemotional communication	X	T1	12	0.25	107.00	0.00	−0.78
		T2	10	−0.53			
	Y	T1	12	−0.35	55.00	0.77	0.08
		T2	10	−0.15			
Task-related communication	X	T1	12	0.18	98.00	0.01	−0.63
		T2	10	−0.65			
	Y	T1	12	−0.38	58.00	0.58	0.15
		T2	10	0.09			

Moreover, socioemotional communication model had co-registration correlations of 0.71 (Pearson) and 0.76 (Spearman) for the first dimension and co-registration correlations of 0.99 (Pearson) and 0.98 (Spearman) for the second. Correspondingly, task-related communication model had co-registration correlations of 0.90 (Pearson) and 0.91 (Spearman) for the first dimension and co-registration correlations of 0.84 (Pearson) and 0.87 (Spearman) for the second. Overall, Pearson and Spearman correlations indicated a strong goodness of fit between the visualizations and the original models.

Figure 3a,b presents the location of centroids at Time 1 (blue) and Time 2 (red) for socioemotional and task-related communication respectively, at a 95% confidence interval. In short, it indicates statistically significant differences between the networks.

Figure 4a,b displays the subtracted graphs depicting the discourse differences between the constructs at Time 1 and Time 2. As it can be seen, both networks present a dense network of connections, but the team made more connections between expressing opinions (SOC_OP), including positive and negative feelings (SOC_POS, SOC_NEG) and brightening up the atmosphere (SOC_LIG) before the membership change, while afterwards it made more links among expressing opinions (SOC_OP), fostering discussions (SOC_EN) and providing support (SOC_SUP) in relation to socioemotional communication. Regarding task-related communication, before the membership change the

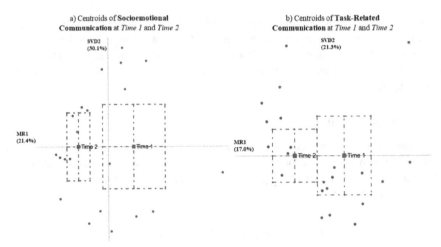

Fig. 3. Centroids of socioemotional and task-related communication at time 1 and time 2. (Color figure online)

team made more connections between informing (T_INF), asking questions (T_QUE), providing details (T_ELA) and showing agreement (T_AGR), whilst it linked more suggestions (T_SUG), questions (T_QUE), clarifying (T_CL) and agreement (T_AGR) after the change. Surprisingly, there are more connections made by the team at Time 2 for both socioemotional and task-related communication. In addition, they appear stronger than at Time 1. That, in turn supports the findings that the team communication has become more complex, reflecting the adjustment period team members experienced. Further, the subtracted models show precisely the tendency of the team to be supportive in light of a membership change as well as their willingness to be inclusive, helpful and understanding.

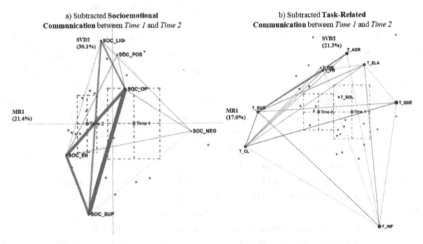

Fig. 4. Subtracted average networks between time 1 and time 2.

4 Discussion

Today's unstable work environment requires increasing flexibility and adaptability from individuals. Acknowledging the challenges related to the regular changes in team allocation, I thus argued that team membership change is liminal due to its ambiguity and transitional nature. Hence, in this paper, I set out to investigate how the team membership change is reflected in the team's collective interactions. I described and analyzed how socioemotional and task-related communication have changed over time in a virtual team.

The findings showed behavioral changes made by employees in a virtual team. Specifically, I found that "finding oneself in a liminal space" [31] makes the communication between team members more complex. As they familiarize themselves with the social context, employees exhibit the need of more support and encouragement to express their opinions. Furthermore, it seems as if the decision-making takes longer time, with each issue or suggestion being thoroughly discussed.

Practically, these findings bring attention to the organizational practices related to team composition, highlighting the necessity of managers to show their compassion for fellow employees experiencing the organizational flux. In other words, greater efforts are needed to diminish the negative effects of the liminal experience for employees. Ensuring appropriate services and support to employees transitioning should be a priority for organizations. A reasonable approach to tackle this issue could be to introduce additional onboarding programs, and increase social activities for teams, both traditional and virtual.

The findings reported in this study indubitably contribute to the scholarly understanding of team composition and its challenges. Methodologically, this research provides useful insights to the literature on quantitative ethnography. By addressing an organizational issue, it extends the current application of the epistemic network analysis to a new field of study.

Undoubtedly, the study shows some limitations, some of which could be alleviated by future research. First, the case selection of a single virtual team limits the generalizability of the findings. As such, a broader examination of several teams is essential for a more thorough understanding of the phenomenon. Second, in my analysis I coded only verbal behavior. Yet, given the nature of interactions, particularly the socioemotional communication can be expressed in a nonverbal way. Finally, to avoid too detailed codes with low occurrence in the dataset, I decided to develop a comprehensive, but more general coding scheme. As such, I am unable to distinguish between, for example, types of questions asked by the team, which could potentially provide more insight into team's interaction patterns. Also, since a single interaction can relate to both socioemotional- and task-communication, the codes are not mutually exclusive, which calls for reassessment in the future research.

Notwithstanding these limitations, this study can help teams, both traditional and virtual, become mindful of functional and dysfunctional interactions in their meetings. The findings call for future research taking into consideration the cultural aspect of unstable membership. For example, it would be interesting to assess any contrast in communication patterns between employees with different cultural backgrounds. Future research should further explore the leadership's role and behavior in assisting team with multiple organizational changes.

References

1. Mathieu, J.E., Wolfson, M.A., Park, S.: The evolution of work team research since Hawthorne. Am. Psychol. **73**(4), 308 (2018)
2. Mortensen, M., Haas, M.R.: Perspective—rethinking teams: from bounded membership to dynamic participation. Organ. Sci. **29**(2), 341–355 (2018)
3. Bell, S.T., et al.: Team composition and the ABCs of teamwork. Am. Psychol. **73**(4), 349 (2018)
4. Santistevan, D., Josserand, E.: Meta-teams: getting global work done in MNEs. J. Manag. **45**(2), 510–539 (2019)
5. Messersmith, J.G., et al.: Turnover at the top: executive team departures and firm performance. Organ. Sci. **25**(3), 776–793 (2014)
6. Groysberg, B., Lee, L.-E., Nanda, A.: Can they take it with them? the portability of star knowledge workers' performance. Manag. Sci. **54**(7), 1213–1230 (2008)
7. Stuart, H.C.: Structural disruption, relational experimentation, and performance in professional hockey teams: a network perspective on member change. Organ. Sci. **28**(2), 283–300 (2017)
8. Kane, A.A., Argote, L., Levine, J.M.: Knowledge transfer between groups via personnel rotation: effects of social identity and knowledge quality. Organ. Behav. Hum. Decis. Process. **96**(1), 56–71 (2005)
9. Feldman, D.C.: Who's socializing whom? the impact of socializing newcomers on insiders, work groups, and organizations. Hum. Res. Manag. Rev. **4**(3), 213–233 (1994)
10. Savelsbergh, C.M., Poell, R.F., van der Heijden, B.I.: Does team stability mediate the relationship between leadership and team learning? an empirical study among dutch project teams. Int. J. Proj. Manag. **33**(2), 406–418 (2015)
11. Pee, L.G., et al.: Mitigating the impact of member turnover in information systems development projects. IEEE Trans. Eng. Manag. **61**(4), 702–716 (2014)
12. Gillespie, B.M., et al.: Team communications in surgery–creating a culture of safety. J. Interprofess. Care **27**(5), 387–393 (2013)
13. Bakker, R.M., et al.: Temporary organizing: promises, processes, problems. Organ. Stud. **37**(12), 1703–1719 (2016)
14. Trainer, H.M., et al.: Team membership change "events": a review and reconceptualization. Group Organ. Manag. **45**(2), 219–251 (2020)
15. Van Gennep, A.: The Rites of Passage. University of Chicago Press, Chicago (1960)
16. Turner, V.: The Ritual Process: Structure and Anti-Structure. Routledge, Abingdon (1969)
17. Cunha, M.P., et al.: Leading and following (un) ethically in limen. J. Bus. Ethics **97**(2), 189–206 (2010)
18. Söderlund, J., Borg, E.: Liminality in management and organization studies: process, position and place. Int. J. Manag. Rev. **20**(4), 880–902 (2018)
19. Concannon, M., Nordberg, D.: Boards strategizing in liminal spaces: process and practice, formal and informal. Euro. Manag. J. **36**(1), 71–82 (2018)
20. Kauffeld, S., Lehmann-Willenbrock, N.: Meetings matter: effects of team meetings on team and organizational success. Small Group Res. **43**(2), 130–158 (2012)
21. Conroy, S.A., O'Leary-Kelly, A.M.: Letting go and moving on: work-related identity loss and recovery. Acad. Manag. Rev. **39**(1), 67–87 (2014)
22. Daskalaki, M., Butler, C.L., Petrovic, J.: Somewhere in-between: narratives of place, identity, and translocal work. J. Manag. Inq. **25**(2), 184–198 (2016)
23. Marks, M.A., Mathieu, J.E., Zaccaro, S.J.: A temporally based framework and taxonomy of team processes. Acad. Manag. Rev. **26**(3), 356–376 (2001)

24. Lehmann-Willenbrock, N., et al.: Understanding positivity within dynamic team interactions: a statistical discourse analysis. Group Organ. Manag. **42**(1), 39–78 (2017)
25. Lei, Z., et al.: Team adaptiveness in dynamic contexts: contextualizing the roles of interaction patterns and in-process planning. Group Organ. Manag. **41**(4), 491–525 (2016)
26. Kauffeld, S., Kompetenzen messen, bewerten, entwickeln: Ein prozessanalytischer Ansatz für Gruppen [Measuring, evaluating, and developing competencies]. vol. 128. Schäffer-Poeschel (2006)
27. Marquart, C.L., et al.: Epistemic Network Analysis (Version 1.7.0) [Software] (2018)
28. Siebert-Evenstone, A.L., et al.: in search of conversational grain size: modelling semantic structure using moving stanza windows. J. Learn. Anal. **4**(3), 123–139 (2017)
29. Shaffer, D.W., Collier, W., Ruis, A.R.: A tutorial on epistemic network analysis: analyzing the structure of connections in cognitive, social, and interaction data. J. Learn. Anal. **3**(3), 9–45 (2016)
30. Wang, Z., et al.: Explaining benefits of employee proactive personality: the role of engagement, team proactivity composition and perceived organizational support. J. Vocat. Behav. **101**, 90–103 (2017)
31. Sturdy, A., Schwarz, M., Spicer, A.: Guess who's coming to dinner? Structures and uses of liminality in strategic management consultancy. Hum. Relat. **59**(7), 929–960 (2006)

Safety First: Developing a Model of Expertise in Collaborative Robotics

Amanda Siebert-Evenstone[1]([⊠]) [iD], Joseph E. Michaelis[2] [iD],
David Williamson Shaffer[1] [iD], and Bilge Mutlu[1] [iD]

[1] University of Wisconsin-Madison, Madison, WI, USA
alevenstone@wisc.edu, dws@education.wisc.edu, bilge@cs.wisc.edu
[2] University of Illinois At Chicago, Chicago, IL, USA
jmich@uic.edu

Abstract. Rapid advances in technology also come with increased training needs for people who engineer and interact with these technologies. One such technology is collaborative robots, *cobots*, which are designed to be safer and easier to use than their traditional robotic counterparts. However, there have been few studies of how people use cobots and even fewer identifying what a user must know to properly set up and effectively use cobots for their manufacturing processes. In this study, we interviewed nine experts in robots and automation in manufacturing settings. We employ a quantitative ethnographic approach to gain qualitative insights into the cultural practices of robotics experts and corroborate these stories with quantitative warrants. Both quantitative and qualitative analyses revealed that experts put safety first when designing and monitoring cobot applications. This study improves our understanding of expert problem-solving in collaborative robotics, defines an expert model that can serve as a basis for the development of an authentic learning technology, and illustrates a useful method for modeling expertise in vocational settings.

Keywords: Collaborative robots · Epistemic frame theory · Epistemic network analysis · Epistemography · Quantitative ethnography

1 Introduction

Rapid advances in technology also come with increased training needs for people who engineer and interact with these technologies. In manufacturing, there is an increase in the automation of repetitive tasks using robots, however, there is also a shortage of workers trained to perform such operations [1]. One robotics technology that is becoming increasingly common in both industrial production and even in maker spaces is collaborative robots. While traditional robots are machines that are programmed to perform a task automatically, collaborative robots, or cobots, are robot systems designed with embedded safety measure that allow them to work with and around workers. Both robots and cobots engage in automation routines, however, the advantage of cobots include their affordability, increased safety, flexible and changeable applications, and easier and scaffolded programming routines [2].

© Springer Nature Switzerland AG 2021
A. R. Ruis and S. B. Lee (Eds.): ICQE 2021, CCIS 1312, pp. 304–318, 2021.
https://doi.org/10.1007/978-3-030-67788-6_21

Nevertheless, there have been few studies of how people use cobots and even fewer identifying what a user must know to properly set up and effectively use cobots for their manufacturing processes. Our long-term goal is to design an authentic learning technology that can teach new and returning users how to use cobots like experts do. But in order to design such a learning environment, we must first identify the critical components of expertise in this emerging area. Therefore, we employ a quantitative ethnographic methodology to enable both qualitative and quantitative representations of what it means to think like an expert in cobots.

In this ethnography, we investigate how experts in implementing and using cobots approach the adoption, integration, and monitoring of collaborative robots in manufacturing settings. Subsequently, we employ a quantitative ethnographic methodology to examine what it means to think like a cobotics expert.

2 Theory

In recent years, the Learning Sciences community has been conducting more research with robots including investigating collaboration in robotics teams [3], engaging students with educational robots [4], as well as teaching students how to program robots [5]. While each of these studies provides insights into educational uses of robots, there is little understanding of how robots are used in authentic settings and less focus on the affordances and uses of the robot itself. Therefore, this study seeks to learn more about robotic automation used in industrial settings and focus on two types of robot: traditional and collaborative.

Traditional robots are powerful and programmed machines that are automated to complete repetitive tasks. Commonly, traditional robots are used on production lines, such as those that manufacture automobiles, to perform routine and high-volume processes [2]. For example, many traditional robotic arms engage in *pick-and-place* applications, where a part is moved from one place to another, or *machine-tending*, where a machine, such as a lathe, is loaded and unloaded.

Robots are used in such contexts because they are faster and more reliable than human workers, and also because they can perform tasks likely to result in injury if performed by humans [6]. But because traditional robots are fast and powerful, like many of the machines they interface with, they must be isolated from human workers to ensure safety. This is often accomplished with caged work cells or other measures to isolate the robots from humans engaged in other parts of the production process.

Whereas traditional robots are fast, powerful, and isolated, cobots are designed with improved safety features that allow them to be deployed without traditional caging and isolation [2]. Cobots are also used in routine and repetitive tasks but are designed to safely work with and around humans. Cobots may work around and in partnership with human workers because they are equipped with embedded safety sensors (i.e. power- and force-limiters) and are built to have rounded components that reduce the risk of operator harm. Consequently, cobots operate at lower speeds and forces in case of an unintentional collision with the human, but they can be incorporated in automation processes without isolation or caging. Cobots were designed with other affordances that allow for varying levels of collaborative interactions with humans including simplified programming, "ease of use," and opportunities for flexible and rapid deployment [7, 8].

Both robots and cobots work with humans in manufacturing settings, however, there are a range of different human-robot collaboration levels. Christiernen [7] outlines four progressively more collaborative levels of human-collaborative interaction: no collaboration, start and stop, interactive, and collaborative. The first level, no collaboration, describes traditional robot activities that occur while physically separated from humans. The next three levels describe increasingly collaborative applications that move from asynchronous work, to synchronous work in the same physical space, and finally to the human and robot jointly working on same task.

Our prior work found that the most common use of cobots by experts in manufacturing was as an "uncaged robot," where cobots were implemented in simple, less collaborative ways but without safety caging [9]. Experts in this study emphasized how traditional robots are faster and more powerful that cobots but are also expensive because they require physical barriers, safety sensors, and programming by engineers. Experts stated that cobots were often used to lower cost and reduce space requirements for simple automation tasks. This study found that the affordances of removing unwieldy and expensive physical barriers was worth the tradeoff in performance for many implementers and companies. At the same time, many common applications for cobots did not use this machine in collaborative, flexible, or synchronous ways promised by cobot designers. That is, cobots were often used like a traditional robot either with no collaboration or start and stop processes [7]. While our previous work focused on understanding how cobots were used, we build on this work in the current project to build an expert model of how experts think about and solve automation problems using cobots in automation.

Researchers have asserted that complex thinking and expertise is characterized by relationships among domain relevant cognitive and social elements, not the isolated accumulation of these elements [10, 11]. Similarly, diSessa [12] describes how novices have "knowledge-in-pieces," unlike experts who display deep and systematic understanding regarding the connections between these disciplinary pieces. Based on these ideas, Shaffer [13] characterizes learning as developing an *epistemic frame*, which is a pattern of associations among knowledge, skills, and other cognitive elements that characterize groups of people who share similar ways of understanding, examining, and problem-solving. Importantly, epistemic frame theory provides a way to view expertise as the relationship between, and not simply the accumulation of, domain elements. Epistemic frame theory has been used to characterize frame elements in a variety of professional contexts including urban planning [14] and biomedical engineering [15], as well as to develop practice-based learning environments based on those elements [16].

To learn more about cobotics experts, we conducted an *epistemography*: an ethnographic analysis of a profession through the lens of epistemic frame theory [17]. An epistemography allows a researcher to observe and describe the components of the epistemic frame for a particular community of practice. Epistemographies have been used to studying professional practica of journalists [17] and urban planners [14]. However, we draw on this method to observe and analyze a profession during, interviews, demonstrations, and factory tours. In particular, we observed the features of and relationships among the epistemic frame for cobotics experts in manufacturing and automation.

The incorporation of cobots is well underway, but we have little sense of how experts understand cobots, how people are trained in cobotic work, and what the implications of the shift are for a range of issues. Therefore, to analyze the epistemic frame of cobot use, we employ a *quantitative ethnographic approach* [18] to gain qualitative insights into the cultural practices of robotics experts and corroborate these stories with statistical warrants. In this epistemography, we interviewed experts in cobot use in manufacturing settings. We then conducted a qualitative analysis of the interviews to identify and understand the key elements of a cobotics experts epistemic frame, and importantly, how these elements are connected to one another. Once key elements were identified, the structure of connections between these elements can be represented as a network of relationships using epistemic network analysis (ENA) [22]. ENA is particularly well-suited to evaluate expert discourse because it can model the structure of relationships between frame elements. This results in a visual representation of the structure, a mathematical model of the structure, and a way to compare the quantified data with its underlying qualitative data. After assessing the epistemic frames of all using ENA, we compared these results to the qualitative findings. Finally, we use the ENA results to reinvestigate the different instantiations and underpinnings of cobot epistemic frames.

3   Methods

3.1   Setting and Participants

Participants ($N = 9$, all male) were from six different institutions including automation sales, manufacturing, and a regional technical college. See Table 1 for a summary of participants, occupations, and organizations. No other demographic information was collected about the participants.

Table 1. Summary of participant employment.

Participant	Occupation	Company	Interview type
P1	Applications Engineer	Automation Sales	Individual
P2	Instructor	Technical College – Robotics and Automation	Individual
P3	Automation Manager	Manufacturing Enterprise	Group A
P4	Application Engineer	Manufacturing Enterprise	Group A
P5	Automation Technician	Automation Sales 2	Group B
P6	Automation Manager	Automation Sales 2	Group B and C
P7	Applications Engineer	Manufacturing Enterprise 2	Group C
P8	Operator	Manufacturing Enterprise 2	Group C
P9	Applications Engineer	Automation Sales 3	Individual

All interviews were conducted at the participants job site and followed an open-ended interviewing approach. Overall, we conducted six interviews in both individual and group settings depending on the availability of participants at the job site and asked questions designed to elicit the expert's ideas about their epistemic frame of collaborative robotics. Each interview lasted approximately one hour. After each interview, the researchers discussed the visit and revised questions for subsequent interviews.

3.2 Data Sources and Analysis

Interviews were recorded and transcribed to provide a detailed record of interactions and were segmented by sentence for the subsequent analysis. We conducted a *grounded analysis* [19] of expert interviews to find meaningful patterns of values, behaviors, and skills. We focused our analysis on identifying common ways experts considered the planning, implementation, and monitoring of cobots in factory settings. First, we read each sentence of the transcript, discussed each interview, and conducted open coding to generate an initial set of qualitative codes that represented common and repeating elements from the expert discourse associated with cobots. We then conducted axial coding by reviewing the data and refining our codes. After reaching saturation, we describe a final set of codes that represent the epistemic frame of cobot expertise (see Table 2).

To code the transcripts, we developed an automated coding scheme that used regular expression matching. We used the *nCoder* webkit [20] to develop automated classifiers for each of the codes in Table 2 and then tested for inter-rater reliability between the human rater and automated classifier. For each code, we achieved a kappa greater than 0.9 and rho was less than 0.05. Rho is a Monte Carlo rejective method that tests the generalizability of a given Kappa to the rest of the data [21]. After validating each code, we applied the automated classifiers to the data set to code the data.

To measure expertise across experts, we used Epistemic Network Analysis (ENA; described in detail elsewhere: Shaffer, Collier, & Ruis, 2016) to identify and model the connections between expert frame elements. ENA measures connections by quantifying the co-occurrence of expert codes within a defined segment of data. In this case, we used a *moving window* [23] of four utterances to measure connections between codes that were within four utterances of one another. Codes that occurred outside of this window were not considered connected. Subsequently, ENA creates two coordinated representations for each unit including the *weighted network graph*, which visualizes these connections as network graphs where the nodes correspond to the codes and edges reflect the relative frequency of the connection between two codes, and a *plotted point*. Thus, we can quantify and visualize the structure of connections among elements of cobot expertise and compare differences across experts, making it possible to characterize an epistemic frame within and across experts. After using ENA, we revisited the qualitative data to further investigate key connections between elements.

4 Results

Our analysis of expert interviews revealed insights into the epistemic frame of expert setup and usage of collaborative robots in manufacturing environments. Our initial review of the interviews revealed that safety was the first and most important consideration

Table 2. Epistemic frame codes from expert discourse about cobots.

Name	Definition	Examples
Application	Referring to the automation task	"Some of the applications that started out with collaborative robots have been machine tending"
Integration	Referring to the process of incorporating a robot and other machinery into a production system	"I guess technology's evolved as well as the mindset behind how to implement and integrate the technology"
Operator	Referring to the employees that initiate or control the cobots and other machines on the factory floor	"Our operators need to know how to edit programs; I don't think every operator needs to know how to edit programs"
Performance factors	Referring to cobot attributes such as payload, cycle time, or speed	"They're also not able to be used for high-speed application, higher pay-load applications"
Programming	Referring to coding, programs, or operating interfaces	"Knowing how to edit the program would be…my biggest concern is knowing how to edit this thing"
Reliability	Referring to errors in cobot operation	"If it hits somebody and then faults out, that's not gonna autorecover"
Safety	Referring to risk assessment for human and cobot interactions	"The way that safety works, is that it's based off of risk assessment"
Trajectory	Referring to the points and/or motion paths of cobot movement	"I always push them to just get a rough program done, your picks and your places"

among elements of cobot implementation, and that in balancing cobots' limited capabilities with their benefits of cost, flexibility and safety, the limited capabilities were often seen as an insurmountable barrier.

4.1 Safety

Safety was core to every expert's perspective. In our interviews, we found that experts considered safety and risk assessment throughout the adoption, integration, implementation, and monitoring of cobots in automation. For example, P9 considered safety as a priority when he stated, "I truly do believe that robots regardless if they're traditional or collaborative, you can't have either of those without an understanding of safety." In such a statement, the expert prioritizes safety for all robots, regardless of the type. This safety prioritization was consistently applied across all experts but implemented in different ways. In the next section, we will present the various ways that experts describe safety of the cobot as a system, safety through sensors, and safety through collaboration.

Safety of the Cobot as a System. One major safety consideration is the safety of the cobot as a system. To ensure safe collaboration, risk assessments of robots must consider the robot, task, and workpiece as a complete system. Nonetheless, experts also stated "the biggest challenge for a collaborative robot is ensuring the entire system is collaborative" (P5). Cobots are manufactured to be collaborative by removing common pinch points and embedding force-sensing capabilities. Another expert, P1, explained how one component of the cobot system could negate those reduced safety affordances, "If your tooling that you're mounting at the end of the arms has sharp points on it and it could be maybe at any level with a person's body, you would definitely have to have some kind of safeguard." While a cobot may be considered collaborative in design, if the system (i.e. relationship between the cobot, task, and part) is not fully collaborative, then the cobot no longer meets the reduced safety rules and must be caged and treated like a traditional robot. In this way, experts must continually assess the interaction between components and processes of the cobot system to make a complete risk assessment.

For each of the experts, the system and application are dynamic. Multiple experts talked about how safety "depends on the application" (P1), "depends on what kind of part you're moving" (P4), and "depends on the brand and how you program it" (P5). In another example, P3 warns about end of arm tool choice, "Well and, I guess we made the point too that it's collaborative until, what are you putting at the end of that arm? You can't have a pneumatic gripper jaw with sharp sides to it, I mean that basically becomes a knife." In a similar case, P5 warns about the part type and states, 'I could buy a collaborative robot, but if I'm moving around steak knives, it's no longer collaborative, so there's no point to using a collaborative robot." In other words, assessment of cobot system safety must consider the relationship between cobot, end of arm tools, and part in each application. As P5 said above, the cobot is only safe when the "entire system is collaborative." As a consequence, a robot is only deemed collaborative if that system can be safely operated around a human. In this way, an expert's epistemic frame for cobots is largely defined by assessing the safety of a cobot through a whole system lens, where individual aspects of the cobot interaction can undermine the safety features inherent in the cobot design.

Safety Through Cooperation. Most commonly, experts set up applications where humans and robots work in close proximity but with low interaction between human and robot. In these cases, the cobot was set up for one application where workers may set up the inputs for a process and then proceed to other activities while the application is running. In the following example, two experts discuss the factors for the set up and operation of a cobot operation,

> "We have like inserts and…it's expensive to get things oriented and aligned where you want…so we'll do that as the operator instead of having this automatic feeder, we'll have an operator just…load it, but we want to be able to load the insert to whatever that robot needs *without really getting in the way*…So, typically they'll be doing some other tasks, like, 'Oh, it's been fifteen minutes, I better put some inserts here so that it keeps running.' So we want to make sure that's in a nice location for the operator, too" (emphasis added).

At first, P3 describes the cost and positioning factors associated with inputs and pallets. He further elaborates by considering the multiple jobs an operator may have in the field. While it is important to consider the specific application, these experts also highlight the broader goals and automation activities that engineers and operators may be a part of. P3 goes on to say that an operator will check back in on the process and see if it is time for him to interact with the process. In this example, P3 uses this human, robot, and system interaction to make sure designs are both safe and convenient for the people that operate them. Importantly, though, the operator mostly interacts with the cobot by setting up, starting, checking on, and/or ending the process and then trying to avoid "getting in the way." Rarely are the operators working synchronously or dynamically with the cobot. Notably, this interaction is much more like cooperation where each entity completes a component separately to complete a joint process, in contrast to collaboration where the human and robot would work together on a joint task.

After the statements above, one interviewer asked, "So not only do you have to program the robot, you also have to design the human interaction?" The other expert in the group interview, P4, responded that,

> "Since we do mold swaps so much, you're machine here (one location), UR always working here (a second location), you might be doing a mold swap over here (a third location), so you need to be able to stay out of their way, as well. Keep it up tight against the press, so you don't interfere with them."

In this conversation, P4 extends his collaborators ideas by highlighting how the different locations affect operator workflow and safety. Here, P4 considers the movement of the operator and the requirements that the operator himself stay clear of certain machine actions. Importantly, it is the onus of the operator to "stay out of their way" indicating that the robot movement gains priority status in the cell. Instead of programming movements that are properly safe and collaborative, the operator should not "interfere with them." And so, while P3 and P4 were two of the experts that described more collaborative interactions than other experts, they too try to keep the cobot and operator separated. The above examples also highlight the need to see the robot and human as components in a bigger line or process, yet the separation between operator and robot task persists in part to improve safety in cases which safety measures may fail. That is to say that an expert epistemic frame considers when and if operators engage in cooperative tasks with cobots.

Safety Through Automation. In contrast to the above cooperative example, some experts viewed human and robot interaction in a different way. One of the goals of automation is to automate tasks that are repetitive and/or harmful for humans to engage in. For some experts, the safest way to use robots is without humans and therefore experts may design processes that keep humans separate from cobots. Two experts in particular, P2 and P5, believed that it was important to automate the easy tasks which would free up that person to engage in other tasks at the factory. These experts argued that companies "who automate are going to want to remove the operator" (P5). This is an important process to do in order to reduce "repetitive injuries" (P5) where "you have people doing [things] that's not very ergonomic" (P5). Likewise, P2 made statements throughout the interview indicating that he believed that automating work using traditional robots was more important than collaborative robots. During his courses, he teaches students primarily about traditional robots because he believes that is what is most important for students to learn to get good jobs in industry. In many cases, he believed that a "collaborative robot just couldn't keep up" and that it was just a "slow robot" (P2). Although he believes that cobots are important enough that he incorporates a cobot challenge into the coursework, he does so only during the final section of coursework. In each of these cases, the expert frame considered the safety of the worker as well as weighing the performance of the robot when thinking about what type of robot would be useful for a certain application.

4.2   Performance Tradeoffs for Cobots

While considering robot systems and applications helps make the work cell collaborative, there are important tradeoffs for these decisions. Experts often discussed how the application may require different capabilities for the robot. During one interview, P1 discussed that "if they need um fairly high throughput one of our robots…we have maybe a couple of robots that might work as far as reach goes and payload goes…but if they need the higher speeds that say, a collaborative robot might not be able to achieve, then we will talk about a traditional robot and then safeguarding that also." Like above, there is a dynamic relationship between robot system and application, and in this case, the experts consider other business goals, efficiency, and performance factors. P2 reflects, "so you've got a, um collaborative robot, co-bot um that is able to work without all of the guarding and next to somebody, but typically the cycle times…are lower." Here, P2 weighs the importance of reduced space requirements in comparison with how long it takes to finish a process. In another case, P6 considers the weight of the product when he says, "so depending on the weight of whatever product you're looking at, you might have to go into say the FANUC collaborative" which is a more powerful type of collaborative robot.

These examples show how experts consider how collaborative robots allow the removal of safeguarding in order to allow a cheaper and less bulky cobot that can more easily work with and around humans. On the other hand, cobots can be collaborative because they do not move as fast or powerfully as traditional robots. In other words, experts work to balance the collaborative benefits and performance tradeoffs for each task, which is an important perspective defining an expert's epistemic frame.

4.3   Epistemic Network Analysis

These qualitative results suggest that an expert epistemic frame depends on the interaction between safety principles, the ability and needs of the workers, the specific applications of cobots, and performance limitations of cobots. Within each application, experts attend to the cobot, programming, sensors, and human collaboration to ensure that the dynamic interactions between these moving components remains safe. When discussing each of these epistemic frame elements, experts switch back and forth between focusing on specific details of a cobot application and broader concerns about the risk of a cobot process. While all participants discussed their expertise in cobot implementation and integration, each expert described cobot use in different ways.

One of the goals of this project was to determine whether and how the qualitative stories we found generalize within the larger set of interviews. Therefore, we used ENA to investigate (1) the types of epistemic frame elements that experts discussed, and (2) how all experts make connections across these frame elements. ENA affords a method to see if the patterns identified in the grounded analysis occur as a systematic pattern across all units. Figure 1 shows an ENA representation of expert discourse when discussing collaborative robots. The figure shows the average plotted points (squares) for each expert, as well as the overall mean plotted point for all experts in the ENA space. The figure also shows an average discourse pattern for all experts, where the thickness and saturation of a connection indicates that experts frequently discussed these ideas together.

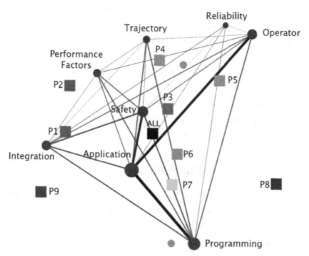

Fig. 1. Mean network points (squares) and overall mean network for the expert model of cobots. Thicker lines indicate higher relative frequency of a given connection between two expert codes.

This model shows connections to SAFETY and to APPLICATION were common across all experts, which reinforces our qualitative interpretation of the interviews. The ENA model also identifies the common ways that experts describe their approaches to setting up robot systems for a specific application. For example, the two strongest connections in the mean network are between APPLICATION and OPERATOR and APPLICATION and PROGRAMMING. Each of these connections provides evidence that experts often consider the two actors in a cobot process: the worker initiating, monitoring, and ending the tasks, and the specific coding and logic that moves the robot through the task. These results support our grounded analyses and provide a quantitative warrant for our qualitative claims that an expert frame focuses on the dynamic interaction between safety and components of application.

These ENA results suggest that experts spend more time talking about specific details of how operators engage with a task and how implementers program the robot system within that task. In this case, ENA can identify that experts consider operators and programming less often than other relationships. It is equally important that through ENA we can see that not all experts discuss cobots in the same way. In the qualitative examples, P9 is very concerned about safety and frequently discussed ways to integrate sensors into each application. And the ENA space positions him farther to the left near APPLICATION, INTEGRATION, and SAFETY. On the other hand, P5 is to the right of the space because he more frequently discussed how the OPERATOR may need to restart a PROGRAM that had issues with RELIABILITY and experienced an error. In this way, ENA allows us to benefit from the variety of expert discourse and classify types of experts. Additionally, ENA affords identification of both expert and researcher blind spots.

However, these results also highlight important gaps in cobot use and additional pieces to the above stories. As researchers we were surprised at the weaker connections to operator, particularly from SAFETY and from PROGRAMMING. For example, as processes incorporate more collaborative interactions, cobot systems need to program for the operator as much as the application. After evaluating these network results, we as researchers dove deeper to learn why some connections were more prominent than we expected (i.e., OPERATOR & APPLICATION), while others were far less prominent than we hypothesized (i.e., OPERATOR and SAFETY or OPERATOR and PROGRAMMING). Based on our review of the literature and our previous work, we would have expected there to be more discussion about ways humans and cobots can safely collaborate, which guided our reevaluation of the qualitative data.

4.4 Challenges in Safety and Collaboration

After investigating our ENA model, we identified qualitative examples that may explain why certain connections were more or less frequent across all experts. Next, we explain how challenges in both safety and collaboration may help us understand these differences and inform future trainings for operators and implementers.

Safety Challenges. Because of the dynamic factors involved in creating safe manufacturing operations, employing good safety practices is still a challenge for experts. Even with the safety standards and physical and electronic barriers separating traditional and collaborative robots from humans, there are still instances of people using the machines unsafely. For example, P9 recounts "traditional robots have always been something that are very high speed. And it's something that you don't want to get yourself within their operational reach. (laughs briefly) Now there's many examples of where I can state people that uh still do that." And so, while traditional robot setups often have stricter rules separating humans from machines, operators may still try to bypass safety precautions in service of their work. For these reasons, P9 believes that,

> "to be honest, if there's weakness right now I think in the automation industry…it's the true understanding and knowledge on how to implement safety correctly. So people when they implement safety, they think if they're doing something and they're putting something there, it's deemed safe. And …that's not necessarily true" (P9).

Even though every expert in our study discusses safety, these conceptions of safety vary in scope, type, and depth as seen in the different positions of experts across the frame elements. Each expert expressed different ways they dealt with safety, although all consistently referenced safety throughout their interviews.

One barrier to safe deployment of all robots and cobots is safety training itself. Above, P9 finds safety to be the most important and yet weakest component in the automation industry. Similarly, P4 expresses this concern and reflects, "I know, from when I was in school, we didn't talk much about safety. At all, when it comes to control systems, so that might be something else that you can start integrating. That they can be aware of safety." Such statements suggest that both engineers and operators would benefit from more opportunities to think about and apply safety techniques in their day to day work.

These results have suggested that safety is the primary lens with which experts consider programming, integration, collaboration, and robot systems. However, this dynamic picture is further complicated and limited by the operator himself.

Collaboration Challenges. An interesting result from our reinvestigation of the qualitative data is how experts talk about operators. People are an important component in a collaborative robot interaction, however, expert attitudes towards the operators may affect how or if collaborative robots are used at all. Some experts see operator agency as an advantage while others see it as a liability. One engineer expressed his desire for more training and assistance for operators. He thought it is a benefit for his workload and for the applications when an operator is trained. For example, P7 says,

> "If [operator name] weren't trained, every time a new error came up that he'd never seen before…we'd just teach them how to reset it and they'd just mindlessly go through and hit the buttons they know to hit to reset it…but if he actually knows what the error means and he knows how to reset it, then he doesn't have to call us, wait for us to come out, reset it".

In this case, operator knowledge and agency would allow the operator to modify programs that could help save both the operator and engineer's time. Knowing how to understand problems would help both individuals.

On the other hand, there were quite a few opinions about what operators should be allowed to do. P6 describes the variety of perspectives that he has experienced working with different companies. He recounts that, "we've had companies say that, 'We want a robot where we can literally let the operator change programs: speed it up, slow it down.' And I've been at facilities where you have to be a trained maintenance or automation technician to get the password to [be] allow[ed] to even unlock the teach pendant." Each of these examples illustrates the wide range of trust that the engineers at a company have for their operators. In some cases, experts even expressed some disdain for employees. P5 asserts that, "If you would ask most owners, they would like to have robots in there doing everything. They don't take smoke breaks, they don't call in sick, they don't intentionally try to sabotage your product if they're having a bad day or weren't treated fairly for X or Y reasons." Even the community college educator states that, "It's not like everybody can move up that pyramid of skills" (P2). And so, it may come as no surprise that P2 and P5 are the two experts that advocate for automation over collaboration to ensure safety and efficiency of work. These examples provide insight into why some experts may be more open to collaboration than others and provide explanations as to why the connections to the operator were less frequent across the entire sample. Some experts may have viewed operators simply as someone that starts and stops an application, treating the humans as one component in the system. Other experts envision a more dynamic role where the operator is an agent that can engage in coding and problem-solving. In either case, an expert frame would consider the interaction between application, cobot system, and operator.

5   Discussion

This study shows how the expert epistemic frame works to assess safety at different levels—from programming logic to the setup of a full automation line. Experts look for how safety depended on the dynamic interaction between the robot system, application, and human actions. These results suggest that experts put *safety first* when designing and implementing collaborative robot interactions.

The epistemic frame outlined in this study can also be used to support novices in learning how to use cobots as well as to support experts' ability to round out their robot expertise. Our future work will leverage the expert model to design and develop a cobot project-based learning simulation. This learning environment will engage students in an authentic cobot application while providing real-time and adaptive supports based on the epistemic frame outlined in this study. Learners will be able to enable components of the frame to see what an expert would see based on the epistemic frame, such as how to consider safety in conjunction with trajectories. We will also explore the design and function of different interface modalities (*i.e.,* teach pendant, desktop simulation, augmented reality) that afford user interactions with the system and how they affect learning the epistemic frame. In this way, a quantitative ethnographic analysis of expertise in a domain can be used to create curriculum and learning environments. Additionally, by creating a representation of expert knowledge through QE and ENA, we can also use the resulting ENA space to evaluate novices and compare their discourse with expert discourse.

This study also provides important methodological implications. When quantifying the qualitative, we must not lose sight of local meanings from discourse. Our analysis highlights the importance of closing the interpretive loop by both scaling our local understandings across the sample as well as investigating how statistical representations shed light on more specific patterns. As seen the two analyses, there were important differences in how experts accounted for safety and collaboration. Some experts addressed safety through fostering more collaborative interactions, while others made the application safer by removing the workers during operation. Future analyses would benefit from learning more about these perspectives and which is more common in the workplace. While the goal of the current study was to summarize all expert perspectives, further analyses could categorize experts based on their perspectives and consider the similarities and differences between these groups.

Our study is limited in both size and diversity of the sample, which would benefit from interviews with more operators, recruitment of female operators, and comparisons across different types of companies. During our data collection, we focused on interviewing implementers and engineers as experts but recognize the need for more understanding about operator uses and interactions with cobots.

However, in the end, this study improves our understanding of expert problem-solving in collaborative robotics, defines an expert model that can serve as a basis for the development of an authentic learning technology, and illustrates a useful method for modeling expertise.

Acknowledgements. This work was funded by the National Science Foundation award # 1822872. Any opinions, findings and conclusions, or recommendations expressed in this material are those of the authors, and do not necessarily reflect those of the NSF.

References

1. National Academies of Sciences: Building America's skilled technical workforce. The National Academies Press, Washington, DC (2017). https://doi.org/https://doi.org/10.17226/23472
2. Faccio, M., Bottin, M., Rosati, G.: Collaborative and traditional robotic assembly: a comparison model. Int. J. Adv. Manufact. Technol. **102**(5–8), 1355–1372 (2019). https://doi.org/10.1007/s00170-018-03247-z
3. Elliott, C.H., Radke, S.C., Ma, J.M.: A focus on contribution towards product performance in collaborative design. In: Kay, J., Luckin, R. (eds.) Rethinking Learning in the Digital Age: Making the Learning Sciences Count, 13th International Conference of the Learning Sciences (ICLS) 2018, pp. 48–55. International Society of the Learning Sciences, London (2018)
4. Kim, Y., Marx, S., Pham, H., Nguyen, T.T.: Designing technology as a cultural broker for young children: challenges and opportunities. In: Kay, J., Luckin, R. (eds.) Rethinking Learning in the Digital Age: Making the Learning Sciences Count, 13th International Conference of the Learning Sciences (ICLS) 2018. pp. 88–95. International Society of the Learning Sciences, London (2018)
5. Starr, E.L., Reilly, J.M., Schneider, B.: Toward using multi-modal learning analytics to support and measure collaboration in co-located dyads. In: Kay, J., Luckin, R. (eds.) Rethinking Learning in the Digital Age: Making the Learning Sciences Count, 13th International Conference of the Learning Sciences (ICLS) 2018, pp. 448–455. International Society of the Learning Sciences, London (2018)
6. Hirschfeld, R.A., Aghazadeh, F., Chapleski, R.C.: Survey of robot safety in industry. Int. J. Hum. Factors Manuf. **3**, 369–379 (1993). https://doi.org/10.1002/hfm.4530030405
7. Christiernin, L.G.: How to describe interaction with a collaborative robot. In: ACM/IEEE International Conference on Human-Robot Interaction, pp. 93–94 (2017). https://doi.org/10.1145/3029798.3038325
8. Djuric, A.M., Urbanic, R.J., Rickli, J.L.: A framework for collaborative robot (CoBot) integration in advanced manufacturing systems. SAE Int. J. Mater. Manuf. **9**, 457–464 (2016)
9. Michaelis, J.E., Siebert-Evenstone, A., Shaffer, D.W., Mutlu, B.: Collaborative or Simply Uncaged? Understanding Human-Cobot Interactions in Automation, pp. 1–12 (2020). https://doi.org/10.1145/3313831.3376547
10. Chi, M.T.H., Feltovich, P.J., Glaser, R.: Categorization and representation of physics problems by experts and novices. Cogn. Sci. **5**, 121–152 (1981). https://doi.org/10.1207/s15516709cog0502_2

11. Bransford, J.D., Brown, A.L., Cocking, R.R.: How People Learn: Brain, Mind, Experience, and School. National Academies Press, Washington, DC (1999)
12. DiSessa, A.: Knowledge in pieces. Constructivism in the Computer Age, pp. 49–70 (1988). https://doi.org/10.1159/000342945
13. Shaffer, D.W.: How Computer Games Help Children Learn. Palgrave Macmillan, New York (2006).
14. Bagley, E.: Epistemography of an urban and regional planning practicum: appropriation in the face of resistance. WCER Working Paper (2010)
15. Arastoopour, G., Chesler, N.C., Shaffer, D.W.: Epistemic persistence: a simulation-based approach to increasing participation of women in engineering. J. Women Minor. Sci. Eng. **20**, 211–234 (2014). https://doi.org/10.1615/JWomenMinorScienEng.2014007317
16. Chesler, N.C., Ruis, A.R., Collier, W., Swiecki, Z., Arastoopour, G., Shaffer, D.W.: A novel paradigm for engineering education: virtual internships with individualized mentoring and assessment of engineering thinking. J. Biomech. Eng. **137**, 1–8 (2015). https://doi.org/10.1115/1.4029235.
17. Shaffer, D.W.: WCER Working Paper No. 2005-8 Epistemography and the Participant Structures of a Professional Practicum: A Story Behind the Story of Journalism 828. Cognition (2005)
18. Shaffer, D.W.: Quantitative Ethnography. Cathcart Press, Madison (2017)
19. Corbin, J., Strauss, A.: Grounded theory research: procedures, canons, and evaluative criteria. Qual. Sociol. **13**, 3–21 (1990)
20. Hinojosa, C., Siebert-Evenstone, A.L., Eagan, B.R., Swiecki, Z., Gleicher, M., Marquart, C.: nCoder (2019). https://app.n-coder.org/
21. Eagan, B.R., Rogers, B., Serlin, R., Ruis, A.R., Irgens, G.A., Shaffer, D.W.: Can we rely on IRR? Testing the assumptions of inter-rater reliability. In: CSCL 2017 Proceedings, pp. 529–532 (2017).
22. Shaffer, D.W., Collier, W., Ruis, A.R.R.: A tutorial on epistemic network analysis: analyzing the structure of connections in cognitive, social, and interaction data. J. Learn. Anal. **3**, 9–45 (2016). https://doi.org/10.18608/jla.2016.33.3
23. Siebert-Evenstone, A.L., Arastoopour Irgens, G., Collier, W., Swiecki, Z., Ruis, A.R., Williamson Shaffer, D.: In search of conversational grain size: Modelling semantic structure using moving stanza windows. J. Learn. Anal. **4**, 123–139 (2017). https://doi.org/10.18608/jla.2017.43.7

Collaborative Learning Analysis Using Business Card-Type Sensors

Shunpei Yamaguchi[1(✉)], Shusuke Ohtawa[2], Ritsuko Oshima[2], Jun Oshima[2], Takuya Fujihashi[1], Shunsuke Saruwatari[1], and Takashi Watanabe[1]

[1] Graduate School of Information Science and Technology, Osaka University, Suita, Japan
yamaguchi.shunpei@ist.osaka-u.ac.jp
[2] Graduate School of Integrated Science and Technology,
Shizuoka University, Hamamatsu, Japan

Abstract. Although most studies have been focused on the language data for investigating cultural practices of learning in the quantitative ethnography, human communication is fundamentally multimodal. The integration of non-language modality data with language data would provide more accurate interpretation of how learners engage in their collaboration. In this study, therefore, we propose Sensor-based Regulation Profiler. Sensor-based Regulation Profiler automatically extracts and visualizes the points that researchers in learning science should notice to support qualitative analysis in collaborative learning. The Sensor-based Regulation Profiler consists of a business card-type sensor that acquires sensor data from each learner as well as a data mining technique that analyzes the acquired sensor data. The proposed data mining technique automatically extracts and visualizes social graphs, learning phases, and speakers during collaborative learning to reduce the costs of qualitative analysis. Experimental evaluations using business card sensors in collaborative learning showed that the social graph, and the learning phase could be automatically extracted and visualized from the acquired sensor data and the speaker identification could be realized with an average accuracy of 77.8% by using the Sensor-based Regulation Profiler. ₎

Keywords: Collaborative learning · Human activity recognition · Sensor-based learning analysis · Sensor networks · Time synchronization

1 Introduction

In quantitative ethnography, researchers have been focused on language data. Based on a variety of theoretical frameworks, learners' cultural practices have been unveiled. Using vocabularies in discourse as nodes of a network, for instance, the state of collective knowledge is represented as a collection of clusters of vocabulary nodes. Its temporal change in the network structure is analyzed for evaluating a group performance [1]. The same discourse data can also be analyzed as epistemic practices by categorizing discourse actions as codes and constructing a network of the codes [2]. Thus, computational approaches would provide new perspectives on cultural practices learners engage

© Springer Nature Switzerland AG 2021
A. R. Ruis and S. B. Lee (Eds.): ICQE 2021, CCIS 1312, pp. 319–333, 2021.
https://doi.org/10.1007/978-3-030-67788-6_22

through their collaboration in different but complementary ways compared with the traditional qualitative approaches such as the conversation analysis [3].

In collaborative discourse practices, however, non-language information is exchanged among participants, and influences how the participants interpret discourse.

Researchers in the qualitative discourse analysis developed several transcribing protocols for expressing participants' actions, voices, and facial expressions. The description of the non-language information makes the discourse transcription richer in that readers can be immersed in the context of collaboration as participants. In learning analytics, the issue has been discussed in the topic of multimodal learning analytics [4]. In multimodal learning analytics, it is assumed that human communication in collaborative learning is fundamentally multimodal such as gaze, body language, actions, facial expressions, speech, and writing and sketching. The technological development to capture the modalities in the learning setting makes it possible for researchers to integrate the modal information for describing practices in more accurate ways.

In this study, we propose Sensor-based Regulation Profiler to quantitatively analyze the activities of learners in collaborative learning and automatically extract and visualize the points of interest for researchers in learning science. The proposed Sensor-based Regulation Profiler consists of a business card-type sensor, namely, Sensor-based Regulation Profiler Badge and a sensor-based learning analysis method. The Sensor-based Regulation Profiler Badges acquire sensor data from the learners in collaborative learning and the sensor-based learning analysis method analyzes and visualizes the collaborative learning activities from the acquired sensor data. In addition, each Sensor-based Regulation Profiler Badge has a RF-based time synchronization module to achieve high-precision time synchronization of sensor data obtained between all the sensors. The proposed Sensor-based Regulation Profiler allows learning science researchers to analyze collaborative learning activities in more detail through the automatic extraction and visualization of the activities from learners' sensor data. We envisage the use of automatic extraction results to find groups whose collaborative learning activities are not working well, and to help researchers navigate the learning activities of those groups in real time.

From experimental evaluations using the proposed Sensor-based Regulation Profiler, we found 1) the time synchronization accuracy between the proposed Sensor-based Regulation Profiler Badges is approximately 30 μs, 2) the proposed method automatically extracts social graphs that represent face-to-face interactions between learners, 3) the proposed method automatically extracts learning phases during collaborative learning activities, and 4) the proposed method identifies which of the three learners spoke with an average accuracy of about 77.8%.

The remainder of this paper is as follows: Sect. 2 describes the requirements for introducing quantitative analysis to collaborative learning environments. Section 3 discusses the related studies. In Sect. 4, we present our proposed scheme, Sensor-based Regulation Profiler. Sections 5 and 6 also present the proposed Sensor-based Regulation Profiler Badge and sensor-based learning analysis. Experimental evaluations are carried out in Sects. 7 and 8 to discuss the performance of the proposed Sensor-based Regulation Profiler Badge and sensor-based learning analysis in collaborative learning. Section 9 finally concludes our paper.

2 Requirements

There are three requirements to deploy a quantitative analysis tool into collaborative learning environments.

1. Easy deployment to learning environments
2. Precise time synchronization across each learner's sensor data
3. Automatic extraction of collaborative learning phases

The first requirement is necessary for the widespread deployment of the quantitative analysis tool. It is impractical to use expensive or poorly available technologies to install in the learning environments. In this study, we design a business card-type sensor that learners can hang from each neck for the purpose of easy deployment to the learning environment. There are several business card-type sensors such as Hitachi's business microscope [5] and MIT's Sociometric Badge [6]. For example, the business microscope enabled a quantitative analysis of communication in the organization. It solved communication issues by analyzing the networks in the organization to understand the walls and unity. However, neither the business microscope nor the Sociometric Badge were available on the market.

The second requirement is necessary as this study focuses on the extraction of interpersonal collaboration. This study analyzes data from the business card-type sensors deployed on various objects, such as learners and learning environments, and confirms the consistency of the data from the sensors. When we analyze data without time synchronization, the analysis may become meaningless because the chronological order of events is broken. As mentioned above, both the business microscope and the Sociometric Badge have been developed to extract the interpersonal collaboration, but there is no mechanism for time synchronization between the sensors. In terms of the accuracy of time synchronization, the accuracy should be less than one-tenth of the sensor's sampling rate. For example, if the sampling rate of the sensor data is 100 Hz, they should be synchronized with the time within 1 ms or less.

The third requirement is necessary to connect qualitative and quantitative analysis in collaborative learning. Ideally, quantitative analysis can automatically extract all of the same results as those obtained in qualitative analysis by the researchers in learning science. However, it is difficult to replace all of the qualitative analysis with the quantitative analysis at present because there is a large gap between the information that can be acquired and processed by machines and humans. As the first effort to connect qualitative and quantitative analysis in collaborative learning, this study focuses on automatic extraction of learning phases and social graphs and speaker identification as automatic extraction in the learning phase.

3 Related Works

Our study relates to the studies on collaborative extraction using business card-type sensors, sensor-based activity recognition, and collaborative learning analysis.

3.1 Collaborative Extraction Using Business Card-Type Sensors

Several studies have tackled to extract the collaboration between users using business card-type sensors on the users. In the business microscope [5], each user wears a business card-type sensor equipped with an infrared sensor. The use of face-to-face information from the infrared sensors has shown that the appropriate frequency of meetings has an impact on work efficiency. In the Sociometric Badge [6], each user also wears a business card-type sensor equipped with an accelerometer, a sound pressure sensor, a position sensor, Bluetooth, and an infrared sensor. By collecting face-to-face information between the users, conversation tone changes, and proximity from the Sociometric Badges, they found that the face-to-face information between the users affects the work productivity and efficiency of the users. In Open Badge [7], the user wears a small sensor with a sound pressure sensor and Bluetooth around the neck. They visualized the face-to-face information between the users based on the sound pressure data and the Received Signal Strength Indicator (RSSI) from Bluetooth.

On the other hand, none of the business card-type sensors are available on the market and it is difficult to obtain them. In addition, since the time synchronization accuracy between the business card-type sensors is from tens to hundreds of milliseconds, the automatic extraction of learning phases in collaborative learning may not be performed correctly.

The business card-type sensor developed in our study, i.e., Sensor-based Regulation Profiler Badge has an acceleration sensor, a sound pressure sensor, and an infrared sensor. One of the major differences from the conventional business card-type sensors is that the time synchronization module can achieve a time synchronization accuracy of several tens of μs. Such time synchronization can improve the accuracy of quantitative analysis, e.g., learning phase extraction, in collaborative learning.

3.2 Sensor-Based Activity Recognition

Some studies have been carried out to recognize a user's behavior by using multiple sensors attached to the user. In the literature [8], the sensor data obtained from attaching accelerometers to the user's wrist, ankle, and chest is transmitted to the cloud. The cloud uses decision tree analysis to classify user's six activities: lying down, sitting, standing, walking, running, and riding a bike. In the literature [9], the user wears a wristwatch-type wearable device with built-in accelerometer, light sensor, thermometer, and sound sensor to classify the user's six activities: sitting, standing, walking, going up stairs, going down stairs, and running. They demonstrated that the classification could be realized in real-time with 92.5% accuracy by using decision tree analysis. Literature [10] uses Zephyr BioHarness Bluetooth to collect acceleration and biometric information on each user and then classify three activities by using the decision tree analysis: running, walking, and sitting. In addition, they showed that the classification can cope with new users without re-learning by learning the data of various users. Literature [11] used fuzzy basis functions for 3-axis accelerometer values worn on the wrist of the user's dominant arm to classify seven activities: brushing teeth, tapping a person, tapping a desk, working on a computer, running, waving, and walking.

Our proposed Sensor-based Regulation Profiler uses sensor data obtained from the proposed Sensor-based Regulation Profiler Badges to visualize collaborative learning and learners' activities. For example, the proposed Sensor-based Regulation Profiler automatically extracts the variations of the learning phase by measuring the network variation among the learners from infrared sensor data mounted on each Sensor-based Regulation Profiler Badge. The automatic extraction of the learning phases can reduce the time for analysis of collaborative learning activities as well as proper navigation in collaborative learning by learning science researchers.

3.3 Collaborative Learning Analysis

A general way to evaluate the learning effects of collaborative learning is to analyze video and audio data corresponding to the activities of the collaborative learning. On the other hand, the above-mentioned way has the following two issues.

1. The cost of detailed analysis
2. The inclusion of the researcher's subjectivity in the analysis

The first issue stems from the transcription of the learners' conversations from the captured video and audio data and the analysis of the conversations considering collaboration using nonverbal behaviors. The second issue stems from the misalignment of notation between researchers when they describe the collaboration that occurs in the learners' conversations.

To solve the aforementioned issues, our study quantitatively analyzes collaborative learning by using the proposed sensor-based learning analysis. The quantitative analysis of collaborative learning allows for detailed and rapid analysis of social graphs, learning phases, and speakers, thus reducing the cost of the detailed analysis. In addition, our Sensor-based Regulation Profiler Badge can represent the learner's condition as the value of each sensor. The proposed sensor-based learning analysis enables the analysis of collaborative learning activities without the researcher's subjectivity.

4 Proposed Scheme: Sensor-Based Regulation Profiler

In order to reduce the cost of qualitative analysis and to provide objective data in collaborative learning, we propose a novel scheme, namely, Sensor-based Regulation Profiler. The proposed scheme consists of Sensor-based Regulation Profiler Badge that acquires sensor data from learners and a learning analysis technique that analyzes the acquired sensor data. Figure 1 shows the overview of the collaborative learning analysis using the proposed Sensor-based Regulation Profiler. The Sensor-based Regulation Profiler supports qualitative analysis of collaborative learning by researchers in learning science as follows:

1. Distribute the proposed Sensor-based Regulation Profiler Badges to learners
2. Conduct collaborative learning between the learners
3. Collect the distributed Sensor-based Regulation Profiler Badges from the learners

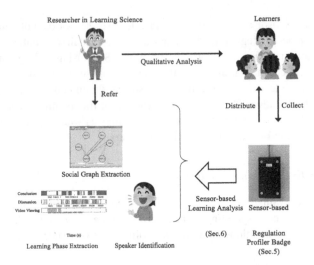

Fig. 1. Overview of collaborative learning analysis using sensor-based regulation profiler.

4. Extract sensor data from the collected Sensor-based Regulation Profiler Badges
5. Automatically extract and visualize the social graph, learning phases, and speakers in the collaborative learning from the sensor data
6. Carry out qualitative analysis of the collaborative learning by learning science researchers using the results of social graph extraction, learning phase extraction, and speaker identification

The proposed Sensor-based Regulation Profiler Badge is described in Sec. 5 and the proposed learning analysis methods of social graph extraction, learning phase extraction, and speaker identification are described in Sect. 6, respectively.

5   Sensor-Based Regulation Profiler Badge

Figures 2 (a) and (b) show the proposed Sensor-based Regulation Profiler Badge (Sensor Node), the block diagram of the Sensor-based Regulation Profiler Badge, and Fig. 3 Sensor-based Regulation Profiler Badge Synchronizer (Sync Node), respectively. The

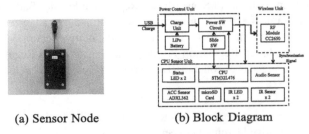

(a) Sensor Node   (b) Block Diagram

Fig. 2. Sensor-based regulation profiler badge.

Sensor-based Regulation Profiler Badge is a business card-type sensor designed to be hung from the learner's neck. The sensor node consists of a power control unit, a CPU sensor unit, and a wireless unit.

Fig. 3. Sync node.

The power control unit has a lithium-ion battery to drive the sensor node. The lithium-ion battery supplies power to the power switch and the Micro Controller Unit (MCU). The sensor node continuously runs for 24 h.

The CPU sensor unit is equipped with STM32L476RGT6 from STMicroelectronics as the MCU, ADXL362 accelerometer from ANALOG DEVICES, OSI5LAS1C1A infrared light emitting diode (LED) from OptoSupply, PIC79603 infrared receiver from KODENSHI CORP., and INMP510 analog microphone from TDK. The 3-axis accelerometer samples 12 bits at 100 Hz and the sound pressure sensor samples 12 bits at 100 Hz. The microSD card connector of DM3AT-SF-PEJM5 from Hirose Electric is used for recording the sensor data. The acceleration data, infrared data, and sound pressure data can be saved in a microSD card.

The wireless unit uses CC2650 from Texas Instruments which contains a wireless synchronization module. The wireless synchronization module transfers the synchronization signal transmitted every 10 ms from the sync node to other sensor nodes to realize time synchronization between the sensor nodes. The CC2650 uses UNISONet, which is also known as Choco [12, 13], to realize precise time synchronization between the sensor nodes. In Choco, an arbitrary sensor node forwards a time-synchronous packet to the neighboring sensor nodes and then propagates the received time-synchronous packet to the destination sensor node. When a sensor node receives a new time-synchronous packet from the neighboring sensor node, it immediately forwards the packet to the neighboring sensor nodes. Each sensor node repeatedly receives and forwards time-synchronous packets by flooding, resulting in fast propagation of time-synchronous packets throughout the sensor nodes.

6   Sensor-Based Learning Analysis

We also propose a novel sensor-based learning analysis method to automatically and precisely extract information of collaborative learning using sensor data obtained from Sensor-based Regulation Profiler Badges. The proposed method consists of social graph and learning phase extractions using infrared data and speaker identification using the combination of sound pressure and acceleration data.

Algorithm 1 Social graph extraction

Require: L, U, t_0
Ensure: G
1: Insert zero into all elements of G
2: **for all** $d \in U$ **do**
3:    $S \leftarrow$ all received IDs in $l_d \in L$ between t_0 to $t_0 + W$
4:    **for all** $s \in S$ **do**
5:       Increment $G[s][d]$
6:    **end for**
7: **end for**
8: **return** G

Table 1. Notation

Variable/Function	Description
U	Set of all the sensor IDs
L	Set of the infrared data obtained from all the sensors
l_d	Infrared data of sensor d
$t0$	Target time for social graph extraction
G	Social graph matrix with the size of $|U| \times |U|$
W	Window size (seconds)

6.1 Social Graph Extraction

In the social graph extraction, we extract social graphs that represent the network of the learners in collaborative learning from the face-to-face relationship between the Sensor-based Regulation Profiler Badges. The face-to-face relationship can be measured from the infrared data of each Sensor-based Regulation Profiler Badge. The infrared data recorded by each Sensor-based Regulation Profiler Badge contains the IDs of the other sensor nodes detected every second. Algorithm 1 shows the procedure of our social graph extraction and Table 1 shows the notation of the algorithm. Algorithm 1 outputs the matrix G which represents the social graph at $t0$ for L from a set of all sensor IDs U, a set of infrared sensor data from all the sensors $L = \{l1, l2,..., l_{|U|}\}$, and a certain time $t0$. The matrix G counts the number of infrared data across all the sensor nodes between $t0$ and $t0 + W$, where the row is the source sensor ID and the column is the destination sensor ID.

For example, we consider that the infrared data of learner 1's Sensor-based Regulation Profiler Badge is as follows.

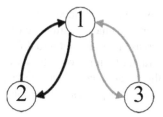

Fig. 4. Example of social graph.

```
900000000, 1, 2
900000001, 2, 3, 2
900000002, 1, 2
```

Here, the infrared data consists of a time stamp, the number of other sensors detected by the infrared sensor since the last time stamp, and ID of each detected sensor. We also consider that the infrared data of learner 2's Sensor-based Regulation Profiler Badge is as follows.

```
900000000, 1, 1
900000001, 1, 1
900000002, 1, 1
```

In addition, the infrared data of learner 3's Sensor-based Regulation Profiler Badge is as follows.

```
900000000, 1, 1
```

In this case, the matrix G is given as follows:

$$G = \begin{pmatrix} 0 & 3 & 1 \\ 3 & 0 & 0 \\ 1 & 0 & 0 \end{pmatrix}$$

The resultant matrix represents the directed graph shown in Fig. 4. Here, a larger value of the matrix indicates a higher frequency of face-to-face interaction between the learners, and thus darker arrows are used in Fig. 4.

6.2 Learning Phase Extraction

The learning phase extraction automatically divides a collaborative learning period into learning phases based on the time variation of the learners' network during collaborative learning. The time variation represents the transition of the learning phase. There are three phases in collaborative learning: video viewing, discussion, and conclusion. During the transition of the learning phase, distinctive changes appear in the learners. For example, learners may increase their attention to different learners/objects or focus on a large number of learners rather than the ones they were facing before. We capture the distinctive changes from the infrared data of each learner's Sensor-based Regulation Profiler Badge to extract the learning phases without analyzing the entire process of collaborative learning.

The time variation of the learners' network is quantified from the time variation of the matrix G. The matrix G of each time $t0$ is extracted according to Algorithm 1. We consider the matrices are extracted at 3-s intervals and the window size W of each matrix is set to 60 s. After creating the matrix G for each window, it regards the residual sum of squares between the matrices of one window and the next window as the time variation of the network.

We use AutoPlait [14] to quickly and automatically extract each learning phase from the network time variation. AutoPlait detects features from large time series data containing various patterns and visualizes the grouping of time series data. The proposed method discovers each learning phase as each time series data group extracted by AutoPlait.

6.3 Speaker Identification

The speaker identification identifies each learner's speech during collaborative learning by combining the sound pressure data and the acceleration data obtained from Sensor-based Regulation Profiler Badges. As mentioned in the previous section, the proposed Sensor-based Regulation Profiler Badge of each learner detects the variation in sound pressure when one of the learners is speaking during collaborative learning. On the other hand, even if the speaker is the same, it is difficult to identify the speaker using only the sound pressure data because the tendency of sound pressure variation depends on the direction of speakers and the voice volume. Our method uses a decision tree analysis [15] to identify the speaker in each speech by using both sound pressure and acceleration data. The decision tree analysis efficiently classifies data by using a tree structure, i.e., decision tree, to analyze the relationship between the objective and explanatory variables. In our case, the objective variable is whether the learner was speaking or not and the explanatory variables are the maximum, minimum, mean, and variance of the sound pressure and 3-axis acceleration.

7 Experimental Evaluation: Time Synchronization Preciseness

We experimentally evaluated the time synchronization accuracy between the sync node and the sensor node in the proposed Sensor-based Regulation Profiler Badge. We set up a sync node and a sensor node at a short distance on a desk and measured the time deviation between the nodes based on the synchronization signals sent from the sync node. We used an oscilloscope to measure the clock rise time at each node to accurately get the time deviation between the nodes. We assumed that the number of samples

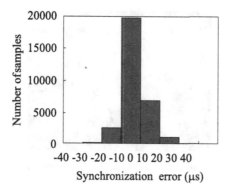

Fig. 5. Time synchronization accuracy.

was 30,003 and the wireless synchronization module of each Sensor-based Regulation Profiler Badge transmits a synchronization signal every 10 ms.

Figure 5 shows the time synchronization accuracy between the nodes. The horizontal axis shows the deviation of the time synchronization and the vertical axis indicates the number of the samples corresponding to the deviation. From Fig. 5, we can see that the time synchronization error was kept within 30 μs. Here, the mean, minimum, and maximum errors are 7.7 μs, 30 μs, and 17 μs, respectively. Since the sampling rate of both the sound pressure sensor and the acceleration sensor on the Sensor-based Regulation Profiler Badge is 100 Hz, the synchronization error is sufficient to meet the required time synchronization accuracy of less than 1 ms. It is also suggested that even if higher sampling rate sensors are used in Sensor-based Regulation Profiler Badge, it is still possible to analyze collaborative learning by combining such sensor data.

8   Experimental Evaluation: Sensor-Based Learning Analysis

We then carried out experimental evaluations to discuss the feasibility of the automatic extractions of social graphs, learning phases, and speakers from the sensor data of each learner's Sensor-based Regulation Profiler Badge during collaborative learning. Figure 6 shows a snapshot of the experiment for collaborative learning. We monitored the problem-solving activities of a group with three learners who possessed Sensor-based Regulation Profiler Badges. We set a sync node at the center of the learners' desk for time synchronization between the sensor nodes. Each learner mounted one Sensor-based Regulation Profiler Badge on his or her chest during the activities. A whiteboard was set up to assist the learners in their discussions. Two Sensor-based Regulation Profiler Badges were put on both edges of the whiteboard. In addition, an iPad was placed on the desk to present learning tasks to the learners and one Sensor-based Regulation Profiler Badge was attached to the top of the iPad.

Fig. 6. Experimental environment for collaborative learning.

8.1 Results on Social Graph Extraction

Figures 7 (a) through (c) show one social graph in each learning phase, respectively. Here, the learning elapsed time [h:mm:ss] is displayed at the upper left corner. In addition, Users 1 through 3 are the sensor nodes mounted on each learner, WB_R and WB_L represent the sensor nodes placed on the right and left edges of the whiteboard, iPad is the sensor node attached on the iPad, and the arrows show the face-to-face data between the sensor nodes.

In Fig. 7 (a), we can see the learners did not face each other during the video viewing phase because the face-to-face data are scarce. Figure 7 (b) shows that User 1, User 2, and the right edge of the whiteboard faced each other and User 2 also faced the left edge of the whiteboard. Since the learner closest to the right edge of the whiteboard was User 1, we think User 1 used the whiteboard for discussion and User 2 saw User 1's writing. In Fig. 7 (c), all the users faced the right edge of the whiteboard and Users 1 and 2 faced each other. The result said that User 1 used the whiteboard to conclude the activities and Users 2 and 3 saw User 1's writing.

8.2 Results on Social Graph Extraction

Figure 8 shows the automatic extraction results of the learning phase using AutoPlait. The three graphs on the top of Fig. 8 show the results of AutoPlait's learning phase extraction. Here, the horizontal axis represents the elapsed time (seconds) and the three graphs show the duration of video viewing, discussion, and conclusion phases, respectively. The bottom graph in Fig. 8 shows the results of the manual extraction of the learning phases by researchers in learning science.

The results of the manual extraction showed that the durations of the video viewing, discussion, and conclusion phases were 110 through 1,173 s, 1,213 through 3,335 s, and 3,360 through 3,844 s, respectively. Although there are some deviations between the automatic and manual extraction results, we can see that the automatic extraction of the approximate learning phase durations from the entire activity of collaborative learning is successful. The factors of the deviations may include the window size of 60 s and deviation due to phenomena that are not observed by humans and sensors.

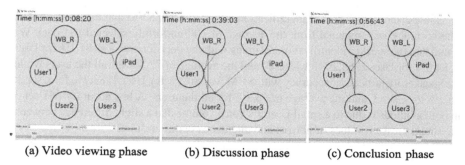

(a) Video viewing phase   (b) Discussion phase   (c) Conclusion phase

Fig. 7. Social graph in each learning phase.

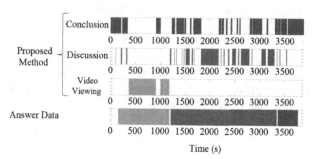

Fig. 8. Automatic extraction result of learning phase.

8.3 Accuracy on Speaker Identification

We finally evaluate the speaker identification accuracy in the proposed method by using the sound pressure data and the acceleration data of each learner in the conclusion phase. There are two reference schemes for comparison: Support Vector Machine (SVM) and decision tree (Our method). In this evaluation, we used 410 s of sensor data, which corresponds to the conclusion phase, as the dataset. The window size was 5 s and the window was moved in 2.5-s increments. Within each window, we labeled whether the learners were speaking. Since 163 samples can be obtained for each learner with Sensor-based Regulation Profiler Badge, we divided the 163 samples into training and test data with a uniform 7:3 ratio and evaluated the accuracy of the speaker identification using the test data.

Table 2. Speaker identification accuracy using SVM and our method

	User 1	User 2	User 3	Average
SVM	80.4%	83.7%	66.2%	76.8%
Our method	81.1%	84.0%	68.2%	77.8%

Table 2 shows the speaker identification accuracy using SVM and the decision tree. The accuracy was obtained from the average of 100 uniformly selected test data. We found that the speaker identification accuracy with the decision tree was 81.1% for User 1, 84.0% for User 2, 68.2% for User 3, and the average of 77.8% for all the users while the speaker identification accuracy with SVM was 80.4% for User 1, 83.7% for User 2, 66.2% for User 3, and the average of 76.8% for all the users. A low accuracy of User 3 in both methods is due to a small User 3's voice volume and a slight difference between the sound pressure values of normal and utterance conditions.

9 Conclusion

In this study, we proposed a Sensor-based Regulation Profiler that quantitatively analyzed learners' activities and automatically extracted and visualized the points that researchers in learning science should pay attention to. It was found that the Sensor-based Regulation Profiler achieves a time synchronization accuracy of approximately 30 μs between business card-type sensors, extracts social graphs showing students meeting during collaborative learning, automatically classifies learning phases during collaborative learning, and identifies speakers out of three learners with an average accuracy of about 77.8% .

Acknowledgements. This work was supported by JSPS KAKENHI (JP16H01718, 18H03231, 19H01101).

References

1. Oshima, J., Oshima, R., Matsuzawa, Y.: Knowledge building discourse explorer: a social network analysis application for knowledge building discourse. Education Tech. Research Dev. **60**(5), 903–921 (2012)
2. Shaffer, D.W.: Quantitative Ethnography. Cathcart Press, Madison (2017)
3. Oshima, J., Oshima, R., Fujita, W.: A mixed-methods approach to analyze shared epistemic agency in jigsaw instruction at multiple scales of temporality. J. Learn. Analyt. **5**(1), 10–24 (2018)
4. Ochoa, X.: Multimodal learning analytics. In: Lang, C., Siemens, G., Wise, A.F., Gaševic, D. (eds.) The Handbook of Learning Analytics, pp. 129–141. Society for Learning Analytics Research (2017)
5. Wakisaka, Y., et al.: Beam-scan sensor node: reliable sensing of human interactions in organization. In: 2009 Sixth International Conference on Networked Sensing Systems (INSS), Pittsburgh, PA, pp. 1–4, June 2009
6. Wu, L., Waber, B., Aral, S., Brynjolfsson, E., Pentland, A.: Mining face-to face interaction networks using sociometric badges: predicting productivity in an IT configuration task. In: Proceedings of International Conference on Information Systems, Paris, France, pp. 1–19, December 2008
7. Lederman, O., Calacci, D., MacMullen, A., Fehder, D., Murray, F., Pentland, A.: Open badges: a low-cost toolkit for measuring team communication and dynamics. In: 2016 International Conference on Social Computing, Behavioral-Cultural Modeling & Prediction and Behavior Representation in Modeling and Simulation, Washington DC, pp. 1–7 (2016)

8. Ermes, M., Pärkka, J., Cluitmans, L.: Advancing from offline to online activity recognition with wearable sensors. In: 2008 30th Annual International Conference of the IEEE Engineering in Medicine and Biology Society, Vancouver, Canada, pp. 4451–4454, August 2008

9. Maurer, U., Smailagic, A., Siewiorek, D.P., Deisher, M.: Activity recognition and monitoring using multiple sensors on different body positions. In: International Workshop on Wearable and Implantable Body Sensor Networks (BSN 2006), Cambridge, MA, pp. 113–116, April 2006

10. Lara, Ó.D., Labrador, M.A.: A mobile platform for real-time human activity recognition. In: 2012 IEEE Consumer Communications and Networking Conference (CCNC), Las Vegas, NV, pp. 667–671, January 2012

11. Kao, T.P., Lin, C.W., Wang, J.S.: Development of a portable activity detector for daily activity recognition. In: 2009 IEEE International Symposium on Industrial Electronics, Seoul, South Korea, pp. 115–120, July 2009

12. Suzuki, M., Liao, C.H., Ohara, S., Jinno, K., Morikawa, H.: Wireless-transparent sensing. In: Proceedings of the 2017 International Conference on Embedded Wireless Systems and Networks, Uppsala, Sweden, pp. 66–77, February 2017

13. Ferrari, F., Zimmerling, M., Thiele, L., Saukh, O.: Efficient network flooding and time synchronization with glossy. In: Proceedings of the 10th ACM/IEEE International Conference on Information Processing in Sensor Networks, Chicago, IL, pp. 73–84, April 2011

14. Matsubara, Y., Sakurai, Y., Faloutsos, C.: AutoPlait: automatic mining of co-evolving time sequences. In: Proceedings of the ACM SIGMOD International Conference on Management of Data, Snowbird, UT, pp. 193–204, June 2014

15. Quinlan, J.R.: Induction of decision trees. Mach. Learn. 1(1), 81–106 (1986)

Student Emotions in the Shift to Online Learning During the COVID-19 Pandemic

Danielle P. Espino[1]($\boxtimes$), Tiffany Wright[1], Victoria M. Brown[1], Zachariah Mbasu[2], Matthew Sweeney[1], and Seung B. Lee[1]

[1] Pepperdine University, Malibu, CA 90263, USA
danielle.espino@pepperdine.edu
[2] Africa Maths Initiative, Kisumu 40100, Kenya

Abstract. The COVID-19 pandemic saw sudden measures to stop the spread of the virus, closing schools and forcing a shift to remote learning. This study examines the emotions exhibited by students around factors of online learning as they transitioned abruptly from in-person instruction. Student responses to a New York Times writing prompt in March 2020 were analyzed using frequencies and epistemic network analysis (ENA) models. About half of the responses contained positive emotional valence, but more than three quarters had negative emotional valence. The strongest connection was observed between negative emotional valence for instructional format and focus. More specifically, anxiety between the format, focus, and workload were strongly connected, indicative of the difficulties faced by students to maintain focus and balance assignments on learning activities while being at home. At the same time, there was a significant connection between positive and negative emotional valence regarding the instructional format, attributed to mixed and changing emotions with adjusting to online learning. When students did exhibit positive emotions, it was interest in the instructional format linked with interest in schedule, indicating that the scheduling flexibility of the online format was the factor students liked most.

Keywords: COVID-19 · Online learning · Emotions

1 Introduction

Learning in online environments had early beginnings in the 1980s, drawing more attention in the decades to follow [6]. While higher education continues to incorporate more online learning programs, this medium is not widely implemented in K12 settings in the United States. However, in early 2020, the world was unexpectedly hit with the COVID-19 pandemic, which abruptly stopped in-person instruction to prevent the spread of the virus. This forced schools to rapidly adopt ways of learning remotely, a format educators were not ready for, particularly in K12 education. Finding ways to manage online learning was a challenge for school districts, teachers implementing curriculum, and more importantly, the students. Students suddenly found themselves switching from school routines and the physical learning environment to education based at home with online

A. R. Ruis and S. B. Lee (Eds.): ICQE 2021, CCIS 1312, pp. 334–347, 2021.
https://doi.org/10.1007/978-3-030-67788-6_23

delivery. This adjustment was an unprecedented experience, with mixed emotions from the students on how the shift was impacting them. This study examines the emotional response of students as they adjusted to online learning during the COVID-19 pandemic.

1.1 Examining the Online Learning Environment

As schools closed for safety, students abruptly shifted from in-person instruction to online learning environments. In considering this adjustment, the Community of Inquiry (CoI) provides a framework for examining learning in the online environment [4]. CoI consists of three factors: teaching presence, social presence, and cognitive presence. Teaching presence refers to how course design and facilitation influences learner's cognitive and social processes under the direction of online learning [2, 4]. Social presence examines the emotional and social connection to others in the online learning environment [2, 4]. Lastly, cognitive presence provides that learners can make meaning of the material and translate such through thoughtful reflection and discussion [2, 4].

Teacher Presence. Garrison et al. describe teaching presence as "[t]he binding element in creating a community of inquiry for educational purposes" [4, p. 96]. CoI acknowledges that teachers play a key role in fostering the social and cognitive presence through instructional design and facilitation in the online environment. In an online learning setting, communication and establishing immediacy can be challenging. Video conferencing can be used for synchronous communication, though it was designed for business communication and not educational instruction and does not completely replicate a physical classroom [13]. Immediacy, or the perception of physical and psychological proximity between people, can also lack in an online environment. Actions to consider in establishing immediacy include addressing students by name or making gestures to encourage engagement [13]. Engaging with peers can cause challenges when video conferencing due to the significant level of exposure in an online setting, which presents intimidation [13].

Social Presence and Peer Interaction. Social presence refers to the ability for participants to establish themselves as "real people" in the online learning environment [4]. Such peer interaction is said to enhance student's motivation, particularly when coping with challenges [10]. Interaction in an online course is explicitly vital in shaping the emotional experience of students [10]. Deficits in student's interpersonal exchanges could result in negative emotions such as anger preventing productive activities like studying, which typically provides peer social support [10].

Cognitive Presence and Emotional Presence. Cognitive presence speaks to the extent that participants are able to make meaning through the communication in the learning environment [4]. This aspect alone cannot sustain learning in the online setting, and best works in conjunction with social and teacher presence.

The learning environment can also influence emotions that connect to motivation [15]. Negative emotions, such as sadness, anxiety, or anger, are known to decrease intrinsic motivation, which in turn impacts performance [12]. Similarly, positive emotions have a significant impact on the development of sustained intrinsic motivation [12].

While emotional responses might factor in with social presence, Cleveland-Innes and Campbell pose that emotional presence be another addition to the original CoI framework. They describe emotional presence as the "outward expression of emotion, affect, and feeling by individuals… as they relate to and interact with the learning technology, course content, students, and the instructor" [2, p. 283].

1.2 Emotions in Learning Environments

Emotions play a vital role in the direction of a student's learning [1, 2, 11, 14]. Learning memories are associated with the emotions experienced during knowledge acquisition [12]. Facets of the learning environment may impact student's emotions, influencing their achievement [8]. Negative emotions may distract from learning, however careful attention to facilitation strategies can help enable emotions that support "thinking, decision making, stimulation, and directing" [2, p. 285].

Students may experience the emotion of anger for various reasons in the online learning context. Aspects such as "the user-friendliness of the online course (technology-related control), the lack of personal contact with the lecturer, or the high demand for self-regulated learning, or trouble with interacting with other students could evoke anger" [15, p. 9]. Additionally, anger can cause withdrawal, which also prevents students from remaining focused [10]. Alternatively, positive emotions that elicit enjoyment and reduce anxiety can support motivation and cognitive processing [10].

In the shift to an online learning environment, the emotional factors of students should especially be considered [1, 2]. Specific to circumstances of crisis, multiple emotions may present themselves simultaneously in response [9]. The current study focuses on examining such expressed student emotions related to aspects of CoI.

2 Methods

The data analyzed in this study consist of student responses to a prompt in the *New York Times* (*NY Times*) on March 30, 2020 about their experiences and perspectives on the transition to online learning as the result of the COVID-19 outbreak. The Learning Network section of the *NY Times* includes articles that seek student opinions on various topics, many of which are related to current events and issues (www.nytimes.com/col umn/learning-student-opinion). The intended audience of these articles are middle and high school students aged 13 and older. New prompts are published daily, and student responses are publicly accessible through the comments window of the article's webpage. Similar to other comments on the *NY Times* website, responses to the articles in the Learning Network are moderated by *NY Times* staff, meaning that only approved responses are posted for public viewing.

This paper examines the comments posted to the article entitled "Has your school switched to remote learning? How is it going so far?" [5]. A total of 395 comments available on May 17, 2020 were downloaded for analysis. This included 35 comments that were in direct reply to a previous comment. Such comments were excluded from the corpus as they constituted reactions to specific issues addressed in earlier posts rather than responses to the original prompt. While these comments might provide additional insights on the perspectives of students regarding online learning, they were removed to maintain consistency in the data. Furthermore, 4 duplicate comments were also omitted, resulting in a final corpus of 356 responses.

The comments were coded for the emotions expressed by students in relation to the different aspects of online learning. Through a grounded analysis of the data, the following six factors of online learning were identified: Focus, Instructional Format, Workload, Schedule, Peer Interaction, and Teacher Interaction. These dimensions are in close alignment with the questions that were posed in the prompt/article. In addition, eight emotions associated with responses to crisis situations were adapted from a study by Kim and Niederdeppe [9], which examined the emotions of college students during the H1N1 influenza pandemic in 2009. Four positive emotional constructs (Gratitude, Interest, Hope, and Compassion) and four negative emotional constructs (Anger, Fear, Sadness, and Anxiety) were included in the codebook along with six factors of online learning (see Tables 1 and 2).

Table 1. Codebook of online learning factors used in analysis.

Construct	Definition	Example
Focus	Related to effectiveness with learning, including ability focus, motivation, level of engagement and productivity	*... it's not always easy to stay focused like I would in class because there are many distractions in the house*
Instructional Format	Related to online learning format/instructional design in general, including technology (medium/platforms), technical challenges and comparisons to in-person learning	*... we were using a platform that was having a few technical difficulties. After only a day of struggling with that, we made the transition to Zoom and I can honestly say it has been very easy to use*
Workload	Related to amount of work (i.e. assignments) or assessments (i.e. grades) with learning	*...we are doing more work at home than we would have been doing in school each day*
Schedule	Related to the timing, scheduling, routine or pace of learning	*I now wake up and hour after I would normally be getting to school... I don't have the structure we used to all get*
Peer Interaction	Related to how students interact with each other in the learning environment	*I have a significant lack of motivation and I miss the thought-provoking discussions I used to have with my classmates during physical school*
Teacher Interaction	Related to how teachers and students interact with each other in the learning environment	*Learning at home is very good when the teacher personal responds and tells you about what you need to work on*

Table 2. Codebook of emotion constructs used in analysis.

Construct	Definition	Example
Anger	Conveying (negative) emotion related to anger, such as irritation and annoyance or even boredom	*It is too much! To elaborate, my teachers are trying to be thoughtful, but there are other teachers that don't grasp exactly how much homework I have. They don't care either*
Fear	Conveying (negative) emotion related to fear (i.e. afraid, scared)	*My biggest fear now is that it is unknown how the new shortened tests will be graded...*
Sadness	Conveying (negative) emotion related to sadness, such as downhearted, or missing something	*I am missing the social aspect of interacting with my friends and peers who make me a more competitive student*
Anxiety	Conveying (negative) emotion related to anxiety, such as concern, worry, stress, confusion, distraction, or struggling with something	*...online schooling has proven to be quite the strenuous task in actuality...*
Gratitude	Conveying (positive) emotion related to gratitude, such as appreciation and thankfulness, or that something is not that bad. Also emotion related to joy, happiness, fun and enjoyment	*I am very grateful for technology allowing me to talk to my friends daily and for allowing my education to continue through this crisis*
Interest	Conveying (positive) emotion related to interest, including "liking" something, alert or curiosity	*In the first days of remote learning have been very independent and I like being able to be on my own routine*
Hope	Conveying (positive) emotion related to hope, including optimism, encouragement, or reassurance	*I feel as if I am still able to communicate with my teachers, ask questions, interact with my classmates and perform other classroom functions*
Compassion	Conveying (positive) emotion related to compassion or sympathy; including acknowledgement or relating to other circumstances	*I feel for my teachers*

The coding process involved annotating each instance when an emotional construct was displayed in connection to a factor of learning. As such, occurrences of different emotions related to the same learning dimension were annotated with multiple codes. Each comment was coded independently by two of the authors, followed by a process of social moderation to reach agreement on its final coding [3, 7].

Analysis of the data was carried out in two stages. The first stage examined the expressions of positive and negative emotional valence in association with the different factor of online learning. For this analysis, responses coded for at least one positive or negative emotional construct were attributed with the corresponding emotional valence.

Comments exhibiting both positive and negative emotional constructs were annotated with both emotional valences. Epistemic network analysis (ENA), a tool in quantitative ethnography for modeling the connections between constructs in data, was used to explore the connections among the pairs of emotional valence and dimension of learning. A single comment was defined as both the unit of analysis and the conversational unit, within which all connections were contained. A minimum edge weight of 0.2 was applied and nodes without connections were removed in the generation of the network model to enhance the visibility of the most salient connections.

The second stage of analysis focused on the expression of individual emotional constructs for the various aspects of online learning. The occurrences of emotional construct for each facet of online learning were tabulated, clustered by positive or negative emotional valence. ENA was then used to examine the co-occurrences among each group of positive and negative emotional constructs. Network models were generated using a minimum edge weight of 0.1, with only the connected nodes included in the display.

3 Results

3.1 Positive and Negative Emotional Valence

Table 3 presents a summary of the number of positive and negative emotional valence expressed in student responses about their transition to online learning in the context of the COVID-19 pandemic. Overall, about half of the 356 students displayed a positive emotional valence in their responses, while a negative emotional valence was contained in more than three quarters of the responses.

Table 3. Number of student responses exhibiting emotional valence.

Constructs	Number of positive responses	Percentage of positive responses	Number of negative responses	Percentage of negative responses
Overall	185	51.97%	268	75.28%
Focus	46	12.92%	141	39.61%
Format	104	29.21%	184	51.69%
Workload	29	8.15%	97	27.25%
Schedule	64	17.98%	64	17.98%
Peer Interaction	15	4.21%	48	13.48%
Teacher Interaction	44	12.36%	73	20.51%

* N = 356 (Total number of student responses)

Examining the emotional valence along the six factors of online learning, positive emotional valence was conveyed most frequently for Instructional Format, which was present in about 30% of all responses. This was followed by Schedule and Focus and

Teacher Interaction, with a positive affect being associated with each in about 18%, 13% and 12% of responses, respectively. Positive valence was displayed least frequently for Peer Interaction (about 4%) and Workload (about 8%).

For negative emotional valence, Instructional Format was also the most prevalent, having been expressed in over half of all responses. Approximately 40% of students exhibited negative feelings about the Focus while for Workload, it was conveyed in around 27% of the responses. Teacher Interaction, Schedule and Peer Interaction was indicated in about 21%, 18%, and 13%, respectively.

Next, ENA was utilized to model how the positive and negative emotional valence for the different factors of online learning are related to one another. Figure 1 displays the mean network model of the student responses, where the nodes represent the positive or negative valence associated with the six elements of online learning and the edges indicate the relative frequency of co-occurrences of the connected nodes within each student response.

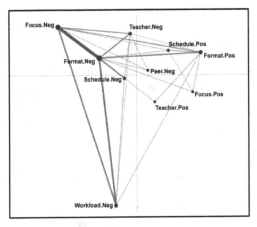

Fig. 1. ENA model of emotional valence and related online learning dimensions.

Overall, thicker edges are present on the left side of the network where the negative emotions are located. Positive emotions, clustered on the right side of the network, show relatively lighter linkages. The strongest connection can be observed between negative emotional valence for Instructional Format and Focus, which is indicative of the difficulties faced by students to maintain focus on learning activities while being at home. These two nodes are also prominently linked to the other negative emotions related to Workload, Teacher Interaction and, to a lesser degree, Schedule. At the same time, there is a significant connection between the positive and negative feelings regarding Instructional Format. This association is reflective of student responses that exhibit mixed feelings about how learning content is organized and delivered via online channels. Positive emotional valence related to Instructional Format is also moderately connected to negative feelings for Focus.

3.2 Emotional Constructs Clustered by Valence

The second stage of the analysis examined how specific emotional constructs clustered by valence were associated with the various factors of online learning in the student responses. Tables 4 and 5 summarize the frequency of occurrence for each of the four constructs clustered along positive and negative valence, respectively. Overall, the expression of negative emotional constructs—with a total of 647 occurrences—was more than twice those related to the positive emotional constructs, which had 314 occurrences in all.

Table 4. Frequency of occurrences for the positive emotional constructs.

Constructs	Gratitude	Interest	Hope	Compassion	Total
Total occurrences	104 (32.70%)	123 (38.68%)	58 (18.24%)	33 (10.38%)	318 (100%)
Focus	8 (2.52%)	2 (0.63%)	8 (2.52%)	131 (41.19%)	145 (22.41%)
Format	21 (6.60%)	22 (6.92%)	16 (5.03%)	1 (0.31%)	47 (14.78%)
Workload	15 (4.72%)	11 (3.46%)	3 (0.94%)	0 (0%)	29 (9.12%)
Schedule	20 (6.29%)	38 (11.95%)	4 (1.26%)	2 (0.63%)	64 (20.13%)
Peer interaction	7 (2.20%)	2 (0.63%)	3 (0.94%)	3 (0.94%)	15 (4.72%)
Teacher interaction	18 (5.66%)	8 (2.52%)	8 (2.52%)	14 (4.40%)	48 (15.09%)

* N = 318 (Total number of occurrences of positive emotions)

Among the positive emotional constructs, Interest was expressed most frequently in the responses, accounting for nearly 39% of the 318 occurrences. This was followed by Gratitude (32.70%), Hope (18.24%) and Compassion (10.38%). Disaggregating the data along the six dimensions of online learning, the positive emotional constructs most often exhibited were Interest in the Instructional Format (6.92%) and Schedule (11.95%) as well as Gratitude toward the Instructional Format (6.60%).

The negative emotions were dominated by Anxiety, comprising approximately 70% of the 647 occurrences. In particular, an overwhelming amount of Anxiety was expressed about Focus (20.25%), Instructional Format (19.94%) and Workload (13.14%). Sadness accounted for about 23% of the occurrences of negative emotions in the student responses, especially toward Instructional Format (8.35%), Teacher Interaction (5.72%) and Peer Interaction (4.79%). Emotions of Anger and Fear were infrequently exhibited, although Anger about the Instructional Format accounted for about 3% of the occurrences, many of which were related to annoyance and frustration stemming from technical difficulties.

Table 5. Frequency of occurrences for the negative emotional constructs.

Constructs	Anger	Fear	Sadness	Anxiety	Total
Total occurrences	43 (6.65%)	7 (1.08%)	146 (22.57%)	451 (69.70%)	647 (100%)
Focus	4 (0.62%)	2 (0.31%)	8 (1.24%)	131 (20.25%)	145 (22.41%)
Format	21 (3.25%)	2 (0.31%)	54 (8.35%)	129 (19.94%)	206 (31.84%)
Workload	14 (2.16%)	2 (0.31%)	2 (0.31%)	85 (13.14%)	103 (15.92%)
Schedule	3 (0.46%)	0 (0%)	14 (2.16%)	50 (7.73%)	67 (10.36%)
Peer Interaction	0 (0%)	1 (0.15%)	31 (4.79%)	16 (2.47%)	48 (7.42%)
Teacher interaction	1 (0.15%)	0 (0%)	37 (5.72%)	40 (6.18%)	78 (12.06%)

* N = 647 (Total number of occurrences of negative emotions)

ENA models were developed to visualize the networks of co-occurrences among the pairings of individual emotional constructs with different aspects of online learning. Figure 2 presents the network model for the positive emotional constructs. The strongest connection can be observed between Interest for Instructional Format and Schedule, indicating that these two constructs were often expressed together in student responses. Similarly, the network also depicts prominent linkages between Gratitude toward the Instructional Format and Schedule and Interest in Focus.

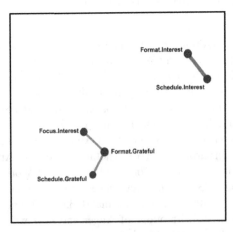

Fig. 2. ENA model of positive emotional constructs and related online learning dimensions.

In the network model for the negative emotional constructs (Fig. 3), the thickest edges can be seen between Anxiety related to Instructional Format, Focus, and Workload. This is reflective of responses that focus on multiple struggles that students have encountered, including the increased amount of assignments, distractions faced at home, and difficulties faced in accessing and interacting with online resources. There are also significant connections between the three aforementioned constructs and Anxiety about Schedule and Teacher Interaction as well as Sadness toward Teacher Interaction, Instructional Format and Peer Interaction. The latter is representative of the longing expressed by many students to return to school-based instruction, including personal contact with teachers and peers in the learning process.

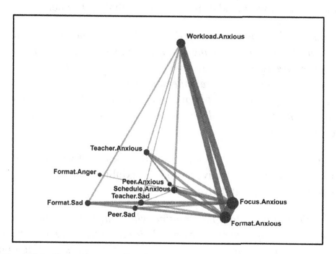

Fig. 3. ENA model of negative emotional constructs and related online learning dimensions,

4   Discussion

This study examined the emotions exhibited around factors of the CoI framework as students transitioned to online learning. In evaluating the frequencies of occurrences, students exhibited more negative than positive emotions with the switch to online learning. More emotions were exhibited around the instructional format, focus, and workload aspects, and less about the schedule and teacher and peer interactions in the learning environment. Strongest connections in the ENA model in Fig. 1 were most notably negative emotions between the instructional format and ability to focus, exhibiting challenges in being able to focus while in the online format:

Having school online has sure been a hassle for me and I have yet to adjust to this new way of "learning." Although it may seem fairly simple as in just checking for assignments and completing the given work, it is quite difficult for many of us... Focusing is also much more difficult because there are so many more distractions, and there's no teacher at your house who will scold you for being off task. Although I do get less work than before, it is more of a hassle to understand and to try and grasp all the information that is given.

The classroom environment is somewhere where I normally thrive, and staying in my room can have some distractions.

The glitches and internet issues really take away from the learning experience and make it really really hard to focus.

Along with instructional format and focus in Fig. 1, students also tended to express negative emotions about workload or interactions with their teacher:

Although online schooling has required a lot of screen time, is a pain to use, and makes focusing hard, I enjoy having my afternoons off. However, I have noticed that my teachers are assigning more homework because of the reduced class time, but it has gotten to the point where I spend all afternoon on my computer. I don't think my teachers understand that I have seven classes to do work for, and I simply do not have the time to spend triple the amount of hours on homework just because we moved to remote learning.

Interestingly, there was a notable connection between positive and negative emotions with the instructional format, indicative of students exhibiting mixed or changing feelings with the new format for content delivery:

It took some time to get into a new routine where all of my subjects are sort of smashed together and spread out into one whole day of learning and review rather than split up into forty minute periods, but by now I think it's starting to work.

While there have inevitably been some downsides to getting accustomed to this unfamiliar way of learning, I have been pleasantly surprised by the various perks...While the internet isn't always the most reliable, I am still able to find alternate ways to learn the material, so we don't fall behind. There is always a bright side.

In examining the individual positive emotions, interest in the format and schedule were closely linked, indicating students liked the online learning format mostly due to the flexibility in schedule:

My first weeks of distance learning have been easier then I thought. I like how I can make a schedule for myself and still have structure to my day. I also can get done my school early in the day and still have a lot of time to relax and do other things.

With individual negative emotions, the strongest connections were seen with anxiety related to the instructional format, focus, and workload. Students expressed struggle with being able to focus and balance assignments in the online learning format.

We're obviously not at school working with our classmates and teachers, so it is hard for me to focus. A problem I have faced with online school is that it is hard to do assignments sometimes...[for] Some teachers it takes me five minutes to complete their assignment but others, it takes me two hours...Overall, online school makes time management extremely difficult and I feel like I'm not even learning in some of my classes.

I live in an area where internet access and WiFi are hard to get and, as a result, I'm not only stressed about school but I'm often anxious that I will not be able to join and maintain access to online classes and assignments. Working at home is hard for me as well since there is no distinct separation of school v.s home. Normally at school, I am able to focus as it is a work environment and I am constantly communicating face-to-face with those around me. At home, I want to get up and go outside and stop staring at my iPad, it gives me headaches and I am tired of looking at it after 4–5 h a day. Many of my teachers have been seemingly understanding of the issues caused by online school, but at the same time, they are continuing to give the normal work-load.

In addition to the emotions regarding the factor constructs examined in the study, students described teachers attempting to conduct direct substitution of in-person class activities within the online learning environment, instead of introducing new forms for creatively completing assignments. This sentiment conveys that there was not much consideration by the teachers to establish different ways for doing assignments that could help sustain the normalcy of students working together in an online learning environment. Efficacy can potentially be improved by teachers rethinking assignment strategies to incorporate feedback and ideas from students on how to be more effective within the online setting.

The negative emotional valence exemplified within the connection between focus and the instructional format environment highlights individual differences amongst students. These differences can be perceived through one's feeling of self-efficacy when adjusting to a new learning setting. When the students' perception of self-efficacy in the online environment is low, stress is heightened and it increases their cognitive load in addition to the task of keeping up with workloads assigned by teachers. The dichotomy between the negative and positive emotions towards the online instructional format address the importance of social interactions within any learning environment [10]. The study focused coding on peer interactions based in the learning environment. While many student emotions related to peers referred to social activities, mention of peer connection was typically stated alongside discussion of the learning environment. The overlap in peer social connection may be indicative of the influence that social relationships have upon psychological development and the ability to navigate challenges in school environments [8]

4.1 Future Study

This study captures the emotions expressed by students related to factors of CoI and the transition to online learning in March 2020, shortly after schools in the United States were closed to in-person instruction. The large frequency of negative emotional valence validates an anticipated response to the abrupt transition, which can be attributed with any sudden change in routine or process. A follow-up study after a sustained period of online learning would provide comparative insights on whether emotions around the online learning environment could change with time, as both students and teachers better adjust to the shift. Further examination into what strategies or factors contribute to any emotional shifts would provide teachers, school administrators, and education researchers with detailed insights on how to better approach online learning.

Additional studies can juxtapose the differences between school districts with more access to resources and technological tools prior to COVID-19 with historically disadvantaged districts to see what type of interventions are needed to ensure all students can continue to thrive. Another direction can examine the nuances of ableism in the online learning environment. Students who may have learning or physical disabilities engage in acquiring knowledge in unique ways and have a host of their own emotions towards learning. Focusing on ableism can expand the conversation from societal views of traditional students to other populations often are overlooked during times of crisis.

References

1. Brookfield, S.D.: The Skillful Teacher: On Technique, Trust and Responsiveness in the Classroom. Jossey-Bass, San Francisco (2006)
2. Cleveland-Innes, M., Campbell, P.: Emotional presence, learning, and the online learning environment. Int. Rev. Res. Open Distrib. Learn. **13**(4), 269–292 (2012). https://doi.org/10.19173/irrodl.v13i4.1234
3. Frederiksen, J.R., Sipusic, M., Sherin, M., Wolfe, E.W.: Video portfolio assessment: creating a framework for viewing the functions of teaching. Educ. Assess. **5**(4), 225–97 (1998)
4. Garrison, D.R., Anderson, T., Archer, W.: Critical inquiry in a text-based environment: computer conferencing in higher education. Internet High. Educ. **2**(2), 87–105 (1999). https://doi.org/10.1016/S1096-7516(00)00016-6
5. Gonchar, M., Doyne, S.: Has your school switched to remote learning? How is it going so far?. *The New York Times* (30 March 2020). https://www.nytimes.com/2020/03/30/learning/has-your-school-switched-to-remote-learning-how-is-it-going-so-far.html
6. Harasim, L.: Shift happens: online education as a new paradigm in learning. Internet High. Educ. **3**(1), 41–61 (2000). https://doi.org/10.1016/S1096-7516(00)00032-4
7. Herrenkohl, L.R., Cornelius, L.: Investigating elementary students' scientific and historical argumentation. J. Learn. Sci. **22**(3), 413–461 (2013). https://doi.org/10.1080/10508406.2013.799475
8. Idsoe, E.M.C.: The importance of social learning environment factors for affective well-being among students. Emotional Behav. Difficulties **21**(2), 155–166 (2016). https://doi.org/10.1080/13632752.2015.1053695
9. Kim, H.K., Niederdeppe, J.: The role of emotional response during an H1N1 influenza pandemic on a college campus. J. Public Relat. Res. **25**(1), 30–50 (2013). https://doi.org/10.1080/1062726X.2013.739100
10. Kim, C.M., Park, S.W., Cozart, J.: Affective and motivational factors of learning in online mathematics courses: factors related to online mathematics learning. Brit. J. Educ. Technol. **45**(1), 171–185 (2014). https://doi.org/10.1111/j.1467-8535.2012.01382.x
11. Linnenbrink-Garcia, L., Pekrun, R.: Students' emotions and academic engagement: introduction to the special issue. Contemp. Educ. Psychol. **36**(1), 1–3 (2011). https://doi.org/10.1016/j.cedpsych.2010.11.004

12. Pekrun, R.: The impact of emotions on learning and achievement: towards a theory of cognitive/motivational mediators. Appl. Psychol. **41**(4), 359–376 (1992). https://doi.org/10.1111/j.1464-0597.1992.tb00712.x

13. Rehn, N., Maor, D., McConney, A.: Investigating teacher presence in courses using synchronous videoconferencing. Distance Educ. **37**(3), 302–316 (2016). https://doi.org/10.1080/01587919.2016.1232157

14. Rientes, B., Rivers, B.A.: Measuring and understanding learner emotions: Evidence and prospects. Learning Analytics Community Exchange. Accessed 28, June, 2020 (2014). http://www.laceproject.eu/publications/learning-analytics-and-emotions.pdf

15. Stephan, M., Markus, S., Gläser-Zikuda, M.: Students' achievement emotions and online learning in teacher education. Front. Educ. **4**(109), 1–12 (2019). https://doi.org/10.3389/feduc.2019.00109

What Do Honor and Face Norms Have to Do with Peer Relations? Adolescents Make Sense of Revenge

Karin S. Frey[✉], Hannah A. Nguyen, Saejin Kwak-Tanguay, and Kaleb Germinaro

University of Washington, Seattle, WA, USA
karinf@uw.edu

Abstract. Historical and experimental research have identified three normative systems that characterize cultures within and between nations—honor, face and dignity. Theory that views culture as situated cognition posits that regionally dominant systems provide environmental cues that preferentially elicit corresponding behaviors and expectations. These shared norms help people coordinate actions and manage conflicts. In the US, waves of colonizers established different regional systems, honor in southern states, dignity in northern states, and face systems in smaller enclaves. The current study used a measure of adolescent norm endorsement to examine the meaning of revenge—a key element of honor culture. Ethnically diverse adolescents described past instances of personal and third-party revenge. Anger over events was closely linked to pride by youth endorsing honor. They cited concerns of security, power and self-direction when explaining their evaluation of personal revenge, and added concerns about benevolence when explaining third-party revenge. Youth endorsing face norms connected anger with feelings of shame when describing personal and third-party revenge. They cited concerns about threats to benevolence, security, and self-direction after personal revenge. The same goals were poised between perceived threat and promotion after third-party revenge, as were concerns about competence. Third-party revenge elicited morally nuanced appraisals. Institutional failure to protect and provide justice to all groups may promote development of honor norms in individuals and groups.

Keywords: Revenge · Norms · Goals · Adolescents · Honor · Face · African American · European American · Mexican American · Native American

1 Introduction

1.1 Cultural Systems Promote Honor, Face or Dignity Norms

Considerable research has characterized the US and Europe as independent (Markus and Kitayama 2010) or individualist cultures (Brewer and Chen 2007) and Japan, China and Korea as interdependent or collectivist cultures. Such broad classifications of cultures have been criticized for failing to recognize that all regions and groups support both

© Springer Nature Switzerland AG 2021
A. R. Ruis and S. B. Lee (Eds.): ICQE 2021, CCIS 1312, pp. 348–361, 2021.
https://doi.org/10.1007/978-3-030-67788-6_24

individualist and collectivist orientations among their citizens (Oyserman 2017). Further, research that has stretched beyond the US and east Asia to include regions like the Middle East and South America has revealed a different type of collectivism, an *honor-based* system that shares some elements with what are sometimes called *face or humility* systems and some elements with *dignity* systems (Leung and Cohen, 2011). Research has also identified regional differences in the United States, divided between the southern and central mountain states (primarily an honor-based system) and the New England, northern Midwest, and Pacific NW (primarily a dignity-based system).

Cultural systems, aka, *normative* systems, provide guidelines for social living. Each one designates behaviors and expectations that (1) enable people to coordinate their actions, (2) promote security and conflict resolution, and (3) impart a sense of self-worth. Each system is thought to have evolved as a logical adaptation to a specific set of social and ecological demands. Variations in conditions are thought to stimulate the development of different social solutions, each one enabling group survival. Even when ecological demands change, and survival no longer requires the traditional adaptations, social norms and power structures support cultural legacies in modern societies (Vandello et al. 2008).

Work that examines the relationship of honor, face, and dignity norms to the behavior and self-evaluation of adolescents is almost non-existent, despite the importance of the work for understanding (1) how youth negotiate conflicts in a multicultural society, and (2) the impact of state-sponsored violence on youth. We first describe theory and research that identifies locations and conditions associated with each of the three types of cultural systems. We then describe our current work examining the meanings associated with adolescent vengeful behavior.

Honor Systems. Honor systems are thought to evolve when rule of law is weak, making it incumbent on citizens to provide security for themselves and their families. They do so by reliably using anger and violence to demonstrate that they cannot be taken advantage of (Aslani et al. 2013). Even minor insults may be a test of resolve and strength. Therefore, it is essential that one be vigilant for threat. Retaliation, even for minor threats, is required to discourage more significant ones. Security is enhanced by mutual defense among family units, clans, and tribes. Honor is needed to secure support, and families must constantly display their trustworthiness. This requires avenging the victimization of any ally (third-party revenge, TPR), even if the risks are greater than benefits (Leung and Cohen 2011). Because effective deterrence depends on the perception that a potential victim will have an "irrationally" vigorous response (Nowak et al. 2016), loss of an honorable reputation, means losing all security. Historic analyses suggest that pastoral groups developed honor systems for self-defense (see Aslani et al. 2013). Contemporary conditions that support honor norms include war—when state protection is non-existent—and oppression of marginalized groups by state-sanctioned enforcers. Groups who are given responsibility for protecting others (e.g., warriors, police) also may adopt honor norms, stressing toughness and the masking of fear (Mandel and Litt 2012).

Face Systems. Face systems (aka humility systems) are believed to have evolved in densely populated areas dependent on joint community labor for crop production. The required cooperation demands a system of rules, self-restraint and a dutiful orientation. Social reputation is as important as in honor cultures. Rather than *compete* for a positive image, however, community members are expected to cooperate to maintain social harmony and everyone's favorable image or *face* (Zhang et al. 2015). Strong social hierarchies enforce rules. Those who occupy superior positions have a social contract to provide protection in exchange for others dutifully discharging their responsibilities.

Dignity Systems. Dignity systems developed in areas with a relative abundance of fertile land (Aslani et al. 2013). Owing to large land holdings, people had to travel to trade excess production for items they did not produce themselves (Aslani et al. 2013). To thrive, market economies need consistent and egalitarian norms of responsibilities and rights that are enforced by reliable institutions. These characteristics encourage trust of trading partners whose reputation for honesty may be unknown. Whereas self-worth in honor and face systems is based on social reputation, self-worth in dignity systems is believed to be intrinsic to the individual. Therefore, insults do not pose the same degree of threat as in honor systems; they can be ignored without harm to one's reputation (Leung and Cohen, 2011).

1.2 Culture as Situated Cognition

What do these variations mean for multi-cultural nations like the United States? Normative systems at the group level reproduce and sustain the status quo. At the individual level, normative systems function as dynamic influences that may promote the dominant social norms at one time and resist or side-step them at another (Oyserman 2017; Wainryb and Recchia 2014). Oyserman's (2017) theory of culture as situated cognition gives central importance to environmental cues that elicit corresponding normative behaviors. Some social roles or situations will preferentially stimulate access to one set of norms versus another. Experimental studies show that being primed with words related to honor, for example, temporarily increases endorsement of honor-related violence among European Americans from predominantly dignity-related regions of the US. Thus, familiarity with multiple systems fosters behavioral flexibility, while the dominant system of a particular region provides environment cues that frequently activate thoughts, emotions and behaviors typical of that system. When social norms are insufficient for maintaining the status quo, state institutions that are meant to provide justice and protection may become instruments of oppression

1.3 Dominant Systems in the United States

Given that the normative orientation of formal and informal communication within a region can be thought of as a constant priming influence, we next consider the dominant systems within the US. We know relatively little about the earliest Indigenous inhabitants, other than they formed a wealth of cultures finely adapted to their environment. It is not clear how applicable the tripart system is to these Indigenous cultures, but some North American tribes (e.g., midwestern US) lived in densely populated agrarian economies and erected massive irrigation systems typical of societies with strong social hierarchies and face orientations (Pauketat 1994). Others lived in nomadic bands and celebrated male courage in ways reminiscent of the "irrational" demonstrations of bravery in honor societies. (Plenty-Coups and Linderman 2002).

The European colonizers of the 17th and 18th centuries also lived within diverse cultural systems. Three waves hailed from different honor cultures. One consisted of non-landowning sons of English aristocrats, descendants of the Norman conquerors. Members of aristocracies, as in clan- or caste-based systems, defend group members and the social hierarchy (Woodard 2011). Landowners in the southeastern colonies used violence to control both enslaved Africans and Anglo-Celt *commoners* (Cohen and Nisbett 1994; Fischer 1989). After the Civil war, many southerners migrated to the western and southwestern frontier (Gaskil 1971), regions where earlier Spanish colonizers lived according to the norms of their own honor culture (Woodard, 2011). Another wave brought honor culture to Appalachia and the hill country of the south from the Scottish borderlands and North Ireland. These regions had endured six centuries of warfare and bands of raiders organized around clans. They brought the same system of violent clan competition to North America. This area remained lawless for generations (Grosjean 2014). Revenge and feuds were the primary defenses against assault and exploitation.

The colonizers who arrived on the northern Atlantic coast embraced rule of law to govern their internal affairs. Early ships often brought entire towns, complete with a constabulary and justices of the peace. Within the community, people expected formal institutions to provide protection, regulate trade, and punish wrongdoers (Fischer, 1989). Despite subsequent waves of migrants, dignity norms comprise the dominant systems in the north Atlantic, northern Midwest, and northwest coast of the US (Woodard, 2011).

Migrants from parts of the world with face systems (e.g., Japan) are more dispersed. Generally, each wave of migrants establish ethnic enclaves where the system of the home country dominates. As people disperse, theory predicts that they will respond to the dominant regional system. Thus, crime statistics reveal important regional differences in violent behavior. Murder rates for European Americans in the south are almost 3 times higher than in the north (Grosjean 2014), and the difference appears in murders after insults to honor rather than murders linked to robbery (Cohen and Nisbett 1994). School shootings are also higher in so-called honor states (Brown, 2016), and adolescents who endorse honor norm report more revenge than those who endorse face norms (Frey et al. 2020b). How is it that 300 year-old regional differences appear to be influential today?

1.4 Potential Mechanisms that Support Revenge

Response to Threat. After insult, Southern European American males show increased cortisol and testosterone levels consistent with preparation for violence, whereas northerners did not. Males from honor regions experience more intense and explosive anger compared to males from dignity and face regions (Cohen et al. 1999; Shafa et al. 2015). To maintain social harmony, face systems prioritize emotional restraint and limited reactivity (Frey et al. 2020b).

Interpretation of Hostility. If you believe (even incorrectly) that your neighbors will respond aggressively to small slights, you must be alert to signs of threat. In live enactments of conflict, southern research participants interpreted the neutral behavior of two others watching the same conflict as encouraging of aggression more than did northern research participants (Vandello et al.2008). Perceptions of hostility from others is higher in countries viewed as honor cultures than in face cultures (Dodge et al. 2015), and among Europeans who endorse honor norms (IJzerman et al. (2007). Inferring greater hostility from others may lead individuals to conclude that they have been victimized by others at relatively high rates. Canadian adolescents who endorsed honor norms reported more victimization than those that endorsed face norms even after controlling for the contributions of ethnicity and gender (Frey et al. 2020b). In a diverse US sample, honor endorsement predicted greater perceived victimization only within European American adolescents. This is consistent with research indicating that a subset of European Americans view themselves as frequent victims of racial discrimination (Norton and Sommers 2011).

1.5 The Current Study

Because the purpose of each normative system is to support the welfare of group members, adherence to those norms regarding emotional and behavioral responses to threat is important for self-worth (Leung and Cohen, 2011). This study examined how adolescents construed their actions and outcomes after they avenged threats to themselves and a peer. Mixed methodologies included ratings of emotions and explanations of how youth evaluated their actions. After participants in our study rated their self-evaluative emotions and appraisals, we asked them to explain their self-critical and self-congratulatory judgements. Rationales were coded to indicate the goals that youth indicated for their actions and whether goals were promoted or threatened. Epistemic network analyses were used to compare the emotions and rationales provided by those whose responses to a norms survey indicated strong endorsement of honor norms versus strong endorsement of face norms.

Networks for honor-endorsing youth were expected to have pride as a prominent feature. While anger is a typical response to victimization, its use as a tool to protect security is a feature of honor systems, suggesting a more prominent role in emotion networks. We expected that goal networks for strong honor-endorsers would provide a prominent role for power and security relative to those associated with face norms, and that revenge would be viewed as promoting desired outcomes.

Personal revenge is clearly proscribed by face norms and we therefore expected that shame and guilt would play a prominent role in that network. While revenge of any kind is discouraged within the in-group (e.g., family, allies), defense of a close other might be less stigmatized. We know of no research on revenge within face cultures that would provide guidance on this point. We expected third-party revenge to show a similar pattern as personal revenge, but to be less dissimilar to the network for high honor-endorsers than personal revenge. For both personal and third-party revenge networks, we expected goal threats to play a more prominent role for those strongly endorsing face than honor.

2 Methods

2.1 Participants

Participants were 270 adolescents (53.7% female) ranging from 13 to 18 years of age. They were African Americans (25.9%), European Americans (24.4%), Mexican Americans (24.4%) and Columbian Plateau Native Americans (25.2%) living in urban, suburban and rural areas in Washington State and Idaho. Participants were paid $20 to participate in an hour-long interview and complete surveys. Interviews were completed during the summer with respect to the previous school year.

2.2 Procedures

Participant recruitment and data collection were conducted in tribal and public schools, community centers, and summer programs. In accordance with institutional review board guidelines and, when applicable, tribal authority research approval, researchers conducting the study obtained participant assent and parent or guardian consent.

Trained research assistants of the same race or ethnicity asked interviewees to describe two events, in which the interviewee (1) retaliated after a peer had been victimized, i.e., third-party revenge, and (2) retaliated after being victimized, i.e., personal revenge. Participants rated how they felt after the event and their appraisal of their action. This study examines emotions linked to moral evaluation of self (pride, guilt, shame) and evaluation of others (anger, cold-heartedness). Following each emotion, interviewees explained their ratings. Participants then completed a survey of honor, face, and dignity norms. Audio-recordings were later transcribed and coded by research assistants who were blind to hypotheses.

2.3 Measures

Emotions. Participants used markers to indicate their emotional experience on a scale of 0–100%. The array of ten emotions included three self-evaluative emotions (pride, shame, guilt), anger, and cold-heartedness. These were used for network analyses. Five other emotions were not analyzed for this study. They were relieved, afraid, sad, excited and grateful.

Goal Codes and Outcome Codes. A system based on Schwartz' circumplex model of human values (1994) coded goals as security, benevolence, competence, power, self-direction, seek stimulation, uphold norms and other (See Frey et al. 2020a). Two codes indicated whether actions promoted the goal or threatened it. Augmented base rates were used to assess inter-rater-reliability. Coding began when Cohen's *kappa* reached 0.60 for each goal and outcome. Tests of rater accuracy were subsequently administered at three-week intervals to prevent coder drift. The mean *kappa* obtained for all goals was .71 and ranged from .61 (uphold norms) to .75 (competence and security). *Kappas* for outcomes, goal promotion and threat, were $k = .72$ and $k = .83$, respectively.

Cultural Norm Endorsement. Confirmatory factor analyses of the survey showed strong factor loadings for honor and face items and acceptable *omegas* (.79 & .69, respectively). Dignity items were weak and not considered further (Frey et al., 2020b). The honor scale had six items (e.g., "You lose respect if you back down from a fight." "People will take advantage of you if you don't show how tough you are.") and the face scale had seven (e.g., "I feel proud when I do my duty without calling attention to myself." "Even when they do something wrong, you shouldn't criticize others.").

2.4 Analytic Plan

For the network analyses, responses for each scale were divided at the midpoint into strong and weak endorsement. This yielded 58 participants who strongly endorsed honor norms and 60 participants who strongly endorsed face norms in the personal revenge condition. Two strong face-endorsers who did not have an example of personal revenge were included in the third-party revenge condition, yielding sample sizes of 58 for honor and 62 for face. No participant was a strong endorser of both honor and face scales.

We performed epistemic network analyses (ENA) using the ENA1.5.2. web tool (Marquat et al. 2018), first on the emotion ratings and then on all lines of explanation associated with emotions and appraisals. Analyses were performed separately for the two actions—personal revenge and third-party revenge. The units of analyses were honor or face norm endorsement with subsets by participant. Networks were aggregated across all participants within each action. Aggregations were created from unweighted summations in which the networks reflect the log of the product for each pair of codes. The ENA model normalized the networks for all units of analysis before they were subject to dimensional reductions, which accounts for the fact that different units of analysis may have different rates of goal codes. For the dimensional reduction, we used a singular value decomposition, which produced orthogonal dimensions that maximize the variance explained by each dimension.

In the graphs of the networks, edges connecting each type of emotion or goal reflect the relative frequency of co-occurrence between two codes, represented as plotted points. The position of the graph nodes for each goal are determined by an optimization routine that minimizes the differences between the plotted nodes and their corresponding network centroids. For a more detailed explanation of the quantitative methodology, see Shaffer et al. (2016). The co-registration of network graphs and projected space, the positions of the plotted nodes—and the connections they define between motives—enables interpretation of the dimensions of the projected space.

3 Results

3.1 Networks for Those Strongly Endorsing Honor Versus Face Norms

Networks of Emotions for Personal and Third-Party Revenge. The centroids presented in Fig. 1 summarize the dimensions of each network. Centroids indicated by boxes and confidence intervals (dotted lines) enable comparisons of networks in their entirety. These can be compared statistically as well as visually. On the x-axis for personal revenge (Fig. 1 A), a two sample t-test assuming unequal variance showed that the centroid for those strongly endorsing honor norms ($M = -0.09$, $SD = 0.40$, $n = 58$) was significantly different at the *alpha* = .05 level from the centroid for those strongly endorsing face norms ($M = 0.09$, $SD = 0.40$, $n = 60$), t (115.3) $= -2.26$, $p = .03$, Cohen's $d = 0.45$). The corresponding values for the y-axis (honor, $M = -0.05$, $SD = 0.37$; face, $M = 0.05$, $SD = 0.42$) was not significantly different, t (114.6) $= -1.32$, *ns*, Cohen's $d = 0.24$. Comparing the placement of the nodes suggests that the x-axis represents approach emotions (anger and pride) versus withdrawal emotions of shame and guilt. The y-axis may represent arousal level.

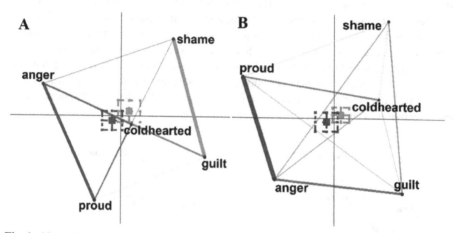

Fig. 1. Networks show differences in patterns of emotion (anger, pride, guilt, shame, coldhearted) experienced by youth endorsing honor norms (red) and youth endorsing face norms (aqua). Networks illustrate personal revenge (A) and third-party revenge (B). Squares show centroids for each group with confidence intervals in dotted lines. (Color figure online)

On the x-axis for third-party revenge (Fig. 1 B), a t-test assuming unequal variance showed that the centroid for those strongly endorsing honor norms ($M = -0.07$, $SD = 0.41$, $n = 58$) was significantly different from the centroid for those strongly endorsing face norms ($M = 0.07$, $SD = 0.32$, $n = 62$), t (107.4) $= -2.07$, $p = .04$, Cohen's $d = 0.22$. The corresponding values for the y-axis (honor, $M = 0.04$, $SD = 0.34$; face, $M = 0.03$, $SD = 0.38$) was not significantly different, t (107.4) $= 1.19$, *ns*, Cohen's $d = 0.22$. Comparing the placement of the nodes suggests that the x-axis again represents approach emotions versus withdrawal emotions, whereas the y-axis is not clearly identified.

Figure 1 provides networks showing differences in emotions for those endorsing honor versus face norms. After personal revenge (Fig. 1A), honor endorsers showed stronger links between anger and pride. Cold-heartedness, a cooler, more strategic emotion, was also connected to pride more strongly among honor endorsers. This suggests that emotions related to both impulsive and strategic retaliation are viewed as consistent with honor norms. These connections were also evident in the network for honor endorsers in the third-party revenge condition (Fig. 1B). In this one, anger was poised between pride and guilt, with pride the stronger link among honor endorsers.

After personal revenge, anger in the network for face-endorsers was more strongly connected to shame and guilt than among honor-endorsers (Fig. 1B). Cold-hearted and shame had stronger connections to guilt than among honor endorsers. Third-party revenge showed similar patterns. Overall, the strongest connections were between guilt and shame, which appeared to play central roles in the emotional experience of face endorsers after they sought personal revenge.

Networks of Goals and Outcomes for Personal Revenge. Networks for youths endorsing honor norms and youth endorsing face norms showed connections between threat and the security motive (see Fig. 2). For those endorsing honor (Fig. 2A), their actions were also perceived to promote security, forming a strong triangle of connections between the three nodes. They also viewed their actions as both promoting and threatening power, competence and uphold norms. Security showed the most connections to other motives: power, self-direction, benevolence, competence and uphold norms. Both networks showed connections between threat and benevolence and self-direction. These were particularly strong for youths endorsing face (see Fig. 2B). As in the honor network, self-direction was strongly connected to security motives.

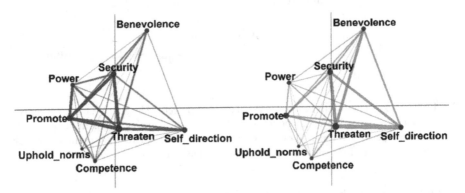

Fig. 2. Networks of goals and outcomes cited by adolescents endorsing honor (red) and face (aqua) norms when explaining their self-evaluation of personal revenge (Color figure online)

Consideration of the placement of the nodes for personal revenge suggests that the x-axis, represents a self-protective focus (power, competence, uphold norms) versus a growth (self-direction) and other-focus (benevolence). Centroids for the two groups showed significant differences on this x-axis (see Fig. 3A). A two sample t-test assuming unequal variance showed that the centroid for honor endorsers ($M = -0.16, SD = 0.44$, $n = 58$) was closer to the self-protective end of the x-axis than the centroid for face endorsers ($M = 0.16, SD = 0.46, n = 60$), $t (116.2) = -3.92, p < .01$, Cohen's $d = 0.72$). Corresponding values for the y-axis (honor, $M = 0.00, SD = 0.41$; face, $M = 0.00, SD = 0.41$) did not differ, $t < 1$, ns.

Networks of Goals and Outcomes for Third-Party Revenge. As shown in Fig. 3B, centroids for honor- ($M = -0.19, SD = 0.58$) and face-endorsers ($M = 0.17, SD = 0.55$)

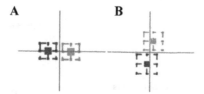

Fig. 3. Centroids for goals cited by youth endorsing honor (red) and face norms (aqua). Figure 3A shows centroids for goals cited after personal revenge; Fig. 3B shows centroids for goals cited after third-party revenge (Color figure online)

differed significantly on the y-axis, $t(116.5) = -3.51, p < .01$, Cohen's $d = 0.64$. The goals at the very top of the y-axis are growth-focused and juxtaposed against protection-focus at he very bottom (See Fig. 4B). The arrangement of other goals between these two nodes do not lend themselves to easy interpretation. Compared to the personal revenge networks, the relationships of goals to each other, and perhaps their meaning has shifted. The x-axis showed no differences for face and honor endorsers, $t < 1$.

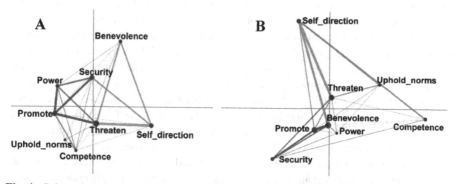

Fig. 4. Subtractive networks illustrating differences in connections between goals and outcomes for youth endorsing honor (red) versus face (aqua) norms. Figure 4A shows the network for personal revenge. Figure 4B shows that for third-party revenge.(Color figure online)

Networks for third-party revenge (see Fig. 4B and Fig. 5) indicated that explanations of honor-endorsers and face-endorsers created links between benevolence and both threaten and promote. Similar links between promote/threaten and both competence and uphold norms were found for each group. Connections between promote/threaten and security were particularly strong for youth endorsing honor, and connections between promote/threaten and self-direction were particularly strong for youth endorsing face.

4   Discussion

This study provides evidence of multiple normative systems among US adolescents. While we expect that most individuals will respond to environmental cues with the

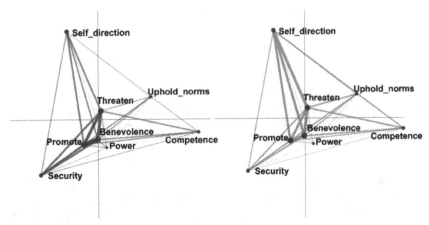

Fig. 5. Networks of goals and outcomes cited by adolescents endorsing honor (red) and face (aqua) norms when explaining their self-evaluation of third-party revenge. (Color figure online)

corresponding perspectives and behaviors, they may have habitual responses that are supported by their environment. Habitual responses may be most likely to emerge under conditions of threat. Even if actions are the same, normative systems place different evaluative lenses on the actions. Thus, personal revenge and third-party revenge yielded contrasting networks of emotions and goals, consistent with face and honor systems. Face norms demand self-restraint and a commitment to social harmony. So anger among youth who strongly endorsed face norms was an occasion for shame. Shame reflects a strongly self-critical evaluation as seen through the eyes of others. Given the importance of reputation in both honor and face systems, having this external perspective is part of proper socialization (Boiger et al. 2014). A person who is shameless would be considered a person who is not properly oriented to reputation and the regard of others. In contrast, anger following a threat was an occasion of pride for youth who strongly endorsed honor norms. Both anger and revenge are tools to bolster group security in honor systems—however risky such actions may be for the individual.

Participants in both groups spoke of their anger in terms of high levels of arousal ("I was so riled up, I couldn't think straight."). High levels of anger were sometimes discussed as threats to self-direction (e.g., "That's not the kind of person I am."), resulting in actions that were not considered indicative of one's *true self* (Thomaes et al. 2017). Anger was cited as a contributor to immediate, disorganized retaliation, whereas cold-heartedness (e.g., "I didn't care what happened to them.") might describe revenge that was carefully planned to have the greatest impact, "It helped me quite a bit, they deserved it…and I just took advantage when they were low in their life…They rubbed me in the bad way so…I was still mad about it."

For youth who strongly endorsed honor, the security motive may have served to organize thinking around revenge. It had the most connections to other motives, and vengeful actions were viewed as both promoting and compromising security. Even when youth proved more powerful than their adversaries, the threat of counter-retaliation remained. In the third-party revenge condition, security promotion was sometimes conceptualized as relationship security. Youth sometimes indicated a greater intimacy with the victim and expected that their friend would defend them if the situation were reversed, "They'd do the same for me if I was in their position." Actions that strengthen alliances by demonstrating one's trustworthiness under threat are strongly encouraged by honor norms. The importance of reputation in honor systems suggests a strong link between third-party revenge and self-worth.

4.1 Limitations

Our participant groups were formed on the basis of a new measure that requires additional revision and validation with a larger sample than the original N of 574. The current study was a cross-sectional design that relied on self-reported thoughts and feelings experienced after the specified action. We do not know which ones were experienced immediately following the actions and which ones developed after considerable reflection.

Using narratives of real events offers ecological validity that is missing when participants respond to hypothetical actions. The disadvantage is the range of events that young people relate. Both the precipitating events and subsequent revenge varied sharply in terms of severity and mode (e.g., relational or physical aggression). Despite this variability, differences between groups were coherent and consistent with theory.

4.2 Implications for Adolescent Development

A unique element of the networks for youths who strongly endorsed face norms was the connection between self-direction and threat. This combination was a common response when youth felt that their actions were at variance with their values (Frey et al. 2020a). Youth, for example, sometimes commented that their past actions were "not me" or that they were not the same person any more. Other times, youth expressed dismay that high levels of angry arousal overcame their efforts to be the persons they wanted to be, as in "you're just not yourself." These reflections are a poignant reminder that adolescents may see themselves in developmental terms. They talk about changes they have made—often in response to what they feel was their own disappointing or misguided behavior.

Other work that has examined third-party revenge has noted that youth's explanations of their subsequent thoughts and feelings reflect sophisticated moral reasoning. Because benevolence to others is clearly youths' most important goal (Frey et al., 2020a), both types of revenge are ultimately incongruent with cherished values, leading to a sense of inauthenticity and incompetence. It is possible that supportive yet challenging conversations about these common, but morally ambiguous actions may be helpful for promoting effective responses to threat that also enhance adolescents' self-concept. As situated theories of cultural systems note, however, normative orientations respond to the environmental cues that youth receive in school and the larger community.

Regional systems, including those that are legacies of colonization, appear to be potent influences either directly, through generational transmission, or through the persistence of environmental factors that elicit particular cognitions and responses. Honor norms evolve when people have reason to distrust law enforcement. Youths who are denied protection and justice by the state may develop traits (e.g., courage, strategic thinking, ruthlessness, ability to form alliances) that may provide personal protection when state institutions do not. When enough individuals in a group are denied state protection and justice, honor norms become the dominant normative system, even if individuals do not personally endorse revenge (Kubrin and Weitzer 2003). While a reasonable response to institutional failures, honor norms are an inadequate substitute for a system that protects and provides justice to all.

Acknowledgements. The research was supported by grants from the National Institute of Justice (2015-CK-BX-0022), National Science Foundation (DRL-1661036, DRL-1713110), Wisconsin Alumni Research Association and University of Wisconsin. Opinions expressed are those of the authors and do not necessarily reflect official positions or policies of the US Department of Justice, other funding agencies and institutions, or other individuals.

References

Aslani, S., Ramirez-Marin, J., Brett, J., Yao, J., Semnani-Azad, Z., Tinsley, C., Weingart, L., et al.: Dignity, face and honor cultures: Implications for negotiation and conflict management. In: Adair, M.O.W. (ed.) Handbook of Research on Negotiation, pp. 249–282. Elgar, Cheltenham, UK (2013)

Boiger, M., Güngör, Karasawa, M., Mesquita, B.: Defending honour, keeping face: interpersonal affordances of anger and shame in Turkey and Japan. Cognit. Emotion **28**, 1255–1269 (2014)

Brewer, M.B., Chen, Y.-R.: Where (who) are collectives in collectivism? toward conceptual clarification of individualism and collectivism. Psychol. Rev. **114**, 133–151 (2007)

Brown, R.: Honor Bound: How a Cultural Ideal Has Shaped the American Psyche. Oxford U Press, New York (2016)

Cohen, D., Nisbett, R.E.: Self-protection and the culture of honor: explaining southern violence. Personal. Soc. Psychol. Bull. **20**, 551–567 (1994)

Cohen, D., Vandello, J.A., Puente, S., Rantilla, A.K.: "When you call me that, smile!" How norms for politeness, interaction styles, and aggression work together in southern culture. Soc. Psychol. Q. *62*, 257–275 (1999)

Dodge, K.A., Malone, P.S., Lansford, J.E., Sorbring, E., Skinner, A.T., Tapanya, S., Uribe Tirado, L.M., et al.: Hostile attributional bias and aggressive behavior in global context. Proc. National Acad. Sci. **112**, 9310–9315 (2015)

Fischer, D.H.: Albion's Seed: Four British Folkways in America. Oxford, New York (1989)

Flannery, K.V.: The cultural evolution of civilizations. Annual Rev. Ecol. Syst. **3**, 399–426 (1972)

Frey, K.S., McDonald, K.L., Onyewuenyi, A.C., Germinaro, K., Eagan, B.R.: "I felt like a hero:" Adolescents' understanding of resolution-promoting and vengeful actions on behalf of their peers. Unpublished manuscript (revise and resubmit). University of Washington (2020)

Frey, K.S., Onyewuenyi, A.C., Hymel, S., Gill, R., Pearson, C.R.: Honor, face, and dignity norm endorsement among diverse North American adolescents: development of three socio-cultural norms scales. Int. J. Behav. Develop., 1–13 (2020) https://doi.org/10.1177/016502542094690

Gaskil, R.D.: Homicide and a regional culture of violence. Am. Sociol. Rev. **36**, 412–427 (1971)

Grosjean, P.: A history of violence: the culture of honor and homicide in the US south. J. Euro. Econ. Assoc. **12**, 1285–1316 (2014)

Henry, D.B., Dymnicki, A.B., Schoeny, M.E., Meyer, A.L., Martin, N.C., MVPP: Middle school students overestimate normative support for aggression and underestimate normative support for nonviolent problem-solving strategies. J. Appl. School Psychol. **43**, 433–445 (2013)

Ijzerman, H., van Dijk, W.W., Gallucci, M.: A bumpy train ride: a field experiment on insult, honor and emotional reactions. Emotion **7**, 869–875 (2007)

Kubrin, C., Weitzer, R.: Retaliatory homicide: concentrated disadvantage and neighborhood culture. Soc. Probl. **50**, 118–157 (2003)

Leung, A.K.Y., Cohen, D.: Within- and between-culture variation: individual differences and the cultual logics of honor, face, and dignity cultures. Pers. Process Individ. Dif. **100**, 507–526 (2011)

Mandel, D.R., Litt, A.: The ultimate sacrifice: perceived peer honor predicts troops' willingness to risk their lives. Group Process. Intergroup Relat. **16**, 375–388 (2012)

Markus, H.R., Kitayama, S.: Cultures and selves: a cycle of mutual constitution. Perspect. Psychol. Sci. **5**, 420–430 (2010)

Marquart, C.L., Hinojosa, C., Swiecki, Z., Eagan, B., Shaffer, D.W.: Epistemic Network Analysis (Version 1.5.2) [Software] (2018) http://app.epistemicnetwork.org

Norton, M.I., Sommers, S.R.: Whites see racism as a zero-sum game that they are now losing. Perspect. Psychol. Sci. **6**, 215–218 (2011)

Pauketat, T.R.: The Ascent of Chiefs: Cahokia and Mississippian Politics in Native North America. University of Alabama Press (1994)

Coups, P., Linderman, F.B.: Plenty-Coups, Chief of the Crows. U of Nebraska Press, Lincoln, NE (2002)

Schwartz, S.H.: Are there universal aspects in the content and structure of values? J. Soc. Issues **50**, 19–45 (1994). https://doi.org/10.1111/j.1540-4560.1994.tb01196.x

Shafa, S., Harinck, F., Ellemers, N., Beersma, B.: Regulating honor in the face of insults. Int. J. Inter. Relat. **47**, 158–174 (2015)

Shaffer, D.W., Collier, W., Ruis, A.R.: A tutorial on epistemic network analysis: analyzing the structure of connections in cognitive, social, and interaction data. J. Learn. Anal. **3**(3), 9–45 (2016)

Thomaes, S., Sedikides, C., van den Bos, N., Hutteman, R., Reijntjes, A.: Happy to be "me?" Authenticity, psychological need satisfaction, and subjective well-being in adolescence. Child Develop. **88**, 1045–1056 (2017)

Vandello, J.A., Cohen, D., Ransom, S.: U.S. southern and northern differences in perceptions of norms about aggression: mechanisms for the perpetuation of a culture of honor. J. Cross-Cult. Psychol. **39**, 162–177 (2008)

Wainryb, C., Recchia, H.: Moral lives across cultures: heterogenity and conflict. In: Killen, M., Smetanta, J.G. (eds.) Handbook of Moral Development, pp. 259–278. Psychology Press, New York, U.S. (2014)

Woodard, C.: American Nations: A History of the Eleven Rival Regional Cultures of North America. Penguin, New York, USA (2011)

Zhang, Q., Oetzel, J.G., Ting-Toomey, S., Zhang, J.: Making up or getting even? The effects of face concerns, self-construal, and apology on forgiveness, reconciliation, and revenge in the United States and China. Commun. Res. **46**(4), 503–524 (2015)

Studying Affect Dynamics Using Epistemic Networks

Shamya Karumbaiah[✉] and Ryan S. Baker

University of Pennsylvania, Philadelphia, USA
shamya@upenn.edu, ryanshaunbaker@gmail.com

Abstract. The study of how affect develops and manifests over time during learning is a popular area of research called affect dynamics. Students' affective states are recorded in authentic settings like classrooms using direct observations by culturally sensitive, trained, and certified coders. A popular approach to studying affect dynamics in the last decade involved a transition metric called the L statistic. However, recent studies have reported statistical errors and other discrepancies with L statistic leading to questions about its reliability. Thus, we turn to epistemic network analysis (ENA), an emerging technique that is gaining popularity in studying the structure of temporal interconnections between codes. In this paper, we present an alternative approach to study affect dynamics by extending ENA to include directionality in the network edges to capture transitions. We also propose a new approach to running significance tests on network edges to identify significantly likely transitions. Then, we apply the two techniques – L statistic and ENA - to a previously collected affect dataset from a middle school math class, in order to better understand the trade-offs between these methods. Our analysis revealed that ENA could be a promising new approach to conduct affect dynamics analysis. In addition to avoiding statistical errors seen in L statistic, ENA offers better visualization which better emphasizes the magnitude of a transition's strength. We discuss the assumptions in ENA that need to be vetted further and the possibility for new kinds of analysis in the future for affect dynamics research using ENA.

Keywords: Affect dynamics · Transition analysis · Epistemic network analysis · L statistic · Temporal sequences

1 Introduction and Motivation

Affect within intelligent tutors and other types of adaptive and artificially intelligent educational systems has been shown to correlate with a range of other important constructs including self-efficacy [17], analytical reasoning [7], motivation [21], and learning [4, 8]. Affect-sensitive interventions have been designed to improve student engagement [22], learning gains [8, 9] and overall experience [10].

Developing effective real-time interventions depends on understanding how affect develops and manifests over time, an area of research termed *affect dynamics* (i.e. [14]), with a large body of research examining how students transition from one affective state

© Springer Nature Switzerland AG 2021
A. R. Ruis and S. B. Lee (Eds.): ICQE 2021, CCIS 1312, pp. 362–374, 2021.
https://doi.org/10.1007/978-3-030-67788-6_25

to the next during learning activities (see [11] for review). These studies have been conducted in a wide range of contexts and demographics, including students in middle school (private), high school (public and private), undergraduate programs and graduate schools, with a particular focus on contexts in the United States and in the Philippines [13].

Identifying student affect for research and to develop automated models is complex and nuanced. Affect data collection in authentic settings like classrooms typically involves direct observations by culturally sensitive, trained, and certified coders, or intensive video data collection and coding procedures [20]. Students are observed using widely-used protocols like BROMP [3] to reduce rater bias and observer effects and enable rigorous quantitative analysis. The output of such a method is temporally sequenced codes representing the field observations of student affect.

A popular transition metric used in affect dynamics research is the L statistic. It calculates the likelihood that a student in a given affective state will transition to a next state, given the base rate of the next state. In 2019, Karumbaiah and colleagues [12] provided mathematical evidence that several past studies applied the transition metric (L) incorrectly - leading to invalid conclusions of statistical significance. They proposed a corrected method which shifts the chance value of L from 0 to a positive value dependent on the number of affective states studied. Although this solution attends to the primary statistical error in past work, it makes the statistic difficult and non-intuitive to interpret. For example, it is possible for an L value to be above 0, but statistically significantly below the chance value, a situation likely to confuse researchers and readers and lead to incorrect conclusions. In addition, a recent study has reported that there are further issues with the L statistic involving states with high base rates [16], frequently seen for the affective state of engaged concentration [2]. Another simulation study with L produced results above chance levels for randomly generated affect sequences, if the sequences were short [5]. These continuing issues with the L statistic suggest an alternate approach may be warranted. We turn to the emerging field of quantitative ethnography for alternative approaches to conduct affect dynamics analysis.

A technique that is gaining popularity to study the structure of temporal interconnections between codes is epistemic network analysis (ENA). ENA models the pattern of association in coded data by building a network of relationships among the codes [23]. For affect dynamics, this means exploring associations between students' affective states during learning. There are five preliminary reasons why ENA could be a useful approach for affect dynamics research. First, the ENA network offers an intuitive way of visualizing probabilistically likely connections between affective states. Second, the edge thickness in the network (representing the strength of the association) offers a straightforward approach to interpreting the magnitudes of the transition strength – an indicator often overlooked in previous work focusing on the statistical significance of transitions. Third, unlike the L statistic, ENA can represent the case where there are multiple affective states occurring during the same time interval (seen more in the use of affect detectors as data sources than in field observation data – i.e. [19]). Fourth, ENA could enable identification of the most salient differences between the transitions observed in different student subgroups or learning activities and visualize them clearly as difference networks. Fifth, ENA could also help researchers study changes in the strength of connections over time.

There are two main limitations of using ENA as-is for affect dynamics analysis. First, we need to go beyond simple associations between the codes to also capturing the directionality of the co-occurrence. For instance, it is not enough to know that confusion and frustration has a strong association. We also need to know whether confusion transitions to frustrations or vice-versa or both. Second, we need to establish ways to conduct statistical tests on the strengths of these associations to identify significant transitions. In this paper, we present an alternative approach to study affect dynamics using ENA, also proposing ways to overcome the current limitations of the ENA tool for this type of analysis. We then compare this method of analyzing affect dynamics to the currently popular method of using the L statistic and discuss the strengths and weaknesses of the two approaches.

2   Affect Dynamics Analysis with L Statistic – Prior Work

Given an affect coding sequence, the *L* statistic [17] calculates the likelihood that an affective state (*prev*) will transition to a subsequent (*next*) state, given the base rate of the next state occurring.

$$L(prev \rightarrow next) = \frac{P(next|prev) - P(next)}{1 - P(next)} \tag{1}$$

The expected probability for an affective state, *P(next)*, is the percentage of times that the state occurred as a next state. The conditional probability, *P(next|prev)* is given by:

$$P(next|prev) = \frac{Count(prev \rightarrow next)}{Count(prev)} \tag{2}$$

where Count(prev → next) is the number of times the prev state transitioned to the next state, and Count(prev) is the number of times the state in prev occurred as the previous state.

The value of *L* varies from $-\infty$ to 1. The sign and the magnitude of *L* has been thought to be intuitively understandable as the direction and size of the association (see [8]). *L* = 0 has generally been treated as chance association, while *L* > 0 and *L* < 0 are treated as transitions that are more likely or less likely (respectively) than chance. To perform affect dynamics analysis across all students in an experiment, first the L value for each affect combination is calculated individually per student. Next, for each transition, a two-tailed one-sample t-test is conducted to test whether the likelihood is significantly greater than or equivalent to zero, across students [1]. More recently, researchers have added a step where a Benjamini-Hochberg post-hoc correction procedure is used to control for false positive results since the set of hypotheses involves multiple comparisons [11].

One special case that is not fully discussed in most of the literature is self-transitions where the student remains in the same affective state for more than one step in a sequence. Close to half of the previous studies have removed self-transitions during the data preparation stage (see discussion in [11]). This straightforward procedure seems quite logical, but violates the statistical assumption of independence between *prev* and *next* states as *next* state can now only take values other than that of *prev* state. Hence, when self-transitions are excluded, P(*next|prev*) $\neq$ P(*next*) for transitions at chance, and for a state space with n affective states (n > 2), the value of L at chance is [11]:

$$L = \frac{1}{(n-1)^2} \qquad \text{if self - transitions are excluded}$$

This finding showed that the L statistic must be interpreted differently depending on how many affective states are being observed; several past published studies which treat chance L as 0 therefore treat relationships significantly less likely than chance as significantly more likely than chance (see [12]). Although adjusting the chance value for L offers a remedy for this error, it complicates the interpretation of the statistic. While running statistical tests or making sense of the transition patterns, researchers have to be cautious about choosing the correct chance L value and interpreting values accordingly.

Additional problems have been revealed in terms of the reliability of the L statistic, based on analysis being conducted at the student-level and ignoring the within-student sample size. A recent simulation study [5] reported that L frequently produced results above chance levels for randomly generated sequences, if the sequences were short. Their study recommends a minimum sequence length of 20 per student for 4 states to avoid invalid values and much longer sequences (in excess of 50) to avoid spurious results. A sequence length of 50 would translate to a minimum observation session of 2.5 h in a typical data collection setting with 10 students and a 20-s observation grain size. This is impractical to achieve in traditional classrooms where a class period is often under an hour long. In other words, L may be unreliable for use with the BROMP data collection where it is currently commonly used [11].

3   Affect Dynamics Analysis with ENA – an Alternate Approach

Epistemic network analysis (ENA) is a method used to identify and quantify connections among elements in a coded data [23]. An epistemic network - originally developed to model cognitive networks [23] - represents the structure of connections and the strength of association among the codes. To interpret situated events, *codes* are used as the socially and culturally organized ways of seeing these recorded actions. In authentic classroom settings, a protocol like BROMP [3] produces a sequence of data coded in terms of a validated list of codes of student affect and behavior. BROMP has been used by over 160 researchers and practitioners in seven countries for field observations with culturally sensitive coding schemes revised for and adapted to different cultural contexts [3]. In this section, we explore the use of ENA to model affect dynamics by capturing the temporal interconnections between the recorded affective codes.

3.1   Capturing Directionality

Traditionally, most ENA research has been interested in the co-occurrences of codes over time and thus focuses on symmetric data where an edge between two codes imply that they are connected to each other, with no explicit consideration of the direction of the connection. When adopting ENA for transition analysis like in the case of affect dynamics, the direction of the connection needs to be established clearly. This can be achieved by extending the approach suggested by Shaffer [23] wherein each code assumes two functions – sending and receiving. These two functions can be represented as two separate nodes in the network. For instance, the affective state of confusion (CON) can be denoted as confusion_sender (CON_S) if it is the current state in the transition and confusion_reciever (CON_R) if it is the next state in the transition. Thus, a transition from confusion to frustration (FRU) will be represented as the codes CON_S (time N) and FRU_R (time N + 1). This change can be captured at the data preparation stage. For an example affect sequence of ENG (engaged concentration)-CON-CON-BOR (bored)-BOR-FRU, Table 1 shows the transformation into the vector encodings representing the 5 transitions in the sequence. Each row has 2 columns that are set to 1 – one for the sender (_S) and one for the receiver (_R). Note that the first state in the sequence is ignored as it does not represent a transition.

Table 1. Vector encodings preserving the direction of the transitions ENG-CON-CON-BOR-BOR-FRU

Affect	Transition	ENG_S	CON_S	FRU_S	BOR_S	ENG_R	CON_R	FRU_R	BOR_R
ENG	–	–	–	–	–	–	–	–	–
CON	ENG-CON	1	0	0	0	0	1	0	0
CON	CON-CON	0	1	0	0	0	1	0	0
BOR	CON-BOR	0	1	0	0	0	0	0	1
BOR	BOR-BOR	0	0	0	1	0	0	0	1
FRU	BOR-FRU	0	0	0	1	0	0	1	0

3.2 Removing Self-transitions

The decision of whether to include or exclude self-transitions depends on the research goals. If some affective states are particularly persistent - for instance engaged concentration [2] - including self-transitions could lower the transition probabilities for transitions to new affective states, and/or in some cases, cause them to become non-significant. In contrast, excluding self-transitions may inflate the frequency of seeing transitions between affective states. Recent research on affect dynamics has focused on between states rather than their persistence [4, 6, 11]. In keeping with this, our analysis within this paper also excludes self-transitions. Self-transitions can be removed from the vector encodings by eliminating all the transitions where the sender (_S) and receiver (_R) states match, such as the third row in Table 1 (CON-CON) where CON_S = 1 and CON_R = 1. The Exclusion of self-transitions could also be done at the beginning of data preparation by collapsing self-transitions in the original sequence into a single state.

3.3 Choosing ENA Parameters

Our unit of analysis is a student. All the affect codes for a student from a single observation session will constitute a conversation, in terms of ENA analysis. Since we are interested in analyzing the transitions between two states, we limit the temporal context for ENA analysis to a single vector encoding a single transition. Thus, the moving window size (grain-size of time for co-occurrence) is set to 1. The resulting epistemic network will not have any edge between the sender nodes (say CON_S and ENG_S) or between the receiver nodes (say CON_R and ENG_R). As we remove self-transitions, there also will not be any edge between the sender and receiver nodes for the same state (say ENG_S and ENG_R). An example epistemic network with three affective states (*Engaged Concentration, Frustration, Confusion*) and without self-transitions is given in Fig. 1. In this example, stronger connections (thicker edges) are seen in these four (of six possible) transitions:

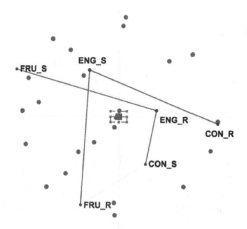

Fig. 1. An example epistemic network

- ENG_S and CON_R - Engaged Concentration -> Confusion
- ENG_S and FRU_R - Engaged Concentration -> Frustration
- FRU_S and ENG_R – Frustration -> Engaged Concentration
- CON_S and ENG_R – Confusion -> Engaged Concentration

3.4 Significance Test for Transition Strength

Most ENA research focuses on network level analysis with statistical tests comparing one network to another. In case of transition analysis like affect dynamics, our focus shifts from the whole network to individual transitions. Thus, it is necessary to quantify the transition strength and establish significance tests on the edges to determine which of the transitions are significant. We do so by extracting the edge weights of the resulting network for each individual student. While the output network in the web version of ENA tool presents the mean strength of the edges (Fig. 1), we can extract the line weights for individual students by clicking each data point and hovering the cursor over the edges of the individual network. This could be time consuming when there is a bigger data set or a higher number of codes. Thus, we recommend extracting the network line weights for individual student networks from the $line.weights variable in rENA - its R implementation [15]. The output matrix will have $\frac{n}{2}C$ columns representing all possible edges, where n is the number of affective states. For instance, if a data set has 4 affective states, there will be weights for 28 possible edges for each student. These include self-transitions (4), transitions between senders (6) and transitions between receivers (6) – all of which are invalid in our network configuration. Thus, we will run a one-sample [two-tailed] t-tests on the normalized transition strengths (line weights) only on the weights of the twelve edges that remain after removing the sixteen invalid edges. Lastly, a Benjamini-Hochberg post-hoc correction procedure is used to control for false positive results since the set of hypotheses involves multiple comparisons.

4   Example Analysis

In this section, we apply the two techniques – L statistic and ENA - to a previously collected affect dataset, in order to better understand the trade-offs between these methods.

4.1   Data

The data used in this analysis was collected through field observations of 838 students using ASSISTments, a computer based learning system for middle school math [6]. The coders used BROMP (Baker Rodrigo Ocumpaugh Monitoring Protocol; [3]) to code 3,127 observations of student affect and behavior. The observation data is highly skewed, with approximately 82% of observations coded as engaged concentration, 10% coded as boredom, 4% coded as confused, and 4% coded as frustration. This affect distribution is consistent with past research on affect prevalence in systems such as ASSISTments.

4.2   L Statistic Result

Table 2 lists the result of the affect dynamics analysis with L statistic. In this case, as there are 4 affective states, the L value at chance is 0.11 (see Sect. 2), and this value is used within the one-sample t-tests. The transitions that are statistically significantly likely than chance (after post-hoc correction) are *Engaged Concentration -> Boredom, Confusion -> Engaged Concentration, Frustration -> Engaged Concentration*, and *Boredom -> Engaged Concentration*. Note that the transitions *Boredom -> Confusion* and *Boredom -> Frustration* are both significant and have an L value greater than zero but are not significantly positive because they both have L values less than the chance value.

Table 2. L Statistic results for ASSISTment BROMP data

Sender State	Receiver State	L	P-value	Adjusted Alpha
ENG	CON	0.171	0.091	0.0333
ENG	FRU	0.153	0.243	0.0375
ENG	**BOR**	**0.349***	**<0.001**	0.0042
CON	**ENG**	**0.539***	**<0.001**	0.0083
CON	FRU	0.049	0.286	0.0416
CON	BOR	0.085	0.683	0.0458
FRU	**ENG**	**0.552***	**<0.001**	0.0125
FRU	CON	−0.003*	0.015	0.0250
FRU	BOR	0.120	0.867	0.0500
BOR	**ENG**	**0.669***	**<0.001**	0.0167
BOR	CON	0.033*	0.022	0.0292
BOR	FRU	0.016*	0.012	0.0208

*All significant transitions
Significantly positive transitions are in bold

Table 3. Significance of transition strengths in the epistemic network

Sender State	Receiver State	Transition Strength	P-value	Adjusted Alpha
ENG	**CON**	**0.099**	**<0.001***	0.0042
ENG	**FRU**	**0.083**	**<0.001***	0.0083
ENG	**BOR**	**0.256**	**<0.001***	0.0125
CON	**ENG**	**0.088**	**<0.001***	0.0167
CON	FRU	−0.027	0.001*	0.0292
CON	BOR	−0.018	0.057	0.0416
FRU	**ENG**	**0.090**	**<0.001***	0.0208
FRU	CON	−0.021	0.053	0.0375
FRU	BOR	−0.015	0.145	0.0458
BOR	**ENG**	**0.240**	**<0.001***	0.0250
BOR	CON	−0.019	0.046	0.0333
BOR	FRU	−0.002	0.907	0.0500

*All significant transitions
Significantly positive transitions are in bold

4.3 ENA Result

Figure 2 and Table 3 present the result of the epistemic network analysis. From the visual inspection of the resulting network (Fig. 2), we can observe that the two strongest connections translate to strong transitions between *Engaged Concentration -> Boredom* and *Boredom -> Engaged Concentration*. There are four other connections that have relatively medium strength - *Engaged Concentration -> Confusion, Engaged Concentration -> Frustration, Confusion -> Engaged Concentration*, and *Frustration -> Engaged Concentration*. Other transitions do not have visibly strong edges.

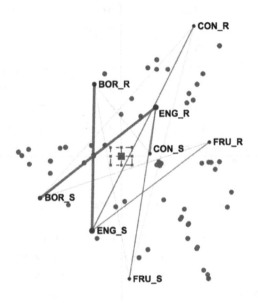

Fig. 2. Epistemic network capturing transitions in ASSISTment BROMP data

While the network provides a visualization to emphasize the relative strengths of the transitions, it is also useful to quantify the transition strength to compare the degree of difference and run significance tests. Table 3 summarizes the method described in Sect. 3.3 to achieve this with rENA. All the visible connections in the network (Fig. 2) have a significantly positive transition strength. The two strongest transitions (*Engaged Concentration -> Boredom* and *Boredom -> Engaged Concentration*) have close to three times the transition strength as the other four statistically significantly positive connections.

There are some similarities and differences between the results of L statistics and ENA-based analyses of significance. In both the results, all the significant transitions are either into or out of *Engaged Concentration* – the state with the highest base rate (80%). Four transitions are more likely than chance within each paradigm. In comparison to the results with L statistics, ENA finds two additional transitions to be more likely

than chance: *Engaged Concentration -> Confusion* and *Engaged Concentration ->
Frustration.* Both of these transitions have positive L values that are above chance (0.17
and 0.15 respectively) but are not significant. They are not among the strongest ENA
results visualized in the network (Fig. 2). Their quantified transition strength is less
than 0.1. Unlike the L results, there is a visually clear distinction between the two
strongest transitions involving *Engaged Concentration* and *Boredom* and all the other
four significant transitions in the ENA results. With L statistic, there is no such obvious
distinction - the significantly positive L values range from 0.35 to 0.67.

5   Comparing L Statistic and ENA Approaches to Affect Dynamics Analysis

Validity. One of the primary concerns with the L statistic is that it breaks down when
self–transitions are removed from the affect sequence. In contrast, ENA does not make
independence assumptions between two states, relying solely on their co-occurrences.
Although ENA has not been traditionally used for transition analysis, this paper has
demonstrated an extension that can serve this purpose. As such, it appears that using
ENA for affect dynamics analysis is a reasonable choice, whether self-transitions are
included or excluded.

Interpretability. Lstatistic offers a simple approach to quantify the transition likelihood, which can be used to run significance tests. However, in the case when self-
transitions are excluded, the results need to be interpreted with a non-zero value for
chance, requiring counterintuitive interpretation. This property has led to incorrect statistical tests being run and incorrect interpretations in past work. In contrast, ENA does
not have an established approach to run significance tests on the transition strength as
such. In this paper, we propose a new approach to do this – the properties of which we
offer initial analysis of but which is yet to be vetted thoroughly.

Visualization. ENA offers a straightforward approach to visualize the results of an
affect dynamics analysis as a network with nodes representing the affective states and
the thickness of the edges representing the strength of the transition between two affective
states. Previously affect dynamics analyses using the L statistic have focused more on the
significance of the transitions than on the magnitude of the likelihood itself. With ENA's
network visualization, it is much easier to see which transitions are most prevalent.

Co-occurring Affective States. Lstatistic requires an affect sequence with a single state
active at a given interval of time. This restricts the possibility that multiple affective states
may occur during the observation interval (e.g., *Confusion* and *Frustration*), and makes
it challenging to handle cases where there is a disagreement between the two coders
who are observing the same student at the same time, or where an automated detector of
affect is unable to distinguish which of two affective states is occurring. With ENA, it
possible to work with data where multiple affective states co-occur as ENA uses vector
encodings for representing transitions instead of the single state representation.

6 Discussion and Conclusions

Affect dynamics is the study of how students' affect develops and manifests over time during learning. Past affect dynamics research has analyzed the likelihood of transition between states using the L statistic. Researchers have identified many limitations to the L statistic. We explore ENA as an alternative approach to model the temporal interconnections between affective codes. In this paper, we extend ENA to include directionality in the network edges to capture transitions. The resulting network represents affect as nodes and the strength of transition as the weight of the edge between them. Our analysis with the affect observation data from a middle school math class reveals that ENA could be a promising new approach to conduct affect dynamics analysis. First, ENA appears to avoid key limitations of using L when self-transitions are removed from the affect data. Second, ENA offers better visualization which better emphasizes the magnitude of a transition's strength. Third, ENA could be used when more than one affective state is active at once.

ENA is an emerging technique, and it needs to be vetted further for its assumptions and implications for different research contexts and practices. Take, for example, the implications of highly imbalanced codes. It is common in affect datasets to have a high base rate for certain states like Engaged Concentration (82% in the data analyzed in this paper). What is striking with the use of ENA is that all the transitions into or out of Engaged Concentration are significantly likely. Further research is needed to analyze the impact of dominant codes in ENA. Mello and Gasevic [18] did some preliminary analysis on this topic and found that excluding dominant codes had drastic impacts on the resulting networks. Unfortunately, removing important codes from the analysis may not be a viable option for researchers but may present a challenge for the use of ENA for some data sets.

One of the contributions of this paper is that it demonstrates the use of ENA for transition analysis with qualitative codes. We also propose a new approach to running significance tests on network edges to identify significantly likely transitions. This has implications beyond affect dynamics. For instance, we could identify the dialog moves that are more likely to precede or follow other dialog moves in a collaborative discourse. It could also be used when the directionality between the epistemic network nodes is important. For example, in a network representing citations between authors – author A's citation of author B is not necessarily the same as author B's citation of author A.

In our current analysis, we see that doing transition analysis with ENA produced significant results for all transitions with a positive transition strength. Further analysis is needed to confirm that the chance value of transition strength in ENA is indeed zero. Along similar lines, further research is needed to investigate if shorter affect sequences could lead to spurious results with ENA, as has been seen for the L statistic (i.e. [5. 16]).

Beyond these potential benefits, ENA opens up the possibility for new kinds of analysis in the future. Traditionally, affect dynamics research has looked at the transitions between two temporally immediately adjacent states. With ENA, we have the provision to examine co-occurrence of states at a coarser level by experimenting with moving window sizes greater than one.

Likewise, ENA offers difference networks (or subtracted networks) to enable identification of the most salient differences between two or more networks. This could be used to identify differences in transition patterns in student subgroups, such as whether there are differences between students in the US vs. the Philippines or between classroom studies and laboratory studies of affect. It could also be used to recognize students' affective trajectories by visualizing difference networks in time intervals or during important moments in learning.

Acknowledgments. We would like to thank the Penn Center for Learning Analytics (PCLA) for supporting this work and the discussions at the 2019 workshop on advanced ENA in the first international conference on quantitative ethnography (ICQE).

References

1. Baker, R.S.J.D., Rodrigo, M.M.T., Xolocotzin, U.E.: The dynamics of affective transitions in simulation problem-solving environments. In: Paiva, Ana C.R., Prada, R., Picard, Rosalind W. (eds.) ACII 2007. LNCS, vol. 4738, pp. 666–677. Springer, Heidelberg (2007). https://doi.org/10.1007/978-3-540-74889-2_58
2. Baker, R.S., D'Mello, S., Rodrigo, M.M.T., Graesser, A.: Better to be frustrated than bored: The incidence, persistence, and impact of learners' cognitive-affective states during interactions with 3 different computer-based learning environments. Int. J. Hum Comput Stud. **68**(4), 223–241 (2010)
3. Baker, R.S., Ocumpaugh, J.L., Andres, J.M.A.L.: BROMP quantitative field observations: a review. Learning Science: Theory, Research, and Practice, McGraw-Hill, New York (2020)
4. Bosch, N., D'Mello, S.: The affective experience of novice computer programmers. Int. J. Artif. Intell. Educ. **27**(1), 181–206 (2017)
5. Bosch, N., Paquette, L.: (under review). What's next? Edge cases in measuring transitions between sequential states (2020, submitted)
6. Botelho, A.F., Baker, R., Ocumpaugh, J., Heffernan, N.: Studying affect dynamics and chronometry using sensor-free detectors. In: Proceedings of the 11th International Conference on Educational Data Mining, pp. 157–166 (2018)
7. D'Mello, S., Person, N., Lehman, B.: Antecedent-consequent relationships and cyclical patterns between affective states and problem solving outcomes. In: AIED, pp. 57–64 (2009)
8. D'Mello, S., Graesser, A.: Dynamics of Affective states during complex learning. Learn. Instr. **22**, 145–157 (2012)
9. DeFalco, J.A., et al.: Detecting and addressing frustration in a serious game for military training. Int. J. Artif. Intell. Educ. **28**(2), 152–193 (2017). https://doi.org/10.1007/s40593-017-0152-1
10. Karumbaiah, S., Lizarralde, R., Allessio, D., Woolf, B.P., Arroyo, I., Wixon, N.: Addressing student behavior and affect with empathy and growth mindset. In: Educational Data Mining (2017)
11. Karumbaiah, S., Andres, J. M.A.L., Botelho, A.F., Baker, R.S., Ocumpaugh, J.S.: The implications of a subtle difference in the calculation of affect dynamics. In: 26th International Conference for Computers in Education (2018)
12. Karumbaiah, S., Baker, Ryan S., Ocumpaugh, J.: The case of self-transitions in affective dynamics. In: Isotani, S., Millán, E., Ogan, A., Hastings, P., McLaren, B., Luckin, R. (eds.) AIED 2019. LNCS (LNAI), vol. 11625, pp. 172–181. Springer, Cham (2019). https://doi.org/10.1007/978-3-030-23204-7_15
13. Karumbaiah, S., Baker, R. S., Ocumpaugh, J., Andres, J. M.A.L.: A Re-analysis and synthesis of data on affect dynamics in learning (2020, submitted)

14. Kuppens, P.: It's about time: A special section on affect dynamics. Emotion Rev. **7**(4), 297–300 (2015)
15. Marquart, C.L., Swiecki, Z., Collier, W., Eagan, B., Woodward, R., Shaffer, D.W.: rENA: epistemic network analysis (2019)
16. Matayoshi, J., Karumbaiah, S.: Adjusting the L statistic when self-transitions are excluded in affect dynamics. J. Educ. Data Min. **12**(4), 1–23 (2020)
17. McQuiggan, S.W., Lester, J.: Modeling affect expression and recognition in an interactive learning environment. Int. J. Learn. Technol. **4**(3–4), 216–233 (2009)
18. Ferreira Mello, R., Gašević, D.: What is the effect of a dominant code in an epistemic network analysis? In: Eagan, B., Misfeldt, M., Siebert-Evenstone, A. (eds.) ICQE 2019. CCIS, vol. 1112, pp. 66–76. Springer, Cham (2019). https://doi.org/10.1007/978-3-030-33232-7_6
19. Nye, B.D., et al.: Engaging with the scenario: affect and facial patterns from a scenario-based intelligent tutoring system. In: Penstein Rosé, C. (ed.) AIED 2018. LNCS (LNAI), vol. 10947, pp. 352–366. Springer, Cham (2018). https://doi.org/10.1007/978-3-319-93843-1_26
20. Okur, E., Aslan, S., Alyuz, N., Arslan Esme, A., Baker, R.S.: Role of socio-cultural differences in labeling students' affective states. In: Penstein Rosé, C. (ed.) AIED 2018. LNCS (LNAI), vol. 10947, pp. 367–380. Springer, Cham (2018). https://doi.org/10.1007/978-3-319-93843-1_27
21. Rodrigo, M.M.T., Anglo, E., Sugay, J., Baker, R.: Useofun-super- vised clustering to characterize learner behaviors and affective states while using an intelligent tutoring system. In: International Conference on Computers in Education, pp. 57–64 (2008)
22. Sanghvi, J., Castellano, G., Leite, I., Pereira, A., McOwan, P.W., Paiva, A.: Automatic analysis of affective postures and body motion to detect engagement with a game companion. In: Proceedings of the 6th International Conference on Human-robot Interaction, pp. 305–312. ACM (2011)
23. Shaffer, D.W., Collier, W., Ruis, A.R.: A tutorial on epistemic network analysis: analyzing the structure of connections in cognitive, social, and interaction data. J. Learn. Anal. **3**(3), 9–45 (2016)

Incorporating Sentiment Analysis with Epistemic Network Analysis to Enhance Discourse Analysis of Twitter Data

Kamila Misiejuk[1]([✉]) [iD], Jennifer Scianna[2] [iD], Rogers Kaliisa[3] [iD], Karl Vachuska[2] [iD], and David Williamson Shaffer[2] [iD]

[1] Centre for the Science of Learning and Technology, University of Bergen, Bergen, Norway
kamila.misiejuk@uib.no
[2] Department of Educational Psychology, University of Wisconsin, Madison, USA
{jscianna,vachuska,dws}@wisc.edu
[3] Department of Education, University of Oslo, Oslo, Norway
rogers.kaliisa@iped.uio.no

Abstract. While there has been much growth in the use of microblogging platforms (e.g., Twitter) to share information on a range of topics, researchers struggle to analyze the large volumes of data produced on such platforms. Established methods such as Sentiment Analysis (SA) have been criticized over their inaccuracy and limited analytical depth. In this exploratory methodological paper, we propose a combination of SA with Epistemic Network Analysis (ENA) as an alternative approach for providing richer qualitative and quantitative insights into Twitter discourse. We illustrate the application and potential use of these approaches by visualizing the differences between tweets directed or discussing Democrats and Republicans after the COVID-19 Stimulus Package announcement in the US. SA was integrated into ENA models in two ways: as a part of the blocking variable and as a set of codes. Our results suggest that incorporating SA into ENA allowed for a better understanding of how groups viewed the components of the stimulus issue by splitting them by sentiment and enabled a meaningful inclusion of data with singular subject focus into the ENA models.

Keywords: Epistemic Network Analysis · Sentiment Analysis · Discourse Analysis

1 Introduction

The emergence of web 2.0 technologies has seen a rise in the use of microblogging platforms such as Twitter and Facebook as means for people to share information, discuss current issues, and express their opinions on almost all aspects of everyday life [1]. Consequently, this shift has captured the interest of researchers, politicians, journalists, and financial and educational organizations to increasingly seek ways to collect and make sense of the vast amount of data produced by users of microblogging platforms to understand and explain different social phenomena. However, analyzing high-volume

© Springer Nature Switzerland AG 2021
A. R. Ruis and S. B. Lee (Eds.): ICQE 2021, CCIS 1312, pp. 375–389, 2021.
https://doi.org/10.1007/978-3-030-67788-6_26

data from microblogging platforms such as Twitter is challenging. This is partly because conversations in such environments are characterized by extensive use of informal language, emoticons, acronyms, and message-length constraints (partly due to the imposed character limit to posts), which could pose interpretative challenges [1, 2]. This implies that the analysis of discourse based on data from microblogging platforms requires the creative use of multiple approaches to gain a richer understanding of the discourse. Sentiment Analysis (SA) is a popular method used to analyse discourse by identifying valence in text data. Another method to model discourse is Epistemic Network Analysis (ENA) that analyzes and visualizes connections among pre-defined codes. In this paper, we argue that ENA and SA, in combination, is a useful addition to the methodological toolbox for analyzing Twitter discourse. We accomplish this through a case study that visualizes the differences in the discourse between tweets directed or talking about Democrats and Republicans from the 26th of March to the 1st of April 2020 following the announcement of the Stimulus package in the USA on the 27th of March. This aid package, the largest in US history, was implemented to mitigate the economic consequences of the COVID pandemic with measures, such as one-time $1,200 direct payments to individuals and business grants to discourage lay-offs [13, 14]. We develop two models combining SA and ENA in different ways and compare them with a model using only ENA.

2 Related Literature

2.1 Sentiment Analysis

There have been many developments in examining and interpreting data produced on microblogging platforms such as Twitter using both qualitative and quantitative approaches. One popular method is *Sentiment Analysis* (SA), also known as opinion mining, that tries to make evident what people think by providing representations, models, and algorithms that extract subjective information to create structured and actionable knowledge [3]. SA determines whether a textual corpus (e.g., document, sentence) tends towards positive, negative, or neutral [1, 4]. One of the significant early efforts for sentiment classification on Twitter data is by Barbosa and Feng [5]. They leveraged sources of noisy labels to train a model and used 1000 manually labeled tweets for tuning and another 1000 manually labeled tweets for testing. Their approach was able to capture more abstract representations of tweets and was more robust regarding biased and noisy data, a common feature of data from microblogging platforms. In another example, Agarwal and colleagues [4] used SA to build models for classifying tweets into positive, negative, and neutral sentiment. They concluded that features that combine prior polarity of words with their parts-of-speech tags are most important for the classification task. Moreover, Kouloumpis, Wilson, and Moore [6] investigated the utility of linguistic features (e.g., informal and creative language) for detecting the sentiment of Twitter messages. Their experiments indicated that part-of-speech features might not be useful for SA in the microblogging domain.

There are, however, some problems with some of the conventional approaches to analyzing Twitter data. For example, even though SA can analyze large volumes of tweets in bulk, questions may arise over its accuracy and the limited depth to the analyzed data

[3]. Further, machine learning-based sentiment classifiers can often prove less efficient in the case of tweets [5, 7], since the latter do not typically consist of representative and syntactically consistent words, due to the imposed character restriction [1]. An additional limitation is that classifiers usually distinguish sentiment into classes (positive, negative, and neutral), assigning a corresponding score to the post as a whole, even though many aspects of the same "notion" may be discussed in a single post [1]. In particular, a key area of exploration includes datasets where there is contention with how people are addressing a given subject. In these cases, one can measure the overall balance in the sentiment of a group of people who mention a single subject, but not what the sentiment is genuinely reflective of. For example, it would be possible to determine that more tweets were negative when mentioning the Supreme Court after a key decision. However, without further exploration, one would not know if the negativity is directed at the decision itself or the case that raised the decision. Therefore, SA alone might fail to provide richer qualitative insights into Twitter discourse, yet these are precisely the types of insights that can be obtained by the use of tools such as ENA which allows for the addition of connections between the subject and details of public discourse elucidating the complexity in the data.

2.2 Epistemic Network Analysis

Epistemic Network Analysis (ENA) is a quantitative ethnographic network analysis technique that analyses logfile data and other records of individual and collaborative learning [8]. ENA consists of a set of techniques that measure connections among coded data elements and represent them in dynamic network models. These models illustrate the structure of connections and measure the strength of association and changes in the composition and strength of connections in a network over time [9]. ENA has also demonstrated flexibility in its ability to combine with other methods. [10] introduced the use of social network analysis as an augmentation of the ENA projection to clarify how social and cognitive factors were influencing collaborative problem-solving. However, while ENA offers powerful mechanisms to analyze collaboration discourse and links among relevant features of collaborative learning [11], it may be challenging to visualize semantic features of different types in the same plot For example, using the previous example concerning the Supreme Court and subsequent ruling, connections projected by ENA using codes describing topics could be enhanced by an understanding of the sentiment behind them. Thus, in this paper, we propose a novel approach that combines SA and ENA to better understand participants' discourse as a response to the potential limitations of individual approaches to the analysis of microblogging data. This proposed approach aligns with Kontopoulos and colleagues [1], who noted that exploring various methods for visualizing the resulting sentiment is necessary to provide comprehensive insights to the users. This paper seeks to explore the following research questions:

1. Can SA and ENA be combined, and if so, how?
2. Can adding SA to ENA models provide different insights into Twitter discourse than ENA models alone?

3 Method

3.1 Twitter Dataset

COVID-19 Tweets Dataset is an open-access dataset published on the IEEE DataPort™ website. With the first tweets collected on the 20th of March 2020, this large dataset includes English tweets filtered by several corona-related keywords including keywords "corona", "coronavirus", "covid", "covid19" and variants of "sarscov2". The model itself monitors Twitter in real-time, and new datasets are published daily. Following Twitter Developer Policy, COVID-19 Tweets Dataset consists of Tweet Ids. To download the "full" tweets, open-source software that handles the Twitter API limits called DocNow's Hydrator was used [12].

In the current study, we focused on the tweets published from the 26th of March to the 1st of April 2020, resulting in a dataset of 2,461,489 tweets. On the 27th of March 2020, President Trump signed a stimulus package. This aid package, the largest in US history, was implemented to mitigate the economic consequences of the COVID pandemic with measures, such as one-time $1,200 direct payments to individuals and business grants to discourage lay-offs [13, 14]. The initial investigation identified key political figures being called into the conversation around COVID and the stimulus package. To reduce the dataset from all available Covid tweets to a more manageable, relevant sample, a text search filter was applied to tweet content, replies, and retweets. Tweets that were direct replies to or retweets of a politician's Twitter handle were considered Direct Mentions of a politician. Tweets that included the politician's Twitter handle, name, or other identifying information were labeled as Indirect Mentions. These mentions were combined with mentions of keywords related to political parties to create two groups: *Republicans* and *Democrats*. The aggregation of filter criteria can be seen in Table 1.

Since each tweet may have more than one politician or group mentioned, a function was applied that moved a given tweet further towards Democrat or Republican based on the number of keywords within the tweet. Tweets containing mentions of both parties in equal numbers were labeled as *Balanced* tweets. Any tweet that was not relevant to a political leader or party was removed from the dataset. A final filter eliminated duplicates from the dataset as we were primarily concerned with original ideas and hoped to avoid a frequently retweeted tweet skewing the sample.

3.2 Qualitative Data Coding and Validation

In order to code the tweets, we used a bottom-up approach and looked directly at the tweets to discover relevant themes [15]. After multiple iterations of 4 coders coding parts of the data, we decided on the coding scheme shown in Table 2. To validate the coding scheme, we used nCoder, a tool that helps develop automated classifiers based on regular expressions. Each code was validated against 2 raters and the automated classifier using Cohen's Kappa and Shaffer's rho [16]. See Table 3 for the validation scores.

Finally, we removed the non-coded tweets from our dataset, which resulted in a dataset of 4,944 tweets that were used in the ENA analysis. Moreover, SA scores were obtained with the help of the *Syuzhet* r package using an AFINN lexicon-based model, which was specifically designed for analyzing microblogs and social media [17, 18].

Table 1. Filters used to identify when tweets were directly related to a subject through response or retweet, indirectly mentioning a subject, and the political content of each tweet.

Politician/Party	Direct mentions	Indirect mentions	Political party addressed
Donald J. Trump	@realDonaldTrump, @POTUS	'Potus45', 'Trump'	*Republican*
Mike Pence	@VP, @Mike_Pence	'Pence', '@vp'	
Ron DeSantis	@govRonDesantis	'desantis'	
Republicans	N/A	'republican', 'republicon', 'GOP', 'trumptard', 'right wing', 'conservative'	
Joe Biden	@JoeBiden	'biden'	*Democratic*
Bernie Sanders	@BernieSanders	'Feelthebern', 'bernie', 'sanders'	
Andrew Cuomo	@AndrewCuomo, @NYGovCuomo	'cuomo'	
Democrats	N/A	'dems', 'democrap', 'democrat', 'leftard', 'libtard', 'liberal', 'DNC', 'left wing'	

Every tweet was assigned one sentiment score in a range from −5 to +5 based on its number of positive, negative, and neutral words. Sentiment scores below zero were coded as *negative*, above zero as *positive*, and equal to zero as *neutral*.

3.3 Quantitative Modeling with Epistemic Network Analysis

Examining the benefits of SA required the construction of three separate types of models, each with different integrations of ENA and SA. Tweets were explored with the Web Tool for Epistemic Network Analysis (webENA). This tool allows users to model connections between codes within their dataset using conversation parameters, window size, and units of analysis. We defined individual tweets as both a single utterance and the entirety of the conversation (and thus window size of one) because we could not identify threads from our data. Furthermore, any attempt to link tweets by date and introduce a moving or infinite stanza would obfuscate the results because individuals came from such far-reaching places. They may have been discussing the same people, and further even possibly centering their discussions around a similar concern, but they were not actively responding to one another, a key component of true conversation. While limiting to the final dataset, it was essential to take each tweet on its own without assuming its connection to the greater body of data.

Table 2. Coding scheme.

Code	Definition	Tweet example
Vulnerable workers	Tweets referring to workers who are disproportionately affected by the COVID situation by an increased risk of infection (e.g., nurses, doctors, essential workers)	*@Mike_Pence @WhiteHouse @GM How are the essential workers going to be compensated?... Amazon workers working in warehouse getting Corona Virus, what about workers on front lines?... Me and my wife are in a factory making $14 a hour putting out essential items. Military gets hazard pay*
High risk people	Tweets referring to groups who are disproportionately affected by the COVID situation by either decreased access to healthcare (e.g., refugees, the poor, homeless, transgender people) and increased chance of death if infected (e.g., elderly)	*Going by the Italian numbers is a gross miscalculation given that 12% of the death certs show corona as the direct cause lol Elderly population, and 1–3 comorbidities doesn't help*
Stimulus action	Tweets referring to the measures against the economic impact of COVID, especially, the stimulus package	*By the way, have any of you caught the Corona Virus. I hope you are taking care of yourselves better than the government is. Trump calling for the only reasonable senator's dismissal is as ridiculous as this stimulus package is*
Reopening	Tweets referring to the re-opening of the economy and going back to work after the lockdown	*@realDonaldTrump It's official!! BREAKING NEWS: OANN and USA government after further intense testing and evaluation just announced that the actual Corona virus death rate is as low as the regular flu (influenza) per Dr Anthony Fauci!! Stop the shutdowns!! Get back to school and work!!*
Lockdown	Tweets referring to lockdown measure (e.g., working from home, quarantine, homeschooling)	*The missing six weeks: how @POTUS @RealDonaldTrump failed the biggest test of his life #coronavirus #CoronavirusUSA #CoronaLockdown #CoronavirusOutbreak #CoronaVillains #Corona #COVID #COVID2019 #Covid_19 #COVIDIOT #TrumpPandemic #TrumpVirus*

(continued)

Table 2. (*continued*)

Code	Definition	Tweet example
China involvement	Tweets discussing China's involvement in the COVID spread or origin	*@realDonaldTrump @POTUS President Trump, don't even talk to the reporters who keep pushing the racist narrative on the Chinese Corona Virus We're tired of hearing this bs! ~ Trump2020*

Table 3. Validation scores.

Code	Rater 1 vs Classifier	Rater 1 vs Rater 2	Rater 2 vs Classifier
Vulnerable workers	Kappa: 0.97*	Kappa: 1.00*	Kappa: 1.00*
High risk people	Kappa: 1.00*	Kappa: 1.00*	Kappa: 1.00*
Lockdown	Kappa: 0.97**	Kappa: 1.00**	Kappa: 1.00**
Stimulus action	Kappa: 1.00**	Kappa: 1.00*	Kappa: 1.00*
Reopening	Kappa: 1.00*	Kappa: 1.00*	Kappa: 1.00*
China involvement	Kappa: 0.97*	Kappa: 0.97*	Kappa: 1.00*

*rho(0.9) < 0.05, **rho(0.9) < 0.01

Table 4. ENA models.

Model	Groups	Conversation	Codes	Sentiment included
1	Republican Democrat Balanced	Individual tweet	Vulnerable Workers, High Risk People, Stimulus Action, Reopening, Lockdown, China Involvement	N/A
2	Republican: Positive, Neutral, Negative Democrat: Positive, Neutral, Negative Balanced: Positive, Neutral, Negative	Individual tweet	Same as Model 1	In grouping
3	Republican Democrat Balanced	Individual tweet	Positive, Negative, Neutral + codes from Model 1	In codes

In this study, three different ENA models were developed, as seen in Table 4. Model 1 focused on comparing units based on the political party mentioned within the context of the tweet. This model served to compare Models 2 and 3 as it was the simplest delineation between groups. Model 2's comparison was based on groups defined by the sentiment directed at a party; this was identified by joining the tweet's sentiment with the political party from Model 1. We chose to append the two together to allow for nine unique groups, including all of the combinations of Positive, Negative, and Neutral with Democratic, Republican, and Balanced. Model 3 reverted to the same groups of comparison as Model 1 but added Positive, Neutral, and Negative to the codes used in Model 1.

The models were analyzed for their ability to differentiate between groups, increased accuracy, enhanced interpretability to the model. For this study, we were looking for interpretability to be enhanced through new relationships not captured by Model 1.

4   Results

Each of the three models produced originated from the same dataset. Due to the short text nature of tweets, the majority of tweets are coded with only one code (4,704 tweets); 240 tweets are coded with two or more codes. More tweets referenced *Republicans* (3,502) than *Democrats* (1,035), and fewer were *Balanced* (407), referencing both parties equally. *Republicans* dominated because there are many tweets directed at or talking about the US president, Donald J. Trump. AFINN sentiment scores classified 2,199 tweets as *Negative*, 1,239 tweets as *Neutral*, and 1,506 tweets as *Positive*. Table 5 shows the distribution of sentiment scores by party. This dataset allows us to address our two exploratory research questions as there is enough variation between the parties and sentiment to observe within an ENA model.

Table 5. Sentiment scores by political affiliation.

Sentiment	Democrat	Balanced	Republican
Negative	476	177	1,546
Neutral	184	65	990
Positive	375	165	966

4.1   RQ1: Can SA and ENA Be Combined, and if so, How?

In this study, we present two ways of incorporating SA into ENA: 1) as a blocking variable (i.e., a qualifier included as a part of the unit of analysis meant to segment the units into more refined categories), 2) as a set of additional "sentiment" codes. All models yielded statistically significant differences between the tweets referencing Democrats and those referencing Republicans on the X-axis. Table 6 shows differences in variance explained by the models and goodness of fit statistics for each model. Model 2 explains the highest variance and Model 3 the lowest. Moreover, Model 2 had the highest co-registration correlation for both dimensions, while Model 3 had the lowest, which suggests weak goodness of fit.

Table 6. Sentiment scores by political affiliation.

	MR1	SVD2	Pearson		Spearman	
			X-axis	Y-axis	X-axis	Y-axis
Model 1	18.7%	24.0%	.96	.94	.86	.79
Model 2*	23.9%	24.0%	.94	.94	.94	.78
Model 3	8.6%	14.5%	.73	.69	.73	.50

*Model 2 statistics originate from the visualized comparison between Negative_Republicans and Negative_Democrats. All other Model 2 visualizations met or exceeded these metrics.

4.2 RQ2: Can Adding SA to ENA Models Provide Different Insights into Twitter Discourse Than ENA Models Alone?

To answer this question, we compare the three models using ENA graphs seeking to highlight differences not only in the plots themselves but also in the tweets underlying the connections.

Model 1 is the base ENA model without SA that compares Republicans with Democrats and only includes the codes from the coding scheme to which we are going to refer as *subject codes*. Model 2 integrates SA and political affiliation into one blocking variable. To visualize Model 2, we produced three graphs: 1) comparing Positive_Democrats with Positive_Republicans; 2) comparing Neutral_Democrats with Neutral_Republicans; and 3) comparing Negative_Democrats with Negative_Republicans. Model 3 incorporates SA as codes in addition to subject codes, and like Model 1 compares Democrats with Republicans. In order to improve the readability of the visualizations and highlight differences between the groups, the Balanced group, though a part of all ENA models, was hidden, and the scale for edge weights was set to 4. The models were rotated by the comparison groups - Democrats (represented by blue) and Republicans (represented by red). Means rotation refers to a reduction of dimensions in order to position both means along a common axis while maximizing the variance between the means of the two groups [19].

Model 1

Model 1, our comparison model which lacks sentiment, shows the main connections between the codes in the dataset (see Fig. 1). Tweets addressing or talking about Democrats have the strongest connections between *Stimulus Action* with *High Risk People* or *Lockdown* and, while tweets addressing or talking about Republicans have the strongest connections between *Lockdown* and *Reopening* or *China Involvement*.

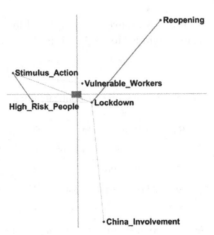

Fig. 1. Model 1 with no SA comparing tweets about or directed at Democrats (in blue) and Republicans (in red). (Color figure online)

Model 2

Model 2 used nine total groups within the model by adding SA as a blocking variable (e.g. Positive_Republican). Model 2 revealed the context in which particular connections were strong and added more nuance to Model 1 (see Fig. 2a−c). The strong connections between *Lockdown* and *Reopening* or *China Involvement* from Model 1 are only visible for positive and neutral tweets directed at or about Republicans, while negative tweets talking about or addressing Republicans have no strong connections among the codes compared with those talking about or addressing Democrats. The relationship between *Lockdown* and *Stimulus Action* seen in Model 1 for tweets directed at or about Democrats is visualized stronger for the polarized positive and negative tweets, but weaker for neutral tweets. Also similar to Model 1, *High Risk People* and *Stimulus Action* are connected strongly for neutral and negative tweets directed at or about Democrats, while only neutral tweets show a strong connection between *Lockdown* with *Vulnerable Workers*.

Adding SA helped highlight the nuances of Twitter discourse not immediately present in Model 1. For example, the sentiment expressed may tell us more about the user's personal political alignment than the policy or subject. For example, in this tweet with negative sentiment directed toward Democrats, the connection between *Stimulus* and *Lockdown* centers around the misallocation of funding to "undeserving" *High Risk People*:

> Why was any of that left in a aid package for the corona virus? This is unacceptable that Congress using their majority in the House should have even been able to add any of these packages. You liberals that support this should start remembering that this is crazy.

It is clear that the user disagrees with the political actions taken and that they do not personally align with liberal philosophies through their choice of, "You liberals". However, in a positive tweet referring to democratic leader Andrew Cuomo, we see the

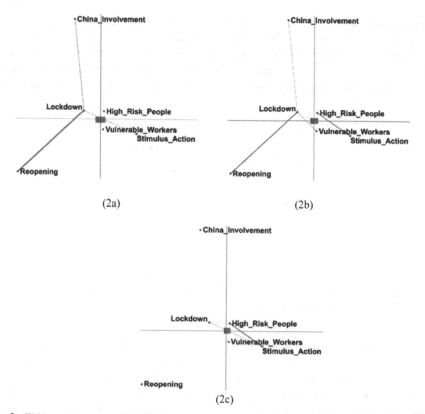

Fig. 2. ENA models comparing tweets about or directed at Democrats (in blue) and Republicans (in red): (a) Model 2a: positive sentiment integrated with the party affiliation, (b) Model 2b: neutral sentiment integrated with the party affiliation, (c) Model 2c: negative sentiment integrated with the party affiliation. (Color figure online)

same questioning of spending, but it is not motivated by political affiliation but rather selective actions.

> @RepLeeZeldin I live in NY & it needs help. But this is a CORONA bill. Cuomo was unprepared. Cuomo spends like a crack addict. Cuomo shut the whole state down. Cuomo wants the federal gov't to bail out NY?

Model 3

Model 3 presents an overview of attitudes expressed in the tweets and their connection to the subject codes, however, the connections seen in Model 1's original codes became less visible by adding the SA codes (see Fig. 3). In Model 3, tweets addressing or talking about Democrats have strongest connections between *China Involvement* and *Positive,* and between *Negative* and *Stimulus Action* or *High Risk People*, while the strongest connections for tweets addressing or talking about Republicans are between *China Involvement* and *Negative* or *Neutral*. Interestingly, some topics are dominated by political affiliation, e.g., *Stimulus Action* is connected to all three sentiments stronger for tweets directed at or about Democrats, whereas *Lockdown* for tweets directed at or about Republicans, while some are divided on the party affiliation, e.g., there is a positive sentiment in tweets that are directed at or about Democrats about *China Involvement*, in comparison to negative or neutral sentiment in tweets directed at or about Republicans.

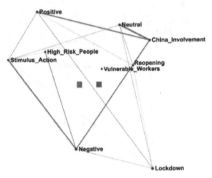

Fig. 3. Model 3 with SA as codes comparing tweets about or directed at Democrats (in blue) and Republicans (in red). (Color figure online)

Using this model, we are able to see how individual subject codes add to the sentiment connections from Model 2. While *Lockdown* is connected to *Stimulus Action* in Model 2a for positive tweets referring to Democrats, the *Lockdown* connection to *Positive* is actually dominated by the Republican group in Model 3. This comes about because there were many additional tweets solely focused on Lockdown that were able to be included in the model by allowing subject code connections to sentiment codes. Tweets express a singular frustration with the lockdown policies,

> 10 thousand new cases of #Corona in America in a single day... #Trump said no to lock down America!!!

Or are connected to concepts otherwise not represented in the model,

> And as of latest figures, usa is now on top in number of cases of Corona virus !! Still Trump is not looking for a full lockdown ! There won't be an economy if there would be no life. #corona #coronaUS #CoronavirusOubreak #CoronaUSA #CoronaVirusUpdates.

Furthermore, the addition of SA as codes added unexpected insights to the model. Nowhere in Models 1 or 2 were tweets referencing Democrats connected to *China Involvement*. In Model 3, there is a clear *Positive - China Involvement* connection that would otherwise go unnoticed.

> @thehill One great thing about the CHINESE WUHAN CORONA VIRUS is that it proved once and for all that the Liberal Socialist Fascist Demoncrats and their MSM cronies are definitely NONESSENTIAL! Remember that come November 2020 people!

The addition of sentiment codes gave greater insights into how people were talking about the subject codes. It allowed for tweets with only one subject code to be included in the model by creating a sentiment code - subject code connection. For example, a tweet solely coded as referencing *Vulnerable People* would fall out of Models 1 and 2, but by connecting *Vulnerable People* and *Positive*, the tweet is able to remain in Model 3.

Model Comparison

Social media is a place where widely disparate views can be shared with a broad audience. In the case of Twitter, users' views are broadcast to the world, leaving them open to critique, support, and overall discussion. In the case of tweets that addressed the economic stimulus package and COVID, connecting the sentiment behind a user's words with the content of their messages was essential to better understanding their intention.

When SA was included alongside the party mentioned in the group described as a blocking variable (e.g. *Neutral_Democrat, Positive_Republican*), it allowed for a greater amount of variance to be visualized in the ENA plots. It also allowed for larger groups to be parsed apart and visualized at once. For example, one could plot both positive and negative tweets directed at republicans and democrats parsed into four groups. This allowed for the identification of commonalities between groups at a macro level. This strategy, sentiment as a blocking variable, was less useful for determining the details of Tweet content through the plot alone, adding SA into the model as sentiment codes allowed for the model to incorporate narrowly focused tweets.

In summary, adding SA as a blocking variable produced a model with most variance explained and the highest co-registration correlation on both axes. The model using sentiment as codes produced a weaker model. However, both models provided more in-depth insights into the rich landscape of Twitter discourse that would be harder to highlight through a model limited to subject codes.

5 Discussion

In this study, we explore two ways that SA may contribute to ENA models using a case-study that included politically charged Twitter data related to Covid-19. We chose to use an external SA tool to determine the sentiment scores for individual tweets, and in doing so, we have demonstrated how SA can be a fast way to obtain information about how discourse is incorporating different subjects and ideas. In other applications, it may be possible to take a grounded approach to develop sentiment codes in a similar way in which we developed codes for subjects within the tweets. In our analysis, there were definite advantages to incorporating SA in that it (1) allowed groups to be better understood by separating the sentiment directed at different groups and (2) allowed data with a singular subject focus to be meaningfully included in the model. There are different utilities for each application, depending on the nature of the dataset. Moreover, this study highlights different ways of including new data into a network, either as a metadata that can help with data segmentation, or as a set of codes that aids exploring different narratives emerging from the data.

This study's limitations are primarily centralized around the case-study itself and secondarily around the nature of SA. The dataset used included several filters that removed tweets that did not include COVID, political mentions, and the subject codes themselves. By working with such a reduced set, it is possible that the importance of sentiment codes was artificially constructed. The same technique may not prove as fruitful in an analysis that lacks such clear "lines in the sand." It will consider those moving forward with integration to test the benefits of SA inclusion in their model. Furthermore, SA, in its purest form, is an automatic coding algorithm. The algorithm we utilized provides a sentiment score, but it is just a number. It can be challenging to determine where to distinguish the numeric score as to what is *Positive* and what is *Negative*. Alongside this observation of the abstraction of sentiment, there is a nuance in natural language processing that can become unwieldy in more casual forums such as Twitter. If SA is used instead of more traditional grounded coding approaches without validation as we have done, it is essential to reexamine the impact that the sentiment is having on one's model and seek to understand how the SA algorithm is manifested in the data.

There are opportunities for the greater community of Quantitative Ethnography (QE) in this challenge to validate both the use of natural language algorithms and the algorithms themselves. Especially in the context of social media data, the amount of available data is ever-growing, allowing researchers to "see" more perspectives and include more voices in their inquiries. The acceptance of more tools that allow us to process data and provide insights into our data rapidly will challenge us to forge new collaborations across fields, integrate more fields into the work of QE, and in turn, continuously develop new methods for the advancement of the field.

References

1. Kontopoulos, E., Berberidis, C., Dergiades, T., Bassiliades, N.: Ontology-based sentiment analysis of twitter posts. Expert Syst. Appl. **40**(10), 4065–4074 (2013)
2. Kumar, A., Sebastian, T.M.: Sentiment analysis on twitter. IJCSI **9**(4), 372–378 (2012)
3. Pozzi, F.A., Fersini, E., Messina, E., Liu, B. (eds.): Sentiment Analysis in Social Networks. Morgan Kaufmann, Burlington (2016)
4. Agarwal, A., Xie, B., Vovsha, I., Rambow, O., Passonneau, R.J.: Sentiment analysis of twitter data. In: LSM 2011 Proceedings, pp. 30–38 (2011)
5. Barbosa, L., Feng, J.: Robust sentiment detection on twitter from biased and noisy data. In: COLING 2010 Proceedings: Poster Volume, pp. 36–44 (2010)
6. Kouloumpis, E., Wilson, T., Moore, J.: Twitter sentiment analysis: the good the bad and the omg! In: ICWSM 2011 Proceedings, pp. 538–541 (2011)
7. He, Y., Lin, C., Alani, H.: Automatically extracting polarity-bearing topics for cross-domain sentiment classification. In: HLT 2011 Proceedings (2011)
8. Shaffer, D.W., Collier, W., Ruis, A.R.: A tutorial on epistemic network analysis: analyzing the structure of connections in cognitive, social, and interaction data. J. Learn. Anal. **3**(3), 9–45 (2016)
9. Shaffer, D.W., et al.: Epistemic network analysis: a prototype for 21st-century assessment of learning. Int. J. Learn. Media. **1**(2), 33–53 (2009)
10. Swiecki, Z., Shaffer, D.W.: iSENS: an integrated approach to combining epistemic and social network analyses. In: LAK 2010 Proceedings, pp. 305–313 (2020)
11. Gasevic, D., Joksimovic, S., Eagan, B.R., Shaffer, D.W.: SENS: network analytics to combine social and cognitive perspectives of collaborative learning. Comput. Hum. Behav. **92**, 562–577 (2019)

12. Documenting the Now: Hydrator [software]. https://github.com/docnow/hydrator. Accessed 27 Apr 2020
13. Kretchmer, H.: Key milestones in the spread of the coronavirus pandemic. In: World Economic Forum. https://www.weforum.org/agenda/2020/04/coronavirus-spread-covid19-pandemic-timeline-milestones/. Accessed 01 June 2020
14. Pramuk, J.: Trump signs $2 trillion coronavirus relief bill as the US tries to prevent economic devastation. In: CNBC. https://www.cnbc.com/2020/03/27/house-passes-2-trillion-coronavirus-stimulus-bill-sends-it-to-trump.html. Accessed 01 June 2020
15. Urquhart, C.: Getting started with coding. In: Urquhart, C. (ed.) Grounded Theory for Qualitative Research: A Practical Guide, pp. 35–54. SAGE, London (2013)
16. Shaffer, D.W., et al.: The nCoder: a technique for improving the utility of inter-rater reliability statistics. Epistemic Games Group Working Paper 2015-01 (2015)
17. Nielsen, F.A.: A new ANEW: evaluation of a word list for sentiment analysis in microblogs. arXiv:1103.2903 (2011)
18. Jockers, M.L.: Syuzhet: Extract Sentiment and Plot Arcs from Text. https://github.com/mjockers/syuzhet. Accessed 05 June 2020

Healthcare Professionals' Perceptions of Telehealth: Analysis of Tweets from Pre- and During the COVID-19 Pandemic

Sarah Larson[1]([✉]) [iD], Vitaliy Popov[2] [iD], Azliza Mohd Ali[3] [iD],
Parameswaran Ramanathan[1] [iD], and Sarah Jung[1] [iD]

[1] University of Wisconsin–Madison, Madison, WI, USA
`{larsonsa,jungs}@surgery.wisc.edu, parmesh.ramanathan@wisc.edu`
[2] University of Michigan, Ann Arbor, MI, USA
`vipopov@umich.edu`
[3] Universiti Teknologi MARA Shah Alam, Selangor, Malaysia
`azliza@tmsk.uitm.edu.my`

Abstract. Telehealth has the potential to improve patient access to professional healthcare. In this paper we examine the publicly held perceptions of healthcare professionals on Twitter regarding telehealth platforms pre and during the COVID-19 pandemic. Sentiment analysis and Epistemic Network Analysis (ENA) were used to investigate whether there were changes in the perceptions and opinions of telehealth expressed on Twitter by healthcare professionals between the time period of January to April 2019 and January to May 2020, during the initial medical system response to COVID-19. Findings suggest that professionals' perceptions shifted from telehealth as innovation during COVID-19 to focus on the pervasive need for safe access and delivery to care. Overall, sentiment on telehealth was found to be positive, with advances made in payment for telehealth care delivery and the easing of some of the restrictions on telehealth practice in 2020, though concerns on access to care through telehealth platforms remain prevalent.

Keywords: Telehealth · Sentiment analysis · COVID-19 · Healthcare

1 Introduction

Telehealth, also known as telemedicine, e-health, and virtual health, uses technology to monitor or consult with patients from a distance without the need for physical contact. According to Zucco et al. [1] telehealth or telemedicine systems provide services to patients, such as consultancy and follow-up, patient remote monitoring, and patient informational visits. In the era of the COVID-19 pandemic, telehealth is an attractive alternative that allows health professionals to continue their patient services without physical contact. For example, chatbots may answer COVID-19 related questions, provide consultation or virtual visits to anyone concerned about COVID-19, and manage healthcare delivery to patients with mild COVID-19 symptoms [2]. In addition to COVID-19 patients, patients with other health problems may also utilize telehealth to

A. R. Ruis and S. B. Lee (Eds.): ICQE 2021, CCIS 1312, pp. 390–405, 2021.
https://doi.org/10.1007/978-3-030-67788-6_27

reduce the likelihood of having risky contacts in the hospital. Zhou et al. [3] reported that COVID-19 has caused panic and fear in the community, resulting in psychological side effects such as depression and anxiety. As such, many patients have opted to seek medical care through telehealth visits for physical and mental health issues. For example, in April 2020, Michigan Medicine [4] reported that there were over 20,000 telehealth related visits across all departments in the hospital. These visits include many telehealth services such as e-visits, e-consults, video visits, and tele-specialty consults to support patients from several departments during this pandemic.

According to Rosenbaum [5], telemedicine is playing a key role in broader communication using robotic devices and camera technology, especially during the pandemic. In the United States, various applications exist for providing ongoing care where physicians are currently using telehealth to care for COVID-19 patients remotely [6]. Telemedicine allows patients to be efficiently screened, is both patient-centered and conducive to self-quarantine, and protects patients, clinicians, and the community from exposure. Additionally, it can allow physicians and patients to communicate 24/7, using smartphones or webcam-enabled computers [7]. As such, telehealth allows for patient to provider virtual connections when in-person connections are not feasible or safe. Given the changed nature of the landscape in which telehealth is currently being employed, we sought to investigate health care providers' publicly expressed perceptions and opinions of telehealth. To do this, we looked at content presented on a popular social media platform.

Twitter is a social media application where people express their opinions, activities, and feelings. Therefore, the content on Twitter contains rich information on people's knowledge and perceptions. According to Talpada et al., [8], Twitter active users are around 261 million and the number of tweets per day averages around 500 million. Text data from the twitter application can be utilized for prediction or classification in such things as movie reviews [9], politics [10], depression level [11] and in telemedicine [8]. One method for investigating opinions or perceptions is through sentiment analysis.

Sentiment analysis or opinion mining is a textual analytics technique that can analyze people's emotions, feelings, and ways of thinking. There are two main categories of sentiment analysis: lexicon-based and machine learning methods [12]. Lexicon-based uses a dictionary-based or corpus-based approach on a set of words associated with a given statement [1]. Techniques used in lexicon-based approaches include WordNet, TextBlob, and SentiWordNet. While machine learning methods consist of supervised and unsupervised learning, in supervised learning methods, datasets have to be labeled for model training. Examples of the supervised algorithms are Support Vector Machine, Naïve Bayes, and Random Forest. However, unsupervised learning methods will use unlabeled data. Clustering is an example of an unsupervised learning method. Sentiment analysis methods can give insight into categories of emotion or general ways of thinking, particularly with regard to positive or negative expressions in the content being analyzed. In this way, it is a useful approach for understanding the general valence of opinions and perceptions expressed on Twitter related to telehealth.

Additionally, there are techniques that can be used to classify tweet content and model this content in ways that allow for interpretations of thee perceptions and opinions to be made. One such technique, Epistemic Network Analysis (ENA), is a quantitative ethnographic technique for modeling the structure of connections in data, while assuming that the way data are connected is meaningful [13]. Though originally developed to address challenges in learning analytics, it has been used to analyze communication among healthcare teams [14, 15]. The key to ENA as a technique is the meaningful structure of connections. Thus, it is a useful method for modeling the connections among tweet content containing information about health care provider's perceptions of telehealth. ENA provides an objective, quantitative method for measuring and comparing perceptions of telehealth over time. We employed both sentiment analysis analysis and ENA to address the question: were there changes in health care professionals' publicly presented perceptions and opinions of telehealth expressed on Twitter between early 2019 and early 2020?

2   Methods

2.1   Data Collection

Data was collected from the Twitter application. Twitterscrapper in python library was used to scrape data from January 2019 to April 2019 and January 2020 to May 2020 to make a comparison. Four keywords were applied in gathering data: Telehealth, Telemedicine, ehealth and virtualhealth. These keywords were selected because they are common terms used virtual contact with healthcare providers. The total raw data was 111,404 from January 2019 to May 2019 and January 2020 to May 2020, but due to redundancy created by retweets, all duplicate values were removed for a final data set of 75,432. In this study, we used the screenname and also text (tweet contents) for analysis.

2.2   Sentiment Analysis

Orange Text Mining software was applied in the dataset to obtain the sentiment analysis score. Orange Text Mining is an open source machine learning and data visualization software which was developed by Bioinformatics Lab University of Ljubljana, Slovenia [16].

The sentiment analysis process begins with importing data in .csv format, then changing the text data into corpus. After that, preprocessing text is applied to clean the data. In the preprocessing part, data is transformed into lowercase, removes accent, url, and detected html text. Then, we applied the tokenization and filtered the data using stopwords and lexicon. The sentiment analysis method is then applied to obtain the sentiment score. There are two methods in Orange Text Mining to perform the sentiment analysis: Vader and Liu Hu methods [8]. In this project, we applied Liu Hu methods. Liu Hu method is a lexicon-based sentiment analysis [17]. This method calculates a single normalized score of sentiment in the text. Negative score represents negative sentiment and positive represents positive sentiment [10]. After getting the sentiment score, the results are viewable in a data table and saved in csv format. Figure 1 shows the sentiment analysis process in Orange Data Mining software. After obtaining the sentiment score, we filtered the data to include tweets only by those identifying as health professionals and specifically physicians, by searching for the keywords Dr and MD in the author column. After the filtering process, data that consisted of health professional's tweets equaled 1479 in 2019 and 1518 in 2020.

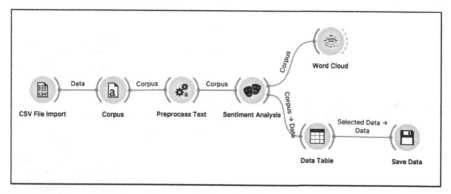

Fig. 1. Steps in conducting sentiment analysis using Orange Text Mining software (Color figure online)

2.3 Qualitative Analysis and ENA

After reviewing the data, three members of the research team developed codes using an inductive process of conventional content analysis [18]. Seven overarching codes were identified, with 12 sub-codes within these overarching codes, depicted in Fig. 2.

Fig. 2. Code and sub-codes tree

Table 1 shows the codes, sub-codes, definitions, and examples of coded tweets. Two researchers coded a random subsample of the data, consisting of 30% of the total dataset. The researchers discussed findings and resolved discrepancies between coders. The final interrater reliability test pooled Cohen's kappa at.88 and Shaffer's rho at 0.034. The two researchers then independently coded half of the remaining dataset.

We applied Epistemic Network Analysis [13, 19, 20] to our data using the ENA1.7.0 [21]. We defined the units of analysis as all lines of data associated with the single value of Year subsetted by Sentiment Valence and Author, and conversations as the previously stated data subsetted by tweet content. The ENA algorithm uses a moving window to construct a network model for each line in the data, showing how codes in the current line are connected to codes that occur within the recent temporal context, defined as four lines within the tweets [22]. The resulting networks are aggregated for each unit of analysis in the model. We aggregated networks using a binary summation.

Table 1. Codes, sub-codes, definitions, and examples

Code name	Sub-code name	Code definition	Example tweet
Access to care		Creating opportunities for better access to care	MedWand is very interesting. Telemedicine appears to have real promise for increasing access to health care, especially in remote areas
Cost to system	Billing from health care system	Issues around payment related to the health care system	Doctors were never paid for telephone calls—not before, and they won't be now. Docs need to educate themselves on how to use/schedule/bill covered #telemedicine services
	Billing of patient	Issues around payment from patients	Yep. My patients already get telemedicine visits at no extra charge. #dpc @dpcalliance
	Cost of infrastructure	Issues around cost of telehealth	More talk less action: the past reality of #digitalhealth. Here's how the pandemic has reversed that philosophy for digital health to live up to its arguments for funding. @es_jensen @hitconsultant

(continued)

Table 1. (*continued*)

Code name	Sub-code name	Code definition	Example tweet
	Insurance coverage	Talking about insurance coverage issues	Two major factors allowed the rapid adoption of #telemedicine: 1. A government mandate that gave the ability to be paid for services and 2. The elimination of #HIPAA requirements for video communication applications - the technology was already in place and #doctors were ready
Innovation in care	New technologies	Discussion of new technologies that can be used for telehealth	Verily's algorithm helps prevent eye disease in India @engadget Last day to come find us in San Francisco! Stop by booth 809 and see what all the hype is about with our new telemedicine platform! #AAAA19 #EHR #Allergists #Telehealth
	Perceived innovation	The tweet is tagged or discussed as innovative by the person tweeting	Yes. #cardiologists support #WorldKidneyDay Just started sending Bluetooth BP cuffs to patients with #coarctation of the #aorta with #hypertension... we can do better! #digitalhealth #innovation #Telemedicine @MassGeneralNews @ACHA_Heart

(*continued*)

Table 1. (*continued*)

Code name	Sub-code name	Code definition	Example tweet
Negative aspects of care delivery	Constraints of physical examination	Issues with doing a comprehensive exam due to not being physically present	Telehealth will likely be limited to certain areas of medicine. In eye care I predict #telehealth will underwhelm, underperform, and largely disappear w/in a year
	Data privacy	Issues around data privacy	Time to open the discussions re:privacy/consent relating to sharing medical info with pts and providers to support expansion of technology in medicine? Would we accept less privacy in return for inc access to our records and telehealth? @CMA_Docs @WebbCharleswebb @DrShelleyRoss
	Technology issues	Difficulty with using technology	There are countless examples of dangerously flawed #eHealth Chatbot triages within the @BadBotThreads
Patient connection		Connecting with patients or healthcare providers	Our providers are able to efficiently and securely communicate with all patients. Staff doesn't feel stressed, and patients continue to receive excellent care. It's a win win

(*continued*)

Networks were normalized before subjecting them to a dimensional reduction. We used singular value decomposition, producing orthogonal dimensions that maximize variance explained by each dimension [23]. Networks were visualized using graphs where nodes

Table 1. (*continued*)

Code name	Sub-code name	Code definition	Example tweet
Safe delivery of care		Delivering care safely	Working hard to ensure my patients receive excellent care with minimal risk
Technology	Platforms for delivery	Discussion of platforms and services for accessing telehealth	#DYK? In Asia, the doctor shortage is fuelling the rapid rise of #telehealth apps such as Halodoc and Doctor Anywhere. With this now available, patients are able to get the care they need
	Resources for access	Having the hardware and software needed to access telehealth	I see the benefits of upgrading your PC – you DON'T look like you're always underwater with a nokia phone
	Skills for use	Having the skills to participate in telehealth visits	That and our current tech can't replicate the important environment of a doctor and a patient face to face. Good medicine requires observational skills that we haven't yet been able to master via telehealth yet. Yet being the key term

correspond to codes, and edges reflect the relative frequency of each connection, between codes. The positions of the nodes are fixed, and those positions are determined by an optimization routine that minimizes the difference between plotted points and their corresponding centroids. ENA can be used to compare units of analysis in terms of their plotted point positions, individual networks, mean plotted point positions, and mean networks, which average the connection weights across individual networks. Networks may also be compared using network difference graphs. These graphs are calculated by subtracting the weight of each connection in one network from the corresponding connections in another and differences are tested using a Mann-Whitney test to the location of points in the projected ENA space.

3   Results

3.1   Sentiment Analysis

Overall, for tweets related to telehealth, there were more positive and negative tweets in the 2019 data than in the 2020 data. In terms of the valence of tweets from healthcare professionals during these times, the numbers of positive and negative tweets were very similar. See Fig. 3.

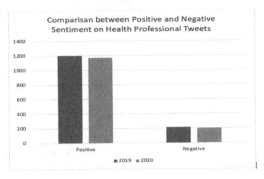

Fig. 3. Comparison of health professional tweets sentiment between 2019 and 2020

3.2   Qualitative Analysis and ENA

In total, 2905 tweets were coded, after removing remaining duplicates. Multiple codes could be assigned to a single tweet. ENA results are summarized in Figs. 4, 5 and 6, which depict the networks for connections between coded trends tweeted about in 2019 and 2020, as well as positive and negative sentiment. Our model had co-registration correlations of 0.87 (Pearson) and 0.77 (Spearman) for the first dimension and co-registration correlations of 0.86 (Pearson) and 0.82 (Spearman) for the second.

Perceived Innovation in Access to Care. Our analysis showed healthcare professionals in 2019 and 2020, and those with positive and negative sentiment, linked telehealth platforms for delivery and perceived innovation in patient access of care. The network for 2019 shows the strongest connections between Perceived Innovation, Platforms for Delivery, and Access to Care, as well as Patient Connection and Access to Care, indicated by the thicker, more saturated red lines across the X-axis in Figs. 4 and 5. These trends are also tweeted about and represented in the 2020 network, represented by the thicker blue lines. This was also apparent in tweets with a positive and negative sentiment, modeled in Fig. 6, though tweets with a negative sentiment were concerned with constraints on the physical examination and data privacy when using telehealth platforms for delivery. Health professionals in 2019 addressed Patient Connection with Constraints of Physical Examination more than in 2020.

Concerns for Care Delivery. Health professionals who tweeted with a negative sentiment connected Access to Care to Insurance Coverage and Data Privacy, whereas positive tweets link Access to Care to Cost of Infrastructure, Billing, and Resources for Access. Healthcare professionals who tweeted with a negative sentiment also connected Platforms for Delivery with Constraints of Physical Examination, which was not apparent in positive tweets. Negative sentiment tweets touched on the subjects of confidentiality and security for patients and physician liability and licensure across state lines in the United States. Technology issues were rarely mentioned, though healthcare professionals noted trends in telehealth care of over-prescriptions and the importance of an in-person physical examination. Generally, telehealth was accepted as an innovative platform for patients to access care, though quality of care was considered higher when providers had a pre-existing connection with patients.

Telehealth Platforms and Costs to the System. 2020 also shows connections between Safe Delivery of Care, Insurance Coverage, and Billing of Patient, which is less apparent in 2019 in Figs. 4 and 5. In 2020, healthcare professionals linked insurance coverage and the billing of patients to safe delivery of care on telehealth platforms, while in 2019 platforms for delivery were associated more with the cost of infrastructure. Many tweets advocated for or lauded insurance coverage of telehealth services on the state and federal level, particularly Medicaid and Medicare programs, for COVID-19 screening and outpatient services as a precautionary social distancing measure that ensures safe access to care. 2020 tweets also promoted investment in telehealth infrastructure and systems in preparation for the anticipated surge of patients due to COVID-19. Healthcare professionals emphasized that patients should not receive "surprise billing" for telemedicine services, particularly during the COVID-19 pandemic.

Telehealth as Safe Delivery and Access to Care. In 2019 there were almost no mentions of the safe delivery of care, whereas in 2020, there were 185. Our analysis showed that healthcare professionals' tweets in 2020 connected platforms for delivery with patient connection, access, and safe delivery of care. The tweets emphasized expanding

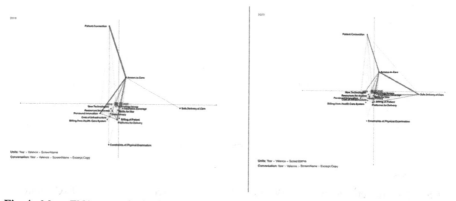

Fig. 4. Mean ENA networks for 2019 (red) and 2020 (blue) tweets about telehealth (Color figure online)

telehealth services during the COVID-19 pandemic in order to implement social distancing measures and mitigate strain and overflow on hospitals. Healthcare professionals also tweeted about telemedicine as a safe way for vulnerable patient populations to bypass safety concerns and barriers, including transportation, weather, and childcare, in order to access care. This included patients who are geographically rural, economically disadvantaged, indigenous, those suffering from chronic pain, mental illness, or substance abuse, as well as gender-affirming healthcare for transgender people and access to contraception. The network for 2020 in Figs. 4 and 5 depicts the strongest connections between Access to Care, Safe Delivery of Care, and Platforms for Delivery indicated by the thicker blue lines across the X-axis.

For a thorough understanding of the themes apparent in our qualitative analysis, we examined the mean networks for 2019 and 2020 tweets, as shown in Fig. 4 and the difference graph comparing the years in Fig. 5. Along the X-axis of Fig. 5, there was a statistically significant difference between 2019 and 2020 (mean $= -0.03$, SD $= 0.08$, N $= 786$; mean $= 0.03$, SD $= 0.18$, N $= 855$; t(1235.53) $= 9.38$, p $= 0.00$, Cohen's d $= 0.45$). Figures 4 and 5 again indicates that healthcare professionals in 2020 tweeted more about Safe Delivery of Care than in 2019, connecting safe delivery to Access to Care, Platforms of Delivery, and Insurance Coverage. By contrast, healthcare professionals in 2019 linked Platforms of Delivery to Perceived Innovation and Access to Care. In 2019 and 2020, tweets focused less on Resources for Access, Skills for Use, and Technology Issues and Data Privacy concerns than on Patient Connection and ensuring Access to Care.

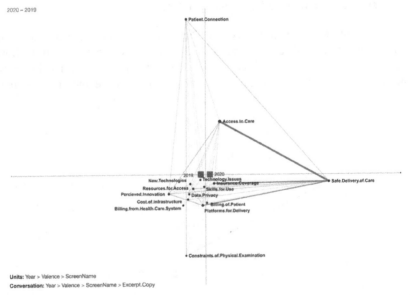

Fig. 5. ENA difference graph for 2019 (red) and 2020 (blue) tweets about telehealth (Color figure online)

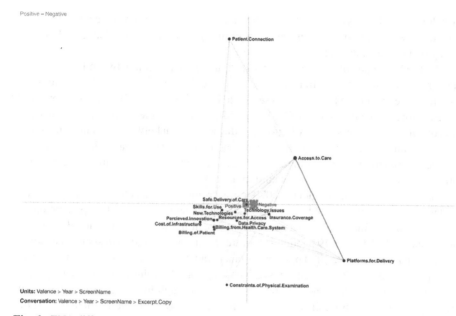

Fig. 6. ENA difference graph for positive (green) and negative (orange) sentiment tweets (Color figure online)

Figure 6 depicts the comparison model with positive and negative sentiment based on our analysis. There was also a statistically significant difference across the X-axis in the model between positive and negative tweets (mean $= -0.01$, SD $= 0.12$, N $= 1136$; mean $= 0.04$, SD $= 0.19$, N $= 326$; t(406.19) $= -4.78$, p $= 0.00$, Cohen's d $= 0.38$). The ENA difference graph in Fig. 6 shows the strongest connection between Platforms for Delivery and Access to Care in tweets with a negative sentiment, depicted by the thicker, more saturated orange line across the X-axis.

4 Discussion

This study compared the publicly-held perceptions on telehealth from healthcare professionals on Twitter in 2019 and 2020 using sentiment analysis and ENA. Our sentiment analysis found a similar valence in positive, negative, and neutral tweets in both years. Overall healthcare professional sentiment in tweets on telehealth was positive. Examination of the epistemic network graphs found significant differences across the X-axis for the 2019 and 2020 comparison and positive and negative sentiment comparison. The COVID-19 pandemic influenced the shift in perceptions on telehealth in 2020. In 2019, the strongest connections between codes were from Platforms for Delivery to Access to Care and Perceived Innovation. In 2020, there were stronger connections between Platforms for Delivery to Access to Care and Safe Delivery of Care. The ENA model comparing positive and negative sentiment found the strongest connection between Platforms for Delivery and Access to Care, indicating underlying concerns of telehealth providing patient access to care despite the majority of tweets conveying a positive sentiment. Issues surrounding access are concerning given the impact that COVID-19 is having on people's mental health in particular [3].

The ENA analysis of the tweets suggests that the connection between Platforms for Delivery, Access to Care, and Innovation in Care in 2019 was due to the lack of wide-scale adoption of telehealth in healthcare systems in the United States. 2019 tweets appeared to focus more on the innovation of building and investing in telehealth technologies as a way for patients to access care. Additionally, the connection between Patient Connection and Constraints of Physical Examination also provides evidence that in 2019, there may have been more focus on the potential drawbacks of not being physically present with a patient as a reason not to adopt telehealth practices.

The comparison ENA model for 2020 more strongly connects Safe Delivery of Care to Platforms for Delivery and Access to Care. This suggests a shift in perception of telehealth from an innovation to a needed instrument in the safe access and delivery of care. Because the COVID-19 pandemic required the implementation of social distancing measures that consist of limited physical contact, and due to concerns of increased strain on hospitals, tweets in 2020 focused on advocating for telehealth systems as a response. They seemed to prioritize practical implementation through focusing on a relaxation of licensing and physician liability, as well as insurance coverage and reimbursement on the state and federal levels, especially pushing Medicaid and Medicare coverage. Several examples of tweets and the associated subcodes are included in Table 2.

Table 2. Examples of connections between coded tweets

Year	Example tweet	Subcode name
2020	#Medicaid must implement this across the nation. The disproportionate burden of disease will undoubtedly fall on the poor & working class. Use cell phones & let docs like me counsel and assess via #telemedicine. There should be a specific funding stream for #FQHCs.#coronavirus	Insurance Coverage, Safe Delivery of Care, Access to Care
2020	Disruptive events that lead to crisis are a source of progress! #COVID19 offer the opportunity to learn, innovate and improve #PatientCare. Great example of how med rec is optimized with Telehealth	Patient Connection, Perceived Innovation
2020	Hospitals and ERs should be adopting a "virtual front line" to deal with this impending #COVID19 crisis. Now is the time for #Telemedicine to serve as a screening tool, prevent exposures, reduce waiting rooms full of both healthy and ill people	Access to Care, Safe Delivery of Care

Although perceptions of telehealth were generally positive and a role for it in healthcare was favored overall, logistical and administrative drawbacks persisted among healthcare professionals. Tweets with a negative sentiment overwhelmingly emphasized telehealth Platforms for Delivery impacting Access to Care, touching on data privacy concerns and lack of insurance coverage for patients and reimbursement for healthcare professionals. Though technology issues were rarely mentioned as a cause for concern, data privacy, security, liability, and confidentiality were trends in 2019 and 2020 in tweets with a negative sentiment. ENA allowed us to examine and interpret the connections among topics that came up in tweets with both positive and negative valence across the two years to better understand how perceptions and opinions have shifted and what affordances and challenges are expressed [13].

Findings from our analysis indicate that COVID-19 impacted healthcare professionals' perceptions of telehealth from a possible innovative tool to a priority to be implemented in order to ensure safe access and delivery of care. These findings are consistent with increased telehealth visits reported by healthcare systems [4]. The publicly held perceptions on telehealth also align with previous work indicating that telehealth can provide effective healthcare delivery to patients exhibiting COVID-19 symptoms and care to those wishing to reduce the likelihood of transmission in the hospital [2]. Data from this study allowed us to explore the publicly held opinions of healthcare professionals on telehealth. A next step is to add more information to our data as to patient public perception on telehealth, which will allow us to better understand their perspectives on access and delivery of care. In addition, exploring differences between healthcare professionals' perceptions based on discipline could provide a more nuanced understanding of which specialties are more conducive and receptive to telehealth.

There were limitations to this study and its conclusions. While Twitter is a social media platform with a variety of users, it is limited by those who use it. There are a small number of healthcare professionals on Twitter, and though they were the focus of this study, we cannot claim to have a full representation of healthcare professionals' sentiments as a whole. A common form of interaction on Twitter are retweets, the reposting of another user's tweet. Despite indicating an agreement with the users tweet, this interaction would be lost in our deletion of duplicates in the data. We are also limited by our tools to gather tweets, which can lack precision in completely scraping Twitter data. Tweets were analyzed and coded based on the scraped text, and we did not investigate articles, images, or any html linked within the tweet. This represents a significant limitation in our contextual and in-depth understanding of the tweet. Additional limitations included the omission of non-English language tweets and our overall small sample size. This limits the generalizability of our findings and emphasizes the need for ongoing research as conversations on telehealth systems continue. It is also important to note that telehealth refers to a variety of platforms and technologies, which were not distinguished in this study. Future research should examine healthcare professionals' sentiment based on technology type and delivery method.

5 Conclusions

In conclusion, this study indicates that healthcare professionals on Twitter have a positive perception towards telehealth overall in both 2019 and 2020. Furthermore, the COVID-19 pandemic shifted the conversation away from potential innovation and drawbacks to push safe access and delivery of care through the infrastructure and administrative expansion of telehealth platforms in the United States. These findings suggest that increasing access and prioritization of telehealth services as a result of COVID-19 may lessen future organizational hurdles in implementation and promote safe delivery and access to care through telehealth.

References

1. Zucco, C., Bella, S., Paglia, C., Tabarini, P., Cannataro, M.: Predicting abandonment in telehomecare programs using sentiment analysis: a system proposal. In: IEEE International Conference on Bioinformatics and Biomedicine (BIBM), pp. 1734–1739 (2018)
2. Moore, J.H., et al.: Ideas for how informaticians can get involved with COVID-19 research. BioData Min. **13**(1), 1–16 (2020)
3. Zhou, X., et al.: The role of telehealth in reducing the mental health burden from COVID-19. Telemed e-Health **26**(4), 377–379 (2020)
4. Virtual Care: Access Michigan Medicine Healthcare Online. University of Michigan (2020)
5. Rosenbaum, E.: Robotic medicine may be the weapon the world needs to combat the coronavirus. CNBC (2020)
6. Smith, A.C., et al.: Telehealth for global emergencies: implications for coronavirus disease 2019 (COVID-19). J. Telemed. Telecare. **26**(5), 309–313 (2020)
7. Hollander, J.E., Carr, B.G.: Virtually Perfect? Telemedicine for COVID-19. N. Engl. J. Med. **382**(18), 1679–1681 (2020)
8. Talpada, H., Halgamuge, M.N., Tran Quoc Vinh, N.: An analysis on use of deep learning and lexical-semantic based sentiment analysis method on twitter data to understand the demographic trend of telemedicine. In: 11th International Conference on Knowledge and Systems Engineering (KSE), Da Nang, pp. 1–9 (2019)
9. Stine, R.A.: Sentiment analysis. Annu. Rev. Stat. Appl. **6**, 287–308 (2019)
10. Kušen, E., Strembeck, M.: Politics, sentiments, and misinformation: an analysis of the Twitter discussion on the 2016 Austrian Presidential Elections. Online Soc. Netw. Media [Internet] **5**, 37–50 (2018). https://doi.org/10.1016/j.osnem.2017.12.002
11. Hassan, A.U., Hussain, J., Hussain, M., Sadiq, M., Lee, S.: Sentiment analysis of social networking sites (SNS) data using machine learning approach for the measurement of depression. In: International Conference on Information and Communication Technology Convergence (ICTC), pp. 138–40, Jeju 2017
12. Zou, X., Yang, J., Zhang, J.: Microblog sentiment analysis using social and topic context. PLoS ONE **13**(2), 1–24 (2018)
13. Shaffer, D.W.: Quantitative Ethnography. Cathcart Press, Madison (2017)
14. Sullivan, S., et al.: Using epistemic network analysis to identify targets for educational interventions in trauma team communication. Surg. (United States) [Internet] **163**(4), 938–43 (2018). https://doi.org/10.1016/j.surg.2017.11.009
15. Wooldridge, A.R., Carayon, P., Shaffer, D.W., Eagan, B.: Human factors case study of task-allocation communication in. ISE Trans. Heal. Syst. Eng. **8**(1), 72–82 (2019)
16. Demsar, J., et al.: Orange: data mining toolbox in Python. J. Mach. Learn. Res. **14**(1), 2349–2353 (2013)
17. Hu, M., Liu, B.: Mining and summarizing customer reviews. In: KDD-2004 – Proceedings of the Tenth ACM SIGKDD International Conference on Knowledge Discovery and Data Mining, pp. 168–177 (2004)

18. Hsieh, H.F., Shannon, S.E.: Three approaches to qualitative content analysis. Qual. Health Res. **15**(9), 1277–1288 (2005)
19. Shaffer, D.W., Collier, W., Ruis, A.R.: A tutorial on epistemic network analysis: analyzing the structure of connections in cognitive, social, and interaction data. J. Learn. Anal. **3**(3), 9–45 (2016)
20. Shaffer, D.W., Ruis, A.R.: Epistemic network analysis: a worked example of theory-based learning analytics. Handb. Learn. Anal., 175–87 (2017)
21. Marquart, C.L., Hinojosa, C., Swiecki, Z., Eagan, B., Shaffer, D.W.: Epistemic Network Analysis [Internet] (2018). http://app.epistemicnetwork.org
22. Siebert-evenstone, A.L., Collier, W., Ruis, A.R., Shaffer, D.W.: In search of conversational grain size: modelling semantic structure using moving stanza windows Golnaz Arastoopour Irgens Wisconsin Center for Education Research University of Wisconsin – Madison, United States University of Wisconsin – Madison. Unite. J Learn Anal. **4**(3), 123–139 (2017)
23. Arastoopour, G., Shaffer, D.W., Swiecki, Z., Ruis, A.R., Chesler, N.C.: Teaching and assessing engineering design thinking with virtual internships and epistemic network analysis. Int. J. Eng. Educ. **32**(3), 1492–1501 (2016)

Governmental Response to the COVID-19 Pandemic - A Quantitative Ethnographic Comparison of Public Health Authorities' Communication in Denmark, Norway, and Sweden

Karoline Schnaider[1]([✉]), Stefano Schiavetto[2], Florian Meier[3], Barbara Wasson[4], Benjamin Brink Allsopp[3], and Daniel Spikol[5]

[1] Umeå University, Umeå, Sweden
karoline.schnaider@umu.se
[2] State University of Campinas, Campinas, Brazil
s072392@dac.unicamp.br
[3] Aalborg University, Copenhagen, Copenhagen, Denmark
{fmeier,bbal}@hum.aau.dk
[4] University of Bergen, Bergen, Norway
barbara.wasson@uib.no
[5] Malmö University, Malmö, Sweden
daniel.spikol@mau.se

Abstract. The Scandinavian countries are often seen as a unity. However, during the COVID-19 pandemic striking differences on how the countries approached the crisis became evident. This quantitative-ethnographic (QE) study aimed to understand political and cultural similarities and differences between the three Scandinavian countries – Denmark, Norway and Sweden – through their crisis communications during the COVID-19 pandemic. Specifically, we focused on how the health authorities of the three countries, in their press releases, treated information about COVID-19 and acted in four fields: reorganization of population behavior, containment of viral transmission, preparation of health systems, and management of socioeconomic impacts. As a methodology, the QE tools nCoder and ENA were applied, respectively: to code the press releases and to correlate the treatment of information with the four fields of action.

Keywords: COVID-19 · Pandemic · Crisis communication · Quantitative ethnography

1 Introduction

Crisis communication is the 'collection, processing and dissemination of information required to address a crisis situation' [4, p. 20]. Studying and evaluating communication strategies in health crisis situations is essential as their effectiveness reduces negative impact and prevents casualties. Research in crisis communication has rarely taken a comparative perspective as most investigations are limited to single case studies [20].

© Springer Nature Switzerland AG 2021
A. R. Ruis and S. B. Lee (Eds.): ICQE 2021, CCIS 1312, pp. 406–421, 2021.
https://doi.org/10.1007/978-3-030-67788-6_28

We take the global pandemic, caused by the SARS-CoV-2 coronavirus (COVID-19) as an opportunity to undergo one of the first comparisons of crisis communication strategies across three Scandinavian countries.

On March 11, 2020 the World Health Organization (WHO) started to characterize the spread of COVID-19 as a global pandemic [28]. During an ongoing pandemic, the media, the government, and public health professionals and institutes play a central role in crisis communication and risk management as they inform the public about the vulnerability to the disease and suggest "measures to control the spread of the disease such as the promotion of individual protection (face masks and hygiene), imposing travel restrictions, and social distancing" [30]. The Trust and Confidence Model suggests that how the public estimates the risk associated with the disease and its willingness to comply with the mentioned countermeasures is strongly dependent on the level of trust and confidence people have in the government and its institution [26]. Research shows that people with a higher level of trust in the government are more likely to comply with what the authorities suggest [19,29,30]. However, groups of people, depending on their socioeconomic, psychological and cultural background, conceptualize risk differently and take different stands towards recommended measures [8,29]. This suggests that how a health crisis is framed and how the public is informed about the risk of a disease and the measures to control it will, to a large degree, depend on the cultural values in a country, as well as the governmental organization and the citizens relation to the state [27]. Thus, a central question is how authorities frame the crisis, communicate the countermeasures, inform about the risks and thus build up that trust among citizens.

As COVID-19 spread around the world, governments reacted in different ways. We analyze the differences in crisis communication of governmental health institutions in Scandinavia at the beginning of the spread of the COVID-19 pandemic in Spring 2020. In particular, we use the press releases published by health authorities between January and April in each country. Scandinavia is a sub region in Northern Europe, covering the three kingdoms of Denmark, Norway, and Sweden. The relation between these countries is characterized by strong historical, cultural, and linguistic ties, which leads to the Scandinavian countries often being considered a homogeneous unity. From a political perspective, the three countries are similar in that they developed a welfare state model where citizens have a high trust in the government [9,11,12]. Despite their salient closeness in culture and politics, during the COVID-19 pandemic significant differences between the countries became evident. While Denmark and Norway seemingly pursued a similar way in terms of their precautionary measures by giving clear instructions for hygiene, social distancing, etc. Sweden's government refrained from taking legally enforced measures such as closing schools, and decided to take a different path with the cost of many more deaths[1]. Acknowledging the differences between the Scandinavian countries, and especially their different reaction to the pandemic, lead to the following research question:

What similarities and differences can be found between the governmental response to the corona crisis in Denmark, Norway, and Sweden through their respective crisis communication strategies conveyed through the public health authorities' press releases?

---

[1] https://ourworldindata.org/grapher/total-deaths-covid-19?country=DNK~NOR~SWE.

To study this question, we use methods from quantitative ethnography to investigate the different responses to the pandemic situation in Denmark, Norway, and Sweden, and people's relationship to the state. During our coding and analysis, two groups of codes – somewhat aligning with Salious' [23] two types of information during a pandemic – were identified as a starting point for understanding the discourses conveyed by the health authorities in the datasets: (1) what sources of information were considered and prioritized by the governments, e.g., statistics on the global spread or information on the symptoms that the virus causes; and (2) the actions taken by the governments e.g., to monitor and regulate people's behavior or equip the healthcare system for the challenge. We developed eight codes and organized them into two frames: four regarding information (sources) and four regarding actions. Our approach revealed significant differences between the countries regarding how the pandemic was framed. While Norway's and Sweden's crisis management followed a clear discourse, Denmark's framing was more difficult to interpret.

We continue by presenting the sociological background of our study as well as relevant empirical work from crisis communication research, before we present our data collection strategy.

2   Background and Related Work

To structure our investigation of how the three Scandinavian countries responded and acted in reaction to COVID-19 we needed to base our interpretation in political culture. This cultural approach was the basis for how we conceptualized the crisis communication the different governments adopted and allowed us to analyze the potential differences between them. Once we grounded our theoretical approach we are able to investigate crisis communication in the three countries.

2.1   Pandemic and Crisis Communication as Political Culture

Throughout the history of the social sciences, culture, in general, has been conceptualized from different perspectives. In the vast epistemological and methodological diversity, Cuche affirms the relevance of this concept to social sciences and explains the diversity of human unity beyond the biological body, by focusing on the ways of acting, thinking and feeling of individuals that are defined by socio-historical dynamics. [5, pp. 9–15].

In this context, the ways that Scandinavian countries treated information regarding COVID-19 and acted in the reordering of population behavior, the containment of viral transmission, and the reorganization of health systems, are under cultural determinations. In specific, in order to understand similarities and differences between Scandinavian countries in how they handled information and acted in relation to COVID-19, it can be considered that press releases from health authorities are relevant because of how they manifest individual variants of *habitus*. These consist of "generative schemes" [2] of ways of acting, thinking and feeling of individuals, as their socialization processes lead to the internalization of values, norms and other social principles, which underlie their readings of the world, their rational choices and other individual and social actions. They are predispositions to act, think and feel, which are "structured and structuring structures" of socio-historical dynamics between individuals in continuous socialization that, because of un-interruptibility of social interactions, keep updating these predispositions.

If we consider a social group in a macro-social perspective, such as the culture of a country, in order to differentiate Danes, Norwegians, and Swedes in responding to the COVID-19 pandemic, we need to consider that the choices of the authorities and the actions of the population are immersed in great social-historical syntheses that are structured as much as they are structuring structures of generative schemes. Thus, we can understand that the decision-making individual, as a health authority, "reveals itself as a 'structural variant' of the *habitus* of its group or class, [and] the personal style appears as a codified deviation in relation to the style of an era, a class or a social group" [18, p. 18]. In this way, governmental and population actions in pandemic situations, such as COVID-19, observed in press releases by health authorities, are empirical sources for studies about *habitus*, and henceforth express cultures of different social groups and countries.

Regarding the Scandinavian countries, the populations' *habitus* are by decades in relation to strong welfare states and high level of trust in government [13–15]. However, these countries' cultural differences have led to distinct polyarchies [6], in this paper addressed especially in the differences between distribution of power within the constitutional monarchies and citizens' relationship with the State. Moreover, elements of the *habitus* of each country are addressed - ethopoliticality in Sweden, to "act fast and with force" in Denmark and the more careful approach to individual rights in Norway.

2.2 Empirical Work in Crisis Communication

Research in communicating health emergencies have identified the need for unique forms of risk and crisis communication. Saliou's [23] investigation in crisis communication singled out two types of emergency information that are most important; preventive and reactive messages. Reynolds and Quinn [21] highlighted trust, creditably, and empathetic communication as essential elements for persuasive communication in influenza pandemics. Multiple studies investigate the risk perception and government trust during epidemics and how public health messages are heard, interpreted, and the responses studied [30]. However, the focus of our study is less on the reaction of the people and more on how authorities communicate information and actions.

The COVID-19 pandemic is still ongoing, however research on crisis communication has been part of a large body published articles investigating all aspects of the epidemic. Early research on crisis communication during the COVID-19 pandemic in the US shows that even within a country, political leaders and media outlets are having divergent ways of framing the crisis and its severity highlighting partisan differences [1]. Many researchers mentioned the problem of the infodemic that accompanies the pandemic: which makes it much harder to build trust in what the government says [10,17].

In summary, it is understood that ways of thinking and acting by government institutions and local populations, which are part of political cultures, in this article observed in the response of Denmark, Norway and Sweden to the current pandemic situation, are intimately linked to socio-historical readings of the world by individuals under "generative schemes" of *habitus*. In specific, the "ways of thinking and acting" are under the eight codes selected to interpret the crisis communication of health authorities in Scandinavian countries: on one hand, information regarding COVID-19 biology, illness, spread and monitoring; on other hand, actions regarding healthcare system, financial system, government response and population response (see Table 2).

3   Data Collection, Processing and Coding

To investigate our research question we decided to use the press releases published by the health agencies of the three Scandinavian countries. The activities of the public health authorities in the three countries were similar in scope and intensity, and therefore considered viable objects for comparison. Thus, we took the press releases from the following three agencies:

Statens Serum Institut[2] (SSI) is under the auspices of the Danish Ministry of Health. The main duty is to ensure preparedness against infectious diseases and biological threats as well as control of congenital disorders. **Folkehelseinstitutet**[3] (FHI), the Norwegian Institute of Public Health, is a government agency under the Ministry of Health and Care Services. FHI provides knowledge about the health status in the population, influencing factors and how it can be improved; they also have competence in infectious disease control. **Folkhälsomyndigheten**[4] (FYI), the Public Health Agency of Sweden, has national responsibility for public health issues and works to ensure good public health. The agency also works to ensure that the population is protected against communicable diseases and other health threats.

3.1   Data Collection

To collect the different press releases, we used Octoparse[5] to scrape the health authorities press releases from their respective web presences over a time frame from the beginning of January to the end of April 2020. In a next step, we used R and the tidytext[6] package to clean and process the documents. First, we deleted non-COVID-19 related press releases and cleaned the remaining text from HTML tags, etc. Moreover, we tokenized the press releases into sentences that we used as stanzas in our coding process which can be considered our window size for looking at connections later. Following the cleaning process we translated each stanza from its respective language into English using the GOOGLETRANSLATE[7] function in Google Sheets. Finally, the two central tools in quantitative ethnographic research, nCoder[8] and Epistemic Network Analysis[9]

---

[2] https://en.ssi.dk/.

[3] https://www.fhi.no/en/.

[4] https://www.folkhalsomyndigheten.se/.

[5] https://www.octoparse.com/.

[6] https://cran.r-project.org/web/packages/tidytext/vignettes/tidytext.html.

[7] https://support.google.com/docs/answer/3093331?hl=en.

[8] http://www.n-coder.org/.

[9] http://www.epistemicnetwork.org/.

(ENA), were employed by coding the press releases in nCoder and visualizing the outcome of the coding process using ENA.

Table 1. Descriptive statistics of the dataset.

Institute	# press releases	avg. # tokens per release	# stanzas (i.e. coded units)
SSI (Denmark)	42	348.1	752
FHI (Norway)	71	257.6	955
FYI (Sweden)	58	249.9	717

Table 1 summarises descriptive statistics of our dataset. All in all, the applied data collection process resulted in a total of 171 press releases with 42 from the Danish SSI, 71 from Norwegian FHI, and 58 from the Swedish FYI. While press releases published by the Norwegian and Swedish health institutes are on average of similar length (FHI 257.6 vs FYI 249.9 tokens), the Danish press releases are quite longer with 348.1 tokens on average. When looking at the number of stanzas the Norwegian FHI accounts for most stanzas in the dataset (955), which aligns with the fact that they also published the most press releases during the period of analysis.

3.2 Coding Process

An iterative four-phase feedback loop guided the coding process. The three initial phases of the coding process followed the circle for interpretation and understanding of the datasets proposed by Shaffer [25]. The fourth, final coding process, followed the test-retest reliability of nCoder [25].

Phase (1), Planning: This phase involved setting team focus, brainstorming, making hypotheses, and development of the first codes. The coding process was initiated from the primary focus of the study, i.e. the differences in crisis communication and the discourse (narrative framing) of the Scandinavian countries with a focus on the peoples relationship to the state. From this overarching focus, two key themes were identified as a starting point for understanding the structure of the discourses in the datasets: (1) the information sources and (2) the response (actions) of the governments.

After the themes were discussed, joint brainstorming sessions were conducted to find keywords, subsequently used in the development of codes. Therefore, the first strategy was to visualize the health press releases from the health agencies in the form of a comparison cloud (Fig. 1) that enabled identification of the most common keywords linked to each country's discourse. Based on the size and color of words, the relative frequency throughout the corpus was visually indicated. However, it should be noted that if a keyword such as "health" or "general" only appeared in one colour, it did not mean that other authorities did not use that word, but that this authority was the one that used the word most frequently. The second strategy was to watch YouTube videos from various press conferences held by the three countries' governments and ministries. Both strategies had the purpose of collecting and defining keywords and

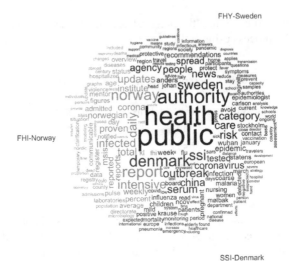

Fig. 1. Comparison wordcloud visualizing the most frequent words used by each health agency.

helping with hypotheses modeling. Thus, hypotheses were created from the two focus themes and the findings made in the brainstorming process. For example, the initial hypothesis concerned how the three countries would differ in how people acted individually and collectively as a response to measures taken, if states were to adopt a proactive or reactive strategy for control, and if the economic status and issues regarding illness, spread, and health care would be other contrasts.

All coding was carried out using the nCoder software and followed the three-step rating process. Thereto, all codes were modeled using a binary (present/not present) decision [7]. In the first phase of the coding process, the following codes were tested: People's response, Duty of the state, COVID-related, Economy, Epidemic, Healthcare, and Sickness. Since the first test did not reach a Kappa > 0.9 for the level of agreement (and with a Rho > 0.05) between human and classifier, a second review of the dataset was conducted.

Phase (2), Refinement of codes: A second review of the datasets belonging to the health authorities was carried out by manual screening. As the same hypotheses still governed the work, the search resulted in more advanced keywords. New codes tested in phase 2 of the coding process were: Healthcare, Government actions, Government response – Financial, Intelligence2, and Peoples relationship to the state.

Phase (3), Additional tests: Phase 3 of the coding process specifically focused on discourse around health-related phenomena. The following codes were selected and tested based on previous examinations of the data sets: Epidemic, Health Care System, Biology of the Disease, and Illness. As test sets from coding phase 2 and 3 did not reach the level of agreement between human vs. classifier with a Kappa < 0.9 (Rho > 0.05), a final, fourth, coding round was initiated.

Phase (4), Test-retest: Through ongoing discussions, a consensus on keywords was reached among the members of the research group, based partly on the research focus and partly on the importance of the keywords in relation to the discourses in the data sets. Therefore, the initial phases were essential in order to enable reliable and valid codes while reducing bias. After a high level of agreement was reached using a specific test-set (Kappa > 0.9 and Rho < 0.05), subsequent steps in nCoder were completed with acceptable values for inter-rater reliability and validity for the entire dataset.

Table 2 presents the results of the four-phase process, i.e. the final coding scheme. In the remains of the paper, codes will be highlighted as seen in this table based on their type as information codes and action codes.

Table 2. The final coding scheme presenting the codes, their description, keywords and type. The codes were used in an automatic coding process via nCoder.

Code	Description	Keywords	Type
Illness	Discourse that addresses the human symptoms and body reactions.	Fever, Respiratory, breath, cough, throat, pain, vomit, asympto, transmit, sick, symptom, flu	Information
Biology of the Disease	Discourse characteristics of nCoV, how it relates to other viruses, and how it is biologically transmitted between people.	Sars, ncov, mers, communicable, virus	Information
Epidemic Spread	Discourse about the spread of the virus on a global and a national level as well as related to social activities and locations.	Abroad, Market, Spread, Outbreak, Epidemi, Pandemi, Contamin, Contageous, Drop, Surface, Crowd, Gathering, Wuhan, China, Fish, Seafood, Abroad	Information
Monitoring Stats	Compilations of cumulative and numerical nature, such as reports, and calculations regarding the number of those hospitalized or ill.	Report, Rate, Statistic, Monitor, Register, Number, Total, Figure, Graph	Information
Healthcare System	Healthcare system-related materiality - entities such as laboratories, doctors, and practices such as intensive care, hospitals, and hospitalization	Microbiolog, Laborator, Nurs, Doctor, Worker, Professional, Admit, Intensive, Care, Hospital, Patient	Action
Financial	Discourse addressing the nations financial situations, and initiatives related to the states economy.	Money, Budget, Unemploy, Financ, Econom, Cost	Action
Peoples Responsibilities Response	Discourse addressing peoples actions to follow recommendations and prevent spread.	Distanc, Distancing, Hygiene, Wash, Soap	Action
Government Response Control	Discourse regarding government's actions to monitor and assess the situation and to recommend and regulate people's behavior	Guideline, Information, Measures, Measuring, Recommend, Recommendation, Monitor, Monitoring, Assess, Assessment, Advice	Action

4 Results and Analysis

To answer our main research question of whether we can identify differences in the health crisis communication of the three Scandinavian countries, we started our analysis by looking at Fig. 2 which showed the three main subtraction networks created via ENA on the basis of our coded data. The subtraction networks show each country's centroid in the form of a square with dotted boxes, which indicate their confidence intervals (CI) in both dimensions of the projection space. A centroid summarises each network as a single point in the projection space and allows for an easy comparison of a large number of networks as the position explains the variance between the networks. The centroids for all three countries are distributed far away from each other with non-overlapping CIs, which was the first indicator that differences existed in how the discourse about the health crisis was framed in each country. Non-parametric Mann-Whitney tests supported this observation statistically. Along the first dimension (x-axis) all three countries are distributed significantly differently from each other. (DK-SE: $Mdn = 0.39$, $N = 58$, $U = 685.00$, $p = 0.00$, $r = 0.44$; DK-NO: $Mdn = 0.19$, $N = 42$, $U = 640.50$, $p = 0.00$, $r = 0.57$; NO-SE: $Mdn = 0.39$, $N = 58$, $U = 514.50$, $p = 0.00$, $r = 0.75$). Along the second dimension (y-axis), only Denmark and Norway showed statistically significant differences ($Mdn = 0.19$, $N = 42$, $U = 2043.50$, $p = 0.00$, $r = -0.37$), that allowed for the conclusion that they also

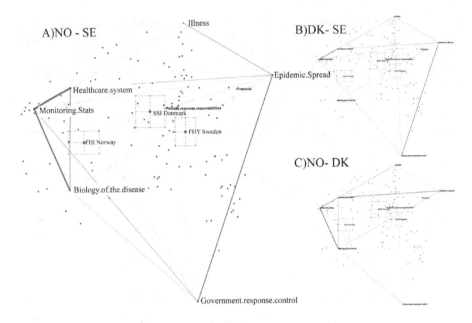

Fig. 2. Subtraction networks for all three country combinations A) Norway-Sweden, B) Denmark-Sweden and C) Norway-Denmark. The distribution of the centroids hints to a clear difference in crisis communication among the three countries.

shared some similarities in how they communicated. All in all, this indicated clearly that Denmark, Norway, and Sweden communicated very differently during the pandemic and had divergent centres of attention in the framing of the discourse, but they also shared some common themes.

4.1   Differences in Crisis Communication

To determine which codes account for the differences between the networks of two countries, two signals were used. First, we looked at the position of the centroids (the bounding boxes) in relation to the position of the codes (dots). Second, we compared the weighted connection (thickness of lines) in each subtraction network. Here we looked for thicker ties (lines), which indicated stronger differences, and the colour of the tie, which provided information on which of the two countries involved has a stronger connection between the two codes. Norway's centroid (compared to DK and SE) sat closer to the codes Monitoring Stats, Biology of the Disease and Healthcare System. Furthermore, in both subtraction plots, we observed thick blue ties between the codes, which indicated that these three codes are highly central for Norway's framing of the pandemic and its health agency's crisis communication. Sweden, on the other hand, is the country whose centroid sat closest to Epidemic Spread. Compared to Norway and Denmark, Sweden's emphasis was positioned clearly on the relation between Epidemic Spread and Government Response Control. A less clear picture emerged for Denmark as its

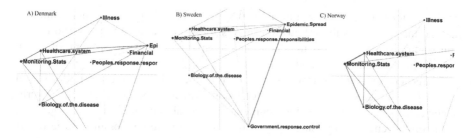

Fig. 3. Close-up views of the mean epistemic networks to illustrate the different relationships between the codes for A) Denmark, B) Sweden and C) Norway.

centroid was between Norway and Sweden (see Fig. 2). Compared to Norway, Denmark placed a stronger focus on Epidemic Spread and Healthcare System, whereas the tie between Epidemic Spread and Monitoring Stats differentiates it clearly from Sweden. To get a clearer picture of what these differences in tie strength mean for the individual countries' crisis communication, Sect. 4.2 takes a closer look at each country's mean epistemic network.

4.2 The Discourse on the Scandinavian Countries' Communication of the COVID-19 Pandemic

An analysis process based on four levels was used to explore each country's crisis communication and discourse around the pandemic. In level 1, we performed a simple visual analysis of the network and took note of the ties between codes. Level 2 relates the codes involved in strong ties to their type, i.e. information or action codes. Level 3 aimed at an even deeper understanding of the ties by relating the codes involved to their descriptions and keywords (see Table 2). In the final and fourth level the interpretative loop was closed by relating the quantitative results to the qualitative data, i.e. quotes from the health agencies press releases (stanzas) as seen in previous quantitative ethnographic work [24].

Norway. Figure 3B) visualises Norway's mean epistemic network. The network indicates a strong relationship between the four codes Healthcare System, Monitoring Stats, Biology of the Disease and Government Response Control. The action code Healthcare System is strongly tied to the sources of information Monitoring Stats and Biology of the Disease and stands in relation to the action code Government Response Control. This can be interpreted as the actions regarding equipping laboratories, the increment of medical staff and admission rates to hospitals, as well as investments in a capacity such as intensive care, were mainly influenced by three factors: (a) accumulated information and facts referring to numbers and figures on the national level such as reports and registers, (b) information on the coronavirus and how it transfers between humans bodies; and (c) actions taken by the government to monitor and assess the situation and to recommend and regulate people's behavior. The information that supplemented the specific actions taken by the healthcare system were publicly presented and communicated to the citizens as the following excerpts show: "there are a total of 166 people with confirmed SARS-CoV-2 that have been admitted to intensive care unit, of which 104 are still hospitalized" (ID:1154).

Moreover, Government Response Control is connected to the source of information Monitoring Stats and the action code Healthcare System. This indicates that governmental actions were mainly fed by accumulated national information (Monitoring stats) on the effectiveness of measures. The following quote exemplifies this: "The report concludes that the measures implemented have reduced infection figures considerably." (ID:1088).

Finally, the following excerpt from the press releases shows how the public was informed about the relation between government actions (Government Response Control) and the effects for the healthcare system (Healthcare System): "such a strategy has four assumptions: increased testing, and improved surveillance, a good understanding of the situation so that we can quickly discover traits that may require adjustments to the infection control measures, and restructuring the business of health care." (ID:855)

Sweden. Sweden's epistemic network (Fig. 3C) indicates a strong tie between Government Response Control and Epidemic Spread, which can be explained by the fact that the government actions were mainly informed by sources of information regarding the spread of the virus. Furthermore, a strong tie between Epidemic Spread and Illness can be observed. This indicates that the actions taken by the government to monitor and assess the situation and to recommend and regulate people's behavior was mainly influenced by the information on the spread of the virus on a global and a national level, as well as related to social activities and locations. Additionally, the information around the spread of the virus was linked to the information gathered around the human symptoms and body reactions (Illness). The information available about the spread was used to inform governmental actions, e.g. actions on creating guidelines and how such measures (Government Response Control) were generally used to prevent contamination between people (Epidemic Spread). The Swedish FYI communicated these guidelines and additionally tried to justify them by adding contextual information that informed the decision making process. This was seen in press release excerpts such as the following: "public health authorities have decided to change the Agency's regulations and general guidelines (HSLF-FS 2020:12) on everyone's responsibility to prevent contamination of COVID-19 and make an exception for children and young people." (ID:1786). However, we also saw that more information did not necessarily lead to any changes in the means to address the disease: "the assessments of risk and the important strategies and measures presented in recent days remain - Now that WHO has now declared that COVID-19 is a pandemic does not make a difference in how we manage the disease." (ID: 2197). The relationship between how the coronavirus spreads (Epidemic.Spread) and how it affected individuals (Illness), is shown by the following example: "Infections, Infectiousness and Infection Risks COVID-19 infects from person to person through drip and contact infections, that is, via drops and secretions from the airways that spread when someone coughs or sneezes, and at close contact between people." (ID: 1968)

Denmark. The press releases published by the Danish authorities, as seen in Fig. 3C), indicate a strong relation between Healthcare System and three codes covering sources of information: Monitoring Stats, Epidemic Spread and Illness. Similar to the Norwegian authorities, the Danes informed the public on how they base the actions taken regarding the healthcare system, i.e. equipping laboratories, the increase of medical staff and investments in capacity such as intensive care were on (a) accumulated information and facts referring to numbers and figures on the national level such as reports and registers, (b) information around the spread of the virus on a global and a national level, as well as related to social activities and location, and (c) the information on the human symptoms and body reactions: "now that it is primarily in patients with severe symptoms who tested positive we work hard to put monitoring systems up that also can follow the spread of infection in the community, such as by random testing of people who have contacted the doctor with mild symptoms [...] confirmed COVID-19 event in Denmark the 1044 cases, 672 men and 372 women aged 0–94 years" (ID: 365). Furthermore, Epidemic Spread has a strong relationship with Biology of the Disease, which indicates that the press releases commented on how the virus spreads on a global and national level through social activities and specific locations (e.g., nursing homes) and linked it to information on how the virus transfers between human bodies. Finally, the analysis of the Danish press releases link Government Response Control to Monitoring Stats, and reveal a mutual relationship to Healthcare System. This indicated that the actions taken by the government to monitor and assess the situation lead to accumulated information and facts referring to numbers and figures in reports and public health registers, which were made publicly accessible. In addition, the actions taken by the government to monitor and assess the situation are linked to Healthcare System, i.e. the actions around equipping laboratories, increment of medical staff and so forth. These activities, carried out to improve the healthcare system, are supported by the government's efforts to mitigate the consequences of viral transmission (Government Response Control), as exemplified by the following quote: "The new guidelines from SST practice this update criteria for suspicious coronavirus infection, and instructions for handling patients and contacts to match the latest knowledge about the disease, infection risk, etc." (ID:608).

However, one has to acknowledge that crisis communication during the corona pandemic was and is still an evolving process where actions by the government might get updated later as compared to earlier reports, as the following excerpt indicates: "the new infections, which is the first in Denmark, does not change the current risk assessment that State Serum Institute and the Board of Health issued on Tuesday, the assessment is that there is low risk that we see widespread infection in Danish society, and low risk that our health care system is challenged." (ID:500).

In the next and final section, we discuss our findings by linking them back to our background and related work presented in Sect. 2.

5   Discussion and Conclusion

In this article, we addressed the question of how different health authorities in Denmark, Norway, and Sweden framed crisis communication during the COVID-19 crisis in early months of 2020 (January through the end of March). We applied a quantitative ethnographic approach by the use of nCoder for the automatic coding of press release data.

Additionally, we visualized the relation of these codes using ENA. Our main results can be summarized as follows: On the one hand, some of the codes that we developed to cover the discourse around the pandemic (e.g., Monitoring Stats, Epidemic Spread, and Healthcare System), occurred much more frequently than others, which hinted at similarities in the countries' press release reports. On the other hand, the subtraction networks (Fig. 2) showed a significant difference in each country's framing, which was surprising given their sociocultural closeness. In the following paragraph, we discuss our findings from the perspective of political cultures and polyarchies, and how the concept of *habitus* can be interpreted as constitutive of generative schemes reflecting peoples ways of acting and thinking.

A central finding is Sweden's closeness to the code Epidemic Spread and the strong tie the code builds to Government Response Control. The frequent co-occurrence of these two codes and the tie they form separated Sweden's discourse strongly from the crisis communication of its neighbouring countries. This characteristic of Sweden's crisis communication can potentially be linked back to the characteristics of welfare states, polyarchy regimes, the resulting autonomy of the Swedish health authorities and the ethopolitical character of Swedish *habitus*. Despite the fact that the three Scandinavian countries are constitutional monarchies, the health authorities in Sweden, have more decision-making autonomy in affecting the behavior of the population, while "the politicians are more directly in charge of the administration in Norway and Denmark" [27]. During the start of the COVID-19 pandemic, this difference in autonomy made it "easier in Denmark and Norway to react quickly with political decisions and even to overrule authorities and their expertise" [27]. Although the three countries' health authorities were initially against severe measures [3,27], the less restrictive measures were applied only in Sweden. To understand Sweden's way of informing the public during the crisis even further, a cultural perspective was applied. Nygren and Olofsson consider [13] that the less restrictive measures taken by this country can further be explained by the biopolitics of "governing of conduct and individual responsibilization" [16]. If one interprets Nikolas Rose's studies on ethopolitics as biopolitics merged with a set of values, practices and moralities on how life ought to be lived by individuals, Sweden's way of communicating the crisis is a good example of how to inform citizens with high autonomy for self-government [22]. It referred to citizenship guided by high trust in the state, in which the conduct of health authorities has historically been marked by routine communication on recommendations for a healthy life. However, this attitude can also be seen as naive, as Swedish citizens are said to blindly follow any recommendation [27].

Sweden differs from Denmark and Norway, which followed a stronger discourse lead around Healthcare System together with accumulated information on statistics, symptoms, and virus characteristics. For instance, in the Swedish political culture the government response to regulate peoples' behavior, appeared more prominently than the less regulatory character of the action code Healthcare System, seen to be stronger in Denmark and Norway. From a ethopolitical perspective, the Swedish health authorities' acknowledgement of the global and national information spread, fed into the actions to create guidelines, disseminate information and make recommendations, and helped to mitigate the consequences of the corona-spread. Hence, such actions reflect the relationship between the state and the people, since milder restrictions convey the trustful relationship between the government and the Swedish citizens' *habitus* of self-governance.

Another central finding was Norway's focus on information around Biology of the Disease, the statistics, numbers and reports on the amount of tested and infected citizens (Monitoring Stats), and the strong connection both had with actions taken by the Health-care System (see Fig. 2A and C). This draws attention to the more inclusive character of the Norwegian polyarchy's decision-making process. According to Christensen, the Norwegian government has a political leadership characterized by bringing together diverse sectors of state and society, such as health authorities, opposition parties, executives and workers [3]. This Norwegian characteristic became strongly evident during the management of the COVID-19 pandemic [3], and the press releases tended to illuminate the inclusive character of the Norwegian *habitus*.

From a cultural perspective, regarding the restrictive measures taken in Denmark and Norway, Olagnier and Davidsen stated that the Danish reaction to COVID-19 can be characterized as "act fast and act with force" [15], due to the fast adoption of restrictive measures and the national speeches to enforce the isolation. Although Norway also adopted restrictive measures and the use of force, Strang highlighted that the political culture of Norway is marked by a greater concern that political changes could limit the individual's democratic rights and weaken democracy [27]. Such political culture can be seen in laws and other regulations taken to ensure that COVID-19 special measures were not threatening democracy and individual rights. For instance, when the Swedish government proposed to empower government officials to take action more quickly, the public debate regarded how it would impact the relationship between government and parliament, not whether it would lead to a risk to individual rights. The Danish strategy "act fast" and the "careful" Norwegian *habitus*, are both important to explain why the former country's actions related to the health care system are informed by Illness, and the latter country's actions related to the healthcare system is informed by Biology of the Disease.

Denmark's crisis communication was much harder to interpret, as it is located centrally between the other two countries, and focuses on information from many sources that inform actions on multiple governmental levels (see Fig. 3A). However, the special role that Denmark represents might be explained by the "fast" reopening (earlier and more permissive than Norway), which led to a greater need to inform the population about the transmission of the virus on surfaces and about characteristic symptoms of COVID-19.

Our study shows that quantitative ethnographic methods can be used to take a comparative perspective in crisis communication research. Yet, we found some methodological challenges with the combination of tools used. For example, using machine translation with Google translate, and possible translation errors of the keywords that could impinge on the construction of codes in nCoder. However, multiple manual screenings of the source file showed only a few errors that were then corrected.

Theoretically, research on *habitus* can contribute to problematize cultural ways of acting. In particular, this study briefly problematized Scandinavian "generative schemes" of acting-thinking regarding the "high trust in State", specifically in the crisis communication during the COVID-19 pandemic. In summary, the particularities discussed – Swedish "ethopolitical life," Danish "act fast and with force" and Norwegian "carefulness" – can signal for attention on, e.g.: the Swedes' and Danes' level of criticality on State measures and the Norwegians' level of tolerance to political changes. These results can contribute to a better understanding of the "generative schemes" and of "high trust in State," and therefore to research and practices on democratic life.

Finally, our findings are only limited to press releases of health agencies, which potentially limits the degree of conclusions we can draw from our study. For example, discourses around the Peoples Responsibilities Response were not salient, which reflects difficulties in finding additional keywords that could enclose this particular code in a good way. Moreover, the discourse around the Financial situation was not present in the press releases why this code could not be related to the actions of the three governments. This perspective is, however, essential as many countries now face economic difficulties due to the enforced lock-downs. As the COVID-19 pandemic is still underway, future work can investigate additional resources such as the speeches of the prime ministers, to gain a more holistic picture on the Scandinavian countries' crisis communication.

References

1. Allcott, H., Boxell, L., Conway, J., Gentzkow, M., Thaler, M., Yang, D.Y.: Polarization and public health: Partisan differences in social distancing during COVID-19. SSRN 3570274 (2020)
2. Bourdieu, P., Nice, R.: Outline of a Theory of Practice. Cambridge University Press, Cambridge (1977)
3. Christensen, T., Lægreid, P.: Balancing governance capacity and legitimacy - how the Norwegian government handled the COVID-19 crisis as a high performer. Public Administration Review n/a(n/a). https://doi.org/10.1111/puar.13241
4. Coombs, T.: Parameters for Crisis Communication. Blackwell Publishing, Hoboken (2010)
5. Cuche, D.: La notion de culture dans les sciences sociales. La découverte (2002)
6. Dahl, R.A.: Polyarchy: Participation and Opposition. Yale University Press, New Haven (1973)
7. Eagan, B., Brohinsky, J., Wang, J., Shaffer, D.W.: Testing the reliability of inter-rater reliability. In: Proceedings of the ICLAK 2020, pp. 454–461. ACM, New York (2020). https://doi.org/10.1145/3375462.3375508
8. Holmes, B.J.: Communicating about emerging infectious disease: the importance of research. Health Risk Soc. 10(4), 349–360 (2008). https://doi.org/10.1080/13698570802166431
9. Hort, S.E.O.: Social Policy, Welfare State, and Civil Society in Sweden [elektronisk resurs], vol. 1 History, Policies, and Institutions 1884–1988 (2017)
10. Hua, J., Shaw, R.: Corona virus (COVID-19) "infodemic" and emerging issues through a data lens: the case of China. Int. J. Environ. Res. Public Health 17 (2020). https://doi.org/10.3390/ijerph17072309
11. Lee, S.H.: Welfare attitudes, political trust and its determinants in Sweden (2018)
12. Lindert, P.H.: Growing Public: Social Spending and Economic Growth Since the Eighteenth Century Vol. 1 The Story. Cambridge University Press, Cambridge (2004)

13. Nygren, K.G., Olofsson, A.: Managing the COVID-19 pandemic through individual responsibility: the consequences of a world risk society and enhanced ethopolitics. J. Risk Res. **0**(0), 1–5 (2020). https://doi.org/10.1080/13669877.2020.1756382
14. OECD: Government at a Glance 2017 (2017). https://bit.ly/2NKWjgU
15. Olagnier, D., Mogensen, T.H.: The Covid-19 pandemic in Denmark: big lessons from a small country. Cytokine Growth Factor Rev. **53**, 10–12 (2020)
16. Olsson, U.: Folkhälsa som pedagogiskt projekt: Bilden av hälsoupplysning i statens offentliga utredningar. Ph.D. thesis, Uppsala University, Department of Education (1997)
17. Orso, D., Federici, N., Copetti, R., Vetrugno, L., Bove, T.: Infodemic and the spread of fake news in the COVID-19-era. Eur. J. Emerg. Med.: Official J. Eur. Soc. Emerg. Med. **27**(5), 327–328 (2020). https://doi.org/10.1097/MEJ.0000000000000713
18. Ortiz, R.: A procura de uma sociologia da prática. Pierre Bourdieu: sociologia, pp. 7–29. Ática, São Paulo (1983)
19. Paek, H.J., Hilyard, K., Freimuth, V.S., Barge, J.K., Mindlin, M.: Public support for government actions during a flu pandemic: lessons learned from a statewide survey. Health Prom. Pract. **9**(4_suppl), 60S–72S (2008). https://doi.org/10.1177/1524839908322114
20. Brandt, P., Woerlein, J.: Government crisis communication during the coronavirus crisis: comparing France, Germany, and The United Kingdom (2020). https://www.sciencespo.fr/cso/fr/content/government-crisis-communication-during-coronavirus-crisis-comparing-france-germany-and-unite.html. Accessed 30 June 2020
21. Reynolds, B., Quinn, S.C.: Effective communication during an influenza pandemic: the value of using a crisis and emergency risk communication framework. Health Prom. Pract. **9**(4_suppl), 13S–17S (2008). https://doi.org/10.1177/1524839908325267
22. Rose, N.: The politics of life itself. Theory Culture Soc. **18**(6), 1–30 (2001). https://doi.org/10.1177/02632760122052020
23. Saliou, P.: Crisis communication in the event of a flu pandemic. Eur. J. Epidemiol. **10**(4), 515–517 (1994). https://doi.org/10.1007/BF01719693
24. Shaffer, D.W., Collier, W., Ruis, A.R.: A tutorial on epistemic network analysis: analyzing the structure of connections in cognitive, social, and interaction data. J. Learn. Analytics **3**(3), 9–45 (1994). https://doi.org/10.18608/jla.2016.33.3
25. Shaffer, D.W.: Quantitative Ethnography. Cathcart Press, Madison (2017)
26. Siegrist, M., Earle, T.C., Gutscher, H.: Test of a trust and confidence model in the applied context of electromagnetic field (EMF) risks. Risk Anal. **23**(4), 705–716 (2003). https://onlinelibrary.wiley.com/doi/abs/10.1111/1539-6924.00349
27. Strang, J.: Why do the Nordic countries react differently to the COVID-19 crisis? (2020). https://nordics.info/show/artikel/the-nordic-countries-react-differently-to-the-covid-19-crisis/
28. Ghebreyesus, T.A.: WHO director-general's opening remarks at the media briefing on COVID-19 - 11 March 2020 (2020). https://www.who.int/director-general/speeches/detail/who-director-general-s-opening-remarks-at-the-media-briefing-on-covid-19---11-march-2020. Accessed 30 June 2020
29. Vaughan, E., Tinker, T.: Effective health risk communication about pandemic influenza for vulnerable populations. Am. J. Public Health **99**(S2), S324–S332 (2009). https://doi.org/10.2105/AJPH.2009.162537
30. van der Weerd, W., Timmermans, D.R.M., Beaujean, D.J.M.A., Oudhoff, J., van Steenbergen, J.E.: Monitoring the level of government trust, risk perception and intention of the general public to adopt protective measures during the influenza A (H1N1) pandemic in the Netherlands. BMC Public Health **11**(1), 575 (2011). https://doi.org/10.1186/1471-2458-11-575

Correction to: Establishing Trustworthiness Through Algorithmic Approaches to Qualitative Research

Ha Nguyen⭕, June Ahn⭕, Ashlee Belgrave, Jiwon Lee,
Lora Cawelti, Ha Eun Kim, Yenda Prado, Rossella Santagata,
and Adriana Villavicencio

Correction to:
Chapter "Establishing Trustworthiness Through Algorithmic
Approaches to Qualitative Research" in: A. R. Ruis
and S. B. Lee (Eds.): *Advances in Quantitative Ethnography*,
CCIS 1312, https://doi.org/10.1007/978-3-030-67788-6_4

In the originally published version of the chapter 4, the name of the author was spelled incorrectly. The author's name has been changed as Ashlee Belgrave.

The updated version of this chapter can be found at
https://doi.org/10.1007/978-3-030-67788-6_4

© Springer Nature Switzerland AG 2021
A. R. Ruis and S. B. Lee (Eds.): ICQE 2021, CCIS 1312, p. C1, 2021.
https://doi.org/10.1007/978-3-030-67788-6_29

Author Index

Printed in the United States
by Baker & Taylor Publisher Services